# COMMUNISM
# in HUNGARY

## HISTORIES OF RULING COMMUNIST PARTIES
Richard F. Staar, editor

# COMMUNISM
# in HUNGARY
## From Kun to Kádár

**BENNETT KOVRIG**

HOOVER INSTITUTION PRESS
Stanford University, Stanford California

*The Hoover Institution on War, Revolution and Peace, founded at Stanford University in 1919 by the late President Herbert Hoover, is an interdisciplinary research center for advanced study on domestic and international affairs in the twentieth century. The views expressed in its publications are entirely those of the authors and do not necessarily reflect the views of the staff, officers, or Board of Overseers of the Hoover Institution.*

## Hoover Institution Publication 211

© 1979 by the Board of Trustees of the
  Leland Stanford Junior University
All rights reserved
International Standard Book Number: 0-8179-7112-2
Library of Congress Catalog Card Number: 78-59863
Printed in the United States of America

DESIGNED BY ELIZABETH GEHMAN

*for*
*Marina, Michael, and Ariana*

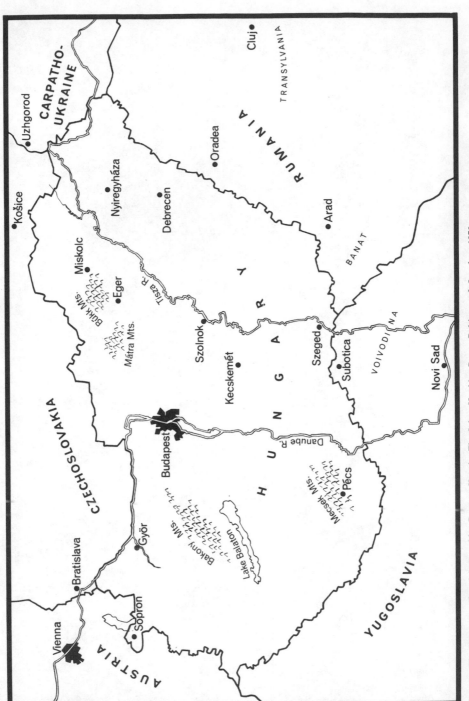

Source: *The Hungarian People's Republic*, Bennett Kovrig. The Johns Hopkins Press, Baltimore & London, 1970.

# Contents

# Editor's Foreword

To the nonspecialist on Hungary, its communist movement at first sight may not appear to warrant a study as long and detailed as this one. Although the Hungarian Communist Party was the first outside Russia to emulate the Bolsheviks—it seized power in early 1919—the Hungarian people tolerated the experiment for only 133 days. The movement (or what little remained of it) played a marginal role during the interwar period, had little effect on the fate of the country during World War II, and would have remained in eclipse if its calculated subversion of the electoral process had not been backed by Soviet armed force.

There is, however, one profound difference between Hungarian communism and that of any other brand. In 1956, as a result of what can only be termed a genuine revolution by the people, the Hungarian Communist Party temporarily lost its monopoly of power. Once again, Soviet arms played a decisive role: communism was restored at gunpoint and the revolutionary leaders, after a period of refuge in the Yugoslav embassy, were kidnapped and executed. No other ruling communist party has experienced anything similar.

The regime that followed the revolution has been forced to tread warily. Under the leadership of János Kádár, it has introduced features that have given it a measure of legitimacy. Hungarian society, in certain respects, has been modernized, and the economy has undergone reforms that were long overdue. These achievements, however, are negated by enforced dependence on the Soviet Union, which continues to treat Hungary as its vassal, and ignores the rights of Hungarian minorities in territories lost by Hungary after World War II. The situation is deeply offensive to the majority of Hungarians, who remain conscious of their unique cultural heritage, and who would opt for a pluralistic form of government if they could. Hungarian patriotism—the spirit of a small, proud nation with powerful neighbors—remains at odds with Hungarian communism.

Professor Kovrig's monograph takes us from the nineteenth-century origins of Hungarian communism in the social democratic movement to the problems of Hungary under communism in the mid-1970s. We become acquainted with the early communist leaders; we are shown why they were able to seize power in 1919; we follow them into exile. The familiar history of the interwar period is viewed from the unfamiliar angle of their underground activities, relations with the Comintern, attempts to form a popular front, and their fate during Stalin's purges. World War II, which aligned Hungary on the side of the Axis, facilitated communist access to power. In brilliant detail, Professor Kovrig describes how the party eliminated adversaries and gained total control. In no other satellite did Stalin's policies inspire such faithful imitation. After Soviet tanks had crushed the emerging Hungarian democracy in 1956, Kádár initiated a less repressive style of one-party rule. Nevertheless, as Professor Kovrig shows with numerous examples, Hungarian society in the late 1970s continues to suffer from problems that official Marxist dogma cannot admit, let alone solve.

As general editor of this series on the histories of ruling communist parties, I am more than pleased that a scholar as well qualified as Bennett Kovrig has applied his special talents to this study of communism in Hungary.

RICHARD F. STAAR
*Director of International Studies*

Hoover Institution
Stanford University

# Preface

Political historians, barring the rare talent cast in the Toynbeean mold, generally yearn for the accolade of definitiveness and shrink from the extensive sweep that carries with it the risk of superficiality. The present work would not have been undertaken had not Dr. Richard F. Staar of the Hoover Institution provided the challenge that raised the temperature of inquiry. In attempting to chronicle the long and tempestuous history of the Hungarian communist party, the author recognized the danger of satisfying no one, certainly neither those who regard communism simply as an abomination to be excoriated nor, at the opposite pole, those who seek only to celebrate its historically preordained liberating function. The truth, inevitably, is more complex but does not necessarily lie at the midpoint between the two extremes of prejudice. Although the author has relied principally on the party's histories and sources to the limits of credibility, it is as well to confirm at the outset that he has not approached the subject of his investigation with the ideological crutch of Marxism, let alone Marxism-Leninism. On the other hand, to consistently apply the convenient benchmark of liberal democracy was tempting but would have been ahistorical in the Hungarian setting. The communists' own proclaimed goals as well as the ascertainable objective and subjective interests of the Hungarian people have served as the more differentiated standards by which the political phenomenon of communism could be evaluated.

The intricate admixture of political, social, economic, and cultural factors, legacies of the past and contemporary forces, can not be fully represented in a single volume spanning some sixty years of a nation's history. A similar economy dictates that only the most directly relevant aspects of the Moscow-centered international movement that begat and nurtured Hungarian communism be related here. Concentration on the communist party, particularly during its long sojourn in the shadows of illegality and exile, imposes a certain distortion of political reality, and it is perhaps superfluous to warn the reader against expecting a comprehensive history of Hungary since World War I. The purpose of the narrower exercise is to survey the party's fortunes, its strategies and tactics, its composition and organization, and its relations with the governed as well as with its Soviet masters, along the road from Béla Kun's fateful espousal of Bolshevism in 1917 to János Kádár's practice of the proletarian dictatorship in the present day.

Students of politics steeped in the contemporary social sciences may miss some of the latter's terminological and analytical conventions. The omission is intentional, for this study is meant as a history rather than as an exercise in comparative politics. The crushing tedium of ideological jargon is more difficult to avoid, and readers will have to brace themselves for the verbal rituals and excesses of the communist movement. Doctrines demand a measure of exegesis, but this study concentrates on the political reality of the communists' quest for and exercise of power.

In addition to the Hoover Institution's sponsorship, financial assistance from the Canada Council, the American Council of Learned Societies, and the University of Toronto's Center for Russian and East European Studies was invaluable and is gratefully acknowledged. The research was facilitated by the cooperation of Radio Free Europe's Hungarian section in Munich, of the National Széchenyi Library and the Institute of Party History in Budapest, and of Canadian and American libraries. Dr. Iván Halász de Béky of the Robarts Library at the University of Toronto deserves special thanks for his unstinting generosity. The conversion of manuscript into book was immeasurably eased by J. M. B. Edwards, a paragon of editors. Finally, it is in full cognizance of current constraints that the author voices the hope that some day this and other Western studies as well as many prewar native works dealing with Hungarian politics will no longer be in the restricted access category at the Széchenyi Library.

# Hungarian Socialist Workers' Party (HSWP)

I. **Politburo**
   Members

   János Kádár
   György Aczél
   Antal Apró
   Valéria Benke
   Béla Biszku
   Jenő Fock
   Sándor Gáspár
   István Huszár
   György Lázár
   Pál Losonczi
   László Maróthy
   Dezső Nemes
   Károly Németh
   Miklós Óvári
   István Sarlós

II. **Central Committee Secretariat**
   First Secretary
   Secretaries

   János Kádár
   Sándor Borbély
   András Gyenes
   Imre Győri
   Ferenc Havasi
   Mihály Korom
   Károly Németh
   Miklós Óvári

III. **Central Control Committee**
   Chairman

   János Brutyó

IV. **Other Committees**
   Chairman, Agitprop Committee
   Chairman, Economic Policy Committee
   Chairman, Youth Committee

   Miklós Óvári
   Károly Németh
   Árpád Pullai

V. **Central Committee Teams**
    Chairman, Co-operative Policy Team          Pál Romány
    Chairman, Cultural Policy Team             Miklós Óvári
    Chairman, Economic Team                Károly Németh
    Chairman, Party Building Team             Béla Biszku ·

## STATE

I. **Presidential Council**
    Chairman (nominal head of state)           Pál Losonczi
II. **National Assembly**
    Chairman                                   Antal Apró

## GOVERNMENT

I. **Council of Ministers**
    Prime Minister                       György Lázár
    Deputy Prime Ministers              György Aczél
                                   János Borbándi
                                   István Huszár
                                   József Marjai
                                   Gyula Szekér

    Ministers
        Agriculture and Food              Pál Romány
        Culture                         Imre Pozsgay
        Defense                        Lajos Czinege
        Education                     Károly Polinszky
        Finance                        Lajos Faluvégi
        Foreign Affairs                Frigyes Puja
        Foreign Trade                 Péter Veress
        Heavy Industry               Pál Simon
        Interior                        András Benkei
        Internal Trade                Vilmos Sághy
        Justice                        Imre Markoja
        Labor                         Ferenc Trethon
        Light Industry                Mrs. János Keserű
        Metallurgy and the Machine Industry    István Soltész
        Public Construction and Urban Development   Kálmán Ábrahám
        Public Health                 Emil Schultheisz
        Transport and Telecommunications      Árpád Pullai
    Chairman (ministerial rank), National Planning
        Office                        István Huszár

## II. Central People's Control Commission
Chairman (state secretarial rank)     József Szakali

## III. Other Chairmen with Rank of State Secretary

| | |
|---|---|
| Central Statistical Office | Mrs. Ferenc Nyitrai |
| Information Bureau | Péter Várkonyi |
| National Bank | Mátyás Timár |
| National Material and Price Control Office | Béla Csikós-Nagy |
| National Water Conservation Office | István Gergely |
| Office for Religious Affairs | Imre Miklós |
| Office for Local Councils | Lajos Papp |
| National Physical Training and Sports Office | Sándor Beckl |

# Abbreviations

AVH      Államvédelmi Hatóság (State Defense Authority)

AVO      Államvédelmi Osztály (State Defense Department)

CPH      Communist Party of Hungary (Kommunisták Magyarországi Pártja)

DEFOSZ   Dolgozó Parasztok és Földmunkások Országos Szövetsége (National Federation of Working Peasants and Agricultural Workers)

DISZ      Dolgozó Ifjúság Szövetsége (Federation of Working Youth)

ESZE      Egyesült Szakszervezeti Ellenzék (United Trade Union Opposition)

FEKOSZ   Földmunkások és Kisbirtokosok Országos Szövetsége (National Federation of Agricultural Workers and Small Proprietors)

HCP      Hungarian Communist Party (Magyar Kommunista Párt)

HSWP      Hungarian Socialist Workers' Party (Magyar Szocialista Munkáspárt)

HWP      Hungarian Workers' Party (Magyar Dolgozók Pártja)

KIMSZ    Kommunista Ifjúmunkások Magyarországi Szövetsége (Hungarian Federation of Young Communist Workers)

KISZ      Kommunista Ifjúsági Szövetség (Federation of Communist Youth)

MADISZ   Magyar Demokratikus Ifjúsági Szövetség (Hungarian Federation of Democratic Youth)

MEFESZ   Magyar Egyetemi és Főiskolai Egyesületek Szövetsége (Federation of Hungarian University and College Associations)

MMTVD   *A magyar munkásmozgalom történetének válogatott dokumentumai* [Selected documents from the history of the Hungarian workers' movement]

MNDSZ   Magyar Nők Demokratikus Szövetsége (Democratic Federation of Hungarian Women)

MOEB    Munkanélküliek Országos Egységbizottsága (National Unity Committee of the Unemployed)

MSZMP   see HSWP

MTI     Magyar Távirati Iroda (Hungarian Telegraphic Agency)

NEKOSZ  Népi Kollégiumok Országos Szövetsége (National Federation of People's Colleges)

NEM     New Economic Mechanism

NPP     National Peasant Party (Nemzeti Parasztpárt)

OIB     Országos Ifjúsági Bizottság (National Youth Committee)

PK      *Párttörténeti Közlemények* [Journal of Party History]

PPF     Patriotic People's Front (Hazafias Népfront)

SDP     Social Democratic Party (Szociáldemokrata Párt)

SHP     Smallholder Party (Független Kisgazdapárt)

SWPH    Socialist Workers' Party of Hungary (Magyarországi Szocialista Munkáspárt)

UFOSZ   Újgazdák és Földhözjuttatottak Országos Szövetsége (National Federation of New Farmers and Land Recipients)

★

# *A Taste of Power*

# PART ONE

*Modern history has dealt harshly with the small nations of Eastern Europe. The Hungarians, located at the crossroads of the continent, have suffered much as their neighbors from the flux and reflux of the imperial ambitions of the Sublime Porte, of Habsburgs and Romanovs, Nazis and Bolsheviks. Foreign rule or intervention has been all the more intolerable for a nation that glories in its past moments of historical greatness and is conscious of its ethnic and linguistic isolation in the heart of Europe.*

*The Magyars entered the Danubian Basin from the east in the last years of the ninth century and proceeded to extend their dominion over an area bounded by the Carpathians, the Transylvanian Alps, and the foothills of the Austrian Alps. In the year 1000 their national kingdom and affiliation to Western Christianity was confirmed by the pope's award of a crown and apostolic cross to King Stephen I. For five centuries the country flourished, surviving Mongol invasions and holding back the tide of Ottoman expansion. Constitutional rule stemmed from the Golden Bull of 1222, which, like the Magna Charta, entrenched certain rights of the gentry at the expense of royal prerogative. Commerce and the arts were fostered by such distinguished monarchs as Louis the Great and Matthias Corvinus. The latter, son of the Transylvanian ruler János Hunyady, who was renowned for his victory over the Turks at Belgrade in 1456, brought the Renaissance to Hungary.*

*The country's development was soon to be arrested. In 1541 the royal city of Buda fell to the Turks. For the next century-and-a-half, Hungary was divided into three parts: a northwestern strip under Habsburg rule, a central area incorporated into the Ottoman Empire, and a nominally independent Transylvania. At the end of the seventeenth century, following the final expulsion of the Turks, a devastated and depopulated Hungary fell under the lasting dominion of the Habsburgs. There ensued fruitless revolts, led by Prince Ferenc Rákóczi, against imperial oppression and religious intolerance. Cultural and economic stagnation prevailed, as imported German and other non-Magyar settlements spread over the territory of the old kingdom.*

*By the turn of the nineteenth century, however, a national revival had materialized. Vienna, anxious for financial support for its imperial wars, granted concessions in what became known as the "reform era." The other national groups in the empire, Poles, Czechs, Slovaks, Croats, and Romanians, all voiced similar demands but to less effect, for Metternich inclined to conciliate the more powerful Magyars. Caught up in the nationalistic wave sweeping Europe at mid-century, the Hungarians reached for independence. In 1848 they rebelled. Despite some early successes under the heroic leadership of Lajos Kossuth, they were crushed the following year thanks to the opportune assistance offered by Czar Nicholas I to his Habsburg ally.*

*Oppressive Austrian rule and passive resistance followed until, in 1867, the militarily weakened imperial power agreed to a compromise that granted Hungary domestic autonomy and established the Austro-Hungarian dual monarchy. The successive reforms of the nineteenth century had liberated the serfs and paved the way for modest industrial development. Political power, however, was exercised paternalistically by the entrenched nobility, while economic power was shared by the landed magnates and an emerging, heavily Germanic urban bourgeoisie. The middle-class liberalism of Western Europe had relatively little impact on Hungary's predominantly agrarian and conservative society. A nationalistic assumption of cultural superiority and attachment to the territorial integrity of the old kingdom spurred attempts to assimilate the non-Magyar ethnic groups. When, towards the end of the century, Jews became a visible and ambitious minority, anti-Semitism also emerged. The small industrial working class was barely touched by syndicalism and socialism, while the huge peasantry remained largely landless; neither enjoyed much political influence, although the latter was revered as the bearer of the traditional culture. Such socioeconomic phenomena were not uncommon in Eastern Europe, but they made Hungary more vulnerable when the tide of liberalism and social revolution finally engulfed the region in the wake of World War I.*

*Defeat in that war shattered the empire into approximate national fragments. Hungary now bore the brunt of minority disaffection and found herself territorially and ethnically truncated. As the old order crumbled, a liberal-democratic regime led by Count Mihály Károlyi stepped into the breach, but it could not remedy the lag in social, economic, and political reform without more time than history gave it. Impotent to extract palatable peace terms from the unsympathetic Entente, Károlyi surrendered power amidst spreading chaos to an impromptu coalition of old social democrats and new communists, the latter led by a disciple of Lenin, Béla Kun. The resulting proletarian dictatorship, a self-styled Republic of Councils, experimented with revolutionary social and economic reforms and waged war against the encircling and vengeful local allies of the Entente. Domestic revulsion at the violent radicalism of the communists and military defeat soon put an end to this Hungarian version of the Bolshevik Revolution.*

# 1. The Socialist Prelude

Every political movement, even one as doctrinally supranational as communism, retrieves from history the evidence that can buttress its claim to national roots and national continuity. In Hungary, for instance, communists have alleged themselves to be the inheritors of such time-honored instances of challenge to established authority as the peasant uprising led by György Dózsa in 1514. These retroactive exercises in historical determinism may serve to embellish a communist regime's facade of domestic legitimacy and ideological superiority. They do not, however, change the fact that communism's progenitor and (eventually) fierce competitor, socialism, was a modern philosophical phenomenon that arose coincidentally with nationalism in the industrializing and increasingly bourgeois milieu of nineteenth-century Europe. Hungarian political history, apart from the momentous events of the late spring and summer of 1919, offered only a marginal role to communism until the intrusion of the victorious Red Army in 1944. The less revolutionary variants of socialism, while also of limited political consequence in Hungary's peculiar circumstances, had nevertheless deeper roots. Their early record, then, must be sketched to indicate the pedigree of the movement that ultimately came to rule over Hungary.

## SOCIALISM AND SYNDICALISM

The manifold strains of utopian socialist and Marxist thought that spread across Europe in the middle of the nineteenth century did not fail to penetrate the Hungarian half of the Habsburg Empire, where they encountered the relatively unfertile ground of industrial underdevelopment and social neofeudalism. The nationalistic and liberal impulses of the 1830s, personified in Hungary by such reformers as Count István Széchenyi and Lajos Kossuth, led—perhaps inevitably—to confrontation with Vienna's conservative rule. On 15 March 1848 the so-called March Youth, galvanized by the radical poet Sándor Petőfi, sparked off the revolution of 1848–49 with a historic demonstration. They called for parliamentary rule and the abolition of serfdom, of the guilds, and of censorship. An uneasy patriotic alliance emerged. It was broad enough to encompass progressive aristocrats such as Count Lajos Batthyány, liberal reformers of the lesser nobility like Kossuth, Petőfi radicals, and even, in the person of Mihály Táncsics, a lone, authentic socialist. Táncsics, a weaver turned intellectual who had returned from foreign parts imbued with utopian socialist ideas, was freed by the revolution from the prison to which his radical writings had sent him; he became a deputy to the new national parliament. An advocate of the redistribution of large estates, Táncsics also assisted the Budapest printers in negotiating the first collective wage agreement in Hungary.

After a brief period of euphoria, during which Hungarian military successes against Austrian and Croatian forces compelled Vienna to make tactical concessions, the revolution collapsed in August 1849 under the overwhelming weight of a combined Austro-Russian offensive. In domestic politics there was much debate over how the nobility should be compensated for their loss of feudal services. The redistribution of land, however, was not attempted, while the guild system was eased but retained. Finally, although the traditional legal distinction between the enfranchised, privileged *populus* and the voiceless *plebs* was erased, the preeminent role of the historic Magyar nation within a multi-ethnic state was confirmed. Nevertheless, in its time the revolution was a notably liberal movement, dominated by a romantic patriotic fervor to which more secular political goals were subordinated.

The victorious Austrians resorted to harsh repression, executing Batthyány and other revolutionary leaders; Kossuth fled into exile. Ironically, the period of direct imperial administration also brought the implementation of a number of revolutionary objectives, including general taxation. Austria's defeats in Italy and in its war against Prussia coincided with the efforts of Ferenc Deák (who became known as "the wise man of the country") and other moderate Hungarians to find a more tolerable modus vivendi. The outcome was the 1867 Compromise, which granted Hungary self-government under a Habsburg king and with joint administration of foreign affairs, defense, and finance.

Over much of the next fifty years Hungary's fortunes were guided by a conservative Liberal Party opposed in parliament by a scarcely less conservative Independence Party that stood for unqualified autonomy. Political power lay in the hands of the landed aristocracy, who were supported by commercial and financial interests and by an impoverished country gentry increasingly being transformed into an administrative class. As late as 1910 the franchise was enjoyed by only 8 percent of the population. Hungary's traditional role had been the breadbasket of the empire, with industrial development the preserve of Austria and Bohemia, and the landed aristocracy was generally satisfied with this state of affairs. At the time of the Compromise the industrial working class, mostly in small and inefficient enterprises, numbered some 300,000 out of a population of 15 million. Subsequently, liberal economic principles and the infusion of mainly Austrian capital did promote some industrial growth, so that by the end of the century the labor force in that sector had expanded to 700,000—still a small proportion considering that in the same period landless peasants alone numbered over 4 million. In the cities the expansion of the proletariat was matched by that of a heavily Germanic and Jewish commercial and professional middle class. In rural areas, where immense estates coexisted with a growing and prosperous freeholder peasant class, a paternalistic form of neofeudalism prevailed.

The Compromise satisfied moderate nationalists, but it could not alter the fact that scarcely half the population was ethnically Magyar. The nationalities law of 1868 was a remarkably liberal charter that granted equal rights to the Slovak, Southern Slav, Romanian and German minorities. It was scrupulously implemented by Deák, then subverted by his more assimilationist successors. Moreover, some of the minorities embraced the nationalism of the age and were incited by their conationals outside Hungary to seek autonomy. Kossuth, in exile, propagated the idea of a Danubian federation to accommodate the multiethnic character of the region, but the proposal fell on deaf ears.

When in 1896 the Hungarians with great pomp celebrated the millennium of their ancestors' arrival in the Carpathian basin, they could take justifiable pride in the political emancipation and economic and cultural revival that had taken place since the darkest days of Austrian rule. The old patriotic axiom, *extra Hungariam non est vita, si est vita non est ita* ("There is no life outside Hungary, and if there is it's not like ours") retained a mystical appeal. The reckoning for its complacency and parochialism was yet to come.

**The Organization of Labor.**   Socialist ideas were introduced into Hungary in the 1860s by German, Austrian, Czech, and Jewish immigrant journeymen, and by Hungarian craftsmen who had learned their trade abroad. These groups derived their socialism mainly from Ferdinand Lassalle, who combined faith in the industrial workers' victory through the ballot box with rejection of any alliance with the peasantry or the petite bourgeoisie, both of whom he lumped with capitalists in a hostile reactionary class. Hungary's socioeconomic structure was not suited to the rapid propagation of radical ideas by a small band of largely foreign-born agitators. What ensued was the isolated implantation of German social democratic ideology in a pale and sickly form.

A blend of Lassalleanism and liberalism inspired the few and small workers' welfare associations that had emerged in the wake of early industrialization. A more radical Marxist strain arrived in the person of János Hrabje, a carpenter and member of the First International's Supreme Council, who was instructed by that body in September 1866 to proselytize for the socialist movement in

Hungary. By 1868 he was at the head of a newly organized socialist group, the General Workers' Association (Általános Munkásegylet). At a mass meeting in Budapest the following year, this group adopted a program calling for freedom of the press and of association, universal suffrage, free schooling, the separation of state and church, confiscation of church property, abolition of the standing army, and the right of self-determination for the national minorities.[1] It subsequently elevated Táncsics to its presidency, but the hapless socialist veteran was relieved of his post when he took the decidedly nonradical initiative of asking the government for financial assistance.

Another group, the Worker Training Association of Pest-Buda (Pest-Budai Munkásképző Egylet) came under socialist influence in 1870 through the activities of Károly Farkas, a machinist who was Hrabje's successor as the First International's chief emissary. It joined the International and established the General Workers' Sickness Fund (Általános Munkás Betegsegélyző- és Rokkantpénztár). The two associations were about to merge when the government banned the Worker Training Association, leaving the older group to carry on a fight now invigorated by news of the Paris Commune. A rash of strikes in April–May 1871 was quelled by the arrest of the ringleaders. When the General Workers' Association mounted a demonstration in protest at these measures, it too was hit by arrests and prosecutions for disloyalty. These measures effectively liquidated it.

Official sanctions, the small size and unorganized state of industrial labor, and the ideological squabbles that fragmented the European socialist movement all militated against the spread of trade unionism and socialism in Hungary. Nevertheless, sporadic attempts at organization continued in the 1870s and 1880s. Upon his return from the International's Hague congress of September 1872, where battle had been engaged with the anarchists, Farkas launched Hungarian- and German-language socialist weeklies. The following March he participated in the establishment of a Workers' Party of Hungary (Magyarországi Munkáspárt). The party was promptly banned.

In 1878 another party, ostensibly nonsocialist to escape prohibition, was founded under the name of the Nonvoters' Party (Nemválasztók Pártja) on the initiative of one Leo Frankel. A former goldsmith, Frankel had played a prominent role in the Paris Commune, worked with Marx in London, and been arrested in Austria, which handed him over to Hungary. There the authorities, in the absence of an extradition request from France, finally set him free. A few months later a competing socialist party, reviving the name of Workers' Party of Hungary, was founded and engaged in an ideological battle with the Nonvoters' Party over the question of collaboration with the liberal left wing of the opposition Independence Party (the Nonvoters' Party favored collaboration but the Workers' Party rejected it on Lassallean grounds). Nevertheless, at a joint congress in May 1880 attended by 113 delegates, the two parties united under the name of General Workers' Party of Hungary (Magyarországi Általános Munkáspárt). Its program encompassed universal franchise, freedom of the press and of association, improvement in working conditions and compensation, nationalization of banks, transportation, mines, and major enterprises, a progressive inheritance tax, and producers' cooperatives. Forbidden by the government to elect a formal leadership, the new party remained under the guidance of the congress organizers on the basis of joint, coequal leadership. It published two weekly papers, one in Hungarian and the other in German. The editor of the German-language paper, Frankel, was imprisoned the following year for breaking press laws and subsequently left the country.

The General Workers' Party was rent by internal squabbles arising from the impatience of a self-styled ''revolutionary-socialist'' faction. It survived long enough, however, to participate in the founding congress of the Second International in Paris in July 1889, where it was represented by Frankel and by the printer Antal Ihrlinger. The factionaries delegated an Austrian socialist to denounce the Ihrlinger leadership at the congress for its tactics of compromise. As a result, a meeting of Austrian and Hungarian socialists later that year at Pozsony (now Bratislava) recommended the replacement of Ihrlinger by the tinsmith Pál Engelmann. The latter then took up the task of consolidating the still sparse and disorganized assortment of local trade and craft unions then existing in Hungary.

**The Social Democratic Party.** Despite official disfavor, labor militancy did lead to mass meetings—notably, one on 1 May 1890—and to occasional strikes. It was a measure of the socialists' growing confidence that, at the General Workers' party congress in December 1890, the name was changed to Social Democratic Party of Hungary (Magyarországi Szociáldemokrata Párt, hereafter SDP).[2] The congress heard a message of greeting from Friedrich Engels and approved a declaration of principles in which it anticipated the abolition of capitalism by a class-conscious proletariat that would be organized into an ''international'' party associated with the Second International. The program, like that of the Austrian sister party, did not confront agrarian and nationality problems.

The practical tasks facing the new party's leadership were rather less dramatic than the defeat of capitalism. In the prevailing Hungarian political and socioeconomic environment the party had to devote its energies to basic union organization, improvements in hours of work and workers' benefits (its efforts in this area did prompt concessions from the government in 1891), and, as a more remote but tirelessly reiterated goal, extension of the franchise. In the later decades of the century, overseas competition aggravated the difficulties of a relatively inefficient agricultural sector. Growing rural unemployment and underemployment precipitated harvest strikes and other outbursts by the agrarian proletariat, occasionally at the instigation of socialists. This prompted the SDP to take up the issue at its 1894 congress and advocate the joint socialization and large-scale operation of industrial and agricultural resources. However, this resolution did not respond to the landless peasants' yearning for their own private farms.

Even the very limited success of the SDP in promoting the interests of industrial labor was regarded by the government as dangerous radicalism to be nipped in the bud. In turn, the growing severity of government repression in the last years of the century exacerbated the divisions within the SDP on the respective merits of compromise and militancy. Factionalism, leadership changes, and secession weakened the party in the mid-1890s. In 1897 an agrarian-oriented Independent Socialist Party (Független Szocialista Párt) was founded by István Várkonyi, a former laborer whose insistence on redistribution of land had resulted in his expulsion from the SDP. The following year, the government outlawed agrarian strikes and unions.

Among the SDP's more positive achievements during this period was a Trades Council, established in January 1898, which served a fragmented union movement with a membership that scarcely surpassed twenty-three thousand. Concurrently works by Marx, Engels, Lassalle, Liebknecht, and Plekhanov made their first appearance in Hungarian translation. In sum, at the turn of the century socialism in Hungary was an ideologically splintered and derivative movement, led in the main by newly assimilated Jewish and other foreign unionists, and resting on the narrow basis of an industrial workers' elite. It existed on the periphery of the political and socioeconomic mainstream of Hungarian life.

After feeling the effects of the Europe-wide economic recession in the first few years of the twentieth century, Hungarian industry underwent a period of rapid expansion and concentration. By 1910 the industrial labor force reached one million. Among the total population of twenty-one million, two-thirds of all workers were still engaged in agriculture. Despite the labor demands of industrialization, agricultural underemployment was endemic; indeed, it led to the emigration of 1.5 million laborers between 1900 and 1914. These economic changes gave impetus to the political mobilization of industrial workers. At the time of the SDP's tenth congress, in April 1903, trade and craft union membership stood at forty-one thousand; there were twelve newly legalized national trade unions.[3] The party's platform, based on the 1891 Erfurt program of the German SDP, was presented by the former bricklayer Dezső Bokányi, a demagogic orator and member of the SDP leadership since 1894. The principal goals remained unaltered, universal franchise by secret ballot being first and foremost among them. In its agrarian policy the party advocated abolition of entailed land tenure to make way for what it called the "revolutionizing" force of capitalism; in general, it stood by its preference for an industrial reform of agriculture instead of land redistribution. On the issue of national independence, the congress accepted party secretary Jakab Weltner's qualified endorsement of so-called customs autonomy and rejected the opposite, free-trade view.* The rights of ethnic minorities received only token reaffirmation. The party's franchise campaign gained unexpected reinforcement from the governmental crisis that erupted in 1905. At the general elections that year the ruling Liberal Party had lost its plurality to the Independence Party, moving Emperor Franz Josef to impose an extraparliamentary administration and, in February 1906, to dismiss parliament. However, popular unrest and political deadlock impelled Vienna to invite the former opposition parties into a coalition government, and at new elections in May 1906 the Independence Party gained an absolute majority of the votes. In the midst of this crisis the interim administration had engaged in discussions with the socialists in order to draw away their support of the opposition with vague promises of electoral reform. Rising to the bait, the SDP organized numerous rallies and, in September 1905, an extraordinary congress and a mass demonstration before the parliament building to petition the coalition parties for electoral reform. The immediate outcome of this manipulation by Vienna was that the opposition, which was basically conservative, merged into a new coalition government.

The thirteenth congress of the SDP in June 1906 could only exhort the party leadership and Hungary's proletariat to prepare for a general strike if the government failed to extend the suffrage (which, incidentally, it did extend in Austria that year). The faction-ridden socialist movement was highly susceptible to manipulation. As early as 1900, a radical faction led by Vilmos Mezőfi had styled itself the Reorganized Social Democratic Party of Hungary (Magyarországi Ujjászervezett Szociáldemokrata Párt). It now adopted the nationalistic line of the Independence Party and was used by the latter until the coalition parties had consolidated their position. The organization of industrial labor reached a plateau in 1906, with twenty-eight national trade unions and close to one hundred and thirty thousand members. As the political crisis dragged on, strikes became more frequent.

On the agrarian front, a National Association of Hungarian Agricultural Workers (Magyarországi Földmunkások Országos Szervezete), led by György Nyisztor, made a brief appearance in 1906 and gathered some fifty thousand members before official persecution virtually destroyed it. Concurrently another, essentially regional, party, the land-reform oriented Peasant Party of Hungary (Magyarországi Parasztpárt), was founded by András Áchim, whose election to parliament in 1906 was nullified on grounds of anticlass agitation.

After 1907, official measures to inhibit industrial and agrarian labor organization multiplied. As a result, the number of strikes declined, as did union membership. The successful showing by the socialists in the Austrian elections

---

*In so doing, the congress aligned itself with the parliamentary opposition, which for years had made "customs autonomy" a rallying cry, and rejected the arguments of Ernő Garami, editor of the SDP newspaper *Népszava*.

of 1907 galvanized the SDP into calling a general strike in support of electoral reform. When the government responded with a draft bill promising only marginal improvement, the desperate socialists turned to the Viennese court for help.

The unshakeable conservatism of the ruling coalition was not the only obstacle facing the SDP. Although the revisionist ideas of the German social democrat Eduard Bernstein and various anarcho-syndicalist tendencies created greater turmoil in the more developed socialist parties of Western and Central Europe, such internal strife also afflicted Hungary's minuscule socialist movement. The central socialist leadership consisted of entrenched trade union bureaucrats possessed of little ideological training and subtlety and generally defensive and cautious in the face of government hostility. Factionalism was the form taken by dissatisfaction with the leadership's patently fruitless quest for political reform. The seeds of mistrust and division then sown would bedevil the fortunes of Hungarian socialism for decades.

One leading opposition figure was Ervin Szabó, a well-educated Marxist librarian who exercised a major influence in left-wing intellectual circles and nurtured many of Hungary's future radical socialists and communists. In his writings and proselytizing activities Szabó criticized the SDP for its rigid trade union hierarchy and overly prudent reformism. He called for an internal democratization that would facilitate a shift to the more radical goals of revolutionary anarcho-syndicalism—goals similar to the ones that had emerged in the French socialist movement. This hybrid ideology encompassed both Marxist socioeconomic principles and an anarchistic hatred of the state. Once the trade unions had been activized not only for economic objectives but also for social revolution, the class struggle would be intensified. At the critical revolutionary moment it would triumph over capitalism and the state and usher in the syndical rule of the proletariat.

The small radical-left faction that emerged within the SDP was of a mainly Jewish, middle-class background. It included such future communists as the journalists Gyula Alpári and Béla Szántó, as well as László Rudas and Béla Vágó. The faction soon aroused the ire of the generally anti-intellectual trade union leadership, which it openly challenged at the SDP's fourteenth congress in 1907. The coup failed, and the radical leftists were excluded from party office. Alpári continued his attacks on the party bureaucracy and, by way of the German socialist press, called for the separation of trade unions and party; this, he argued, would make the latter more militant. Amidst violent controversy the party expelled him at its 1910 congress. Some dissident socialists dispatched Alpári to the Second International's Copenhagen congress later that year, but despite support from Lenin and Rosa Luxemburg his mandate was not recognized.[4]

At its Stuttgart (1907), Copenhagen, and Basel (1912) congresses, the Second International made efforts to forge a genuinely supranational alliance of socialists against divisive imperialist wars—or, at least, to exploit such conflicts to the disadvantage of the dominant system. The congresses produced more rhetorical declarations than anything else, for those parties that already enjoyed parliamentary status were inexorably drawn by the lure of national interest. In Hungary, the government responded to the increasingly unstable Balkan situation with bills for greater military preparedness and expenditures. These measures, in turn, gave rise to initiatives for a rapprochement between the SDP and the Justh Party, a parliamentary opposition group that had seceded from the Independence Party. At the SDP's 1911 congress Garami presented the leadership's proposal for support of the Justh Party's antimilitary stand and of its clearly opportunistic espousal of universal suffrage. The motion was passed over the reservations of the railway workers' representative, the lawyer Jenő Landler. Despite their obviously different priorities, the two parties thereupon joined forces to organize public meetings.

**Liberals and Radicals.** This summary of the fortunes of Hungary's socialists in the early years of the century should not leave the impression that they represented anything but a marginal irritant to the conservative establishment. More significant, at least in the short run, was the activity of the reformist parliamentary splinter groups and of what became known as the "second reform generation" (to distinguish it from that of the 1830s), a diffuse and heterodox collection of intellectuals and literati whose significance in a society that venerated poets and writers surpassed its numbers and low rate of political participation.[5] Both of these groups played a part, sometimes unwittingly, in bringing Hungary to the brink of social revolution.

One rallying point for progressive intellectuals was the Society of Social Sciences (Társadalomtudományi Társaság). Launched in 1901, it was soon caught up in debates on which directions and methods of reform were desirable in what was still in many respects a neofeudal society. Its more radical wing, which included, besides the socialist Szabó, the crypto-Marxist Gyula Pikler (a law professor) and the anti-Marxist Oszkár Jászi (a sociologist with federalist views), mounted educational programs in collaboration with the SDP. Within a few years, at a time when the government's nationality policy was turning even more assimilationist, the multicultural and federalist schemes of the radicals sounded so out of tune with orthodox opinion that a leadership struggle erupted. The result was that Pikler, Szabó, and Jászi were left to preside over a rump society. Their Jewishness and leftist leanings, together with their stand on the nationalities issue, had combined to isolate if not to silence them.

Another outlet and rallying point for the more literary reformist intellectuals was the review *Nyugat* (West), founded in 1908 and designed, as its name implied, to bring Hungary into the mainstream of modern European philosophical and literary trends. Among its contributors were such intellectual luminaries as the poet Endre Ady and a budding idealist philosopher named György

Lukács. Finally, a discussion group for radical undergraduates, the Galileo Circle, was founded by Pikler in 1908 and became over the years a seedbed of increasingly revolutionary ideas.

All these initiatives served to supplement the honest but inward-looking trade-unionism of such SDP leaders as Garami, Sándor Garbai, and Zsigmond Kunfi. Through the medium of debate and educational programs for students and workers, these leaders received an infusion of progressive concepts that extend from democratic liberalism to the revolutionary extremes of Marxism. Such concepts stood in antithesis to the dominant orthodoxies: political paternalism by a historical ruling class and its allies; Magyar nationalism and cultural superiority; and a clericalism that dominated education. Like their bourgeois-radical and trade union purveyors, the various strains of socialism and liberalism were regarded with suspicion and distaste by the overwhelming majority, who were imbued with a somewhat xenophobic, anti-Semitic, and fervently patriotic conservatism. Nevertheless the middle-class radicals invigorated intellectual life and would undoubtedly have served as useful social catalysts had Hungary been allowed to evolve peacefully into a modern industrialized and democratic society. Instead, the war and two successive revolutions would briefly raise and then dash the hopes for orderly and measured change that the moderate reformist intelligentsia shared with the socialist leadership. For this tragic setback the domestic revolutionaries and external forces were as much to blame as Hungary's conservative elite.

## DOMESTIC POLITICS AND WORLD WAR I

While Hungary enjoyed a period of rapid industrialization and intellectual ferment in the years preceding the Great War, her political system remained dominated by a tug-of-war between a dynastically oriented government, essentially satisfied with the outcome of the 1867 Compromise, and an opposition that professed loyalty to the nationalistic ideals of 1848.[6] The two sides took turns baiting each other with demands for universal suffrage. Both, however, did so with ambivalence, since both represented the interests of the traditional ruling elite of aristocrats and country gentry. Both, too, feared the consequences of a democracy that would allow for the participation of the urban and rural proletariat and, more significantly, of the non-Magyar minorities who threatened the nationalists' vision of a sovereign Magyar nation. At the fringes of political life and based in Budapest could be found the Jewish-liberal Democratic Citizens' Party led by Vilmos Vázsonyi, which had token representation in parliament, and Garami's SDP, which had never succeeded in electing a single deputy. The former generally sided with the nationalist opposition. The latter, together with much of the republican and left-leaning intelligentsia, had initially been repelled by the nationalistic, county-based opposition. In the absence of any support from the Habsburg court, however, it was seduced into collaboration by the lure of electoral reform.

When the government of the old ruling coalition, renamed "Party of National Work" took office in April 1912, it was determined to overcome parliamentary obstruction of the defense bill. The opposition parties sought a compromise: trimming their objections to the defense bill, they proposed a limited electoral reform extending the franchise from 1.2 to 2.5 million voters. They also invited the SDP to lend its approval. The socialists responded on 23 May with a general strike that precipitated a bloody clash with the police on Parliament Square. Perhaps frightened by its own unaccustomed militancy—certainly, the immediate calls for interdiction and martial law came as a shock—and disillusioned by the aloofness of the Justh Party (in whose aid the strike had been called), the SDP leadership cancelled the strike that same afternoon. Amid violent opposition protests the government rammed through the defense bill on 4 June.

Progress on electoral reform proved painfully slow. In March 1913 the parliament passed a government bill extending voting rights to 1.9 million citizens and limiting the secret ballot to urban areas. The opposition parties withdrew from the sitting in protest, and the SDP leadership used the withdrawal as an excuse to avoid calling another general strike. The parliamentary opposition was nevertheless undergoing a certain radicalization in face of the government's obduracy. In June a new Independence Party coalesced under the leadership of Count Mihály Károlyi from the Justh Party and other disaffected groups. The count was not alone among aristocrats in perceiving the need for democratization, but he went farther than any of them in fostering a working relationship with the Vázsonyi liberals and with the socialists, notably Kunfi. Socialist contacts influenced his intellectual drift to the left. Regrettably, Károlyi's progressive ideas were not bolstered by good political judgment, as his later career was to testify. The socialists, meanwhile, continued to concentrate on the franchise issue and to tailor their tactics to the momentary demands of the parliamentary opposition. This strategy always had its ideological and political opponents within the party. At the SDP's October 1913 congress a delegate from the Transylvanian city of Kolozsvár, the journalist Béla Kun, challenged Garami's policy of alliance with the Károlyi group. But the moderates held sway in the SDP leadership, and the outbreak of the Great War found both Károlyi, the magnate turned democrat, and Kunfi, the socialist firebrand, lecturing Hungarian-Americans on the merits of independence and democracy for their ancestral home.

In Hungary, as in other European countries, the war was greeted with a patriotic jubilation, mingled with a certain psychic relief, that encompassed all social classes. The supranationalist and pacifistic illusions of the Second International were shattered. The SDP, until the very last minute, opposed the

Austro-Hungarian punitive attack on Serbia. Faced with the reality of war, however, the party retrenched into a posture of patriotic cooperation with the regime and exhorted its members to preserve their organizations through the troubled times. A year later, doubts about Germany's ability to lead the alliance to victory had dissipated much of the early euphoria. The more radical politicians, Károlyi foremost among them, began to seek ways of snatching a negotiated peace from the jaws of defeat. As usual, they carried the SDP on their coattails. With the support of German and Austrian socialists, the SDP did make some attempts to organize a meeting with its sister parties of the Triple Entente. The latter, however, refused to negotiate with the parties of occupying powers.

The efforts of Károlyi and like-minded liberals to press the case for wider suffrage, customs autonomy, and a separate Austro-Hungarian peace initiative received some impetus from the accession of Charles I to the throne in November 1916. Within six months the monarch named a new minority government in Budapest. It was led by Count Móricz Eszterházi and included such liberal politicians as Károlyi and Vázsonyi. The SDP, though still unrepresented, regarded it with favor; so did Jászi's National Radical Party. Shortly before this government assumed office, a so-called Suffrage Bloc had come into being on Károlyi's initiative. It consisted of his own party, those of Vázsonyi and Jászi, and the SDP, which contributed Garbai as vice-president of the bloc. Although the new government professed support for electoral reform, its early implementation was still precluded by the distribution of power and interests in parliament.

The socialist leadership divided its attention between the franchise issue, the economic hardships caused by the war effort, and peace feelers. A delegation led by Garami participated in the socialist preparatory conference at Stockholm in May 1917, and held forth, along with Victor Adler's Austrian group, on the territorial inviolability of the monarchy. However, the absence of Entente socialists turned the meeting into an exercise in futility.

**The Rise of Radical Leftism.**  As the war progressed, there were shortages of fuel and other essentials. Urban housing facilities, already inadequate, were stretched to breaking point by masses of Transylvanian refugees and Galician Jews. The social stress that resulted, particularly in Budapest, was exacerbated by the contrasting self-enrichment of profiteers and speculators. The growing discomfort of the working and lower-middle classes had the effect of reviving the trade union movement, whose membership rebounded to some two hundred thousand by late 1917. Low public morale at home and the mushrooming desertion rate in the armed forces emboldened the more radical elements, both within and outside the SDP, to launch an underground offensive for peace and social revolution.

The key group, in the wake of the Bolshevik coup in Russia, adopted the name of Revolutionary Socialists. It attracted members of the Galileo Circle and syndicalist socialists such as Szabó. Finding inspiration in the celebrated pacifist manifesto of 20 March 1917, the group launched an illegal pamphlet campaign that November.* The pamphlets called for war on war ("the slogan of the Petrograd and Moscow proletariat who now call on us in the name of peace") by sabotageing the military effort of the imperialist ruling classes. This movement was joined by an anarchist group of future communists that included Ottó Korvin (a former bank clerk), János Lékai, József Révai, and Imre Sallai. Instruction in conspiratorial techniques was provided by one Vladimir Justus, a Russian bolshevik émigré. The Revolutionary Socialists became the Hungarian forerunners of a pro-Bolshevik orientation that rejected both the status quo and social democracy.[7]

The SDP was moved by the new Soviet regime's peace proposal to call for a public demonstration on 25 November 1917. Later that day, however, the leadership, having called an extraordinary congress, showed itself more concerned with the immediate problem of the food shortage and with the right of assembly and association. At the initiative of Landler and other radical leftists, the congress did instruct the leadership to resort to drastic measures if the government failed to proceed with electoral reform. In his concluding remarks Garbai responded to the mood of militancy by proclaiming it the duty of all socialist parties to hitch on to the "locomotive of revolution that has started in Petrograd," but neither he nor most of his colleagues were sanguine about the prospects or desirability of a similar revolution in Hungary.[8]

In the meantime, the Revolutionary Socialists stepped up its antiwar agitation and advocacy of workers' councils. The first council was brought into being on 26 December 1917 by two syndicalist shop stewards, Antal Mosolygó and Sándor Ösztreicher, and there followed planning by various extremist groups for more such organizations as well as a general strike. On 12 January 1918 the government intervened by banning the Galileo Circle and having most of its members arrested on charges of sedition.

News of Germany's harsh peace terms at the Brest-Litovsk negotiations and of a strike at Wiener Neustadt in Austria emboldened the syndicalists and those members of the Revolutionary Socialists still at liberty to seize the initiative from the SDP leadership and engineer a massive strike on 18 January. One demonstration after another rang with calls for a separate peace, for workers' councils, and for sabotage. The SDP executive had initially endorsed the strike, but the radical tone of its instigators and the government's hurried promises to alleviate the workers' plight, to seek peace, and to eventually implement an

---

*The manifesto had been drawn up by the Zimmerwald International Socialist Committee and relayed to Hungary by a student member of the Galileo Circle, Ilona Duczynska.

electoral reform impelled them to call it off. When two large unions refused to comply, the executive threatened to resign. By this tactic it momentarily succeeded in restoring its authority. It did not, however, resolve the deep cleavage that separated it from such radical union leaders as Landler and Béla Vágó.

Significantly, the socialists' friend Vázsonyi, who was now minister of justice, had led the attack against the pro-Bolshevik underground and had topped the arrests with even stricter press censorship. But the social-revolutionary illusions inspired by Lenin's coup and the democratic pacifism of President Wilson's Fourteen Points fueled the flames of radical leftism, which in turn exploited the disillusionment of a war-weary populace. A signal instance of spreading unrest was the short-lived sailors' mutiny at the Austro-Hungarian naval base at Cattaro (now Kotor), in the course of which the red flag of revolution was flown by the rebels.

The arrests did not stop the Revolutionary Socialists, now headed by Korvin, who had managed to escape arrest, from sustaining a vitriolic leaflet campaign that heralded a proletarian revolution and called for the formation of a Budapest Workers' Council. Sensing the precariousness of their posture of collaboration, the SDP leaders called for an extraordinary congress on 10 February. A proposal at that congress to sever the party's links with the Vázsonyi and Károlyi groups earned them a vote of confidence. The timing of this submission to the militant left's demands was not without irony, for it coincided with the Károlyi party's withdrawal from the government and its open advocacy of a separate peace. In May a new police raid swept up some fifty syndicalists and members of the Revolutionary Socialists, but not the slippery Korvin. For the time being, the radical surge had been halted. A second major strike broke out on 22 June. Initiated by Landler's railway workers' union after a clash between troops and railway factory workers demanding wage increases, the strike was endorsed by the SDP executive but called off five days later when the government promised to investigate the incident and the grievances. The radicals were not pacified, however, for the compromise left Landler and other instigators in jail.

With the inevitability of defeat increasingly apparent, and the negotiation of a separate peace improbable, power in parliament shifted to the uncompromising forces of Count István Tisza. The disintegration of the empire was foreshadowed by the appearance of national secessionist bodies, notably (in July) the Czech National Council, in Prague. Critical food and fuel shortages, runaway inflation, speculation, and widespread desertion were other symptoms of impending collapse. The socialists campaigned for the release of political prisoners (they did win Landler's freedom) and, anticipating major political changes, held a party congress on 13 October. Acting as the centrist leadership's chief spokesman, Kunfi dismissed the strategy of "all power to soldiers', workers' and peasants' councils" as unsuited to Hungarian circumstances. The party, he argued, was not strong enough to impose its program unilaterally, and should therefore pursue a renewed alliance with the liberal parties, an alliance in which it would now lead rather than follow. Rejecting the device of personal union, he called for an independent Hungary, raising the possibility of federation as a means of assuaging the hostility of the minorities and preserving the country's territorial integrity. Socialization of the means of production he regarded as a long-term objective. Some delegates demurred, urging the creation of workers' councils and immediate and extensive political and economic reforms. Landler challenged Kunfi's depreciation of the socialists' strength and, without rejecting outright the option of collaborating with the liberal parties, called for unstinting battle against all parties not accepting the SDP's program. With this amendment, the leadership's proposals were endorsed by the congress.[9]

## THE KAROLYI REVOLUTION

By the end of October the Czechs, Slovaks, and Croats had all proclaimed their secession, and Count Tisza had admitted to parliament that "Károlyi was right": the war was lost, and he no longer opposed universal suffrage. King Karl hurried to Budapest to appoint a new and more conciliatory government. Such palliatives, however, could not halt the debacle. On 25 October the formation of a Hungarian National Council was announced by Károlyi, who included in the council not only his party but also the SDP and Jászi's National Radical Party. Installed at the Astoria Hotel, the council issued a proclamation calling for an immediate ceasefire; the election of a democratic government by universal, secret ballot; the freeing of political prisoners; land reform; measures to curb speculation; and the abolition of censorship (which in fact had already lapsed). On the critical minorities question, the council offered the forlorn promise of cultural and local administrative autonomy. The three parties regarded the proclamation as the program of their anticipated coalition government and requested Károlyi's appointment as prime minister.

Left-wing activists, including Landler, Korvin, and Béla Szántó, rallied to this countergovernment. An ad hoc Soldiers' Council came into being, as did a Budapest Workers' Council under the aegis of the SDP. The scent of revolution was in the air; even the state police threw in its lot with the National Council. When word spread of the impending arrival of loyalist troops, Korvin and other extremist elements launched a virtual armed uprising that caught even the National Council by surprise. Anarchy ruled as the streets teemed with disoriented but euphoric demonstrators. Many of them were soldiers who sported little chrysanthemums (called autumn roses in Hungary) in their gun barrels, giving rise to the name "revolution of autumn roses."

Still hoping to save the monarchy, the king on 31 October called on Károlyi to form a new government, and the socialists Garami and Kunfi were named, respectively, ministers of commerce and public welfare. The revolution—largely bloodless, with the notable exception of Tisza's murder—had triumphed.[10] The question of the monarchy, which was preferred in a constitutional variant by Károlyi's party but opposed by the republican socialists and radicals, was left to a future constitutional assembly. The new government hopefully declared the revolution concluded and called for order. However, the voices of republicanism were so vociferous—mainly in the capital, with the left-wing socialists loudest among them—that on 16 November, a few days after similar developments in Germany and Austria, the National Council proclaimed Hungary a republic.

**Coalition amidst Chaos.**   The initial revolutionary enthusiasm that gripped many Hungarians soon gave way to recognition that the problems facing the coalition regime were gigantic if not insurmountable. The attitude of the victorious Entente powers remained one of uncompromising hostility; Romanian, French, and Yugoslav armies advanced on Hungary from the east and the south. The overtures of Jászi, the new minister for national minorities, went unheard as the empire rapidly disintegrated into its national units. To most Magyar Hungarians military defeat was far less painful than the spectre of national and territorial truncation. The government's vicissitudes were in turn exploited by militant left-wing elements, a development that placed the SDP, in particular, in an increasingly difficult position. The moderate socialist leadership, having finally won a share of power, attempted to restrain the radical dissidents. Kunfi had appealed for a truce in the class war, and in establishing the Budapest Workers' Council the SDP leaders had attempted to exclude the more recently radicalized leftists.

The socialists also endorsed the government's decision not to publish a congratulatory message from the Russian Bolshevik regime. The telegram, sent on 3 November and signed by Lenin, Sverdlov, and Kamenev, greeted Hungary's workers, soldiers, and peasants, and enjoined them not to stop at the substitution of Hungarian for Austrian capitalist rule but to establish their own revolutionary government.[11] When agitation by the Revolutionary Socialists finally compelled the SDP daily *Népszava* to print the telegram, the editors appended a rejection of the "socialist republic" concept in favor of a consolidation of the new "people's republic" proclaimed two days earlier. The SDP leadership by and large shared the government's wish to restore order, a goal that, in the midst of anarchic conditions and sporadic outbursts by farm laborers and repatriated soldiers, could not be accomplished without forceful emergency measures. In these and other ways, after decades in the political wilderness, the socialists were earnestly seeking to establish their credentials for respectability and moderation. In the process, and almost by accident, the initiative slipped into the hands of a new breed of revolutionaries. For if Lenin's Bolsheviks had fathered Hungary's communists, the midwife that delivered them was the Social Democratic Party.

# 2. The Communist Party

The many irretrievable consequences of Europe's internecine quarrel, the Great War, can be viewed as either tragic or sublime, according to one's philosophical preconceptions. By creating conditions propitious for the Bolshevik Revolution, the war unleashed an international civil conflict that endures to this day. The most resounding external repercussion of that revolution occurred in Hungary, where domestic chaos made way for the first successful attempt at transplanting Lenin's marriage of Marxist theory and political power.

By 1917 the vast expanse of the tsarist empire held over half a million Hungarian prisoners of war as well as two million captives of other nationalities. Tens of thousands had already succumbed to the harsh climate and to the deprivations of the minimal existence that the prisoners shared with the indigenous masses. The rank and file spent their time working for the Russian war economy and thus came into contact with local socialists of all hues. In their camps the men were under the discipline of career officers, who were exempt from labor and showed little tolerance for socialist ideas and for those short-term officers who were socially inferior or, worst of all, Jewish. For those who were either (or both) and for the wretched rank and file who were already susceptible to the lure of socialism, the burgeoning revolution would serve both as an inspiration and as an escape from the intolerance, hardships, and tedium of camp life.

## THE MAKING OF A REVOLUTIONARY

The most famous Hungarian graduate of the Bolshevik Revolution, Béla Kun, was born in 1886 in the small Transylvanian village of Szilágycsehi, the son of a Jewish clerk. A good student, Kun acquired an early taste for socialist ideas and joined the SDP at the age of sixteen. He pursued a journalistic career that led him to Budapest. When he failed to get a staff job with *Népszava* he returned to Kolozsvár (now Cluj), the scene of his early career, to work in the workers' insurance office while continuing with part-time socialist journalism.

When war came Kun was drafted. He reached the rank of reserve lieutenant before being captured in early 1916 and sent to a prisoner-of-war camp near Tomsk. There he met old socialist friends and made new ones, notably Ferenc Münnich from the SDP organization of Kassa (now Košice) in northeast Hungary. With them he began to study Marx and Engels and to learn Russian. In the spring of 1917 Kun, Münnich, and another socialist, Ernő Seidler, seized the occasion of a clash in the Tomsk camp over the unequitable distribution of Red Cross parcels to agitate for a more representative system of self-administration. They were disciplined by an officers' court. In April Kun made an overture to the Tomsk branch of the Russian Social Democratic Workers' party, inflating his past party status and signing himself "president" of the Kolozsvár Workers' Insurance Bureau. Granted freedom to move beyond the confines of the camp, Kun and his friends joined the Bolsheviks in May and acquired administrative and agitprop functions over his fellow prisoners. He also wrote a series of simplistic articles for the Tomsk socialist paper hailing Lenin's revolutionaries and anticipating the spread of proletarian revolution to Germany.[1]

Concurrently, in other camps, links were forged between the local Russian socialists, mainly the Bolsheviks, and Hungarian junior officers of a predominantly Jewish and socialist or Galileist background. Some of them shared in the early armed actions of the October Revolution and reached positions of leadership. Hundreds of others were galvanized by that event into enrolling in the various Bolshevik Red guard units. In Omsk, József Rabinovics, a former goldsmith who became a social democratic union organizer, and two comrades were named deputies to the city soviet and in February 1918 they founded the Hungarian International Social Democratic (Bolshevik) Party.[2]

In December 1917 Kun was ordered to Petrograd, where he served under Karl Radek in the international propaganda department of the People's Commissariat for Foreign Affairs and edited the Hungarian and German newssheets that propagated the Bolshevik peace program among both prisoners of war and the enemy armies during the Brest-Litovsk negotiations. He soon became a leading figure in the recruitment of Hungarians to the Bolshevik cause and in coordinating the work of the various ad hoc prisoner-of-war organizations. His Hungarian Bolshevik team in Petrograd and later in Moscow included Endre Rudnyánszky, a former lawyer and cavalry officer who had married Bukharin's sister; Tibor Szamuely, a young firebrand socialist journalist; Károly Vántus, a more moderate trade union and SDP functionary; Rabinovics, Münnich, and a few others. The hyperactive Kun impressed Lenin and his associates with tireless organizational work and journalistic skills. He also showed himself to be excessively forceful, overbearing, and, even in the circumstances, uncompromising: he sided with Bukharin for immediate world revolution against Lenin's prudent advocacy of the Brest-Litovsk peace.[3] This zealot's unprepossessing mien was depicted by the British diplomat Harold Nicolson on the occasion of the Smuts mission to Budapest in April 1919: "A little man of about 30; puffy white face and loose wet lips; shaven head; impression of red hair; shifty suspicious eyes; he has the face of a sulky and uncertain criminal.'"[4] The little man Kun was nevertheless to leave a big mark on history.

**A Party Is Born.** On 24 March 1918, ten days after the Moscow conference of so-called International Social Democratic Prisoners of War, a meeting chaired by Béla Kun founded the Hungarian section of the Russian Communist Party (Bolshevik—the first foreign group to take this step. Kun was chosen chairman of the section, Ernö Pór, a former SDP functionary, secretary, Szamuely commissar for military organization, and Rudnyánszky commissar for press and publications. The group thereupon addressed a formal request to the Central Committee for recognition, promising to disseminate communist ideas among the prisoners of war and in Hungary and to train agitators for dispatch to Hungary, where they would serve as liaison with the left wing social democrats.[5] (Initially, Kun and Szamuely also undertook to organize revolution in the United States through the Hungarian immigrant community.) The creation of this Hungarian revolutionary vanguard received Lenin's enthusiastic approval.[6]

While only a small minority of the Hungarian prisoners of war rallied to the red flag, by Soviet accounting they played a disproportionately large role in the revolution.[7] This was owing partly to the uncommonly effective activism of Kun's group, and partly to the relatively little practical effect in Hungarian prisoner-of-war camps of the Brest-Litovsk treaty's prohibition against agitation and propaganda. The Soviet leadership concentrated its revolutionary guns on Germany, but it was encouraged by Kun's group to regard Hungary also as a fertile field. The Hungarians earned their spurs by devoted service to the Bolshevik Revolution. The military exploits of Münnich and Máté Zalka, the contribution of Szamuely and students from the agitator school to the defeat of the leftist social revolutionary uprising in Moscow, the election of Kun to the presidency of the Bolsheviks' Federation of Foreign Sections—all testify to their prominence.[8]

The Hungarian section established agitator schools in Moscow and Omsk to train former socialists for agitprop and officers and noncoms for service with the Red Army. By November 1918 some five hundred liberated prisoners had passed through these crash courses, which included both basic Marxism and field practice. Apart from the creation of this instant communist elite, the Hungarian group devoted great energy, notably through Szamuely's diatribes in their journal *Szociális Forradalom* (Social Revolution), to indoctrinate the mass of prisoners of war and incite them to revolutionary action against their government and the prevailing social system. Meanwhile, through the summer and early fall of 1918, Kun elaborated his views on the prospects for revolution in Hungary. He concluded that conditions did not allow for peaceful change. The bourgeois regime would be forced to resort to force to repress the workers' dissatisfaction. As in Russia, this would lead to a disintegration of the regime's authority, to the assumption of power by the armed proletariat, and to the completion of social revolution under the latter's dictatorship. Such a revolution would entail wholesale nationalization, including that of agricultural land, and the adoption of the political principles of the new Russian Soviet constitution.[9] The leading figures in the Hungarian section, Kun, Szamuely, and Rudnyánszky, were close to Bukharin and Radek and shared their anticipation of immediate revolution in the west. They also maintained contact with Lenin, who was informed by Szamuely that cooperation with the Hungarian social democrats would be impossible.[10]

All signs were pointing to the imminent collapse of the Austro-Hungarian monarchy when the Hungarian section met at Moscow's Hotel Dresden on 25 October. The time for revolution and armed uprising had arrived, declared Kun, and a Communist Party of Hungary modeled on the Russian party had to be established.[11] The Károlyi revolution opened up new possibilities, and Kun found a ready analogy in the Russian experience. He wrote in *Pravda* at the end of October that "the masses may not immediately find the straight road," but he compared Károlyi to Kerensky in predicting that "Hungarian opportunism will soon get its own October."[12] An enlarged meeting reconvened on 4 November and instructed all Hungarian members of the Russian party to "leave the territory of the Russian Soviet Republic as soon as possible and place their strength in the service of international revolution in Hungary." It proclaimed the creation of the Communist Party of Hungary (Kommunisták Magyarországi Pártja, or CPH) as an integral part of the "international communist party." The meeting chose a nine-man Central Committee that included Kun, Pór, Vántus, and representatives of the Slovakian, Romanian, and southern Slav communists. It also chose a seven-man External Committee under Rudnyánszky to serve as the Moscow link when Kun returned to Hungary. Rudnyánszky succeeded Kun as president of the Federation of Foreign Sections when the latter left Moscow.[13]

In the course of November some two hundred communists drifted back to Hungary in small groups, bringing with them their newly acquired revolutionary skills and a conviction that they were following the iron laws of history. Disguised as a repatriated army surgeon, and carrying a large sum of money, Kun arrived in Budapest around 17 November.[14] The socialist functionary turned professional revolutionary was on the road to power.

## DILEMMAS OF LIBERALISM

The returning Bolshevik agitators were momentarily the least of the problems confronting Károlyi's liberal democratic regime. Its peaceful accession to power had been facilitated by the collapse of the old order and the readiness of much of the population to welcome far-reaching domestic reforms. However, fulfillment of this mandate depended in large measure on time and a normalization of Hungary's international status. In the event, neither condition obtained. The Entente powers' minor allies, namely, the Romanians, Czechs, and south Slavs, were all impatient to settle old scores with their former masters and to establish or expand their nation-states. The Belgrade armistice, signed by Károlyi on 13 November, placed under foreign control half of Hungary's territory. As winter approached, tens of thousands of repatriated soldiers and refugees from the occupied areas accentuated the already critical food shortage caused by inadequate transportation. The fuel problem was equally critical, since Hungary had lost four-fifths of her coal mines to what became known as the successor states.

There was, moreover, a multiplicity of more-or-less competing centers of power. In practice, the coalition government shared administrative authority with its progenitor the National Council, with the Budapest Soldiers' Council, which was led by József Pogány and other radical officers, and with the Budapest Workers' Council. The SDP's nominal rule over the last two organizations and its one-million-strong trade union constituency made it momentarily the sole organized political force in Hungary, and the only one with potentially useful foreign connections. The moderate socialist leadership chose not to exploit its new power unilaterally but to pursue close collaboration with the liberal aristocrats and middle-class elements in Károlyi's government. Nevertheless, the vacuum left by the abdication of the old regime could not be rapidly and adequately filled by this inexperienced and ideologically heterodox group.

The government's initial program envisioned national independence, electoral and land reform, protection of basic freedoms, and a more equitable distribution of wealth. Acceptance of what were basically bourgeois liberal reforms implied a certain compromise of socialist principles, however, and it alienated the leftists from the SDP leadership. Within the party itself the left wing was led by Landler, Pogány, Nyisztor, and Jenő Hamburger, the last-named a doctor who had been jailed briefly for antiwar agitation. Other radicals like Alpári, Rudas, and János Hirossik (formerly a construction worker, now an editor and union organizer) had earlier severed their links with the SDP but remained uncertain as to alternative routes. The Revolutionary Socialists' antiwar passion dissipated with the armistice, but their syndicalist orientation led them to pursue the goal of workers' councils and of radical land reform. Heading in the same direction was the small band of young intellectuals of the Galileo Circle, Korvin, Lékai, and Sallai being the most radical among them. These various extremist groups, united in their dissatisfaction at the moderation of the Károlyi coalition, were groping for more revolutionary courses of action. At the initiative of Rudas and Hirossik a secret meeting of some fifty leftists was held on 17 November. The compromises made by the SDP leadership were roundly denounced, but Rudas's proposal for a new political organization was greeted with general reserve. It was agreed simply to form a radical debating circle named after Ervin Szabó, who had died in September.[15] The old concern with the preservation of working-class unity was still strong and the left radicals, at least in the short run, were not prepared to endanger the SDP's newly won political status.

**The Communists in Hungary.**   The energetic Kun arrived in the midst of this chaos like a whirlwind. Armed with the prestige of his Bolshevik experience and with a simple and purposeful plan of action, he exerted himself to draw the more radical leftists to his new party. He met in coffee houses with Béla Vágó and other socialist dissidents (taking time out on 19 November to carry a message from Lenin to Adler in Vienna), rallied the repatriated graduates of the agitator schools, and sought to forestall alternative organizing initiatives. "These were wonderful days of negotiations," he has recalled, but it was "very difficult to convince the majority of the necessity of a party" against counterarguments favoring action within the SDP, and syndicalist preferences for trade union supremacy.[16]

Among Kun's earliest adherents were the idealistic young intellectuals Béla Fogarasi, József Lengyel, as well as Lukács and Révai. Persuasion, not to mention bribery in kind and promises of future high office, induced a few syndicalist shop stewards to throw in their lot with the communists. Kun held what he must have known would be fruitless discussions with such moderate SDP leaders as Kunfi and Weltner. Later, after the fusion of the two parties, he would claim that "our goal was not the party, but the liberation of the class" and that "if unified revolutionary action had been possible four months ago within a unified Social Democratic Party . . . we old fighters of the old SDP would not have seceded."[17] The gap between Kun's Leninism and internationalism and the prudent socialism and patriotism that predominated in the SDP was insurmountable; Kun was already committed to the creation of a truly revolutionary party.

On 24 November, in a private apartment in Buda, a conference of repatriated communists and local leftists acceded, without a vote but not without reservations, to Kun's urging that the CPH be established.[18] The precise composition of the Central Committee chosen at that meeting is uncertain, and in any case it underwent repeated changes. It included the repatriated Bolsheviks Kun (as chairman), Vántus, and probably György Nánássy, a young agitator school graduate who later became a police informer and fled the country. Subsequently coopted were Seidler, Rabinovics, Pór, Ferenc Jancsik (an active Bolshevik and union organizer), Szamuely after his return from missions to Switzerland and Germany on behalf of the Russian party. Also elected were Korvin and such left-wing socialists as Vágó and Szántó. Of twelve certain members (including Szamuely) and nine probable ones, eight had some Russian experience, and most had been active in the SDP.[19] The majority, excluding such less certain quantities as shop stewards and intellectuals of the Lukács variety, were political activists of proven ability. They were a predominantly youthful group, ranging in age from twenty-four (Korvin) to forty (the social democrat lawyer Jenő László), and mostly Jews. After the heady days of power, fewer than half would die peaceful deaths. Eight, including Kun, fell victim to Stalin's purges; Korvin and László were executed, and Szamuely committed suicide.

The CPH made its official public appearance with the first issue of *Vörös Ujság* (Red Gazette) on 7 December. "Capitalism is ripe for its downfall," began the lead article. The SDP had betrayed the proletariat by allying itself with the bourgeoisie and claiming that the revolution had been won. "This," the article continued, "is why we communists present ourselves to the Hungarian workers, to prepare them for the inevitably forthcoming, indeed already present new proletarian revolution." The party would detach the workers from the ruling classes and lead them in the struggle for international proletarian revolution in alliance with Russia's Bolsheviks.

The immediacy of revolution and the practical bent of the CPH leaders precluded a more rigorous Marxian analysis of the situation. Kun's retrospective views on the class power basis of the Károlyi regime would undergo some change over time. In 1920 he would write that the government's nonsocialist parties "represented not special class interests but the private property system in general." Later he would identify finance capital as the power behind the regime.[20] In December 1918 he contented himself with the belief that he was predestined to lead the proletariat to power, and that the moment for bold action had arrived.

The communist strategy was simple enough: to undermine the already precarious stability of the coalition government, particularly the position of the social democrats and their hold over the industrial workers, and to build up strength for the proletarian revolution that Kun and his comrades confidently regarded as imminent not only in Hungary but throughout Europe. For tactics, they applied their Bolshevik experience in party organization and recruitment, in carefully devised and differentiated propaganda, in the infiltration of mass organizations susceptible to radicalization, and in the mobilization of apparent mass pressures to weaken the regime's authority. On the burning patriotic issue of the day they could offer little comfort. Their agitators were instructed to denounce as social chauvinism the SDP's inclination to defend territorial integrity; instead, they were to stress the "total internationalism" of the communist program.[21] Doubting, with some justification, whether it could achieve victory by peaceful means, the party began to purchase and stockpile arms and gird for civil war.

As convinced internationalists the communist leaders considered Hungary to be only one of many interconnected battlefronts. A courier service maintained the link with Moscow, so that Lenin and his associates regularly received news from Kun and from his intermediary Rudnyánszky. They in turn sent advice and substantial sums of money to the fledgling Hungarian party and used the latter's services for communicating with the Austrian party. Before his return to Hungary on 3 January 1919, Szamuely had attended the German Communist Party's founding congress and had conferred with Karl Liebknecht and Rosa Luxemburg. The Germans provided additional financial assistance. Rudnyánszky represented the CPH at the Comintern founding congress (Kun had dispatched Rudas, but he arrived too late), which was delayed until March 1919 because of the crushing of the Spartacus uprising, and the Hungarian party was honored with membership on its Executive Committee.[22] From the vantage point of Moscow, Kun's party was an integral and important part of the revolutionary wave sweeping Central Europe.

**The Building of a Party.** From the start, according to Kun, the CPH adopted the Bolshevik model of a closed, centralized party. In the event, the building of a fully developed vanguard party was aborted by fusion with the socialists and accession to power, and up to that point the party functioned primarily as a propaganda organization.[23] The interim organizational statutes, published in *Vörös Ujság* on 28 December, restricted membership to physical workers and landless peasants (with provision for exceptions nominated by two members) and required members to pay dues, subscribe to *Vörös Ujság*, establish local cells, and strictly obey central instructions. It provided for district and factory committees while assigning executive powers to the Central Committee until a party congress could be held.

Within a few weeks the party had set up an elaborate central organization and eventually managed to expand beyond Budapest to a few provincial cities and mining centers. For security reasons the full Central Committee met for only brief and furtive sessions, leaving individual members and sections of the committee with wide latitude in the discharge of their special responsibilities. The secretariat, with a few paid employees, was directed by Korvin.[24] Compared to its orthodox political competitors, even this modest conspiratorial machine would prove highly effective in pursuing the main task of agitation and propaganda.

The members of the fledgling party were instructed to adopt the "snowball" system of recruitment: each of them was to draw eight to ten susceptible colleagues into a cell, and each new member was to continue the process. At the same time, the Central Committee warned against massive recruitment, insisting on convinced and conscious revolutionaries. In fact, the organizational statutes' membership qualifications were not rigidly applied, and the membership reportedly reached some ten thousand by January 1919.[25] The principal targets for both recruitment and radicalization were the trade unions in heavy industry around Budapest and the miners and steelworkers of the Miskolc-Salgótarján area, in the northeast, and of western Hungary. Other targets were the Budapest Soldiers' Council and the associations of noncommissioned officers, war veterans, and disabled soldiers. An "association of the unemployed" came into being largely on communist initiative. Radical youth and lumpenproletariat elements were also fertile fields for recruitment.

All these groups had grievances or weaknesses that invited selective exploitation. The more militant union members had become disillusioned over the years with the SDP's cautious tactics, but the majority of organized labor and their leaders were largely satisfied by the political influence and collective agreements secured under the Károlyi regime. The accommodation of organized labor to a reformed capitalist economy was regarded by the socialist-unionist leadership as a far more realistic step than insistence on immediate socialization. Among the communists a minority favored boycott of the unions (citing as precedent the decision of the German communists at their December 1918 congress), but Kun argued successfully for infiltration and subversion of the emerging "industrial truce." The communists fought a stiff and initially successful battle to win permission for members of the key metalworkers' union to join their party. Through December communist cells were organized in several other old unions, but they constituted in all cases a small minority. In some of the newer unions they managed to acquire greater influence. Szántó became president of the office clerks' association, whose central committee also included Korvin and Vágó.[26] The latter also headed the communist faction in the Budapest Workers' Council.

The head of the Budapest Soldiers' Council, the demagogic József Pogány, regarded the CPH as superfluous but pursued a similar line of opposition to the government. Meanwhile, Szántó and other communists concentrated on the returning soldiers and managed to recruit a few hundred among them. The party won most influence with the most dissatisfied and volatile elements, namely, the war cripples, the unemployed, and the demobilized noncommissioned officers' organizations. The SDP-inspired National Federation of Working Youth, founded on 30 November, fell under communist control within a few weeks thanks to the agitation and manipulation of young Lékai (who had earlier made an unsuccessful attempt to assassinate Tisza) and other communists.

The radical intelligentsia was courted through lectures, seminars, and the party's theoretical journal *Internationale.* The historic significance of the Bolshevik Revolution, the superiority of Lenin's proletarian internationalism over the currently prominent Wilsonian principles of national self-determination, and, in general, the ethical and economic aspects of communism were earnestly propagated by Kun and his more intellectual comrades, such as Lukács and Fogarasi, and eventually taken up by sympathizers such as the socialist economist Jenő Varga. Many radical and anarcho-syndicalist intellectuals, notably a group around the artist-writer Lajos Kassák and his review *MA* (Today), responded with some enthusiasm to the call for a purifying revolution, but few among them submitted to party discipline.

**Communist Tactics.** Despite its small numbers, the party succeeded in imposing its presence with a veritable deluge of pamphlets, public orations, and impromptu or staged street-corner debates. The indefatigable Kun delivered up to twenty speeches a day while other Bolshevik-trained agitators fanned out to carry the message of revolution. "There was hardly a worker," recalled Révai with some accuracy, "who was not at some time and in some way exposed to communist propaganda."[27] All this feverish agitation brought relatively few converts to the Bolshevik creed, but in the prevailing conditions of political, social, and economic chaos it served to accentuate tensions and imprint on the public's consciousness at least the possibility of the revolutionary alternative that was sweeping their neighbor to the east.

The communists' appearance on the Hungarian political stage was regarded with alarm not only by Károlyi and his liberal reformers but also by the SDP leadership. Even the left opposition within the SDP, including Landler, Nyisztor, and Hamburger, regarded the creation of a competing party with disapproval, although they sympathized with some of its radical objectives. By the end of November the government decided to increase its vigilance over the CPH. Kunfi reported to the cabinet that he had promised Kun there would be no police persecution if the communists kept their activities within legal bounds. He added—somewhat disingenuously—that if continued SDP participation in the coalition tied the government's hands in the fight against extremists, the socialist ministers could formally withdraw.[28]

The communists meanwhile exploited the potential for institutional conflict by infiltrating the Workers' Council, which had 365 members and was dominated by the SDP. Vágó's small faction managed to introduce the CPH's policy alternatives into the council's debates. Against the socialist compromise proposal for a limited redistribution of land with compensation, the communists, while making a tactical allowance for the retention of small private farms, advocated expropriation and the organization of the rural proletariat into councils. Another communist campaign was for so-called democratization of the factory workers' councils, which were under firm SDP control and included few representatives of the more radical persuasion. An early communist tactic was to demand supervision of production by the factory councils. In a few instances, notably at the huge Manfred Weiss steel works, the communists did succeed in engineering the seizure of control from management. By these tactics, coupled with proposals to improve wages and welfare benefits, the communists strived to radicalize the council against the socialist leadership's necessarily more responsible pursuit of reforms within the government.

As economic conditions worsened, Kun stepped up his agitation. On Christmas Day, 1918, bands of demobilized soldiers went on the rampage in Budapest. As the year drew to a close Kun, accompanied by communist soldiers, made the rounds of army barracks (at one he was shot at and momentarily put under arrest) calling for "all power over the troops to the Soldiers' Council." Their immediate target was the conservative Count Sándor Festetics, Károlyi's brother-in-law, who had just been appointed minister of defense and was making secret plans for a military strike against the communists. Thanks to its exposure in *Vörös Ujság* and a show of force by Pogány's Soldiers' Council, the scheme misfired and Festetics was replaced.[29] However, when in January 1919 communist-led miners took over the mines at Salgótarján, the government's reaction was vigorous indeed. It declared martial law in the district and dispatched the SDP secretary of the miners' union, Károly Peyer, to restore order, which he did, at a cost of at least sixteen lives.

Domestic unrest remained less of a problem for the beleaguered Károlyi regime than the progressive occupation of Hungarian territory by French and allied armies. The Entente powers' disdain for Hungary as an enemy state and their distaste for the burgeoning left-wing radicalism were strengthened by the influence of the successor state lobbies with Clemenceau and the British. The Czechs were the most forceful in arguing that military occupation of Hungary had rendered superfluous the democratic preconditions of Wilsonian self-determination. While pitiful waves of refugees streamed into Budapest, Károlyi desperately pursued both a tolerable peace settlement and the containment of internal dissent, the latter now including pressure from conservative officers and politicians appalled at the spread of anarchy.

## THE COLLAPSE OF LIBERALISM

On 5 January Kun wrote to Lenin asking for money and warning that "in all probability an exclusively social democratic government will be formed in the next few days, which will mean that during their rule the counterrevolution will rise against us."[30] Indeed, Károlyi had told the socialists that without their support the government could not withstand the conflicting pressures from left and right and restore order. The SDP executive, meeting on 7 January in an atmosphere of crisis, split on the question. Garami argued for a temporary withdrawal from the government while assuring it of socialist support; Pogány and other left-wingers advocated an SDP takeover. The SDP's options, as presented by Károlyi, were to either assume the reins of government or remain in the coalition and accept two more portfolios. That day's issue of *Vörös Ujság* thundered that the "only way to avoid [a fratricidal struggle] is to separate reformists from the followers of the revolution. . . . Let us choose!"

The divided socialist leadership put the alternatives before the Budapest Workers' Council the following day. The case for a purely socialist government was presented by Garbai and endorsed by Vágó, who also called however for rule by councils. Garami stuck to his belief that Hungary was not ripe for socialism and urged that, in preparation for the planned election, the socialists win back those seduced by Bolshevism. The meeting initially endorsed Garbai's proposal, but the latter demurred in light of the small majority and threw his support behind a compromise proposal by Kunfi that the party ask for the additional portfolios of interior and defense. Although the council finally adopted this compromise, the divisions within the leadership and the council itself testified to the radicalizing impact of the communists. The latter had also instigated a delegates' petition for a joint commission to resolve the two parties' differences. Despite the leadership's veto this too indicated the remarkable self-assertion of the minuscule CPH.[31]

On 5 and 6 January the Spartacus Revolt suddenly erupted in Berlin and was as suddenly liquidated. Liebknecht and Luxemburg were killed. These events may have provided an additional impulse for the SDP leadership to remain in the coalition. With socialist participation assured, the government was reorganized on 18 January under the premiership of Dénes Berinkey. Károlyi was named provisional president and remained effectively in command. Although the interior portfolio was withheld from the socialists, they did increase their representation: Vilmos Böhm got defense, Kunfi education, Gyula Peidl public welfare, and Garami, as before, commerce. The struggle against the communists became progressively more overt and bitter.

On 22 January the CPH issued a call for a rent strike. In the event, the initiative was followed in all of ten buildings, but the government responded with a general rent reduction. Public demonstrations by the unemployed, refugees, disabled soldiers, and students, often under communist guidance, became an almost daily occurrence. Mobs wrecked the offices of two newspapers which had denounced communist agitation. In the factories, communist-instigated wage demands and seizures hampered production. As Rudas would report to the Comintern, the party tried to exploit the most immediate and concrete difficulties in order to demonstrate the impotence of the crumbling capitalist system.[32]

Despite these successes in fomenting unrest, the Central Committee had to recognize that the socialist-bourgeois coalition was gradually entrenching itself.

Indeed, it seemed likely to emerge from the general elections with a strong mandate, in which case the new government, backed by the burgeoning conservative associations, would not suffer the communists' rampages for long. Already on 28 January the SDP leadership had won the Workers' Council's approval to expel Vágó's faction, and the decision was immediately implemented, by force. New legislation was prepared with a view to curtailing the excesses of the factory workers' councils.

**The Communists under Attack.**   "I will handle things firmly in a Marxist manner," Kun had assured Lenin in early January. There would be no putsch of any kind, he added; when the Hungarian communists seized power, no one would be able to take it away from them.[33] Yet a month later the party in some desperation launched a frontal assault that culminated, on 3 February, in *Vörös Ujság's* absurdly premature call for "all power to the councils of workers', soldiers', and poor peasants' deputies." Identifying the government with counterrevolution, the CPH invited the proletariat to take up arms. The newsprint distribution center, under Garami's jurisdiction, had already tried to withhold supplies from the communist paper; now the police raided its editorial offices. Six days later the socialists called an extraordinary party congress which approved a resolution to purge communists from the SDP and the trade unions (the resolution was amended, on a motion by Landler and Pogány, to request a purely social democratic administration if the government failed to repel the counterrevolutionary challenge from the right). The communists fought these attempts to isolate them; party members were instructed to avoid any clash with trade union leaders that might provide a pretext for their exclusion.[34] In the event, the more exposed communists—notably in the metalworkers' union— were expelled but there followed no wholesale purge of the unions.

The conservative reaction was most evident in the countryside. Impatience at the government's procrastination with land reform had led to a rash of spontaneous seizures of land by poor peasants. The aroused rural gentry responded to the threat of revolution and the government's leftward slide by raising local militias and, notably in the city of Székesfehérvár, by seizing local administration. The coalition parties and the Budapest Workers' Council had endorsed the basic principles of limiting the size of landholdings and of compensating dispossessed owners. After much debate the land reform bill was promulgated on 16 February. A week later, amidst great publicity, Károlyi himself launched the redistribution on his estate at Kápolna. His example inspired little enthusiasm among other landowners, most of whom diffidently divested themselves of their least productive acres.

The countermeasures of the government and the SDP were already impelling the communists to retrench when on 20 February the opportunity for a decisive strike against the latter presented itself. After being harangued by Kun before the offices of *Vörös Ujság*, a mob of jobless demonstrators proceeded to the *Népszava* building to protest the socialist paper's hostile reporting. On their way they met a police cordon and shots were exchanged. Most of the fatalities were policemen, but the CPH immediately disclaimed any responsibility for the outrage and blamed agents provocateurs. Whatever the truth, the government that same night ordered the arrest of the communist leadership. By the end of February fifty-five communists had been detained and warrants issued for twenty more; other known communists were kept under close observation. The SDP endorsed these measures and staged a show of strength: at a mass meeting of several hundred thousand before the parliament building the communists were roundly excoriated. Even the left-wing socialists approved of the arrests, although they also seized the opportunity to press new demands on the leadership, Pogány calling for a purge of the military, Varga for nationalization, and Hamburger and Nyisztor for the collectivization of agriculture.

In jail Kun was repeatedly interrogated and beaten. He refused to divulge his party's secrets, but his comrade Nánássy told all. Press reports of police brutality did arouse some public sympathy, notably among the Galileists, who held a protest rally and successfully lobbied Károlyi for an investigation. Wrote Lukács in a flier: "This is all in vain. Truth is on its way, and the persecution of its propagators can only speed its arrival."[35] The government had designed its forceful intervention partly to win sympathy from the Entente powers. For good measure it also confirmed its proscription of the leading right-wing organization, Magyar Országos Véderő Egyesület (Hungarian Association of National Defense, or MOVE), and interned a few prominent conservative notables, including a bishop. On 8 March, having apparently received from Lenin a threat of reprisals against Hungarian prisoners of war, Károlyi gave instructions that the detained communists be designated political prisoners and given preferential treatment, including the right to receive visitors. Thereupon Kun and his companions in captivity resumed their activities in relative comfort and turned the Gyüjtőfogház (collector jail) into the functioning headquarters of the CPH.[36]

While the socialist leadership invited communists at large to rally to the SDP, some left-wingers, Pogány among them, urged the government and the SDP to establish contact with the Russian regime and party. Moscow sent a telegram inviting the socialist leader Manó Buchinger, and a letter of recommendation was secured from the imprisoned Kun, but that was the end of it.[37] With the decimation of the party leadership many of the CPH organizations collapsed, while others survived in semilegality. Several competing central committees emerged. The authoritative second Central Committee, which included Fiedler and Lukács, at first considered liquidating the party, then decided to continue the struggle. In collaboration with the fugitive Szamuely it labored to revive party activity and managed to publish *Vörös Ujság* once again on 1 March. The Budapest area party groups, emboldened by the government's lenience, were meeting again by 8 March, disseminating leaflets and agitating in the streets.[38]

**Drift to Anarchy.** While the seemingly irrepressible communists returned to the fray, the seedlings of anarchy that they had nurtured began to develop an independent life. Through March land seizures and looting by farm laborers, led in some instances by radical socialists like Hamburger, occurred with increasing frequency. Concurrently workers' councils under leftist influence began to flex their muscles outside the capital. On 10 March the workers' council of Kaposvár seized power over the city and asked for recognition from the government. These disturbances bore little relation to the communist objective of a proletarian dictatorship, but they did challenge the authority of the government. The latter tried to still the unrest by appointing new, socialist district commissioners. At its meeting on 7 March the Budapest Workers' Council approved a motion by Varga calling for an investigation of the possibilities of socializing industry. Four days later the council proclaimed its support for the coalition until the elections, prompting *Vörös Ujság* to mock the socialist leftists. However, the SDP leadership was gradually drifting toward the conclusion that anarchy could not be stemmed without some understanding with the communists.

Kun had early on begged Landler and Hamburger—the most sympathetic socialists—to visit him in jail, but the first tentative contacts were made through the syndicalist worker Ignác Bogár on behalf of the metalworkers' union. At the latter's invitation Kun drafted a memorandum on 11 March setting out the communist position. After explaining the historical necessity for splitting the socialist movement and the "dialectic inevitability" of its eventual reunification, Kun spelled out his conditions. Among them were abandonment of class cooperation and of the policy of territorial integrity. His transitional steps to socialism included a centralized republic of councils instead of a parliamentary republic; a class army of the proletariat; the expropriation, without redistribution, of all land in favor of the state (even agricultural cooperatives would have to be regarded as a "short-term temporary phenomenon"); the nationalization of banks and confiscation of deposits; the socialization of industry, transportation, foreign trade, and wholesale commerce; immediate implementation of the SDP's social welfare program; and the secularization of schools. Kun called for a conference of "revolutionary elements" to adopt this program and join the Comintern. He proudly admitted having received financial aid from Lenin and the German Spartacists and concluded pointedly that in Russia "it was not the Bolsheviks who embraced the Menshevik platform."[39]

By the time this letter was written, Kun and other imprisoned leaders were once again pulling the strings in the party; Szamuely's second Central Committee had been relegated to an implementing role.

Kun's matchless arrogance in demanding ideological surrender from the SDP stunned that party's moderate leaders, and its electoral proclamation, published on 13 March, was anything but conciliatory. It denounced the CPH's leaders as adventurers, its tiny membership as wretched rabble, and its goal as the "creation of a bitter world with wild barbarian methods, with murder and devastation." The socialist platform called for an exclusively SDP government to complete the land reform and carry out sweeping nationalization; on the minority question it voiced the hope that non-Magyar voters would opt for Hungary.[40] In a letter to one of his critics Károlyi allowed that "Bolshevism was never strong here" and speculated that the socialists might gain an electoral majority and use it against the communists.[41] On the other hand, there were widespread apprehensions that the emboldened socialists would seize power whatever the election's outcome. It was in protest against this prospect that the Radical Party withdrew from the campaign.

Faced with the hopelessness of Hungary's international situation, most politically conscious Hungarians were lapsing into a desperate fatalism. Some, however, reacted with an equally desperate lunge toward communist salvation. Strikes and demonstrations multiplied, some of them directed against the socialists. Among Kun's numerous visitors was a delegation of shop stewards who, on 16 March, promised to return within a week to liberate the communists, if necessary by force. The promise was endorsed at a mass meeting of steelworkers two days later. In an attempt to defuse the initiative the government released twenty-two of the less prominent communists on 19 March. In the meantime, the Central Committee had approved the plans for Kun's liberation. A leaflet was issued calling on all class-conscious proletarians to assemble before the parliament building on 23 March.[42] The communists were growing confident of their ability to rule the streets.

**The Entente's Ultimatum.** The coup de grace was delivered on the morning of 20 March by Colonel Vyx, the head of the Entente missions in Budapest.[43] The aide-memoire he handed to Károlyi arose from a 26 February ruling of the Paris peace conference that had been inspired, in all essentials, by the French general staff. It provided for a further advance by the Romanian army and for Hungarian evacuation and creation of a neutral zone under French and allied military supervision in the northern, eastern, and southern reaches of what remained of Hungary. Earlier, Károlyi had apparently brushed off Western suggestions that he participate in the anti-Bolshevik intervention, whereas the Romanians, in particular, were fully cooperative and expected their territorial demands to be fulfilled.[44] The Romanians were essential to the Entente's strategy against the Red Army, which in the Ukrainian theater was within 300 kilometers of the Hungarian frontier—a proximity that also excited the imagination of Kun's communists.

If the ultimatum was not accepted within a day, said Vyx, the Entente missions would leave Budapest, the implication being that more forceful measures might follow. The shattered Károlyi observed that the demands were politically impossible and that the Entente might as well occupy all of Hungary. Böhm, who was also present at this climactic interview, warned that the ultimatum could only serve the communists' interests, but the French messenger replied, unsympathetically but candidly, with the German phrase, *Das ist mir ganz egal* ("It's all the same to me").

At a meeting of the SDP leadership that afternoon, Böhm proposed that the party assume the reins of government. As a matter of strategic necessity, he argued, and in order to gather the entire country's support, it should conduct negotiations with the Bolsheviks and "conclude a pact under which the latter would, if only passively, support the government." The leftist Landler volunteered to serve as an intermediary, observing that he had already conferred with Kun, but a concrete decision was deferred pending that evening's cabinet meeting.

A tearful Károlyi reported to that gathering that "the Entente was organizing against the Bolsheviks. It will not declare war, but will use the Romanians, Serbs, and Czechs against them, for which it will pay mercenary wages with our territory. The Paris peace conference does not abide by Wilsonian principles. . . ." The government, he said, had therefore no choice but to resign and make room for a social democratic administration in order to avoid anarchy and Bolshevism. Károlyi's nominee for the premiership, the moderate Kunfi, suggested Vyx be warned that, if the Entente did not relent, a new socialist government would inevitably drift toward communism. The other ministers, however, were in too defeatist a mood to reconsider, and professed confidence in the capacity of the moderate social democrats. On Károlyi's motion, the cabinet thereupon resigned in protest at the Entente's dictate.[45]

Whatever the faults of Károlyi, and they included indecisiveness as well as a politically naive tolerance, conditions could not have been less propitious for the stabilization of a liberal democratic order. The heavy weight of an authoritarian political culture, the wild expectations of the underprivileged, the intoxicating revolutionary currents, the disastrous economic and political repercussions of war and defeat—all conspired against such an outcome. The government's collapse in face of the ultimatum left a political void that had to be filled. Kun's small band of Bolsheviks grabbed for power in the name of their own laws of history.

# 3. The Republic of Councils

The abdication of the Berinkey government left the social democratic leaders in a quandary. When they met on the morning of 21 March, Kunfi, Böhm, and Weltner voiced willingness to attempt the formation of a socialist government with implicit communist backing.[1] Garami, Buchinger, and Peidl were profoundly sceptical and refused to serve in any government based on an accord with the communists. Buchinger argued that the coalition should be revived and the Entente dictate fulfilled. Debate was raging when Landler appeared and reported excitedly that he had reached agreement with Kun.

It is not entirely clear whether Landler had informed the surprised Kun that the socialists were ready for a merger and the proclamation of the dictatorship of the proletariat, or whether Kun had merely been asked for passive support and had rejected that option. Nor does it appear that the delegation hurriedly dispatched to Kun's prison was armed with firm instructions. One of its members, Kunfi, proposed cooperation between the two parties rather than unification, but Kun remained adamant. (He wrote subsequently that such a coalition "would have fallen apart within two weeks, whereupon the dictatorship would also have collapsed.")[2] In any case, Kun behaved as if the socialists depended on him to assume power rather than the reverse, and his disconcerted interlocutors found themselves accepting his terms.

Probably, Kun's apparent revolutionary skills, his financial resources, and the promises of Russian assistance relayed by him were instrumental in securing socialist acquiescence. The differences were reduced to the name of the new party. Kun suggested retention of his own party's name, but it was finally agreed to use "Socialist Party of Hungary" pending a final ruling by the Comintern. The draft agreement, which was to be submitted to a joint meeting of the party executives later that day, declared that the new party would without delay "take over all powers in the name of the proletariat." It continued:

> The dictatorship of the proletariat is exercised by the workers', soldiers', and peasants' councils. Therefore the plans for parliamentary elections are naturally

abandoned. A class army of the proletariat must be raised without delay, removing all armed force from the hands of the bourgeoisie. To secure the rule of the proletariat and resist Entente imperialism, the fullest and most intimate armed and spiritual alliance must be established with the Soviet Russian government.[3]

The accord was not sealed without a certain fatalism on the part of the socialists. Their spokesman, Weltner, reportedly remarked that "we will make the dictatorship, and in two weeks we will give up the ghost and all be hanged. But at least we will not have destroyed one another."[4]

## THE DOMESTIC POLITICS OF THE COMMUNE

Kun and the Central Committee immediately set to the task of persuading their comrades of the necessity for the merger. Indeed, it was not easy to convince the more passionate revolutionaries such as Szamuely that accommodation with yesterday's enemies was tactically imperative. The merger, recalled Lukács years later, "aroused general dissatisfaction" among the communists. At a meeting of activists on the twenty-second, opposition to the merger, particularly among the younger zealots, was so vehement that another meeting had to be called four days later to extract obedience to the central ruling. "Even if not in open street battles, we have nevertheless won," insisted Kun.[5]

Party discipline and the lure of power prevailed, but many bewildered veterans would not fully reconcile themselves to such an unprincipled step. Szamuely, Révai, and other members of the second Central Committee had apparently been making plans, unknown to Kun, for an armed uprising in May. Their resentment at not being consulted in the interparty negotiations would fester and be only aggravated by Kun's subsequent tactical concessions at their expense in the new government. While the ultraleftist communists did not alter the course of the revolution, they would repeatedly mount overt and conspiratorial actions to steer the regime leftward. The departure from revolutionary precedent tortured Kun as well. On the morrow of the merger he confessed to Béla Szántó: "I could not sleep all night. I kept wondering where we made the mistake, because something is wrong here. It went too smoothly."[6]

While the two parties' leaders were formally ratifying the agreement, Pogány's Soldiers' Council also endorsed the change, assumed command over the Budapest police, occupied the collector jail, and dispatched armed bands throughout the capital to intimidate potential opponents. Szamuely emerged from hiding and marshaled the flood of communists at the party's Visegrád Street headquarters to key points such as the telephone exchange. In the evening the Budapest Workers' Council approved the merger, whereupon the SDP leadership convened to formally dissolve itself. When one socialist refused to take part in the compromise, Weltner burst out: "You madman, you want to leave these wild beasts on their own, they would destroy everything."[7]

The meeting, joined by Kun and his acolytes, agreed to create a Revolutionary Governing Council under the presidency of Sándor Garbai. Only two communists were named as people's commissars, Kun for foreign affairs and Vántus as one of four commissars for agriculture. The rest were socialists, mainly leftists like Pogány (defense), Landler (interior), and Varga (finance). However, nine out of thirteen deputy people's commissars were communist, including Lukács (for culture, under Kunfi, with whom he would have a difficult relationship), Szántó and Szamuely (defense), and a twenty-seven-year-old graduate of a Russian agitator school who would one day become Stalin's most devoted viceroy, Mátyás Rákosi (commerce). It was further agreed that the council would assume the unified party's leadership pending a congress. A single secretariat would administer the party's affairs. Böhm proposed that Károlyi remain as head of state, and indeed the latter was awaiting the call, but the communists would not hear of it and disseminated a falsified letter of resignation that Károlyi chose not to challenge.[8]

The first two decrees of the Revolutionary Governing Council instituted the death penalty for armed resistance and a total prohibition of alcohol consumption. After a day's absence newspapers reappeared carrying the proclamation, drafted by Kun and Pogány, of the proletarian dictatorship and the Republic of Councils. (The latter is often also referred to as the Soviet Republic or, more loosely, as the Commune.) It looked forward to the nationwide creation of councils; to the nationalization of large estates, industry, banks, and transportation; to the creation of a proletarian army for defense not only against Hungary's capitalists and landowners but also against "Romanian boyars and Czech bourgeois"; and to alliance with Russia's proletariat. Workers of the world were invited to join the struggle against international imperialism.[9]

Kun was realistic enough to recognize that his success in consolidating the dictatorship against internal and external enemies would depend in large measure on the progress of the "international proletarian revolution," whose prospects he however wildly overrated.[10] A circuitous wireless telegraph connection was established between Moscow and Budapest on the twenty-second, and Lenin, whose party was in the midst of its eighth congress, lost no time in sending a message of congratulations and received fraternal greetings in return. In his congressional address, Lenin mistakenly gave credit to the Hungarian bourgeoisie for recognizing the historical necessity of proletarian dictatorship. "The seed sown by the Russian revolution," he exulted, "is germinating in Europe." In a telegram to Kun on the twenty-third he warned against the indiscriminate imitation of Russian tactics but inquired: "What actual guarantees do you have that the new Hungarian government will be truly communist and not simply socialist, that is, one of social traitors?" Kun replied that the leftist and centrist socialists had accepted his platform, which accorded with Lenin's and Bukharin's theses. He added that his personal influence over the Revolutionary

Governing Council was such that the firm dictatorship of the proletariat was assured; the masses, too, were behind him.[11]

Daily wireless contact was maintained with the Russian commissar for foreign affairs, Chicherin, who found the Hungarians useful: they could inform him about developments in Central Europe, and they could transmit messages such as Lenin's greeting, on 7 April, to the short-lived Bavarian Soviet Republic. The link with Moscow was also served by couriers, who carried money as well as instructions. When, in May, Szamuely made an adventurous flying trip to Moscow, Rudnyánszky was appointed Hungary's ambassador. The Russians in their isolation rather overestimated Kun's utility; for instance, Chicherin telegraphed him on 6 April that he was "in a position to do much against the campaign of lies that is still raging against us."[12]

Kun needed little encouragement from Moscow to style himself the leading purveyor of revolution in the Danubian basin. He was hampered in this role, however, by the wave of nationalism that was sweeping the former ethnic minorities. The Hungarian communists tried to assist the sister parties in the surrounding areas. Within Hungary they promised local autonomy for the Slovak, Ruthenian, and German minorities within a Soviet-styled federal structure, but they could not overcome the more powerful pull of national particularism.[13] In Hungary itself, it was a nationalistic despair more than any other factor that brought about the collapse of the Károlyi regime. Even the socialists were far more susceptible to the patriotic call for territorial integrity than to the vague Marxist internationalism that they nominally subscribed to. Kun's communists had made the choice for international revolution over national interests, but in the weeks to come they too would have to dilute ideological purity for the sake of an essentially national military enterprise.

The international significance of the Hungarian coup was underscored by the appeal of the Comintern's Executive Committee to the workers of Europe, "In Paris the imperialist robbers are sharpening their knives to strike down the young Hungarian Republic of Councils." The future of other European revolutions hung in the balance: "Hurry, brothers, to the aid of the Hungarian workers and peasants."[14] Such appeals were futile but they impressed Kun. His best chance for a supporting revolution, he believed, lay in Vienna, where through his ambassador, Elek Bolgár, he provided the Austrian communists with propaganda and substantial financial assistance. The Austrian social democrats had chosen meanwhile to join the liberal coalition. Their leader, Victor Adler, sent a self-serving explanatory message to Hungary's proletariat claiming that he was a slave to the Entente, which controlled Vienna's food supply. In spite of this, Kun remained obsessed with the idea of an Austrian coup. On 27 March he told the Governing Council that such a coup would allow for the extension of the revolution to France's borders.[15] After Adler's disappointing response he set his hopes on the tiny Austrian communist party, which would ultimately be driven into a suicidal uprising by his emissary Ernő Bettelheim. In the meantime, some eighteen hundred Austrian communists were lured to Hungary to assist in the armed defense of the revolution and share in its spoils.

**Communists and Socialists.** Kun's reassurances to Lenin were valid insofar as they indicated his preeminent role in the Revolutionary Governing Council. Even there, however, he would have to accommodate himself to the apprehensions of the centrist socialists. And power at the apex did not provide the communists with effective control over the organization and membership in which their own party had become submerged. The alliance could not create even the impression of ideological unanimity, for the morning *Népszava* and the afternoon *Vörös Ujság* continued to represent the competing moderate and revolutionary orientations of the founding parties. In the new party secretariat the moderate socialists held sway despite the presence of Rabinovics and Hirossik. Its activity was largely propagandistic, and it failed to exercise systematic supervision over the local councils and the state administration. Compared to the affairs of state, the Budapest Workers' Council, and the Red Army, party matters enjoyed low priority. Left to his own devices to propagandize for the party, Rabinovics resorted to the recruitment of assorted zealots for an agitprop campaign that on balance only alienated the population. On one occasion he even dispatched sixty orthodox rabbinical students to preach socialism in the predominantly catholic city of Székesfehérvár.[16]

During the life of the Commune, the unified party's nominal membership rose from 800,000 to over 1.5 million (out of a territorial population of some nine million). This rapid expansion brought an inevitable dilution of the party's working-class character. Numerous new unions had come into being encompassing most occupations and social strata, and white-collar workers soon outnumbered the old trade union membership in the party.[17] The more radical communists, notably Révai, protested bitterly at the influx of "petty bourgeois fellow travellers" and appealed for "pure proletarian politics" even if, as Rabinovics conceded, the state might be compelled to make tactical concessions to the right.[18] The concurrent decline or disappearance of the various associations of unemployed and demobilized soldiers only further eroded the communists' organized constituency. They were more successful in retaining organizational if not ideological control over the merged youth organization, renamed the Hungarian Federation of Young Communist Workers (Kommunista Ifjúmunkások Magyarországi Szövetsége, or KIMSZ). The federation had some one hundred and twenty thousand members, most of them industrial and commercial apprentices whose cultural deprivations made them good revolutionary material. At its congress between 20 and 22 June Lukács exhorted the young delegates to adhere to an uncompromising line and set a "moral standard" for the revolution.[19]

The communists' failure to convert the party into a servant of their revolutionary ideology was most striking in that central component of the socialist movement, the trade unions. The old leadership of the Trades Council and of the majority of trade unions viewed the revolution with great reserve and resolutely excluded radical leftists from their ranks. They preserved an autonomous existence separate from the ruling group of government and party, and would exert a powerful anticommunist pressure that ultimately contributed to the collapse of the Commune. Many leftist communists, particularly the Szabó-inspired young intellectuals who predominated in the short-lived second Central Committee, would only strengthen this conservatism with their argument that the unions had become superfluous and should be liquidated, all power properly belonging to the workers' councils. Kun denounced such extreme and impolitic views but could not prevent clashes between the ultraleftists and the unions.[20]

From the very beginning, therefore, communist power rested on the fragile base of alliance with a predominantly moderate socialist movement. Among the latter's centrist leaders, Kunfi and Böhm were sincere advocates of the councils system and socialization, but others like Weltner and the old union bureaucrats were the most reluctant of partners in a revolution they regarded as doomed from the start. Meanwhile rightist socialist leaders like Garami simply withdrew from office and bided their time.

Initially the symbiotic alliance of Leninism and social democracy was abetted not only by radical socialists of Landler's ilk but also by such centrists as Kunfi and Böhm. From below, the more radical intellectuals, engineers, and industrial workers offered guarded support and awaited the fulfillment of their assorted vested interests. The rest of the population took cognizance of the lightning revolution in amazement tinged with fear at the real and rumored depredations of the communist "terror units" that roamed the capital. Following Budapest's example, old and new local councils, reinforced with communists, assumed full powers in the towns and villages. In the countryside, and particularly in Transdanubia (western Hungary), counterrevolutionary resistance simmered from the outset and would passively or actively subvert central authority. In the occupied areas, notably in Pozsony, in Szeged, and in Pécs, administered respectively by the Czechs, the French, and the Yugoslavs, the foreign military authorities made short shrift of attempts to form revolutionary directorates.

The Revolutionary Governing Council was a heterodox collection of communists whose competence lay mainly in agitprop and of socialists who generally possessed greater political realism and administrative or professional expertise. In order to strengthen the communists' position, Kun had the distinction between full and deputy commissars erased, and in the council reconstituted on 3 April thirteen of the thirty-four people's commissars were communist. To demonstrate his moderation, Kun did shift the violent and inflexible Szamuely to a nominal, less sensitive post in culture, and kept most other extremists out of the government. The social and occupational profile of the Governing Council was decidedly unproletarian. Only twelve were of working-class origin, and most of these had long ago abandoned physical labor for party or union office. The others were middle- or lower-middle-class professionals, intellectuals, and white-collar workers.[21]

The fact that over half the people's commissars were Jewish was only the tip of an iceberg that activated popular prejudices against what was perceived as the racial character of the revolutionary regime. Anti-Semitism in the years of the Dual Monarchy had been fed by a rapid influx of Jews, who became concentrated in the occupations most readily open to them—finance and commerce, the professions, certain trade union bureaucracies, and the retail trade. During the war, when new waves of Galician Jews streamed into Budapest and became identified in the popular mind with speculative small trade, Jews accounted for one-quarter of the capital's population. With the onset of revolution, the regime's urgent need for politically reliable public servants to supplant the old, conservative state administration was met in large part by the more adaptable and easily radicalized Jewish professionals, intellectuals, and lower-middle-class elements who felt perhaps the least attachment to the old order. The young fanatics in the communist political police and terror bands included a preponderance of Jews, who also figured prominently in all the regime's administrative, judicial, enforcement, and propagandistic spheres of activity, partly through the flagrant practice of nepotism. While this characteristic of the radical left was not unique to Hungary, the coincidence of its visibility and the latent anti-Semitism of the milieu gave rise to widespread rumors of a gigantic Jewish plot against the Hungarian nation. The Jewish factor palpably reduced the legitimacy of the regime and served the interests of the counterrevolution.[22]

**The Economic Revolution.**   Although the acquisition of power had been miraculously easy, Kun soon realized that professional revolutionaries did not necessarily possess the requisite skills for planning and administration. This was all the more galling because the socialists could draw on the services of enthusiastic experts in economics and other technical fields. As a stopgap, Kun urgently cabled Chicherin for a full set of the Russian regime's legislation.[23] Kun's reading of Marx and of the Russian Bolsheviks' early measures led him and the more radical socialists to the blithe assumption that Hungary was ripe for a socioeconomic transformation leading to communism. They appraised the government's wartime emergency measures as useful psychological conditioning of the populace for a planned economy.[24] Indeed, hardly had the proletarian dictatorship been proclaimed than a veritable deluge of decrees and regulations began to issue from the regime.[25]

The scheme for the comprehensive institution of a centrally planned economy was drawn up by Varga and two socialist engineers, Gyula Hevesi and József Kelen. The first decrees, replicating in some respects the concurrent "war communism" of the Russian regime, appeared on 25 March.[26] They covered the socialization of industry, banks, and transportation; the freezing of bank deposits; the nationalization of rental housing (with a rent reduction for small apartments); the seizure of food stocks; and the general right as well as obligation to gainful employment. There followed the imposition of state control over insurance companies, the requisitioning of gold, jewelry, works of art, and large apartments, and the extension of sickness and accident insurance. After protracted debate it was decided to temporarily set the lower limit of nationalization at enterprises with more than twenty employees. In many instances smaller concerns were spontaneously seized by their workers. Within a month some twenty-seven thousand industrial enterprises were socialized, leaving for the future the doctrinally required nationalization of the remaining mass of smaller producers. The country's precarious international status induced the government to forgo the nationalization of foreign-owned concerns, although these too were placed under the supervision of workers' councils.

This rapid series of measures received chaotic implementation. Pending the appointment of so-called production commissars, the socialized banks and factories fell under the supervision of their workers' councils. Employees in commerce and small industry were charged with overseeing their managers. A decree of 24 March, issued apparently by the impetuous Rákosi (a merchant's son who had earlier studied commerce on a scholarship), nationalized virtually all commercial establishments. The decree was almost immediately rescinded, but the ensuing massive inventory taking effectively paralyzed commerce. To Varga's protests Rákosi retorted impatiently: "You appointed me people's commissar because I knew how to shut down the shops. Now appoint someone else who knows how to reopen them, because I don't."[27] The impact of such arbitrary measures on the merchants was aggravated by numerous cases of theft by real or fake inspectors. Toward the end of the Commune plans were being drawn up for the consolidation of all retail trade into a cooperative network.

An intensive socialization program like the one attempted by the Republic of Councils would have led to at least temporary dislocation in the best of times. In the circumstances of 1919, it inevitably accentuated the economy's financial and productive weaknesses. Decrees could not replace careful central planning and direction. Eventually, the government established a People's Economic Council, to coordinate the work of the various related agencies, but this, like most of the regime's reforms, hardly had a chance to prove itself. In the meantime, productivity declined, not least because of the time-consuming conflicts between works councils, trade unions, and production commissars, all of whom were jealous of their uncertain prerogatives. The inaccessibility of essential raw materials in the occupied territories, the inclination of foreign firms to regard the Commune as transitory and untrustworthy, the eventual economic blockade by the Entente, and the already disorganized state of production also played their part in impeding recovery. At least equally significant was the unenthusiastic response, to the point of outright sabotage, of both the alienated owners and managers and much of the labor force. Many of the more radical workers were drawn into nonproductive political activities or into the Red Army. A new wage scale favoring the unskilled also undermined morale and productivity, while the general atmosphere of sustained crisis was hardly conducive to disciplined work. Although Kun and Varga subsequently claimed that these problems were on the way to being resolved, the temporary lapse of capitalism only accelerated the economic slump.

The challenge of simultaneously reforming and managing a war-worn and disrupted economy was complicated by the monetary situation. Because of the currency shortage, the Károlyi government had introduced "white money" (so named because it was printed on one side only), which was generally regarded as of little real value. The communists lacked the resources to create a stronger currency. The inflationary spiral was fed by the regime's politically motivated allocation of increases in workers' wages and other benefits, and by an acute shortage of goods, particularly foodstuffs in urban areas. Rationing, communal kitchens, barter, hoarding, and so-called bag trading by peasants was the order of the day. The government's inability to improve the standard of living dealt a heavy blow to its already limited prestige even among the favored proletariat.

The social welfare initiatives of the regime were essentially an extension of plans drawn up by its liberal democratic predecessor.[28] Already before the March revolution the workers had extracted sizeable wage increases from the Károlyi administration. Subsequently, the workers' councils expected and demanded even more from their self-appointed vanguard. As a result, the nominal value of wages grew by an average of 100 percent between the start of the first and the end of the second revolution. Real wages, however, grew hardly if at all. The eight-hour work day was introduced, along with compulsory health insurance; divorce was made easier; the equal rights of illegitimate children were affirmed; and a variety of benefits were allocated to working-class mothers and children.

The nationalization of apartment buildings and family houses was already an unpopular step, but it was outdone by what followed. Probably no other single measure aroused such horror among the middle classes as did the requisitioning of space in their homes for the proletariat. The first head of the central housing office was such a crude and aggressive communist that his replacement by Vágó and the ubiquitous Szamuely was regarded as a move toward moderation. Under this program, over one hundred thousand of the most ill-housed proletarians in Budapest became unsolicited tenants. The practice was extended to the towns and villages. Housing conditions for the mass of workers and the hordes of refugees were unquestionably pitiful, but the arbitrariness of this palliative, not to speak of the culture shock, struck deep.

Both communist and other postmortems have identified the republic's agrarian policy as a tactical mistake of catastrophic proportions.[29] The ruling elite of urban socialists and communists had little understanding of the economic and social dimensions of agriculture. Their ideological preconceptions led them to ignore the signals that redistribution was the poor peasants' deepest desire. In the first days of the revolution even the Russian Bolshevik press anticipated that redistribution would be the regime's line of reform. Kun, however, had been misled by the rash of land seizures. On 27 March he called for nothing less than an agrarian revolution. His watchword was "We should be able to do it better than the Russians."[30]

On 3 April, after a week-long debate, the Governing Council issued a decree expropriating all large and medium estates and expressly forbidding the redistribution of land and equipment to individuals or groups. Instead, the land was to be turned over for collective cultivation by the agrarian proletariat. The measure affected a little over half the arable land in unoccupied Hungary. In practice, it generated not genuine producers' cooperatives but rather a centrally administered system of state farms. As in the nationalized industries, immediate supervision was vested in an appointed production commissar and a generally subordinate workers' council. Since the regime had no alternative reserves of expertise, in many cases the former estate bailiff or even landlord was named production commissar. The laborers, on the other hand, were treated as industrial wage earners rather than as profit-sharing members of a cooperative.

For Kun, even this measure was a weak compromise, and he did not conceal his view that ideally agriculture ought to be converted into a socialized state industry.[31] However, the enacted version of collectivization clearly stood little chance of winning the loyalty and the labor of the peasantry, and a strictly confidential directive was therefore issued allowing for fractional redistribution where absolutely necessary. In refusing to depart substantially from their ideological rejection of private farming, Kun and like-minded socialists underestimated the peasants' powerful hunger for land. The communists held that only by socializing agriculture could they forge the necessary alliance with the rural proletariat and pit the latter against the peasant smallholder class. This doctrinaire assumption overestimated rural class antagonisms, which paled in significance beside the common dream of a private farm.

The agrarian proletariat's disappointment with its new status was intense. The production commissars were no better than their old masters, and the improvement in their wages was purely nominal. The dwarf landholding peasants (i.e., those whose farms were too small to afford more than a marginal living) were equally disappointed. Together with their more affluent neighbors they resented the emergency requisitions of food for the cities. The regime had abolished land taxes—an expedient measure, aimed at winning the tolerance if not support of peasant proprietors—but the proprietors only regarded this concession as a prelude to confiscation. Not surprisingly, agricultural productivity declined during the brief life of the Commune.

Of more immediate consequence was the political alienatioñ of the bulk of the peasantry from the regime, a circumstance that greatly facilitated the organization of the counterrevolution in the countryside. The irate landless laborers, who would have been the regime's most likely rural constituency, organized themselves into an Association of Agrarian Workers. Their congress, held during the first two days of June, turned into an open confrontation with the government. The official agenda, which precluded any discussion of redistribution, consisted of a proposal by the agricultural commissariat to erase the distinction between state and collective farms. It was designed to emasculate the authority of the workers' councils in the latter. The meeting rang with protests at bureaucratic harassment and the retention of the old estate overseers. The official proposal met with such hostility that the party's agrarian radicals, Hamburger and Nyisztor, had to admit defeat and hurriedly dismiss the delegates. At the subsequent national assembly of councils the provincial delegates formed a similarly aggrieved opposition to the urban socialists.[32] In the event, the formation of collective farms progressed so slowly that they ultimately encompassed less than one-fifth of the nationalized land. However, the communists' failure to redistribute land had an enduring impact, for even after the 1945 land reform the peasants remained deeply suspicious of the party's intentions—rightly so, considering the subsequent brutal imposition of collectivization during the Rákosi era and again at the end of the 1950s.

**The Cultural Revolution.**  The cultural pluralism that flourished during the Károlyi interregnum was greeted with enthusiasm by the more liberal intellectuals, particularly by the avant-garde writers and artists who had chafed under the orthodoxy of the old order. Their disposition toward the second revolution was governed in large measure by its tolerance of creative freedom and diversity. After a few early paeans to the revolution, even the liberal writers soon realized that communism demanded unprecedented ideological submission and uniformity. Amidst mounting excesses, they withdrew into passive hostility. A few, including Béla Illés and Andor Gábor, began their journey toward communism, while the occasional early convert, such as József Lengyel, abandoned literature for revolutionary activism.[33]

A noteworthy dissonant chord in the cultural life of the revolution was struck by Kassák and his review *MA*. He and his young followers, known as the Activists, propagated through the review a Futuristic style and an ultraleftist ideology of permanent and absolute revolution. The fiercely independent Kassák, whose activities as poet, painter, and writer-publicist made him practically a one-man movement, regarding the two parties' merger as a dilution of pure revolution and refused formal association with any party or institution. Socialist reservations and the need to provide an ideological definition of revolutionary culture were giving Lukács enough trouble without the Kassák group's demand that their brand of Futurism be anointed the official artistic form. When Kun in the course of the party congress dismissed the *MA* style as a product of bourgeois decadence, Kassák responded with an open letter that galvanized his youthful supporters at the subsequent congress of working youth. He had also bypassed the censors in disseminating a brochure that contained the attack on Kun together with other Activist writings. The regime thereupon added *MA* to what was to be its final list of suspended publications.[34]

Creative intellectuals were notoriously difficult to please, and in any case the cultural commissariat was more concerned with educational reform.[35] In a major transformation, begun under Károlyi, the majority of church-administered educational facilities were nationalized. Tuition fees were abolished and schooling made compulsory until the age of fourteen. Kunfi placed the University of Budapest under the direction of a committee headed by the Galileist mathematician Pál Dienes. He closed down the university's hostile law faculty, and suspended the more unsympathetic professors to make way for new instructors, most of whom, surprisingly enough, were well qualified. The conservative Academy of Sciences was abolished and its building requisitioned for the Red Guard.

The cultural commissars, particularly Lukács, were most active in the sphere of popular education and propaganda. Literacy programs and lecture series were mounted for the working class, which was also induced to attend special musical and theatrical performances, normally preceded by propagandistic lectures. All theaters, cinemas, and film studios were nationalized. Authentic communists formed only a small minority in the propaganda department, and its output displayed more of an earnest radical socialist than a Leninist character. Oral propagation of the new creed was furthered by agitator schools and countless meetings, while the printing presses busily churned out streams of leaflets as well as a few theoretical works of Marx and Lenin. Over the life of the Commune, 680 leaflets, 334 pamphlets, and 84 posters were reproduced in immense quantities that rapidly depleted the dwindling paper stocks when the blockade cut off external supplies.[36] As March drew to a close, Kun exploited the shortages as an excuse for eliminating the nonsocialist press. A few newspapers were effectively suppressed on 2 April, but while Kun and Lukács continued to agitate for a total ban, the socialist centrists Kunfi and Weltner argued instead for censorship, to save the jobs of journalists and printers. Lukács's order that all articles be signed had already inhibited the regime's critics, and when in early May the remaining nonsocialist papers hazarded some nationalist sentiments against Austria's active campaign to annex part of western Hungary, the communists seized the occasion to shut them down.

Formal separation of church and state was to have been followed by a ban on teaching religion in the schools. However, the Governing Council recognized the sensitive nature of the issue and left the decision to the local councils. The regime's undisguised prejudice against organized religion was manifested in a more aggressive manner by its wilder agitators, who harassed priests, desecrated churches while advocating their conversion into socialist houses of culture, and scandalized their audiences with praise of free love. It hardly needs saying that from the very beginning the clergy was a dedicated and, particularly in the countryside, highly influential enemy of the revolution.

**Democracy and Terror.** Early in the life of the Commune a number of provisional district councils, a few under communist direction, had organized themselves in Budapest. On March 31 their delegates and those of party organizations were convoked to approve the proposed provisional constitution of the Republic of Councils.[37] This draft outlined the modalities of the forthcoming council elections. The franchise, with the right to candidacy, was granted to men and women over eighteen who were in socially useful employment. Others, including employers, merchants, and clergymen, were disenfranchised.* Approximately half the republic's population was thus qualified to vote, and nearly half of these exercised their right, the proportion being highest in Budapest and lowest in the villages.

The elections of 7 April were conducted on a single-list basis. Most of the urban candidates were industrial workers and most of the rural ones agrarian laborers. Nevertheless, the election was bitterly fought, with numerous arrests and casualties. The electoral restrictions were subverted in many instances, opposition lists materialized, priests and other "class enemies" actively campaigned against the ruling party, and a number of clearly ineligible candidates such as landowners were elected. In Budapest conflicts arose between the communists and centrist or rightist socialists. Only one-sixth of the councilors who formed the capital's "Workers' and Soldiers' Council of 500" were communist, and socialists also predominated in its executive committee. In Budapest's eighth district, the anarcho-syndicalist opposition used force to prevail against the official slate; the government prevailed by nullifying the result. In three other districts the communists tried to seize control but had to content themselves with a generous share of the common list.[38] With all the agitation and rigged rules, the ruling party could hardly claim to have won a genuine mandate from the population. Nor was it confident of the new councils' sup-

---

*In contrast, the Berinkey government's electoral law had contained no class restrictions and had set the minimum age at twenty-one for men and twenty-four for women.

port. In late May it constrained their autonomy with centrally appointed, plenipotentiary commissars.

In the election's aftermath political power remained effectively divided between the Governing Council, the Council of 500, and other loosely controlled councils, and the Trades Council and its unions. Kun and his communist aides tried to retain the initiative in the first body, but even there the numerical weight of the socialists proved a hindrance. On 12 April the Governing Council named a five-man political committee consisting of the communists Kun and Fiedler, their close collaborator Landler, Böhm, and Garbai to facilitate speedy executive action. Their sessions lengthened as domestic and external difficulties multiplied. In late June, upon Szántó's suggestion, the people's commissars all moved into the luxurious Hungaria Hotel, which became known as the "Soviet House." Security was as important a consideration as ease of communication, so a special detachment of the Red Guard protected the commissars.[39]

The ambitious socialization programs of the regime required the state bureaucracy to be doubled.[40] The influx of new "red" civil servants was greatest in the economic branches, in education (where the complement expanded from 494 to 1,786, to cope with the all-important task of propaganda), in the foreign propaganda section of Kun's commissariat, and in the department of the interior (where one-third of the original staff was replaced). The holdovers from the old civil service showed little enthusiasm for the revolution; indeed, they resorted to systematic obstruction of its measures. The new recruits, on the other hand, compensated for their inexperience with zeal and arbitrariness. Authoritarianism, cliquishness, nepotism, and, as noted earlier, a preponderance of Jews were the distinctive features of the new red bureaucracy.[41]

The suddenness of the second revolution made the creation of a reliable enforcement agency problematical. Despite sharp demurrals from Kun, Szamuely, Szántó, and Fiedler the government saw little alternative to absorbing the old police force into the renamed Red Guard.[42] Led for a time by Münnich, the Red Guard would demonstrate little loyalty to the regime. The communists therefore established their own terrorist detachment, the notorious gang of some two hundred so-called Lenin boys, recruited from the CPH headquarters guard, sailors, and common criminals. Clad in leather jackets and armed to the teeth, this unsavory band was led by József Cserny, a friend of Szamuely's who had been trained in Moscow.[43] The depredations of the Lenin boys may not have included all the murders of which they were subsequently accused, but they did succeed in striking terror in the hearts of the citizenry with their razzias and their proclivity for kidnapping affluent notables for ransom.

The five-hundred-man political department of the interior commissariat functioned autonomously as the communists' secret police under the direction of Korvin, whose fanaticism (not to mention his repulsive physical appearance) were never put to better use.[44] Relying on a pervasive network of informers, Korvin's men resorted to all the vicious tools of arbitrary and preventive arrest, interrogation under torture, and intimidation that became identified with the imposition of communist rule in Russia and elsewhere. From the communist point of view, such measures were made necessary by the ever-present threat of counterrevolution. As the Romanian offensive got under way, the threat mounted. On 21 April Szamuely took personal charge of the maintenance of order behind the front lines. He received full freedom to use all necessary sanctions and to bypass the "revolutionary tribunals."* Szamuely and his armed detachments would speed through the countryside by armored train bringing summary justice to those who dared challenge the revolution.

The terroristic excesses of the communist security organs dismayed moderate socialists like Weltner. Violent debates erupted over the rash of arrests and house searches; the latter were often an excuse for theft, and even Böhm's apartment had been ransacked by the Lenin boys. Socialist protests compelled Kun to make some concessions. By May the Red Guard had been placed under the command of the socialist József Haubrich. The more irrepressible Lenin boys, with such communist activists as Münnich and Rákosi were transferred to the front; the purpose was both to pacify the socialists and to propagandize the troops.

## THE COMMUNE AT WAR

Chaos reigned in the organization of the Commune's defenses.[45] The first commissar, Pogány, became intoxicated with his new power and clashed with the equally radical Szamuely and Vágó. Fearing for the future of the Red Army, which was little more than a phantom force, the Governing Council on 2 April replaced Pogány with Böhm and transferred Szamuely to culture, where he retained responsibility for propaganda in the military recruitment campaign. When Szamuely's extremist friends mounted a demonstration by several thousand leftist soldiers to protest these demotions, the Governing Council reconvened in some confusion. Kun tactically deprecated the significance of the volatile crowd outside, and finally agreement was reached on a five-man defense directorate consisting of Böhm, Fiedler, Haubrich, Kun, and Szántó.[46]

These disputes were hardly papered over when at dawn on 4 April a special

---

*The revolutionary tribunals, presided over mainly by leftist workers, served as the Commune's official judiciary. Thousands of cases of counterrevolutionary crimes were brought before these courts, and 153 formal death sentences were delivered. The total number of executions during the Commune (apparently including common criminals as well as political dissidents) has been estimated at 590, most of them occurring in the final weeks, when counterrevolutionary outbursts became more frequent. See Béla Sarlós, *A Tanácsköztársaság forradalmi törvényszékei* (Budapest: Közgazdasági és Jogi, 1962), pp. 232–33; and Albert Váry, *A vörösuralom áldozatai Magyarországon* (Budapest; n.p., 1923).

train carrying the Entente's envoy, General Smuts, pulled into Budapest. During his day-and-a-half visit Smuts remained on the train in order to avoid giving the impression of formal diplomatic recognition. He brought the proposal that in exchange for Hungarian acceptance of the Vyx terms, which had been marginally amended, the Entente would lift its economic blockade. Kun, like Károlyi before him, warned of anarchy and suggested that representatives of the Hungarian, Austrian, Czech, German, Romanian, and Yugoslav governments be convened to work out a territorial and economic settlement. In a report cabled to Paris, Smuts endorsed Kun's suggestion, commenting that the regime's weakness would force it to "swallow much and submit to terms which it would be difficult to make [Hungary] agree to otherwise."[47] At the peace conference the counterproposal aroused little interest and did not impede the French general staff from marshaling the allied forces for intervention. That forceful option was also preferred by the so-called Anti-Bolshevik Committee of Hungarian émigrés in Vienna, a group that included the future prime minister Count István Bethlen.

**The Romanian Attack.** The Romanians were eager to win territorial concessions even greater than those provided by the secret wartime Treaty of Bucharest. The French commander of the eastern allied armies, General Franchet d'Espérey, worked out the details with them and with the Czechs. On 16 April the Royal Romanian Army launched a frontal attack against the Hungarians. The Red Army's strength stood at fifty-five thousand, less than at the end of March, for the recruitment of proletarian volunteers had met with little success. Böhm quickly curtailed the purge of the officer corps begun by Pogány and took steps to restrain the disruptive activities of the newly appointed political commissars. The career officers were ready to serve the motherland but, needless to say, had little love for the Commune. Facing the Romanians was a Transylvanian division, under General Károly Kratochvil, whose officers and men did not disguise their contempt for the red regime. On all fronts, north, east, and south, the Hungarians faced overwhelming numerical odds.

As resistance to the Romanian offensive began to falter, Kun and his acolytes fantasized about forestalling disaster. If they could survive long enough, they hoped, the coincidental riots in Vienna and the communist coup in Bavaria would somehow produce a revolutionary alliance, and the Russian Red Army would relieve the pressure. "We will soon be in direct contact with you," Chicherin had cabled Kun on the twenty-sixth.[48] While new battalions of volunteers were hurriedly dispatched to the front, close to five hundred hostages were rounded up by Cserny's gang and their rural counterparts. "Let our bourgeoisie understand that from today we regard it as a hostage," raved Pogány.[49] The ideological confusion that reigned even within communist ranks was illustrated by Lukács's protest at the measure. He criticized class terror and produced an idiosyncratic theory: the merger had created a new type of party that was itself a transitory phenomenon, pending the full flowering of the proletariat's class consciousness. After the revolution, these notions required abject recantation.[50] Counterrevolutionary plots and insurgencies multiplied in the wake of the Romanian attack, necessitating Szamuely's first punitive forays. Concurrently, the interior commissariat issued a conciliatory decree guaranteeing freedom of religion and the safety of places of worship. At the same time, it ordered the socialization of other church property.[51]

Neither carrot nor stick were of much avail, however. While Kun, before a meeting of the Council of Five Hundred on 25 April, denounced the proletariat's lack of class consciousness and reluctance to enlist, the Transylvanian Division was preparing to secure a separate cease-fire, and retreat turned into rout. At President Wilson's urging the peace conference instructed the Romanians to stop at the Vyx line, but their compliance was uncertain when the Governing Council met on 26 April. Kun reported that he had sent to Paris by way of an American observer, Professor Philip Brown, a request for a meeting in Switzerland to negotiate a "Brest-Litovsk peace." His proposal entailed the lifting of the blockade and the withdrawal of Romanian forces to the demarcation line in exchange for the dismissal of the extremists Szamuely, Pogány, and Vágó, the release of hostages and the curtailment of terror, and the cessation of propaganda among enemy soldiers. The council rejected the view of its deputy chairman, the socialist Antal Dovcsák, that the time had come to liquidate the proletarian dictatorship, and endorsed Kun's initiative.[52]

On the twenty-seventh the Romanians advanced beyond the neutral zone toward the Tisza River, looting and shooting communists on their way, while the Yugoslavs in the south and the Czechs in the north launched their own minor offensives. Two days later, Szamuely and Pogány were officially replaced as people's commissars by Bolgár and Weltner, and Kun sent a personal appeal to President Wilson as well as peace feelers to the Czech, Romanian, and Yugoslav governments.[53] Meanwhile, the peace conference had ordered the Romanians to stop at the Tisza and not press on to Budapest as they had requested. At the end of April a deceptive calm descended on the eastern and southern battlefronts.

Fireworks lit the sky over Budapest when, on 1 May, a delegation of union leaders presented itself at the Soviet House to demand the transfer of power to a trade union directorate. The political committee decided to put the question before the Governing Council and the Council of Five Hundred the following day. After a night-long debate, Kun confronted the rightist union leaders Peyer and Ferenc Miákits at the enlarged meeting of the Governing Council. Kun seemed a broken man, ready to resign. Szamuely, Landler, and Szántó argued against surrender, but the socialist majority was in a defeatist mood, and it was finally agreed to let the Workers' and Soldiers' Council decide on the regime's future and on the military defense of Budapest. When the council met that evening there were scenes of wild debate and virulent criticism of the communists and their terroristic and administrative misdemeanors. The ultimate, grudging endorsement of the government owed far more to the entreaties of the socialists Böhm and Haubrich than to the passionate pleading of Kun, who had now recovered.[54] Awaiting the outcome, the panicky commissars had sought assurances of asylum from the Austrian government.

Nevertheless, the workers' spokesmen had been rallied for one last effort. Under trade union direction the raising of new battalions proceeded apace; by 14 May an additional forty-four thousand men were put under arms. The peasantry stubbornly refused to share in the defense of a regime that had offered it so little. The Commune's opponents, meanwhile, continued to organize. A countergovernment formed in Romanian-occupied Arad by Count Gyula Károlyi (much more conservative than his namesake) moved on 9 May to Szeged, in southern Hungary—a more hospitable base because it was under French administration. Károlyi's group established contact with the Viennese émigrés, some of whom in turn attempted an abortive armed incursion from Bruck across the Leitha River into Hungary. At its meeting on 17 May the Revolutionary Governing Council rather superfluously condemned these distant enemies and ordered the confiscation of their property.

**The Commune Counterattacks.**   The crisis of 1 and 2 May had reminded Kun how tenuous his power really was. He could not long survive a combination of popular dissatisfaction at communist excesses and the stigma of being unable to defend the country against the Entente. (On 8 May the Entente's foreign ministers had agreed on the final delineation of the new Hungarian boundaries, but this was not yet known in Budapest.) Centrist socialists like Böhm and Kunfi, whose initial support had been at best ambivalent, were drifting towards a hostile position that Weltner voiced openly in *Népszava*. They and rightist social democrats like Garami began to seek out the various Entente representatives in Budapest and Vienna, who in turn were more than ready to exploit dissension among the Commune's leaders. The conservative trade union bureaucrats had already demonstrated their opposition to the regime and maintained their pressure on it.

The first congress of the unified party was scheduled for the second week in June. Kun was desperate for some concrete success to restore his fading political credibility. There being no suitable outlet on the domestic scene, he concentrated on military and foreign schemes. Both Kun and, upon occasion, Lenin, overrated the isolated successes of the Red Army in the Ukraine against the Romanians. In like manner, they would reinforce each other's dream of a simultaneous offensive that would link up the two armies of Bolshevism. The Ukrainian nationalist uprising and the offensive in late May of Denikin's White

Army in eastern Ukraine would tie down the Russian Red Army. In the meantime, however, Kun made plans for his own military thrust. Despite the evident military and political advantages of a northern offensive against weak Czech forces, he chose the target of Miskolc in the northeast on the road to eastern Slovakia. The goal was to establish a Slovak Soviet Republic and to press on to meet the expected advance of the Russian Red Army. Meanwhile, Kun sent Bettelheim to Vienna, ostensibly as the Comintern's emissary, with instructions to drive the Austrian communists into an uprising slated for 15 June. The Austrian party leaders refused to play Kun's game, and Bettelheim was forced to dismiss them before developing plans for the suicidal venture.[55] Victory in Austria and Slovakia, speculated Kun, would confirm his revolutionary genius.

The prelude to the northern campaign, under the command of the career staff officer General Aurél Stromfeld, was set in motion on 20 May with an advance that soon liberated Miskolc. A day later Szamuely flew to the Ukraine to assess the military situation and then proceeded by special train to Moscow.[56] Upon arrival he reviewed in Lenin's company a parade of armed workers and held discussions with the Bolshevik leaders on the urgent question of military assistance. He did not return to Budapest until 31 May. In the meantime Kun had asked Lenin for a public endorsement to forestall socialist defection and counter reports in the Viennese press of Lenin's displeasure. Szamuely was still in Moscow when Lenin complied with a "Greeting to the Workers of Hungary." The message, informed by Szamuely's account, was suitably exhortative and adamant. Lenin confirmed that in the given situation only a proletarian dictatorship could lead to socialism, and that force had to be used in the altered but continuing class struggle. "Be firm. And if wavering appears among the socialists who joined you yesterday, or among the petite bourgeoisie, repress such vacillations ruthlessly. Execution by shooting—that is the just desert of the coward in war."[57]

On 30 May the reinforced Hungarian Red Army launched an unexpectedly successful offensive that within a week had captured Kassa (Košice) from the Czechs. The latter eventually mounted a counteroffensive from Pozsony. On this front Hungarian resistance was weakened by the determination of the Governing Council to follow the northeastern thrust with an attack against the Romanians across the Tisza. On the home front, a rash of counterrevolutionary insurgencies erupted. Transportation in much of Transdanubia was paralyzed by a strike of railroad workers. The Governing Council designated that region a war zone, and the freshly returned Szamuely had to resort to armed force and hangings to quell the general unrest (the railroad workers were pacified with a wage increase). When Lenin's greeting, brought back by Szamuely and translated by Kun, was published over socialist objections in *Népszava* on 1 June, the more moderate socialists were incensed. Even Kunfi pointedly dissociated himself from Lenin's more violent cadences.[58]

The Paris peace conference was taken aback by the Hungarian army's prowess. On 7 June Clemenceau sent a memorandum demanding the immediate cessation of hostilities and promising in return that Hungary's delegates would be invited to receive the peace terms. In his reply Kun, in effect, accepted an offer that seemed to hold out the promise of recognition. He explained that the Czechs, by occupying Slovakia without a formal settlement, had contravened the Belgrade armistice. His own government, he asserted with diplomatic ambiguity, was not wedded to the principle of territorial integrity.[59] Kun, like Clemenceau, was playing for time. While Stromfeld hurriedly consolidated his defenses along the entire northern front, the party made final preparations for its congress.

**A Divided Congress.** Whereas on the eve of unification the CPH, with perhaps thirty thousand members, could be considered a centralized, closed party, its successor did not accord with the Leninist prescription for a revolutionary vanguard. Instead, what had emerged was a heterogeneous mass party in which opportunism and a moderate version of socialism predominated. Many of the new members and unions were motivated by self-interest rather than ideological conviction. Official policies often meant very little. In one local party organization, for instance, 43 out of 53 members resigned in protest at the regime's anticlerical measures.[60] Moreover, the party hardly functioned as a political force distinct from the loosely coordinated local councils and the autonomous trade unions. Friction between the unions and the communist extremists had poisoned the atmosphere. Although, thanks to Landler's opposition, a communist proposal to divorce the party from the trade unions had been rejected by the Governing Council on 14 April, the damage was already done. The first month of council rule had only confirmed the union bureaucrats' suspicions. By early May an opposition group of rightists such as the miners' Peyer and the metal-workers' Miákits began to coalesce in open anticipation of the regime's collapse.

As the time of the congress drew near, the communists revived their campaign to sever the party from the unions and to purge the party itself. The doctrinaire Révai argued in the pages of *Vörös Ujság* that the unions' role be limited to the pursuit of the material welfare of their members.[61] In his lectures on the proposed party program, Kun tried to mitigate the effect of Révai's impolitic outbursts by praising the unions' historical merits and their current participation in the administration of socialist production. On the other hand, he argued, the party should not "be allowed to accept everyone but [should] be solely the organization of the avant-garde, of the elite of the proletariat." At the same time, he stressed, the party was not superior to the workers' councils, which represented "the entire class."[62] Reconciling political power with the schematic prescriptions of ideology was clearly not an easy task.

An essential source of popular support for the Commune had been the hope that it could find a tolerable modus vivendi with the Entente. When this prospect failed to materialize, the simmering differences over the exercise of power erupted into open confrontation within the ruling circles. The opening salvo was fired by Weltner in *Népszava* as the congress was about to convene on 12 June. He delivered a blistering attack on Lenin's advocacy of violence and charged that the new state bureaucracy was full of incompetent young extremists who outdid their predecessors in shameful excess.

The 321 delegates attending the congress included 25 former CPH leaders, but the socialist trade union officers formed a large majority. Over half the delegates came from the Budapest area, the nomination process having effectively limited peasant representation and, in consequence, debate of the contentious agrarian policy. A short party program had been drafted by Kun, who had modeled it on the one adopted at the Russian party's eighth congress but with the tactical ommission of the latter's severe censure of social democracy.[63] It advanced the general principle of a proletarian dictatorship arising from the defeat of capitalism and imperialism. In his opening address Kun anticipated that socialization of the economy would propel Hungary to the forefront of developed countries and voiced "tremendous pride" at the agrarian reform.

The vapid generalities of Kun's program did not seem to arouse the congress, which adopted it without debate. In contrast, acrimonious disputes were sparked by two more immediate issues: the party's name, and the practice of dictatorship. Kun relayed the Comintern's recommendation that the name "communist" be retained. Lenin and Bukharin, reported Rudas upon his return from Moscow, were disturbed at the socialists' reluctance to adopt this name when they had already agreed on more substantive points. Kunfi rejected imitation of the Russian example as unnecessary, Weltner dismissed the Comintern's ruling as one based on ignorance of the Hungarian situation, and other socialists warned that, for the population at large, the term "communist" connoted atheism, Jews, and terror.[64] The congress finally compromised with the name "Hungarian Party of Socialist-Communist Workers."

On the practice of power, Kun declared that "all wavering and gentle exercise of the dictatorship lowers its prestige." The "active minority" ruled legitimately on behalf of a "largely passive" working class, said Kun defensively, and the new bureaucracy should not be hastily censured for its mistakes. The principal opposing spokesman, Kunfi, called for a more humane and tolerant exercise of the dictatorship, if only, he tactfully explained, because the international revolution on which the radicals pinned their hopes for preventing counterrevolution had not yet emerged. Claiming that he and his colleagues had originally acquiesced in the proletarian dictatorship with great reservations and only to avoid a fratricidal struggle, Kunfi asserted that terroristic methods and intolerance in the arts and sciences ran against the wishes of organized labor. In conclusion, he advised the communists to stop aping their Russian comrades and resorting to police terror to inhibit intraparty dissent.[65] The gulf separating the two camps was laid bare when a slanging match ensued between the supporters of Kun, including Rákosi, Szamuely, and Lukács (who argued against moderation) and their socialist detractors.

On the second day of the congress, deadlock over the communist proposal to purge the party and dissociate it from the unions forced postponement of a decision on the organizational statutes. The socialist speakers rose in defense of an organic link with the trade unions and disparaged the Russian model of a closed vanguard party. Said one delegate: "We shall not allow a gang of young, decadent, psychologically disturbed degenerates to write our party literature or carry out party agitation."[66] The predominantly urban and essentially nationalistic socialists were no better disposed towards the claims for greater representation of the poor peasants and of the ethnic minorities.

The final, climactic confrontation arose over the election of the party's leadership. The nominating committee's slate consisted of five communists (Kun, Pór, Rudas, Vágó, and Vántus), four leftist socialists (Ferenc Bajáki, Bokányi, Landler, and Nyisztor), and four moderate socialists (Böhm, Garbai, Kunfi, and Weltner). When it came to a vote, however, Kunfi and Weltner engineered the substitution of more conservative socialists for Bokányi, Pór, Rudas, and Vágó. The communists refused to accept this outcome, and a tearful Kun threatened violent reprisals. When the prudent socialists failed to secure a promise of support from the capital's military commander, the opportunistic Haubrich, Landler emerged once again as conciliator. Communist obduracy combined with socialist timidity to win the day. The original slate was reintroduced for congressional approval, Böhm stressing the need for unity at a time of national peril.[67] The deliberations of the two-day congress had made clear, however, that if the socialists were still prepared to make concessions to the overbearing communists, the latter had alienated most of their reluctant allies and would have to wage a constant struggle for political survival.

## THE FALL OF THE COMMUNE

On 15 June Kun's fanciful hopes for world revolution suffered a setback with the swift and bloody repression of the attempted communist putsch in Vienna. A confidential message from the Vienna mission warning of the coup's slim chances had been leaked to the congressional delegates, and the entire affair only damaged Kun's prestige.[68] That same day a new memorandum arrived from Clemenceau indicating the peace conference's ruling on Hungary's future borders and requesting withdrawal of the Red Army to these lines (in practice, in the north); upon compliance the Romanians would also pull back to the new frontier. At the party leadership meeting the more radical leftists initially opposed a military withdrawal, but in the end only Rudas (generally regarded as the Comintern's envoy) voted against it. In his formal response to Clemenceau, Kun protested at the injustice of the territorial dictate and reiterated his call for a general conference of the Danubian nations. To gain time, he suggested military negotiations on an orderly mutual withdrawal.[69]

Kun's reply was on its way to Clemenceau when on 16 June the Slovakian Republic of Councils was proclaimed in eastern Slovakia. This, like the Viennese farrago, was Kun's brainchild. Its leading figures, including the president, Antonin Janoušek (leader of the Hungarian party's Czechoslovak section), were former CPH members, some originally from northern Hungary; other familiar names were Hirossik, Pór, Szamuely, and, as commander of the embryonic Slovakian Red Army, Münnich. A week earlier Chicherin had relayed Lenin's concern that unless the Slovaks were offered self-determination the occupation would provoke a nationalist reaction, but Kun had replied: "Our nationality policy is Leninist."[70] In the event, this Hungarian-inspired satellite regime would no more fulfil Kun's expectations than had the Viennese adventure, for it collapsed within two weeks, as the Hungarian forces pulled back.[71]

Amidst these international reversals the National Assembly of Councils, attended by elected delegates of the county and city councils and of the trade unions, gathered on 14 June for a ten-day-long session. The assembly indulged in protracted and, in the circumstances, rather irrelevant debates on long-term economic questions as well as on minor matters of local concern. The government's immediate dilemma was far removed from such mundane matters. The Entente's ultimatum and the collapse of the Viennese coup left Kun with but a single hope, and that a remote one: Russian aid. To bolster his eroding prestige, Kun had begged Lenin to dispatch Bukharin to the Hungarian party and council conferences. The Bolshevik leader replied on 18 June that the request could not be fulfilled; instead, he was sending Manuilsky (who never arrived). He went on to endorse Kun's decision to negotiate with the Entente, but with a warning: the Entente powers wanted only "to gain time to be able to strangle you and us too." Kun's riposte was remarkably immodest for a disciple: "It fills me with pride that I am one of your best students, but I think that in one sphere I am even superior to you, and that is in the matter of *mala fides* ["suspiciousness"]. I think I understand the Entente very well. I know that it is waging an implacable struggle against us. In this battle the best that can ensue is an armistice, not a peace. This is a life-and-death struggle."[72]

In the meantime, the Hungarian Red Army on the northern front had launched a new offensive that faltered quickly as the weary and demoralized troops began to desert in droves. Hoping to rally their soldiers with more patriotic symbols, the officers requested permission to fly the national colors instead of the red banner of revolution. The communists, however, were too attached to the latter to let the government say yes. In these circumstances Kun saw no alternative but to recommend to the Assembly of Councils on 19 June that the military withdrawal demanded by the Entente be carried out. He stressed that the compromise would be no more enduring than that of Brest-Litovsk. The imperialists would divide among themselves in grabbing for a Hungarian colony, he prophesied, while in Germany the forthcoming peace treaty would lead only to proletarian revolution, all of which would ultimately confirm the wisdom of his tactical retrenchment. Hungary, he insisted, was not wedded to the principle of territorial integrity; she upheld the right to self-determination of workers of all nationalities within a "federative republic of councils." The protests of the ultraleftists Szamuely and Pogány at this betrayal of world revolution were dismissed by Kun as "left-wing defeatism." Kunfi endorsed the withdrawal on more pragmatic grounds and, to Kun's dismay, disclaimed any responsibility for proletarian revolutionaries in Slovakia or elsewhere. In the end the assembly unanimously ratified the proposed compromise.[73]

Four days later another ultimatum arrived, from the French Marshal Foch, demanding an immediate ceasefire and withdrawal by the twenty-eighth from the territories assigned to Czechoslovakia. The Hungarians promised to comply. The Weimar assembly having ratified the peace terms for Germany, Clemenceau could now concentrate on eliminating the Hungarian irritant.

In its penultimate act, the Assembly of Councils on 23 June approved a draft constitution loosely based on the Russian instrument.[74] It confirmed the proletarian dictatorship's transitional function: to eradicate exploitation by means of wholesale nationalization on the way to the classless and stateless utopia. To stress the familial link with similar political initiatives elsewhere, the new state's name was to be the "Allied Socialist Republic of Hungary." In specifying the rights and obligations of workers the constitution restricted the political freedom of the bourgeoisie. It provided for a council system of government, operating on the principle of democratic centralism, with the National Assembly of Councils (meeting twice a year) at the apex of political power. Continuity of supervision over the Governing Council (the chief executive organ) would be served by a 150-member "Federal Central Executive Committee," which was in fact elected by the June assembly. The composition of this executive committee reflected the political profile of the assembly; of the Budapest members one-third were communist, the others socialists of various hues. Two-thirds of the general membership came from the Budapest area, while the peasantry enjoyed only token representation. The committee met on 24 June to choose a new Governing Council. As a compromise both Kunfi and Szamuely were excluded, while Garbai continued as president and Kun as foreign affairs commissar. The communists and left socialists held a nominal majority.[75]

**Betrayal and Defeat.** The counterrevolution meanwhile raised its head in Budapest. For days the countryside had been aflame with local risings. In the Kalocsa district the regime's opponents seized power from the workers' councils. Village after village in Transdanubia and the southeast saw the peasants, gentry, priests, and the old rural gendarmerie joining forces to oust their bewildered rulers. Szamuely's armored train once again raced from one flashpoint to another, spreading terror by public hangings. In Budapest a group of conspirators tried unsuccessfully to win Stromfeld and Haubrich to their cause. Nevertheless, on 24 June an attack was launched by the Danube flotilla, which opened fire on the Soviet House, and by cadets from the Ludovika Military Academy. Leaflets issued by the conspirators called for a truly national government. At least one factory's workers joined the rebels, and for a few hours the capital's citizenry awaited the tyrants' fall with patriotic excitement. In the end, Korvin managed to marshal sufficient forces to quell the ill-conceived and disorganized rising and win a brief surcease for the Commune.

The communists now demanded that a central agency modeled on the Russian Cheka be created under Szamuely's direction to consolidate their reign of terror. The official communiqué hinted at a bloodbath. "In view of the fact that the moderate exercise of the dictatorship had encouraged the bourgeoisie to counterrevolutionary behavior instead of bringing it to its senses, it has been decided to apply the dictatorship of the proletariat to the fullest with merciless measures . . . and, if necessary, to drown the bourgeoisie's counterrevolution in blood."[76] The process of converting these threats into action was cut short when the Entente's representative and General Stromfeld intervened, but it had already been slowed by the socialists' subversive leniency, which saved the captured rebels from execution. Szamuely and Korvin began to rebuild a terrorist force similar to the disbanded Lenin boys, but Kun could not prevent the government from sending a military unit to disarm and disperse this budding Hungarian Cheka. Although Rákosi was eventually appointed commander of the Red Guard, the communists had been put on a leash.

The increasing self-assertion of the moderate socialists, already evident at the party congress, produced the inevitable reaction on the extreme left. While young doctrinaire intellectuals like Lukács and Révai earnestly debated how to restore the purity and momentum of the revolution, the more pragmatic Szamuely, with Kun's tacit approval, devised a plan to create a new network of secret cells that would eventually seize control within the party, trade unions, and councils. His preparations were outpaced by the disintegration of the Commune, but he may also have been involved with an anarchist group that proceeded (with the active participation of two Ukrainian officers) to plot an armed uprising against the government. The conspiracy was smashed on 19 July, two days before the planned coup. The communists—or at least their radical wing—had suffered another propaganda defeat.[77]

When on 30 June the military withdrawal on the northern front was set in motion, Kun defended its necessity more in terms of what he called "our internal disorganization" than because of external imperatives.[78] Stromfeld resigned in protest at this nullification of his military successes. For three weeks the

Republic of Councils enjoyed a relative but deceptive calm. The regime made plans to deport the wealthier middle classes from Budapest but only got as far as repatriating several thousand Galician Jewish refugees, a step calculated to appease the public's anti-Semitic hostility toward the government. But while Varga's National Economic Council elaborated new schemes to revive industrial production, including unpaid overtime in the guise of "socialist work competition," the regime's popular legitimacy was fast eroding. The journalists' union was the stage on 8 July of an open challenge to the government's abrogation of freedom of the press. Mihály Károlyi finally decided to leave the country, as much out of fear at the apparently inevitable counterrevolution as from disgust with the communists and their withdrawal in the north.[79]

The centrist and rightist socialists multiplied their precautionary contacts with the Entente in Budapest and Vienna. Kunfi met with his friend Otto Bauer, Austria's social democratic foreign minister. They discussed the possibility of Austrian aid in saving socialist achievements in Hungary from the foreseeable reaction against the communists. Böhm, for his part, convened a representative gathering of social democrats, including the leftists Hamburger and Pogány, to propose a military coup that would oust the communists but preserve the rule of councils. The sceptical Weltner's dissent aborted the scheme.[80]

Meanwhile, on 2 July, the Romanian government advised Clemenceau that it would not recognize the Budapest regime and therefore refused to fulfil its half of the bargain and evacuate eastern Hungary. At this critical juncture the communists and their allies, desperate to regain some prestige, decided to resort to one last military venture and made plans for an offensive across the Tisza River. Kun implored Lenin to put pressure on the Romanians on the Bessarabian front, but the Russian Bolsheviks had their hands full with various White and nationalist enemies. Kun reminded the peace conference of the promise to evacuate eastern Hungary. But his case was hopeless. The conference replied that it would not negotiate until the Red Army's complement was reduced in accordance with the armistice agreement.[81] The Entente was aware of the Hungarian plans for a new offensive and made its own preparations. In Szeged the countergovernment intensified its nationalistic agitation to good effect among the Red Army's officer corps and began to organize its own armed force under Miklós Horthy, an admiral of the defunct Austro-Hungarian fleet.

Playing his last card, the exhausted Kun tried to rekindle the flame of patriotic resistance. On 12 July compulsory military service was decreed. On 20 July, as the Red Army was crossing the Tisza, the party issued a pathetic appeal to the world's proletarians: "We stand like a lonely rock amidst the encircling imperialist tide." The Comintern called upon the workers of Europe to strike in solidarity with the Russian and Hungarian Soviet republics.[82] Kun expected much from the international strike action scheduled for 21 July, but the eventual limited work stoppages in Austria and a few other countries were hardly sufficient to weaken the Entente's resolve. That same day Kun had to relay another piece of bad news to the Governing Council: the peace conference had decided to award Austria the westernmost region of Hungary.

Böhm assumed the post of ambassador to Vienna on 21 July. Amidst news of the Hungarian offensive, he tried to persuade the head of the British military mission, Colonel Sir Thomas A. A. Cuninghame, to accept at least temporary retention of a councils regime headed by Böhm and two other centrist socialists. Böhm was ready to sacrifice the communists in order to preserve the councils system and its economic reforms. But while the Romanians counterattacked against the outnumbered and dispirited Red Army, the peace conference declared on 26 July that the blockade would be lifted and peace secured only with respect to a government that represented the Hungarian people and did not rest on terror. Peyer and Weltner now joined Böhm in Vienna and the negotiations veered in the direction of a moderate social democratic regime that would pave the way for restoration of a pluralistic political system.

The distraught Kun complained to Lenin that the Russians' uncooperativeness was responsible for the Romanian onslaught. Lenin replied by way of Rudnyánszky that the Bolshevik regime was doing everything possible to help "our Hungarian friends," but that its strength was limited. He rejected Kun's allegation that the dispatch of Rakovsky to create order in the Ukraine had been counterproductive.[83] The ship of revolution was sinking fast. On the twenty-ninth the Trade Union Council convened to prepare the ouster of the government, with which Haubrich now concurred. The following day, while the Romanians crossed the Tisza towards Budapest, Kun met with Böhm on the Austrian border but stubbornly refused to surrender the dictatorship.[84]

Kun and the Red Army's political commander, Landler, conferred one last time with the military staff on 31 July. They insisted against all evidence of defeat on sustaining the struggle. Meanwhile, Weltner had informed the Trade Union Council of the Viennese negotiations, and the council by a vote of 43 to 3 decided to ask for the government's resignation. Kun gradually realized the hopelessness of his position, but along with Szamuely, who had rushed back from the front, he pleaded for one more attempt to rally the workers' councils and to throw all reserves into battle. The two men brought this proposal before a joint meeting of the Governing Council and the party executive on 1 August. But the socialist commissars and their associates had had enough. Declared Peyer: "Corruption is the cause of [the government's] downfall. Bourgeois rule will follow . . . . The trade unions and their resources must be preserved."[85] Even such fervent radicals as Rudas and Varga bowed to the inevitable. After Haubrich threatened to mobilize the workers, the Governing Council resigned.

That afternoon the Budapest Workers' and Soldiers' Council met to hear the centrist Zoltán Rónai report on the regime's abdication. He anticipated that the

Entente would prevent a counterrevolutionary terror and explained that the requisites for the revolution's success—world revolution, Russian aid, and the Hungarian proletariat's readiness for self-sacrifice—had failed to meet expectations. Béla Kun himself made an appearance at the meeting to deliver a farewell address. His remarks were suffused with bitterness against the proletariat, which would need, he declared, "the most cruel and merciless dictatorship of the bourgeoisie" before it learned how to be revolutionary. After a transitional period, "with renewed strength, greater experience, under more realistic and objective conditions, and with a more mature proletariat," he and the party faithful would engage in a new battle for the dictatorship of the proletariat, and "inaugurate a new phase in the international proletarian revolution." He informed Lenin of the collapse:

> Today a right-wing socialist government has been created in Budapest, composed of trade union leaders, enemies of the dictatorship, and of trade union functionaries who until now had shared in the dictatorship. This turnabout was caused primarily by the disintegration of our army, and secondly by the antidictatorship mood of the workers. This occurred in circumstances where all struggle to preserve the proper but wavering dictatorship would have been useless.[86]

The 133-day revolution had run its course.

**A Premature Revolution.** The fall of the Commune released a flood of rationalization, recrimination, and self-justification by the Hungarian communists and their Russian mentors. Over the years, as the next chapter will relate, these retrospective debates departed more and more from the reality of the revolution and came to reflect, instead, the ideological shifts and factionalism of the communist movement. A key target of criticism was the merger with the socialists. It was adopted in December 1919 by Rudnyánszky's External Committee in Moscow to explain the absence of the preconditions for a proletarian revolution. Lenin, who never directly blamed Kun for the debacle, reflected in February 1920:

> Undoubtedly some of the Hungarian socialists were sincere in joining Béla Kun and professing to be communist. But this in no way alters the essence of the matter: he who "sincerely" professes to be a communist, but instead of following an implacable, steadfast, self-sacrificingly brave and heroic policy (the only policy suited to the dictatorship of the proletariat) is fainthearted and wavers . . . is as guilty of betrayal as the outright traitor.[87]

In a similar vein, Zinoviev wrote after the Commune's fall that "the old official social democracy is our mortal foe. This is the lesson to be derived from the Hungarian events." Abandonment of the homogeneous vanguard party and ultimate defeat were also attributed, notably by Trotsky, to the undesirably peaceful seizure of power.[88]

In fact, the various allies that Kun's bolsheviks had acquired on the road to power—ranging from politically prudent trade union bureaucrats to anarcho-syndicalist workers and intellectuals eager for utopia—impeded organizational and ideological cohesion as much as did the eventual merger. Thereafter the conservatism of a Peyer, the opportunism of a Haubrich, the impatient reformism of a Lukács or Varga, the obsession with force and terror of a Szamuely all conspired to undermine the stability of the Commune. Kun himself failed to fully appreciate and apply some of the Russian Bolsheviks' tactical accommodations nor did he permit himself their reliance on patriotism against foreign imperialism.[89] His political skills were demonstrated in the exploitation of the momentary weaknesses of the Károlyi regime, but they were not up to the complex demands of exercising power.

Although many of Kun's communists and fellow travellers were no better than common thugs and adventurers, others were men of superior intellect. Their revolutionary ethics were circumstantial or ideological, but necessarily unconventional. A great gap separates the pitiless fanaticism of Szamuely and Korvin from the distorted humanistic fervor of Lukács or the professional zeal of the economist Varga. For many the revolution offered a unique opportunity to exercise skills and expertise that formerly had been constrained by social prejudice. As always in politics, some sought power for its own sake, and others more as an instrument for the realization of their utopia. In a dictatorial setting shorn of traditional and constitutional restraints, personal ambition and revolutionary zeal converged in the immediate exploitation of power. As a result, corruption in the Commune's government surpassed the deficiencies of the old regime.

Rudas concluded in 1920 that "the mistake lay not in unification. The mistake was in the communists' abandonment of the struggle to captivate the masses."[90] It is most unlikely that even a closed vanguard party could have accomplished that task given the very limited popular sympathy for Bolshevism. However, some of the regime's actions and willful omissions were undoubtedly counterproductive. A year after the debacle, Kun assured Lenin that "our greatest achievement was the socialist agricultural large-scale industry." Five more years were to pass before he would concede—finally adapting himself to Russian practice—that "eventually we would have been compelled to redistribute land, like it happened in Russia."[91] The alienation of the peasantry and of much of the urban population by the forced pace of economic socialization, by terroristic methods, and by anticlericalism could hardly have been remedied by a communist vanguard free of socialist restraints.

Mistakes in the regime's domestic policy were all the same of less weight than external factors in its early downfall. In March 1920 Kun would still reproach Lenin that "the council rule did not have to collapse, but the assistance of the Russian comrades did not come." Years later he admitted that in agreeing to withdraw from Slovakia instead of pursuing dilatory negotiations he had fallen into Clemenceau's trap.[92] But even had he been blessed with the greatest diplomatic acumen, Kun could not have prevented the Entente from exerting its preponderant power against the spread of Bolshevik infection into central Europe. Hungary's geographic position, the distribution of power in Europe, and the defensive retrenchment imposed on the Russian Bolsheviks precluded any other outcome.

By any criterion, the Commune was a disastrous failure. To ask whether, in a less hostile international environment, it could have survived and flourished is no more fruitful than to assert that in other circumstances it would not have come about. A Marxian persuasion is required to see in such phenomena the relentless impersonal march of the forces of history. The strains of industrialization and of war in Europe were resolved in differing ways according to local conditions and the vagaries of political leadership. Three years after the event, Varga could concede that the Commune had been historically premature because "the struggle against the trade union bureacracy was not carried to the end, and there was no solidly organized, closed Communist Party." "The revolutionary process in the surrounding countries," he added, "had not reached a stage that would facilitate the expansion of proletarian revolution."[93] Such tautological explanations skirt the inescapable fact that neither in 1919 nor in more recent history has communist ideology and rule been espoused in any country by the freely expressed will of the popular majority.

In Hungary, where reform—social, economic, and political—was unquestionably overdue, the communist experiment had the regrettable long-term consequence of discrediting not only itself but also the burgeoning liberal democratic alternative that unwittingly paved the way for the Republic of Councils. Whether in the absence of Kun's Bolsheviks the Károlyi regime, resting as it did on a narrow sociocultural basis, could have acquired lasting popular legitimacy cannot be conclusively demonstrated. What is certain is that fickle fortune had deserted Hungary's communists and would not beckon again for twenty-five years.

★★

## *The Years of Impotence*

# PART TWO

*The Commune's fall ushered in a conservative reaction that drove communists into exile or illegality until the penultimate year of World War II. The political ideology of the restoration regime was one of counterrevolutionary conservatism and irredentist nationalism, values that guided Hungary's fortunes until the next war definitively shattered the old order. Their popular appeal stemmed from general revulsion at the Commune's excesses and abhorrence of the catastrophic Treaty of Trianon. In reducing Hungary's territory by more than two thirds, the treaty had not simply liberated the old minorities from Magyar jurisdiction. It had also transferred millions of ethnic Hungarians to the inimical rule of the successor states; wreaked economic havoc by depriving Hungary of most of her mineral resources, severing old commercial links in the process; and added the burden of masses of destitute refugees.*

*Confronted with penury and chaos, the conservative regimes that came to govern Hungary under the regency of Admiral Horthy tried to foster economic revival, muting their irredentism to win external assistance. An early and modest attempt at land reform enlarged the peasant smallholder class but left agriculture dominated by large estates. To ameliorate the lot of the industrial proletariat, a few welfare measures were enacted. A political compromise was reached when the Social Democratic party, after purging itself of radical elements, was granted participation in political life and modest latitude in the organization of urban labor. In exchange, the party offered a common front against radicalism. The general economic distress of postwar Hungary affected most social strata, and the numerically still small industrial working class, tainted by the dictatorship so recently exercised in its name, could expect no special favor.*

*Despite the nominal pluralism of the political system, a limited franchise backed by a nationalistic consensus left power in the hands of an expanded social elite that ruled with a blend of paternalism and authoritarianism. It dealt mercilessly with real or apprehended left-wing radicalism, and recoiled even from democratic liberalism. The communists bore the brunt of this persecution. The "White terror" that followed the Commune decimated their ranks, leaving a few scattered groups abroad or in hiding.*

*The party was revived by the indefatigable Béla Kun, first in Vienna and Moscow and then in Hungary itself. Throughout the interwar period, however, it remained incapacitated by chronic factionalism and the vigilance of the Hungarian authorities. Divided over tactics, the émigrés were among the more doctrinaire and impatient revolutionaries of the Comintern, which had to intervene repeatedly in the internecine disputes. Factionalism arose from divergent views, all of them overoptimistic, regarding the prospects for a second revolution in Hungary. Since the reconstructed social democrats were determinedly anti-communist and preserved their hold over organized labor, the few home communists were driven to marginal agitation in illegality. In 1925 communists and a few left-wing socialists launched a legal, crypto-communist party, but it failed to draw support away from the Social Democratic Party and soon disintegrated.*

*Rent by factionalism, unable to offer credible panaceas to the workers, dogmatically committed to agricultural collectivization despite the peasantry's hunger for private land, prevented by ideologically preordained internationalism from espousing irredentism, the minuscule communist party failed to exploit even the economic stresses and mass unemployment of the Great Depression. In the mid-1930s political radicalism in Hungary took the form of a nationalistic and peasant-oriented populism, which the communists tried unsuccessfully to convert to their own ends. Later, an extreme right-wing movement materialized that, like the Populists, was far more successful than the moribund communist party in attracting disaffected elements. The ruling elite had little difficulty in suppressing or isolating these new radical tendencies, but it was drawn inexorably into the embrace of Nazi Germany and fascist Italy by the lure of markets and investment, sympathy for revisionism, and common anticommunism.*

*In the short run this alignment brought tangible benefits: an acceleration in economic growth and the return by Italo-German arbitration of parts of Slovakia and Transylvania. Hungary thereby became wedded to the Axis and to war against the Soviet Union. The wartime governments tried to limit military participation and for a time preserved a degree of sovereignty that allowed Hungarians, and in particular, Jews, to avoid the horrors of Nazism. But the fortunes of war dashed hopes that defeat, now seen as inevitable, would bring Western rather than Soviet occupation. In March 1944 the Germans occupied Hungary. After an interval of seven months they seized Horthy, and imposed a fascist regime, thus exposing the country to Nazi excesses and, ultimately, to "liberation" by the Red Army. Thus Berlin's imperialism made way for Moscow's. The Hungarians, along with their East European neighbors, were once again grist in the mill of Great Power rivalry.*

*As for the communists, those in exile devoted their energies to a variety of Comintern assignments, notably the Spanish civil war. By the time that the Comintern, serving as Stalin's agent, had adopted an antifascist popular front policy in the mid-1930s, the Hungarian party was in such disarray that it was powerless to take up the challenge, neither its leaders nor the social democrats being eager for alliance. Concurrently, many of the émigrés, including Kun, perished in Stalin's purges.*

*With the onset of war the survivors rallied in Moscow under the leadership of the recently liberated Mátyás Rákosi. They mounted a propaganda campaign and infiltrated a few partisan groups. An isolated handful of home communists pursued their own struggle through propaganda, occasional sabotage, and another short-lived front party. They also forged links with an emerging legal opposition movement that did not survive German occupation. As the war ground to its conclusion, both groups made plans for reintroducing the party and its creed to Hungarians, this time with the anticipated sponsorship of the victorious Russians. After twenty-five years in the political wilderness, Hungary's communists were hungry for power.*

# 4. Exile and Factionalism, 1919–1924

The Peidl government, composed in the main of moderate trade union leaders, assumed office on 1 August 1919 and proceeded to dismantle its predecessor's work.[1] It did so in order to accommodate not only the Entente but also the powerful domestic revulsion at the Commune's excesses. Although the new regime had initially announced that the revolution's legislation remained in force, the councils were soon replaced with a more orthodox democratic structure and the more radical measures abrogated. The imprisoned enemies of the Commune were set free; the prerevolutionary judiciary and police were restored; all nationalized property was returned to its former owners; rents were raised to their former levels; and a new "people's republic" was proclaimed. Workers were instructed to remain in their plants. Throughout the unoccupied territories, communists were relieved of all administrative functions.

## OCCUPATION AND COUNTERTERROR

The Entente's promise of recognition and ceasefire did not prevent Romanian forces from occupying Budapest on 4 August. Concurrently, so-called officers' detachments of the counterrevolutionary high command at Szeged moved into Transdanubia to organize a White army and begin the hunt for communist sympathizers. The Peidl regime lasted a bare six days. On 6 August, a group of monarchist officers led by a former undersecretary of state for defense, István Friedrich, compelled it to resign. With the approval of British and Italian emissaries, Archduke Joseph Habsburg appointed a new government under Friedrich, thereby preempting the competing Szeged group, which was sponsored by the French. The Archduke was soon forced to withdraw from the scene, but Friedrich remained in office. Though momentarily pursuing the mandatory counterterror, he showed some promise of reviving the liberal democratic precepts of the Károlyi interregnum.[2]

During the chaotic weeks of restoration, while political factions jockeyed for power, the spirit of revenge dominated governmental and military activity. At its extreme, the so-called White terror was perpetrated by the officers' detachments, more or less welded into a national army headquartered at Siófok on Lake Balaton, which engaged in a merciless hunt for real and alleged communists in the countryside. The Romanian forces shared in the pogrom while indulging in indiscriminate looting. For a pogrom it was. The fact that a large proportion of the communist leaders and activists were Jews inspired a vengeful anti-Semitism that remained a feature of the nationalist ideology that would dominate Hungary's interwar political system. Hundreds of communists and suspected sympathizers fell victim to the officers' detachments. The Friedrich government for its part issued instructions for accelerated trials and stiff sentences for communists and set up several internment camps. Apart from the summary justice meted out by the military, the official measures rested on a legalistic rationale first advanced by the Peidl government: the Republic of Councils had represented not legitimate political rule but the seizure of power by armed individuals. The economic and security enactments of the Commune were thus construed as common crimes of theft and murder and their perpetrators were prosecuted accordingly. The restoration regimes had more time than their predecessor to pursue political dissidents. It has been estimated that some five thousand were executed and seventy-five thousand jailed for their activities during the Commune. Another hundred thousand chose exile, most of them not communists but socialist and liberal political activists and intellectuals, including many middle-class Jews.[3] Among the more lasting legacies of the Commune were official and popular attribution of its genesis to the weakness and incompetence of the Károlyi regime and a consequent general deprecation of liberal democracy.

The socialist leaders remaining in Hungary lost no time in disengaging their party from its disastrous alliance with the communists and in minimizing its role in the Commune. The old SDP was formally reconstituted at an extraordinary congress on 24 August. The party retrieved its 1903 program and rejoined the Second International. Those present, said Peyer, "refuse to identify themselves with the acts committed by the dictatorship of a small group."[4] He urged that the communists be punished in exemplary fashion and that the party be purged of all those associated with the defunct regime. The congress adopted a staunch anticommunist line from which the party would not depart for over two decades.

While the reaction of the majority of socialists against revolutionary excess was genuine, its proclamation was made imperative by the requisites of political survival..In the emerging system socialism was to be merely tolerated, and within strict bounds. Only long-established trade unions were authorized by the Friedrich government. All the ones created during the Commune were effectively emasculated while the government made attempts to promote alternative "Christian socialist" labor organizations. In the meantime, amidst growing inflation and unemployment, the regime revoked the Commune's provisions for unemployment benefits and shorter working hours and reduced industrial wages. A miners' strike against these regressive measures in early September had to be quelled by force of arms. Vivid memories of the Commune together with evidence of the country's bankruptcy did not dispose the leaders of the restoration to sympathy for a numerically still modest industrial proletariat.

When in October the Entente's intervention against the Soviet Red Army faltered, the Romanian forces had to be redeployed in a hurry. This, in turn, required that Hungary be secured against a communist revival by a strengthened White army and by a government that included the SDP. Following the Romanians' withdrawal on 16 November a national army, led by Miklós Horthy mounted on a white horse, entered Budapest—a "sinful city," thundered the admiral. A week later, with the advice of the Entente's representative, Sir George Clerk, a coalition government was assembled under Károly Huszár; it encompassed a "Christian bloc," the SDP, and a few liberals such as Vázsonyi. For the socialists, the price of participation was unqualified anticommunism and the suspension of militancy. Although Peyer received the public welfare portfolio, the conditions for collaborating with a fundamentally conservative regime decimated the ranks of the socialist leadership. Böhm, Kunfi, and Garbai were already in Vienna. They were now joined in emigration by Buchinger, Garami, and Weltner. Bokányi, Haubrich and others languished in jail along with hundreds of communists. For the latter, the long night was only beginning.

## COMMUNISM PROSCRIBED

The tentative agreement for the liquidation of the Commune hammered out between Sir Thomas Cuninghame and Böhm in Vienna in the last days of July anticipated the curtailment of all communist activity in Hungary. To this end, the Austrian government was persuaded to offer political asylum to a number of leading old and new communists, including Kun, Landler, Pogány, Pór, and Varga. Before their departure the leaders conferred on the party's future in Hungary. Korvin and Lukács volunteered to stay behind in order to salvage what remained. The others boarded two special trains with their families, arrived in Vienna on 2 and 3 August, and were promptly interned in Karlstein Castle.[5] Subsequently, many less prominent communists also sought asylum in Austria. Szamuely, who had been refused an entry permit, attempted to cross the border illegally and apparently committed suicide when challenged by Austrian police.

With most of their comrades driven into exile, imprisoned, or executed, the communists still at liberty drew back from any idea of once more forming an illegal party.[6] A few stalwart activists in Budapest hoped that party cells might be sustained within the SDP. This was a modest expectation, but they had little organization to preserve, their initially small numbers having been dispersed in the united party during the Commune. The latter did bequeath them some tangible assets. As early as April the commissar for finance, Gyula Lengyel, had transferred a sizable sum from the Austro-Hungarian Bank into private safekeeping, and a stock of false documents had also been amassed. In the event, these precautions came to naught. Most of the money was surrendered to the government by its guardians, communication among widely known activists proved to be impossibly hazardous, and on 7 August Korvin himself was arrested. The gathering White terror compelled Lukács and other exposed communists to flee to Austria in September.

Even emigration did not guarantee security. On 16 August, the Friedrich regime requested the extradition of Kun and his associates. Only after a violent domestic debate did the Austrian government refuse to comply. Hungarian right-wing groups then launched a series of attempts to murder or kidnap the communists. They succeeded in enticing a few across the border and managed to infiltrate what was left of the movement in Hungary.

The émigrés lived and planned in expectation of an early return to the fray. Already in September their printed propaganda was appearing under the auspices of the Austrian party. Those in Vienna, including Lukács and Szántó, busily conferred with the Karlstein group. By November a Provisional Central Committee had come into being; it consisted of Hamburger and Lukács, the still interned Kun, Landler, and Pór, plus Hirossik, who remained in Hungary. By December Kun was assuring Lenin that illegal activities were being pursued in Hungary. Indeed, a few former members of the KIMSZ (including Pál Demény, who would later lead a dissident leftist faction) did manage to evade arrest and remain in touch with each other, clinging to the dream of a proletarian dictatorship in the face of even socialist and unionist hostility.

The trial of Korvin and the Lenin boys opened on 24 November. The émigrés made repeated efforts to save them. It was suggested that the Soviet government select hostages from among the prisoners of war, and a plan was hatched to liberate Korvin by force. The latter scheme only led to further losses, for a courier between Vienna and Budapest turned out to be an informer whose contacts were soon put under arrest. Korvin and twenty-two others were executed. Another group, which had produced the first communist leaflet since the Commune's fall, was also arrested thanks to the same informer.[7]

**Reappraisals of Theory and Practice.**    While the White terror decimated communist ranks in Hungary, the émigrés indulged in historical and ideological reassessments, beginning with Kun's essay "From Revolution to Revolution."[8]

In their search for the causes of the Commune's disintegration, the émigrés focused on the weaknesses of the ruling party although, as will be seen later, differences in interpretation, particularly of Kun's failings, would generate factional polemics. The proclamation of a Republic of Councils was not premature, argued Kun. The bourgeoisie had admitted its incapacity to rule, while the social democrats felt unable to take the reins alone. A further imperative was the need to provide at least moral support for the struggling Soviet regime. The problem had been that before the communists had had the chance to build a strong party, they were driven by circumstance to join forces with the socialists, and in the united party they operated as a minority faction. The socialist-communist party was too amorphous, ideologically too eclectic, to serve as the necessary revolutionary vanguard. The cardinal sin, which for Kun and others became a shibboleth, had been to share power with reformist, right-wing socialists. The latter diluted ideological purity, beclouded class consciousness, and ultimately served the interests of the enemy. Some émigrés, notably Lukács, now recanted their view, expressed during the Commune, that once the dictatorship of the proletariat was proclaimed, there was no longer any need for a communist party.

Apart from such reconsiderations, the émigrés blamed the proletariat's insufficient revolutionary class consciousness for their failure. They left momentarily unchallenged the possibly counterproductive measures of the Commune, such as its agrarian policy, and stressed as the main task for the future the development of grass roots support among the industrial working class. Kun, ignoring the obvious appeal of social democracy among the workers, rejected outright the parliamentary route to power. In this, and in their dogmatic dismissal of the possibility of cooperation with centrist socialists, Kun and a few like-minded comrades drew in some measure on the experience of the Commune but in the process placed themselves on the extreme left of the communist movement. Their position made collaboration with the Hungarian socialist émigrés unthinkable.*

In their speculations on the Hungarian party's experiences and prospects, the émigrés inevitably became enmeshed in the ongoing debate within the European socialist movement. Fueling the controversy were the writings of Karl Kautsky and Eduard Bernstein, who in defense of German social democracy and the parliamentary process denied the general applicability of the dictatorship of the proletariat. The Comintern's position, published in a circular on 1 September 1919, was that parliamentary politics could only serve as a means to create a soviet system, a proletarian dictatorship that would necessarily entail

---

*The principal organization of centrist social democratic émigrés, formed in Vienna in April 1920, was named "Világosság," after their periodical. Led by Böhm and Kunfi, it had close links with the Austrian Social Democratic Party.

the destruction of bourgeois parliamentarism. Further guidelines, issued by the Comintern's West European Secretariat in January 1920, recognized that the pace of revolution was slowing. Warning against rash action, the guidelines instructed communists to win over the most important elements of industrial labor in preparation for the civil wars that would pave the way for authentic revolution.

Kun was too flushed with his brief success to abandon hope for more rapid revolution. With the counterrevolution momentarily in the ascendant in Hungary, he anticipated eagerly that proletarian revolutions in Germany and Italy would provide the impetus for his party's return to power. He wrote to Lenin in December 1919 that "as soon as revolution begins somewhere in the West, Hungary will go along."[9] Some of his comrades in Vienna felt that conditions were not yet ripe. Most, however, awaited with unwarranted optimism the outbreak of a German revolution and were devastated by the German communists' acquiescence in a socialist regime in March 1920. The outbreak of Soviet-Polish hostilities the following month kindled hopes of a Red Army victory and of the westward advance of revolution—again, with direct consequences for Hungary.

In a letter written in the spring of 1920, Kun begged Lenin not to restrain him with public statements that the Bolshevik method was not immediately applicable in Western Europe. Such cautionary advice, he complained, would be used by the Kautskyites to deprecate revolutionary action. He also reported that he opposed the inclination of some comrades to issue a call for land reform, and asked for Lenin's views on the matter.[10] But by then Lenin was mounting a campaign against the "leftist" rejection of legal methods. In June 1920 he singled out articles by Lukács and Kun denouncing the German compromise (they had appeared in the Comintern's review *Kommunismus*). Lukács's views were "very leftist and very bad," observed Lenin, while Kun had missed "that which is the most essential in Marxism, which is Marxism's living soul—the concrete analysis of a concrete situation." With irony, he congratulated Kun: "Bravo, bravo comrade B.K.! When you defend antiparliamentarism, you deliver a more devastating blow against this stupidity than I with my critique."[11] Lenin's famous tract, *"Left-Wing Communism": An Infantile Disorder of Communism*, written in preparation for the Comintern's second congress, was directed in part at the doctrinaire stance of the Hungarians and took stock of the lessons of the Commune.

At that congress, which convened on 19 July 1920, the Hungarian party was represented by Rudnyánszky and by Rákosi, the latter having been recently released from Austrian internment. Rákosi presented a report on the CPH, reviewing organizational shortcomings during the Commune and indicating the problems of reconstruction under the White terror. His was a standard account of the Commune and of its errors, notably, the error of collaboration between

Socialists and communists. Lenin himself was acutely aware of these dangers. His demand to the congress for reorganization of the Comintern into a nucleus of ideologically unified, disciplined, "pure" parties on the Bolshevik model was directly inspired by the Hungarian debacle.

The "Twenty-One Conditions of Admission into the Communist International" adopted by the congress both explicitly and implicitly drew on the Hungarian experience. The preamble instructed that no communist should forget the "lessons" of the Commune: "The alliance between the Hungarian communists and the so-called left social democrats cost the Hungarian proletariat dearly." The prescriptions for Comintern parties called, inter alia, for purging reformist elements, curtailing factions, maintaining party cells in trade unions and workers' councils, and winning over the agrarian proletariat, in all of which Kun could have been deemed deficient.[12] The congress specifically criticized the Commune's agrarian policy and in general reflected Lenin's indictment of leftism. Kun, however, would continue to cling to his uncompromising line.[13]

In August 1920, as the prospect of Soviet victory over the Poles receded, Kun, who had recently arrived in Moscow, adumbrated a new strategy focusing on the chances of revolution in southeast Europe. His optimism in this regard was fed by the view, shared notably by Lukács, that the fragmentation of the Austro-Hungarian Empire had not produced economically viable and ethnically homogeneous states, and that only a federative soviet republic could resolve these problems. The Hungarian proletariat, opined Kun, had lost its power of initiative, but it stood ready to follow the lead of the surrounding nations, which were ripe for the launching of a second phase of socialist revolution. In the event, a band of activists was infiltrated into Slovakia, and Kun expected much from the repatriation to the successor states of suitably radicalized Hungarian war prisoners. His fanciful schemes, however, succeeded only in sowing the seeds of discord among the communist émigrés.[14]

In appraising the Hungarian situation, the émigrés recognized that the revolutionary experience had strengthened the class consciousness of the bourgeoisie, whereas the Commune's demise had debilitated the organized proletariat. What, then, was the momentary locus of power? On this they were divided. Did it rest solely with the military under Horthy? With the petite bourgeoisie? With the capitalists and landowners? They did agree on the objective of a second Republic of Councils, dismissing the intermediate step of a bourgeois democracy as having had its brief historical run and being now superseded. But they could not reach consensus on the tactics best suited to the confusing political situation, both in Hungary and internationally, and to the dispersed state of the party. Lukács, meanwhile, was earning his ideologue's spurs with a series of essays that gave the fullest expression to the idea of a close-knit vanguard party, ideologically pure and deserving of every sacrifice, which possessed a truth that even the proletariat could never by itself comprehend.[15]

**The Resumption of Agitation.** The reconstruction of a closed, centralized party was the émigrés' most urgent task. The provisional organizational statutes, drafted by Kun and issued in mid-1920, proclaimed the CPH to be the Comintern's Hungarian section, outlined rules for a structure and membership based on democratic centralism, and singled out the trade unions as the most suitable battleground. To facilitate recruitment and preserve security, the statutes allowed for a category of "sympathizer members." To encourage the home communists, the illegal paper *Proletár* reported on an agitprop conference in Moscow attended by three thousand Hungarians who had been admitted to the Soviet party.[16] The Provisional Central Committee at this time consisted of Kun, Landler, Lukács, Szántó, and Hirossik, who was still in Hungary. Hungarian émigrés operating in Slovakia collaborated with the Viennese colony in preparing propaganda material and smuggling it into Hungary.

Another area of activity was the city of Pécs in a region of Hungary that remained under Yugoslav occupation until August 1921. At communist instigation, the local branch of the SDP converted itself into an independent "Socialist Party" aligned with the Comintern. It maintained contact with the Provisional Central Committee and turned Pécs into a center of revolutionary agitation. The party leadership urged the Pécs communists to do everything to prolong Serbian occupation, knowing full well that once the area reverted to Hungarian administration their relative freedom of action would disappear.

Within Hungary a few isolated groups of communists engaged in sporadic activity, mainly the dissemination of leaflets, through 1920 and 1921.[17] Their work was hampered by internal disputes and haphazard communications with the émigré leaders. They would variously receive guidance from Lékai, the Youth Comintern's representative in Vienna, from Lukács and Landler, and from Hirossik. In December 1920 two young recruits, Erzsébet Andics and Andor Berei, tried to draw together the dispersed communists and even managed to acquire printing facilities. Within a few months, their group was under arrest, and a new law confirmed the proscription of the party.[18] The police regularly rounded up disseminators of communist leaflets, which in mid-1920 concentrated on attacking the regime's alleged intention of aiding Poland in its war against the Soviet Union.

Externally, the communists were more successful in mounting a propaganda campaign against the Hungarian government. Its repressive measures had already aroused criticism in progressive foreign circles. Representatives of the British Labour and Italian Socialist parties visited Hungary as guests of the government in April and May 1920, but their reports did little to assuage foreign criticism. That summer, the International Transport Workers' Union and the International Federation of Trade Unions ordered a two-month boycott designed to cut all communication links with Hungary. The boycott was only fractionally implemented and, within Hungary, was denounced even by the SDP.

## CONSERVATIVE RESTORATION, COMMUNIST DISPUTES

By 1920, the process of political consolidation in Hungary was well advanced. The political values that came to predominate in interwar Hungary were irredentist nationalism and counterrevolutionary conservatism. Both were sustained and propagated by a succession of governments. The first rested on a consensual abhorrence of the Treaty of Trianon of June 1920, by which Hungary lost two-thirds of her territory and over three million ethnic Magyars to the surrounding states. *Nem, nem, soha* (*"*No, no, never*"*), a slogan rejecting the finality of this dismemberment, reflected the patriotic rage that gripped all classes and layers of Hungarian society. Numerous secret societies and paramilitary organizations emerged during the 1920s. With their blend of revisionist and anti-Bolshevik ideology, they played an influential role in the political system. Such linking of revisionist nationalism with the maintenance of the prevailing social order, following on the recent painful experience with Bolshevism, greatly helped the ruling elite in its task of conservative consolidation. The middle classes, swollen by the influx of refugees from the lost territories, readily shared the political values of the ruling aristocrats and gentry. A modest land reform enacted in 1920 redistributed some 13 percent of the arable land, thereby enlarging a rural smallholder class that was loyal to the regime and enjoyed token representation in parliament with the Smallholder Party (Kisgazdapárt, or SHP). Although most people in the countryside now owned land, the prevalence of both vast estates and dwarfholdings left social tensions in the countryside unresolved.

The first postwar national assembly was elected in 1920 by secret ballot on the basis of a franchise extending to 3,042,000 voters; the SDP, which was still in disgrace, did not participate. The assembly reestablished the old constitution of the kingdom of Hungary and named Admiral Horthy regent and acting head of state. In 1921, the deposed Charles I made two attempts to return to Hungary and claim the crown. He was rebuffed: the opposition of antilegitimists, backed by the Western and successor states, was too strong. The Habsburg link was definitively severed, and Hungary remained a kingdom without a king. That same year, Count István Bethlen, a conservative Transylvanian, was appointed prime minister. His paternalistic but by and large capable administration guided Hungary's fortunes over the next decade.

The most urgent problem facing Bethlen's government was the state of the economy. Inflation, lost industries and markets, reparations, massive unemployment—such were the consequences of defeat and dismemberment. Desperately short of capital, the regime pragmatically muted its irredentism and in 1924 negotiated a foreign loan that brought with it League of Nations supervision of the country's finances. The resulting reconstruction program bore fruit, and by 1930 a favorable balance of trade had been achieved. Unemployment among middle-class professionals and administrators was resolved by the expedient of inflating the government bureaucracy. Industrialization and a declining birth rate in rural areas served to alleviate the hidden unemployment plaguing the agricultural labor force.

A major task of consolidation was to reach a modus vivendi with the industrial workers (numbering 464,000 in 1920), or at least with their official representatives, the trade unions and the SDP. By October 1920, the trade unions felt free to hold a national conference. Between 1921 and 1930 a series of social measures were enacted covering social insurance, pensions, minimum age of workers, and working conditions, all in partial satisfaction of long-standing socialist demands.[19]

In its determination to forestall a new radical politicization of the proletariat, the regime resorted to both legislated repression and compromise. A 1921 law proscribed subversive activities, confirming the de facto prohibition of the communist party. The regularization of the SDP's status took the form of a secret agreement concluded by Bethlen and Peyer in December 1921. The pact delineated the role of the party in the interwar political system. The SDP was allowed to seek representation in parliament and pursue normal party and union activities in Budapest and other urban areas. In exchange, Peyer agreed to limit strikes, support the government's foreign policy, and forego any attempt to unionize civil servants, railway workers, or agricultural laborers. Bethlen promised to limit internment to communist agitators, and indeed by the time of the pact, most of the socialists had been set free. In December 1920, the trial of ten former people's commissars had ended with death sentences for Bokányi, Haubrich, Vántus, and Péter Ágoston, and life imprisonment for the rest. However, the Soviet government had interned a thousand Hungarian officer prisoners of war and selected ten as hostages. After months of negotiation the condemned commissars and several hundred other communists were exchanged.[20]

**The Factional Battles Begin.** The communist émigrés meanwhile persisted in largely theoretical debates on strategy and tactics. A conference of Hungarian communists in Russia was convened in September 1920. Anticipating an intensification of the White terror and therefore of class conflict, Kun waxed optimistic: "Our policy must be one of active offense vis-à-vis all levels of the society in order to replace the White terror and bourgeois dictatorship with the dictatorship of the proletariat." To achieve this, expanded Kun, they could easily find, among the prisoners of war about to be repatriated, two thousand reliable communists who would proceed to subvert the trade unions, lead strikes, and launch an armed uprising.[21] The gap between Kun's fantasy and Hungarian reality did not escape even the procommunist prisoners. Many of them chose to ignore the leadership's instructions, while others asked to be assigned to Germany or Austria. Landler and Hirossik therefore urged Kun in December 1920 to place under Vienna's direction only the most dedicated activists.[22] The Hungarian authorities, for their part, shepherded the repatriates into a holding camp. There, through interrogation and denunciation, the communists were soon identified and were subsequently kept under close observation by the police.

Undeterred, Kun continued to advocate that a home-based party be reestablished at all cost. To attempt this from the outside would be futile. "All those whose chances of annihilation are no greater than 60 to 70 percent must somehow return to Hungary," he wrote in January 1921. In a contemporary article, the equally impatient Rudnyánszky disparaged the more cautious disposition of the party's Viennese leadership.[23]

It is not uncommon for political émigrés to engage in internecine squabbles, and the revolutionary and conspiratorial ethos of the communists only exacerbated this general tendency. By late 1920, a vicious factional struggle had erupted between Kun, who was supported by Rudnyánszky, Vágó, and Varga, and a collection of opponents that included the Landler group in Vienna, Lukács, Szántó, and Rudas, and such free-wheeling ultraleftists as Bettelheim and Bolgár. Decades later, Lukács recalled that "on the great philosophical questions of the revolution, I remained the advocate of ultraleft tendencies, while as a member of the Hungarian party leadership I became the bitter opponent of Kun's kind of sectarianism." His own sectarianism, argued Lukács, was one of the pure "messianic" variety, whereas Kun represented a modern "bureaucratic" sectarianism. At the same time, however, Lukács was a passionate defender of the so-called March Action, a German uprising in which Kun played a leading part (see below).[24] The anti-Kun polemics covered a broad field and were steeped in personal animosity. The ultraleftists blamed Kun's tactics for the fall of the Commune and even accused him of embezzlement.[25] The Landler group challenged him on future tactics and condemned both the publication and substance of Kun's and Rudnyánszky's critiques.

Landler and his associates formulated their complaint in a memorandum sent by special courier at the end of March 1921 to the Comintern. Kun, they protested, would have done better to discuss his reservations privately with them prior to his departure for Moscow. Public quarrels only harmed the party's work in Hungary. The immediate calling of a party conference and establishment of a leading center in Hungary was totally unfeasible. Even overt communist agitation in the trade unions would lead to immediate arrest. The

Viennese Provisional Central Committee therefore rejected Kun's call for repatriation of the party, adding that not all available activists were qualified for the special conditions of illegality. They also dismissed the suggestion that the Soviet Union was the only suitable base for émigré activity, pointing out Vienna's various advantages. Nor did they accept Rudnyánszky's allegation that they had adopted a nationalist-irredentist posture. On the contrary, they had restrained Rákosi from attempting to organize a Slovakian party separate from the Czechs. And they disagreed with Kun's proposal for development of a concrete plan for revolution at a time when the international revolutionary momentum had not yet acquired a clear direction. They would therefore pursue their current tasks until the Comintern's Executive Committee made a ruling on the matter.[26]

Kun, ever the man of action, devoted only part of his time to such theoretical debates. The short-lived Commune had endowed him with an aura of revolutionary experience and expertise, and he wanted to serve on the current battlefronts of Bolshevism. When, in November 1920, Wrangel's White Army was defeated in the Crimea, Kun, as a member of the Red Army's revolutionary council, negotiated the surrender, promising amnesty to the survivors. When he thereupon coldly ordered the massacre of thousands of prisoners, Lenin was driven to recall and censure his zealous Hungarian disciple.[27]

Kun was next assigned by the Comintern's chairman, Zinoviev, to mastermind revolution in Germany. Pogány and Münnich were also dispatched to Germany as agents of the Comintern. It was largely at Kun's instigation that, in March 1921, the German party called for a general strike and launched an armed rising (known as the March Action). On the orders of social democratic ministers, it was quickly suppressed. The German communist leaders Clara Zetkin and Paul Levi (who subsequently defected to the socialists) wrote to Lenin protesting at Kun's promotion of the March Action. The Bolshevik leader replied: "With regard to the latest strikes and uprising in Germany, I have read nothing about them. I can readily believe that the representative of the Executive Committee defended the stupid, overly leftist tactic of immediate action 'in the interest of helping the Russians'—this representative is frequently too leftist."[28] (The argument for helping the Russians presumably derived from the Soviet regime's concurrent embarrassment at the Kronstadt Rebellion, which took place from 28 February to 18 March.) Kun had acted on orders from Zinoviev, who took a rather proprietary view of the Comintern, but it is difficult to believe that Lenin was unaware of the proposed action. The Comintern had sent not only advisers but also money and probably arms to the German communists. Since the uprising had ended in fiasco, however, Kun was a convenient scapegoat. In his analysis before the Comintern's Executive Committee, Lenin would repeatedly refer to *les bêtises de Béla Kun* ("Béla Kun's stupid mistakes").[29]

The Hungarian émigrés seemed uncommonly predisposed to dogmatism. When, in January 1921, Rákosi was sent by the Comintern to the Italian Socialist Party's congress in Leghorn, he managed to split off its left wing by insisting on the letter of the Twenty-one Conditions.[30] Two years later, Lenin and his associates persuaded themselves that conditions had ripened for revolution in Germany. Kun, still regarded as a German expert, was once again involved in the preparations, this time under the supervision of Karl Radek. Concerted uprisings leading to a coup d'etat were planned for 23 October 1923. At the last minute Radek decided to postpone the venture but neglected to inform the Hamburg leader, Ernst Thälmann, who launched a rising that was quickly and bloodily suppressed. Back in Moscow, violent arguments ensued, notably between Kun and Thälmann, over who had disobeyed instructions and "betrayed" the German revolution. Finally, Radek's responsibility was confirmed.[31]

When Kun returned to Moscow in April 1921, after the first German fiasco, he reacted to his Viennese comrades' offensive by forming with Pogány a faction under the name of "party builders" and composing a countermemorandum to the Comintern.[32] The basic premise of his riposte was that the Viennese majority on the Central Committee were no longer the decisive voice in the party but merely a faction at odds with the three-thousand-strong party section in Russia and the newly formed party-builder faction. The petty protests of the Landler group, he continued, arose from their remoteness from the mass movement and were reminiscent of what he called "Paul Levi's indignation." Rejecting the current incremental tactic of developing communist cells within the SDP, the party builders called for the creation of a distinct communist party in Hungary and the detachment of the trade unions from the SDP, initially by withholding party dues from the latter. They criticized the Viennese for neglecting the Hungarian scene in their review *Proletár* and for failing to produce an action program. There was a need for conferences to develop such a program and debate the agrarian question.

Thus the lines were drawn between the Landler wing, which recognized the ongoing political consolidation in Hungary and the consequent difficulty of a communist revival, and the Kun faction, which questioned the consolidation and urged immediate action. Accusations of rightist and leftist deviation colored by personal animosities embittered the émigrés' relations. The Central Committee in May rejected the party builders' charges and proposed suspension of the dispute until the Comintern's forthcoming third congress. The same sentiment was echoed in Moscow by Varga, who wrote in *Vörös Ujság* that "an illegal movement cannot be established through public debates."[33]

**"Party Builders" versus "Liquidators."** In mid-June Landler, Lukács, and Hirossik left Vienna for the Comintern congress, sending ahead a second memorandum. In this they repeated that conditions in Hungary prevented the creation of a leading organ. They described the party's tasks as follows: the cautious development of an illegal, centralized, closed party based on cells; the gradual infiltration of trade unions leading to communist control; propaganda among the rural proletariat; "disruptive activities" to divide the ruling classes; and, more generally, activities attuned to the workers' immediate concerns, all in aid of an eventual seizure of power.[34]

The Hungarian party was represented at the congress by Kun, Lukács, Pogány, Rákosi, Rudnyánszky, Szántó, Varga, Hirossik, and three others (two additional delegates, Ernő Gerő and Frigyes Karikás, had been arrested in transit at the Austro-German border). The congress convened on 22 June. The Hungarians had initially nominated Kun, Landler, and Szántó to their presidency and Szántó as their secretary in charge of liaison with the Comintern's Executive Committee. By 2 July, however, they had divided into openly antagonistic factions.

At the plenary sessions debate raged over the tactics best suited to a time of revolutionary relapse. Although the March Action was widely criticized, Zinoviev's and Trotsky's general appraisals were sufficiently ambivalent to embolden the Austrian, German, and Italian delegates to introduce an amendment favoring a militantly offensive tactic. This was promptly endorsed by Kun's faction. Thereupon Landler, Lukács, and Hirossik proclaimed their support for the Leninist "Russian theses" and protested that, despite the Executive Committee's decision to grant equal votes to the two Hungarian factions, Kun pretended to speak for a majority. Lenin, as we have seen, was acutely aware of certain Hungarians' extremism, and he profoundly embarrassed Kun at an Executive Committee meeting on the French party. "I came to speak against Kun's views," he began his address, "for I am certain that when Kun opens his mouth he will undoubtedly defend the 'leftists'."[35] The congress ultimately endorsed the Leninist theses, which anticipated a protracted struggle to win over the working class, with the slogan "into the masses." This was subsequently elaborated into the concept of a worker-peasant alliance and government.[36] Rudnyánszky was elected to the Executive Committee and to its five-man presidium.

Following the congress, a commission composed of the Comintern nominees Radek, Bukarin, and Thalheimer and of representative Hungarians met to investigate the factional dispute. The two positions were expounded by Hirossik and Pogány, the latter asserting that the Hungarian regime was on the brink of collapse. Among the less committed protagonists Varga now moved closer to the Viennese faction, while Alpári, the editor of the Comintern's *Inprekor*, joined Rákosi in siding with the party builders. The three non-Hungarians, without approving the party builders' proposals in their entirety, denounced the Landler group as "liquidators" and branded their activities as "Menshevik." After prolonged and acrimonious debate the commission produced a set of resolutions, which were ratified in August by the Executive Committee and issued as the Comintern's directive to the CPH.

Asserting that conditions in Hungary had become more propitious with the attenuation of the White terror, and noting that while the party was proscribed the trade unions enjoyed a certain freedom of action, the directive concluded that the latter provided the best field for communist activity. It would therefore be counterproductive to deny payment of dues to the SDP, although the class traitors leading that party had to be unmasked. The existing loosely organized propaganda cells were deemed insufficient. Instead, a centralized illegal party had to be constructed with local and works cells as well as trade union cells and with a leading organ located in Hungary. (The directive did not, however, endorse the massive repatriation proposal.) All propaganda had to be clearly identified as issuing from the communist party.[37]

Concurrently, a new Central Committee was appointed, still designated provisional pending a regular party congress. Proposed by Radek, its membership gave a four-to-three majority to the party builders Kun, Pogány, Rudnyánszky, and one Dezső Szilágyi, who confronted Landler, Lukács, and Hirossik. Kun remained in Moscow as a member of the Comintern's Executive Committee. The others left for Vienna. One of them, Rudnyánszky, seized the opportunity to defect. After denouncing the CPH in a letter to Zinoviev, he fled to Romania, reportedly absconding with sizable Comintern funds. Five years later, he returned to the Soviet Union, where he was promptly clapped in jail.

The dispute had produced deep rifts in the party, and in September the new Central Committee launched an attempt to reintegrate the various factions in Vienna and Berlin. Meanwhile, in the spirit of the Comintern resolutions, *Proletár* issued the call "Communists, into the trade unions!" The reconciliation proved to be ephemeral. For one thing, the Comintern's directive was with slight exaggeration promoted as a vindication of the party builders. Wrote Kun in October: "After the Comintern's decision there would be no room for factional dispute even if the 'party builder' faction's program had not prevailed." The ostensible victory of Kun's faction only embittered the internecine battles. The squabbling reached a new peak when Pogány wrote an article condemning the activities of the alternate Central Committee during the leaders' absence at the Comintern congress.

The alternate Central Committee had over the summer incited the communists and workers in Hungary to sabotage. Instead of restraining the activists in Pécs, who were toying with the idea of proclaiming a Soviet Republic to challenge the impending return of the district to Budapest's administration, the committee invited the local miners to flood their mines. The factional positions were thus turned about, with Pogány denouncing irresponsible adventurism and his opponents, notably Gyula Lengyel and Rudas, arguing that the revolutionary conditions were favorable, but the end result was total paralysis of party work. Pogány, who was endorsed by coopted members to take Rudnyánszky's place on the Central Committee, and Szilágyi, who was frequently absent, represented one faction. The Landler faction controlled the party apparatus (the Viennese secretariat under Landler himself, the illegal one under Hirossik) as well as the journal *Proletár*. Both factions proceeded to proselytize, not infrequently with the inducement of a paid post in the apparatus. At a Central Committee meeting on 12 October, Landler, Lukács, and Hirossik reacted to Pogány's charge of sabotage by threatening to resign. Arguments dragged on over allegedly missed opportunities for action on the occasion of Charles I's second attempt to return to Hungary. Finally, on 24 October, Landler and his supporters made good their threat and appealed once again to the Comintern.[38]

When Pogány attempted to purge the apparatus, a strike broke out among party employees and the vindictively personal vendetta only intensified. Vituperative outbursts in *Proletár*, now the party builders' organ, and the opposition's *Vörös Ujság* (Vienna) compelled the Comintern on 21 December to interdict further polemics with a threat of expulsion (and indeed Rudas was expelled from the party for a particularly virulent attack on Kun). The émigré leaders were ordered back to Moscow. Unable to impose harmony, the Comintern's Executive Committee in January 1922 ordered all Hungarian factions to be disbanded and their fractious members to be integrated into the parties of their host countries. A new provisional Central Committee was designated; consisting of Hirossik, Szilágyi, and Seidler, it was to be located in Budapest and aided by a Moscow-based "editorial committee."[39] In March, it was Bettelheim's turn to be expelled from the movement for a pamphlet attack on Kun.

In the event, the members of the new Central Committee persisted in the old disputes, convened only infrequently, and remained in exile, most frequently in Berlin. The few communists left in Hungary possessed little organization and enjoyed only irregular contact with the emigration. A three-man "executive committee" dispatched from Vienna in late 1921 reported on the existence of 30 party cells with some 250 activists.[40] They found that what opposition existed within the SDP and the trade unions was inspired by the centrist socialist group in Vienna led by Kunfi and Böhm. In February 1922 the three fact finders were seized by the police. Typically, their arrest led to the denunciation of numerous other communists.

Shortly thereafter, Landler delegated Ernő Gerő, a twenty-four-year-old former economics student who had joined the party in 1918, to revive the young-communist-worker movement in Hungary. Gerő managed to contact a few activists who had escaped arrest thanks to their fortuitous isolation from the defunct "executive committee," and the painstaking conspiratorial task of organizing cells began anew. Only once, in April 1922, did Gerő have the opportunity to report to the Central Committee, at one of the latter's rare meetings in Berlin. Over time, despite all these setbacks, a few left-wing social democrats like István Vági, the SDP secretary in the northwestern city of Győr, came under communist influence. For eight months, from February 1922, an illegal newssheet appeared bearing the name *Kommün*. Its issue of 5 March instructed that ''an illegal and closed communist group must be created in each trade union. . . . The trade union groups must strive to gather around themselves the dissatisfied, revolutionary elements in the trade unions and to organize opposition to the social democratic leadership.''

## SOCIALIST ORTHODOXY AND DISSENT

In the aftermath of the Bethlen-Peyer pact, the SDP decided to participate in the general elections of spring 1922. It succeeded in winning 15.3 percent of the popular vote, its support being concentrated in Budapest (new electoral laws had now restored the open vote in all but a few urban areas). The communists, although they were already vaguely aware of the secret pact, urged voters to vote socialist. Their concurrent attempt to propagate the idea of a republic, implicitly in the interest of broader, if bourgeois, civil rights, aroused no response.

The freedom of action allowed the SDP by the pact and by representation in parliament served not only to legitimize its position but also to consolidate the conservative Peyer leadership. This in turn prompted socialist emigration — the centrists as well as Garami's separate faction—to redouble their efforts at developing an opposition group within the party. In March 1922 the Comintern had officially authorized its sections to seek collaboration with socialists. In Hungary, however, this had little relevance, for the staunchly anticommunist Peyer denied the very existence of the admittedly minuscule and illegal CPH. The communists therefore chose to concentrate on infiltrating the SDP's left wing in the hope of eventually converting it into a separate legal party. Their agitation against the Peyer leadership and social democracy in general momentarily fell on deaf ears. In September 1922 a massive police sweep rounded up over a hundred communists and once again virtually annihilated the party. The leading figures, including Gerő, were expelled to the Soviet Union in a prisoner exchange in 1924.

Just when, in organization and membership, the CPH was nearing its nadir, an opposition movement emerged within the SDP. Rapid inflation in the years 1922 to 1923 and a concurrent decline in real incomes affected all salaried classes. By 1924 the growth in production and the League-supervised loan allowed Bethlen to introduce a financial reorganization program that did promote industrial recovery but that, in its deflationary austerity measures, at first only aggravated penury and unemployment among the middle as well as working classes. The acute distress of industrial labor led to a rash of strikes. When they proved futile, the socialist union leadership was in turn criticized for its complacency and failure to provide instant panaceas. Unemployment and disaffection reduced the ranks of unionized labor from 202,956 in 1922 to 127,526 at the end of 1924. It was in these circumstances that a few frustrated socialists coalesced into an opposition faction within the SDP. They were influenced initially by the Viennese "Világosság" group, centrists who criticized Peyer's policy of accommodation with the regime. Instead, they urged a more militant pursuit of socialist objectives, notably a republican-democratic political system. At the same time, the centrists held the communists responsible for the 1919 disaster and would brook no talk of a proletarian dictatorship. In sum, the émigrés and their supporters in Hungary stood for authentic social democratic principles untainted by compromise with the Bethlen regime and its self-serving definition of national interest.

In March 1923 two communist agitators, Károly Őri and Nándor Szekér, arrived from Vienna with instructions from Landler and the Youth Comintern's Viennese resident, Imre Sallai, to reestablish contact with the dispersed communists and to explore the possibility of bringing the socialist opposition movement under communist guidance. By the end of the year, their overtures had met with some success; several socialist radicals were drawn to the communist line, and two prominent figures, Vági and Aladár Weisshaus, even joined the CPH. The illegal party had to remain in the shadows, leaving overt direction of the radical opposition faction to ostensibly noncommunist socialist and union activists. Communist guidance was provided by the "troika" of Őri, Ignác Gőgös, and the veteran Kató Hámán along lines laid down by Landler. A more broadly based "executive committee," including the troika as well as Vági, Weisshaus, and other radicals, served as the semilegal organizing and recruiting arm.

The SDP's twenty-second congress, held from 20 to 22 April 1924, saw the first formal appearance of the crypto-communist opposition.[41] The party's official program remained true to the goal of social democracy by peaceful parliamentary means. It reiterated the demands for universal, secret franchise, progressive taxation, unemployment relief, land reform with compensation, and amnesty for socialist political prisoners and exiles. The approximately thirty-strong opposition faction decided to introduce an alternative program in the hope of arousing sufficient dissent to force the ouster of the Peyer leadership. The declaration of the "opposition group of the SDP," presented by Vági, called for a militant policy of class struggle and denounced the "opportunism" of the socialist leaders (who steadfastly denied the existence of a secret understanding with Bethlen). The faction's premiere turned into a fiasco. The "Világosság" group's followers refused to have anything to do with the radicals, and the SDP leadership invited Vági and his acolytes to leave the party if they rejected its commitment to parliamentary democracy. Vági's precipitous retreat took the wind out of the extremists' sails for several months. The SDP and trade union leaders, alerted to their new opponents, mounted a campaign to isolate and if necessary expel them.

Five years after the Commune, communist influence was indeed at a low ebb within the confines of Hungary. The émigrés quarreled and danced to the changing tunes of the Comintern. Given the doctrinal inevitability of revolution, failures in the political arena would impel the Comintern to shift from one tactical formula to another, each resting on a denunciation of its predecessor and the latter's hapless proponents. While in its early years the Comintern had been dedicated to the general task of fomenting proletarian revolution, by the mid-1920s it was caught up in the Soviet party's factional struggles. Soon it became simply an instrument of Stalin's foreign policy.[42]

# 5. The Search for Relevance, 1924–1932

By 1924, the CPH was moribund. At home it could account for all of 120 members, mostly metalworkers, carpenters, and printers from the Budapest area. Its Central Committee had ceased to function.[1] In Vienna, Landler and Hirossik, ignored by the Comintern, were reduced to sporadic communication with the home troops. In these dismal straits, the Moscow émigrés decided to petition the Comintern for revival of its Hungarian section. Kun, who from 1921 to 1923 had served as the Soviet party's Urals bureau chief, and then became its representative in the Komsomol, addressed a letter to Otto Kuusinen, a Comintern secretary, requesting a conference on the future of the CPH. Landler and Hirossik concurred that the Hungarian section be revived, but insisted that leading communists from Hungary be involved in any planning.[2]

The first concrete steps were taken in mid-1924 on the occasion of the Comintern's fifth congress, which the Hungarians (including Weisshaus and Szekér) could only attend in an unofficial capacity.[3] Preliminary discussions produced sufficient consensus to warrant a formal request to the Comintern's Executive Committee: Would it once again recognize its Hungarian section and name an organizing committee, pending a party conference? The signatories proposed that the various émigré party committees be allowed to reorganize in order to provide systematic aid for the home movement.

The Comintern acquiesced. It had already appointed a five-man committee (Frunze, Umschlicht, Kuusinen, Piatnitsky, and Anvelt) to reconsider the Hungarians' factional dispute.[4] In July, an "Organizational Committee" composed of Alpári, Kun, and Landler proceeded to develop a six-month work plan. In essentials, it endorsed the current party tactics in Hungary, and instructed the Vági faction to insist that the SDP run independently of the bourgeois liberal parties in the Budapest municipal elections of spring 1925.[5] In the meantime the Comintern congress, held from 17 June to 8 July (the first since Lenin's death), exhibited a certain leftward turn: basically, it rejected the tactic of imposing a united front from above, since it judged that capitalism was entering a phase of temporary and partial stabilization. Communist parties were accordingly instructed to infiltrate and preserve existing trade unions and promote united fronts from below. Zinoviev, however, beclouded the issue by asserting that social democracy had become a branch of fascism.[6] The Hungarian party would pay dearly for the Comintern's ambiguities.

The Organizational Committee met in Vienna in early November 1924 to hear reports by Öri and Weisshaus on some forty factory party cells.[7] The communist-led opposition faction's activities encompassed attempts to organize the unemployed and incite resistance to rent increases. Perhaps inspired by Zinoviev's reservations regarding alliance with the social democrats, both Kun and Landler concluded that the time had come to split the SDP and create a new legal party. The committee composed a program of demands that for the first time included land reform with compensation for the dispossessed proprietors, a departure from established CPH policy that was designed to aid the party in gaining a hitherto elusive foothold in the countryside. The first step would be to establish links with the left wing of the Federation of Agricultural Workers (Földmunkásszövetség), an organization whose membership amounted to a grand 3,851 out of over 500,000 farm laborers. The committee recommended that the Federation of Young Communist Workers also seek a legal cover for its mobilizing efforts. The party's young activists did in fact achieve some success in infiltrating a variety of sport and cultural organizations.

The émigré leaders lived in fear that the radical opposition faction would slip away from communist control. They therefore overrode the heated objections of home representatives and dispatched Hirossik and Rákosi to Hungary to assist in the implementation of the new program. Their task was hampered as usual by the vigilant SDP leadership, which counterattacked by denouncing the opposition as communist and expelling (in late 1924 and early 1925) Vági, Öri, Gőgös, and other troublemakers. In the meantime, the rumor campaigns of the radicals and the socialist émigrés finally compelled the SDP leadership to publish details of the Bethlen-Peyer pact in the issue of *Népszava* for 31 December 1924. After an investigation, the Second International censured the SDP for the pact. The Peyer leadership responded airily that the party was no longer bound by it and would exercise greater tolerance in future with respect to internal dissent.[8]

## A COVER PARTY AND A CONGRESS

The SDP's embarrassment at the disclosure of the pact was only one of the factors that impelled the communists to launch a competing party; Bethlen's new economic program, for instance, had proved to be painful medicine. In November 1924 the bourgeois liberal parties and a few legitimist deputies were joined by the SDP in forming the Democratic Bloc of Opposition Parties. Their militancy was only accentuated by the government's electoral reform bill, which proposed further restriction of the franchise, and by revelations implicating official circles in the 1920 murder of two socialist journalists. Appraising the apparent vulnerability of both the government and the SDP, the radical faction issued an appeal to the latter to abandon the bourgeois parties. Predictably, the appeal was futile. On 14 April 1925 the faction broke away, styling itself the Socialist Workers' Party of Hungary (Magyarországi Szocialista Munkáspárt, or SWPH).

The decision was not reached without much debate. Kun would argue retrospectively that while conditions in the SDP and the unions were not optimal, the favorable domestic atmosphere had to be exploited. The Organizational Committee had decided earlier that the radical opposition should demonstrate its offensive capability by nominating candidates in the municipal elections. For this a legal party was necessary.[9] The authorities were closely following the evolution of the opposition movement and had subjected it to some harrassment. They nevertheless recognized the new party, presumably because they hoped it might weaken the SDP and aid in the detection of subversive elements.

Officially independent, the SWPH was of course conceived and financed by the CPH. Neither Zinoviev nor the CPH's émigré leaders expected it to enjoy a long legal existence. They regarded it as a cover organization, a temporarily useful outlet for the proscribed communists. The Comintern's relevant directive prescribed that the "workers' party leadership must be firmly in the hands of the communist party, but its committees must not consist solely of communists. Their majority must be communist to ensure the correct line. Communist leadership must be exercised not by coercion but by ideological persuasion." The CPH link was maintained by Öri, Gőgös, and Hámán, and by periodic illegal visits from Rákosi, Hirossik, and Révai. The Central Committee, unlike the general membership, was predominantly communist. It included Vági, the railwayman Weisshaus, the chemical worker Hámán, and the engineering instructor Dr. László Váradi, as well as a teacher, a boilersmith, a carpenter, a stonemason, a cobbler, a shop assistant, and a locksmith. By June, the party's membership had risen to about fifteen hundred, most of them industrial workers from the Budapest area. The goal of the SWPH, reduced to its essentials, was to raise the proletariat's consciousness of its "objectively" timely task of seizing power, initially by fighting for a democratic transformation of Hungary's political system.[10]

The SWPH presented no great challenge to the well-entrenched SDP, but the socialist leaders lost no time in denouncing the dissidents as Bolsheviks and occasionally, for good measure, as right-wing agents provocateurs. The domestic and émigré centrists also deplored the split and tried to return the new party to the path of social democracy. At the spring municipal elections, the SWPH could not even round up sufficient signatures to nominate its own candidates and had to content itself with calling on workers to vote for the Democratic Bloc. Fearing that its child was stillborn, in July the CPH Organizational Committee instructed its remaining SDP cell, led by Dr. József Madzsar, to work toward a further secession in favor of the new party.[11] That summer, a number of promising SWPH activists attended a CPH party school in Vienna. A typical participant was the twenty-two-year-old Károly Kiss, a socialist shoemaker who had joined the CPH in 1922. Active in his factory and union cells in promoting wage demands and strikes, Kiss was expelled from the SDP and became one of the founders of the SWPH. He and his six comrades (including a police informer, József Oancz) were lectured by Kun, Révai, Landler, Szántó, and Lukács on party history and conspiratorial techniques. Kiss was assigned to agitprop work in the metalworkers' union. His arrest in September 1925 led to the first of many imprisonments.[12]

The SWPH's activity in mid-1925 consisted of the distribution of leaflets, of meetings, frequently dispersed by the police, to protest the franchise bill, and of attempts to avoid expulsion from the trade unions. In July, the CPH and the Comintern decided to have the SWPH seek recognition from the Second International at its Marseilles congress the following month. The SWPH delegation, consisting of Váradi and the cobbler Benedek György (with Alpári along as adviser) arrived late from the overlapping CPH conference in Vienna. The SDP took advantage of the delay to block their recognition, but thanks to the intercession of Kunfi, Böhm, and Garbai, and of Austrian social democrats who doubted the communist character of the new party, the decision was reversed. After this initial victory the SWPH delegates distributed an anti-SDP memorandum, but their plea for membership in the Second International failed to receive consideration.

**The Reorganizing Congress.** Since the autumn of 1924 the CPH leadership had been making plans for a party conference. After a series of preparatory meetings, twenty-two comrades gathered on the premises of a small library at Glockengasse 6 in Vienna on 18 August 1925. In attendance were the five members of the Organizational Committee, Kun, Alpári, Landler, Rákosi, and Hirossik (the last two recently coopted); fourteen delegates from Hungary, including Hámán, Öri, Gőgös, and Váradi; and three other émigrés, Révai, Zoltán Szántó, and Zoltán Weinberger, alias Vas. A questionnaire survey provided a profile of these revolutionaries. The oldest, Landler, was fifty; the youngest, both twenty-two, were Vas, a self-described "terror boy" during the Commune, and Lajos Samuel, who was a police informer. Almost all had joined the CPH prior to the Commune, had at some stage adhered to the SDP, were active in trade unions, had taken an active part in the Commune and served in the Hungarian Red Army. Their reported occupations included "professional revolutionary," shoemaker, chemistry teacher, and farm laborer, the predominant background being industrial working class. At least thirteen had a police record.[13]

Declaring themselves to be representative of the entire Hungarian communist movement, the participants designated their meeting the first, reorganizing congress of the Communist Party of Hungary.[14] For the sake of discretion, they agreed to forego the ritual singing of the "Internationale." The purpose of the conference, declared Kun at the outset, was to finally liquidate the factional dispute. The long agenda (previously approved by the Comintern) included reports by Alpári on the international situation and the Comintern; by Öri on illegal activities in Hungary; by Váradi on the SWPH; by Kun on the general political situation in Hungary and the party's tasks; by Landler on the trade unions; by Kun on the peasant question; by Landler on the economic situation; by Rákosi on party organization; and by Vas on the communist youth movement.

Discussion on the first topic revolved around social democracy and the need to disabuse Hungarian workers of this fantasy from the "cultured West"; on the need to promote a Soviet-Hungarian commercial agreement for its ideological as well as economic benefits; and on irredentism. Kun did acknowledge the important place held by the latter in Hungarian opinion, and he denounced the Treaty of Trianon as an imperialist dictate. Otherwise, however, he wallowed in generalities on the desirability of consultation with the communist parties of the successor states regarding the Hungarian minorities' right to self-determination.

Öri gave an account of the party's strength in Hungary: from sixty to sixty-five members in twenty-two plant cells and from ninety-five to a hundred others working in legal organizations, including from twelve to fifteen within the SDP. The congress approved the maintenance and expansion of the SWPH with a program distinct from that of its parent party.

Kun's theses described the Hungarian political scene as dominated by property and capital, with finance capital reaching for leadership. Domestic finance capital, in the process of restoring budgetary order, was delivering the country into the hands of foreign finance capital. The ruling classes were united by their fear of revolution. Kun laid stress on the threat of a Habsburg restoration and the legitimists' tactical use of democratic slogans. The urban middle classes had been alienated by the Commune's measures against private property; they were irredentist and generally unsympathetic to the workers. Some of the intellectuals and middle-class Jews were also repelled by the counterrevolutionary excesses. The wealthy peasant class was influential, irredentist, and a firm supporter of the regime. The smallholder class had been partly won over by the limited land reform, but its political leaders served the regime. These, and the even more disgruntled dwarf landholders, were potential allies of the proletarian revolution. The "oppressed" industrial working class had expanded since the revolution, and its newer members were less affected by the defeat of the Commune and less loyal to the social democrats. The newer generation of landless farm laborers, according to Kun, felt closer to their urban proletarian brothers and were susceptible to political radicalization.

The social democratic and liberal parties, continued Kun, contented themselves with parliamentary criticism. The CPH's general strategic objective must therefore remain the revolutionary dictatorship of the proletariat, in close alliance with the poor peasants. For tactical reasons, communists should participate in the campaign for immediate, partial political and economic reforms, but not for a bourgeois democracy as such. The latter goal should, on the other hand, be advocated by the SWPH. On the agrarian question, the congress finally acknowledged the tactical inappropriateness of the Commune's policies and adopted the slogan of redistribution without compensation. In the short run, this could be amended to the less revolutionary pursuit of land reform. The party, agreed the congress, must attempt to develop rural cells, but its main organizing sphere remained the trade unions.

New organizational statutes, based on the Comintern's latest directive, were approved for the party-in-reconstruction. The hypothetical pyramid rose from works and village cells through local and district organs (as well as fractions within legal parties and trade unions) to the ultimate forum, the party congress. In conditions of illegality, the election of various organs might prove unfeasible and be replaced by appointment from above. Continuing direction was to be provided by the Central Committee, some of whose members would serve as a Secretariat operating in Hungary, and others as an External Committee responsible for Comintern and other international links and for ideological and financial aid for the home movement.

The newly elected Central Committee consisted of Kun, Landler, Alpári, Gőgös, Imre Komor, József Mitterer, Öri, József Weiss, Rákosi, Váradi, Vági, and Weisshaus (the last two having been under arrest since the end of June). At its meeting following the congress, the Central Committee assigned Mitterer, Öri, and Rákosi to the Secretariat, and Kun, Alpári and Landler to the External Committee. Kun remained the party's representative with the Comintern. The congressional resolutions appeared shortly thereafter in *Új Március* (New March), a new theoretical review based on Vienna. A further initiative was the establishment of the Hungarian section of the International Red Aid, an agency designed to aid imprisoned communists.

If the congress had formed a partially accurate picture of the political situation in Hungary (leaving aside Kun's misplaced concern with a Habsburg restoration), it grossly exaggerated the tiny communist movement's potential for acquiring mass support. Admittedly, the CPH leadership entertained no illusions about the prospects for an early proletarian dictatorship. The party, wrote Kun in *Inprekor* in October 1925, "is fighting in this period between two revolutions not for the immediate seizure of power but to win the support of the majority of the working class and to build the foundation of an alliance with the peasantry.'' But even these goals were patently unrealistic, for the CPH leadership overestimated the extent of dissatisfaction among organized labor and so its susceptibility to radicalization.

**The Perils of Illegality.** The problems of ideological conversion and recruitment paled beside those of official persecution. The vigilance of the authorities made the survival of an illegal party contingent on the most sophisticated conspiratorial methods. These, particularly in the context of a legal cover party and in light of the inexperience of new adherents, were seldom sufficient to avert detection. From its very inception, the SWPH was suspected of being a communist contrivance, and in late June 1925 the police launched a series of arrests against the party's activists on charges of incitement and disseminating communist propaganda.

The communist connection was made easier to expose by informers, notably young Samuel, who took an active part in the Vienna congress. A devastating blow fell on 22 September when the entire resident communist leadership as well as all the graduates of that summer's Viennese party course were rounded up by the police. Among those arrested were Rákosi, Gőgös, Hámán, and Öri, who at the initial interrogation admitted that the SWPH served as a cover for communist activities. Together with Vas, they were charged with subversion and in November were brought before a summary court. There, however, they retracted their earlier confession (claiming that it had been extracted under torture) and succeeded in having the case transferred to a normal judicial proceeding.

In the meantime, the CPH and the Comintern had developed a plan of action. The External Committee, Béla Szántó in the Comintern's Hungarian committee, Pogány in the Comintern's agitprop department, and *Inprekor* editor Alpári, made concerted efforts to arouse an international outcry against the forthcoming trial, primarily by mobilizing progressive Western intellectuals and politicians.

A notable recruit to this campaign was Mihály Károlyi, who after many peregrinations had settled down in Paris in 1925 to pursue his political vendetta against the Horthy regime.[15] Exile and the regime's calumnies had driven Károlyi further to the left, not so much in terms of his vague socialism as in a pragmatic quest for allies against the common foe. After failing to come to terms with Kunfi's socialist group, Károlyi and the communists engaged in sporadic and ambivalent negotiations. In a letter to Lenin dated 4 May 1920, Kun indicated that the majority of his comrades favored such contacts. While he himself opposed intimate collaboration with Károlyi, he did allow for the possibility of exploiting Károlyi's alleged popularity among the peasantry. (Kun also reported Károlyi's wish to visit the Soviet Union.) When, a few years later, Károlyi accepted the honorary presidency of the Paris-based League of Human Rights, a loose coalition, backed by Freemasons, of Hungarian émigré socialists and liberals, the local communists denounced both him and the league. Nevertheless, it was with Comintern approval that the Organizational Committee held talks with Károlyi in Vienna in early August 1925, prior to the party congress. The communist tactic was to avoid a damning public identification of Károlyi with the party but to encourage his independent advocacy of revolutionary land reform. Károlyi, for his part, considered the CPH to be a useful partner in forging an alliance between workers and peasants. He reserved the right to sever his links with the communists if less revolutionary channels materialized, and a secret agreement was concluded to this effect.

In the event, this bizarre compact between two equally impotent interlocutors proved to be of no practical consequence. Károlyi tried to unify the fractious émigrés in the League of Human Rights, but earned only criticism from the French Communist Party's ultra leftist Hungarian group, which was led by Gerő. He would occasionally comply with communist requests, notably when he appealed to the SDP in 1926 for greater militancy, and also when he participated in the various Comintern-inspired campaigns on behalf of the persecuted Hungarian communists. Kun reported on a June 1926 meeting with Károlyi in Berlin that the latter was "willing to follow our instructions, and we must merely compensate for his helplessness." But the personal antipathy between the two men, the internal divisions among the communists, and above all the dearth of opportunities for constructive joint action prevented this opportunistic alliance from ever amounting to much.

The mass trial of fifty-three communists opened on 12 July 1926.[16] Their counsel, sponsored by Red Aid, instructed the accused to follow two tactics. Rákosi and the exposed communists were to admit their party affiliation and deny responsibility for the SWPH. Vági, Weisshaus, and the other known SWPH leaders were to deny the communist connection and proclaim that theirs was a centrist socialist party. The defendants'followed this advice and made use of their courtroom appearance to deliver tirades against the regime. Two leading SDP witnesses amended their earlier testimony and described the SWPH as essentially noncommunist. As a result, the court found the evidence against the SWPH insufficient to demonstrate communist subversion. Thirty among the accused, including Rákosi and Vas, received prison sentences of up to eight years. (Rákosi was reportedly accused by Kun of having denounced some of his comrades to save himself, and his party membership was suspended by the Comintern.)[17] Vági, Weisshaus, and another SWPH member received lighter penalties, and twenty others were set free.

**The Legal Experiment.** While some SWPH activists now advocated a return to the SDP fold, and others urged more radical action, the CPH decided to try to preserve the existing cover party. Its attitude was, as Kun told the Comintern's Hungarian committee in November 1925, that "everything must be done to maintain a legal party as long as possible.'' Such a party, Kun wrote at the time of the trial, ''is the most suitable recruiting centre for future communists. . . . In present conditions, without a legal party, we could not pursue agitation and operations, we would be condemned for a long time to limit ourselves to propaganda work.''[18] In December, the SWPH turned to the SDP and the Trade Union Council with an open letter proposing joint action, but the socialist leadership did not even bother to reply. The radicals' earlier accusation that the SDP was no longer a working-class party caused not a ripple at the socialist congress that month. The concurrent disclosure of a bizarre plot, hatched by irredentist notables close to the regime, to pass large amounts of forged French francs caused the Bethlen government serious international embarrassment and momentarily galvanized the opposition. In January 1926, the SWPH resorted to a leaflet campaign and yet another fruitless overture to the SDP. By the following spring, its recruitment drive had been rewarded with the creation of all of four new factory cells and some marginal interest in a number of rural districts.[19]

While the SWPH managed to barely survive as the radical gadfly in Hungarian politics, the CPH attempted to rebuild its decimated leadership. Zoltán Szántó, Béla Lándor, and Révai made illegal visits in the course of 1926, and Kun received the Comintern's permission to devote more of his time to guiding the CPH from Vienna and Berlin. The Central Committee, at its June 1926 meeting, set as the two parties' immediate objectives the struggle against the Bethlen regime and against a Habsburg restoration, amnesty for political prisoners, the shifting of taxes to the wealthy, a commercial treaty with the Soviet Union, and a democratic land reform.[20] Recognizing that the SWPH held negligible attraction for the masses, the Central Committee stressed the need to concentrate on minor but politically rewarding grievances in order to build grass-roots support. The meeting instructed the SWPH to seek united-front accords at all levels of the SDP and the trade unions, and to urge urban and rural workers to join the unions and the Federation of Agricultural Workers.

Asserting the communist line in the SWPH became more of a problem after the September arrests. Weisshaus had become the center of a faction that blamed the party's misfortunes on the communist connection and argued that its legal activities would be facilitated by greater autonomy. By the late summer of 1926 this faction had acquired a dominant position in the SWPH leadership, and in September Weisshaus publicly denied the party's commitment to revolution. The CPH External Committee thereupon branded Weisshaus a ''liquidator,'' expelled him from the CPH, and engineered the recapture of the SWPH leadership by more docile elements, including the recently released Vági. The purge was completed with the expulsion from the SWPH in December of the dangerously popular Weisshaus and his supporters.[21] There followed new efforts to indoctrinate reliable activists. In mid-1926 Kun, Landler,

Gyula Lengyel, Révai, and Varga led a party course in Berlin. Meanwhile, Lenin's *"Left-Wing Communism"* finally appeared in Hungarian with a laudatory preface by one of its original targets, Béla Kun.

Now that the CPH was firmly in control, the cover party could persevere with recruitment. By 1926 it was claiming 9,648 members, most of them noncommunists. It also followed a program of agitation, which met with some success particularly among younger workers and agricultural laborers.[22] In the autumn of 1926, as its rallying cry in the forthcoming general elections, the SWPH issued a call for a republic led by a worker-peasant government. The communists were still motivated by the unfounded fear of a monarchical restoration, and it was explained to activists that the republic, far from being a strategic objective, "represents for us a minor station through which passes the whistling train."[23] The new battle cry also served to move the SWPH from a position of mere antagonism to the SDP. At the communists' instigation, as noted above, the exiled Mihály Károlyi called on the SDP to forge a common proletarian front in pursuit of a republic and land reform. At its twenty-fourth congress in October, the SDP, under the slogan of a "new October," did advance proposals for a plebiscite on the question of a republic. But this was mainly for tactical reasons, for the SDP leadership ignored the SWPH's latest feelers for a joint electoral campaign.

The SWPH's independent electioneering was effectively paralyzed by official harassment. The party leadership, despite the External Committee's advice in favor of a voter boycott, chose to urge workers to support the SDP. The outcome of the December elections was disappointing for the socialists. Their support fell to 124,000 votes, less than half the 1922 level. The SDP's secretary, Árpád Szakasits, reflected bitterly that the Vági group had drawn away the support of the masses, particularly of the young.[24] While this overstated the influence of the radicals, it did reflect a malaise within the ranks of democratic socialists.

## NEW TACTICS AND OLD REALITIES

The CPH Central Committee met in Vienna from 29 to 30 December 1926 in order to reassess the Hungarian situation. Its new membership consisted of Kun, Landler, Varga, Zoltán and Béla Szántó, Lukács, Révai, Lándor, Sándor Poll, and Imre Komor; the youth wing, which had eighty-one members, was represented by Sándor Löwy.[25] The meeting was an attempt to prepare for the renewed persecution of the SWPH that was anticipated as a result of the governing party's electoral success. Noting that the Comintern was shifting to the view that cover parties were a right-wing deviation, the plenum blithely branded the SWPH's land reform slogan as "social democratic" and insisted that an undiluted communist line prevail in the cover party. The communists' task was to "subordinate the party's legal agitation and slogans to the strategic battle plan for proletarian dictatorship, and prevent the emergence of democratic illusions." The accentuated militancy of the plenum derived from the Comintern, from the plenum's own disappointment with the SWPH's record, and also from some distorted perceptions of the Hungarian scene. These included not only expectations that the Habsburg restoration issue would divide the ruling classes but also fanciful assessments of potential support for the illegal communist movement (as encompassing, for instance, all the urban and rural workers who had abstained from voting). Kun wrote in *Inprekor* in January 1927 that "whatever the sacrifice, the struggle must now be intensified."[26]

The Hungarian émigrés were once again showing an excess of zeal. At the plenum of the Comintern Executive Committee, when it met from late November to early December 1926, Bukharin had referred to a foreseeable revolutionary situation emerging in Central Europe. Subsequently, however, the Comintern disparaged the Hungarians' fixation on the restoration issue and instructed the CPH to sustain the cover party even with distinctive slogans and tactics.[27] Despite such cautionary advice, extremism among the Hungarian communists only waxed over the next two years.

**The Conspirators Unmasked and Divided.** The official campaign to extirpate subversion in Hungary reached its peak in the first quarter of 1927, when some 550 real and suspected communists, including the CPH Secretariat (Zoltán Szántó, Kocsis, Poll), Löwy, and SWPH secretary Vági were picked up by the police. Informers helped, but the communists' conspiratorial ineptitude made their persecutors' task an easy one: they were most enlightened by the contents of a briefcase, left inadvertently in a taxi in Vienna, which provided detailed information on the CPH and its front organization. (One member recalls protesting at the émigré leadership's insistence on receiving full written reports even on low-level meetings.)[28] The so-called Szántó case closely followed the pattern of the Rákosi trial: initial confessions, abortive summary proceedings, mobilization of foreign protests by Lukács and Alpári, a regular trial with retraction of confessions and inflammatory speeches by the accused, all leading on 9 November to the conviction for subversive activity of thirty-six of the sixty-eight defendants. The court displayed remarkable judicial impartiality in ruling that the common identity of the CPH and the SWPH had not been adequately demonstrated. Nevertheless, the SWPH was to all intents and purposes liquidated, nominally lingering on until it issued a final leaflet in October 1929.

The periodic decimation of the Hungarian communist movement received new impetus from the arrest in Vienna of Béla Kun and three comrades on 26 April 1928.[29] As a member of the Comintern Executive Committee and head of its agitprop department, Kun was devoting only half his time to party affairs. He had traveled to Vienna illegally to pull together the External Committee after Landler's death and to make preparations for a party conference. Budapest promptly demanded Kun's extradition and the Comintern launched a propaganda campaign for his safe return. But the moderate Austrian government was inclined to refuse Budapest anyway. In the end, Kun was charged with possession of forged papers and with illegal organizing activity. After a brief imprisonment, he was escorted out of the country and reached the Soviet Union at the end of July. Of greater consequence was the seizure of the External Committee's files and their partial transmission to the Hungarian authorities. The External Committee was the fulcrum of all party activity, and the vast documentation so obtained provided a full picture of illegal membership, organization, and tactics. Evidence of the party's internal squabbles was gleefully reported in the press of the two countries, but the rest of the information was kept secret and used by the Hungarian police to infiltrate the party and deliver paralyzing blows in 1929 and 1930.

With plans for a congress scotched by Kun's arrest, the Central Committee met in Prague in July 1928.[30] It appraised the international situation as favoring the left and issued the militant slogan "Class against class." The committee still endorsed the maintenance of unity in the trade union movement and reaffirmed the need for a legal front. It therefore instructed the SDP's communist faction to engineer a split in that party to aid the moribund SWPH. These were mere émigré fantasies, however, for the successive arrests had eroded the communists' hold over the cover party. As the latter disintegrated, many of its members drifted back to the SDP, while the most militant rallied to the CPH.

Shorn of its legal cover, the CPH devoted undivided attention to its cells and influence within the SDP and the trade unions and among young workers. Particularly in rural areas, the loss of the SWPH forced the communists to rebuild almost from scratch. In September 1927 the party had launched a legal cultural review, *100%*; ten months later, it began to issue the underground newssheet *Kommunista*. The efforts to reach workers through cultural and sports organizations met with some success, but the activities of extremist factions led by Demény and Weisshaus in opposition to the CPH and its youth wing fragmented the radical left, and the party gained few recruits.

The party's work in the trade unions was complicated by the secessionist initiatives of unionists disgruntled with the socialist leadership. The established CPH policy, as we have seen, had been to preserve the unity of the trade unions. When a number of minor secessions nevertheless occurred in the fall of 1928, the Central Committee decided that the party might as well seize the opportunity to assume a leading role; the breakaway unions might well become the germ of a red trade union movement.[31] The Central Committee's rationale for this shift was that the SDP–trade union bureaucracy represented a "social fascist" orientation with which no compromise was possible. When, in January, Révai brought this "open visor" plan of action to the home comrades, however, he found no enthusiasm for Red trade unions, and long debates ensued. The dismal failure of the long-planned May Day demonstration only strengthened the local communists' resistance to more aggressive and overt tactics.[32]

This shift in union policy reflected two developments: the new outbreak of factional disputes in the party following Landler's death in February; and the message of the Comintern's sixth congress, held in the summer of 1928. The dominant themes at that congress were the alleged drift of social democracy toward fascism—Stalin denounced the two as "twin brothers"—and the impending imperialist war against the Soviet Union. The congress had also drawn a distinction between different stages of capitalism: in semideveloped capitalist systems such as Hungary, intermediate stages of revolution, from bourgeois democracy to worker-peasant "democratic dictatorship," were now conceivable on the road to proletarian dictatorship.[33]

Divergent interpretations of the new Comintern line split the already faction-ridden Hungarian party. Returning to Moscow after his brief sojourn in an Austrian jail, Kun moved to confirm leftist domination of the leadership. Accordingly, the External Committee's majority denounced Béla Szántó and Alpári as "right opportunists" for their views. These were, in brief, that the Horthy regime was not a fascist dictatorship; that the SDP was not "social fascist" but an authentic opposition party; that the Hungarian proletariat was atomized and not ripe for revolution; and that therefore the communists needed an incremental strategy.[34] Kun's opponents, in turn, regarded him (in the words of a fellow revolutionary) as a "remarkably odious figure. He was the incarnation of intellectual inadequacy, uncertainty of will, and authoritarian corruption."[35]

**The Blum Theses.** While the two factions proselytized and outdid each other in extravagant polemics, Lukács was commissioned in September 1928 to prepare a new political program for the forthcoming CPH congress. The result of his labors, known from his pen name as the "Blum theses," was never implemented but remains a noteworthy appraisal of the Hungarian situation by one of the party's few intellectuals.[36] These "draft theses on the Hungarian political and economic conditions and the tasks of the CPH" considered the dominant feature of the Bethlen era to be the relative entrenchment of capitalism and industry within a still largely agrarian economy. The ruling capitalist and landowning elites were collaborating in the modernization of agriculture and forging a broad political basis, partly by exploiting the SDP's urban bias.[37]

Nevertheless, continued Lukács, the Bethlen regime was facing a crisis that had arisen from the failure of its British and Italian oriented foreign policy. The aim of this policy had been to win territorial revision and consequent economic benefits—objectives that had mass support. Pursuit of similar national goals had activated a liberal democratic opposition, including the SDP. From the communist perspective, however, both orientations served only the interests of bourgeois consolidation. The petite bourgeoisie was aligned with one or the other dominant wing, while the peasantry remained largely disorganized. Since all the parties were revisionist, anticommunist, and anti-Soviet, no foreseeable democratic reorganization, in Lukács's view, could produce genuine bourgeois democracy.

The working class, meanwhile, was suffering from a decline in the standard of living and was deserting the trade unions, whose leadership was becoming integrated into the capitalist economic and state structure. From the communist point of view, genuine opposition to the regime was manifested only in spontaneous strikes and demonstrations by the unemployed. The SDP bureaucracy found such opposition all the easier to contain because even the centrist socialist exiles favored a peaceful transition to liberal democracy and socialism. As result, the communist SWPH had failed to rally even leftist workers to its banner, and communist leadership was currently nonexistent. There were, on the other hand, signs that the disaffected and atomized proletariat was seeking salvation on the extreme right of the political spectrum.

Lukács regarded the miners' strike at Salgótarján in the spring of 1928 as a decisive step in the party's development.* He claimed that the CPH was slowly overcoming the antagonism of the leftist workers but noted the weakness of the party cells, the incompetence of its activists, and the uncertain leadership. The caution and pessimism behind this weakness he attributed to the rightist deviation exemplified by Alpári and Béla Szántó, an attitude that had induced a timid withdrawal into illegality by the party members in Hungary.

This general appraisal led Lukács to the conclusion that in Hungary the CPH was the only party seriously struggling for bourgeois democracy. The party had to expand this battle into a broad mass campaign extending beyond the proletariat. The struggle was one that aimed at the overthrow of the entire Bethlen system. Its slogan should be "The democratic dictatorship of the proletariat and the peasantry." Accordingly, the working class and the party had to be persuaded of the tactical desirability of bourgeois democracy. Democratic dictatorship was the "most perfect realization of bourgeois democracy." Since it was "in principle incompatible with the retention of the economic and social dominance of the bourgeoisie," democratic dictatorship was a "concrete transitional

---

*The strike was inspired in part by a secret communist meeting attended by Kun in early March at Losonc (Lučenec) across the Slovakian border.

phase through which bourgeois revolution [would be] transformed into proletarian revolution.'' Party members should therefore be instructed not to reject democracy but to appraise it in light of the class interests that it momentarily served.

Despite a popular fixation on the Western democratic model, argued Lukács, its successful American variant could not be replicated in Europe. The Hungarian regime's political consolidation was allowing it to move toward more liberal democratic reforms, but this was a deception that concealed fascistic tendencies. The communists would therefore pursue the goal of democratic dictatorship by calling for a republic, bourgeois freedoms, the abolition of compulsory arbitration, and the confiscation and redistribution of land. At the same time, Lukács rejected the applicability of the ''democracy-fascism'' antithesis, substituting the slogan ''Class against class.'' Such a strategy could pave the way for the ultimate seizure of power by the proletariat.

Within the trade unions, wrote Lukács, the fascistic tendencies of the bureaucracy had to be fought from within and, if necessary, by the creation of new labor organizations. The unions had to be detached from the SDP, which would thereby be destroyed—a necessity, in view of its service to the regime and its latent fascism. The centrist socialist orientation was the communists' most dangerous enemy and an obstacle in the way of the democratic dictatorship strategy. It had therefore to be isolated.

Finally, since the Soviet Union's enemies were preparing for war, the party had to dispel false expectations that such an imperialist crusade would bring territorial revision in Hungary's favor. Principally, the party could propagate the Soviet regime's peaceful intentions and progressive domestic achievements. If the war could not be forestalled by a proletarian revolution, it had to be converted into civil war; the Soviet Union, ''the bastion of proletarian revolution and the home of the proletariat,'' had to be defended at all cost. Instead of boycotting the military, the party should infiltrate the armed forces and arms industries to agitate against war and sabotage the war effort.

The workers, concluded Lukács, were the party's first and ultimate concern. The new strategy had to be built on the works cells. ''The factory must be our fortress.''

Riddled with semantic obfuscation, ideological contradiction, and erroneous appraisals, the Blum theses departed from both the "pessimism" (that is, the realism) and dogmatic leftism of the two principal émigré factions. When the draft was submitted for debate in early 1929, it aroused some enthusiasm among a few younger members, notably Révai, who had been a leading light in Landler's faction. However, the decisive reaction was harshly negative, partly because of the sharp criticism of "right-wing dangers" that had materialized within the Comintern while Lukács was composing his submission.[38] Lukács found himself isolated. According to his own account, he temporized.

The group around Kun saw in the theses the clearest opportunism; my own faction's support was decidedly lukewarm. Thus when I learned from a reliable source that Béla Kun was preparing to have me expelled from the party as a "liquidator," knowing of Kun's influence in the Comintern, I gave up further struggle and proffered a "self-criticism." I remained firmly convinced of the correctness of my views, but I also knew . . . that expulsion from the party at that time would have precluded my active participation in the approaching battle against fascism.[39]

The factional struggles for power and ideological supremacy were Byzantine in their complexity. Another survivor has argued at length that Lukács was sincere in his self-criticism and dutiful adoption of the official line. What is clear is that following Kun, Révai took the lead in denouncing the theses' "opportunism." The party's earlier strategy and the SWPH's republican appeals, which Révai had once endorsed, were now appraised by him as "deviating in the direction of democratic revolution." The chastised Lukács thereupon acknowledged that "a second Hungarian revolution could in no way be of a lower type than the first, i.e., *after* a proletarian dictatorship a democratic dictatorship is inconceivable." He now realized that "in Hungary collaboration with the entire peasantry in the battle against feudal remains is out of the question." His opportunistic advocacy of democracy as the optimal battlecry for the workers, confessed Lukács, would have in effect liquidated the party's policy of social revolution. The debate on Lukács's mistakes (or prescience) was revived in the mid-1950s, but his stillborn theses bore only a faint resemblance to the Comintern's eventual popular front strategy.[40]

**Gradualism Rejected.** Following Lukács's ignominious surrender, Kun, aided by Révai and another young comrade, Sándor Szerényi, composed a new directive at the request of the Comintern. Their premises, carefully differentiated from the Blum theses, were that there was only one ruling class in Hungary, finance capital, which dominated the alliance of big capital and big estates. Therefore the immediate rather than once-removed task of the revolution was the destruction of the capitalist system. Class contradictions other than the bourgeois-proletarian antithesis did not alter the essence of the revolution. The middle peasantry and the urban lower middle classes would simply have to be neutralized.

In the fall of 1929 the Comintern, under the title of "Open letter to All CPH Members," issued a denunciation of the Blum theses. In Hungary, it declared, the only proper strategic goal was the dictatorship of the proletariat (if only, argued Kun, because of the historical precedent). The remnants of feudalism notwithstanding, the time had passed for a democratic revolution. The party's former policy had been right-wing deviationist, and any factional defense of it would be punished with expulsion. Although the economic crisis had not yet brought about the preconditions of revolution, the party would have to raise its profile among the masses, notably by means of the newly established, illegal Red trade unions. Social democracy was veering towards social fascism.* Accordingly, a united front could be attempted only from below.[41]

The open letter also rectified the party's policy on revisionism. Since the fall of the Commune, the émigré leaders' contribution to this burning issue had been to advocate a Danubian confederation of soviet republics. The communist parties of the successor states saw no need for hypothetical schemes to accommodate Hungarian irredentism, and the Comintern diplomatically refrained from issuing a directive on the question. The CPH, however, in keeping with the national preference for revisionism, nevertheless felt compelled to take a position. In 1927 its review *Új Március* carried the advice that "the responsibility of revolutionary workers is to link the slogans of Trianon's revolutionary overthrow [i.e., repudiating the Treaty of Trianon] and the right of self-determination of the Hungarian people with the cause of the Soviet Union's defense." This line was elaborated in the spring of 1929 by Révai, who argued that territorial revision was the exclusive interest of the ruling classes and their dependent petite bourgeoisie. "Down with revision!" trumpeted a contemporary leaflet written by Révai. But the Comintern's open letter warned that such slogans would only drive the workers into the arms of the fascists and weaken the anti-imperialist movement. Révai had to issue a self-criticism in which he accurately observed that "it is not an easy thing to give the workers a clear and popular explanation of how one can be at once against Trianon and against imperialistic revision."[42]

## A MORIBUND PARTY

Once again, the emigration was locked in battle over ideological nuances. With the Central Committee inoperative, the small band of home communists, mostly young post-Commune recruits, soldiered on as best they could. The Secretariat coordinated the Budapest party committee, the KIMSZ, the Red Aid, and the rural and trade union departments. The party possessed eleven district organizations, five of them in the capital area. Small cells existed in a few provincial industrial centers, notably around Salgótarján, where the communists helped to instigate another miners' strike in November 1929 (it lasted four weeks). But central direction of the dispersed cells, with a reported combined membership of close to one thousand, was haphazard.[43]

---

*The fascist epithet served many ends. In the same period, a new understanding between the government and the SDP allowed Garami to return from exile. He promptly denounced the communists for being not radical socialists but fascists on the left.

**The Second Congress.** Under the direction of a Comintern committee headed by Dmitri Z. Manuilsky, the Hungarians made preparations for the party's second congress, which was duly held at Aprilovka, near Moscow, from 25 February to 15 March 1930.[44] Twenty-two delegates completed the perilous journey from Hungary to join the émigrés at the congress. The majority were youngish industrial workers who had joined the party within the past five years and had already paid the price of imprisonment. The principal reports were delivered by Kun (on the political situation in Hungary), Szerényi (on trade union questions), and Révai (on agrarian policy). The congress essentially confirmed the line of the 1929 open letter. As usual, the weakness of the regime was overestimated by Kun, who anticipated that the deepening economic crisis would soon lead to revolution. The wealthy and middle peasants were beyond redemption, declared Révai. The principal slogans adopted by the congress were overthrow of the "fascist" system and creation of a worker-peasant government (synonymous here with proletarian dictatorship); a seven-hour working day; reduced taxes for the peasantry and redistribution of large estates without compensation among poor peasants and farm laborers; struggle against imperialist wars; and revolutionary defense of the Soviet Union.* The party, agreed the delegates, should be strengthened by expanding its membership and the cell network and by more effective agitprop among women and youth. It should try to seize control of the trade unions and, in some trades, to create red unions.

Impatient with the interminable factional disputes, the Comintern had ruled that the CPH should be led primarily by the home Secretariat and repatriated Central Committee members, with the External Committee relegated to a supporting role. The newly elected Central Committee reflected this wish: only Kun remained from the old guard, and even he was replaced as the party's representative to the Comintern. The fourteen other members, mainly workers and veterans of the SWPH and imprisonment, were all from the home movement. They were all too young to have been active in the Commune; the new secretary, Szerényi, was only 26 years old. From the outset, relations between Kun and the newcomers were strained. They mistrusted him for his role in the debilitating internecine battles. He, in turn, regarded the domestic activists as dangerously inexperienced and possibly infiltrated.[45]

Kun had not forgiven Révai for his earlier adherence to the Landler faction and for his initial support of Lukács. He fought hard before and during the congress to have Révai removed from party work. In the event, he succeeded

---

*One participant who subsequently rose to prominence, the émigré agronomist Imre Nagy, was reportedly compelled to exercise self-criticism at the congress for having earlier refused to "stand at attention before the Comintern," that is, by clinging to rightist-opportunist views. See *Népszabadság,* 9 March 1957.

in dropping Révai from the Central Committee, but at the other comrades' insistence Révai remained as editor of *Új Március* and a member of the External Committee.[46] Lukács himself was suspended from party work and spent the next three years directing a communist writers' group in Germany. The stinging rebuke over the Blum theses convinced him of his political ineptitude and allowed him in good conscience to withdraw to the realm of theoretical work.[47]

The party's misfortunes in Hungary were due in no small part to the aftereffects of Kun's Austrian arrest. József Oancz, the former metalworker, had been persuaded by the police to infiltrate the CPH. His career there was meteoric, reflecting presumably the paucity of available talent: he became Budapest party secretary and eventually a member of the Central Committee. Thanks to his services, the police swept up the Secretariat and other activists in the fall of 1930. Later that year, he was finally unmasked, lured to Moscow, and killed in a Russian jail. The Moscow leadership now thought that the coast was clear. Révai was sent back to once again rebuild the party, but at the end of December he, too, was arrested. As if all this were not trouble enough, the CPH had to cope with the activities of a newsboy by the name of Iván Hartstein, who with Trotskyite-anarchist slogans organized young workers into a short-lived "Federation of Hungarian Left-wing Communists" that denounced the CPH and the Soviet Union.

Despite the Comintern's strictures against factionalism, by early 1931 the new Central Committee had disintegrated. Internal strife, as well as the tangible demonstration of Kun's suspicions, added fuel to the flames of mutual recrimination. Once again, the Comintern intervened. The latter's Executive Committee expelled Szerényi from the Central Committee, and in 1933 he was jailed on what were later generically termed "fabricated charges," though he survived to serve the party after the war. At least one other member, József Bergmann, was also purged and disappeared in 1933. The activist Szekér was imprisoned from 1933 to 1941. All this was merely a foretaste of the great purges perpetrated under Stalin's rule.

From March 1931 to May 1932, the Comintern laboriously reconstructed the Central Committee. Apart from Kun, the new members included four émigrés assigned to salvage the home movement, Ferenc Huszti, Géza Gold, Karikás, and Sallai; other members were Sándor Fürst, György Kilián, Kiss, Sándor Poll, Pál Sebes, and József Tóth.[48] Huszti became the de facto head of the CPH and its External Committee. The thirty-seven-year-old lawyer-journalist had acted as a revolutionary prosecutor during the Commune, had been active in occupied Pécs, and subsequently worked on various assignments for the Russian party. He was directed by the Comintern to stay out of Hungary, but most of the other Central Committee members rotated every three months between the External Committee and the home Secretariat.

**The Communists and the Great Depression.** While the CPH Central Committee was being rebuilt, Bethlen, overwhelmed by the difficulties of coping with the deepening depression, resigned and was replaced in August 1931 by the government of Count Gyula Károlyi, who had led the short-lived Szeged countergovernment in 1919. Károlyi was less of a compromiser than his predecessor. On 17 September the railway bridge at Biatorbágy was blown up under the Budapest-Vienna express, causing twenty-two deaths. The outrage was committed by a madman named Szilveszter Matuska, but the government nevertheless blamed the communists and invoked martial-law provisions against the party. (The latter, in turn, blamed right-wing elements linked with the Austrian Heimwehr.) The pursuit of communists was stepped up, and in the summer of 1932 the police captured the members of the Secretariat, Sallai, Fürst, Karikás, and Kilián, and also arrested Kiss and Poll.[49]

The usual international protest campaign was organized against the government's obvious intent to apply the full rigor of martial law against the communists. Prominent progressive literati and politicians from Thomas Mann to Léon Blum were induced to collaborate in the protest, as was Mihály Károlyi. In Hungary, a few middle-class radicals led by the lawyer Rusztém Vámbéry were mobilized by the Red Aid. The protests availed little. After a summary trial, Fürst and Sallai were executed on 29 July to become revered martyrs of the movement. The others subsequently received prison sentences.[50]

Internal divisions and official persecution had virtually incapacitated the CPH at the very time when economic and social conditions in Hungary were beginning to provide a more fertile field for radical agitation. The symptoms of the worldwide economic depression—a precipitous fall in industrial production leading to massive unemployment—were replicated in Hungary. The party did manage to instigate a few demonstrations by the unemployed, calculating that the latter were potential adherents and would be radicalized by the experience. However, these operations were frequently ill-conceived and ill-timed, depending more on the Comintern's symbolic dates than on particularly favorable local circumstances.[51]

In late 1929 the home communists had created a National Unity Committee of Unemployed (Munkanélküliek Országos Egységbizottsága, or MOEB) which through a number of local committees attempted to outdo the SDP in agitation and the organization of protest meetings. At a secret meeting of these committees in January 1930, the phenomenon of unemployment was identified as an integral part of capitalism and therefore eradicable only by the dictatorship of the proletariat; pending that solution, public demonstrations were the most appropriate channel to advance demands for unemployment compensation, tax relief, reduced working hours to spread employment, and for conversion of the ad hoc committees into official labor exchanges.[52] The largest demonstration instigated by the communist-led MOEB occurred on 26 January, when some three thousand unemployed clashed with the police in Budapest.

The External Committee next proposed a major hunger demonstration for 1 November, and the Secretariat proceeded to lay the groundwork. In the meantime, the Trade Union Council decided to call a general work stoppage and peaceful protest march for 1 September. The SDP was suffering from the erosion of its traditional constituency, trade union membership having declined to 87,000, and it took up the cause of the jobless masses. The CPH decided to join this initiative in the hope of turning it into a more militant protest, although the party was desperately short of funds and had been virtually annihilated outside Budapest.[53] The truly massive demonstration on 1 September was the scene of occasional, mainly communist-instigated violence, prompting *Népszava* to denounce the "Bolshevik detachments" as the deadly enemies of the working class. The Central Committee, meeting in Vienna from 19 to 23 September, gloated that the "social fascist" SDP had been dealt a stinging blow. It was the police, however, who delivered the decisive blow by rounding up over one hundred communists in September and October and effectively forestalling the hunger demonstration set for 1 November.[54]

The arrests also prevented the party from implementing a plan to have Madzsar's cell within the SDP secede and run independent candidates in the December municipal elections. The remaining members of the Central Committee met in Vienna on 12 November to review the party's tactics.[55] Concluding that the "action policy" of repeated demonstrations was unrealistic in view of organizational and conspiratorial weaknesses, they blamed the old Central Committee and Secretariat for inadequate party building and overblown slogans and objectives. In fact, the party's troubles arose in equal measure from police infiltration and the Comintern's own action policy imposed through Béla Kun.

During 1931 the CPH was unable to initiate a single public protest. For symbolic and agitprop reasons it attempted to participate in the June general elections under the guise of a "Socialist Workers' Bloc," but its weakness and the countermeasures of the SDP and the government aborted the halfhearted exercise. Illegal communist posters advised voters that any vote served bourgeois interests and urged workers to spoil ballots with the slogan "Work, bread, freedom!"[56] In the event, the SDP managed to retain its fourteen electoral mandates, although its base of support shifted somewhat toward the lower middle class.

Reasonably enough, the CPH continued to seek support among the unemployed and organized a petition campaign.[57] In the autumn of 1931 it collected thirteen radical union factions under the umbrella of a United Trade Union Opposition (Egyesült Szakszervezeti Ellenzék, or ESZE).[58] The latter issued an action program calling for a variety of social and economic reforms and relief measures, for the amnesty of political prisoners, and for diplomatic and commercial relations with the Soviet Union. Although the communists attempted to create the illusion of a major opposition movement, notably by publishing a series of radical newssheets for various trades, the ESZE remained a marginal force in organized labor; in fact, it could claim credit for only one strike, by dockworkers in the spring of 1932.[59] With a membership hovering between two and three hundred, exercising influence over a few thousand workers, and locked into a dogmatic adversary relationship with the SDP, the party's political impact on the Hungarian scene was minimal.

In March 1932 the Central Committee issued what is called a "battle program."[60] Apart from restating the goals of the second congress, it advanced such patently unrealistic objectives as a 50-percent wage increase. Its principal demand was for suspension of the martial-law provisions against communists. The Central Committee also reviewed the party's agrarian policy, adding to the goal of redistribution a series of piecemeal measures to ease the peasants' lot.* But in the countryside the proscribed communists enjoyed less freedom of action than even the SDP.[61] In the cities, meanwhile, the frustration of trying to organize the unemployed drove impatient young communist activists to foment occasional looting although party leaders advised against it.

**Agents of the Comintern.** The perennial misfortunes of the home movement did not prevent the exiled communists from soldiering on elsewhere in the cause of revolution. Vienna, Berlin, Prague, Paris—all had their émigré groups, but most of the communist refugees sought haven in the Soviet Union, and a few rose to prominence in the Comintern and the Soviet state apparatus. The economist Jenő Varga frequently addressed the Comintern on his specialty and from 1927 headed the Institute of World Economy and Politics. Bokányi first worked for the Comintern, then for the labor commissariat of the Soviet government. The journalist Lajos Magyar, who had come to the Soviet Union in the 1922 prisoner exchange, worked for *Pravda,* served in the Soviet embassies in Berlin and Peking, and became Otto Kuusinen's deputy in the Comintern's Far Eastern section. In 1922, the Comintern dispatched Pogány to the United States to organize and in effect lead the local party. He rose to alternate membership of the Executive Committee and served on the Comintern's key political commission. In 1928 and 1929, however, he came under fire, ultimately from Stalin himself, for erroneous appraisals of the American working class and was dismissed from the Comintern.

---

*At its twenty-seventh congress in September 1930, the SDP had finally issued its own moderate land reform program. The government had persistently obstructed the SDP's attempts to organize in rural areas. Accordingly, the party scheduled a demonstration and strike for 7 April 1932, but the heavy-handed Károlyi regime responded by briefly suspending *Népszava* and squelched the protest.

In the early 1920s Rákosi was responsible for Italian communist affairs in the Comintern, and in 1935 was elected in absentia to the Executive Committee. Landler was sent on missions to Central and Western Europe in 1924. Gerő was also active in Western Europe, serving as the secretary of the French party's Hungarian section between 1926 and 1928, and later as a Comintern instructor with the French and Belgian parties. He assisted Manuilsky, the secretary of the Executive Committee's presidium, with the preparations for the seventh congress, was a key Comintern envoy to Spain during the civil war, then returned to Moscow as Manuilsky's secretary. Rudas taught at the Comintern's Lenin School and later worked in the Marx-Engels-Lenin Institute. From 1926 Hirossik was assigned to the German party and as Berlin correspondent of *Inprekor*; his membership lapsed in 1933 and he never rejoined the party. As for the ubiquitous Kun, he was a regular member of the Executive Committee (and of its presidium in 1931) and was put in charge in 1929 of the Comintern's Balkan secretariat. Most of the Comintern's foreign activists had acquired Soviet citizenship and doubled as agents of the Soviet secret service.

Whatever their assignment, the majority of the émigrés retained their links with the CPH and shared in its factional disputes. Those who were not sent on Comintern missions found employment according to their talents in the Soviet economy and kept in touch through Hungarian-language publications such as *Sarló és Kalapács* (Hammer and Sickle). Factional friction and the consolidation of Stalin's autocratic rule made the émigrés' life increasingly one of fear and suspicion. As soon as the young Károly Kiss arrived in Moscow in 1931 to attend the Lenin School and work with Profintern, the Red trade union international, he was cautioned by Kun: "You must be conspiratorial in Moscow, too, be particularly wary of the Hungarians, don't seek them out." When an old acquaintance hailed Kiss at the Moscow Hungarian Club, the former was reproved by Kun: "You see, this is your great weakness, this is why you were not admitted to the CPSU." And when, before his purge, Szerényi wrote an article in *Új Március* under the pen-name of "Aczél" (meaning "steel," a direct imitation of Stalin), Kun was furious: "This sort of thing is noticed."[62] This oppressive atmosphere tested the revolutionary ardor of the émigrés, but it must have been preferable to persecution by the Hungarian police.

**Proletarian Realism.**    The cultural line issuing from Moscow and adopted with varying consistency by the party's far-flung publications reflected the leftist dogmatism of the Kun faction.[63] The principal émigré journal was the Moscow *Sarló és Kalapács,* published from December 1929 until March 1937. In Budapest, a number of literary and critical periodicals appeared with covert communist· sponsorship, notably *100%* (1927–30) and *Társadalmi Szemle* (Social Review, 1931–33), the latter edited by Dr. Madzsar. The talented writer Zoltán Fábry edited *Az Út* (The Road, 1931–36) which was nominally published in Bratislava. Other Hungarian communist reviews appeared in Paris and New York.

Apart from propounding the achievements of Soviet education and culture, these journals generally propagated a cultural line that, inspired by the goal of a second Commune, rejected all literary manifestations departing from the cult of the proletariat. This, at a time when the Hungarian party was in dire need of progressive allies, largely excluded cooperation with the socialist, liberal, and peasant-oriented Populist wings of the literary opposition. The stylistically avant-garde and ultraleftist line of Kassák, who had returned from exile, was denounced by the communist press as Trotskyite. The liberal urbanist writers around the review *Nyugat* were criticized for their middle-class, apolitical stance, while the romantic peasant nationalism of the emerging populist movement was denigrated as regressive and unproletarian.

Only a purely proletarian, class literature was deemed acceptable in the service of revolution. This dogma was forcefully preached by a group of leftist émigrés in Moscow led by Béla Illés, the general secretary of the International Bureau of Revolutionary Writers. They compensated for their relative lack of talent by an extremism that placed the Hungarian group on the extreme left wing of the Moscow Federation of Proletarian Writers. In the spring of 1931 this group adopted a platform for Hungary's proletarian literature: in the revolutionizing circumstances of the economic depression, there was no need for compromise with other reformist tendencies. Since only active party members could be true proletarian writers, a qualification that effectively excluded virtually all contemporary Hungarian writing, the platform accordingly proceeded to excoriate the latter. Concurrently Lukács was expounding on the concept of "proletarian realism" (known subsequently as socialist realism) and the necessity of integrating reportorial observation into an ideologically sound world view.[64]

Apart from Fábry, the Hungarian communist movement could claim one outstanding literary figure, the young poet Attila József. Imbued with a vague anarchist idealism, he had returned in 1926 from a sojourn in Paris to join forces with the short-lived SWPH. He turned to communism while taking one of Madzsar's leadership seminars, adhered to the party in 1930, and became the leading literary champion of the working class. The party's reward was the epithet of "fascist" (presumably for his earlier flirtation with nationalist circles) in the above-mentioned Moscow platform. József responded with the charge that the émigrés were out of touch with Hungarian reality, notably in their assumption of the crisis of fascist dictatorship when the latter was only in its initial stages. Nevertheless, in 1933 *Társadalmi Szemle* carried a new attack on József's poetry. His independent spirit irritated the party's leaders, including Madzsar, while other activists slavishly parroted the orthodox critiques. József drifted away from the CPH (by some accounts he was expelled.)[65] Without ever losing his passionate empathy with the working class, he revised his views of Marxism, doubting the viability of a proletarian dictatorship. Mentally disturbed, the tragic young poet took his own life in 1937. Within a few years he would be elevated to the pantheon of Hungarian communism and extolled as the poet laureate of the working class, but the party could never fully expiate its shabby treatment of this rare luminary.

## THE FRUSTRATIONS OF IRRELEVANCE

In the final analysis, the variations in the tactical line of the Comintern and its Hungarian party in the 1920s carried little practical significance in the Hungarian context, where no ideological acrobatics could remedy the movement's isolation and irrelevance. The communists were consensually regarded as antinational (in their ideology and their subordination to the Soviet-led Comintern) and, by virtue of their Russian parentage, pro-Slav. These values were of course antithetical to the prevailing political ethos. In the interwar period, the home party's membership never exceeded one thousand, and the movement was only marginally more successful in recruiting adherents among the oppressed and alienated Magyar minorities in Slovakia and Romania.[66]

Yet the émigrés persevered, intoxicated with the doctrinal inevitability of revolution and its promise of power, and constrained in their choice of career by advancing age and international opprobrium. They stubbornly inflated the achievements (as well as the failures) of the tiny home movement, and immersed themselves in the organizational minutiae of reports and directives and in casuistic quarrels. Meanwhile, their predominant ultraleftism alienated their most likely working class constituents and intellectual allies. Party historians disagree about the sins of omission and commission, but one of them has written:

> The home communist movement, very weak in influence and organization, and representing little more than a potential force, was in the time of the depression at one of the low points in its history. Misreading the distinctive features and possibilities of the era, the communist party clothed its revolutionary voluntarism in rigid dogmatism. The sectarian indictment of social democracy and other "centrist" forces; the rigid rejection of ideological explorations; the inability to provide a differentiated analysis of cultural complexities; the linkage of these ideological-political weaknesses and the growing bureaucratic-authoritarian tendencies in the Comintern, which had a particularly profound impact on the small illegal movement of a small country—all prevented the communist movement from becoming the proponent and active nucleus of a new left-wing alternative.[67]

The popular front tactic promulgated at the Comintern's 1935 congress rectified these earlier mistakes. But it still could not propel the party to the center of Hungarian political life.

# 6. Popular Front, Hungarian Front, 1932–1944

The year 1932, the depression's deepest point, found the communists in disarray. Their leadership had been decimated by successive arrests, and for a long period the External Committee had lost contact with home base. Madzsar, the party's principal figure in the legal sphere, had been expelled from the SDP the previous year and was subsequently also arrested and jailed. The party's secret printing press and propaganda apparatus had been annihilated. The jobless movement petered out from the weariness induced by futile demonstrations and the CPH's own incapacity to lead.

Concurrently the regime underwent a shift to the right when, in September 1932, the former defense minister, General Gyula Gömbös, was called to form a new government. Gömbös launched a series of initiatives to deal with the economic crisis. His projects ranged from work camps and welfare jobs to the creation of an entire corporatist system. To organize the rural and urban working classes became the goal not only of Gömbös's corporatist National Labor Center (Nemzeti Munkaközpont) and the Christian socialists but also of extreme right-wing groups such as the Arrow Cross Party. At the SDP's twenty-ninth congress in January 1933 the Peyer leadership expressed alarm at these attempts to encroach on its traditional constituency and vowed to fight against the regime's corporatist schemes.

## THE PARTY SHATTERED AND OUTFLANKED

In late 1932, yet another reorganization of the CPH was set in motion. The revived and normally dispersed Central Committee included Kun, Huszti,

Gold, and Sebes, with the addition of two new members, the journalist Komor and, from 1934, the former upholsterer and KIMSZ secretary Dezső Nemes. The External Committee, momentarily led by Huszti, was located in Berlin. The constant threat of arrest impelled the Central Committee to forego the recreation of a home Secretariat. It chose instead to rely on the periodic repatriation of one of its members, beginning with Sebes, who was instructed, in rebuilding the home movement, to exclude the more exposed activists. But the party continued to suffer reverses, for by the summer of 1933 its renascent rural branch was destroyed through a combination of ineptitude and police vigilance.[1]

Realistically, the Central Committee dismissed the possibility of collaboration with the SDP leadership. In March 1933, however, the Comintern called for an antifascist, proletarian united front, and the Central Committee complied by proposing joint action at the lower party levels. Even this modest initiative brought down the wrath of the socialist leaders, who feared that the authorities would seize the excuse of Bolshevik infiltration to further curtail their party's freedom. Declared the SDP's general secretary, Illés Mónus: "We can't even discuss a united front, because by doing so we would recognize the legitimacy of a Bolshevik party. We don't acknowledge them, so there is no one with whom a united front could be forged."[2] Nevertheless, the CPH was inspired by the Comintern's new line. At that time, its one covert foothold was in the youth organizations under the SDP's National Youth Committee (Országos Ifjúsági Bizottság, or OIB).

In mid-1933 the Comintern instructed the CPH to abandon the Red union alternative and concentrate exclusively on legal trade unions. The Central Committee complied by issuing the slogan "Into the trade unions!" It also liquidated the two small Red unions, which were in the construction and leather industries. Debates continued in the Central Committee on the desirability of drawing union members into shadow opposition factions within the legal trade unions. By the end of the year, however, the Comintern had imposed its view that the "reformist" trade unions could and should be led to class-conscious militancy.[3] The SDP and the Trade Union Council responded in September with a determined campaign against the "united front" infection. To impose the CPH's presence the resident Central Committee member, Géza Gold, took it upon himself to call a one-day general strike for 22 October. The affair turned out to be such an utter fiasco that Gold was expelled by the Comintern's International Control Committee, while the trade unions were only strengthened in their resolve to extirpate communist agitators from their ranks.

The Gömbös regime meanwhile completed its corporatist scenario, which entailed compulsory membership in so-called chambers for all workers and employers, and entered into secret consultations with Peyer. The communists seized upon the scheme to encourage the SDP to collaborate with them. In

December 1934 the Central Committee appealed to the SDP leadership to publicly join a united front. The following spring they advanced the politically more realistic proposal, transmitted by the left-leaning socialist Szakasits, for a secret meeting of the two parties' representatives. Once more the communists were rebuffed. In the event, Gömbös' corporatist scheme foundered on the shoals of widespread opposition within the ruling circles.[4] In his foreign policy the prime minister would continue to pursue collaboration with Mussolini and Hitler, partly out of ideological empathy with the former and partly to win support for territorial revision. In this, of course, he was adamantly opposed by the encircling Little Entente of Czechoslovakia, Romania, and Yugoslavia, and by their French ally.

At the March 1935 elections the CPH again resorted to the promotion of a cover organization, the so-called Antifascist United Workers' Front, which as usual failed to reach the ballots. The SDP retained its votes but its representation fell by 3 to 11 seats; Gömbös' National Unity Party won 170 seats, the Smallholder Party 23, the Christian Party 17, other liberal opposition parties 10, and the far right Arrow Cross 2. The communists managed to run an opposition slate in the April elections to the representative council of the National Social Insurance Institute (Országos Társadalombiztosító Intézet, or OTI) and received 5 percent of the vote.

By the spring of 1935, amidst the first signs of economic recovery, strikes were becoming more frequent. Communists and left-wing socialists collaborated in mounting a four-week-long strike by construction workers in July. The party group within that union included two future communist leaders, László Rajk and Antal Apró. The twenty-six-year-old Rajk had joined the CPH in 1931 as a university student and after repeated arrests had found work as a building worker. Apró, aged twenty-two, became a party member the same year as Rajk; a painter by trade, he had been temporarily suspended from the union during the 1934 drive against opposition agitators. Concurrently, young KIMSZ activists associated themselves with a student movement, the Tuition Reform Committee (Tandijreform Bizottság), which was agitating for financial aid for poorer students.

At its thirtieth congress in September 1935 the SDP came out in open opposition to the regime's corporatist overtures but continued to dismiss the very idea of collaboration with communists. The CPH, on the other hand, had to modify its former stand. In keeping with the emerging Comintern line, it now advised workers to vote for the SDP in parliamentary by-elections that fall. In January 1936 the party liquidated its shadow front organization, the United Trade Union Opposition (ESZE), and abandoned attempts to organize cohesive opposition factions within the trade unions. From now on, it began to concentrate instead on infiltrating communists into the trade union bureaucracy. The CPH also launched a new legal monthly of social and literary criticism, *Gondolat*

(Thought), to replace the defunct *Társadalmi Szemle*. In February the party made another of its fruitless secret overtures to the SDP. It called for limited joint action that would defend the legal workers' party and the unions, oppose the regime's German and Italian orientation, and protest the persecution of radical activists.[5] The latter concern was prompted by the arrest the previous month of a number of communists including the Central Committee member Zsigmond Kiss.

In the mid-1930s the party entered a new phase of disintegration, dispersal, and individual liquidation. The outbreak of the Spanish Civil War brought over a thousand Hungarian volunteers, mainly émigré communists, to fight in the international brigades. The more noteworthy among them were Zalka (alias General Lukács), who commanded the Twelfth International Brigade, Münnich, and Rajk, who served as commissar of the Thirteenth International Brigade's Rákosi Battalion. Gerő (alias Pedro) was one of the principal Comintern instructors in Spain and controlled the Catalan Communist Party. He played a leading role in the liquidation of anarchists and of the POUM in May and June 1937.[6] Several hundred Hungarian volunteers lost their lives in the civil war. Most of the survivors either returned to the Soviet Union or adhered to West European communist movements until they met again in Hungary after World War II.

**The Elusive United Front.**   The overture to the great purges, sparked by Kirov's murder, was already resounding when the Comintern effected a major tactical shift, away from the "sectarianism" that had characterized its policies since 1928. The new line was elaborated and confirmed at its seventh congress, held in Moscow between 25 July and 20 August, 1935.[7] In his keynote address Dimitrov identified the immediate peril, fascism, as the dictatorship of the most reactionary and imperialist capitalistic circles. Given this threat to bourgeois democracy, the task of communists was to rise to the defense of the latter by forging a united workers' front. That in turn required the consolidation of orthodox and Red trade unions and an alliance or even merger with the social democrats—as long as the latter recognized the ultimate imperative of replacing capitalism by a proletarian dictatorship on the Soviet model. That goal was in no way compromised, argued Dimitrov, by resort to a transitional and momentarily useful popular front. The social democratic parties were thus converted overnight from loathsome "social fascists" into desirable allies.

Béla Kun's revolutionary dogmatism surfaced once again, and at great cost to the CPH. As a member of the congress's preparatory commission, Kun had already demurred at the new tactic. Other members of the Central Committee followed his lead. After the congress, they advised their comrades in a letter dated 18 September that their party's policy of late had followed such a correct line "that the congressional resolutions do not require a sharp turn from us."[8] Seven years had elapsed since the party had rejected the transitional tactic of the Blum theses, and while the leadership had made tentative moves after 1933 toward collaboration with the SDP, its failures had only reinforced its leftist inclination. Among the leading émigrés it was the budding ideologue Révai who showed the greatest prescience. Having emerged from three years' imprisonment, he had prepared in mid-1934 a brief study for the Comintern's Executive Committee which, admidst the usual theoretical convolutions, managed to suggest the possibility of alternative transitional tactics for reaching a proletarian dictatorship. Significantly, as Stalin's purges engulfed the communist movement, Révai was in charge of the CPH within the Comintern's Central European Secretariat.

On 20 November 1935 the Executive Committee's presidium was informed by Otto Kuusinen that many parties had not risen to the challenge of the seventh congress. "In most cases," he complained, "they are pursuing general united-front propaganda instead of a concrete united-front policy."[9] There followed more direct urgings from the Comintern Secretariat that the CPH revise its policies. The January 1936 meeting of the Central Committee was marked by heated debate in the course of which Kun felt compelled to exercise self-criticism. The committee passed a resolution acknowledging that the party had been dilatory in adopting the new orthodoxy.[10] A "comradely letter" sent to all CPH members outlined a "democratic battle plan expressing the common interests of all working people" for an antiwar, antifascist, anticapitalist alliance. The letter conceded that the CPH's former negative evaluation of the SDP and other parliamentary opposition groups had been incorrect. The communists, it continued, attached no preconditions to joint action against fascism, capitalist exploitation, and war, nor did they insist on written agreements or on open negotiations and agreements. They did not even expect the "legal organizations oppressed by fascism" to side openly with the CPH. On one point, however, they could insist, namely, that "in the interest of the common struggle . . . the slandering of the CPH and the Soviet Union be curtailed."[11]

For Stalin's Comintern, all this was too little too late. On 8 May the Comintern Secretariat averred that the Hungarian leadership's sectarian opposition had persisted beyond the December warnings. The Central Committee was summarily dismissed.[12] Zoltán Szántó was instructed to form a provisional Secretariat whose task would be to implement the new tactic and prepare a party congress at which a more accommodating Central Committee could be elected. A coincidental directive, apparently issued unilaterally by the Comintern's cadre department, ordered the infiltrated home party to be dissolved in order to make tabula rasa for the united front. Accordingly the Budapest party organization (with some four hundred activists) and the other district organs were dismantled. By the following spring the party's illegal propaganda had been suspended and the KIMSZ disbanded; the party's Vienna office was closed down. Members were instructed to join legal workers' organizations and await further instructions.[13] Total confusion reigned in the ranks of the home communists.

In these circumstances there was no realistic prospect of calling a party congress. The provisional Secretariat, which settled in Prague in July 1936, therefore converted itself into a provisional Central Committee. Its leading figure, Zoltán Szántó, probably owed his elevation and survival to his only recent reappearance in Moscow after eight years' imprisonment. Originally a clerk, he had joined the party in 1918 and served as a commissar in the Hungarian Red Army. István Friss, a thirty-three-year-old economist who became a party member in 1928, had been attending the Lenin School after spending the years from 1929 to 1934 in jail. Two other Central Committee members were recent adherents to the party. Lajos Papp, aged thirty, was a stonecutter; he joined in 1928 and played a leading role in the KIMSZ and the ESZE until 1935. The locksmith Ferenc Bozsóki, aged thirty-two, was recruited in 1929 and had been sent to the Moscow party school five years later. He returned to party work in Hungary in 1936 before being summoned to the Central Committee in Prague. In the spring of 1937 Révai, too, was ordered to Prague to reinforce the Secretariat. One common denominator of these men was their absence from Moscow during at least part of the recent "sectarian" disputes.

In its first policy statement, issued 23 June 1936, the provisional Secretariat had developed the theme of the above-mentioned comradely letter.[14] The party's objectives were, first, a popular front, through active collaboration with the SDP, in defense of democratic liberties against fascism and in the interest of a Hungarian democratic republic; the fight for peace and against the regime's revisionism; a land reform without compensation; and improvement in the daily lot of the workers. The duty of Hungarian communists was to strengthen the trade unions and the SDP, and turn the latter into a true party of the proletarian class struggle.

Given the inhospitable conditions in Hungary and the disbandment and demoralization of the home party, the conversion of theory into practice was clearly going to be a formidable challenge. Through György Vértes, the editor of *Gondolat*, Szántó managed to make contact with a student activist named Ferenc Donáth, and repeated attempts were also made to restore communication with trade union communists and organize the distribution of party material. Second thoughts about the wisdom of disbandment finally led the Comintern to instruct Szántó in March 1937 to reconstitute an illegal party center in Hungary and, as a preparatory step, to publish a new underground newspaper.[15] Accordingly, in April the party launched *Dolgozók Lapja* (Workers' Paper); it was based in Prague and edited by Friss. The paper's first issue relayed the Comintern's popular front directive to the dispersed activists, confirming that the immediate task was not to create a republic of councils or even socialism in Hungary but to unite all social strata in a broad democratic front against fascism.[16] Within a few months its distribution network was annihilated by the police, while the "illegal party center" remained a fantasy.

It was during this period that Révai emerged as the party's chief ideologist. In a series of articles and monographs published outside Hungary he elaborated the Hungarian application of the new tactic and its implications for the future transformation of Hungarian society: "The character of the transformation," he prophesied, "will surpass bourgeois democracy in the measure that the masses will not shrink from intervening in their own interest in the ownership of monopoly capital, and that socialist labor will become the most reliable, organized, vigilant, and determined pillar of that transformation, in other words its leading force."[17] In order to expand the basis of an eventual united front, the party had to steer clear of the concept of agrarian revolution (which would mobilize only the lowest peasant classes) and to promote general land reform.

**Populism and the March Front.**   Agrarian policy had to be emphasized because, despite the rapid industrial recovery and expansion of the mid-1930s, Hungary remained a country dominated by agriculture; half its labor force, in fact, was employed in that sector. Amidst overpopulation and underemployment, the extremes of vast estates and dwarf landholdings remained typical.[18] The parliamentary Smallholder Party, whose leader, István Nagyatádi Szabó, had been associated with the limited redistribution of land after the Commune, represented the self-satisfied, propertied peasant class and had neither the power nor the determination to promote more extensive land reform. Though hardly privileged in economic terms, the peasantry was venerated as the truest embodiment of the virtues of the Magyar race. For the regime, this romantic conception of the peasant served to legitimize the agrarian status quo, and indeed the countryside was ruled by conservatism and tradition. The peasantry's assigned role in the dominant nationalist and anti-Bolshevik ideology was as a counterrevolutionary bulwark against the liberal and proletarian elements that infested the cities.

Much intellectual soul-searching was devoted to the problems and destiny of postwar Hungary. One stimulus to debate was an exploration by the prominent historian Gyula Szekfű of the antinomies in Hungarian society: not only Magyars versus Jews and Catholics versus Protestants but the differences between generations, landholders, Magyars in Hungary and those in the successor states.[19] Another stimulus was the urban-rural cleavage, whose literary protagonists became known as the urbanists and the populists. The former and their parties (the Liberal Party and the SDP) were only marginally interested in agrarian reform and were in any event hamstrung by the regime's efforts, notably by retaining the open vote outside the cities, to isolate the countryside from subversive ideas. The urban and largely Jewish liberal intelligentsia coalesced around the reviews *Nyugat* and *Szép Szó* (Fine Word, 1936–39), the latter counting Attila József among its founders and directors. The socialists had *Népszava* and the monthly *Szocializmus* (Socialism); their communist counterpart was *Gondolat,* acquired by the CPH in 1936. The urbanists generally advocated progressive ideas but had little sympathy for the romantic view of the peasantry and for the anti-Semitism occasionally associated with it.

The agrarian question nevertheless imposed itself on political and intellectual life. By the late 1920s a broad and heterodox literary movement, generically known as Populism, had emerged to espouse the cause of the rural masses. Much of it materialized from the moderate right, exemplified by György Oláh's rousing exposé *Three Million Beggars,* and indeed a decade later the rural proletariat would show itself susceptible to the call of right-wing political movements. The writings of Dezső Szabó, who proclaimed the peasantry's racial purity and dismissed both rightist and leftist ideologies as alien to Hungary, had wide popular appeal particularly with the younger generation.[20] Young intellectuals concerned with rural problems congregated in the Miklós Bartha Society (founded 1925), the Agrarian Settlement Movement at Szeged, and other associations.

Poets, writers, sociologists, and agronomists shared in this revival of interest in rural life. During the early 1930s, their investigative forays came to be known as "village exploring." In his review *Tanu* (Witness) the writer László Németh, excoriating both capitalism's neglect of human values and the supranational pretensions and aridity of Marxian analysis and prescriptions, called for a "revolution of quality."[21] The brilliant poet Gyula Illyés, whose political contacts ranged from *Nyugat* liberals to the communists, raised the alarm at the numerical decline of the Magyar race and wrote a moving account of peasant life on the Transdanubian Plain, where he had been raised.[22] Imre Kovács, Géza Féja, Ferenc Erdei, and Péter Veres were also among the two dozen or so intellectuals, mainly of peasant origin, who formed the Populist Movement and generally sought a national and peasant oriented third road between the secular ideologies of right and left.

The so-called new intellectual front of 1934–35 was an attempt to consolidate the various Populist orientations. The writer Lajos Zilahy, who sympathized with the Populists and also expected much from Gömbös's radicalism, arranged a secret meeting between a few writers and the prime minister. The latter tactically endorsed their goals, but the government's inaction soon disappointed the Populists, and the front evaporated. In the meantime, in 1934, a few Populists founded their own review *Válasz* (Answer). The broader public's interest in Populism was aroused by the publication, in 1936, of Kovács's book *Néma Forradalom* (Silent Revolution). This was followed by a "Discovery of Hungary" series of sociographic studies that was launched with Féja's account of a depressed rural region known as the Viharsarok (Stormy Corner).

The significance of the Populist Movement within the context of a history of Hungarian communism is twofold. First, as an indigenous reformist movement it had an immediate public impact that far surpassed that of the communists; indeed, it endured well into the postwar era as a powerful noncommunist literary-political force. Second, the communists soon sought to associate themselves with the movement and decades later would claim to have played a leading role in its politicization and sustenance.[23]

Prior to the emergence of the new Comintern line the Hungarian communists had denigrated Németh and the other Populists, and their subsequent involvement with the movement came about through the activity of a number of young university students and intellectuals more or less under the party's control. Typically, they were recent recruits to the party and from a middle-class, Transylvanian background. Until he departed from Hungary in 1936 to fight in the Spanish Civil War, the principal manipulator of the party's intellectual wing was Rajk. Others drifted into the party through the tuition reform movement, one of whose activists was the law student Ferenc Donáth. At the University of Debrecen, the major city in the great plains, the communists Sándor Zöld and Gyula Kállai formed a nucleus of sympathizers and on the occasion of a student assembly in March 1936 succeeded in sparking off a heated debate with their proposed program of democratic left-wing reforms. Only in the autumn of that year was regular contact established between Party Secretary Szántó, on a surreptitious visit from Prague, and Donáth (the latter was instructed to engineer a united front of reformist intellectuals and students).

The regime at this time was confronted not only with the democratic sloganeering of the socialist youth organization and certain student groups, but also with the extreme right-wing student federation Turul. Led chiefly by German-Hungarians, the federation conducted anti-Semitic forays that brought down official sanctions. It was in this atmosphere of intellectual and political ferment that in 1937 a group of Populists led by Kovács and Féja conceived the idea of a formal proclamation of desirable reforms. They scheduled it for the national holiday, on 15 March. Donáth and the Debrecen communists promptly associated themselves with what became known as the "March Front" and helped to propagate it in university circles.

The twelve-point proclamation of the March Front, drafted by Kovács and Féja, was issued at a mass meeting in the gardens of the National Museum, where on the same day in 1848 the poet Petőfi had galvanized a similar youthful assembly into nationalistic fervor. The demands encompassed a democratic transformation: the guarantee of such basic rights as universal suffrage by secret ballot; the prohibition of conflicts of interest for members of parliament; the expropriation of large estates; curtailment of the economic power of banks, cartels, and monopolies; progressive taxation; full employment, the forty-hour work week, and a decent minimum wage; the unrestricted organization of labor in defense of its economic interests; and better access for the poorer classes to higher education. The final point dealt with the issue of revisionism. It called for free choice by the peoples of the Danubian Basin as to their national and state affiliation, and for a confederal structure to resist pan-German and pan-Slav imperialism. These desiderata were compatible with the communists' united-front program with one important exception, the allusion to the threat of pan-Slavism, which they tried unsuccessfully to have expunged from the proclamation.

When the Debrecen group activized a broader circle of students, including such subsequent party members as Lajos Fehér and Géza Losonczy, into public endorsement of the March Front, the government ordered the suspension of the student organizations. Veres was beaten up by the police in the course of interrogation, and Féja and Kovács received short prison terms for the alleged anti-class incitement in their sociographic writings. Despite these repressive measures, which were prompted in part by an overestimation of the communists' influence in the front, the Populist proclamation had a national impact. The majority of the writers, Féja foremost among them, wished to preserve the front as a purely intellectual movement, while the more leftist ones, notably Erdei and József Darvas, and for a time, Kovács himself, favored its transformation into a peasant oriented political party.

The communists tactically endorsed the front's democratic demands, but they insisted, as Révai wrote in *Gondolat,* that "an 'intellectual movement' could only expand into a popular movement by association and involvement with current politics."[24] Donáth was sent on a tour of provincial towns to drum up support among intellectuals, and in October 1937 a meeting of Populists at Makó reiterated the March proclamation. The Debrecen communists meanwhile launched a short-lived review, *Tovább* (Further), urging radicalization of the March Front. "We must work in gray daily battles for the creation of a common front of workers, peasants, and progressive intellectuals," appealed Kállai.[25]

The communists' urgings went largely unheeded. In the protracted debate on the choice between movement and party the Populist majority, including Illyés, rejected the latter route, which was also regarded with apprehension and hostility by the SDP. The front's last proclamation, issued in March 1938, was only marginally adapted to the left's desires: it suggested more active propaganda and subsumed the pan-Slav threat in a general reference to "great-power imperialism." The authorities withheld permission for another public assembly and laid charges against the document's five Populist authors. *Válasz* ceased publication that summer, while *Tovább* was banned and its communist editors brought to trial.

Thus the March Front, which never became more than a loose intellectual coalition, effectively dissipated. Populist ideas, however, had put down deep roots. Their proponents, apart from Erdei and Darvas, never accepted the Marxist alternative, but the movement served to radicalize many young people and indirectly aided the communists' own proselytizing efforts, notably at the

Bólyai (later Győrffy) College, a residence established in late 1939 to accommodate poor university students mainly of peasant origin. The front's original young communist fellow travelers, on the other hand, were themselves influenced by the nationalistic and peasant orientation of the Populist mainstream. Many among them would reach high party and state office after the postwar communist takeover, suffer from the Cominform purges, and play a prominent role in the genesis of the 1956 revolution. As will be seen later, the Populist-communist dichotomy was never to be fully resolved, for reasons that were partially adumbrated in Révai's postmortem on the March Front: "'They could not clarify their essential relationship to the workers, the workers' movement, and proletarian socialism. They vacillated between 'anti-Marxist' hostility and a platonic sympathy for the workers. They dared not, would not, could not educate the peasantry in the spirit of militant alliance with the working class."[26]

That class, at least for the moment, was almost equally impervious to the lure of communism, if only because successive waves of arrests continued to incapacitate the home party. The provisional Central Committee in Prague could maintain only intermittent contact with activists in the trade unions, the socialist youth movement, and intellectual circles. Although *Népszava* steadfastly denounced communism and the Soviet Union, the communist members of the SDP were compelled by the logic of the united front to participate in the party's subscriber and recruiting campaigns. In its application to Hungary, the popular front tactic had effectively destroyed the CPH as an organized political movement.

## THE GREAT PURGES

While the party was reduced to these peripheral activities in Hungary, the dark night of Stalin's terror was descending upon its émigré colony in the Soviet Union. Possibly the first Hungarian caught up in the wave of liquidations—the first, that is, since the party's 1933 purge—was Lajos Magyar, who was arrested in the wake of Kirov's murder in late 1934 and never reappeared. Between 1936 and 1939, as the purge gathered momentum, party members began to disappear in increasing numbers; the majority were arrested in 1937 and 1938. The veterans of the party were particularly hard hit. Accurate statistics are not available, but to judge from a selective listing in the party's encyclopedia of the most prominent communists, over fifty were purged in this period, and very few survived.[27] Most of the party's founders (Kun, Ede Chlepkó, Fiedler, Jancsik, Pór, Rabinovics, Vágó), prominent survivors of the Commune (Bajáki, Bierman, Bokányi, Hamburger, Haubrich, Karikás, Gyula Lengyel), more recent émigrés (Madzsar, Öri, Vági)—in all, at least sixteen former Central Committee members—were among the victims. Some of the early ones were apparently denounced by Kun himself in revenge for their opposition.[28]

**The Liquidation of Kun.**   Béla Kun had been removed from the Comintern's Executive Committee and from the leadership of the CPH in the summer of 1936, ostensibly because of his resistance to the line adopted by the seventh congress. Granted an audience with Stalin, he requested that if he was barred from Hungarian party work he be given some practical assignment instead of a desk job. Stalin urged that he remain in the Comintern, but Kun complained that he could not collaborate with the capricious and hypocritical Manuilsky. He asked instead to be appointed head of the Red Army's Political Department so he could prepare the forces for the war against fascism. When Molotov objected that his notoriety made him unsuitable for the post, it was agreed that he would be employed in the Soviet party's Central Committee office. The details were to be worked out with N. I. Yezhov, then head of the Orgburo but soon to become the interior commissar in charge of Stalin's purges. Months later Yezhov convoked Kun and proposed that he write a pamphlet against the "people's enemies." Kun refused and was put in charge of the economics publishing house.[29]

One day in early June 1937 Kun told his wife about a chance encounter with Varga. To the greeting "How are you?" Varga had replied apprehensively: "For the moment, free." Kun could hardly have been unaware of the terror engulfing all foreign as well as Soviet communists, but he commented irritably: "To think that even an intelligent man like Varga can say such stupid things!" Shortly thereafter, Stalin telephoned and cheerfully asked Kun to issue a public denial of allegations in the Western press that he had been arrested.[30] Kun complied, but a few days later he was summoned by Dimitrov to what amounted to a trial before the Comintern Executive Committee. He was accused of dangerous deviations, of ideological concordance with the discredited Trotsky, Bukharin, and Zinoviev, in sum, of opposition to Stalin. Kun, recalled a witness in 1956, "roared like a wounded lion: 'This is a terrible provocation, a conspiracy to get me murdered. But I swear that I have not wanted to insult Comrade Stalin. I want to explain everything to Comrade Stalin himself.' " He was defending himself cleverly when Varga delivered a stab in the back by alleging that in 1919 Kun had undermined the Commune and betrayed communist principles.* The outcome of this sordid charade was of course predetermined. As Kun left, "two NKVD men took him away. Nothing more was heard of him and his case was not discussed at Comintern meetings again."[31] By his wife's account, his last words to her were: "Don't worry. Some misunderstanding. I will be home in half an hour."[32] Interrogated and tortured at Lefortovo Prison, Kun confessed, was transferred to Butyrka Prison, and died, presumably by execution, on 30 November 1939. His wife and his son-in-law, the writer Antal Hidas, were also arrested and deported but survived.[33]

---

*Other participants in the trial were the German Wilhelm Pieck and the Italian Palmiro Togliatti.

The purges were the culmination of the factional struggle within the Soviet Communist Party. Through them Stalin's megalomania and paranoia were fully and brutally expressed. In such an atmosphere the colony of expatriates was particularly suspect. For the Hungarian émigrés, this was a time of unmitigated terror, denunciation, and pervasive suspicion, of ideological recantation and appeals to sacrifice for the nebulous good of the party. "It became apparent," a survivor has written, "that there was no fact, no action which—given the will—could not be construed in a light totally at odds with reality. . . . Some maintain that if one survived the Soviet emigration without arrest, this was inexplicable. It was all a matter of chance. Some were lucky, others—the majority—were not."[34] Initially, many of the émigrés believed uncomprehendingly that their closest comrades had been in some mysterious fashion traitors to the cause, so that as the ring of suspicion closed in on them they would commonly plead for a chance to confirm their loyalty to Stalin. When the absurdity and arbitrariness of the holocaust became inescapably obvious, the survivors withdrew into a self-preserving, terrified isolation. As one of the fortunate few asserts, "the true revolutionary remains a revolutionary even if he receives an unjustified slap from the revolution," and indeed most of them remained loyal to the movement.[35] What comfort they could derive from the faith helped them to persevere in a career from which by this time there was little real possibility of escape. The road to the historically inevitable revolution, they rationalized, was full of hardships and pitfalls from which lessons could be gleaned for the future. The operative lesson seemed to be the imperatives of discipline and obedience to the Soviet Union and the party, for in their years of power these hardened veterans would replay the same sinister scenario of terror for the benefit of other hapless comrades.

## THE FATEFUL ALLIANCE

As the Nazi whirlwind began its sweep across the continent, the power vacuum created by the Versailles treaties in East-Central Europe exacted its price. In the spring of 1938 came the Anschluss; in the fall, the Munich Pact. Both testified to the Western powers' lack of resolve to maintain the status quo. The exposed neighbors of the Third Reich drew their own conclusions, and irredentist Hungary was inevitably drawn into the German-Italian orbit. In the words of a liberal historian: "With a social structure, foreign relations, and official mystique such as Hungary's, no country could have reacted differently to Hitlerite expansion and the subsequent World War."[36]

**Revision and Nationalism.** The government of Kálmán Darányi, which had taken office following the death of Gömbös in October 1936, reacted with some alarm to Austria's fate and launched a major rearmament program. It also passed a *numerus clausus* ("restricted number") law in order to limit the access of Jews to the civil service and certain professions. In May 1938 Darányi was succeeded in office by the former finance minister, Béla Imrédy, who was himself replaced the following year by the popular scholar-politician Pál Teleki. None of these men was ideologically attuned to Nazism and German imperialism, but they could not alter the fact that Hungary's geopolitical situation made reliance on the Western democracies unproductive, at least for the foreseeable future. While at Munich Chamberlain and Daladier acceded to German demands backed by German power, they felt no such compulsion with respect to Hungary's request that the predominantly Magyar-inhabited areas of Slovakia be ceded back. This impasse proved to be decisive, for it strengthened the hand of those who had argued all along that Hungary's fortunes lay with the Axis powers. Germany and Italy agreed to arbitrate the territorial dispute, and by the Vienna Award of November 1938 a strip of Slovakia was actually returned to Hungary.

By that act, however, the die had been cast. Hungary became increasingly committed to the Axis. Early in 1939 she signed the Anti-Comintern Pact, left the League of Nations, and occupied Ruthenia, the easternmost region of Czechoslovakia inhabited mainly by Ukrainians but with a Hungarian minority. An effort to effect a realignment toward the south produced, in December 1940, the domestically popular "pact of eternal friendship" with Yugoslavia, but that eternity proved to be short-lived. Earlier in the year a second Vienna Award had returned part of Transylvania to Hungary. Given the ethnic mix in the region, arbitration could only produce an imperfect compromise that left sizable Romanian and Magyar minorities on the two sides of the new border. As a quid pro quo Hungary adhered to the German-Italian-Japanese Tripartite Pact. When a military-nationalist coup d'état in Belgrade precipitated German occupation, Teleki felt powerless to prevent the Wehrmacht from crossing Hungarian territory. He committed suicide—an act that, as Churchill observed, absolved his name before history but could not extricate his people from the embrace of the Axis.[37]

The powerful passions of nationalism now swept up Hungarians of all political persuasions. As the spirit of fascism spread across Europe in the late 1930s, the extreme right emerged in Hungary as the main radical challenge to the established order. The Arrow Cross Party propagated a confused racism and anti-Semitism mixed with a vague social reformism. This ideology appealed to a wide spectrum of disgruntled elements ranging from Habsburg archdukes to the lumpenproletariat. White-collar workers constituted the bulk of the Arrow Cross's membership, and not a few former communist sympathizers adhered to the party, seeing in it a legal outlet for their social-revolutionary aspirations. On 12 November 1938 Arrow Cross gangs raided a number of socialist establishments, impelling the SDP leadership to appeal to the authorities to maintain order. The conservative regime, however, showed little sympathy for either the Arrow Cross or the socialists and attempted to constrain the activities of both. At the May 1939 general elections, conducted under a new electoral law that gave the vote by secret ballot to just over two million citizens, the SDP fell back from eleven to five mandates, while the extreme right managed to elect fifty deputies. Much to the dismay of the SDP, a significant part of organized labor had shifted its support to the Arrow Cross.

The socialists, too, had responded to the upsurge of nationalism. Conviction played no less a part in their thinking than self-preservation. At its January 1939 congress the SDP expunged the adjective "Hungarian" from the party's name in order to stress that it was truly national and not the branch of an international movement. The Peyer leadership called for the development of links with the Western democracies and for the preservation of Hungarian independence in the face of growing German economic and political influence. Gyula Kulich, the communist secretary of the SDP's youth organization, the OIB, introduced a motion in favor of a more positive action program on behalf of national independence, the workers' interests, and land reform. But the leadership shied away from the politics of confrontation, fearing that this would only provoke more repressive measures against the party.

Meanwhile, a group of Populists acquired the journal *Szabad Szó* (Free Word) and in June founded the National Peasant Party (Nemzeti Parasztpárt, or NPP). Their program was an amalgam of demands for land reform and nationalistic warnings against "external enemies and internal traitors," the latter being identified as the Germanic and Jewish middle classes. The NPP's leaders included the left-leaning József Darvas and Erdei, who had links with the underground communists, as well as Kovács and Veres; all were sociographers of the "village explorer" school.

**The Party Rebuilds.** The CPH was already suffering from the dismantling of its Hungarian apparatus and the liquidation of much of its émigré leadership. The German occupation of Bohemia put an end to the faltering activity of its provisional Central Committee in Prague. Révai, Zoltán Szántó, and Friss fled to Moscow, while Papp spent the war years in France. In 1938 the party had assigned Ferenc Rózsa, a thirty-two-year-old architect who had become a member six years before, to spur the revival of the home movement.[38] Among his more unsavory tasks was the extension of Stalin's purge to Hungary. This was accomplished by the simple expedient of denouncing to the police the alleged "Trotskyite sectarians." Many threatened comrades saved their lives by fleeing to the West. Thus purified, the rump home party was led by Rózsa along with the textile worker László Gács and the construction worker István Kenéz. In early 1940 a police sweep rounded up Kulich and other OIB activists as well as several hundred members of the Czechoslovak party in the reannexed territory. The police report noted that Kulich had been receiving instructions and funds from Paris, and that the communists had been preparing to sabotage the war industries.[39]

The party's latest slogan, "Peace, bread, land, freedom," was propagated in leaflets and by the illegal *Dolgozók Lapja,* printed in Kassa, which had reappeared in March. Apart from such marginal propaganda, the party's drive to foster debate in favor of a broad anti-German independence movement was served by the accession of a few communists to the editorial staff of *Népszava* and by the occasional planting of an article in the NPP's *Szabad Szó.*

The Russo-German Nonaggression Pact of August 1939 gave new cause for consternation and ideological confusion among the rank and file. It was followed in September by the restoration of diplomatic relations between Moscow and Budapest. A year later the two sides negotiated an agreement exchanging Hungarian flags captured by Tsarist armies in 1849 for the most prominent imprisoned communists, Rákosi and Vas. Rákosi's time in jail had increased his standing with the party. In 1935, as soon as he had finished serving his initial sentence, the Hungarian authorities put him on trial again, this time for his crimes during the Commune. In Moscow, Kun recommended that this measure of dubious legality be exploited to the fullest. Stalin apparently agreed that Rákosi should be reinstated to the party and international protests mobilized on his behalf.[40] Although Rákosi received a life sentence, the communist-led propaganda campaign gave him a prominence that would subsequently serve his ambitions for the leadership. Back in jail, he applied himself to the study of languages and other subjects. Reportedly, he also insinuated himself into the prison governor's good graces; in any case, he took pains after the war to liquidate the witnesses of his incarceration.

On 1 November 1940 the remnants of the Hungarian colony gathered at Moscow's Kiev Station to welcome the liberated Rákosi and Vas. Rákosi had learned in prison of Kun's arrest, but he was appalled to discover how few of the party's activists had survived. "The whole party has fallen apart," he complained almost in tears. "We have to begin rebuilding from scratch. And with what? Fifty people, if that many, with whom we can start."[41] Rákosi was hardly the obvious candidate for the task. Although he had been named in absentia to the Comintern's Executive Committee, Stalin initially held him in low esteem and had reportedly referred to him as a British agent, presumably because he had lived for a while in England before World War I.[42]

In the first panicky days of the Russo-German war a new wave of arrests hit the émigrés. Among the victims were László Rudas (who had been arrested once before, in 1938) and Lukács. "The blow," recalls a witness, "struck all the Hungarian communists. We all felt that our love and loyalty for the Soviet Union—which had been complicated by the events of the last few years, but restored by the new danger that now threatened it—had again been unthinkingly mocked." Lukács and Rudas were soon released. It was rumored that Rákosi, who until then had not stood up for a single arrested comrade, had finally been galvanized into forceful intercession.[43]

The task of rebuilding the émigré party fell on the one hand to Rákosi and Vas and on the other to such experienced Comintern agents as Gerő, Révai, Sándor Nógrádi, and Mihály Farkas, the last-named a veteran of the Czech party and the secretary-general of the Communist Youth International. In Moscow they lived at the old Hotel Lux on Gorky Street, a self-contained Comintern residence since World War I. Together with what remained of the old guard—Andor Gábor, Imre Nagy, Ferenc Münnich, and the Szántó brothers, Rezső and Zoltán—they were instructed by the Russians to concentrate on radio and print propaganda. Stalinist orthodoxy was absolute. When Zoltán Szántó argued with the Soviet radio editors regarding the suitability of Russian material for a Hungarian audience, he was accused of anti-Soviet sabotage and replaced by Münnich, who confided to Endre Sik that "it is not always advisable to seek the truth."[44] Sik, who became Hungary's foreign minister in 1958, worked at that time as a translator. In his memoirs, published in 1970, he recalls that in their major project, a Stalinist party history, Gerő insisted that the translation had to be verbatim with no alteration even in the word order. Russian editors chose the works to be translated, many of which, notes Sik, "were not well suited to arouse the sympathy of Hungarian readers for the Soviet Union and the Soviet people."[45] These were the historical and literary works that after the war would serve the party's indoctrination and cultural russification policies.

The leadership question was not resolved until well into the war. Gerő's obvious ambitions were set back by Rákosi's unexpected reappearance. Over time their Soviet masters apparently came to the conclusion that Rákosi would be a more familiar and engaging candidate for Hungarian consumption than the austere and arrogant Gerő, much of whose Comintern and NKVD career had been devoted to extra-Hungarian pursuits.* According to one account, the decision was revealed to the party only in March 1942 at Ufa, where the leading émigrés had been evacuated during the German drive on Moscow. At a celebration of Rákosi's fiftieth birthday Gerő, in his toast, indicated that the former had to be considered the party's leader. "Everyone had to take this seriously," Nógrádi later recalled, "for it was spoken by the comrade who—as some thought—was also a contender for the title." Nógrádi never heard the émigré leaders discuss the prospect of collaboration with the home comrades after their

---

*One of Gerő's wartime assignments was as political adviser to the National Committee for Free Germany, and a contemporary asserts that he "undoubtedly played an important part in laying down the policy of Communist Parties in other countries." Wolfgang Leonhard, *Child of the Revolution* (London: Collins, 1957), p. 253.

eventual return. The latter were generally disparaged, and the External Committee considered itself to be solely qualified to direct the postwar party.[46]

Meanwhile, the Comintern and its Hungarian section continued to wrestle with the problem that had dominated official and public consciousness in interwar Hungary, namely, that of territorial revision. In the spirit of the seventh congress's call for an antifascist united front, the provisional Central Committee in 1936 had denounced the forcible alteration of the Trianon dictate; instead, the committee urged peaceful cooperation with Hungary's neighbors against the immediate threat of German imperialism.[47] Whatever their theoretical merits, such urgings went unheard amid the rejoicing that greeted the reannexations. The Comintern's directives in 1939 and 1940, developed by Révai in consultation with two refugees from the Czechoslovakian party, Zoltán Schönherz and József Skolnik, designated national independence as the primary slogan of the CPH; the reannexations, according to these directives, were merely false successes engineered by the imperialist ruling classes. The directives also emphasized the right to self-determination of Hungary's enlarged Romanian, Slovakian, and Ukrainian minorities. The context here was one of working-class unity, but it was clear that the minorities were being appealed to because they were thought to be momentarily more susceptible to radicalization than the Hungarian workers themselves.[48]

The Comintern's directive of 5 September 1940 also called for the reconstruction of a centralized Budapest party organization without the old party activists. This recommendation, inspired by considerations of security, turned out to be unrealistic and was largely ignored when, later in the year, Schönherz and Skolnik returned to Hungary. In January 1941 they reconstituted a Central Committee with Gács, Rózsa, and a certain Mihály Tóth. The "reactionary governing party," instructed the directive, was a more important and immediate enemy than the Arrow Cross fascists. The earlier popular front strategy was now expanded to encompass all potential allies against the Axis. The party accordingly issued its ideologically anodyne, enduring wartime slogan, "For an independent, free, democratic Hungary!"[49]

## HUNGARY AT WAR

On 26 June 1941, four days after the German invasion of the Soviet Union, unidentified aircraft bombed Kassa and a few other localities in northeastern Hungary. The government of premier László Bárdossy eagerly interpreted this as a Soviet provocation and declared war the following day.[50] The roundup of suspected communists was intensified, notably in reannexed northern Transylvania.

The Central Committee met on 28 June and responded to the state of war by issuing slogans for a separate peace and "not a single soldier for Hitler."

Another meeting on 1 September resulted in a circular letter to all political groups, including the governing party. This called for withdrawal from the anti-Soviet war and for the defense of Hungarian territory; retention of adequate food supplies for the population at the expense of exports to Germany; and industrial expansion to provide more consumer goods for the peasantry. The party promised to "direct its entire activity, mass influence, and organizational strength exclusively against the common enemy, the German expansionist power, until the common national goals are realized." Germany's defeat was inevitable, it asserted, and Hungary would pay even more dearly than at Versailles for her misalliance.[51] Similar messages were propagated by the Hungarian service of Radio Moscow and, from late September, by the new Radio Kossuth, which was sponsored by the Comintern.

In July a press and propaganda committee had been formed, consisting of Kállai, Aladár Mód, and Ferenc Földes, to generate public debate on these objectives. Their targets were the opposition newspapers—*Népszava, Szabad Szó*, and the liberal *Magyar Nemzet* (Hungarian Nation). The campaign was facilitated by the presence on the *Népszava* editorial staff of the above three as well as two other communists, Losonczy and András Kasztel; the editor, SDP Secretary-General Szakasits, and other socialist journalists were on the left wing of their party. A press debate developed through the summer of 1941 on the need for national unity and the respective roles of the working class, the middle class, and the peasantry. Notable contributions were made by Kállai, the moderate Populist Kovács, and the historian Szekfű. Kállai, for instance, would respond to Kovács's Populist definition of national unity by cautiously stressing the primacy of industrial workers in a united front.[52] The debate reflected in fact a general intellectual ferment regarding the future of Hungarian society and national independence, and it was only marginally advanced by communist manipulation.

Within its own ranks the CPH was experiencing some difficulty in explaining the logic of the popular front and the tactical need to use patriotic slogans and appeals to national historical traditions. The lapse in the party's organizational life between 1936 and 1940 made the task of reorienting members more difficult. A faction led by Demény and enjoying some support in Budapest's industrial districts rejected the popular front tactic as an opportunistic betrayal of the workers' interests; proletarian dictatorship, it insisted, was the only possible and immediate objective.[53]

The risks of illegality had become so great with the onset of war that in late 1941 it was decided to no longer hold regular meetings of the five-man Central Committee, or of the three secretaries among them. Effective leadership of the party was delegated to Skolnik until, a year later, he was arrested. Concurrently, and for the same reasons, recruitment policy was modified. In the reconstruction phase since 1938 recruits had to be approved by the top leadership, but this ponderous process increased the risk of detection, and local cells were therefore given the authority to induct new members. Provision was made for a category of candidate members who did not participate in cell meetings and undertook the more perilous tasks of disseminating leaflets and painting slogans on walls.[54] The party also initiated a fund-raising campaign—similar to the Red Aid, which had been terminated in 1936—on behalf of imprisoned communists.

**The Communist Search for Allies.** Although the Peyer leadership remained impervious to communist cajolery, and repeatedly urged SDP members to avoid contacts with communists, the Central Committee decided in the fall of 1941 to make a preliminary overture to the socialist left wing. Rózsa and Schönherz instructed Márton Horváth (a former architect who had joined the party in 1931 and had already spent five years in jail) to sound out Szakasits on the possibility of joint action.[55] Szakasits demurred, fearing that the proposed antiwar agitation would imperil the already precarious existence of the SDP. Indeed, his party was suffering not only because the authorities' tolerance for it was limited but also because its membership declined after the economy was placed on a wartime footing. The SDP and the trade unions had drawn most of their members from medium and small industries, and accounted for just over 15 percent of the industrial labor force in 1938. By 1942 the proportion had been depressed to under 8 percent by the expansion of large war industries where unionization was officially discouraged. The largest decline in union membership occurred in the mining sector, where the Arrow Cross made significant inroads. In these circumstances the CPH's own chances of expanding its membership were minimal. It remained entrenched in the OIB and the odd SDP and union local, but the party's cells were few and far between. By one rough estimate, in 1942 there were 400 to 450 full and candidate communist party members in Budapest.[56]

In the fall of 1941 the communists launched a series of minor but symbolic demonstrations commemorating the 1848 revolution. The implicit message was the need to resist Germany's threat to Hungarian independence. The OIB's new communist secretary, Endre Ságvári, mobilized a few hundred young workers to hold a brief demonstration on 6 October at the statue of Count Batthyány. The next peaceful demonstration, held at the graves of Kossuth and Táncsics on 1 November, drew representative figures from the various opposition parties. Such protests, a series of literary-cultural evenings organized by the communist theater director Ferenc Hont, and efforts at press agentry such as the Christmas 1941 issue of *Népszava* all reflected the tactic of a nonideological emphasis on patriotic solidarity and national independence.[57] Although these initiatives reinforced debate among politically conscious intellectuals of various persuasions, they had little impact on the mass of Hungarians, most of whom delighted in the recent territorial revisions and supported—with some foreboding—the war against the unanimously detested Soviet Union. Those notables who, like Szekfű and the smallholder deputy Endre Bajcsy-Zsilinszky, sympathized with the burgeoning independence movement were inspired by a profound patriotism. They defended the integrity of Hungary's enlarged territory, abhorred Nazism, and entertained few illusions about the outcome of the war. While recognizing the need for a democratization of Hungarian society and politics, they totally rejected the Soviet alternative. What they hoped for was a separate peace with the Western allies, which might allow for a peaceful evolution toward their various political and socioeconomic objectives.*

In January 1942 secret negotiations were resumed between Horváth and Szakasits. The communist proposal was for a joint committee to direct the independence front activities and for industrial sabotage, but Szakasits rejected it on the same grounds as before. A new illegal paper, *Szabad Nép* (Free People), edited by Rózsa, was issued at the beginning of February with an initial run of eighty copies; it was designed to instruct party members in the complex politics of the united front. Later that month the communists and their sympathizers on *Népszava* and *Szabad Szó* formed a Hungarian Historical Memorial Committee (Magyar Történelmi Emlékbizottság) with the ostensible purpose of propagating the ideals of the 1848 revolution. Numerous political and cultural figures—Bajcsy-Zsilinszky and Zoltán Tildy from the SHP, Darvas and Veres from the NPP, Illyés, Szekfű—initially endorsed the committee's aims. Some, including Szekfű, broke with the committee upon realizing that it was communist-directed and designed to foment unrest.

The communists, for their part, overestimated the domestic difficulties of the Bárdossy government. Under fire for atrocities committed by Hungarian forces in the occupied Bácska district of Yugoslavia, it was also in the midst of complying with Germany's request for the dispatch of a Hungarian army to the eastern front. The Central Committee concluded that antiregime and anti-German feelings were spreading, and that therefore a mobilized independence movement could topple the regime. "The hour of action has struck," Radio Kossuth thundered. In the event, the coincidental replacement of Bárdossy by Miklós Kállay on 7 March and official warnings to the SDP leadership to avoid provocation served to deflate the various opposition groups. The demonstration planned for 15 March turned out to be a minor event, attended largely by communists.[58]

The Kállay government, which survived until the German occupation in March 1944, pursued a persistent if ultimately futile balancing act. Constantly appealing for national unity against the Soviet Union, it raised the specter of

---

*The United States, after a six-month delay, acknowledged a technical state of war with Hungary on 5 June 1942.

another internal disintegration like the one in 1918. German demands were fufilled minimally, in a manner consistent with the preservation of Hungarian sovereignty. Meanwhile Kállay made repeated secret overtures to the Western allies for a separate peace that would preserve Hungary's territorial integrity and political stability. Although the fortunes of war soon showed this moderate and determinedly Western-oriented strategy to be unrealistic, it nevertheless drew the support of all shades of political opinion save the extreme right and left and effectively isolated the CPH from its independence front associates. As for the Memorial Committee, official harassment and the SDP's denunciation of the demonstration held on 15 March led to its early demise.

**The Party Is Crippled Again.**   At its April 1942 meeting the Central Committee recognized the dangers in the Kállay strategy's popular appeal and urged communists to exert themselves in party building. Anticipating renewed persecution, and observing that many party members were afraid of illegal work, the Central Committee insisted on strict observance of conspiratorial rules.[59] Nevertheless, a police sweep that began on 30 April rounded up several hundred communists, including Rózsa, Schönherz, and virtually all the leading cadres. Concurrently, the authorities in the Ruthenian territory liquidated the local communist organization. A decree prohibiting young men of military cadet age from membership in political associations prompted the SDP to disband the communist-led OIB. The communists on *Népszava* were also arrested, as was Szakasits, whose contacts with the CPH had become known to the authorities. But the government, unlike the military, wanted to stop short of destroying the SDP, and Szakasits was released within a few days. Having been roundly condemned for his secret initiatives by Peyer, he was replaced in the post of secretary-general by the more moderate Ferenc Szeder but left nominally in charge of *Népszava*. The SDP leadership confirmed its determination to purge the party of communist sympathizers and to resist Bolshevik agitation in the trade unions.

In late July, when this latest wave of arrests came to an end, the remaining communist leaders met to assess the damage. The Central Committee now consisted of Gács, Skolnik, and the recently coopted János Kádár. The last had taken a road to communism that was in many respects typical of the party's working-class recruits. Born János Czermanik in the then-Hungarian Adriatic port of Fiume (now Rijeka) in 1912 and promptly abandoned by his father, he settled with his mother in Budapest and earned a penurious living as a machinist. By his own account he was first drawn to communism through reading Engels' *Anti-Dühring*, which he won in a chess competition. Caught up in the September 1930 general strike, he joined the KIMSZ and worked for the party within the SDP. Twice jailed, he collaborated in the reconstruction of the party from 1940 and adopted the nom de guerre Kádár.[60] The communists managed to induce some generous, liberal-minded notables to appear as defense witnesses at the first military trial—Szekfű conceded that even communists could be good Hungarians—but the indictment for subversion brought down the death sentence on Schönherz. That fall over two hundred other communists were tried and imprisoned; most of them subsequently perished in German concentration camps. The party would not recover from this crippling blow until the end of the war.

In addition to Kádár, the Central Committee coopted the recently released István Kovács; subsequently, Pál Tonhauser and István Szirmai were also added to its roster. These two had had long experience as communist organizers in the reannexed territories, Tonhauser in northern Hungary (Slovakia) and Szirmai in Transylvania.[61] Arguments ensued over the causes of the party's virtual liquidation. Kovács insisted that the historical phase of bourgeois revolution had come to an end in 1918 and that therefore the current objective of an independent democratic Hungary was inappropriate. Moreover, he argued, the party's cell system should have been based on factories and districts rather than on legal labor organizations. Although these views were rejected in a resolution entitled "The Lessons of the Arrests," which blamed conspiratorial slackness on overconfidence in the possibilities of overt action, disagreements and mistrust persisted among members of the Central Committee.[62]

The task of drafting a general policy statement was entrusted to Skolnik and to László Orbán, the latter a thirty-year-old lawyer who had joined the party in 1938, had directed the work of the party cells within the SDP, and since May had been living in illegality. After lengthy discussion this statement was delivered in early November to party members as well as to a few left-wing socialists and other sympathizers. It essentially reiterated the party's advocacy of a "national fighting front" led by the working class but encompassing also the peasantry, progressive intellectuals, and all other political groupings willing to cooperate in toppling the forces of reaction from their "narrow base." The left-wing elements within the SDP and trade unions and in the SHP and its affiliated Peasant Federation would have to be mobilized.[63]

To reconstruct the party almost from scratch was an impossibly hazardous task under the prevailing conditions of illegality and wartime vigilance, but the surviving faithful soldiered on.[64] Following the dissolution of the OIB, Ságvári tried to assemble young workers into "action groups," and some modest proselytizing was accomplished among university students at the Győrffy College and in the Jewish Students' Federation. Attempts were made to bring back to the fold a faction led by György Deák and Arnold Mayer which, like the Demény faction, was ultraleftist and was preempting the CPH in the large industrial suburbs of Budapest. Party organizations were also revived in northern Hungary and Transylvania.

In addition to these efforts to rally the dispersed remnants of the party, propaganda activities were resumed thanks to a printing press that had been saved from seizure. A few communists, including Kállai and Mód, who had been arrested but escaped prosecution, returned to *Népszava*. Active on the NPP's *Szabad Szó* were Donáth and two new recruits, both teachers, Lajos Fehér and Ferenc Iliás. Radio Kossuth meanwhile pursued its largely unheard propaganda campaign and was the first source to report the disaster that befell the Hungarian Second Army at Voronezh in January 1943, shortly before the German surrender at Stalingrad.

The military setbacks only reinforced Kállay's interest in an escape that would place Hungary within the Western sphere of influence. Internally, the growing strains of a wartime economy, due in large measure to German demands, had aroused unrest among miners and industrial workers. The government attempted to alleviate some of the discontent with a new economic program promulgated in mid-1943. Recognizing that Hungary's dilemma was due more to geopolitical realities than to the regime's failings, and that in wartime Central Europe Hungary had managed to preserve more domestic freedom (notably for the Jews) than any of her neighbors, the major opposition parties refrained from frontal attacks on Kállay. The leaders of the SDP and SHP were particularly wary of communist infiltration, but a few sympathizers could be found on their left wings, notably Szakasits and György Marosán in the SDP and István Dobi and György Pálffy in the SHP. Marosán, a former baker's assistant, became the SDP's rural organizing secretary in 1943. Pálffy was a cashiered career officer who gravitated to the CPH in 1942. When, in June 1943, the SHP decided to expand beyond its smallholder constituency and establish a *polgári tagozat* ("citizen section," in the sense of "bourgeois," "middle-class") under the aegis of Bajcsy-Zsilinszky, Pálffy was instructed to join it together with another officer turned communist, László Sólyom. In the Peasant Federation, an organization set up in 1941 by Ferenc Nagy and other SHP and governing-party politicians for the benefit of peasant proprietors, left-wing pressures led in May 1943 to the creation of an agricultural laborers' section. This was led by the procommunist Dobi, himself a former farm worker, and the CPH member Iliás.[65]

The party had hardly begun to recover from the arrests of spring 1942 when, the following winter, a new razzia caught over two hundred suspected communists, including István Kovács and Skolnik. The vestigial CPH was left with little alternative but to try to incite noncommunist groups to take up the cause of secession from the Axis. On 28 December 1942 Radio Kossuth broadcast an "independence front" program developed by the Moscow émigrés.[66] The program was endorsed by Mihály Károlyi, who was busily organizing a so-called Movement for a New Democratic Hungary in London. It consisted of repudiation of the Axis through a separate peace and of desiderata for the democratic transformation of Hungary, including a "national" government, basic democratic and minority rights, an "independent" industrial policy, and the redistribution of large estates. The following April the domestic Central Committee issued its own version of the program, stressing the aspects, such as the economic burdens of war, that were most likely to win public sympathy. It warned again that Hungary, "as Hitler's comrade in arms, could expect dismemberment, occupation, and ruin at the conclusion of peace."[67] Among the opposition parties, the SDP drafted a moderate reform program designed to avoid a repetition of the disastrous transition from war to revolution in 1918 and 1919. The SHP followed suit but in even more cautious terms, although the party maverick, Bajcsy-Zsilinszky, urged more radical change in order to forestall the danger of anarchy and a slide into Bolshevism. Eventually these two parties came to an agreement on a loose parliamentary alliance.

**The Peace Party Gambit.** In May 1943 the CPH made one last attempt to reach some understanding with the socialist left, but the discussions between Szakasits and Kádár ended in an impasse over the former's insistence that the communists abandon illegal methods. Faced with the rejection of all political groupings, the Central Committee engaged in heated debate in June on the option of converting the party into a superficially new political entity. The dissolution in May of the Comintern, argued the tactic's proponents, allowed its former sections to adopt any means to pursue the antifascist struggle. It was finally agreed to publicly proclaim the dissolution of the CPH and temporarily suspend all illegal activity. An expanded meeting of the Central Committee attended by Kádár, Szirmai, Tonhauser, Donáth, Orbán, and Gábor Péter (a former tailor and party member since 1931) baptised the new party Békepárt (Peace Party) and promptly converted itself into its Central Committee. Their hopeful calculation was that the ostensible liquidation of the CPH would alleviate official persecution and that the Peace Party would be a more successful bridge to the other opposition groups. In the event, the authorities never doubted that the Peace Party was a communist front and did not relax their pursuit; nor did the opposition groups rise to the bait. The communist rank and file, on the other hand, was once again disoriented by the tactical dissolution and the temporary suspension of activity.[68]

Both the Peace Party and Radio Kossuth, notably in Révai's broadcasts, endorsed the coalescence of opposition parties initiated by the SDP and SHP while urging that it be expanded to include the communists. When the party began to issue thousands of leaflets (one telling peasants to withhold their produce from "Hitler and his hireling Kállay government") retribution was not long in coming. Beginning in September, a nationwide police operation rounded up many Peace Party communists, including Szirmai and Tonhauser, and led to the seizure of their illegal printing press.

Meanwhile various political groups, including one around former prime minister Bethlen, were lobbying the government in favor of an immediate separate peace—even at the price, argued Bajcsy-Zsilinszky, of military confrontation with Hitler. A joint SDP–SHP resolution forwarded to Kállay on 12 September 1943 argued that a declaration of Hungary's neutrality and withdrawal from the war carried more palatable risks than persistence in his cautious balancing act.[69] Caught between the millstones of German Nazism and Soviet communism, the leading figures in the regime—Horthy, Kállay, Interior Minister Ferenc Keresztes-Fischer—preferred to avoid dramatic steps, such as a purge of the largely pro-German general staff, which would inevitably bring about German occupation. Rather they multiplied their overtures to the Anglo-Saxon allies in neutral capitals from Ankara to Bern.

That these tactical differences did not arise from any revolutionary disaffection from the political system is clear from the following episode. A youth conference was held in late August 1943 at Balatonszárszó with the tacit support of Keresztes-Fischer. It was attended by Populist writers and other opposition figures. Those who advanced socialist-communist views on the nation's future—Erdei, Darvas, Dobi—attracted far less support than the writer László Németh and other proponents of the so-called third road, which opposed both fascism and communism and took a moderate national line. Even this relatively progressive assembly shied away from military confrontation with Germany and from the long-range prospect of integral socialism.[70] The ideologues in Moscow, Révai and Lukács, quite properly regarded Populism as an important reformist movement but despaired of reconciling it with communism. Their numerous analyses and critiques, notably Révai's "Marxism and Populism" (which was smuggled into Hungary by Losonczy and published under Kállai's name) expressed the inevitable reservations regarding the diffuse movement's nationalistic and racial overtones and its neglect of the proletariat.[71]

Most Hungarians remained impervious to the lure of political extremism. The crypto-fascist parties, including the Arrow Cross, had initially enjoyed a surge in membership to some three hundred thousand in 1940, but they rapidly lost ground thereafter. Prime Minister Kállay only confirmed their isolation when, on 4 December 1943, he publicly excoriated the rightist radicals' subordination of Hungary's interests to those of Nazi Germany. Concurrently the trade unions began to revive, as did the SDP, which was attracting growing numbers of lower-middle-class, white-collar members.

Undaunted by their unpopularity and periodic waves of arrests, the communists persisted with marginal agitation. The Peace Party dismissed as unrealistic any strategy that ignored the Soviet Union and concentrated exclusively on accommodation with the Western powers, and it endorsed Károlyi's call in December 1943 for a national uprising. The communists besieged opposition politicians with pleas for a united antifascist front and even launched a new illegal propaganda organ, *Béke és Szabadság* (Peace and Freedom), in March 1944. By then the Red Army was approaching the foothills of the Carpathians. The government was compelled to face the prospect of negotiating with the Russians even while preparations were under way for a last-ditch defense of the national frontier. Hungary's wavering and the need to bolster a crumbling Ukrainian front drove Hitler to take a preemptive step. On 18 March 1944, while Horthy was visiting the Führer at Klessheim, the German army proceeded to occupy Hungary.

## OCCUPATION AND RESISTANCE

Along with German occupation came the Gestapo and Eichmann's Sonderkommando and the end of even qualified democracy in Hungary. A German ultimatum compelled Horthy to appoint as prime minister his former ambassador to Berlin, the pro-Nazi Döme Sztójay. The opposition parties and their press were banned and their leaders arrested. Among the latter were Peyer, Mónus, Ferenc Nagy, Bajcsy-Zsilinszky; Keresztes-Fischer and other anti-Nazi government officials suffered the same fate. Kállay sought refuge in the Turkish embassy. Following the confiscation of Jewish property and other discriminatory measures, massive deportations began in mid-May. By early July over four hundred thousand Jews and other anti-Nazi Hungarians had been transported to the concentration camps of the Third Reich. Few survived. The Arrow Cross and other far right groups meanwhile enjoyed the material support of the occupiers and shared in their depredations.

**The Hungarian Front.** The Peace Party's Central Committee (Kádár, Donáth, Horváth, Orbán, and Péter) and Radio Kossuth promptly issued futile calls to armed resistance and sabotage. The Central Committee's concurrent proposal to the dispersed opposition for creation of a so-called Hungarian Front was only marginally more successful. By the end of March agreement in principle was reached with a few left-wing socialists around Szakasits, but the Trade Union Council leaders Lajos Kabók and Sándor Karácsony refused to involve organized labor in illegal activities. The SHP's Béla Kovács, who was secretary of the Peasant Federation, and Bajcsy-Zsilinszky, now in prison, also rejected collaboration on the communists' terms. Nevertheless, at a secret meeting in mid-May between Szakasits, the smallholder Gyula Dessewffy, the legitimist Count György Pallavicini, and a Peace Party representative, a joint proclamation entitled "To the Hungarian Nation" was discussed. The final version disseminated by the communists in early June ignored the other parties' reservations regarding an unqualified denunciation of the regent and the Kállay government. Alleging betrayal of the nation by a twenty-five-year-old counter-revolutionary reaction, the proclamation called for an armed uprising against the Germans and a separate peace, and insisted that the Soviet Union was not an enemy but a defender of Hungarian independence. Purposely omitted from the appeal was any adumbration of the communists' views on the future transformation of Hungarian society. A July issue of *Béke és Szabadság* did claim, however, that the working class had the leading role in the Hungarian Front and was fighting not for some sham bourgeois democracy but for "authentic government by the people."[72]

The dubious representativeness of the Hungarian Front and the constraints of illegality ensured that the communists' propaganda campaign remained unilateral. In July Pálffy was charged with agitation among the military. Ságvári tried to forge partisan groups from young sympathizers but was killed resisting arrest on 27 July. The communists clearly had neither the numbers nor the credibility to rally resistance. With the Russians at their doors and the Germans encamped in their houses the majority of Hungarians still looked to the Horthy regime for some magical formula that would avert disaster.

Since the beginning of the war the home communists had had no direct contact with the émigré leadership. It was, then, partly in order to profit from the air link between Tito's headquarters and Moscow that, in mid-April, Kádár volunteered to attempt the perilous journey to the Yugoslav partisans' base. Arrested en route, he was lucky enough to be taken for a deserter and was imprisoned on that charge. Meanwhile the External Committee, under Rákosi's leadership, pursued its propaganda activities both through Radio Kossuth and in the war zone. The work at the front, directed first by Gerő and then by Farkas, consisted in both intelligence and recruitment. The reports on morale were scarcely encouraging to the communists. While the Hungarian soldiers' resentment at the Germans was growing, desertions were few, and it was generally agreed that the defense of the Carpathian line was in Hungary's national interest. The politics of national survival was regarded as Horthy's responsibility and not the task of some alternative, anti-German resistance movement. One report noted: "It never even enters the soldier's mind that there will be a change in regime after the war." The troops were motivated above all by fear and hatred of the Soviet Union.[73]

The communists nevertheless pursued indoctrination activities among prisoners of war and set up a partisan school that eventually trained some three hundred volunteers; most of them were eventually parachuted into Hungarian territory. An attempt in 1943 to organize a "Hungarian legion" had been blocked by the prisoners' officer corps. Strident calls for sabotage, strikes, armed resistance, and the formation of local "national committees" continued to be issued by Radio Kossuth and in millions of leaflets, but this propaganda barrage fell on deaf ears. To overcome what they regarded as passivity, the External Committee decided in May to offer a more tangible inducement by announcing (in the name of their own "Hungarian National Independence Front") that active partisans would receive as a national reward land and property seized from traitors.

In the weeks following D-Day the group around Horthy redoubled its covert attempts to negotiate with the Western allies. It received some encouragement from momentary revival of Churchill's proposals for a southern thrust that might bring Anglo-American forces through the Ljubljana Gap towards Hungary. The defunct Kállay government had already assured the allies of its willingness to surrender as soon as the first Western soldier set foot in Hungary. Horthy, who had earlier protested to Hitler at the deportations, replaced Sztójay with the more loyal General Géza Lakatos on 25 August. The rapid advance of the Red Army, Romania's switch to the Soviet side on 23 August followed by that of Bulgaria on 8 September, Finland's capitulation on 4 September—all heightened the urgency of seeking an armistice. A secret special bureau within the foreign ministry served as the policy organ for these penultimate attempts and maintained contact with a proliferation of spontaneous groupings (notably the Hungarian Independence Movement led by the Nobel Prize–winning scientist Albert Szent-Györgyi) that encompassed most leading noncommunists intent on a separate peace.

**The Communist Party Revived.** In September the Central Committee decided that the Peace Party tactic had run its course and that the time had come to officially reintroduce the communist party. This was all the more necessary since the Demény faction had in the interim taken to speaking in the name of the CPH against a national front and for a proletarian dictatorship. On 12 September a leaflet announced the revival of the Communist Party; the qualifier "of Hungary" had been dropped in order to reflect the dissolution of the Comintern. The leaflet indicated that the party's ultimate goal remained "socialism" and its immediate objective a "democratic" Hungary. Hungarians were exhorted to demonstrate, strike, and rebel against the Germans. Concurrent instructions to party members lamented that the appointment of the Lakatos government had raised popular hopes and urged organized, mass action by the working class.[74]

László Rajk, who had just emerged from prison, stepped into Kádár's shoes as secretary of the reorganized Central Committee. Its other members were Horváth, Kiss (also recently released from internment), Apró, and Bertalan Bartha (a locksmith who joined the CPH in 1933), the last two having useful contacts among construction and metal workers. Led by the energetic Rajk, the party became activized in various spheres. At the end of September the illegal *Szabad Nép* reappeared. A military committee under Pálffy generated some front-line propaganda and spurred the formation of a few small partisan groups; those in Budapest were under the guidance of Fehér.[75] A number of works cells coalesced in the capital's industrial belt, in the mining districts, and in the industrial region of Miskolc and Diósgyőr, where the Anti-Nazi Committee of Hungarian Communists (Magyarországi Kommunisták Antináci Komitéja, or MOKAN) managed to foment a sizable antiwar demonstration on 21 September. The communist groups also perpetrated some isolated acts of industrial sabotage.

The new leadership exerted itself to turn the elusive Hungarian Front, which was at least based in Hungary, into an effective political alliance. The initial plan developed by Kállai and Rajk in late September envisaged a unified workers' party devoted to the creation of "radical people's democracy." This concept, however, was watered down in an attempt to go beyond Szakasits's left-wing clique in rallying the SDP and the Trade Union Council (TUC). Discussions with the centrist socialist Antal Bán and TUC leaders proved once again fruitless, partly because they still preferred supporting Horthy's separate-peace strategy to the risks of illegality. Consequently, the joint action document signed on 10 October by Kállai and Szakasits, which postponed to peacetime the question of merging the two parties, hardly reflected official SDP policy.[76] Two weeks earlier the NPP, represented by Imre Kovács, had been invited to join the Hungarian Front, as was the SHP's left-leaning Zoltán Tildy. The noncommunist participants entertained visions of a pluralistic democratic system and mistrusted the communists, fearing that the latter would exploit the Red Army's eventual presence to install a proletarian dictatorship. Hoping to dispel these apprehensions, Rajk and Kállai prepared a draft program aiming to clarify the communist version of democracy. The program included references to the participation of all "working strata" in a worker-peasant democratic dictatorship. However, the rapid course of events prevented discussion of this scenario by the Hungarian Front's executive committee.[77]

At the end of September a communist-drafted memorandum calling for war against Germany and for a Hungarian Front coalition government had been forwarded to Horthy; it was signed by Kállai, Szakasits, and Tildy. Preliminary discussions ensued between the two sides. Rajk urged the arming of workers and, impatient with the regime's apparent hesitation, decided on a symbolic gesture. On 8 October a partisan group blew up the statue of General Gömbös near one of the Danube bridges in Budapest.

**The Nazi Coup.**    By then the Red Army had penetrated into Hungarian territory and secret negotiations were being conducted by Horthy's envoys in Moscow. The armistice agreement initialed on 11 October provided, inter alia, for Hungary's evacuation of the reannexed territories and her adherence to the anti-German alliance. Apprised of these plans, the Germans took military precautions and mobilized their Hungarian supporters for a coup. Horthy in turn was aware of the threat and delayed proclamation of the armistice. At a meeting with Tildy and Szakasits on 11 October he allegedly agreed in principle to arm reliable workers and to have the Hungarian Front call a general strike six days later in order to signal Hungary's switch.[78] In the event, when on 15 October Horthy's armistice proclamation was broadcast, the Germans were ready. After overcoming the desperate resistance of the regent's guard detachment, they seized Horthy and planted in his place the Arrow Cross leader Ferenc Szálasi, who proceeded to impose a Nazi-style rule of terror. The commander of the First Army, General Béla Miklós, defected to the Soviet side with part of his staff and some ten thousand soldiers; and he was soon followed by the chief of staff himself, General János Vörös. The Germans and their quislings meanwhile managed to maintain a semblance of order in the shrinking territory under their control.

Although the regime's attempts at switching sides had been foredoomed, the underground Central Committee reacted violently to this demonstration of its impotence. In an "open letter" on 28 October the committee charged that the Horthy regime had not been able to overcome the reactionary notions with which it had been born twenty-five years ago. "Militarily they wanted to lead the country out of war, but politically they feared the Red Army and the democratic forces of the Hungarian people. They wanted to accomplish their task without the reorganization of the army and without the Hungarian democratic forces. This caused the pathetic collapse of their efforts." The committee did not shrink from self-criticism: "Propaganda alone is not sufficient to propel the masses into battle. Propaganda must be accompanied by patient, determined organization. The Hungarian Front failed to do this, and for this reason the masses were, and remain, unprepared for battle. Unfortunately even the CP was not entirely free of this error."[79] The committee also appealed for Hungarian Front action to organize partisan groups and armed resistance by the army and the workers, to sabotage production, and to obstruct the removal of industrial equipment and stock by the Germans. And indeed the party's military committee continued to coordinate a handful of partisan groups in the Budapest area and to infiltrate a few communists into the civilian auxiliary units. On 28 October the communist youth federation was revived and some 350 young people were marshaled into propaganda teams.

**The Liberating Committee.** While the Szálasi regime decreed total mobilization, arrested all overt opponents, and collaborated in the resumption of deportations, the groups that had pinned their hopes on Horthy's strategy now gravitated to the Hungarian Front. Fearing the "dilution" of the already heterogeneous front, the communists resisted its expansion and proposed a new umbrella organization. On 9 November the "Liberating Committee of the Hungarian National Uprising" (Magyar Nemzeti Felkelés Felszabadító Bizottsága) was established under the presidency of Bajcsy-Zsilinszky, who had been freed on 15 October (he thereafter went into hiding, as did most opposition politicians who had managed to escape arrest). The committee incorporated representatives of all interested groups and drafted an ideologically anodyne program calling for resistance to the Germans, a free, independent, democratic Hungary, preparations for certain social reforms, and collaboration with Hungary's neighbors, including the Soviet Union.[80]

Bajcsy-Zsilinszky insisted that the deported Horthy remain Hungary's head of state. He also made clear that, as far as he was concerned, the independence movement derived from the earlier SHP–SDP alliance and only marginally from the efforts of the communists. This caused debate, but the communists finally swallowed their pride. The Liberating Committee's manifesto to the Hungarian people on 10 November branded Szálasi's rule unconstitutional and claimed legal continuity for the committee. An underground military staff was formed led by the retired Lieutenant-General János Kiss; it developed ambitious plans for a coordinated armed rising. Rajk opposed the scheme, arguing that it was unrealistic (and, implicitly, a threat to communist claims of leadership in the country's liberation) and proposing more prudent, partisan-style operations. The Liberating Committee also planned to make contact with Marshal Malinovsky's Red Army headquarters and designated a delegation, headed by Professor Szent-Györgyi, to carry a letter to Soviet Foreign Minister Molotov. The message, composed by Bajcsy-Zsilinszky, recommended among other things the preservation of the existing civil administration and police in the liberated areas.[81]

All these plans were aborted when a series of arrests, beginning on 22 November, swept up Bajcsy-Zsilinszky, the military staff, and even László Rajk. After a summary trial Bajcsy-Zsilinszky, János Kiss, and several other plotters were executed. Rajk was sentenced to death but escaped execution thanks to his Arrow Cross brother and was deported to Germany. The Liberating Committee thus collapsed, and the Hungarian Front ceased any meaningful activity. At the concurrent negotiations in Moscow on the constitution of a new government in the liberated territories, conducted on the Hungarian side by Generals Miklós, Vörös, and others, the Hungarian Front had at least token representation in the person of a staff officer, Ernő Simonffy Tóth, who had worked with the Liberating Committee and managed to reach the Soviet Union. But in Moscow these Hungarians were mere suppliants compared to the exiled communists.

Before the arrests, the communists had been much exercised by the competing activities of the Demény faction. In the wake of the Szálasi coup the latter issued leaflets in the name of the CPH calling for a general strike and hailing the impending creation of a "Soviet Hungary." Demény effectively prevented the formation of orthodox communist cells in his district. Together with other local extremist organizers, he engaged in preliminary discussions with the Liberating Committee and its military staff on the preparation of an uprising. This threat to its already weak influence—indeed, to its very identity—moved the communist leadership to initiate discussions with the Demény group in early November. Although one condition had been that Demény himself would be absent from the talks, it was later revealed that he had been present under an assumed name. The faction proposed a joint leadership of the two communist groups, but this was rejected by Rajk and Péter, and the agreement published in the December issue of *Szabad Nép* recommended the dissolution of the extremist faction, whose members would have to prove their worth before being admitted to the party. Demény and some of his followers ignored the agreement and paid dearly for their heresy after liberation.[82]

Following the downfall of the Liberating Committee the remaining communists continued to perpetrate minor acts of sabotage and to exhort the workers to resist evacuation and the dismantlement of their factories. A few Soviet-dispatched Hungarian partisan groups began operating in the countryside, including one in the north commanded by Nógrádi. In all some 2,500 partisans were active during the last year of war in Hungary. Subsequently inflated into a myth of heroic communist resistance, these actions were of little military significance and were only minor elements in the chaos that was engulfing the country. While the Hungarian army's strength declined and the Szálasi clique retreated to the Austrian border, the Germans methodically shipped machinery, stock, and other valuables out of the country and reinforced their defense of northwestern Hungary.

In late December 1944 the Red Army encircled Budapest. During the siege, which lasted two months, much of the city was destroyed. Huddling in their shelters, the population waited for deliverance from war while remaining profoundly apprehensive about the Soviet version of liberation. The small band of underground communists, in contrast, awaited the Red Army's advance with eager anticipation. Freed from the shackles of their conservative masters, the people of Hungary would finally be free to choose the faith advocated with such extraordinary persistence by a minute and persecuted band of true believers. As for the Hungarian communist cadres in Moscow, the long years of humiliation, imprisonment, and exile were coming to an end. Exhilarated by the scent of power, the marginal men were preparing to come home.

★ ★ ★

# *Return to Power*

# PART THREE

*Hungary emerged from the Second World War devastated—and occupied by the Red Army. The old political elite had led the country into a perhaps inevitable but fateful alliance and was thereby discredited, at least in the eyes of the victorious powers. The prevailing popular mood favored political, social, and economic reform while fearing the revolutionary impact of Soviet influence. There was wide consensus on the need for pluralistic democratic institutions, for land reform, and of course for economic reconstruction. The prospects for all this depended on the balance of political forces both within and outside Hungary.*

*Stalin was intent on fostering compatible regimes in his newly acquired sphere of influence, but in the case of Hungary he proceeded more cautiously than in Bulgaria and Romania. Following his advice, and conscious of the Hungarians' mistrust of communism, the party's Muscovite leaders developed an incremental strategy: initially, they laid stress on the creation of a progressive and multiparty interim government, on Hungarian participation in the final battle against Hitler, on the redistribution of land, and on reconstruction. Accordingly, the new government formed at Debrecen in December 1944 included not only the communists and their allies but also old opposition groups, notably the Smallholder and Social Democratic parties.*

*When the Muscovite and home leaderships merged, it became clear that the former, led by Rákosi, would call the shots. Putting on a conciliatory mask, they called for national unity and set the pace for the implementation of the land reform and the relief of Budapest's population. At the same time they sought to expand their power base by indiscriminate recruitment, by seizing a dominant position in the Trade Union Council and the police, and by creating a political police to pursue their enemies.*

*The other parties all favored reform, to differing degrees but short of the apprehended communist objectives of a wholly socialized economy and proletarian dictatorship. The Smallholder Party rapidly became the non-Marxist rallying point, while the social democrats divided over the desirability of collaborating with the communists. Despite the advantages of a concrete program and Soviet aid, the communists suffered a stinging rebuke at the relatively free elections in October–November 1945. Part of the working class and some radical intellectuals and white-collar workers had rallied to the party, but the social democrats retained the allegiance of most of organized labor, while the National Peasant party won only modest rural support. The bulk of the middle classes and the peasantry turned to the Smallholder Party, which emerged with a clear majority.*

*At Soviet insistence a coalition government was maintained, and the disappointed communists intensified their struggle from above and from below. Control over the interior ministry helped them to purge their opponents from the state administration, to persecute their enemies at large, to disband noncommunist youth organizations, and to harass workers into joining the party. In the ostensible interest of reconstruction they pressed for economic reform at the expense of the private sector. At the same time, while rejecting Western aid, they would not countenance criticism of Russian pillage, of the heavy burden of reparations, and of disadvantageous commercial deals with the Soviet Union. With what Rákosi called "salami tactics," they progressively incapacitated the Smallholder Party, whose leaders had hoped to outlast Soviet occupation, and subverted the Social Democratic Party.*

*The Western allies proved powerless to counter the Soviet-communist assault on the elected majority. At the August 1947 elections the communists resorted to fraudulent practices but won no better than a plurality. Shortly thereafter Stalin created the Cominform and the communists were encouraged to abandon any pretence at parliamentary rule. Private banks and industry were nationalized and, in June 1948, the left wing of the Social Democratic Party was absorbed into the renamed Hungarian Workers' Party. Liberal democracy and free enterprise were thus liquidated, although the new "people's democracy" momentarily appeared to accommodate private farming as well as a vestige of nominal pluralism within a communist-led "people's front." Thanks to terror, manipulation, and, above all, Soviet aid, the communists had overcome the preference of the majority of Hungarians for orderly change and seized dictatorial power.*

# 7. The Party as Liberator, 1944–1945

Battle was still raging over Hungary when the HCP's émigré leadership in Moscow set to devising an action program that would serve as its political overture to the Hungarian people. No precise information is available regarding the advice that the émigrés received from their Soviet sponsors and the shadow Comintern. It is safe to assume, however, that they were informed in their deliberations by the probability that the Soviet Union's influence would be preponderant in the territories occupied by the Red Army.

## SPHERES OF INFLUENCE

The first Russo-German war had paved the way for the Bolshevik Revolution; the second brought the armies of Russian communism into the heart of Europe. The evolution of Stalin's designs on East-Central Europe cannot be described here in any detail.[1] Publicly, of course, he subscribed to the principles of unimpeded self-determination contained in the various wartime statements, from the Atlantic Charter to the Yalta Declaration on Liberated Europe. His fundamental outlook, on the other hand, was perhaps more authentically reflected in his observation to the Yugoslav communist Milovan Djilas that a novel feature of the current war was that "whoever occupies a territory also imposes on it his own social system."[2] In this he was considering not so much communist ideology as the Soviet national interest, of which, in Soviet foreign policy, ideology had always been the servant. Thus while in all probability no definitive blueprint was ever conceived for Soviet domination of East-Central Europe, Stalin's policy, particularly after Stalingrad, was clearly directed toward the fullest possible extension of Soviet influence consistent with preserving the Grand Alliance.

The tactics of constructing a subservient buffer zone varied with local circumstances and Allied diplomatic priorities. Compared to the problems of Poland and Germany, the disposition of Hungary's political future received relatively little attention or sympathy in the Allied councils. At the Anglo-Soviet discussions in Moscow in October 1944, Churchill had presented Stalin with a proposal adumbrating in percentage terms their respective shares of influence in certain liberated countries: 10–90 percent over Greece, in favor of Britain; 50–50 percent over Yugoslavia and Hungary; and, in favor of Russia, 75–25 percent over Bulgaria, and 90–10 percent over Romania. Molotov, Eden recalled in his memoirs, "showed a disposition to haggle over the percentages for [Bulgaria and Hungary]. Finally I told him that I was not interested in figures. All that I wanted was to be sure that we had more voice in Bulgaria and Hungary than we had accepted in Rumania." In the case of Hungary such calculations proved to be ephemeral. The U.S. State Department's Yalta briefing paper anticipated that American and Soviet policies "may not be in harmony if the Soviet Union uses its position as the power in actual control of the execution of the armistice to intervene in Hungarian domestic affairs, to dominate Hungary, or to pursue a severe policy on the reparation question which would cripple the Hungarian economy." Listed as policy objectives were maximum Western participation in the Allied Control Commission; a level of reparations compatible with economic recovery; and a territorial settlement with respect to Slovakia and Transylvania that would take account of Hungarian ethnic claims. However, the United States "would not, of course, take the position of supporting Hungary against the Soviet Union." Here the language became delicately equivocal: "The United States government recognizes that the Soviet Union's interest in Hungary is more direct than ours. . . . We do not, however, consider that the Soviet Union has any special or dominant position in Hungary." By the time of the Potsdam Conference in July 1945, Soviet exploitation of the Allied control commissions in the countries occupied by the Red Army showed the Yalta principles to be a dead letter. As Stalin commented informally, freely elected governments in the liberated areas would be anti-Soviet (meaning, in fact, insufficiently docile), "and that we cannot allow." He did, however, offer assurances that he had no intention of sovietizing these countries.[3]

**The Gradualist Strategy.**   That the émigré communists, as faithful servants of Stalin's ideologically construed strategy, would be catapulted from the distant periphery to the center of Hungarian political life was never in doubt. Their small numbers, limited popular appeal, and the momentary requisites of Allied cooperation impelled them to develop gradualist tactics. In a series of expanded meetings in September and early October 1944 the External Committee debated programmatic proposals introduced by Révai and Gerő.[4] There was general agreement that conditions were not ripe for the immediate revolutionary imposition of a proletarian dictatorship. The modalities of the alternative "democratic transformation" occasioned more debate. Révai cautioned that the action program must be tailored to the existing power relations in Hungary. He therefore advocated a national, anti-Nazi common front, which could serve as the instrument of democratic revolution initially in the governing structure and in land tenure. The construction of a national-democratic state would therefore take precedence over revolutionary socioeconomic change.

The structural and class dimensions of this democratic transformation were still nebulous. Gerő pointed out that the class struggle would not disappear merely because, after liberation, every party would necessarily be "democratic." The communists' limited direct support and their foreseeable difficulties in a multiparty democratic coalition would demand organized pressure from below. The party would have to create revolutionary organizations such as local national committees, works committees, and land-distribution committees and mobilize them if necessary against the government. The future relation between these organizations and the government was left undecided. As Révai put it: "This is a question of class struggle. Which is more advantageous for us: for the state to control [these organizations] or for the latter to control the state? Where will the party exercise greater influence? We cannot give an answer ahead of time." Observed Lukács: "Circumstances will determine where our strength lies."

The concept of democracy had acquired new meaning and class content. In 1919, recalled Gerő, the term had been an antisocialist battle cry. In the mid-1930s it had become the defensive slogan against fascism. In the current final battle against fascism and, ultimately, against imperialism, the operative concept was that of "people's democracy," which rested on the cooperation of other classes with the proletariat in the exercise of power.

Debate on the nature of this preliminary tactic of an antifascist united front took priority over detailed exploration of longer-term tactics for achieving socialism. It was sufficient to recognize, said Lukács, that "peaceful transition" was "in principle possible." A truly democratic state, observed Gerő, would not have to be destroyed to realize socialism. In any event, he continued, to proclaim at the outset the Leninist objective of converting the bourgeois revolution into a socialist revolution would only arouse opposition. The party was not giving up its ultimate objective, but it was essential that the eventual confrontation between the working class and some of its allies be delayed until the party's position was sufficiently strong.

Several factors were seen as both facilitating and necessitating a longer, more gradual phase of transformation. The "new role of the Soviet Union" and the greater acceptability of communist parties in general were positive new elements. Today, Gerő argued, they would have to start farther back than in 1918, but they could move ahead on a much broader front with allies (i.e., the increasingly anti-German ruling classes) that they did not and could not have back then. Since, in their view, the Great Powers would probably continue to collaborate, progress toward socialism would have to be slower. Révai wrote in August 1944 that "anything else would be an adventurist policy."[5] Such expectations may have been encouraged by Stalin's uncertainty regarding Western interference in the political disposition of East-Central Europe. The Soviet Union, however, as Stalin's policies in Bulgaria and Romania would soon indicate, was determined to fully exploit its position of strength. In Hungary the momentary concessions to Allied sensibilities and the initial weakness of the communists militated in favor of gradualism.

## THE COMMUNISTS RETURN

As the Red Army fought its way toward Budapest, the question of political reorganization became urgent. The immediate goal of the Soviet Union was to enlist Hungary in the final battle against Germany, and to this end the modalities of governance were subordinated. Whether the conversion of Hungary from enemy to ally would occur by way of a provisional government or of some ad hoc national committee of antifascist forces remained an open question. While Molotov held sporadic discussions in Moscow with the armistice delegation led by General Faraghó, the émigré communists began their slow homeward journey.

For several weeks Zoltán Vas had been exploring Hungary on Rákosi's behalf behind the advancing Red Army. In mid-October 1944 he reached Szeged, where he made contact with local communists and social democrats, requisitioned a building for the party, and issued the party's first newssheet, *Népakarat* (People's Will). When he telephoned Rákosi to inquire why Gerő was so long in being repatriated, he was told that Stalin's personal decision was necessary. Finally, in the first days of November, Gerő, Révai, Farkas, and Imre Nagy arrived in Szeged to formally revive the Hungarian Communist party (Magyar Kommunista Párt, or HCP) and assess the political climate. Vas was informed that the new home leadership would consist of these four men, who had been approved by Dimitrov and Manuilsky. Why Farkas and not me, he wondered; Farkas was a former Czechoslovakian party member who had not the slightest familiarity with Hungarian conditions.[6] But the command of the ostensibly disbanded Comintern was not to be questioned.

**The Party's Overture.**    Gerő and his comrades promptly sought out the dispersed representatives of the old Hungarian Front parties to launch a new antifascist front, now genuinely under communist guidance. "There will be a Hungarian rebirth," he proclaimed at a ceremonial gathering on 7 November, the anniversary of the Bolshevik Revolution. But the great task lying before the Hungarian nation could not, he insisted, be fulfilled by the communists or any other single party. The HCP sought no monopoly and invited the other parties to join forces with it. Gerő took pains to denigrate the radicalism of some reactivated home communists: "Some communists, looking to the Soviet Union, think that the order of the day in Hungary is to establish socialism. This is not the position of the HCP. It is not a correct viewpoint to urge the construction of socialism upon the rubble of defeat." Instead, he said, the communists were joining with other progressive parties and organizations to activate national committees that would launch the nation's revival.[7] The comforting image projected by the Moscow emissaries was apparent in the contemporary account of the smallholder János Gyöngyösi. The communists, he wrote, "do not seek any privileged status for themselves, and in the questions of private enterprise and of economic and social structure they hint at a progressive but bourgeois compromise." Around 20 November, Rákosi telephoned from Moscow to the communists in Szeged that the party's program and the option of a coalition government had received Soviet approval; negotiations with the Faraghó mission had been broken off. The communists gathered the available representatives of the opposition parties and the trade unions into a Hungarian National Independence Front and issued in its name a program that had been drafted in Moscow.[8]

Published in the Debrecen *Néplap* (People's Gazette) on 30 November under the heading "The Program of Hungary's Democratic Revival and Reconstruction: The HCP's Proposal," the communist program was formally proclaimed three days later. The occasion was a general meeting of the Szeged national committee, which included representatives of the HCP, SDP, SHP, NPP, Citizens' Democratic Party, and the "free" trade unions. Its main thrust was the need to join battle against Nazi Germany. On the domestic front the designated enemies were the Arrow Cross and other pro-German elements; significantly, the defunct Horthy regime was at this point spared from direct denunciation. These elements, the program insisted, should be removed from the civil administration, the judiciary, the police, and the military, and tried by people's courts—a set of demands that reflected the party's tactical, relatively narrow definition of the internal enemy. The same outlook was evident in its proposal for land reform, which was to be implemented as soon as possible, with the active participation of the future beneficiaries. Unlike its predecessors, the new formulation avoided elaborating on the extent of expropriation, but merely specified that the necessary land would be seized from traitors, war criminals, members of the Volksbund (the association of German-Hungarians), and those who had served in the German armed forces.

The program further anticipated the nationalization of mines, oil fields, electrical power plants, and insurance companies, together with state supervision of banks and industrial cartels. On the other hand, it called on private enterprise to contribute to economic revival. A variety of social measures, guarantees of basic political and religious freedoms and of the right to trial by jury, and the cleansing of cultural life from nationalistic and racist influences also found place in the program. It further proposed the formation of national committees which, as the local political organs of the Independence Front, would supervise civil administration. Friendly relations with all neighboring countries and with the United States and Great Britain, and "close friendship with the mighty Soviet Union, defender of people's freedom and independence," summed up the party's goals for Hungarian foreign policy. The former opposition parties, the trade unions, the Peasant Federation, partisan groups, and "all Hungarian patriots" were invited to adopt the communist program.

These proposals represented the party's initial minimum program, that of the "people's democratic revolution." In its cautious treatment of the old regime and of land reform, and in its avoidance of other potentially contentious matters, such as workers' control in industry, the program aimed for the widest possible appeal. As such it differed in tone and content from the draft program completed by Rajk and Kállai on 2 October, which was designed to serve a similar purpose. The latter program was generally more radical in its advocacy of a people's republic, in excluding inimical social classes from power, in its anticapitalist measures, and in the leading role it allotted to the masses, notably through workers' control. However, the German coup and the arrest of Rajk prevented it from being submitted for approval by the Hungarian Front. This tactical divergence between the party's two leading centers was a reflection of their different environments and mutual isolation, which in turn inspired a notable mistrust on the part of the Moscow leadership. In the course of the meetings in September and October Gerő would allege that the home party had slackened its discipline and would deprecate its political effectiveness. The émigrés were particularly critical of the home communists' futile Peace Party initiative.[9] Viewed from the relative security of Moscow, the home communists seemed foolish and impotent.

Such disharmonies were of less immediate significance than the spontaneous radicalism of the dispersed communists in the liberated territories. Coordinating them was no easy task, although as early as 9 November Gerő had called together a number of local activists to lay down Moscow's line. On 26 September, a few days after the Red Army's entry into Hungary, the first ad hoc national committee had come into being at Makó. Since then, both the local communists and the repatriated émigrés had devoted great energy to the creation of such committees behind the advancing front. Under the general authority of the Red Army, these national committees were designed to serve as a temporary civil government and as the building blocks of a new political system. The quest for an antifascist regroupment made it necessary to involve the other

Independence Front parties in the committees. In order to strengthen communist influence, Rákosi sent instructions in November to include the communist-led "free" trade unions as a distinct and equal form of political organization in both the front and the national committees.[10] At first, the committees were largely dominated by local communist journeymen who indulged in vengeful and arbitrary measures and behaved as if the dictatorship of the proletariat was imminent. Their excesses became so embarrassing that the provisional Central Committee eventually was forced in some cases to intervene.[11]

**Final Preparations.** The Gerő group initially assumed the seat of the new regime would be Szeged, but it had been the birthplace of the counterrevolution in 1919. Moscow therefore ruled in favor of Debrecen which, as the scene of Kossuth's declaration of independence, had the more positive historical associations. On 30 November Gerő and Imre Nagy were summoned back to Moscow, where they joined Rákosi in meetings with Molotov and his deputy V. G. Dekanozov to work out the details of the coalition government. Dekanozov was arguing for a national liberation committee patterned on the French precedent when Stalin appeared and endorsed the Hungarians' proposal for a provisional government. When the question of constitutional continuity arose, Stalin observed that Horthy had "committed political suicide" in allowing the Germans to depose him and that a new source of political legitimacy had to be devised. He went on to recommend that a new national council be formed, with representatives of local government and, if possible, of the trade unions; for the moment, the communist party should take no direct part in it. The government should not include those communists exchanged before the war, he advised, for they would be regarded in Hungary as Moscow's hirelings. As for the members of the inactive armistice delegation, they would have to be told to participate in the new government or face the consequences of a more left-wing regime. The Soviet officials also insisted on the importance of including comprehensive land reform in the inaugural program.[12]

These Soviet directives were incorporated in the plans developed between 1 and 5 December, with the amendment that a preparatory commission, helped by the national committees, would conduct elections in the liberated territories for a provisional national assembly. It would then fall to the latter to "elect" the provisional government. The composition of the government was predetermined. The Russians recommended Generals Miklós, Vörös, and Faraghó as, respectively, prime minister, defense minister, and minister of food supply. The émigrés proposed Imre Nagy for agriculture and József Gábor for commerce and transportation. Besides these names they anticipated two portfolios each for the SDP and SHP and one for the NPP.[13]

Stalin also exercised a decisive influence over the tone of the proposed declaration by the provisional government. He urged the émigrés to lay greater stress on the protection of the property of ordinary people and on their right to private entrepreneurial initiative. He recommended less rigid formulations, notably with respect to the purge of the civil service.[14] Stalin's moderating advice throughout the meetings was clearly inspired by the immediate tactical desirability of marshaling the broadest spectrum of Hungarians into an antifascist coalition that would both satisfy the democratic sensibilities of the Western Allies and contribute to the early conclusion of the war. The resulting revisions of the Rákosi group's already gradualist action program included a calculatedly sympathetic reference to the deportation of Horthy, "our country's governor"; an emphasis on private property and omission of any reference to nationalization; and an avoidance of harsh words for the nonfascist ruling classes. The Russians and the émigrés both understood that these concessions were tactical and had no bearing on the political future of Hungary.

Molotov thereupon convoked Horthy's armistice delegation, including Géza Teleki, the deceased premier's son, who was allocated the culture portfolio. They had little choice but to accept their designated role. "When Hungary is fully liberated," said Molotov in response to their reservations, "a legal and constitutional government can be formed on a democratic basis. We assist the provisional government, the rest is up to your conscience and sense of responsibility."[15] Horthy's former envoys and generals, a few communist émigré leaders, G. M. Pushkin, later Soviet ambassador to Hungary, and General Susajkov, who was to act as liaison with Marshal Malinovsky, all entrained at the Kiev Station and after a slow journey arrived in Debrecen at dawn on 12 December. It was also the dawn of a new era in the political life of Hungary.

## THE PROVISIONAL GOVERNMENT

Under the supervision of the Allied Control Commission's chairman, Marshal Voroshilov (who was also a member of the Soviet Politburo), the proportions of party representation in the provisional assembly were determined and the deputies selected. The latter were then transported to Debrecen by the Red Army. Official nomination of the delegates was generally staged by the local national committees, which held public meetings in celebration. In order to lend respectability to the national committees and the provisional assembly, the Soviet security police actively aided the HCP in recruiting local notables, resorting when necessary to threats of deportation. A prominent victim of such blackmail was Péter Veres, a Populist who escaped prosecution for his rightist writings during the war by accommodating himself to crypto-communist dominance in the NPP.[16] The communist Sándor Nógrádi arrived in Debrecen by Russian military transport after terminating his partisan forays and learned there that he had been "elected" in his absence by the city of Miskolc, where no one knew him personally.[17]

Of the 230 delegates who assembled on 21 December, 71 represented the HCP, 55 the SHP, 38 the SDP, 16 the NPP, and 12 the Citizen's Democratic party (Polgári Demokrata Párt, or CDP, a liberal urban middle-class group). There were in addition 19 mostly communist representatives of the "free trade unions" and 19 independents, some of whom were also communist sympathizers. (By social background, 81 were industrial or agricultural workers, 36 smallholder peasants, 39 businessmen and merchants, 60 white-collar workers and intellectuals, and 14 others.) At its inaugural two-day session, the assembly endorsed the amended Independence Front program and the appointment of a government headed by General Miklós. In addition to the assignments determined in Moscow, the crypto-communist historian Erik Molnár became minister of public welfare; the social democrats Ágoston Valentiny and Ferenc Takács received justice and industry; the smallholders Gyöngyösi and István Vásáry, foreign affairs and finance; and the NPP's Erdei, who was procommunist, the interior portfolio. Erdei had been told by Gerő that he would put Voroshilov in "a very difficult position" if he declined the offer of this critical ministry, since the HCP could not cede it to the SHP, while the latter and the generals would not accept a communist.[18] Speaking to the government's program, Révai appealed for "unity, unity, and thirdly, again unity." What united them—the liberation and reconstruction of the homeland—was, he said, a thousand times more important than what divided them. The other delegates performed according to the Soviet script; reportedly, even their speeches were prepared by the Russians and transmitted by General Susajkov.[19]

Having performed their legitimizing function, the delegates were sent home. The provisional government remained in Debrecen under close Soviet supervision and was prevented from communicating directly with the representatives of the Western Allies. It declared war on Germany on 28 December and sent a delegation to Moscow to receive the final armistice terms. The agreement, signed on 20 January 1945, nullified the Vienna Awards and other territorial acquisitions and stipulated reparations of $200 million for the Soviet Union and $100 million for Czechoslovakia and Yugoslavia, all to be paid in commodities over a period of six years. The Allied Control Commission, charged with overseeing the execution of these terms, included British and American representatives but was placed under the general direction of the Soviet high command. The armistice also provided for Hungarian participation in the final battle against Hitler. In the event, however, the state and morale of those Hungarian forces available in the liberated territories did not allow fulfillment of this undertaking.

The failure of Miklós and Vörös to marshal even a belated, token military effort was one of several issues on which cleavages soon materialized in the provisional government. Others were the proposed land reform, the purge of the civil service, the role of the national committees, and the reorganization of the police. As a mere servant of the occupying power, the government had little choice but to issue decrees legitimizing the national committees (4 January 1945), the screening committees for the civil service (5 January), and the people's courts (5 February), the last-named being under direct Soviet control. Nevertheless, disputes arose. These, wrote Gerő to Rákosi on 7 January, were "signs that the battle against reaction [was] becoming accentuated." "We anticipated this," he continued, "and although we do not want to push it artificially fast, we will begin shortly to exercise the necessary pressure on the government from above and from below."[20]

In the first eleven liberated counties the post of *főispán* (i.e., of top administrator) was filled by four communists, three smallholders, two social democrats, and two NPP members. The HCP's urging for a purge of insufficiently progressive civil servants met with stiff resistance at all levels and in all areas not under direct communist control. There could be little open protest, however. The Red Army's wild rapine and pillage went largely unchecked. Over 600,000 military personnel and civilians were transported to the Soviet Union for reconstruction work, and a third of them never returned.[21] The communists, relying on their link with the occupiers, acted with equal impunity. In one instance, in the spring of 1945, a communist mob took over the administration of Gyömrő near Budapest, killing a score of people in the process, but the other parties and their press had to remain silent. When in December the smallholder deputy justice minister finally ordered the arrest of the principal suspects, Rákosi intervened and the case was closed.[22] The summary purges conducted by the more radical national committees impelled the government's noncommunist members to urge that they be dissolved; they had become superfluous, these members argued, with the restoration of civil administration. The communists repulsed this attack, although later they themselves would allow the national committees to wither away.

**Land Reform.**    In early January the Debrecen Central Committee launched the long-heralded land reform campaign. Its intermediary was the NPP, whose leading figures included both crypto-communists like Erdei and more democratically inclined Populists like Imre Kovács.[23] Although some party members urged immediate collectivization, the official, Soviet-endorsed line confirmed that redistribution was the order of the day. Ostensibly it was an NPP proposal, published on 14 January, that the communists embraced and promoted. The reform envisaged the outright expropriation of estates over 1,000 *hold* (1 *hold* equals 1.42 acres) and the seizure of all but 100 *hold* of the smaller estates, except for those belonging to the wealthy peasants (soon identified with the Russian word kulak), whose political neutrality was courted by an allowance of 200 *hold*. Communist agitators thereupon fanned out in the countryside to recruit landless peasants into "land-claimant committees," which in turn were mobilized to prepare for redistribution and put pressure on the government.

There was no opposition within the government to the principle of land reform, but debate dragged on over its timeliness when not all of Hungary had been liberated. In fact, everything about it was debatable—the schedule, the amount of land to be retained, and the agents who could execute it. The SHP, for instance, wanted a higher and economically more viable ceiling on retained land and execution by experts rather than by the ad hoc land-claimant committees. The communists saw greater political advantage in awarding land, no matter how small, to all claimants, while converting some large estates into state farms to form the embryo of a socialized agricultural sector. Initially the HCP had projected completion of the reform by 1 October, but in early 1945 an even tighter schedule was requested by Voroshilov, who hoped that redistribution would generate popular support for the final military push against the Germans and their remaining Hungarian allies. Impatient at the deadlock, he publicly invited the peasantry on 15 March to seize land, then convoked party representatives to Debrecen. Ruling out further discussion, he imposed a draft that, formally introduced by Agriculture Minister Nagy, was issued as a governmental decree on 17 March.[24]

The reform so hastily introduced was implemented by over three thousand land-claimant committees, the majority of whose members were new recruits to the HCP and the NPP, with the active participation of the Soviet military. The process was hampered by what one "Muscovite" (the term applied to the repatriated communists) identified as the peasants' "traditional mistrust of communism." "Weeks, even months passed," he recalled in the 1960s, "and in many places the land was neither distributed nor tilled."[25] The committees, on the other hand, did succeed in dispensing rough justice, in many cases seizing far above the specified acreage from gentry landowners and kulaks alike. By the end of June nearly 35 percent of the arable land had been reallocated to 642,342 laborers and dwarf landholders or consigned to communal property. The reform still left some 300,000 landless peasants, and it could not by itself assure the efficient productivity of the newly landed farmers. The latter would subsequently show little gratitude to the HCP, while the excesses of the land-claimant committees left a wake of mistrust and litigation and alienated the wealthier peasantry from the left-wing parties. Notwithstanding these negative consequences, the reform had finally destroyed the predominance of vast private estates in Hungarian agriculture. The comparative efficiency of small private farming was not to be fully tested, however, for the peasantry's fears of forced collectivization were realized within a few years.

The HCP gave high priority to land reform because most social and political groups already supported it, at least in principle. Equally urgent was the food supply problem, particularly in the capital. Battle raged over Buda until 13 February, but in liberated Pest a national committee was formed on communist initiative on 23 January, and the smallholder János Csorba was named mayor, with socialist and communist deputies. Neither the new city administration nor

Faraghó's food supply ministry in Debrecen could find a ready solution to the problem of feeding and protecting from disease the population of the devastated capital. On 5 January the HCP decided to mobilize its forces and demonstrate its superior capability by providing relief for the workers of the northern industrial region and of Budapest. It engineered the appointment of Vas as the capital's commissioner of food supply; in May he also replaced Csorba as mayor. Party activists, the national committees, and the partisan support of the Red Army were all mobilized to bring food to Budapest. In late March the Russians loaned the starving citizenry a large quantity of foodstuffs.[26] The HCP, which had been deprecating Faraghó's own efforts, hailed this as a demonstration of its political and administrative superiority and of Russian magnanimity. The loaned supplies were in fact a small fraction of the immense quantities of grain and livestock that the Red Army had confiscated.

## THE COMMUNISTS REUNITED

While the home party's underground leaders remained trapped during the long siege of the capital, the Muscovite provisional Central Committee (known at the time as the "Central Leadership") moved from Szeged to Debrecen and proceeded to revive the party. Thus Nógrádi, after a week in Debrecen, was dispatched by Gerő to Miskolc to organize the party in northern Hungary. He was even allocated a car, an unheard-of luxury at the time, and the local Soviet commander provided a building for the party. Violent arguments ensued with local party zealots who anticipated a proletarian dictatorship and saw no need for other parties, but eventually good relations were established with the city's leftist social democratic organizer, Sándor Rónai. (The latter had begged Farkas to be admitted to the HCP, only to be told that he would be of greater use in the SDP.)[27] In the political vacuum of late 1944 the communists enjoyed a certain appeal that derived from their seizure of initiative and from the fact that they alone among the revived parties enjoyed the unstinting support of the occupying power. The moderate reformism of their program and their calculated muting of ideology contributed to this favorable image. One new adherent told Nógrádi: "Only the communists know what they want!"[28]

The battle for Budapest was only beginning when in mid-November István Kossa was sent by Farkas from Szeged across the front line to seek out the communists in the capital. Kossa, a former social democratic union secretary, had defected to the Russian side during the war to join the HCP and become a Red Army officer. His mission was to incite the Budapest communists to rise in arms. The message, the first official communication between the two branches of the party in several years, was received by Károly Kiss, whereupon Apró set out for Debrecen. As was related in the previous chapter, the Liberating Committee's plans for an uprising had been nipped in the bud, and the underground communists in the capital were hardly in a position to take up the challenge. The next contact occurred on 5 January when Vas, with Soviet assistance, reached the industrial suburb of Kőbánya. Upon his arrival a national committee was set up under the chairmanship of the local priest, and a communist was appointed police captain. This was, recalls Vas, their common practice: to seek out a reasonably progressive and popular individual to head the civil administration, and to ensure communist control of the police "so that communists [would] no longer be jailed, so that *we* could decide who [was] the enemy." Kádár and Donáth had meanwhile set out from their hiding place in Budapest. After some difficulties, owing to their ignorance of Russian, they finally met Vas.

In their initial discussions they agreed that in a few years, perhaps sooner, the party would become the ruler of Hungary, and that until then it would be the driving force in the Independence Front. When the home comrades proposed to secure two rooms in a union headquarters, Vas dismissed that as nonsense and asserted that as soon as Pest was liberated they would occupy one of the largest and soundest buildings for the party's offices. (Rákosi and Gerő would later ironically refer to the "two-room spirit" of the Budapest comrades.) Within a few days they took over the former Volksbund headquarters on Kálmán Tisza Square. On 19 January the first recorded meeting was held of a second ad hoc Central Committee; it consisted of Apró, Bartha, Horváth, Kádár, Kállai, Kiss, Kossa, István Kovács, and Vas. Following the pattern set in the liberated areas, they had conferred with a few immediately available members of the opposition parties and that same day published the Independence Front proclamation in Budapest's first postwar communist newssheet, *Szabadság* (Freedom).[29]

The tactics of gradualism did require some explanation, for the Budapest communists were incensed at the number of "Horthyites" in the provisional government and particularly at the choice of General Miklós. When subsequently challenged on this point in the Central Committee by Horváth, Gerő retorted that they had had to accept Miklós because of the "international situation," that it had been a condition of the armistice agreement, in other words a concession to the Western Allies.[30]

While the Germans continued to hold out in Buda, in liberated Pest the communists seized the organizing initiative; they were helped by the Soviet commander, General Zamercev. Gerő soon arrived to marshal the troops. He entrusted the trade unions to Kossa, the city administration to Vas, and the Budapest police to Kádár, who eventually became deputy police chief under Münnich, a Muscovite; István Kovács and Kiss were assigned to party organization and cadre work.[31] Finally, on 21 February, Rákosi himself arrived in Budapest, and two days later the party's two leading groups officially coalesced into a single Central Committee. Rákosi assumed the title of general secretary;

the thirteen other members included such Muscovites as Farkas, Gerő, Kossa, Nagy, Révai, and Vas, and the home communists Apró, Horváth, Kádár, Kiss, Kovács, and Péter. The rough numerical balance between the two wings in no way reflected the distribution of power, for from the start the top Muscovites—Rákosi, Gerő, and Farkas—were in undisputed control.

The repatriated communists, less than two hundred in number, were generally older, more experienced, and had the inestimable advantage of speaking Russian and having direct access to the Soviet leadership. They were also distinguished by a generally Jewish, lower-middle-class background, whereas their home comrades were more typically of the working class or Transylvanian middle class. A further characteristic, and one that the home comrades acquired only gradually, was unquestioning loyalty to the Soviet Union. The Muscovites were all Soviet citizens, many had Soviet military rank and affiliation with the Soviet secret police, and they could conceive of no Hungarian interests that departed from those of their adopted country. Upon their return they were totally subordinated to the authority of Voroshilov and his assistants.[32]

**Leaders and Followers.**   The party's leader, Rákosi, was a squat, bald man, undeniably clever, capable of disarming charm, and inclined by choice to seek a middle position between the rightist and leftist tendencies in the reconstructed party. While Rákosi would occasionally pander to national sentiment, the austere and authoritarian Gerő was the archetypical apparatchik. Farkas, Rákosi's closest acolyte, lacked the intellectual gifts and Hungarian experience of the other leading Muscovites. The intense, bespectacled Révai performed as the party's theoretician and mobilizing agent among the intelligentsia. An obviously less influential Muscovite was the faintly avuncular agronomist Imre Nagy, whose Radio Kossuth scripts had reportedly been criticized by Rákosi for their excessive nationalism.[33] His persistent preference for redistribution over collectivization, together with his relative moderation and administrative incompetence, soon relegated Nagy to a secondary level in the hierarchy.

The most commanding home communist was Rajk, who upon his return from a German concentration camp in March 1945 was appointed secretary of the important Budapest party organization. Later that year he was named deputy general secretary of the party. The intelligent and volatile Rajk was a tireless and occasionally impatient leftist who enjoyed a following among young communists. The less gifted but more disciplined Kádár was the leading home link with the industrial proletariat. He would succeed Rajk, first as Budapest secretary and then as deputy general secretary, when the latter devoted his energies to the interior ministry. Another noteworthy home figure was Péter, who had reportedly received NKVD training in the 1930s and thereafter served as the home party's security specialist. At war's end the Russians put Péter in charge of the political police, which he dutifully modeled on the NKVD as the key agency of communist terror.

The Muscovite–home communist dichotomy had less practical significance during the immediate postwar period than the tactical differences that arose within both groups. The impatient fanaticism of Rajk jarred with the disciplined leftism of Gerő, while both overrode the relative moderation of Imre Nagy. But even these differences were submerged in the pressing tasks of building a mass party and imposing communist predominance. Indeed, the new leadership—Muscovites and home communists alike—was ostensibly unanimous in stressing the dangers of "left sectarianism" manifested by some of the indigenous veterans. The most troublesome factional leaders of the preliberation era, Aladár Weisshaus and Pál Demény, were disposed of in short order. Despite the 1944 accord, Demény had persisted in promoting his own ultraleftist version of the party. When he was arrested in early 1945 (shortly after emerging from an Arrow Cross jail), his followers at Csepel promptly agitated for his release. Rajk led the action to persuade Demény's supporters to rejoin the HCP, while Demény himself was convicted of conspiracy. Imprisoned until 1957, he was then granted legal but not "political" rehabilitation.[34] Weisshaus suffered a similar fate. With the elimination of these marginal mavericks, the HCP easily confirmed its monopolistic position in the Hungarian communist movement.

Since the party's pitifully small membership had to be expanded, the tight controls and ideological requisites of the years of illegality were now relaxed. The experienced core consisted of the Muscovites, the home communists, and the "Westerners," including some who had fled the purge of so-called Trotskyites. The prospect of electoral competition and proportional allocation of positions in the bureaucracy impelled the leadership to launch an indiscriminate recruiting campaign. Former Arrow Cross members and the urban lumpenproletariat were as welcome in the party as the SDP's industrial workers and as the agricultural laborers. Anyone even remotely associated with the wartime resistance was assiduously courted in order to enhance the party's patriotic image. The seduction of the intelligentsia was primarily Révai's task, and he worked hard at it. He was rewarded by the early adhesion of a number of budding intellectuals. Alienated from family and society and eager for radical change, these young recruits, many of them Jewish, were intoxicated by the power and material benefits bestowed upon them by the party. The expansion of the network of people's colleges, which served the more gifted rural youth, was also abetted by the party despite their Populist and autonomist flavor.

In order to overcome their numerical weakness the communists initially proposed the creation of multiparty mass organizations for youth and women. In December 1944 they established in Debrecen the Hungarian Federation of Democratic Youth (Magyar Demokratikus Ifjúsági Szövetség, or MADISZ) in collaboration with the NPP. When the SDP and SHP decided to form their own youth wings, the MADISZ remained as the purely communist successor to the KIMSZ. The Democratic Federation of Hungarian Women (Magyar Nők Demokratikus Szövetsége, or MNDSZ) followed the same course.

Initially the revival of the party had gone hand in hand with the creation of national committees. At the repatriated Central Committee's first meeting in Szeged on 7 November 1944 it was decided to conduct a purge of "questionable elements" in conjunction with the distribution of party cards. The party organizations were first directed to restore order, create new, "popularly based" administrative and security services, explain the national unity policy to party members, and extirpate opportunists from the membership.[35] The HCP, counting in particular on the adhesion of left-wing socialists, went all out to create an instant mass party. At the same time, it avoided giving the impression of reaching for monopoly power and indeed urged the revival of the other Independence Front parties. From February 1945 strict vetting was gradually abandoned in favor of mass recruitment, and in consequence membership increased from some 30,000 to 220,000 in July. In August, at the beginning of the electoral campaign, virtually all controls were dispensed with. Within three months the party's ranks swelled to 500,000. This roughly equaled the membership claimed by the SDP, and meant that some 40 percent of the industrial workers in greater Budapest belonged to one or the other of the two left-wing parties.[36]

Party membership in the immediate postwar period entailed little sacrifice while bringing tangible benefits. It provided security from arrest (notably for the former minor fascists) while assuring employment and a certain sense of power. Ideological indoctrination had low priority compared to other pressing demands on the few trained communist cadres. The momentarily loose hierarchical organization of the HCP allowed unusual autonomy at lower levels, where the party committees were freely elected and received only limited guidance from the permanent secretary. This relaxation of the restrictive aspect of democratic centralism, together with the ostensible moderation and constructiveness of the official party line, persuaded not a few Hungarians to join the party that seemed most purposeful in serving the national tasks of reconstruction and reform.

The rapid expansion of the membership could not, however, supply the need for trained activists within the party apparatus and in public service. The low caliber of hurriedly recruited communist functionaries proved a persistent embarrassment to the party, particularly when the more experienced social democratic activists and members of other parties reentered the political arena. Many of the initial communist appointees had to be replaced. Nógrádi reported in June 1945 that they would have to put up "a very determined struggle" if the party's prestige in the northern territory was to be preserved.[37] He was not the only one who thought so. When a repatriated Muscovite complained about his assignment, Rákosi exploded: "We have to fight for every position, for every inch of ground. I have no idea how I am going to fill the hundreds of positions with suitable and reliable people who will stand their ground amidst all the difficulties of this coalition chaos."[38] Indeed, while the top leaders impressed all comers with their competence and preparedness, the dearth of trained middle cadres would undermine the party's effectiveness and prestige for years to come.

How could a tiny underground party gain in size and influence so rapidly, asked Gerő rhetorically at a meeting of activists in March 1946. Some said it came about because the communists were clever in exploiting chaos and the disorganization of the other parties, because they seized the initiative, occupied important positions in the police and the civil administration, and possessed the best propaganda tools. There was no denying, allowed Gerő, that they were better prepared and had a head start. In the same lecture Gerő felt compelled to address the Jewish question. The party supported the rightful demands of the Jewish lower classes for restitution, he said, but it opposed the Jewish councils that wanted to turn the Jews against the Hungarian people and to create a separate Jewish state within the state.[39] The issue was in fact a sensitive one for, much as in 1919, popular anti-Semitism was inflamed by the preponderance of Jews in the party, particularly among its leaders (Rákosi, Farkas, Gerő, Révai, Vas) and in the new secret police. Rákosi, by all accounts himself an anti-Semite, was aware of these risks. He would repeatedly caution the ranks against exacerbating racial tensions, referring to elements who committed "grave mistakes in the course of our mass actions."[40] Many survivors among Hungary's Jewry did gravitate to the HCP. The Jewish community at large, however, received little preferential treatment and suffered equally from the excesses of a party whose leaders readily ignored their own Jewishness.[41]

**Compromise and Its Limits.**   With the old militants reactivated and party membership expanded, the Central Committee launched an educational campaign to explain the official strategy. This was all the more imperative since many of the initially autonomous party groups in the liberated areas had taken it upon themselves to promote a far more radical line against the old administration, a line that favored immediate socialist revolution. At party meetings and in a series of "seminar brochures" the leadership propagated the line developed in Moscow. The immediate pursuit of proletarian dictatorship would be a narrow, nationalist policy, wrote Révai, and one that could provoke conflict between the Soviet Union and its Western partners, whose alliance was destined to endure. Moreover, the popular majority would not support a party fighting for proletarian dictatorship. Therefore the HCP had devised a transitional policy for the next several years. From another perspective, Révai defended gradualism with the argument that their support from the Soviet Union would render the methods of 1918/19 unnecessary in the drive toward communism. Such rationales reflected the party's total subordination to Stalin. As a communist historian notes, the HCP leaders were immersed in daily politics, had little time for independent ideological explorations, and were disposed in any case to rely on Moscow's guidance.[42]

In a speech on 11 February 1945, Rákosi announced that the first task of the new Hungarian democracy, the creation of a central authority to conclude the armistice and proclaim a general program, had been fulfilled. Now, he said, the time had come to launch the second phase, that of program implementation, under the slogan "Land, bread, liberty!"[43] Until the end of 1944 the domestic enemy had been identified as the Arrow Cross and other traitors. By February 1945 the Central Committee was ready to launch a frontal attack on "reactionaries," especially those in government, but the Russians counseled restraint. The party thereupon issued the slogan "A strong and democratic government!" and urged that the seat of power be transferred to Budapest—which, on 12 April, it was. The party also demanded that Faraghó and the other "Horthyite" ministers be replaced. Concurrently its press began to vilify Horthy as a war criminal and to denounce his regime and its supporters. The circle of war criminals and other antisocial elements liable to prosecution was extended, while Révai explained: "Reaction means one thing when the fight for liberation is the main task and another when the task is the consolidation of democracy." A reactionary he defined variously as an anticommunist; one who wanted to set village against city; one who claimed that the country could not be rebuilt by its own strength; and one who manifested pseudo–left-wing demagogy.[44]

What Révai had called the "Szeged handshake" was thus superseded by a less conciliatory line that intensified the struggle against reaction and capitalism while momentarily exploiting the latter in the interest of reconstruction. The task of reconstruction was identified by Rákosi as "the most urgent and the most important party program" for political as well as economic reasons. Taking Lenin's NEP policy as his model, Révai declared on 14 May at a miners' congress that the capitalists' profit was a price worth paying for their participation in the country's economic revival. The essential corollary of cooperation with those capitalists who did not sabotage production was the staunch defense and steady expansion of the party's positions of power.[45]

**The Battle from Above.** Their successful launching of land reform and their efforts to seize the initiative in economic reconstruction were only one dimension of the communists' drive for power. Other dimensions were the promotion of national and works committees; the prosecution of loosely defined "fascists"; attempts to purge the civil service, police, and army; and total control over the political police. In the sphere of party politics the communists would try to forestall competition with the SDP by preaching "working-class unity" and suborning the other parties' left wings while attacking their more rightist members.

The task of pursuing hostile political elements was initially performed by the NKVD agents who arrived in Hungary with the Red Army. It was then assumed in part by the newly formed Hungarian political police, acting under

Soviet direction. The Russians made sure that the political police, known universally as the AVO (from Államvédelmi Osztály, meaning "State Defense Department") was from the start the exclusive preserve of the communists. Led by Péter, its complement was a politically bizarre mixture that included former Horthyite experts and Arrow Cross thugs as well as many Jewish survivors of concentration camps disposed to seek revenge. From the AVO's headquarters at 60 Andrássy Street, formerly occupied by the Arrow Cross, Péter's men and their Soviet advisers conducted razzias against the "enemies of the people." Their activities were above the law and beyond the jurisdiction of all but the HCP leadership and the Soviet authorities.

Péter exercised such absolute control over the political police that when, in late January 1945, the nucleus of the interior ministry's political security department, headed by another communist, moved from Debrecen to Pest, he initially refused to admit them to his Andrássy Street headquarters. Under Erdei's nominal authority the key public security departments in the ministry were supervised by communists led at first by Zöld and then by Farkas. Gradually, other departments responsible for personnel and the armistice provisions also fell into communist hands.[46]

The rebuilding of the state administration was marked by fierce competition between the parties for positions at every level, from the ministerial to that of local police captain. The communists, initially constrained by their small numbers, concentrated on gaining control over the enforcing arms of the state. They also assiduously promoted "people's courts" as an alternative to the old judiciary. The government was compelled to legalize these courts, and by April 1945 they had rendered judgment over nearly ten thousand Arrow Cross and other political criminals. Communist transformation of the military was more problematical at this early stage; the HCP cadres were insufficient and the other parties resisted the idea strongly. However, Pálffy was put in charge of the defense ministry's military-political department, as the Russians and the HCP insisted, and his "orientation officers" carried out indoctrination under direct HCP control. Nevertheless, the major communist drive for predominance in the armed forces was launched only in 1946. Similar factors along with bureaucratic sabotage hampered the work of the communist-inspired but multiparty political screening committees in the purge of the civil service. While no recognized party objected to the expulsion of outright fascists from the various state organs, the communists' increasingly broad definition of what it was to be an undesirable reactionary met with widespread resistance both active and passive.

**The Battle from Below.** The drive for power from above went hand in hand with the battle from below. Originally the HCP had conceived of the national committees as a key weapon at this level, with the dual task of radically implementing government policies and mobilizing mass pressure on the government in the guise of an independent popular opposition.[47] The HCP did not, however, intend the committees to become the building blocks of a new revolutionary state, and it accepted the government's decision of 4 January to restore the old administrative structure. The national committees thereupon degenerated into local coalition organs exercising an uncertain advisory and supervisory function. Prime Minister Miklós and the majority in the government deplored the anarchic excesses of the committees, but the HCP continued to pay lip service to their significance as an authentic grass-roots political force.' On 12 February Gerő praised them as being far more solidly democratic than the government itself and described their function as the exertion of leftward pressure on the central and local administration. The external and domestic situation, wrote Horváth in *Szabad Nép* on 31 May, required "a pace of democratic transformation" that lagged behind "the instinctive hopes of the masses." The party's ambivalence was reflected in Rákosi's argument at a meeting of the communist-socialist liaison committee that to enhance and centralize the power of the national committees concurrently with the newly announced reconstruction program would arouse the fears of the middle class.[48] A multiparty National Council of National Committees did come into being in September 1945; it was designed to foster mutual reinforcement of state and national committee activities. But the continuing friction between the two forced the communists to make a tactical choice: in order to implement the economic reconstruction program, they settled for a reformed central government.[49] A further and perhaps more compelling reason for the HCP's virtual abandonment of the national committees was the progressive revival of noncommunist political activity throughout the country and the relative decline in communist strength even on the committees themselves.

The other weapon from below, the works committees, materialized both spontaneously and at communist instigation in the factories of liberated Hungary. The committees frequently consisted of extremists who seized their plants on the pretext that a second commune was about to abolish capitalism, and then proceeded to conduct their own purges of unsympathetic managers and workers. Such impatient radicalism was out of tune with the HCP's initial program. A decree issued on 18 February and legitimizing the works committees restricted their sphere of activity to defense of the workers' social and economic interests and to a supervisory but not controlling function over management. Communist pressure through the Trade Union Council resulted in a second decree on 5 June that prescribed the formation of works committees in all plants with at least twenty employees but officially put an end to the existing committees' independent purges.[50]

The generally self-appointed and communist-led works committees did contribute in some measure to the revival of industrial production, but subordinating them to the party's coalition tactics required many a stern admonition. At the May HCP conference, Kossa observed that the communists in the trade unions and the works committees did not yet understand or believe that socialization was not on the day's agenda.

> Many mistakes arise from this in trade union work. . . . Those comrades who work, and play a decisive role in the works committees, do not fully comprehend that the party's political line is the recognition of private property. They interpret this line as being transitory and do not consider it worthwhile to hand back the plants and remove them from works committee control for the brief interval during which the party stands for private property.[51]

On the same occasion Rákosi blamed leftist sectarianism for such excesses. A conference of works committee representatives, called by the Trade Union Council for 12 and 13 July, again reflected the divergence between grass-roots radicalism and the party's inclination to marshal the works committees for the task of reconstruction.[52]

## PARTY POLITICS AND ELECTIONS

With its narrow political base, the HCP needed to look for allies within the coalition. The NPP had been activated with communist support to counteract the rural appeal of the SHP and serve as the advocate of land reform. Despite this, it had never been, nor was it developing into, a mass party.[53] The SDP, on the other hand, was an important competitor as well as potential ally, since its traditional constituency was among the industrial proletariat and its popularity with the lower middle class was increasing. There was much historical animosity to overcome, for the official socialist dismissal of the communists as a negligible band of fanatical outlaws had been only partially expiated in the tentative accord concluded by Szakasits and Kállai in October 1944.

**The Social Democrats.** At the time of the creation of the Debrecen provisional government, much of the old socialist leadership was still dispersed, in hiding, or in concentration camps. When their friend Szakasits finally reappeared, the communists were visibly relieved. Ideologically on the left wing of the SDP, Szakasits possessed a streak of decency but was a hopelessly indecisive and timorous figure. He was, along with many other noncommunist politicians, a potential subject of blackmail, for the Russians and the HCP had promptly assembled a file of his wartime anti-Soviet utterances.[54] A provisional agreement on close cooperation between the two working-class parties was concluded and subsequently confirmed by SDP and HCP representatives in Pest on 21 January. Thereupon a joint liaison committee was formed to coordinate the two parties' activities. The communists both feared and needed the SDP's large and experienced apparatus and therefore devoted great effort to win the socialists' support in the name of working-class unity. When, in Budapest on 19 February, the SDP's national leadership was reconstructed, it included under Szakasits the leftists Marosán and István Ries, the centrist Bán, and the more conservative Imre Szelig, Anna Kéthly, and (in absentia) Peyer. Marosán and Szakasits were from the start in regular contact with the communist leaders. Occasionally they were repelled by the latter's arrogance and expressed fear for the survival of an independent SDP, but they nevertheless generally served the interests of the HCP.

The communists initially put on a conciliatory mask. On 21 February Rákosi proclaimed that the collaboration was "not provisional and transitory but . . . designed for long years to come." Such reassurances stood in sharp contrast to the behavior of the more radical communist cadres, whose dictatorial exuberance and contempt for the SDP soon embittered interparty relations to the extent that the communist leaders had to at least go through the motions of counseling restraint. The ambivalence in their relationship was clearly voiced by Rákosi when he told a meeting of activists on 17 May that a middle road had to be followed. He criticized the excessively hostile stance of some communists, but allowed that he was "even more concerned" when he heard that comrades were getting along really well with the social democrats.[55]

Similar problems prevailed in the SDP, where many of the more moderate leaders and functionaries could not overcome their deep suspicion of communist designs. For the next three years the party would be torn and debilitated by debates on the appropriate relationship with the HCP and the other parties. The communists, for their part, were not prevented by the slogan of working-class unity from active recruitment among SDP members, nor did they cease to pursue control over the trade unions and the works committees. One of the major battles on the HCP's road to power was for official representation of the industrial working class. The nominal alliance with the more popular SDP was merely a tactic designed to incapacitate and ultimately liquidate the communists' historical rival.

The social democrats correctly identified the works committees as a communist challenge to their hold over the industrial workers, which they hoped to consolidate through the traditional trade unions and shop steward system. But there, too, the communists had seized the initiative. When the Trade Union Council was revived in early February 1945, pressure from the Russians and the Hungarian communists ensured the appointment of Kossa as secretary-general under the titular presidency of the left-wing socialist Ödön Kisházi. The communists quickly acquired a two-to-one majority on the council's secretariat and departmental staff. Although the majority of union members rallied to the reorganized SDP, the two parties agreed on equal allotment of trade union offices. Even so, a bitter and protracted struggle ensued.[56] The communists were determined to secure a commanding position in the unions and readily denounced unsympathetic socialists as traitors to the cause of working-class unity.

Communist tactics in the two parties' official relations consisted of courting left-wingers like Marosán and Szakasits and denouncing those leaders who saw through the communists' self-serving advocacy of working-class unity and their pro-Soviet line. The left-wing socialists were soon shown to represent a small but not ineffectual minority in the SDP, the majority of whose leadership remained attached to the philosophy of democratic socialism exemplified by the British Labour Party. In January the socialist spokesmen still favored the national committees, but by March the reorganized leadership was clearly hostile to the idea. Valentiny, the SDP justice minister, made attempts to mitigate the internment system and the excesses of the national committees. Meanwhile, the SHP's Ferenc Nagy replicated, with Tildy, the communists' efforts to draw the SDP into an alliance. An HCP report noted: "The social democratic right wing is showing growing inclination to concert with the reactionary wing of the SHP, and this makes all the more necessary the strengthening of the united front from below."[57] In other words, the anticommunist leadership of the SDP had to be undermined.

**The Communists Gird for Election.**   By the time the HCP held its first national conference in Budapest on 20 and 21 May, membership had risen to 150,000, and some 1,500 basic party cells were in existence. The 145 delegates heard reports on the political situation and party tasks by Rákosi, on trade union policy by Kádár, on amendment of the provisional party statutes by Gerő, and on the election of a new Central Committee by the recently repatriated Rajk.[58] Under the slogan "Battle for reconstruction," the conference laid stress on the party's leading role in reviving the economy, notably through restoring rail transport, nationalizing coal mines, and prosecuting speculators. It hailed cooperation with the "democratic forces" in the Independence Front and the consolidation of a united workers' front with the SDP. The conference also confirmed the expanded definition of the reactionary enemy and the need for more rigorous screening procedures in the public service. Some of the speakers, including Farkas, acknowledged the low competence of the communist-dominated police and the deluge of complaints at the arbitrary internments and other abuses, but it was argued that the alternatives were a fascist police and anarchy.

Both right-wing deviation, i.e., unreserved cooperation with other parties, and left-wing sectarianism, i.e., the radical advocacy of a proletarian dictatorship, were identified as divisive phenomena requiring correction by an intensive educational program. Rákosi branded the old comrades, the so-called 1919-ers, as politically backward and chiefly responsible for the left-wing distortions.

Indeed, under Rákosi's leadership the party's old guard would suffer from official disfavor. Kun would be mentioned seldom, and only disparagingly; his son-in-law Antal Hidas would be prevented from returning from the Soviet Union until 1957. The reasons for this depreciation of the veterans could be found in Stalin's purge of the Kun leadership and the latter's political shortcomings and inopportune radicalism; in Rákosi's own megalomania, which demanded the fictional embellishment of his minor role in the Commune at the expense of his erstwhile masters and comrades; and in the calculated rejection of extremism to enhance Rákosi's image as a reasonable centrist.

The conference enlarged the Central Committee to twenty-five members and created an eleven-member Politburo and a five-man Secretariat. The Politburo was composed of Rákosi, Farkas, Gerő, Horváth, Kádár, Kiss, Kovács, Kossa, Nagy, Rajk, and Révai. Apart from General Secretary Rákosi the Secretariat included Farkas, Kádár, Rajk, and Révai. The Muscovites were in a small numerical majority but continued to call the shots.

The HCP's leaders had become alarmed in early spring at the rapid expansion of the SHP. The latter, they concluded in April, was abandoning its "class party" role and becoming the collector party for reactionary elements who, in alliance with the kulaks, might gain control and leave Tildy and his left-liberal associates in a minority. Indeed, as the population began to recover from the horrors of war its overwhelmingly anticommunist predisposition asserted itself within the new political structure. Nevertheless, the communist-organized mass rallies on May Day persuaded Rákosi that the HCP's electoral chances were excellent. The rallies, he told the Central Committee four days later, were "successful beyond our expectations" and showed that the party's mass support was far greater than its organized complement. He predicted a "colossal communist–social democratic" success if municipal elections were held in Budapest. An additional consideration was that the food supply would be better in the fall (when in fact the Russians released new stocks) than the following spring. The HCP district secretaries, pressed to estimate local support, responded with wildly optimistic predictions, and despite some expressions of doubt the Secretariat was instructed to organize the electoral campaign.[59]

Moved by the calculation that their electoral chances were best in the Budapest area, the HCP leaders were adamant that the municipal elections come before (and, they hoped, favorably affect the outcome of) the national vote. The decision to hold general elections arose both from the communists' estimate of success and from the Soviet decision that Hungary should fulfill this precondition of Western recognition, which was made explicit by U.S. Secretary of State James Byrnes at the September meeting of the Council of Foreign Ministers in London. By midsummer the worsening economic crisis and the growing political strength of the noncommunists was making Rákosi apprehensive, and some of his colleagues urged postponing the elections. Even Soviet

Ambassador Pushkin and General Zamercev did not think that the HCP would receive more than 20 percent of the vote. The party leadership, however, continued to hope for a more favorable outcome.[60] At the same time, Rákosi decided to shift some of the party's energies away from reconstruction and toward the fight against reaction.

As public outrage mounted at the excesses of the AVO and the communist-dominated police, Justice Minister Valentiny proposed in late June the creation of a "judicial police" under his ministry's aegis to replace the AVO. This was readily accepted by the majority of the government, but the communists and the left-wing social democrats counterattacked and with Soviet support forced the withdrawal of the decree and Valentiny's resignation. He and the communists' other target, Faraghó, were replaced on 21 July by two left-wing socialists, Ries and Rónai.[61] In other changes, on 11 May Gerő took over commerce and transportation and the smallholder Ferenc Nagy reconstruction; on 1 June, Bán assumed the industry portfolio; and on 21 July, the smallholder Imre Oltványi took finance. In balance these shifts favored the left.

**The Smallholder and Third Road Challenges.** Rákosi's alarm was justified, for by the autumn of 1945 the SHP was emerging as a formidable political force attracting the support of a broad spectrum of the population. From its prewar status as a small opposition party representing the interests of the landed peasantry it had evolved into the principal rallying point of the anticommunist middle and upper classes and of the peasantry. The latter remained the party's mass basis, and at its conference on 20 August its members echoed their discontent at the prevailing compulsory delivery system amidst calls for a peasants' strike. The SHP leaders—including Dezső Sulyok, Béla Kovács, Ferenc Nagy, and Béla Varga—were united in their advocacy of a Western-style pluralistic democracy based on a mixed economy but preserving private property. They also hoped that, with temporary concessions to Soviet and HCP demands, the party could survive the period of occupation.

The smallholders' chronic inability to exploit their soon-to-be-demonstrated electoral strength was due to many factors. From the very beginning the party was constrained by the dictates of the occupying power. With Soviet support the HCP had gradually acquired a stranglehold over law enforcement agencies and most organs of local government, and this rendered the SHP visibly impotent. The social heterogeneity of the party's membership, ranging from peasants to bankers, militated against a coherent political strategy, and the communists exploited the more leftist inclination of a few leading smallholders such as Tildy, Gyula Ortutay, and Dobi. The last-named, an uneducated former laborer, was initially courted by both the SHP and the NPP but was advised by Rákosi that he would be most valuable if he joined the former.[62] Nor did the Russians and the communists shrink from the crudest forms of pressure to cow the smallholder leaders. Dredging up incriminating evidence from the political and private past of such prominent figures as Ferenc Nagy, Varga, Tildy, and Lajos Dinnyés, they repeatedly resorted to blackmail with varying success.[63] Summary trial, followed by deportation, was no idle threat in the circumstances of occupied Hungary.

Prevented from publicly exposing the extensive economic depredations and political blackmail of the Russians, and continually on the defensive in the face of Soviet-communist initiatives, the smallholders nevertheless labored to develop a realistic program. The party's avowedly pro-Western leadership considered reconstruction to be contingent on four factors: revival of the private sector; Western credits; return of confiscated property; and reduction of the costly Soviet army of occupation. The sympathetic but limited efforts of the American and British delegations to the Allied Control Commission were systematically obstructed by the Soviet authorities and denounced as unwarranted interference by the Hungarian communists, who by the middle of 1945 scarcely concealed their hatred of the Western powers.

The NPP was widely regarded as a branch of the HCP. The latter did little to dispel this impression, although it hoped that the NPP would draw away rural support from the smallholders.[64] Its Populist leadership was divided between those who, like Erdei and Darvas, were covert communists, and others, notably Imre Kovács and István Bibó, who leaned toward a Western-style social democracy adapted to the needs of the peasantry. Bibó sparked off a public debate in late 1945 with his advocacy of a third road between the Western and Eastern versions of democracy. He argued that a democratic, reformist alliance of the NPP and the SDP could forestall a destructive polarization between the communists on the left and the more conservative smallholders on the right. The democracy was in a state of crisis, wrote Bibó, for it lived in fear; he compared the arbitrary methods of the police to the excesses of the Horthy regime. In their prompt rebuttals, Révai and Lukács denounced such center-democratic consolidation as a fantasy favoring the right and asserted that the intelligentsia would follow the camp that showed the greater strength. Révai charged Bibó with aiming at the isolation of the HCP; ''as long as the major issues in a country's history [were] unresolved,'' he insisted, polarization was inevitable.[65] The HCP was able to exploit the equally realistic views of some other notables. The historian Szekfű, for instance, argued that Hungary could ignore neither the dominant proximity of the Soviet Union nor the reformist wave that was sweeping Europe. He was appointed ambassador to Moscow.[66] But the concept of a genuine third road, which enjoyed some currency also in social democratic circles, was consistently denigrated by the communists as an ahistorical illusion.

Within the SDP even Szakasits would claim after the Budapest election that his party was the democratic center between the two extremes, a center at which Eastern and Western democracy would be reconciled. But in the summer of 1945 many socialists were still susceptible to the HCP's professions of moderation and identity of purpose. This circumscribed sympathy was manifest at the party's 1945 congress, held from 18 to 20 August, which confirmed Szakasits as secretary-general. Despite widespread opposition, the left-wing socialist leaders managed to extract grudging acceptance of the communist proposal for a common list in the municipal elections due on 7 October.[67]

**Two Elections, Two Defeats.** The hopes of noncommunists for international supervision of the elections were dashed by the Russians, but they did succeed in reducing the franchise restrictions proposed by the HCP.[68] Meanwhile, on 7 August the HCP's Secretariat drew up plans for the training and mobilization of some fifteen hundred activists under Rajk's general direction for the conduct of house-to-house agitation. At the same time the party intensified its recruitment campaign at the expense of the more populous SDP. Harassment and intimidation became the common techniques for drawing the hapless industrial workers to their self-appointed champion.

The HCP's electoral platform, published in *Szabad Nép* on 23 September, proclaimed a three-year reconstruction program. This entailed the reduction of inflation by means of price and delivery controls on essential goods; a more progressive system of taxation; central control of bank credit; the return of Hungarian gold and currency reserves removed by the Germans; priority for the restoration of transportation facilities and of the mining and textile industries; implementation of the original proposals for partial nationalization and central control of industrial production and foreign trade; assistance to small industry; the full implementation of land reform; and support for the creation of collective farms. In the sphere of foreign policy the party urged implementation of the Potsdam Agreement on the expulsion of German-Hungarians; deplored "foreign interference in Hungary's internal affairs . . . which offers support to Hungarian reaction"; and condemned the Prague government's disposition to expel the Hungarian population of Slovakia, even making passing reference to the Kossuth ideal of a Danubian confederation.[69]

In the heat of the campaign, antagonism between the HCP and the SHP went beyond the level of vituperation as the communists resorted to violent disruption of their enemy's meetings. Relations between socialists and communists also degenerated into open hostility, although their parties were officially allied. Confident of success and fearing unnecessary international repercussions, the HCP negotiated a temporary electoral truce with the SHP on 26 September.

Rákosi had expected that the communists' mass agitation and their electoral alliance with the SDP would produce a resounding victory in the heavily working-class Budapest area. He was wrong. On 7 October the SHP won a clear majority (50.54 percent) of the votes, while the "United Workers' Front" received only 42.76 percent. Voroshilov was furious; reportedly, he slapped Rákosi in the face.[70] A smallholder victory celebration the next day was quickly followed by communist counterdemonstrations denouncing the forces of reaction. The new communist slogan was: "The worker's fist is a fist of iron, it will strike where necessary!" The electoral truce was over.

Meeting on the morrow of the election, the Politburo concluded that the party would have to adopt an even more aggressive stance with respect to the SHP and that propaganda and agitation at all levels would have to be intensified. The Central Committee meeting on 11 October found the principal reason for the poor results in the severe economic crisis. It also blamed the right-wing socialists, the anticommunist and anti-Soviet attitude of the middle classes, the influence of the churches, and the unreasonably broad franchise. The party retained its original program, but tried to tailor its campaign more to everyday practical issues.[71] The SDP leadership, for its part, came to the unanimous conclusion that the united front was to blame for the defeat. On 12 October it was decided that the SDP would run separately in the November general elections. Proclaiming the party to be the "bridge between East and West," the leadership anticipated that it would emerge as a dominant, centrist force in the new government.

On 16 October Marshal Voroshilov convoked the leaders of all parties to recommend a single-list electoral alliance and predetermine their shares in the national assembly. He proposed 40 percent for the SHP and made wild threats to enlarge the occupying army from 600,000 to 3 million and starve the country. The smallholders rejected even his final offer of 47.5 percent. Concurrently, a warning from the Western powers that they would withhold diplomatic recognition aborted the stratagem. Voroshilov did extract a tentative acquiescence that the coalition government would be preserved regardless of the election outcome.[72] Hoping to bolster the noncommunist forces, the United States recognized the provisional government on 2 November.

Millions of posters, huge placards bearing Rákosi's image, mass demonstrations, and protest strikes characterized the HCP's campaign, which benefited from Soviet-supplied funds and transportation that far surpassed the resources of the other parties. A handbook for repatriated prisoners of war claimed that "through Rákosi's intercession you came home before the conclusion of peace." It added: "Never forget this."[73] The communists were most infuriated by Cardinal Mindszenty's pastoral letter of 18 October in which he threw the full support of the Roman Catholic church behind the SHP, thereby abandoning its earlier promotion of various marginal Catholic parties. In contrast to the HCP and NPP, the smallholders were permitted an only limited campaign effort. Overt displays of anticommunism were repressed; both the Russians and the AVO arrested those who took part in them.

Although more Hungarians voted in the election of 4 November than ever before in the nation's history, the franchise was nevertheless restricted by the exclusion, on generally specious political grounds, of over 1 million names from the provisional list of 5.75 million.[74] Those prevented from voting were, it is safe to assume, all in the noncommunist camp. Even so, the SHP emerged as the dominant party, with 57 percent of the vote and 245 mandates (out of a total of 409). The HCP received 17 percent, including close to 180,000 in the Budapest area, and 70 seats, while its former partner, the SDP, gained 17.4 percent and 69 seats. The NPP won 23 seats and the Citizens' Democratic party 2. The SHP received a plurality in all 16 and a clear majority in all but 3 electoral districts. Even the socialists outperformed the HCP in 9 districts, including Budapest, where the communists predictably exceeded their national average.

**The Political Balance.**    It is hazardous to go beyond generalities in assessing the ideological significance of the election's outcome. All parties were committed to reconstruction and social and economic reform. The bulk of the SHP and SDP favored evolutionary change through a pluralistic democracy, the fostering of private enterprise or at least of a mixed economy, and resistance to Soviet and communist influence. The NPP's Populist orientation subsumed a vague agrarian socialism and an anachronistic preference for cottage industries, while its leaders' (and presumably its supporters') instrumental biases ranged from pluralistic to more revolutionary models. The HCP, as we have seen, was committed to industrial and agrarian socialization and to the leading role of the proletariat. These strategic goals, however, were subordinated at this stage to public advocacy of economic reconstruction by a "national unity" government that would be cleansed of what were vaguely defined as "reactionaries." Nevertheless, the HCP clearly presented itself as the party of radical social and economic change.[75]

However, these variations on the theme of modernization were overshadowed by popular perceptions of Soviet influence, of Hungary's national interests, and of the HCP's position on these issues. The wave of indiscriminate rapine and looting that accompanied liberation by the Red Army had surpassed the more selective depredations of the Gestapo and the Wehrmacht. It hardly alleviated the Hungarians' traditional hatred, already accentuated by the Horthy regime's propaganda, for Russia and its Bolshevik regime. Police terror and manipulated mobs seemed to confirm that the communists were intent on importing Stalin's political methods despite their occasional professions of moderation and tolerance. In these circumstances the HCP's Soviet parentage, its unstinting praise for the liberators, and its insistence that any aid for reconstruction was dependent on Soviet friendship and should not be sought from the capitalist West, could only arouse popular antagonism. The SHP, on the other hand, was perceived as the principal bulwark against Soviet influence and as the most likely defender of Hungary's territorial and ethnic interests. These included retention of at least part of the Magyar-inhabited areas lost at Trianon, regained by the Vienna Awards, and provisionally surrendered once again in the armistice agreement.

The SHP drew its support from all socioeconomic layers but most heavily from the urban middle class and the landowning peasantry (including, to the communists' chagrin, many recent beneficiaries of the land reform). The SDP's votes came mainly from organized labor, white-collar workers, and the left-liberal intelligentsia. The NPP's support was concentrated in the more impoverished rural areas. The HCP was thus left with the more easily radicalized elements of the industrial proletariat. It also enjoyed scattered support among the white-collar members of the lower-middle classes, including a large proportion of Jews, and with some radical young intellectuals. Révai, with disarming candor, had attempted to persuade the intelligentsia that the communist program was the only philosophically coherent and practically comprehensive answer to Hungary's problems. Calling for a new intellectual front, he wrote: "If we wanted to move ahead only with those who always stood on the left and without those who shifted from the right to the left, we would have hardly any fellow travellers beyond a handful of men."[76] Very few responded to his siren song.

## COALITION IMPOSED

The smallholders soon discovered that electoral success could not readily be translated into political power. Although Voroshilov now diplomatically told the SHP leaders that the Soviet Union "wishes to base its friendship with Hungary on its relations with the Smallholder party," he backed the communists in keeping concessions to a minimum.[77] The party's rank and file clamored for an exclusively SHP government, but Tildy ignored them and acceded to communist demands that the SHP receive only the premiership and half the cabinet posts. The smallholders were initially successful in nominating Béla Kovács to the interior portfolio. As the days went by, however, the communists raised their requirements for a "stronger government." The dispute was once again settled by the intervention of Voroshilov, who called the party leaders together on 14 November. At the last minute Rákosi had threatened to withdraw from the coalition if his party did not get the interior ministry, which it allegedly needed both in order to "lead the fight against reaction" and for its own protection.[78] Tildy caved in, with consequences that were accurately predicted in a telegram of protest from a smallholder county secretary to the party leader: "Loss of interior portfolio will mean death of SHP. Our further work is futile."[79] At the grass roots, victory seemed ephemeral indeed. In one instance, when the smallholders attempted to organize a mass meeting of peasants at Miskolc, Nógrádi and the SDP representative applied "moral pressure" to have it called off.[80]

In the cabinet approved by Voroshilov, Tildy became prime minister, while Dobi, Szakasits, and Rákosi were named ministers of state. Of the fourteen departmental portfolios the SHP received seven, the SDP and HCP three each, and the NPP one. The coveted interior ministry was given to the communist Imre Nagy, Gerő took transportation, and Erik Molnár public welfare. The SDP ministers, Szakasits, Bán, Ries, and Rónai, belonged to the left or left-center of the party, as was the case with Dobi and Tildy in the SHP. In its political coloring the Tildy government was hardly an accurate reflection of the popular will, but it was nevertheless more representative than the governments imposed on Bulgaria and Romania.

The program announced in parliament by Tildy on 30 November ostensibly demonstrated the coalition's unity of purpose in the pursuit of objectives that actually differed little from the HCP's electoral platform. The ensuing debate skirted controversy apart from the sharply differing views of Rajk, who demanded the purge of the civil service, and of noncommunists denouncing the undeniable excesses of the "democratic" police. But the real struggle for power was only beginning. Its character would be determined by the HCP's assessment of Soviet wishes and of domestic factors. In his postmortem on the election, Révai allowed that compared to those in Bulgaria and Yugoslavia it had been more democratic in form, but not in substance, since the right had been allowed to win. He blamed the deep roots of Hungarian reaction, the unexpectedly lasting influence of the Horthy regime on public opinion, the absence of a domestic revolution, and the historical weaknesses of the left. The votes cast for the HCP were, he claimed, qualitatively superior and homogeneous. Looking to the future, he called for alliance with the other parties against their right wings. No single party or class could solve Hungary's burning problems, he reasoned. National unity was essential for survival; therefore the coalition leadership had to be homogeneous; therefore the coalition parties would have to rid themselves of those who stood in the way of homogeneity and unity. "Who isolates whom: only a struggle can decide this question, and the battle is far from over."[81]

Confident of Soviet support, the communists would act as if they, and not the SHP, had received the endorsement of the majority of Hungarians. There was no need for bargaining, declared Rákosi later. "If" he trumpeted, "for twenty-five years no one could destroy us, no enemy could tear the red banner from our hands, now that we have the direct support of the Soviet Union, the outcome of the struggle cannot be doubted."[82] The people of Hungary had simply failed to recognize the desirability and inevitability of communist rule.

# 8. The Tactics of Attrition, 1945–1947

Massive rejection by the electorate spurred the HCP to what Rákosi would proudly describe as "salami tactics": the progressive slicing up and debilitation of the organized majority. "We communists," he said at a lecture at the party's political academy on 19 January 1946, "understand by democracy the decisive influence of workers, peasants, and the progressive intelligentsia on the government and administration of a country." The reactionary enemy constituted a "resilient stratum accustomed to a century of governance, self-confident, attached to traditions that reject democracy." The transition to democracy would be a slow and difficult process. Secular expertise would have to take second place to political convictions and class background in the staffing of the public service, notably the police. Hungarian "fascists" had adopted the tactic of infiltrating certain legal parties, and the latter should not take umbrage when other parties exposed this great peril. The HCP desired democracy and independence, he asserted; it did not wish to turn Hungary into a Soviet satellite.[1]

## THE COMMUNIST OFFENSIVE

The ideological context remained that of people's democracy, but the official interpretation of this elusive concept underwent a certain alteration as the Kremlin reassessed its relations with the Western powers. The signals sent by Stalin to his East European disciples indicated the need both for tactical flexibility and for a clearer expression of the ultimate goal. The Bulgarian communist leader Dimitrov proclaimed in February 1946 that "the peoples will reach socialism not along a uniform, stereotyped road, not exactly on the Soviet road, but along their own particular roads."[2] The lessons of this address were drawn to Rákosi's attention in a letter dated 4 April from the party's representative in Moscow, Rezső Szántó. The latter criticized Révai for arguing that, since the party's weakness and Soviet foreign policy required collaboration with other political forces, the immediate goal was not socialism. It would be better to emphasize, wrote Szántó, that "in the current phase the battle [was] for the creation of the preconditions of socialism."[3]

Publicly, at least, Révai continued to maintain that while formerly communists had considered the proletariat, first in revolt and then as dictator, to be the only bringer of socialism, "this distinction between social democracy and communism was in the process of disappearing from history's agenda." The party's objective remained a people's democracy, which was not synonymous with socialism but was a variant of bourgeois democracy. That such semantic convolutions served at least in part the purpose of obscuring the party's strategic goal was conceded by Révai when, in 1949, he observed that in the midst of the struggle for power it had been appropriate "not to uncover our cards."[4] Referring to the coalition's place in party strategy, Rákosi would explain years later that "we could not inform [the party rank and file] about these questions in 1945, and only within very narrow circles did we discuss these problems. We did not mention this to the party members at that time, since to assert even theoretically that our goal was the dictatorship of the proletariat would have created great difficulties for our winning the support of the petite bourgeoisie and even that of the majority of workers."[5]

Rákosi would exult in November 1948 that "seldom in history has a program been implemented so exactly as was the November 1944 program of the HCP."[6] Assertions of this sort were designed to demonstrate the inexorability of the party's march to monopoly power, but they probably understated the element of chance. As was noted earlier, Stalin had personally recommended a coalition format for the party's reentry into Hungarian political life (it was, of course, a time when the Grand Alliance was still in existence). Thereafter, the HCP leadership did indeed work in close collaboration with Voroshilov and the other resident Soviet officials to expand its power. Questions of long-term strategy, however, were Stalin's domain, and his instructions, as far as can be ascertained, were infrequent and elliptical. Stalin's subordinates may have occasionally forced the pace of consolidation of communist power in Hungary and the rest of East-Central Europe, but the Soviet leader himself probably had no blueprint for the timing and modalities of political change in the area.

The Soviet Union's determination to secure a sphere of influence that included Hungary was never in real doubt. Ambassador Pushkin once remarked in the presence of the social democrat Antal Bán: "We have shed our blood for Hungary and we do not want to loosen our grip on her."[7] But the immediate communist tactics appeared to be improvised accommodations to domestic developments, accommodations that were informed by only short-range guidance from the Soviet authorities. The concurrent and precipitous disintegration of the wartime alliance was due only in part to the West's dismay—voiced eloquently in Churchill's "iron curtain" speech at Fulton, Missouri, on 5 March 1946—at

Stalin's proprietary view of East-Central Europe. It is nonetheless clear that the consequent hostility impelled the Soviet leader to accelerate the consolidation of his Western approaches.

The HCP was therefore instructed to intensify its drive to hegemony. Rezső Szántó's criticism helped to set the process in motion. Rákosi reacted by informing the Central Committee at its meeting of 17 May that while in the beginning it had been necessary to restrain hotheads who advocated instant socialism and a soviet republic, "the time had come to remind our party and the working class that we are also socialists." The time was drawing near, he asserted, when socialism could be realized. International considerations were no longer regarded as a major constraint.[8]

In practice, the message from Moscow only reinforced the decision, adopted by the party leadership on 22 November 1945, to stage a counterattack. The presence of communists and sympathizers in the new government, as well as communist acquisition of the interior portfolio, would serve the struggle from above; so, too, would the creation of a supreme economic directorate to exercise an "economic dictatorship." The battle from below would meanwhile demonstrate the grass-roots support for communist objectives. "There is a place in a democracy for spontaneous acts of the masses," said Rákosi, "and it is only right that the people should take justice into its own hands when it sees fit."[9]

Concurrently the party organization was revamped to turn it into a more disciplined and unified weapon. A three-man "high secretariat" was created; it consisted of Rákosi and two deputy secretaries-general, Farkas and Rajk. A Central Control Committee was instituted with the task of extirpating corruption and strengthening party morale. Regional committees were replaced by county committees; the idea was to adjust the party's line of command to the levels of state administration, which was based on counties. A euphemistically named Organizing Guard (Rendező gárda) was formed to serve as the HCP's paramilitary security force. Organized under the supervision of the Soviet General Zabersky, the guard included by the summer of 1946 some twenty-five thousand activists, many of them former Arrow Cross thugs and assorted criminals. New central departments were created to coordinate the work of communists in the state administration and the major industries. Although the policy of indiscriminate mass recruitment was retained, steps were taken to improve the new adherents' indoctrination. They were also encouraged to play a more active part in internal party affairs as well as in the party's public campaigns, notably those for coal production and for the purge of reactionaries. The Secretariat decreed that all party units had to hold one membership meeting, two "party days" (i.e., special days of party activities), and one cultural evening each month.[10]

**Who Speaks for the Workers?** Since the supremacy of the industrial working class was ideologically preordained, it was imperative for the HCP to assume the role of its sole legitimate spokesman. By late 1945, the fifty-odd organizations under the umbrella of the Trade Union Council counted close to a million members. The largest, with a membership of 160,000, was the National Federation of Agricultural Workers and Small Proprietors (Földmunkások és Kisbirtokosok Országos Szövetsége, or FEKOSZ). The HCP had succeeded in implanting a communist majority in the leadership of most unions, which in turn facilitated control over the works committees. In others they shared the leadership with the SDP, and only in a few professional unions were the communists in a clear minority. Most of the communist positions were acquired through manipulation and intimidation; the wishes of the rank-and-file majority and of their socialist leaders were overridden. Nevertheless, the HCP would claim the backing of organized labor and ensure that at the national congress of trade unions, held on 2 December 1945, the majority of delegates were communist. The more moderate SDP leaders failed to have their party boycott the congress and withdraw from the Trade Union Council (which was led by Kossa), but they did intensify their campaign for a more realistic allocation of union posts and for the election of works committees. At the HCP's instigation the congressional resolutions surpassed the party's own program, notably in the demand for nationalization of more industries. This was only one example of the communist stratagem "from below": the artificial generation of radical group or mass demands that would then be used to buttress the party's pressures on the enemy.

Distributing posts and preserving its influence over organized labor and working youth were tasks that much exercised the SDP. Its former leader, Károly Peyer, attempted in late January 1946 to sever the party from the Szakasits clique, but the left-wingers, thanks to communist support, managed to repulse this challenge with appeals to working-class unity. The hotly contested works committee elections, which lasted until the end of March, increased the representation of social democrats. Overall, however, the communists still held a narrow majority of the offices. Socialist protests at the abuses perpetrated by communists in the conduct of these elections impelled the HCP leadership to make conciliatory gestures and blame individual zealotry, but this scarcely altered the outcome.[11]

The communists' aggressive recruitment in industry—not only of workers but also of technical and managerial staff—only exacerbated the two parties' relations in this key sector. A national conference of social democratic rail workers at Cegléd turned into a bitter attack on the HCP's brutal recruitment practices and on the Szakasits leadership. The consternation at SDP headquarters reached new heights. Marosán was sent to negotiate with Rajk on the most sensitive issue, the distribution of posts in the interior ministry. He complained that communist recruitment frequently took the form of ''join the party or lose your job,'' and that ''when a minor fascist joined the communist party, he automatically ceased to be a fascist.'' According to Marosán, Ambassador Pushkin spent hours ''brainwashing'' him on the iniquities of the SDP right wing and on the need for collaboration between the two parties. The same themes were pursued by his communist interlocutors, Révai indicating to him that the road led to a coalescence of communists and leftist socialists.[12]

When the prospect of fusion was aired by Rákosi at a joint meeting of the two parties' functionaries on 29 April, the socialist reaction was anything but favorable. At a Central Committee meeting on 19 May, Rákosi acknowledged that the proposal had been ill received and concluded that it would have to be kept alive as only a remote objective.[13] Nevertheless the alarm had been sounded, and the SDP moderates eagerly took this cue to rally the troops. There was plenty of evidence that at the grass roots the HCP was not immune from its own weapons of street protest. The communist propaganda campaign against profiteers backfired. At Miskolc, in particular, a demonstration by miners and other workers on 30 July not only acquired anti-Semitic overtones but also resulted in the killing of a communist officer. The anticommunist tone of an SDP mass meeting in Debrecen strengthened the resolve of the more conservative socialist leaders, including Szeder and Kéthly, who in mid-1946 began to agitate in favor of abandoning the alliance with the HCP and exploring an alternative collaboration with the SHP.[14]

**Tests of Strength.**   After the November 1945 general elections a wave of overt anticommunism had swept the country. Many local HCP organizations saw their membership decline or, in a few cases, disappear entirely.[15] The emboldened smallholders urged proportional reapportionment of administrative and police posts, which the communists resisted momentarily by defending the status quo. From the highest to the lowest levels of the public service, the parties fought bitterly for these ''positions of power.'' Even village cinemas were a subject of apportioning disputes. Having acquired the interior portfolio, the HCP was able to sustain and expand its initial advantage in the police forces. It therefore gained a wide degree of control over the central and local administrative apparatus of the state, effectively isolating the population from the noncommunist majority in the government. Nevertheless, restoration of order had brought about a certain dilution of communist predominance, and by the end of 1945 only 19 percent of the Greater Budapest police forces' complement belonged to the HCP.[16] There, and in the civil service, drastic measures were clearly necessary if the party was to remain a potent political force.

The stakes were equally high in the armed forces, whose anticommunist orientation remained largely impervious to the efforts of the HCP's indoctrination teams. The problem was resolved by the simple expedient of disbanding one army and creating another. In October 1945 the Soviet head of the Allied Control Commission had directed that the armed forces be reduced from the 70,000 permitted by the armistice to a maximum of 20,000. Within a few months the dismissals, which aimed first and foremost at the pro-Western officer corps, lowered the complement even below that ceiling. At the same time, the frontier guard was doubled in size to 10,000 and converted into a communist armed force under Pálffy. The defense ministry's military-political department, also headed by Pálffy, meanwhile arranged for untrained but politically reliable recruits to be promoted to officer rank. By June 1946 some 60 percent of the truncated regular army's officers and noncommissioned officers were party members or sympathizers.[17] The entire operation was coordinated by the HCP's new Military Committee under Farkas. The party, however, had been less effective in subverting the armed forces than the Soviet-directed Allied Control Commission (the authority of the Hungarian defense minister, who was a smallholder, counted for very little).

In rural areas the NPP's right wing also reached for independence from the communists by moving toward a more positive relationship with the SHP. The latter took up the cudgels for those who had been unfairly dispossessed during the precipitous implementation of the land reform and urged judicial review of the innumerable contested cases. The HCP responded by calling the land-distribution committees' communist members to a national conference that proclaimed the slogan "Land we will not return!" (*Földet vissza nem adunk*). The communist-manipulated mass protests persuaded the smallholders in the government that the land reform, for all its arbitrary injustices, was best left as a fait accompli, and legislation confirming this was duly passed. On 23 February, Prime Minister Ferenc Nagy made a further concession in replacing the moderate Béla Kovács with Dobi as minister of agriculture.

The battle for the peasantry's political allegiance was not so easily resolved. In the summer of 1946 the HCP initiated a "village visitor movement" in which workers' brigades, led by trained agitators, descended on the countryside to bring political enlightenment. The party had earlier launched the National Federation of New Farmers and Land Recipients (Ujgazdák és Földhözjuttatottak Országos Szövetsége, or UFOSZ). This federation was designed both to supplement the FEKOSZ, whose laborer image repelled most newly landed farmers, and to compete with the Peasant Federation, which had been reorganized by Ferenc Nagy and was also recruiting among the beneficiaries of the reform. The group around Imre Kovács tried to steer the NPP toward affiliation with the Peasant Federation, but the left-dominated leadership opted for the communist UFOSZ. In spite of this, the UFOSZ was a failure. "The bulk of the peasantry," reported Révai, "stands behind the SHP, and we have not been successful in setting the poorer peasants against the kulaks."[18] Another aspect of the rural battle concerned the national producers' cooperatives, the principal and oldest of which, the Ant (Hangya), was under SHP control. The communists' initial attempt to replace the Ant by a new network failed after protracted parliamentary and grass-roots skirmishes. Only in March 1947, when the SHP had been largely incapacitated, did the government legislate a single institutional cooperative framework that served the HCP's interests.[19]

One of the least controversial acts of the new government was the proclamation of a republic on 31 January 1946. There was some debate regarding the powers of the presidency and its first incumbent. The communists and their allies advocated restricted powers, fearing exploitation of the office by the SHP, and they promoted the candidacy of the most congenial smallholder, Zoltán Tildy, who was duly acclaimed on 1 February. (The centrist and right-wing SDP leaders and the fringe Hungarian Radical Party had put forward the candidacy of Károlyi, but Rákosi was adamant, arguing that the latter had lived in England too long and had probably been influenced by the capitalistic ethos.)[20] The smallholders' first nominee for the premiership, the capable and popular Sulyok, was vetoed by Voroshilov, and the less gifted and experienced Ferenc Nagy was consequently appointed to succeed Tildy.

If the SHP exercised a nominal preeminence in the government, the communists ruled the streets. Here their ability to mobilize mass protests was unrivaled; although the noncommunists, with the instrumental aid of Cardinal Mindszenty and the clergy, would mount their own public rallies, notably a massive one in Budapest on 10 February. The mass-movement tactic devised by the HCP in early 1946 was intended to serve the party's immediate objectives, which Rákosi at a public meeting on 16 February enumerated as fighting inflation, implementing the nationalization program (and introducing production controls), purging the civil service, and legally confirming the changes in land ownership. There followed a series of communist-organized mass meetings, often degenerating into violence, that were designed to give the impression of mass support. On 23 February, Kossa led a Trade Union Council delegation, with several thousand demonstrators in its wake, to demand that Prime Minister Nagy conduct the purge of the state bureaucracy with the participation of trade union advisers.[21]

**The Left-Wing Bloc.**   These "mass movements" were then utilized by the HCP to exert pressure from above on the majority party. At its meeting of 28 February the Politburo decided that the party should "alter its former stand and openly blame the reactionaries in the SHP for the state of the nation and demand a settling of accounts with the reaction as the indispensable precondition for financial reform and the country's reconstruction."[22] The communists thereupon engineered the formation of a so-called Left-Wing Bloc consisting of the HCP, the SDP, the NPP, and the Trade Union Council. On 6 March the bloc proclaimed its unwillingness to cooperate with the SHP's ''reactionary right wing'' and its readiness to mobilize workers and peasants in defense of the land reform and against capitalist sabotage. It also reiterated the Trade Union Council's demand for a supervised purge and urged further nationalization (the coal mines had already been brought under state control on 1 January), plus state supervision of the banks. The following day 300,000 demonstrators were marshaled under the slogan ''Out with the people's enemies from the coalition!''

The SHP leadership was unable to withstand the left's offensive and agreed to expel twenty of the party's deputies, including such prominent figures as Sulyok and Vince Nagy. In its efforts to appease the Left-Wing Bloc it later made other changes in personnel; Gyula Dessewffy, for instance, was replaced as its newspaper's editor. With these successes in hand, the Politburo decided on 12 March to suspend its mass agitation, which had already provoked serious friction within the bloc and had also backfired against the local communists in many districts.[23]

Although Dobi and five of his fellow leftists in the SHP had issued a statement concurring with the bloc's demands, a report to the HCP Central Committee on 17 May admitted that communist attempts to organize a leftist faction within the SHP had been a signal failure. The Central Committee nevertheless decided that further efforts from above and below were imperative in order to move the equilibrium leftward in the SHP.[24] The communists further hoped that a purge of the SHP's rural organizations might lead to a shift in peasant support toward the HCP.

The smallholders counterattacked on 21 May with a memorandum to the other parties requesting a more proportional allocation of administrative posts and the early calling of local elections. The latter proposal embarrassed the HCP leadership, which feared that reactivating the nationwide agitation necessary for such elections would only further undermine the party's popularity. They therefore adopted a delaying tactic on the pretext that ''those who want elections impede reconstruction.''[25] At the same time the communists turned a deaf ear to the vociferous SHP campaign in parliament against the illegalities perpetrated by the police and accused the smallholders of economic sabotage and anti-Soviet propaganda.

The socialists' mounting dissatisfaction, and also, to some extent, the wavering within the NPP, impelled the HCP to organize a mass meeting at Kaposvár on 26 May for a public show of left-wing unity. With the participation of Rákosi, Bán, and Veres, the assembly confirmed that the defense of democracy could not be left to a heterogeneous, disunited, insufficiently purged SHP but had to be shouldered by the Left-Wing Bloc. A few days later, at a meeting of the bloc's executive committee, Rákosi outlined a response to the SHP memorandum. Reapportionment, he argued, should be rejected as untimely in view of the concurrent preparations for the Paris Peace Conference and for financial reform; while local elections could be accepted in principle, effectively they would be postponed. Some participants, including Rajk and Marosán, held that even this was too much of a compromise with the enemy.[26]

**The Abuses of the Interior Ministry.** In the midst of these political maneuvers the purge of the state administration was proceeding apace. From the very beginning the HCP, realizing that the overwhelming majority of civil servants were anticommunist, had assigned high priority to this task. All the parties in the Independence Front had originally agreed to a housecleaning, and the provisional government had decreed on 4 January 1945 that state employees should be politically screened. The communists were disappointed with the outcome, for in the course of 1945 only a small fraction of the central and regional administrative complement were dismissed on grounds of demonstrable fascist collaboration.[27] The hopes of the SDP and the NPP for a massive entry by their members into the ranks of the civil service were similarly unfulfilled. The smallholders, on the other hand, found themselves defending the apolitical expertise of the old civil servants against unwarranted allegations of political unreliability.

The plan developed by the HCP in late November 1945 linked the political goal with the generally recognized economic necessity of trimming the bureaucracy. From the party's perspective, the savings were clearly less important than the replacement of inimical administrators by reliable communists. The party therefore launched a nationwide campaign on behalf of the proposed purge. "The purge of reactionary civil servants from the machinery of state," proclaimed a resolution of the Budapest party conference in early January 1946, "is the touchstone of Hungarian democracy and the precondition of its further development."[28] Since Marosán took part in the interparty discussions superficial agreement on communist terms was achieved without too much difficulty. At bottom, however, the socialists feared for their recently acquired positions and regarded the purge with ambivalence. The smallholders, for their part, could not deny the economic imperatives but suggested that the less-qualified civil servants were the redundant ones. These happened to be mainly the postwar plants of the left-wing parties.

While the national committees controlled by the left were mobilized to agitate for the purge, the HCP leadership came to the conclusion that Imre Nagy was unequal to the task of converting the interior ministry into an effective communist weapon. On 8 March the Politburo nominated László Rajk as his replacement; the switch was implemented twelve days later. Through the energetic Rajk the party thus secured effective control over local and regional administration, the police, and citizenship matters, a supervisory function over the press and all recognized social organizations, and a critical role in the drafting of legislation.

Organized pressure from below and from the newly formed Left-Wing Bloc compelled the SHP to seek a compromise. A tentative draft, prepared in mid-March by Finance Minister Ferenc Gordon, a smallholder, and Justice Minister Ries, a socialist, provided for the placing on "B-lists" of both antidemocratic and unqualified civil servants (excluding judges and elected administrators) by an orderly screening system that pointedly ignored the request of the Trade Union Council for a voice in the purge. The communists rejected the proposal both for its threat to recent recruits and for its slow and purely administrative selection process. The B-list decree that was finally promulgated on 19 May provided both for a ceiling on the dismissal of postwar appointees and for trade-union participation (which in the circumstances meant additional communist participation) in the screening committees.

By that time the purge was well under way thanks to the initiative of Rajk, who ensured that the interior ministry's organizing function would be an exclusively communist preserve.[29] Rajk was well placed to engineer the appointment of communists and left-wing socialists to the screening committees, whose task was to ascertain whether an individual's work "positively served the democratically inspired reshaping of the country." The purge led to the suspension of some sixty thousand civil servants and was marked by absurd communist excesses, including the indiscriminate dismissal of virtually all rural public notaries and, in at least two districts, the liquidation of the entire administrative apparatus. Many civil servants had hurriedly joined the SDP in the hope of saving their jobs. A notable feature of the purge was quarreling between the two working-class parties.

Indeed, the communists' blatant exploitation of the B-list operation aroused such violent antagonism within the coalition and the Left-Wing Bloc that the HCP was compelled to agree to a partial revision later that summer. Although in a few instances the smallholders and the social democrats succeeded in turning the revision against communist incumbents, it was preordained that the purge would benefit the HCP. Within the already communist-dominated police, the net result of the dismissal of some five thousand men was a relative increase in communist strength.[30] Addressing the party's third congress in September, Rajk observed: "It is not in our program, nor even in our established customs, to promote our people's progress on the road to democracy necessarily by forcible and painful measures. . . . However, if progress cannot be ensured by gentle methods, . . . then the great cause of the people compels us to implement the kind of painful operation that was the B-list."[31] In fact, the purge had been a two-edged sword, for it dealt a blow to the prestige of both the HCP (particularly among the intelligentsia) and the SHP, which had proven incapable of imposing orderly and equitable procedures.

The Left-Wing Bloc's Kaposvár declaration had only heightened tensions within the coalition. None of the parties, however, was eager to break the coalition and assume sole responsibility either for the formidable task of economic reconstruction or for the thankless pursuit of a palatable peace settlement. At a meeting in Tildy's country villa on 5 June the coalition party leaders hammered out a modus vivendi encompassing joint elaboration of a one-year government program, the eventual holding of local elections, and the concession of a few additional administrative and police posts for the SHP. The prospect of local elections momentarily galvanized the SHP, for it reasonably expected that the outcome would confirm its popular majority.[32]

The communists returned to the attack with the Bloc's "Open Letter to SHP Members," published on 23 June, which called on the smallholders to loyally implement the agreement of 5 June and warned them against exploiting their hold over the discontented peasantry. While conceding that the SHP's protests at the imperfect application of the majority principle were technically not unfounded, the letter insisted that the only valid expression of majority was one that included the Left-Wing Bloc. Concurrently, the communists revived the idea of a left-wing fusion by proposing the formation of unified local committees of the bloc parties. But the SDP leadership (apart from Marosán) rejected this out of hand.

When the initial, relatively unbridled persecution of political opponents by the communist-led police was superseded by a more orthodox state administration, the necessity arose for new legal pretexts to justify the political pursuits of Rajk's interior ministry. In December 1945 the SHP had endorsed the need for a new legal formulation of the defense of democratic freedoms against both left and right extremism, but the draft presented by Justice Minister Ries in January focused on incitement against the democratic state (replacing the Horthy regime's proscription of "anticlass incitement") and on the jurisdiction of the notorious people's courts. The debate over the operative definition of "democratic state system" reached its climax at the same time that the Left-Wing Bloc was formed and Sulyok and other diehard anticommunists were expelled from the SHP.[33] Bowing to Soviet and leftist pressure, Ferenc Nagy endorsed the bill for the protection of the republic and public order, and it was promulgated on 12 March.

Armed with what became popularly known as the "executioners' law," Rajk instigated a campaign of harassment that brought, for instance, police searches of parochial schools and the discovery of planted weapons, all of which was designed to demonstrate the antidemocratic machinations of the Roman Catholic church. In June 1946 the murder of a Russian soldier (apparently by one of his comrades) was blamed on a member of a Catholic youth organization. The communist-led bloc promptly called for a pursuit of right-wing extremists and for an investigation of the organizing activities of the clergy.[34] The Soviet head of the Allied Control Commission thereupon sent a note to the government demanding the dissolution of all organizations that could be suspected of involvement in actions against Red Army personnel or in agitation against the people's democracy. Rajk happily complied by ordering the disbandment, between 4 and 6 July, of some 220 "right-wing" organizations, including the Boy Scouts and the Catholic young peasants' movement. When at a meeting of coalition leaders on 8 July the SHP representatives protested at this excessive fulfillment of the Soviet request, Rákosi retorted that the hostile right wing of the SHP also had to be liquidated. As long as this was not done, he added, there could and would be no tranquillity.[35]

At subsequent interparty discussions, which at the left's insistence were also attended by the compliant Tildy, Rákosi dismissed the idea of holding local elections in September on the usual pretext of allowing for undisturbed financial stabilization. Révai offered to make apportioning concessions as soon as the SHP conducted a new purge of its membership. Fearing the HCP's ability to activate public violence, Prime Minister Ferenc Nagy once again complied, and a new compromise agreement was reached on 16 July. The official communiqué acknowledged that reactionary elements had exploited the country's difficult situation, called for a sustained fight against them within and outside the coalition, and anticipated the preparation of administrative and electoral reforms that would allow local elections to be held that autumn. But the desperate Ferenc Nagy had to recognize that he had no effective influence in the most critical spheres of government. When in August he made a futile attempt to regain some control over the interior ministry, Rajk haughtily protested at this "unwarranted lack of confidence" in him and his party.[36]

## ECONOMICS AND FOREIGN RELATIONS

The acquisition of "economic dictatorship" was a key component in the strategy developed by the HCP leadership. This assumption of responsibility was perhaps inescapable for a party whose ideology allegedly rested on superior economic insight, so that it claimed to possess the remedy to the plight of the working masses. The task was nevertheless unenviable in light of the lamentable state of Hungary's economy.

**The Price of Defeat.** By rough estimate the material loss attributable to war damage and German removals amounted to 40 percent of the national wealth at its 1944 level. In addition, over 600,000 Hungarians had lost their lives in the war and in German concentration camps. These immense losses were capped by the economic costs of liberation by the Soviet Union. The massive looting by the Red Army as invader paled in significance beside its organized pillage as occupying power. Over the nine months from November 1944 to July 1945 that Hungarian enterprises were under military management, some 75 percent of industrial output was requisitioned by the Russians for military and reconstruction purposes. Soviet management was distinguished by arbitrariness, confiscation of liquid assets, depletion of stocks, and nonpayment of workers.[37] The Russians later loaned back the confiscated liquid assets at high interest rates. The government was also compelled to convert Soviet-printed Hungarian currency by February 1946. All these measures contributed heavily to the inflationary spiral. The seizure of booty from a defeated power is of course a time-hallowed practice, but the Soviet Union thereby tarnished its image of liberator and complicated the task of its communist servants. At the same time, however, the debilitating effect of military management on the private sector served the anticapitalist interests of the HCP. In the agricultural sector, as noted above, the Russians seized most of the livestock and accumulated produce.

The reparations agreement allocated $200 million to the Soviet Union and $100 million to Czechoslovakia and Yugoslavia. However, the foregoing massive confiscations were not deducted from these amounts. Moreover, the use of unrealistic exchange rates at least doubled and possibly quintupled the actual cost of reparations.[38] In the 1945–46 period almost 90 percent of heavy industrial production was allocated to reparations. The following year, when to aid the HCP's financial stabilization scheme the Soviet Union rescheduled the reparations over 8 instead of the original 6 years, they still absorbed 60 percent of that production. (After the communist seizure of power in 1948 the Soviet Union reduced by half the outstanding reparations.) The pressure to finance reparations by expanding the money supply was irresistible, with the inflationary consequence that by the end of 1945 the cost of living was increasing at the rate of 15 percent per hour. Fear of antagonizing the occupation authorities and recognition that reparations were the price of defeat led to suppression of official comment on these causes of inflation, although a few noncommunist politicians, notably Sulyok, would dare to raise the issue in passing.

The Allied allocation of German and Italian assets to the occupying power had a major impact on Hungary, where between 1938 and 1942 German ownership had increased dramatically. The Soviet Union thus acquired 201 formerly German-owned enterprises. (These assets, with an estimated value in 1952 of $900 million, were subsequently repurchased by Hungary for roughly half that sum.)[39] The disposition of partially German- or Italian-owned assets was settled when, at the Russians' invitation, a Hungarian delegation led by Commerce Minister Gerő visited Moscow in August 1945. Taking advantage of a virtual carte blanche from the inexperienced prime minister, General Miklós, Gerő agreed not only to a comprehensive trade pact but also to the creation of Soviet-Hungarian joint-stock companies based on the remaining German and Italian assets.[40] The two countries held equal shares in the five companies that were formed in early 1946, but the latter were in practice Soviet managed and had to be granted various concessions, exemptions, and additional Hungarian capital. These joint-stock companies dominated Danubian shipping, civil aviation, the bauxite-aluminum industry, and the petroleum industry. The aggregate Soviet gain from various forms of exploitation is difficult to estimate, but it may have amounted to as much as $3 billion between 1945 and 1955. In the same period, the wealth extracted by the Soviet Union from its sphere in East-Central Europe was roughly equivalent to the Marshall Plan aid for Western Europe.

The provisional government endorsed the Soviet-Hungarian trade agreement on 15 October 1945 with the qualification that it was in no way discriminatory against other states. Although individual smallholders continued to voice reservations, it was ratified by the new government on 20 December. In the meantime, the United States and Great Britain had delivered a barrage of notes protesting the apparently exclusive provisions of the trade and economic cooperation pact. The Americans did not conceal their view that Hungary's economic problems derived in large measure from Soviet occupation policies, and they proposed a tripartite commission to develop a rehabilitation program. Although the SHP and the senior noncommunist administrators were eager for such multilateral assistance, neither they nor the Western allies could overcome the opposition of the Soviet Union and the HCP. In fact, even Washington was decidedly ambivalent, on the one hand expecting the smallholders to stand firm against communist encroachments, and on the other, in the words of Ferenc Nagy, urging Hungary ''to cultivate, at all costs, the friendship of Russia.''[41] Hungary did receive $4 million of UNRRA aid as well as a $10 million credit for the purchase of U.S. military surplus stocks. But Finance Minister Gordon's urgent plea for credits to assist the revival of Hungary's trade with the West was refused. Washington was reluctant to bail out a country that was paying reparations, and presumably shared the pessimistic view of its minister to Budapest, H.F.A. Schoenfeld, that Hungary was becoming a Soviet economic colony dominated by a communist minority.[42]

Marshal Voroshilov was at once head of the Soviet high command and chairman of the Allied Control Commission. He generally ignored the advice of the British and American delegates, and his directives frequently and conveniently omitted to specify the precise status of the issuing authority. In these circumstances, and faced with the ever-present threat of communist-fomented chaos, Prime Minister Ferenc Nagy could derive small comfort from the Western powers' intangible expressions of sympathy. His one hope was that the SHP could hang on to some vestige of formal power until the ratification of the peace treaty, which he expected would terminate both Soviet occupation and direct Soviet intervention on behalf of the HCP.[43]

**Economic Reform.**   By the winter of 1945 the economic crisis, marked by runaway inflation and food shortages, had become so severe that a rash of protest strikes erupted; not infrequently, they were directed at the HCP. Industrial production stood at less than half the 1938 level. Fearing for its support among the workers, the party leadership made a concerted effort to develop remedial measures. Jenő Varga arrived from Moscow to provide expert guidance, and at its meetings of 1 and 8 October the Politburo outlined the modalities of government intervention to brake inflation. At the same time, the viability of private industry was to be progressively undermined. Observed Rákosi: "Our economic policy must in many respects resemble the NEP [Lenin's 'New Economic Plan']. We must produce partial solutions. . . ."[44] In other words, economic stabilization ought not to consolidate the private sector.

To achieve this dual objective and bring all key economic activity under its control, the HCP engineered the institution of an all-powerful Supreme Economic Council in mid-December 1945. Although this was ostensibly a coalition body, consisting of Tildy (later, Ferenc Nagy), Gerő, and Bán, effective initiating and implementing power rested with the Secretariat. The latter, under general secretary Zoltán Vas, was communist dominated, so from its very inception the council was an agent of HCP policy. It enjoyed almost limitless authority over taxation, trade permits, credits, price and wage policy, and the allocation of raw material supplies. This power was to be used, reveals a secret party memorandum, to exploit the reliance of private enterprises on state credits and compel them to surrender shares to the state—all pending the opportune imposition of wholesale nationalization.[45]

The first priority in the nationalization program was the coal mines. American opposition to any nationalization before the peace treaty was accommodated by the subterfuge of bringing the mines under so-called state management on 1 January 1946. (In any event, the Politburo was adamant that compensation for nationalized property "not represent a significant burden for the state in the coming years.")[46] The HCP thereupon launched an intensive "battle for coal," led by State Secretary for Industry Sándor Nógrádi to raise production and demonstrate the superiority of state control.

The party's financial stabilization scheme was endorsed by the Politburo on 11 February and adopted in its essentials by the Supreme Economic Council on 18 March. The program, developed by Varga and others, envisaged the accumulation not only of foreign exchange and gold reserves but also of consumer goods which, together with a Soviet loan, would back up the introduction of a new currency on 1 August. A less unbalanced state budget, to be achieved through the B-list dismissals and selective tax increases, wage-and-price controls, and a trade-expansion program, would subsequently help to brake inflation.

The SDP's economic experts (including the British Labour Party's Hungarian-born economist Thomas Balogh) considered the communist projections of state income unrealistically high and insisted on the need for foreign credits or for a reduction in reparations. Similar objections issued from the SHP. Debate dragged on over technicalities among the coalition parties, but the communists had demonstrated their capacity for initiative in the economic sphere, where all recognized the necessity of rapid and drastic action. The Soviet Union came to the aid of the communist program with various loans and concessions, including the rescheduling of reparations, while in June the United States agreed to return the National Bank's gold reserves, which had been removed by the retreating Germans. A multiparty agreement led to the creation of a rather special organization, the "West-Orient Trading Company," which resorted to unorthodox and illegal methods to secure imports in aid of the stabilization program.[47]

With the introduction of the new currency, the forint, on 1 August the inflationary spiral was brought under a semblance of control. The economic situation remained precarious, reparations still absorbing nearly two-fifths of the state budget, and Soviet-communist predominance steadily increased. For instance, trade with the Soviet Union was controlled by the Soviet-owned Hungarian Commercial and Industrial Bank, and all commercial currency transactions were administered by a National Bank department headed by László Háy, a Muscovite. Rákosi reported to the Central Committee on 2 August that "the class struggle [had] focused on financial reorganization in the past few weeks," and indeed for the HCP the stabilization was not an end in itself but the first major step on its road to economic dictatorship.[48] The party mobilized thousands of activists into "forint defense committees" to seek out infractions of the new economic controls. The village visitor program to radicalize the peasantry was carried on through the summer. And lesser initiatives, such as the "workers for science, scientists for workers" program, which provided some assistance in the reconstruction of educational and research institutions, aimed at the seduction of special interest groups.[49]

**Hungarian Interests and the Peace Conference.** While in the economic sphere the HCP had forcefully taken the initiative, in the realm of foreign policy it deliberately adopted a low profile. The pursuit on ethnic grounds of territorial revision remained an intensely patriotic cause that drew virtually unanimous public support and gained the active endorsement of all noncommunist parties. The HCP was restrained from following suit by the Soviet Union's preferential patronage of the two interested successor states, Czechoslovakia and Romania. The party, in fact, said as little as possible about the matter. One of the rare exceptions to this policy was an article by Révai in *Szabad Nép* on 25 December 1945; it condemned chauvinism and lack of realism for harming Hungary's relations with the neighboring countries. Such pronouncements only aroused popular antagonism. Outrage at the official persecution of the Magyar minority in Slovakia finally compelled the HCP to intercede, for in late December or early January 1946 Gerő, Révai, and Apró met with the representatives of the Slovakian party, Gustáv Husák, Viliam Široký, and Daniel Okali. According to Široký, a notorious Stalinist who was not purged until 1963,

"Gerő and Révai tried to convince us with dogmatic, theoretical arguments; we turned to the living practice—Stalin—and he said we were right."[50]

Thus the task of preparing Hungary's brief to the peace conference was left largely to the foreign office professionals and the SHP. The proposals, completed in February 1946, essentially reiterated the injustice of the Trianon dictate and asked for its modification along ethnic lines in Transylvania and Slovakia. The HCP's Politburo debated foreign policy at a series of meetings in March. It reached no substantive conclusions, however, beyond recommending that a delegation led by Ferenc Nagy visit Moscow, and that the party renew its contacts with its Romanian and Yugoslav counterparts (an indication of how isolated the East European parties were from each other).[51]

Negotiations in December 1945 between Czechoslovakia and Hungary ended in deadlock: the former proposed to expel the Slovakian Magyars while the latter held out for the transfer of predominantly Magyar-inhabited territory. Two months later the two governments did reach agreement on a balanced exchange of population, but the threat of expulsion still hung over the heads of the far more numerous Hungarians in Slovakia. Even Rákosi felt compelled to rise to the challenge by telling the visiting Czech foreign secretary, Vlado Clementis, that the HCP could not agree to the wholesale expulsion of Hungarians; such a measure, he warned, would bring about the collapse of Hungarian democracy and strengthen the forces of reaction. The HCP also joined in the criticism of the propagandistic excesses of the Czechoslovakian Resettlement Commission among Hungary's Slovakian minority.[52]

Prime Minister Ferenc Nagy, accompanied by Gerő, Gyöngyösi, and Szakasits, held talks in Moscow from 9 to 18 April with Stalin and Molotov. On the ethnic-territorial question, the Russians made vague promises to defend the rights of the Slovakian Magyars and, implying support, suggested that the Hungarians initiate bilateral negotiations regarding Transylvania with the Romanian government. The latter, as the Russians expected, refused. The final blow was yet to come. At its meeting in Paris on 7 May the Council of Foreign Ministers recommended the award of all Transylvania to Romania. The appalled Nagy was told by the Americans that while they had favored some adjustment in favor of Hungary, Molotov had adamantly opposed it. In a March memorandum on the Transylvanian question Schoenfeld had reported to the State Department that it was more important for the United States to consider the effect of a frontier revision on Hungarian internal politics than on Romanian internal politics. "Hungary," he explained, "is still a twilight zone in respect to Soviet expansion whereas the shadows falling on Rumania are already of a deeper hue."[53] Similar considerations presumably led the Kremlin to the opposite conclusion.

The resulting public uproar drove Nagy to make a last, largely symbolic effort. In June, with Rákosi in tow, he set off for Washington and London. The communists were by now fully aware of, and reconciled to the Soviet stand, but they diplomatically refrained from objecting to the trip. In Washington Nagy offered to support the American stand on international control of Danubian navigation, and he was promised the return of the gold bullion and an increase in credits for war surplus. With regard to Transylvania, however, Secretary of State Byrnes allowed only that American support might be forthcoming if the Russians chose to reopen the issue. Passing through Paris on his way home Nagy learned from Molotov that this was out of the question.[54] After Nagy had reported to a despondent parliament on his failure, the HCP's Gyula Kállai declared that the Western trip's most important consequence was that it dispelled illusions regarding the ability or willingness of the United States and Great Britain to counterbalance the Soviet Union in matters affecting Hungary.[55]

The final preparations for the peace conference, and the conference itself in Paris in August, were for Hungary anticlimactic exercises in futility. An American proposal to ease Hungary's economic distress by reducing the reparations burden by one-third was voted down. The loss of Transylvania was confirmed; the Romanians, in turn, had to stomach the cession of northern Bukovina to the Soviet Union. A Czechoslovakian request for a further fragment of Hungarian territory across the Danube from Bratislava (which at preliminary discussions even Révai termed totally unacceptable) was approved. However, the conference rejected in principle the expulsion of the remaining Hungarian minority from Slovakia and invited the two governments to settle the dispute bilaterally.[56]

In November the Hungarian government directed a final appeal to the Allied powers warning that if the reparations clause in the treaty were not amended, the country's economy might collapse. In the absence of a positive response it had no choice but to sign the treaty in Paris on 10 February 1947. In the meantime, the minority problem had been aggravated by the Czech government's decision to transplant thousands of Hungarians to the formerly German-inhabited Czech territories. Rightly or wrongly, the communists received much of the public blame for the government's failure to prevent these punitive measures, and Révai felt compelled to condemn the Prague regime in an article entitled "We Protest."[57]

The Soviet Union's opposition to Hungary's brief to the peace conference stood in sharp contrast to its close collaboration with the Romanians, Bulgarians, and Czechs, whose governments were either communist-dominated or tactically pro-Soviet on all issues. The SHP, as the principal Hungarian party with a Western orientation, lost some popular prestige with this demonstration of its impotence. The HCP's passive acceptance of Soviet disfavor did not enhance its patriotic image, but the party, as it blamed Hungary's reactionary past for the Allies' unquestionably harsh treatment, could at least claim to have been the more realistic prophet. The communists gloated over the discomfiture of the pro-Western parties. Of his western journey Rákosi noted with undisguised satisfaction that everywhere he and Nagy had gone, they had been made to understand that in their part of Europe the decisive voice belonged to the Soviet Union. "Capitalism," he concluded, "is toying with the idea of a world war, but it is unlikely to attempt it."[58] The lesson was clear: the HCP could pursue with impunity its progressive decimation of the opposition.

Communist policy regarding the disposition of Hungary's German minority served both Soviet and HCP interests. Although the Potsdam Agreement provided for the expulsion of German minorities from Czechoslovakia, Hungary, and Poland, in the case of Hungary this had been purely a Soviet initiative, resting partly on the calculation that it would facilitate the transfer of Slovakian Magyars to Hungary. At first the Nagy government made only half-hearted attempts to implement the directive, but the communists endorsed it all the more enthusiastically since they knew that the German minority was overwhelmingly anticommunist. When Rajk (himself of German extraction) took over the interior ministry, he accelerated the expulsions despite American and domestic protests. Ultimately, over two-thirds of Hungary's Germanic population was summarily deported to Germany.[59]

**Peasant Days.** Meanwhile, fearing a leftist coup, the beleaguered smallholders made a final attempt to demonstrate their mass support by organizing what they called National Hungarian Peasant Days in Budapest from 7 to 9 September 1946. Concluding that this initiative was directed against the workers' parties, the HCP leadership took measures to dissuade peasants from coming to the capital, mobilized the works committees for agitation among the visitors, and placed the party's security forces on alert. The HCP and the SDP declared jointly on 6 September that the "workers of Greater Budapest" would not allow any provocation, and that they believed this was also the firm intention of the "working peasants" coming to Budapest. They then affirmed their faith in a worker-peasant alliance.[60] The SHP mass meeting drew some one hundred thousand from the capital and the countryside, and the "peasant days" passed without major clashes.

Concurrently the SHP had put before parliament a draft bill for the creation of a National Agricultural Federation to represent the interests of the various peasant groups. The left-wing parties, led by the HCP, feared that such a body would serve to consolidate the hold of the SHP over the rural population and registered their dissent. The last word belonged to the Soviet head of the Allied Control Commission: he declared that the proposed federation was of a corporatist character and therefore incompatible with the armistice terms.[61] The bill was deferred sine die.

The financial stabilization program had only worsened the so-called agrarian scissors dilemma of the peasantry, the fall in price of their produce and the rise in price of manufactured goods. Even Jenő Varga had to admit publicly that this was a necessary, if transitory drawback, and he pointed to the comparably reduced real incomes of industrial workers.[62] The HCP saw the hopelessness of winning over the disgruntled landed peasantry and concentrated on the remaining rural proletariat and its recent graduates to the proprietor class. On 14 August the Politburo reaffirmed its resolve to "break into the ranks of the SHP from above and from below." Twelve days later it decided to promote the idea of nationalizing the flour mills, but despite the usual manipulated mass agitation the other coalition parties showed no interest.[63] The communists' attempts to turn the UFOSZ into a politically active mass organization also floundered. A frontal attack on the majority party appeared to be an easier task than the seduction of its constituents.

## THE DESTRUCTION OF THE MAJORITY

The HCP's third congress, its first since 1930, met between 29 September and 1 October 1946. "Everyone is conscious," wrote Révai a few days before the event, "that we are at a crossroads."[64] Financial stabilization and the peace treaty would usher in a new phase of political development. As Rajk told the congress, "we have stopped halfway, for if we are not merely a bourgeois democracy, neither are we as yet a people's democracy. . . . We must decide which we want."[65] The choice was rhetorical, for people's democracy, notwithstanding its variable content, was clearly the preordained communist goal in all of East-Central Europe. Its achievement, in Révai's formulation, required four steps: nationalization, at least to the extent of the coalition program; aid for the poorer peasants and the new proprietors, preferably through collectivization; improvement in the standard of living of the working people; and a government in which the decisive voice belonged to the peasants' and workers' delegates.

The congressional resolutions elaborated the next stage in the piecemeal destruction of capitalism: state supervision of production and credit, the banks, foreign trade, nationalization of flour mills and of factories whose owners obstructed economic growth, and the development of a three-year plan. The long-term goal was clearly stated to be the construction of socialism, although the relationship between bourgeois democracy, people's democracy, and socialism received varying interpretations at the congress. Progress to socialism through a people's democracy, said Révai, was unquestionably slower than under the Commune. Nevertheless, he continued, for the sake of "the entire working nation," the HCP would gladly advance to socialism slowly and painlessly rather than faster but at the price of civil war. The party, Rákosi confirmed, was establishing a people's democracy so that it could advance to build "our common desire, socialism." In Hungary today the battle was not between two social systems, said Imre Nagy, but lay within capitalism, between democracy and reaction. And there would be a characteristically Hungarian road. Rákosi made the same promise: while drawing on international experiences, Hungarian socialism would be homegrown, tailored to Hungarian conditions.[66]

The most pressing political task in the unified people's democracy was indicated by the congressional slogan "Out with the people's enemies from the coalition!" A multiparty Independence Front could only be preserved it if was thoroughly purged of the bourgeoisie; the SHP would therefore have to be reduced to a purely peasant party. Révai explained that

> people's democracy is a type of bourgeois democracy which curtails profit-oriented exploitation by big capital and places under the working people's supervision the democratic state, with workers and peasants exercising the decisive influence. In a people's democracy the peasantry is the equal ally of the working class against the economic exploitation and political reaction of big capital, whereas in an ordinary bourgeois democracy the peasantry is the defrauded and subservient tool of big capital against the working class.[67]

The congress accordingly stressed the critical role of the peasantry in the redistribution of power while studiously skirting the question of collectivization.[68]

In other resolutions the congress called for the social transformation of the civil service by the elevation of workers and peasants; denounced criticism of the "democratic" police and urged the exclusion of "people's enemies" from its ranks; and invited various educational reforms, including the extension of the people's colleges. In her foreign relations Hungary should "progress sincerely and decisively on the road of economic and political cooperation with the peoples of the Danubian Basin, principally with the Soviet Union."[69]

The congress confirmed the policy of mass recruitment by approving organizational statutes that dispensed with the requirement for nomination by two members. All workers, peasants, and intellectuals who professed support for the party's objectives were welcome. Party membership at the time of the congress officially stood at 653,300 (6.7 percent of the population) distributed among 4,799 basic cells. Its occupational profile, by rough estimate, was 42.6 percent workers, 39.4 percent peasants, 4.8 percent intellectuals, and 13.3 percent others, including shopkeepers and craftsmen.[70]

An Organizing Committee chaired by Farkas was established to coordinate the work of the expanding party apparatus. Otherwise, however, the existing pyramidal structure was retained: basic works and local units, intermediate city and county committees, and, overall, the Central Committee and Central Control Committee, formally elected by the congress. The new Politburo, chosen from the ranks of the thirty-one-member Central Committee, consisted of Apró, Farkas, Gerő, Kádár, Kossa, Imre Nagy, Rajk, Rákosi, and Révai, the Muscovites outnumbering the home veterans by two to one. Rákosi remained general secretary, and Farkas and Kádár were appointed deputies, the latter replacing Rajk but remaining well behind the Muscovites in effective power.

**The Opposition Falters.** On the eve of the congress the SHP newspaper had carried a leader by the party's general secretary, Béla Kovács, headed "There Is No Democracy Without Us."[71] The SHP remained publicly committed to pluralistic democracy and the preservation of private property and private enterprise, and proclaimed its appeal to all social classes. While counting the days until ratification of the peace treaty, the SHP leaders realized that without some consolidation of anticommunist strength the race would be lost. A more forceful exercise of their nominal majority, cooperation with the conservative, extracoalition Freedom Party (Szabadságpárt) formed by Sulyok in November, possibly a rapprochement with the SDP and NPP, and the holding of the much-delayed local elections might, they hoped, compel the communists to accept a role more commensurate with their electoral strength and constrain the power that they exercised through the interior ministry.[72]

The communists and their allies shrank from another electoral campaign, fearing the political effect of the peace treaty, the "agrarian scissors," and the general economic malaise. The HCP therefore insisted on a new and more discriminatory franchise reform as well as on administrative reform that would extend the purge begun with the B-lists. In mid-November the Politburo decided to propose a number of stringent measures to combat price inflation; in communist eyes, its roots were in corruption, speculation, and ineffective application of the stabilization controls. Meanwhile, from below, the party organized the usual mass protests.[73]

Within the NPP, a virtual ultimatum had been addressed to Péter Veres, the party president, by Imre Kovács, Gyula Illyés, and others demanding in effect an internal purge and a shift away from the communist line. In late October a related attempt was made to bring about a fusion between the SHP and the NPP. When Révai denounced this at an HCP parliamentary caucus meeting on 28 November as a reactionary plot to break up the Left-Wing Bloc and bring the poor peasants under kulak dominance, the NPP's pro-communist wing effectively blocked the initiative.[74]

As for the SDP, in early December Peyer and a few other conservative social democrats delivered a memorandum to the leadership branding the party's alliance with the communists as destructive of its influence and power of initiative, and protesting at the leadership's pro-Russian orientation. The disorganization and debilitation of the party was widely blamed on the leftist leaders, but Peyer's memorandum could not overcome the latters' distaste for the party's prewar line and leadership. At the SDP's thirty-fifth congress, held from 1 to 3 February 1947, the left wing extracted a denunciation of Peyer's "party-splitting'' activities in exchange for temporarily abandoning its initial demand for his expulsion. The more moderate Kéthly-Szelig wing managed to have the congress acknowledge the possibility of closer cooperation with the SHP, but Szakasits was confirmed as general secretary while Marosán and Ries were elected as his deputies. Ideologically confused, divided on tactics, the SDP proved chronically incapable of mustering its potential strength in defense of social democracy.[75]

Peyer's defeat, however, was not the end of the story. Socialists and communists continued to fight as hard as ever for jobs and influence. Towards the end of 1946 the socialists began to prepare energetically for the next round of works committee elections. The communists were justifiably apprehensive about the outcome, and on 12 December the Politburo instructed its union activists to campaign for postponement. When the socialists proved adamant, the Trade Union Council was compelled to schedule elections to begin on 4 January 1947. The Politburo charged Kádár and Apró with the campaign. Their instructions were that in those enterprises where communist predominance was assured, the vote should be held early in the lengthy election period. To maximize support for the communists, congenial social democrats and nonparty candidates were to be put on HCP lists. Thanks to advantageous scheduling and an extraordinarily vicious campaign of coercion and intimidation (including threats of dismissal and harassment by the secret police), the communists achieved favorable results in the first week of the elections. They thereupon persuaded the appalled SDP leadership to have the remaining elections suspended for a year. As a minor concession the HCP allowed the ''rectification'' of a few of the most flagrant abuses in the abbreviated elections, but its grip over the works committees and trade unions was only strengthened by the exercise.[76]

**Plot and Counterplot.**  Another reason for postponing further works committee elections was the concurrent culmination of a plot to decapitate the majority party. Communist victories in the contrived Bulgarian and Romanian elections that autumn had left Hungary out of step. The smallholders and their allies doggedly refused to acknowledge the inevitability of left-wing rule. Accordingly, the HCP was driven to seek some new maneuver for implementing its congressional pledge to expel the enemies from the government. ''It depends on the SHP's democrats,'' threatened Márton Horváth in October, ''whether the plotters of big capital leave the political stage with or without them.''[77] As the pressure built up, *Szabad Nép* thundered on 12 December: ''The time has come to abandon negotiations that promise no concessions. We must speak out: the SHP is unwilling to break with reaction, unwilling to conduct an internal purge that admits of no delay.'' By then communist agents were busily amassing the ammunition for a crippling blow.

In mid-1946 the Soviet authorities had seized two SHP secretaries at Gyöngyős. Claiming to have uncovered evidence of an anti-Russian conspiracy, they proceeded to arrest and deport scores of other smallholder activists. Further investigation by the political and military secret police agencies, both under close Soviet supervision, identified a group called the Hungarian Community (Magyar Közösség), which traced its roots to the wartime anti-Nazi, noncommunist opposition movement.[78] In September 1946, reacting to the purge of the armed forces, this group (together with a cadre of senior officers that became known as the Underground General Staff) began to develop an action program to facilitate the orderly restoration of a genuinely democratic government and administration after the expected Soviet military evacuation. Certain prominent smallholders were evidently privy to these preparations. It was this alleged "conspiracy against the republic" that Rajk's and Pálffy's operatives uncovered in mid-December.

The Politburo closely monitored the investigation and held its fire until sufficient incriminating evidence had been assembled or fabricated. Ferenc Nagy ordered Defense Minister Bartha to have the arrested officers (who included General Lajos Veres) released. He was told that Pálffy sabotaged all such attempts and was himself protected by the HCP (in fact, he was protected by the Soviet general Sviridov of the Allied Control Commission).[79] On 5 January, the day when the interior ministry gave official notice of the affair, *Szabad Nép* launched a public offensive: "It is already evident that the conspirators tried to establish contact with the SHP's reactionary wing and to use the SHP as a legal cover. That this could happen indicates that the SHP leadership is less than innocent." The report to the Central Committee's meeting from 11 to 12 January anticipated that the alleged conspiracy might be portentous enough to change the party's entire strategy for 1947: "A heavy stone is in flight and we don't know where it will stop."[80]

The interior ministry's dossier implicated Ferenc Nagy's key aide, Kálmán Saláta, an SHP minister, and several deputies. After one smallholder had been kidnapped by the Russians and several others summarily arrested, the SHP leadership felt compelled to bypass parliamentary procedure and suspend the immunity of the fourteen accused deputies. Saláta escaped to the West, but the others were arrested and deported to the Soviet Union, where one of them "confessed" that Béla Kovács was the leader of the conspiracy. Confronted with this evidence by Sviridov and Pushkin on 24 January, Nagy wavered. The HCP leaders told him that Kovács had to resign and submit to interrogation, and that furthermore the SHP had to abandon its catchall-party role and become the progressive, democratic party of the peasantry.[81]

Nagy sent Kovács on leave, and on 4 February expelled another group of deputies from the SHP, but the communists did not relax their pressure. Révai, speaking in parliament two days later, charged Kovács with criminal responsibility. He was echoed by Mihály Károlyi, sitting as a special nonparty deputy, who speculated on the terrible consequences that had been luckily avoided by the exclusion of Kovács from the interior portfolio. There ensued a protracted tug-of-war. Kovács resigned from his party offices on 19 February. The following day Marosán and Farkas introduced a motion lifting his parliamentary immunity, but this was defeated by the smallholder majority. Finally, Kovács was prevailed upon by Ferenc Nagy, whose better judgment had been overcome by Rákosi and Szakasits, to submit voluntarily to questioning by the secret police, or, by another account, was tricked into doing so by his smallholder colleagues.[82] In any case, when he presented himself to the secret police on 25 February, he was beaten but refused to confess to complicity. Tiring of this useless charade, the Soviet authorities seized Kovács that same evening. When a smallholder delegation visited Rákosi to seek redress, the latter laughed and said that he would like to help but that the matter was in the hands of the Russians.[83]

In the face of this frontal assault, Premier Nagy sought Western support. In March the United States and Great Britain delivered a series of notes to General V. P. Sviridov protesting at the concerted Soviet-communist attack on a popularly elected majority party. Sviridov dismissed the protests and announced that Kovács had "fully acknowledged his crimes against the Soviet Army."[84] Kovács was spirited away to the Soviet Union and returned only nine years later, his health permanently damaged by imprisonment. With Russian help the communists had disposed of a dangerously able and popular opponent.

At interparty conferences each concession by Nagy only elicited new demands by the HCP for changes in personnel and ideology. At the Politburo's instigation the Left-Wing Bloc issued a declaration blaming the prime minister for the alleged fruitlessness and ultimate suspension of these conferences. Caught between the left's attack, which within the SHP had the support of Dobi and Ortutay, and the counterpressures of an alarmed SHP group led by Zoltán Pfeiffer, Nagy offered to resign. Dissuaded by President Tildy, Nagy proceeded to make new concessions in reconstructing the cabinet and expelling from the party Pfeiffer and four other conservative deputies. The coalition was thus superficially preserved, but the surcease was to be of short duration.

"The reaction's unity has disintegrated," crowed the Central Committee on 4 April, "the government's composition has altered in favor of the democratic forces." But this was only a partial victory; it had to be completed by sustaining the struggle against the remaining SHP reactionaries and the new, emergent enemy, Sulyok's Freedom Party, which wanted to regroup the anticommunist forces.[85] Moreover, these successes "from above" had not aroused mass support, particularly among the peasantry. The SHP's political decline was reflected in the atrophy of the party's local organizations, but had not produced a significant shift in peasant support to the communists, while it had benefited the SDP and the NPP, if only marginally. The increasingly evident fiasco of Nagy's delaying tactics was leading to a realignment of the noncommunist political groups and their masses. The Freedom Party and another faction, István

Barankovics's Catholic Democratic People's Party (Demokrata Néppárt), were rapidly gathering strength as the new champions of anticommunism.

Another rallying point was the Roman Catholic Church. Its head, Cardinal Mindszenty, possessed a respectable anti-Nazi record and was a profoundly conservative and inflexible advocate of what he held to be the inalienable rights of church and believers alike. His campaign in March against making religious instruction in the schools optional was his opening salvo in defense of the church's traditional dominion over Hungarian education. The cardinal's riposte and the ensuing mass demonstrations by Catholics put the left, including the new minister of religion and education, Ortutay, momentarily on the defensive.

On the economic front the HCP had worked out its proposals for a three-year plan in December 1946.[86] There followed negotiations with the socialists, who favored greater investment in industry and less in agriculture, and counted on substantial Western economic aid, which the communists in turn refused even to consider. A compromise (which included a capital levy) was reached in late March and was tentatively accepted by the cowed smallholders. Thus encouraged, the Politburo decided on 8 May to launch the next stage in its drive to destroy capitalism and called for the nationalization of banks. Even the SDP was taken aback by this move, and Ferenc Nagy rose in opposition to further nationalization, whereupon the communists mobilized the street mobs. On 28 May the Supreme Economic Council, as an interim measure, put the banks under its direct supervision.

The American protests over the Béla Kovács outrage and the publication of the Truman Doctrine on 12 March had momentarily revived the hopes of noncommunists for Western support; Sulyok even introduced a motion in parliament calling for Hungary's "eternal" neutrality. The Politburo rose to the challenge on 20 March by insisting on a pro-Soviet orientation that, following the coming into force of the peace treaty, would formally and exclusively bind Hungary to the Soviet Union and the other people's democracies.[87]

Ferenc Nagy, in his *The Struggle behind the Iron Curtain*, has recalled counting the days until ratification and the termination ninety days thereafter of Hungary's status as an occupied country.[88] The adjournment sine die of Allied negotiations on an Austrian peace treaty would, however, preserve the Russian pretext for maintaining troops in Hungary, namely, to guard communication lines to the Soviet zone in Austria. Before leaving for a holiday in Switzerland on 14 May, the prime minister had addressed a note to the Soviet Union requesting the surrender of Kovács. After the arrival of the predictable Russian refusal, Rákosi in his capacity as acting prime minister called an extraordinary cabinet meeting. He presented Soviet-supplied evidence purporting to show Nagy's own complicity in the "conspiracy" and received authority to recall him.[89]

The Politburo drew up plans to consolidate the Left-Wing Bloc's position on the matter in case Nagy did return, but the precaution was superfluous. Seeing his fate sealed, Nagy chose exile; his letter of resignation was exchanged for his five-year-old son on 30 May. He was soon followed by Béla Varga, Imre Kovács, and other prominent anticommunists, while the Hungarian ambassadors in Washington and other Western capitals abandoned their posts in protest. (The ever-gullible Károlyi was persuaded to take over the Paris embassy and served the communist-dominated regime until June 1949.) They joined in emigration the thousands of Hungarians—civil servants, professionals, businessmen, dispossessed peasants—who had been fleeing the country since the beginning of the communist offensive, braving official restrictions and the communist-led Frontier Guard.

**Power Shifts to the Left.** The communists did not want to alter immediately the formal outline of the coalition, but Oltványi, the SHP nominee to replace Nagy, was dismissed by Sviridov with the remark: "You gentlemen know that Marshal Voroshilov does not like him." Instead, the choice fell on the more compliant Dinnyés; as the NPP's Péter Veres observed, they "did not have much to choose from."[90] President Truman denounced the coup as an outrage, and the American representative on the Allied Control Commission was instructed to demand evidence for the allegations against Nagy, but as each side dug in for the cold war such protests had little but propaganda value. In July the Hungarian government published a "white book" on the conspiracy that construed any personal contact of the conspirators with Western officials as treason.[91]

In his maiden speech before parliament on 10 June Dinnyés insisted on the constitutionality of the shift and on his government's devotion to individual and property rights and to national independence. Révai put a finer point on the last question:

> Hungary must primarily adopt a foreign policy of friendship with the Soviet Union and our democratic neighbors, not only because we live along the Danube and not in Mexico, but also because in today's international politics it is the Soviet Union and the East European democracies that make up the camp which stands for peace, democracy, and the independence of nations, and against all aggressive colonialist efforts.[92]

Only Sulyok had the courage to observe that Hungary had become a "veritable police state."[93] After days of debate, the left-wing forces barely managed to ram through a bill for the three-year plan, which provided not only for the nationalization of banks but also for a Planning Council and a National Planning Office to facilitate economic socialization. The HCP decided that despite the stunning success of its salami tactics it needed to consolidate its growing influence through general elections for a new government. The struggle was not over, but its outcome would not be left to the free expression of popular will.

# 9. The Party Triumphant, 1947-1948

In communist historiography the period from early 1947 to mid-1948 is known as "the year of the turning point" (*a fordulat éve*). This encompasses the liquidation of the "conspiracy," the launching of the three-year plan on 1 August, the national elections of 31 August, the failure of the SDP moderates to regain control of the party, the progressive nationalization of banks and other private enterprises, and the merger, in June 1948, of the two major left-wing parties. With this phase, recalled Révai in 1950, Hungary "crossed the Rubicon between a bourgeois and a people's democracy."[1]

The party's leaders, a communist historian has written, "knew that the battle could not be fought with parliamentary instruments alone, and correctly . . . did not delay the turning point until all significant strata and groups had been drawn to the party's policy."[2] The deterioration in East-West relations, the evident inability of the Western powers to influence Hungarian developments, and the removal of even the legal pretext for joint Allied supervision after ratification of the peace treaty all prompted the Kremlin to give the HCP the green light to resort to bolder measures in its drive for power. "Our conception," Rákosi told a party meeting in February 1947, "is that we will develop the strength of the communist party and of the forces of people's democracy and reduce the mass basis of reaction and break up, neutralize, or annihilate its forces until, at the appropriate moment, we can shift to a general offensive and with or without the utilization of mass actions drive them back through new elections." This, he anticipated, would restore the preponderant influence that the left had lost in the 1945 elections.[3]

The HCP, partly from tactic and partly due to genuine uncertainty, did not promote wholesale replication of the Soviet model. "The principle of a people's democracy . . . ," Lukács wrote in the spring of 1947, "is only in the early stage of implementation, and even if it is realized, it does not aim to abolish the capitalist system of production and therefore cannot aim at the creation of a classless society.'' The immediate purpose of such disclaimers was of course to disarm internal opposition and, to a decreasing extent, to pacify Western opinion, but they also reflected the ambiguity of the directives from Moscow. Back in the Soviet Union, Jenő Varga suggested that the political rule of the workers might be ''feasible along with the retention of the outward forms of parliamentary democracy,'' and that a people's democracy was neither a bourgeois nor a proletarian model but an entirely new sociopolitical system.[4] This ambiguity presumably arose from a degree of flexibility in Moscow regarding the ways and means of implanting subservient regimes in East-Central Europe. The ideological rationales prevailing in the year of the turning point were ostensibly gradualist and, in some measure, pluralistic. They would be exploited by the party in the 1960s to demonstrate its early devotion to socialist democracy and dismiss the ensuing totalitarian horrors as a regrettable but brief historical aberration.

## MANDATE FOR POWER

The Dinnyés government was formally an extension of the coalition regime, but it represented a clear shift in power to the left. Leftist smallholders like Dinnyés himself (who also held the defense portfolio), Dobi (minister of state), Ortutay, and Ernő Mihályfi (foreign affairs and information) were susceptible to communist influence, and there were now two deputy premiers in the persons of Rákosi and Szakasits. ''It is clear that this government,'' said Révai in parliament on 11 June, ''is in its coalition character, program, and personal and party composition a continuation of the old government. Nevertheless, this government represents a very important turning point in the development of Hungarian democracy.''[5] The major change lay of course in the emasculation of the SHP. Dobi, the party's new leader, could be relied upon by the communists to try to convert it into a leftist organ of the peasantry. The seizure of the SHP leadership by a handful of leftists impelled the majority of orthodox smallholders to mount a rearguard action by styling themselves the ''defenders of the constitution.'' They were promptly and ominously denounced by Rákosi as a semilegal faction collaborating with the bourgeois forces of Sulyok and Pfeiffer.[6] With the purge of the SHP the extracoalition forces in parliament had acquired both numbers and a sense of responsibility as the main opposition to the communist-dominated government. Their minimum demands, as voiced by Béla Zsedényi on 12 June, included parliamentary investigation of political persecution by the police and the people's courts, the use of Western loans to finance the three-year plan (Secretary of State Marshall had delivered his historic Harvard address on American aid for European reconstruction on 5 June), the curtailment of government by decree, and the postponement of new elections.

The opposition's last two demands arose from its recognition that despite the purges the 1945 parliament remained in majority anticommunist. That same perception was impelling the HCP to seek a more favorable parliamentary basis for implementing its program. The Central Committee concluded as early as 4 April that general elections ought to be held by autumn at the latest.[7] The final decision on the timing was made public by Gerő in a speech at Győr on 20 July, when he announced that the elections would take place on 31 August. The notice was purposely short. The Freedom Party's meetings were systematically disrupted by communist thugs. After Rajk's chilling advice that the police could not guarantee the safety of the meetings from the "just anger of the people against the enemies of democracy," Sulyok saw no alternative but to disband the party.[8] Having thus disposed of their main organized opponent, the communists wanted to leave as little time as possible for their enemies to regroup.

**A New Electoral Law.** The subversion of the majority party within the coalition, the SHP, and the systematic persecution of Sulyok's party were not sufficient to make the communists confident of electoral success. In May Rajk and his assistants accordingly began work on a modification of the electoral law. The HCP's initial proposal was to withdraw the franchise (and, of course, the right to candidacy) from deputies and candidates of the preliberation governing party, from members of the mass organizations disbanded by decree in 1946, from all those who had been interned for any length of time since liberation, from those who had been placed on the B-lists, and from most of the Slovakian expellees—a potentially sweeping disqualification that would damage exclusively the electoral chances of the SHP and other anticommunist groups.[9] The personal disenfranchisement of Sulyok was one symbolic communist objective. The HCP managed to win the SDP's tentative support for these proposals, but at interparty discussions beginning on 8 July both the smallholders (despite Dobi's inclination to compromise) and certain NPP representatives, including Veres, raised objections against potential injustices. Rákosi dismissed the smallholder reservations as "reactionary" and complained that the party was led by the "defenders of the constitution" rather than by its (leftist and unrepresentative) Political Committee.[10] After some minor left-wing concessions on the order of Rajk's offer of police protection for all candidates in the two weeks preceding the elections, and with President Tildy's endorsement, the proposals were rammed through parliament on 23 July.

Under the interior ministry's guidance registering committees were constituted to draw up the electoral rolls and rule on the exclusions. The first struggle was for representation and, in the case of the HCP, for preponderance on the committees. The competition was most acute between the SDP and the HCP, not least over the allegiance of trade union representatives, the majority of whom turned out to be communist. Although the HCP's Secretariat issued instructions that "in the matter of exclusions agreement must be sought with the organizations and leaders of the SDP," the activities of the registering committees were marked by bitter interparty rivalry and outrageously partisan application of the new electoral law.[11] In a number of districts collusion between socialists and smallholders prevented the communists from applying the discriminatory clauses to the fullest extent, and in a few isolated instances the committees even excluded communists from the rolls. But the HCP's determination to disenfranchise the maximum of opponents generally prevailed, upon occasion through the simple expedient of barring smallholder representatives from committee hearings. The screening operation excluded 893,662 from the 6 million otherwise eligible voters.[12] The fraudulent performance of the registering committees prompted outraged protests from the noncommunist parties and the public at large, but the somewhat embarrassed communists could draw comfort from having arbitrarily reduced the size of the opposition.

**The Electoral Campaign.**   While the various emerging opposition groups awaited formal recognition by the Nationwide National Committee, which moved at a dilatory pace, the coalition parties launched their electoral campaigns. The HCP had wavered between the tactics of preserving a united coalition front and enhancing its own profile. The Central Committee resolution of 13 June leaned toward the latter option:

> Taking into account the evolution of the domestic situation . . . and of the international situation, primarily the events in France and Italy, i.e., the two countries' communist parties' withdrawal from the government, the party has decided that while retaining the existing coalition, workers' unity, the Left-Wing Bloc, and the worker-peasant alliance, it will broaden its direct influence and mass base. In contrast to, but without abandoning, the prevailing general national unity policy, the party has accentuated the class character of the struggle.[13]

The HCP's attempts to turn the coalition into a solid left-wing phalanx foundered on the shoals of its own excesses. In early June the party proposed an electoral alliance to its coalition partners. The latter reacted so negatively, however, that only on 29 July was an anodyne agreement concluded proclaiming the devotion of the Independence Front to both orthodox democratic principles and a mixed economy. Hailed by Révai as a nonaggression pact, this electoral alliance of reluctant bedfellows could neither prevent nor conceal profound political cleavages.[14]

The HCP electoral platform, published on 3 August, was a model of pragmatic moderation. In its advocacy of the three-year plan (officially launched two days earlier) it emphasized the immediate benefits that would accrue to workers in the form of lower unemployment and a higher standard of living. To the newly landed peasantry it promised material aid, legal confirmation of their holdings by 1 October, and the option of independent farming: "The future of Hungarian agriculture lies in the strengthening of peasant property and private cultivation and in the vigorous development of the agricultural cooperative movement." The property of the "little people" was deemed by the platform to be "sacred and untouchable." The right to private enterprise within the bounds of public interest was affirmed, as was religious freedom. (At most ten percent of the workers understood and shared the fundamental communist view of religion, commented Rákosi, and the party had to avoid alienating the others.)[15] In foreign policy the stress was on national independence couched in anti-Western terms and confronting the "internal reactionary villains and their foreign masters."[16] Recognizing that the fate of the Slovakian Magyars was a powerful political issue, the HCP had once again approached the Czech party on their behalf, and had once again been rebuffed with the argument that a communist initiative in favor of greater tolerance would only strengthen the Czech nationalist bourgeois forces.[17]

Tailored to the immediate requisites of the election, the platform skirted the question of integral socialism. The short-term outlook, wrote Horváth in *Szabad Nép* on 27 July, was "not for an imaginary socialist Hungary but for a country belonging to the little people." In Révai's rendition, the two great tasks before them were "creation of the constitutional basis and appropriate power configuration" for implementing the three-year plan without too much fuss and, as a result, "to deliver a decisive blow against those reactionary forces who . . . obstruct democratic consolidation."[18]

The party's appeal to the middle-class intelligentsia was delivered by Révai at the Academy of Music on 12 August.[19] He identified three types of consolidation in the postwar world: the Greek road of civil war, in which the reactionaries enlisted the foreign imperialists to impose their rule by force; the English road, which was to delay necessary reforms and restore the old order with external financial assistance; and the Hungarian road of self-help. To counter the widespread belief that American aid was necessary for reconstruction, Révai argued that this would have "inevitably led to civil war and turned that loan into military aid as in Greece." He complained that doubts regarding the permanence of democracy and suspicions of communist intentions were more prevalent among the intelligentsia than within the population at large. Contrary fears, that the communist democracy would collapse as it did in 1919, were unfounded, he said, in light of the land reform and Hungary's "external friends."

For those who felt guilt for their service to the old regime Révai promised forgiveness and a chance to test their abilities against the new intelligentsia emerging from the working classes. They were all needed for implementation of the three-year plan and would benefit from it. The archetype of the old intelligentsia was the lawyer, he observed, but now the need was for doctors, engineers, and pedagogues. The HCP—undivided, strong, determined, committed to democracy—deserved their support. Révai's pleas evoked little response. In fact, a sprinkling of intellectuals had been drawn to the HCP by its aura of purposeful reformism, but the bulk of the middle classes remained profoundly hostile to both the philosophy and recent practice of the party.

The official political orientation of the other three coalition parties remained essentially unchanged, although Dobi, claiming to speak for the SHP, would proclaim in the middle of the campaign that his enemies were on the right and not among the left-wing parties. The Nationwide National Committee issued its list of authorized parties on 30 July, one month before the election. These included two existing fringe groups, the Citizens' Democratic Party, an urban liberal group whose leader had recently fled to the West, and the Hungarian Radical Party, an urban, progressive, and traditionally Jewish intellectual group that had been largely taken over by Peyer and a few other conservative socialists after their departure from the SDP.

The communists' determination to divide and weaken the opposition was reflected in the official authorization of four additional parties. The Hungarian Independence Party (Magyar Függetlenségi Párt) which was led by Pfeiffer seized the moderate conservative-nationalist torch of the defunct Freedom Party. István Barankovics's Democratic People's Party, nominally in existence since March 1945, was a Hungarian variant of the Christian democratic orientation that had emerged in postwar Western Europe and enjoyed the support of the Roman Catholic Church. A third opposition group was officially called the Independent Hungarian Democratic Party (Független Magyar Demokrata Párt) but generally known by the name of its leader, István Balogh. The latter was an opportunistic priest and former smallholder rumored to have been blackmailed into Soviet service. He had gathered around him a motley collection of noncommunist figures, including Imre Kovács, lately of the NPP. There was, finally, the Christian Women's Camp Party of Margit Slachta.

With variations in emphasis, these new and old extracoalition parties professed opposition to the communists' concept of a people's democracy, to the politics of class struggle, to the further socialization of the economy, and to an exclusively pro-Soviet policy. In their liberal-democratic orientation they were the successors of the old SHP, many of whose members gravitated to the opposition parties after the leftist seizure of the leadership. That leadership was powerless to prevent the remaining local smallholder organizations from pursuing the party's established anticommunist line, and although the HCP Politburo resolved on 7 August to strengthen the electoral alliance with the SHP, the two parties' electoral campaigns were sharply competitive.[20]

As for the SDP, the majority of its leaders momentarily united in one last effort to rally the industrial working class and the middle class to the banner of social democracy. The long-exiled Vilmos Böhm had returned from Sweden that spring to aid the party in the election campaign, and the "third road" idea was revived in *Népszava*. The two parties had agreed to avoid the question of amalgamation during the campaign. When, in an election address on 1 August, Rákosi nevertheless referred to that prospect, Szakasits felt compelled to proclaim the slogan "Workers' unity forever, fusion never!" Its socialist counterpart became "The road is wide, there is room for both of us."[21] But internal squabbles and communist assaults had left the SDP with a weak organization and a reduced and disoriented membership. Professions of alliance to the contrary, the communists spared no effort to win over the SDP's supporters; they even spread a rumour that Marosán had joined the HCP. When at the last minute his associates persuaded him to refute the allegation in a radio broadcast, Rákosi remarked: "Never mind, it won't make any difference now."[22]

As the vigorously fought election campaign drew to a close, the communists could find little encouragement in the performance of either their left-wing allies or the mushrooming opposition parties. There was, in fact, a notable absence of unity or collaboration among both groupings. The HCP's election posters attempted to humanize the image of the party; one credited Rákosi with the return of some prisoners of war, while another showed a child thanking "Uncle Gerő" for being sent to a holiday camp. Rákosi resorted to both carrot and stick: on the one hand, he promised to bring the remaining prisoners home and to secure Soviet economic concessions; on the other, he warned that if the HCP did not get mass support the Soviet Union would intervene.[23] The non-communist parties, in contrast, denounced the terroristic methods of the HCP, encouraged fears of collectivization, and branded communism as alien to Hungarian history and culture. By 22 August an apprehensive Révai would warn publicly: "Pfeiffer's party is the party of big capital and Hungarian reaction and is the enemy of the three-year plan."[24]

**A Fraudulent Plurality.** Not content with the results of the disenfranchisement drive and with its vastly superior campaign resources, the HCP resorted to a massive exploitation of the notorious "blue slips," the registration cards issued by Rajk's ministry to voters who would be absent from their home constituency on election day. Estimates vary on the extent of the fraud. Sulyok claims that 500,000 blue slips were reserved for communist use. Antal Bán reports that 400,000 were printed and that the conmunists cast about 300,000 illegal votes. The SDP leaders were also offered a share but did not use them, assuming apparently that fraud would be unnecessary. According to Sulyok, the NPP was allocated 100,000 blue slips to inflate its own electoral results. Finally, a party historian allows that a mere 63,000 blue slips were misused, with only marginal impact on the election's outcome. The last is in all likelihood a gross underestimation of the huge fraud that was actually perpetrated. In the days preceding the election the AVO made numerous arrests and traded its victims' release for surrender of their blue slips, so that only a few thousand of the slips were put to proper use.[25]

On election day truckloads of communist activists sped around the countryside voting repeatedly for their party. In one instance, 156 blue slips were found on a single communist. The counting of the votes by Rajk's ministry allowed for further adjustment in favor of the communists. Even before the tally was completed, Pfeiffer's party reportedly accounted for over 1 million votes, whereas its final share was only 670,547. Moreover, the absentee ballots of prisoners of war and others were processed by the communists alone.[26] Since all of these manipulations vastly inflated the electoral record of the HCP (and of the NPP), the official results, published five days after the election of 5 September, offer a highly unreliable profile of the popular will (see table 9.1).

TABLE 9.1
VOTE IN HUNGARIAN NATIONAL ELECTIONS, BY PARTY, 1945 AND 1947

|  | 1945 | | 1947 | |
| --- | --- | --- | --- | --- |
|  | Votes | % | Votes | % |
| Hungarian Communist Party .............. | 802,122 | 16.95 | 1,113,050 | 22.3 |
| National Peasant Party ................... | 325,284 | 6.87 | 415,465 | 8.3 |
| Social Democratic Party ................. | 823,314 | 17.41 | 744,641 | 14.9 |
| Smallholder Party ....................... | 2,697,508 | 57.03 | 769,763 | 15.4 |
| Citizens' Democratic Party .............. | 76,424 | 1.62 | 50,294 | 1.0 |
| Hungarian Radical Party ................ | 5,762 | 0.12 | 84,169 | 1.7 |
| Democratic People's Party[a] ................ | ............... |  | 820,453 | 16.4 |
| Hungarian Independence Party[a] ........... | ............... |  | 670,547 | 13.4 |
| Independent Hungarian Democratic Party[a] .... | ............... |  | 260,420 | 5.2 |
| Christian Women's Camp[a] ............... | ............... |  | 69,536 | 1.4 |

SOURCE: Adapted from Sándor Balogh, *Parlamenti és pártharcok Magyarországon, 1945–1947* (Budapest: Kossuth, 1975), pp. 98, 525.
a. Not on 1945 ballot.

According to the official statistics, the coalition garnered 60.8 percent of the vote, while the three more Marxist parties within it received 45.4 percent. The biggest change was the dramatic decline in SHP support, which was roughly equivalent to the new-found strength of the opposition parties. The HCP could claim the overall plurality as well as a local plurality in five out of sixteen electoral districts, including Budapest. The redistribution of land had once again brought disappointing results, for reportedly only 40 percent of the beneficiaries voted for the HCP.[27] Thus if the communists achieved their objective of becoming officially the strongest single party, their victory hardly represented a major shift in support among the electorate. Indeed, when the various frauds are taken into account, the number of authentic HCP supporters may even have declined since the 1945 election. Barankovics's Democratic People's

Party won an outright majority in the traditionally Catholic and conservative western counties of Zala and Vas and a plurality in four other districts. A provision in the electoral law for national as well as constituency mandates favored the winning coalition, giving it 271 (or 66 percent) of the 411 parliamentary seats.

Although the election had debilitated the anticommunist forces within the coalition, reduced the SDP's support, and divided the opposition, it hardly provided a convincing mandate for the HCP to implement a radical transformation of the political and economic system. But such legalistic obstacles were no longer of much consequence, for Stalin was about to give the signal for the undisguised seizure of monopoly power.

## THE COMINFORM LINE

Stalin's decision to impose tight coordination on the international communist movement led to the hasty convening of a conference of representatives of nine parties (the Soviet, Bulgarian, Czechoslovak, Hungarian, Polish, Romanian, Yugoslav, French, and Italian) at Szklarska Poreba near the Polish city of Wroclaw between 22 and 27 September 1947. The Soviet delegates, Zhdanov and Malenkov, delivered the guidelines and orchestrated the deliberations so as to produce a united front against the imperialist threat and the discredited tactics of the French and Italian parties. Révai and Farkas were present on behalf of the HCP.

In his opening address Zhdanov appraised the Truman doctrine, the Marshall Plan, and the pro-Western orientation of the French and Italian governments as evidence of Washington's imperialistic designs. The whole world, he proclaimed, was now divided into two antagonistic camps. The dissolution of the Comintern had been interpreted in such a way as to loosen the ties between the fraternal parties. The danger of war and of American aggression now demanded a common determination of policy and action. The East European parties, continued Zhdanov, had seceded from the imperialist system and had created a

> new type of state, the people's republic, in which power belongs to the people, major industries, banks, and transportation belong to the state, and the leading force is the bloc of the working classes, with the industrial proletariat in the vanguard. When all is said and done, the peoples of these countries not only freed themselves from imperialism, but also laid the foundations of the transition to socialist development.[28]

Malenkov followed with an account of the Soviet party's domestic achievements that was clearly designed to serve as the Stalinist model to be adopted by the other parties.

The other delegates then delivered reports on the fortunes of their parties. Révai's turn came on 24 September.[29] Reflecting on the recent elections, he observed: "We have taken a step forward; but our plan was not as successful as we expected. . . . Our influence within the working class is not yet overwhelming. In certain plants and mines the socialists are stronger than us." The HCP had raised the prospect of fusion to persuade workers that they might as well shift their support to the communists right away. The socialists thus became the weaker party and could no longer legitimately demand important posts in the army and the police. The HCP was well entrenched in the new government, asserted Révai; the secretary of the NPP was a communist, and the majority of its deputies were communists or sympathizers. The circulation of the party press was greater than that of all other publications. The party controlled 230 out of 400 movie theaters. Twenty percent of doctors, 25 percent of engineers were communist. Control of the 1.5-million-strong union movement was assured by a 15 to 7 majority on the Trade Union Council's central committee. In the regular and political police all leading positions were held by communists. Nearly all senior army officers were communists, former partisans, or Spanish civil war veterans. This final accounting was received with brisk applause.

Turning to the future, Révai asked rhetorically: "Will Hungarian democracy be popular or bourgeois? Nothing is yet decided. Will Hungary become one of the people's democracies or will she be drawn into the Anglo-American orbit? Hungarian democracy is a blend of popular democracy and bourgeois democracy." The party was working to overcome Hungary's economic difficulties (Révai noted that 50 percent of the budget was swallowed up by reparations), to strengthen the left wing of the other coalition parties, and to consolidate its position in the armed forces. The reactionaries were regrouping, but the most immediate threat was not the influential Roman Catholic Church or the Barankovics party: "The destruction of Pfeiffer's party is indispensable; we will manage it by police methods."

In the sphere of foreign policy Révai followed Zhdanov's line. "The Hungarian communists have proclaimed that the struggle against Germany was linked to the friendship of the Slavic peoples. We opposed the chauvinist line that aimed to recover for Hungary all Magyar-inhabited territories. We endorsed some minor complaints. As soon as the peace treaty is signed we believe there will be no more room for any kind of revisionism." He did observe that the situation of the Hungarians in Slovakia was unsatisfactory, but Rudolf Slánský, the Czech party's secretary-general, would later explain that this was historically understandable and momentarily unavoidable.[30] Révai affirmed Hungary's friendship toward the Yugoslavs and her determined hostility toward the United States, as demonstrated by her refusal to attend the Paris Conference on the Marshall Plan. He boasted: "We are inciting hatred of the Anglo-Americans among the Hungarian people." The Politburo, he concluded, had instructed them to inquire whether the Anglo-American menace was merely a blackmail attempt or a tangible threat requiring military preparations: "Must our party take measures in domestic policy that would allow us to come to the aid of the neighboring democratic peoples?"

The time approached for the opening salvo in the premeditated denunciation of the Italian and French parties. Edward Kardelj began on the twenty-fourth with a triumphant account of the Yugoslav party's assumption of power without the encumbrance of parliamentarism, and continued the following day with an attack on the opportunism and caution of the two Western parties. (At the June 1948 Cominform meeting Togliatti would repay the Yugoslavs by enthusiastically supporting their expulsion.) The script called for Farkas to rise after Kardelj and denounce the timidity of the French and Italian comrades; he accused the Italian Luigi Longo, who was present, of "parliamentary cretinism." Alluding to the Hungarian example, Farkas advised: "One can always confront a parliamentary majority with the masses, one could well form a minority government which would dissolve parliament." The Hungarian communists had sought advice from Stalin, Tito, and Dimitrov, and more regular interparty contacts, which Rákosi had proposed a year earlier, were imperative to coordinate action against Anglo-American imperialism.[31] With an abjectly self-critical speech by Jacques Duclos the prescribed unanimity was achieved. At the final session the decision was made to establish a Communist Information Bureau, to be located in Belgrade in order, as Gomulka put it, to forestall calumnies that Moscow was calling the shots.[32]

The Szklarska Poreba conference served to enshrine the new Stalinist orthodoxy. This consisted of establishing single-party dictatorships at all costs; of rejecting the possibility of democratic road to socialism; of concentrating fire on social democrats susceptible to imperialist influence; and of identifying the Americans, with their Marshall Plan, as the great immediate peril.

**The Drive to Hegemony.** In their report to the Politburo, Révai and Farkas noted with satisfaction that the conference had included Hungary without qualification in the list of people's democracies.[33] The Cominform platform, they concluded, did not necessitate a major shift in HCP policy, but it did require the party leadership to supplant tactical pragmatism with more elaborate planning. The "basic principles" of Hungarian people's democracy and HCP policy had not been adequately elaborated. The shift in the international balance of power meant that "following the defeat of Hitler-fascism American imperialism [had] become the principal enemy of socialism and democracy." As a consequence, those former allies of the working class who were now supporters of American imperialism, i.e., the rightist social democrats, had become the most dangerous enemy. The conference had modified the guidelines of the Comintern's seventh congress, reported the HCP delegates. In the pressing battle for hegemony, parliamentary tools had to be supplemented by other methods of consolidating and acquiring power, notably a popular front modeled on the Yugoslav single-party experience.

The party's immediate tasks, as they arose from the founding meeting of the Cominform, were summed up as follows: first, the accelerated creation of a "new coalition"; second, a review of economic policy aiming at the gradual exclusion of the bourgeoisie; third, reform of the old administrative structure and of the armed forces, and the expansion of the latter; fourth, enhancement of the party's fighting spirit and ideological and organizational unity along with preservation of its mass character; fifth, a review of mass organizing work to forestall bureaucratic ossification in the trade unions and the consequent danger of isolation from the masses; and sixth, to remedy deficiencies in theoretical work. All these steps were designed to facilitate the rapid acquisition of monopoly power.[34]

The Politburo promptly endorsed the report and appointed three commissions to review general policy, economic policy, and party and mass organizational work. The resulting guidelines for economic policy were ratified by the Politburo on 12 February 1948; an elaboration of agricultural policy was approved the following April.[35] The objectives outlined included the elimination of private capital and extension of the state sector, support for the voluntary development of the cooperative movement in agriculture, and efficient state planning for the completion of the three-year plan. Private banks would have to be absorbed into the central state banking system. Other specific immediate objectives were nationalization of the bauxite-aluminum and electric power industries, the acquisition of control over other enterprises by trading state credit for a controlling share and by close state supervision, the merging of small industries and craftsmen into cooperatives, state control over internal commerce in essential consumer goods and raw materials, and state monopoly in foreign trade. In agriculture, "general measures against the kulaks" were not seen as timely, for these would have negative economic consequences and also alienate the middle peasants. The kulaks' influence would accordingly have to be curtailed by progressively heavier taxation, by the development of model state farms, and by gradually extending the cooperative movement. The cooperative was pictured as the "weapon of the working class" that would expunge bourgeois influences and allow for the modernization of agriculture.

The draft guidelines had provoked some internal debate on ideology. One view, advanced apparently by Imre Nagy, held that since people's democracy was a variant of bourgeois democracy it was compatible with residual capitalism. This perspective, ruled the Politburo on 18 December 1947, was obsolete. As usual, the party took its cue from the Soviet Union, where Jenő Varga, who had a similar understanding of people's democracy as an essentially political transformation, had come under attack and been forced to recant.

Within the HCP it had been Gerő's task to subject the economic aspects of people's democracy to ideological revision. The shift in emphasis to the socialist content of people's democracy was evident on 10 January 1948 at the third HCP activists' conference, whose slogan was "The country is yours, you are building it for yourself." But Gerő was hard pressed to make a distinction between people's democracy and proletarian dictatorship. In both cases, he argued, the government was one of workers and peasants, but the former was a "worker-peasant state" while the latter was a "workers' state." Soviet victory made it possible for Hungary to progress toward socialism without its own proletarian dictatorship.[36]

**Instant Nationalization.** Events outpaced the incremental pace of nationalization and collectivization anticipated in the guidelines. In October and November the banks were nationalized, a measure that brought under state control over half the major industries. There followed the conversion of the banking system to the Soviet model. The communist-dominated National Planning Office and Planning Council began to collect data on the entire industrial sector. When on 25 March 1948 a Central Committee plan for nationalization of all enterprises employing more than 100 workers was put before the cabinet, the latter's approval was a mere formality. Already the management of the 600 affected enterprises had been taken over by specially selected communist activists, physical workers whose total lack of managerial expertise was overshadowed by their political reliability. This abrupt nationalization, proclaimed with the slogan "The factory is yours, you work for yourselves," put 83.5 percent of industrial workers in the state sector.[37] Gerő had explained the rationale for this radical move to the Politburo on 3 March:

> The domestic and international political situation has made possible a new and serious forward step in the nationalization of industry and, in part, of commerce, although this departs from our original conceptions. As is known, our original plan was to nationalize by the "dry road." However, at that time we did not count on the rapid development of the internal political situation, nor did we take into account the Czechoslovakian and other events. In my view it would be a mistake to adhere to the original schedule and not exploit the favorable conjuncture.[38]

Clearly the consolidation of the noncommunist forces in Western Europe and the Soviet reaction required that socialization in Hungary be accelerated.

For the industrial working class, the party's radical measures brought little tangible advantage. The takeover of management by ill-prepared workers simply subordinated the enterprises to the central planning authorities. In May 1948 twenty industrial directorates of the various branch ministries were set up to administer the nationalized industries. Not only did the workers not gain effective control of their enterprises, they also lost their traditional trade union rights. A decree abolished the right to strike, wages and production quotas were centrally determined, and an iron discipline was imposed. Rákosi told the workers of the Csepel Island industrial complex in February 1948 that they were "producing much less for our democracy than they did for Horthy" and called for "order." Wildcat strikes at Csepel the preceding October had brought swift repression and the execution of the leaders. As Rákosi explained to the workers, while striking in France was "a necessary and corrective battle," in Hungary it was a "reactionary manifestation."[39]

With nationalization the works committees also lost their usefulness to the HCP, although many of the new worker-managers were drawn from their ranks. Their supervisory role was abruptly terminated in the spring of 1948 on the pretext that "the works committees are an outdated institution." Within a few months they were absorbed by the trade unions.[40] In August 1948 the communist head of the Trade Union Council, István Kossa, became minister of industry. His appointment symbolized the shift to a command economy and the superfluity of labor unions and self-management in a nominal workers' state.

**The Liquidation of Pluralism.**   As the capitalist economy was rapidly dismantled, pluralistic politics were effectively eliminated. In the immediate aftermath of the 1947 election the noncommunist parties made a last show of defiance against HCP dominance. Within the SDP, anger at the communist frauds led to a decision on 2 September (even before publication of the election results) to withdraw from the coalition, and the SDP ministers abandoned their offices in protest. When delegations of incensed workers descended on the party headquarters, the distraught Marosán tendered his resignation. He was finally persuaded to reconsider by Ambassador Pushkin and by Rákosi, who pleaded: "Please trust us! We will never forsake you or negotiate without you. Hold the [SDP] left wing together."[41] Even the left-wing socialists felt that the price of future collaboration was a larger share of power. Debates raged at the conference of SDP activists from 8 to 9 September and at subsequent meetings on how desirable it was to collaborate with the communists and on what terms. General Sviridov warned Antal Bán that no change in the leadership was permitted, and the left-wing–centrist group complied by defeating attempts to dismiss Szakasits and Marosán and to leave the coalition. The party's harassed moderate-conservative faction set up a separate headquarters and, supported by much of the rank and file, continued the hopeless struggle.[42]

Similar convulsions shook the SHP. At its meeting of 11 September the general council of the party revolted. Anticipating a common front with the opposition, it withdrew its confidence from Dinnyés, Ortutay, and Dobi. At Sviridov's request, Marshal Voroshilov hurried to Budapest and indicated that if the decision were not reversed he would dissolve the party. The council reluctantly complied and endorsed the status quo, but the SHP became a mere shadow of its former self, nominally represented in the corridors of power by Dobi and a handful of other figureheads.

The HCP redoubled its efforts after the election to conjure up the elusive "workers' unity" and to destroy the reactionary enemy. Pressure from below took the form of a huge mass demonstration on 6 September. On 23 September, after much haggling within the coalition, a new government was formed in which the communists and their fellow travelers were predominant. The former included Rákosi (deputy premier and minister of state), Rajk (interior), Gerő (transportation), Erik Molnár (foreign affairs), and Károly Olt (public welfare); among the latter could be counted Szakasits (deputy premier and minister of state), Erdei (minister of state), Darvas (construction and public works), Péter Veres (defense), and Ortutay (religion and education). Dinnyés remained as prime minister. Other appointments in state administration mirrored the expansion of communist power. The new government, concludes the party history, was "the popular front–style coalition of the accelerated transformation, the government of direct transition to proletarian dictatorship."[43]

Already on 1 September the Politburo had delivered the verdict that the Hungarian Independence Party was the "heir and continuance of Dezső Sulyok's party, whose antidemocratic machinations we will thwart." The AVO immediately proceeded to round up the signatories of the original petitions on behalf of the Pfeiffer and Barankovics parties.[44] Confessions of forgery were extracted under torture, charges of conspiracy and espionage were laid, and, as a result, in October the two parties lost 106 out of their 109 mandates—to the benefit of the HCP, which had been the runner-up. The Hungarian Independence Party ceased to exist and its leaders fled into exile. Barankovics's Democratic People's Party momentarily survived but was publicly challenged to choose between democracy and reaction. The remaining anticommunist forces attempted to regroup around the last institutional bulwark, the church. But the communists would not countenance organized dissent. "We must put an end to the untenable situation in which the bulk of the people's enemies hides behind the mantle of the churches, principally of the Roman Catholic Church," roared Rákosi at a meeting of party functionaries on 10 January 1948.[45] Meanwhile, even the semblance of parliamentary rule had become superfluous for the impatient communists. On 15 November 1947 the national assembly had delegated its powers to the cabinet and did not reconvene for over a year.

## THE WORKERS' VANGUARD

With the various "bourgeois" parties destroyed or rendered powerless, the last battlefield for communist predominance lay within the SDP. The commu-

nists' obvious determination to seize monopoly power drove the moderate socialist leaders to make a penultimate attempt to regain control of the party and preserve an authentically social democratic and, in the international context, "third
road" alternative to the HCP. Renewed communist invitations to merge, brutal
pressures to coerce ordinary SDP members to switch to the HCP, the urgings of
the dispersed opposition and of Western social democrats—all impelled a clar-
ification of the party's role. The SDP functionaries of the Budapest area delivered a memorandum on 15 October attacking the left wing's predominance
in the central office and suggesting that the alternative to restoration of a truly
independent line was outright dissolution of the party.

**The SDP Disintegrates.**   Meanwhile the socialists persisted in demanding
proportional allocation of posts in the interior ministry and the police force. The
communists replied with a classic subterfuge. An interior ministry decree on 3
November 1947 prohibited policemen from membership in party organizations.
The HCP thereupon dissolved its party units in the police force, at the same
time making sure of communist dominance over the ostensibly apolitical Police
Association, in which membership was made compulsory for all policemen.
This key sphere of power was thus effectively rendered immune to apportion-
ment.[46]

Rajk also played a central role in the resolution of the final battle between
the SDP's procommunists (including Marosán, Pál Justus, Géza Révész, Imre
Vajda, and an increasingly bewildered Szakasits) and such defenders of the old
party as Szelig, Kéthly, and the now anticommunist Bán. His secret police
mercilessly harassed the more inimical social democrats, whose dismissal was
meanwhile demanded by the HCP as the price for stopping an organized campaign that had turned the transfer of members into a veritable landslide. The
latter left out of fear as well as recognition that there was indeed no further use
for a party whose leaders, like Vajda, argued that there could be no social
democratic third road and that if necessary dictatorial methods could be
employed to achieve socialism.[47]

In late December a left-dominated SDP group in Budapest passed a pro-
Soviet, procommunist resolution that served as the pretext for a concerted attack on the remaining centrists. While Rajk generously provided safe-conducts
out of Hungary for Bán and other terrified socialists, Marosán, by now the
party's de facto leader, reached agreement with the HCP on a timetable for
unification. "The fratricidal struggle has ended," crowed Révai. In mid-
February Szakasits had accompanied Rákosi to Moscow to discuss the merger.
Concurrently, the Soviet Union promised to repatriate the over 100,000 remaining prisoners of war on the implicit condition that the two parties settle their
differences. Upon his return Szakasits protested that there could be no forcible
merger, but he soon bowed to the inevitable. On 18 February a meeting of

leftist socialists announced that the centrist leaders had "resigned." The party's congress, which took place from 6 to 8 March, only confirmed that the communist-directed coup had succeeded. The congress approved the expulsion of the moderate leaders, including Kéthly, and formally called for negotiations on fusion with the HCP. As in 1919, but more definitively, the latter had succeeded in destroying the party of social democracy. The veteran Vilmos Böhm had warned Marosán that the deceitful communists would swallow their party without leaving a trace, but from the safety of a second exile he telegraphed his redundant approval of the merger.[48]

A Politburo resolution on 11 March hailed the SDP congress for having overcome the split in the "workers' movement" brought about by the treachery of the foreign and domestic social democrats. Since the goal was no longer to shift members to the HCP but to work out the modalities of unification, the party arrested the landslide by temporarily suspending the admission of new members. On 10 March a joint Politburo and a joint Organizing Committee had been set up.* They were followed by similar committees at lower levels with two-thirds communist and one-third socialist membership, to oversee the transition to unification.

To aid the reorganization of the HCP after three years of indiscriminate recruitment, the Politburo had ordered a party card exchange on 20 November 1947. This exercise, when completed some months later, showed that real membership stood at 752,672, which in light of the influx of new members in the interim meant that earlier claims had been inflated by some 200,000. Some 12,000 undesirable members were dropped in the course of review. The card exchange also indicated that the membership was composed of 41.5 percent industrial and transportation workers, 32.8 percent peasants, 2.3 percent intellectuals, and 23.4 percent white-collar workers and others. The concurrent shift of SDP members to the HCP was only momentarily halted by the moratorium on new memberships between 21 February and 15 March. The communists had vigorously promoted this shift, but they also wanted to prevent the SDP's total disintegration before the ceremonial union of the two parties. Over 100,000 switched prior to the merger, at which time the HCP's strength stood at 887,472. With the merger, the membership of the renamed Hungarian Workers' Party was 1,128,130. Some 25,000 SDP members had been expelled in the purge of the right wing, while another 180,000 or so evidently chose not to rally to the new flag. The social composition of the membership underwent a notable change due to the different profile of the SDP contribution, the proportion of peasants dropping to 18.2 percent and that of white-collar workers rising to 37.5 percent.[49]

---

*For the HCP: Farkas, Gerő, Rajk, Rákosi, Révai (Politburo); and Apró, Farkas, Kádár, István Kovács (Organizing Committee). For the SDP: Marosán, Rónai, Szakasits, Vajda (Politburo); and Marosán, Ferenc Révész, József Harustyák (Organizing Committee).

These swings owed less to the changing convictions of the masses caught in the political maelstrom than to the communist leadership's quest for statistical evidence of the party's supremacy among the urban and rural proletariat. In the process the HCP far outstripped the other East European parties (with the exception of the Czechoslovakian) in the proportion of the population, 9.7 percent, that it claimed as its members. With the merger, this rose to 12 percent. The decision for mass recruitment spelled an end, for the time being, to the elite, vanguard party concept, and although this was rhetorically revived by Rákosi in April 1948 it was not applied again until after the merger. As a temporary palliative, the Politburo decided to identify a core of activists as "party workers." At the time of the merger over 100,000 members possessed special party worker cards.[50] The beginning of the real purges was still some months away.

**The Unequal Union.** From April 1948 onwards the communists conducted a massive propaganda campaign within the two parties to prepare for the merger; in particular, they established accelerated training programs for new party functionaries. By 12 June, when the parties held their last separate congresses, all their lower organizations had already been merged.[51] After the two congresses had ratified the merger, the first congress of the united Hungarian Workers' Party (Magyar Dolgozók Pártja, literally "Hungarian Working-People's Party", or HWP) was convened that same afternoon. The programmatic statement of the congress declared that power lay with the working class and the allied peasantry, the former being the leading class in the Hungarian society. Although big commerce and small industries were still in the capitalist sector, the new realities of power would facilitate their subjection. The capitalist sector in agriculture, represented by some sixty thousand kulak farms, also had to be brought under central supervision and control; while the program did not call for the elimination of kulaks, it did urge the defense of working peasants against village exploiters. Voluntary collectivization and the mechanization of agriculture were other immediate objectives. Artisans, tradesmen, and small merchants were free to serve the national economy. The three-year plan had to be completed and a new five-year plan developed, the standard of living raised, and work competition encouraged to improve productivity. The program further recommended the final purge of the state administration and its democratization by the employment of workers and peasants; the reorganization of the Independence Front, led by the HWP and encompassing all other parties, trade unions, cooperatives, and women's and youth organizations; a cultural policy designed for the masses; progressive extension of social insurance to all workers; a new constitution; and alliance with the Soviet Union and the other people's democracies. The new party, it was stated, represented the victory of Marxism-Leninism over reformism and opportunism.[52]

The program had been introduced to the 443 delegates (294 communist, 149 socialist) by Rákosi and Szakasits, while the new organizational statutes were presented by Farkas. The congress elected a 66-member Central Committee and other governing bodies: a 14-member Politburo consisting of 9 communists, Apró, Farkas, Gerő, Kádár, Kossa, Nagy, Rajk, Rákosi, Révai, and 5 socialists, Harustyák, Marosán, Rónai, Szakasits, and Vajda; an 8-man Secretariat with 6 communists, Farkas, Gerő, Kádár, Rajk, Rákosi, and Révai, and 2 former socialists, Marosán and Szakasits; and a Central Control Committee. Szakasits was named party president and Rákosi secretary-general, with Farkas, Kádár, and Marosán as deputies.

This fusion or, more accurately, absorption of the social democrats by the communists, was replicated throughout Eastern Europe. The Romanians took the step on 21 February, the Czechoslovaks on 27 June, the Bulgarians on 11 August, and the Poles on 15 December. In later years Hungarian party historians would depict this shotgun marriage of communism and social democracy and the new program of their offspring, the HWP, as indicative of a positive people's democratic orientation that was later perverted into the dogmatic excesses of Stalinism. This is allegedly borne out by the party's avoidance of compulsory collectivization, the stress on the standard of living, and by the preservation of some vestigial pluralism in the Independence Front and the postponement of proletarian dictatorship.

In fact, external impulses drove the party to hegemony so rapidly that the formulation of ideological rationales fell behind. At its meeting of 12 February 1948 the Politburo had approved a critical memorandum. "There are serious defects and omissions," it ran, "in our party's theoretical work. The Politburo itself has not analyzed from a Marxist-Leninist perspective the theoretical problems of the development of Hungarian democracy and the questions of people's democracy. As a consequence incorrect views have emerged in the party, even in the Politburo, regarding the significance of people's democracy and the qualitative changes in Hungary's economic structure."[53] But the party leaders were so busy complying with Stalin's order to seize power that they had neither the time, nor indeed the independent authority, to develop lasting definitions of the forthcoming political system.

The fate of the Independence Front was a case in point. In March Rákosi anticipated that a new "people's front" would be established in the fall, and that the other parties within it would retain some formal organization only in Budapest; in the countryside, where peasant support for the communists was sparse, the HCP and its successor would enjoy a monopoly position (and indeed in the spring of 1948 a campaign concentrated on the recruitment of middle peasants). But even if the original conception of the people's front allowed for the symbolic retention of a few "allied" parties, it left no doubt that the HWP would exercise undivided power.[54] The argument that the party was engaged on a path of democracy and tolerance until Stalinism reared its ugly head perverts historical evidence, which shows that at no time were the communists in a position to acquire power and implement even gradualist policies except by coercion.

**The Uninvited Revolution.**  With the inestimable support of the Soviet Union, a handful of communists had become the masters of Hungary. Their growing domination of the national scene owed far less to some ideologically defined historical inevitability or to the inherent dynamics of domestic politics than to the evolving calculations of Soviet national interest. Révai himself put it in a nutshell: "At every critical juncture our party could rely on the guidance and advice of the Soviet Bolshevik Party and personally of comrade Stalin."[55] At war's end the preconditions for economic and social reform were present in Hungary. The returning communists managed to seize the initiative in exploiting this popular desire for change. With Soviet assistance they kept the noncommunist forces on the defensive and always one step behind in a political chess game in which one side could arbitrarily change the rules. "Though we were a minority," boasted Révai, "nothing important could happen without us or against us in government; we could dictate the rate of change, and through control of armed power deal with conspiracy inspired by the coalition majority."[56] Alone among the postwar parties they managed to convey an image of discipline, purposefulness, and reformist zeal, all of which proved seductive to some of the underprivileged, to intellectuals in search of planned utopias, and, principally, to those attracted by raw power.

Yet not even at its conciliatory and cajoling best could the party command the allegiance of more than a small fraction of the Hungarian people. From the communist point of view, the diffident majority was simply untutored in the correct reading of the laws of history and would have to be led to the inevitable outcome of the class struggle. Only for a brief moment in 1945 did a few of the communist leaders entertain the illusion that victory could be theirs through the free contest of political values. Fortunately, they possessed alternative means. In Révai's words: "We never lost sight of the importance of power, and one assurance of our success was our move, immediately after liberation, to gain control of the armed enforcement agencies of the state and to later refuse any 'coalition' dilution of the communist direction of this armed power."[57] Dictatorships, whatever their political coloring, rest on the threat or exercise of force, and the Soviet Union and its communist servants enjoyed a monopoly of that essential commodity in Hungary.

★ ★ ★ ★

# The Corruption of Power

# PART FOUR

With the onset of the cold war and the Soviet-Yugoslav schism, Stalin moved to consolidate his new domain. Since the Stalinist prototype had to be replicated, an army of Russian advisers ensured that the satellites would march in step. Thus hardly had the Hungarian communists seized power than they abandoned all pretence at gradualism and respect for local conditions. In agriculture collectivization was the order of the day. Pursued with ruthless determination, it totally alienated the peasantry and created economic disaster. The precipitous expansion of heavy industry was equally ill conceived. Trade was reoriented, on exploitative terms, to the Soviet Union. Management of this socioeconomic transformation was entrusted to indoctrinated but incompetent workers and laborers. Not surprisingly, the standard of living declined from its already low level and the promised equality of affluence turned out to be an equality of misery.

Regimentation, cultural russification, and brutal class discrimination characterized the regime's totalitarian attempt at creating socialist supermen. Trade unions became agents of state control, while mass organizations served to mobilize people for ritualistic obeisance to the infallible leaders Stalin and Rákosi. The iron curtain sealed off Hungarians from the West, and Western and national culture were supplanted by communist and Russian panegyrics. The resistance of the churches was broken by the show trial and imprisonment of Cardinal Mindszenty. With the aid of the ubiquitous secret police, Hungarian society was atomized into terrified submission.

Concurrently the party itself underwent convulsions in consequence of Stalin's cold-war, anti-Tito hysteria. The Muscovite and home veterans had been joined by idealists as well as careerists, but now the party had to be purified of all elements other than the Soviets' trusted agents and the newest, most mal-

*leable recruits. The party's decimation began with the show trial and execution of the alleged Titoist László Rajk and continued with the arrest of countless other home communists (including the future leader János Kádár), of socialist fellow travelers, and of early postwar adherents. What little internal party democracy had existed gave way to the tyrannical rule of the foursome of Rákosi, Gerő, Farkas, and Révai. Their triumph created a spiritual wasteland in party and nation.*

*After Stalin's death in March 1953, concern at the stresses induced in his empire (as manifested in riots in Czechoslovakia and East Germany) led his uneasy heirs to seek compromise. Rákosi was compelled to cede the premiership to a less doctrinaire comrade, Imre Nagy, and to adopt a "New Course" of greater tolerance and economic rationality. Rákosi remained at the helm of the party while his new rival attempted to implement the liberalizing "June resolutions," abandon forced collectivization and industrialization, release imprisoned communists, and establish a more humane rapport with the masses. Some disillusioned communists rallied to Nagy, but the wily Rákosi obstructed and intrigued until, in early 1955, the Kremlin withdrew Nagy's mandate.*

*Although Rákosi had eliminated his competitor, the winds of change were not blowing in favor of restoring his Stalinist tyranny. His Soviet masters began to preach peaceful coexistence, even with his arch-enemy Tito. The masses remained voiceless, but the party's iron discipline had been broken, the integral validity of its totalitarian methods put in question.*

# 10. The Totalitarian State, 1948–1953

By absorbing the disintegrating SDP, the communists had eliminated the last tangible challenge to their claim of being the spokesmen of the working class and thereby the sole legitimate repository of political power. The political structure for the exercise of that power and the tactics for imposing socialism were still in a state of flux, however, when in late June 1948 the festering Soviet-Yugoslav controversy erupted into open confrontation and led to the expulsion of Tito's party from the Cominform. Stalin's fury at the Yugoslav comrades' refusal to pay obeisance knew no bounds. The disease of Titoism, with its alleged symptoms of anti-Sovietism and right-wing, nationalist deviation, was soon identified as a region-wide threat that had to be stamped out.

Communist leaders afflicted by this disease were accused of having failed to anticipate Stalin's new axiom, that in the transition from capitalism to socialism the class struggle necessarily becomes accentuated. This in turn required sharpened vigilance and the merciless application of what were euphemistically known as "administrative measures" to root out the internal enemy. Along with these paranoid suspicions Stalin was exhibiting a megalomania that demanded recognition of his infinite wisdom and therefore rigorous replication of the political and economic model that he had constructed in the Soviet Union. The Polish Central Committee subsequently passed a resolution on its leadership's deviations. These were identified as inadequate understanding of the proper rate of progress to socialism; failure to appreciate the Soviet Union's pre-eminent experience and leading role in constructing socialism; and liberal tolerance of inappropriate and erroneous theoretical formations. The resolutions of the Cominform and the Polish party were to serve as Stalinist guidelines for the other East European parties.

## FROM PEOPLE'S DEMOCRACY TO DICTATORSHIP

The founding conference of the Cominform had endorsed the Yugoslav political model, and Rákosi was thus caught unaware by the Stalin-Tito split. According to one account, when Rákosi was summoned by Stalin in late 1947 to report on his recent visit to Yugoslavia, his eulogy of Tito was received by Stalin in silence. Nevertheless, the HCP, like its sister parties, promptly imitated the Russians in sending critical letters to Belgrade in the spring of 1948.[1] Rákosi, Farkas, and Gerő were present at the June 1948 meeting of the Cominform in Bucharest that denounced Tito's heresy.

Thus no sooner had the two working-class parties merged and adopted a relatively gradualist program than modifications were imposed by the revised Cominform line. Now there could be no Hungarian road to socialism distinct from the Soviet model; the class struggle had to be waged more vigorously, notably in agriculture, and a political monolith had to be forged at the expense of the semipluralistic facade envisaged in the new Independence Front.

The full elaboration and impact of this orthodoxy emerged only gradually. As late as September 1948 Révai would present an obsolescent formulation of the nature of state power to the HWP's educational conference: "Historically," he began, "the people's democratic state belongs to the same category as the Soviet state: the state-type of the transition from capitalism to socialism." In this context the new Independence Front was essentially "the unique political structure that [linked] the leading workers' class with the allied masses of working people, primarily with the peasantry, and also with the urban lower-middle class and intelligentsia, in circumstances where differences still [prevailed] among classes of working people and therefore apart from the workers' party other democratic parties [retained] roots among the masses." It would be falsely radical and self-deceiving, warned Révai, to liquidate other parties before the disappearance of class distinctions. He also indicated that collectivization of agriculture was still in a preliminary, preparatory stage. Learning from the Soviet party did not mean servile imitation: "Stalin does not do our thinking, nor does he act in our stead."[2] Such gradualist convolutions were out of step with the new Stalinist dogma. By the November 1948 meeting of the Central Committee, Rákosi was anticipating the "liquidation of the allied parties," the expropriation of kulak lands, and the collectivization of agriculture within three to four years. He concluded: "Whoever among us clings to institutions or measures because we ourselves initiated them two or three years ago will, with the best of intentions, cause harm."[3] The dogmatic imposition of proletarian dictatorship was around the corner.

In mid-December the Polish and Bulgarian party congresses proclaimed the identity of people's democracy and proletarian dictatorship. It was allegedly during his Warsaw visit that Gerő absorbed the full implication of Stalin's line.

In his letter of 26 December to the Secretariat he indicated that the HWP "must draw a lesson from comrade Stalin's latest, theoretically highly significant pronouncements." According to Gerő, the Stalinist definition that "a people's democracy fulfills the basic functions of a proletarian dictatorship" meant that "a people's democracy is essentially a variant of proletarian dictatorship brought about by special circumstances of historical evolution." Gerő's practical conclusion was that socialism could not be built without dictatorship: "We must strengthen the dictatorial character of people's democracy, we must strengthen the role of party and working class in the state, the economy, and the political and cultural life of the country."[4]

The HWP leadership hurriedly endorsed the new line. Rákosi noted defensively that the party's former orientation had not amounted to a revision of Leninism but had simply not been fully developed. Rákosi, Révai, and Gerő all stressed to each other that the shift to dictatorship should not be overdone or accomplished by excessively repressive measures. They debated further the problem of reconciling the nominal sharing of power with the peasantry, as well as the existence of other parties (no matter how impotent), with the requisites of proletarian dictatorship.[5] For public consumption Rákosi wrote an article explaining that the people's democracy was "a state through which, thanks to the victory of the Soviet Union, the working people, led by the working class, progress from capitalism to socialism." True, the people's democracy would function as a proletarian dictatorship, but "without a Soviet structure."[6]

At its March 1949 meeting the Central Committee confirmed the operational implications of the new dogma. The Independence Front would serve not to concentrate allied forces but to liquidate them and, ultimately, itself. The kulak class would have to be destroyed in order to "win over" the middle peasants.[7] In sum, compulsion and repression were to be the tools of dictatorship by a single party. Révai belatedly trimmed his sails to the new wind. "Recognition that people's democracy is a variant of proletarian dictatorship," he explained, "arms us with the knowledge that we must even more determinedly and uniformly develop those organs of state power most suitable for the use of force against the class enemy."[8] The die was cast for one of the most pitiless exercises of state power in modern history. "The first test for a communist," János Kádár reflected many years later, "is when he faces the enemy, the second when he acquires power. Rákosi stood the first test remarkably well, but he failed the second."[9] What Kádár left unsaid was that Rákosi fulfilled the most basic requirement of a communist in East-Central Europe, blind obedience to the Soviet Union regardless of the consequences.

**The Stalinist Model.** In a lecture published in 1950 Révai outlined the main components of the latest phase, which he described as stretching from the creation of the HWP to the inauguration of the first five-year plan in January

1950. These included the beginning of socialist industrialization; the conversion of socialist worker competition into a mass movement (shock-worker brigades, the Stakhanov movement, and so forth); the building of rural socialism by repression of the kulaks, forceful promotion of collectivization, and development of machine-tractor stations; consolidation of the hegemony of the working class and of the party's rule; a cultural revolution; the battle against clerical reaction; the purge from the party of imperialist agents and Titoist conspirators; the vigilance campaign; and the use of techniques of criticism and autocriticism.[10]

Indeed, the Procrustean imposition of Stalin's version of proletarian dictatorship resulted in a radical transformation of the entire political, social, and economic system. Rákosi and his associates showed extraordinary zeal and single-mindedness in replicating the Stalinist model down to its most trivial aspects. Although the assistance of an army of Soviet experts was invaluable, the party's leaders acted not under compulsion but out of a conditioned and unconditional loyalty to their Russian masters. The possibility that Hungary's interests might not fully coincide with those of the Soviet Union was never entertained by men who long ago had divested themselves of any patriotic sentiments and intellectual independence in favor of the iron discipline of service to a Soviet-defined communist cause.

**The Cult of Personality.**   A critical adjustment to the Stalinist model occurred in the sphere of leadership. Rákosi swiftly dropped the mask of genial politician which he had worn with some discomfort for three years to emerge as a pitiless autocrat who visibly enjoyed the exercise of unbridled authority and wished only to emulate his Soviet ideal. As Tolstoy once observed, revolutionaries in power always behave worse than those they replace because they come fresh to it. The myth of proletarian dictatorship could scarcely conceal the reality of Rákosi's autocracy. A foretaste of this "cult of personality" came at an election rally in April 1949, as Gerő thundered: "When we say Rákosi, we mean the Hungarian people. And when we say the Hungarian people, we mean Rákosi."[11]

The cult was carried to the most absurd extremes. Each public mention of Rákosi (and, of course, of Stalin) was received with the obligatory thunderous applause started by a party claque. "The party leader," recalled a Muscovite comrade in the mid-1960s, "had turned into a 'sage' who not only interpreted but also advanced Marxist-Leninist theory."[12] Deified as the infallible leader, Rákosi became the object of fulsome praise. Although he was not known to have written as much as a couplet, he was lauded by a young party versifier as the greatest poet in Hungary's literary history.[13] While the Muscovites were long accustomed to such sycophantic panegyrics, the home comrades were somewhat taken aback by the dimensions of the personality cult. But such misgivings were easily submerged in the exhilarating exercise of power, and were in any event constrained by the conversion of the party from a relatively loose organization into a disciplined tool of the Muscovite leadership.

Rákosi stood alone at the apex of power, jealously reserving to himself the right to formulate general policy. The other members of the leading quadrumvirate, Gerő, Farkas, and Révai, enjoyed more restricted spheres of authority. Their membership in the inner circle suggests a collegiality that did not preclude mutual suspicion and rivalry. All had their private ambitions and their own Soviet contacts or patrons. It is not unlikely that Stalin fostered the tensions between them to preserve an element of insecurity similar to that afflicting his own entourage. Decision making took place in an atmosphere of secrecy and conspiracy. Beyond Rákosi, and perhaps Gerő and Farkas, the party leaders and the functionaries in the central apparatus were encapsulated in narrow spheres of responsibility and with correspondingly narrow access to information. Such fragmentation and isolation served, of course, to facilitate Rákosi's autocratic exercise of power.

His chief acolyte and potential rival, the gifted, ascetic, abrasive Gerő, was given the risk-laden job of constructing the economy. As chairman of the People's Economic Council, Gerő wielded an immense power that was only marginally shared by two other Muscovites: Vas, who headed the State Planning Office, and Friss, who was in charge of the Secretariat's economic department. The armed forces and internal security were the preserve of Farkas, who had been appointed defense minister in August 1948. Since these were the spheres under most direct Soviet control, Farkas enjoyed little latitude, but his eagerness to fulfill orders unthinkingly made him a fearsomely efficient agent of that control. Utterly ruthless and amoral, Farkas was, in the words of his principal aide Nógrádi, the type of man who under no circumstances should be given power.[14]

One rung below Gerő and Farkas in the hierarchy stood Révai, the party's cultural czar and self-styled theoretician. As ideological spokesman he had the thankless task of anticipating or at least reformulating the changing Stalinist guidelines. Time and again he would find himself out of step and have to draft new theoretical rationalizations. Unimpeachably loyal to the party and the Soviet Union, Révai, as minister of culture, was also implacable in his imposition of cultural russification. He was nevertheless the least secure and influential member of the foursome. Other notable Muscovites in Révai's sphere were Zoltán Biró, head of the Secretariat's education department and Rákosi's brother, and Erzsébet Andics, a party historian and occasional cultural dictator.

There was, finally, that anomalous Muscovite, the veteran Imre Nagy. A devoted and loyal party member, he was generally kept on the periphery of decision making. He had proven unequal to the task of reconstructing and activizing the interior ministry and, as will be described later, he expressed deviant views on collectivization that led to his expulsion from the Politburo in

August 1949. Nagy then withdrew to academe, where he established a rapport with some concurrently disgraced left-wing Populists. After exercising self-criticism he was reappointed to the Politburo and became a secretary at the time of the HWP's second congress in February 1951. He also served a stint as minister of crop collections and, in November 1952, became one of the five deputy premiers. Whether or not his survival and rehabilitation were linked to the coincident rise of Malenkov, his influence in the party remained negligible until the climactic changes following Stalin's death.

With the onset of Rákosi's dictatorship, the always circumscribed influence of the old home communists rapidly waned until most of them fell victim to the purges. Nominally most powerful among them was Kádár, who while retaining his post of deputy secretary-general succeeded Rajk as interior minister in August 1948. In June 1950 he was appointed head of the Central Committee's party and mass organization department. Despite these high functions Kádár was little more than a dutiful apparatchik, and it was the more talented Rajk who paid for his flamboyance by being chosen for the inaugural show trial that launched the purges. The colorless Apró showed a talent for survival and little else. Kállai replaced Rajk in the ceremonial post of foreign minister in June 1949 before his turn came to be purged. The doctrinaire journeyman Károly Kiss survived the purges as chairman of the Central Control Committee, in which capacity he was theoretically responsible for party discipline and sanctions. His influence in that post and others he held concurrently (foreign minister in 1951/52 and deputy premier in 1952/53) was inconsequential compared to that of the Muscovite leaders.

**The Centralized Party.**    Formal titles and party structure gave little indication of the locus and distribution of power in the Rákosi era. The Secretariat, modeled on the Soviet version of 1948, encompassed departments dealing with agitprop, cadres, the various sectors of state activity, and a section linked to the AVH. It functioned as the servant of the leading foursome. The organizational hierarchy reached down from the triennial congress and the Central Committee through district committees to the primary units in factories, collective farms, and all spheres of employment. Even individual apartment buildings had their party trusty and AVH informer. This army of ordinary members, activists, and full-time secretaries was a mere tool of the leadership, for the principle of democratic centralism, in its application by Rákosi, invited no advice, let alone dissent. The careful selection of delegates to the congresses and of Central Committee members ensured unquestioning obedience. Recalled Imre Nagy in the mid-1950s:

> Rákosi and the Party leaders, Gerő, Révai, and Farkas, seriously impaired the effectiveness of the Communist principle of criticism and self-criticism within the Party and government. They generally considered criticism from below as the

voice of the enemy and acted accordingly. They did not criticize one another but shielded each other from criticism. They took even the mildest form of criticism as a personal insult. According to them, mistakes could be made only at the lower echelons. They themselves were infallible and could do no wrong.[15]

Decision making was therefore the exclusive prerogative of Rákosi's clique and not of the full Politburo or of the Central Committee. The last met only infrequently for formalistic approval of Rákosi's perfunctory reports. According to one member, "for years there was no debate at Central Committee meetings, at most there were a few comments designed to underscore the 'correctness' of the report."[16] The rare independent interjection was quickly dismissed as ill-informed. The clique thus withdrew into isolation not only from the masses but also from the party itself. Not surprisingly, this style of leadership inspired a form of subservience in party and government that concealed or falsified all that did not suit the preconceptions of the rulers.

Thus Rákosi's autocratic style permeated the entire party and converted it into a bureaucratized and centralized servant of the leadership. In late 1948 the official emphasis was still on decentralization and the elimination of overlapping jurisdictions between the party apparatus, mass organizations, and the state administration. In practice, however, any autonomy in the latter spheres and at the lower levels of the party was rapidly eliminated. The always rather illusory principle of intraparty democracy was jettisoned in favor of the personal authority of county and district secretaries, who thereby became local petty tyrants in the image of Rákosi. The Muscovite writer Gyula Háy recalls that when once asked to chair a party meeting, he was "handed a printed sheet which not only laid down the exact contents of my speech but also prescribed the cheers that were to interrupt it and the respective intensities of the applause that was to greet each mention of Rákosi's or Stalin's name."[17]

The party's central control reached into all spheres of economic, social, and cultural activity. By a resolution of the Organizational Committee on 15 June 1950, new party cadres, who were automatically elected local secretaries but operated under central direction, were sent into the factories to spur implementation of the five-year plan. Concurrently, worker-cadres were dispatched to the countryside to lead district party committees in the collectivization campaign. That campaign outpaced the expansion of party cells, since in early 1951 only half the new collective farms had any form of party organization. Political direction was not lacking, however, for the machine-tractor stations had their own party units, with the secretary serving as political deputy to the manager.

Confronted with a general deterioration in party life, the Central Committee on 10 February 1950 called for new elections at all party levels, for self-criticism and for a rejuvenation of the leadership. In conjunction with the elections the committee imposed a certain structural decentralization, which expanded the number of basic units from 9,500 in 1950 to over 16,000 in 1952.

But the main thrust of organizational policy remained the activization of the membership and not the democratization of party life. Amendments to the party statutes ratified at the second congress eliminated the earlier provision that basic units develop local policy, limiting their function to the implementation of directives from above. In aid of the latter they were now formally assigned supervisory authority over production.

The dominant feature of party life in the Rákosi era was an almost ceaseless purging of cadres and of the general membership. In the words of a central directive: "A considerable decline of vigilance in recruitment has created a situation in which, while the leading organizations are progressively exposing and expelling the enemy, in the factories and offices the latter is penetrating the party's ranks and is thereby reaching leading functions in the party, state, and economic mass organizations."[18] As a result, 46.4 percent of middle and lower party leaders were replaced on the occasion of the elections of October–November 1951. These purges served not so much to eliminate the incompetent as to convert the party's complement of cadres into a body totally subservient to Rákosi. That goal required replacement of the older generation of 1919 veterans, home communists, and "Westerners" with a new breed of raw recruits who would know no communism other than that dictated by Rákosi, who would have no loyalties beyond their dependence on the latter's favor. Rákosi thus purposely and effectively destroyed what little pluralism and creativity had existed in the postwar party to create a spiritually and intellectually barren apparatus alienated both from the old movement and from the population at large.

While Rákosi and the small Muscovite contingent consolidated their hold over the key positions of power, some 100,000 new cadres were inducted into a secondary party elite that staffed the central apparatus and the security arms of party and state. As in the Soviet Union, the party elite enjoyed blatantly "bourgeois" perquisites of power in accordance with the individual's precise status, all far above the dismal living standard of the rest of the population. The cynical materialism and careerism that suffused party life were only accentuated by the climate of fear in the years of the purges.

**The Rise and Fall of the People's Colleges.**    A notable victim of the drive to destroy all remnants of heterogeneity and autonomy within the party was the people's college movement. The broader Populist movement had been the party's most dangerous if unorganized rival ever since the 1930s. Initially, as was noted earlier, the communists attempted to ride on the Populist coattails and turn the movement leftward, but its nationalistic and peasant orientation could not readily be reconciled with the communists' pro-Soviet and urban-proletarian line.

During the war a younger generation of peasant youth attending the Győrffy College came under Populist influence, and the illegal communist party through Lajos Fehér managed to convert a few of them—notably András Hegedüs—to communism. In the spring of 1946 a group of these students called for the creation of a network of similar colleges, devoted to the democratization of education in general and to the political and cultural enlightenment of young peasants in particular. The HCP endorsed the idea all the more enthusiastically since it promised to serve to radicalize the peasantry and detach it from smallholder influence. Since the old universities remained under orthodox state and church control, the people's colleges could serve as counterinstitutions susceptible to communist guidance.

At first only a few of the Győrffy students were avowed communists, but many others eagerly took part in implementing the land reform and threw themselves unstintingly into the establishment of embryonic people's colleges. By the fall of 1946, with the active support of the HCP and the NPP, forty-four barely viable colleges began operation with 1,627 students under the aegis of the Győrffy-led National Federation of People's Colleges (Népi Kollégiumok Országos Szövetsége, or NÉKOSZ).[19] From the start their relation to the HCP and communist ideology was anomalous. Their stress on the inculcation of democratic principles and national cultural values was consonant with left-wing Populism, and the communists, notably Révai, qualified their endorsement with reminders that the colleges should explain the leading role of the working class.[20] László Rajk became the colleges' most influential advocate, declaring that his party did not insist on the primacy of Marxism-Leninism in their curriculum, and indeed the HCP tactically accommodated itself to the NÉKOSZ leaders' insistence that self-government and freedom from any party's control were essential to the people's college movement.

Most other parties and the churches soon came to regard the people's colleges as the training ground for communist "janissaries" and reserved their support for the traditional universities and residential colleges. The SDP established the competing Endre Ady College. In fact, the people's colleges represented more a spontaneous student movement than an orderly pedagogical service. Their programs consisted of innovative experiments in communal learning and in earnest explorations of peasant life and traditions at the expense of rigorous academic work. Most of the students became members of the HCP or the NPP, but party discipline was steadfastly rejected in favor of collegiate autonomy. At the same time, the ideological tendency within the colleges was largely determined by the communists and left-wing Populists although it remained leavened by a healthy eclecticism.

The movement prospered, and in September 1947 100 people's colleges opened their doors to 6,000 students. Most of the colleges provided a variegated remedial program for teenage youths of mainly peasant stock; 19 claimed to perform postsecondary functions. Activism and youthful enthusiasm sustained the momentum of the movement and induced an esprit de corps and a consequent contempt for party authority, but it failed to provide a disciplined preparation for future employment. The HCP's Youth Secretariat only aroused the organizers' hostility by trying to impose party rule, while the party's leaders, notably Révai and Rajk, showed a tactical permissiveness toward the movement.

From the beginning of 1948 the HCP's guarded tolerance evaporated as the party reached for monopoly power. In the immediate task of marshaling the universities to train proletarian youth for the transformation of economy and society, the people's colleges, with their relatively anarchic and peasant character, were more hindrance than help. Only some 11 to 12 percent of their students came from the industrial working class, and their leaders persisted in pursuing independent objectives, such as the creation of a new social science university. The axe fell shortly after the Cominform split. At its September 1948 meeting the Politburo passed a resolution condemning the NÉKOSZ organizers for neglecting the party, for propagating a confused anti-Leninist ideology and tolerating a cult of the peasantry, for isolating the colleges from the young workers' movement, and even for private immorality. In their last year of operation over 160 colleges enrolled some 10,000 students, but the process of integration was under way, and in mid-1949 the colleges were absorbed as ordinary student residences into the fully nationalized and centralized educational system. According to the official rationale, when working-class power was imposed on the state, the difference between state colleges and the people's colleges disappeared. Thus, the autonomy of NÉKOSZ could not be allowed to disturb the creation of a new, communist intelligentsia.[21]

Despite their academic shortcomings, the people's colleges had performed a certain liberating function for thousands of young people, inculcating them with an independent, radical, national Populism that the party leadership could not countenance once the struggle for power was concluded. With the colleges disbanded and their leaders dispersed, the movement was swallowed up in the new totalitarian state. Their organizers and alumni, however, carried with them an enduring nostalgia and a sense of comradeship. Rákosi regarded them, with some justification, as a dangerously undisciplined and unconventional breed within the new Stalinist party, and many neo-Populist communists would fall victim to his purges. The liquidation of Rajk, their principal communist mentor, can be seen as both cause and effect of the final disgrace of the people's college movement. One of the accusations levelled at Rajk was that of persistent cooperation with the Populists, notably their right wing, in the wake of the German-Soviet Pact.[22] In Rákosi's demonology, Populism became as abhorrent an evil as Titoism.

## THE PARTY PURIFIED

Stalin's determination to isolate the Titoist heresy and shore up his western defenses against the imperialists demanded total subservience on the part of the satellite parties. In order to secure this obedience, he resorted characteristically to the exercise of terror by means of a meticulously synchronized area-wide purge of alleged Titoist traitors and imperialist agents. In Hungary the choice of chief scapegoat was made by Rákosi and Farkas. It fell on László Rajk. To all appearances, Rajk had been the most devoted, indeed fanatical of communists, a tireless and pitiless manager of the party's brutal grab for power. Nor could he be faulted for nationalism: "Every man has his compass and mine is the Soviet Union," he would proclaim.[23] But his personal magnetism, his attraction for young radicals, and the fact that he was not a Muscovite set him apart from the leading foursome.

Rajk's relative popularity was particularly irksome to Farkas, who aspired to become the party's security overlord and perhaps even to lead the party. As a former colleague reportedly described him, Farkas "was the worst. The others were probably 'sincerely evil.' Farkas was just ambitious. He wanted Rákosi's job and he was determined to destroy any man who might stand in his way."[24] Friction between Rajk, on the one hand, and Gábor Péter and Farkas on the other, had already prompted the last-named to accuse Rajk in December 1947 of antiparty behavior (the charge was that he reorganized party groups within his ministry). "The interior is not in the party's hands!" thundered Farkas when Péter complained of his minister.[25] The charge was dismissed by the Secretariat, but Rákosi shifted Rajk to the foreign ministry the following August.[26] The bewildered Rajk soon became aware that a sinister web of suspicion was descending around him. He took to spontaneously assuring visitors that rumors of his estrangement from the Muscovites and of his sympathy for Tito were hostile and totally unfounded.[27] In January 1949 the wily Rákosi sent Rajk off to Moscow, anticipating that his complaints against the apparent Muscovite conspiracy would only damn him in the Russians' eyes. The stratagem worked, and the painstaking preparations for the human sacrifice were set in motion.

**The Rajk Trial.** The long series of purges was launched in 1949 with show trials orchestrated by the MVD's Lieutenant-General Fedor Bielkin and Gábor Péter, backed up by their army of Russian and Hungarian specialists. The entire vigilance campaign was directed from Moscow by Beria's secret police, whose operations in Hungary were covered by a February 1949 agreement on close cooperation in security matters. Rajk and his wife were arrested on 30 May along with other "accomplices." *Szabad Nép* still reported on his official activities on 1 and 4 June, and only on 16 June was his expulsion from the party made public, with news of his arrest following three days later. The charges included spying for Western intelligence, conspiring with Tito to murder Rákosi, Gerő, and Farkas (who had reportedly asked for the honor of having his name placed second!), and informing for Horthy's police and the Gestapo.[28] Tortured and brainwashed, Rajk withheld the confession he knew led to death. Finally Rákosi dispatched Kádár, the then interior minister, who appealed to his friend's loyalty: "The Party has chosen you for the role of traitor, you must sacrifice yourself to the Party. This is terrible, but after all you are an old militant and cannot refuse to help the Party." Kádár promised Rajk and his family anonymous exile in the Soviet Union, but said that the public would have to be told he had been executed.[29] Rajk ultimately gave in and learned his part for the trial, while an assortment of witnesses (including the American Noel Field) were coerced and coached to testify to his alleged misdemeanors. An attempt was made concurrently to link the most exposed member of the foursome, Révai, to Rajk. Révai reportedly abstained in the Politburo from approving Rajk's death sentence, and was then compelled to compose the official indictment.[30]

At the trial, which opened on 16 September, Rajk confessed that he had served as an informer for Horthy's secret police; that he sabotaged the Republican effort in the Spanish Civil War; that as a Gestapo agent he led the wartime party toward merger with the Arrow Cross; and that he then brought the party under Populist control. After the war, he confessed, he brought fascists and criminals into the Organizing Guard to alienate the masses, then was blackmailed by the Americans into perpetrating the blue-slip fraud to discredit the party and into serving as Tito's agent.[31] The verdict was predetermined. On 15 October, Rajk was hanged in Budapest, as his wife Julia followed the proceedings from a nearby cell. Among the other home communists liquidated in this first purge were armed forces' Inspector-General Pálffy and the head and deputy head of the Secretariat's cadre department, Tibor Szőnyi and András Szalai. The social democrat fellow traveler Pál Justus was also purged, but survived.

The intended demonstration effect of the show trials was spelled out by Gerő: "Anyone who is reluctant to pay homage to the leading role of the Soviet fatherland and its great leader, comrade Stalin, is guilty of treason against the party."[32] After Rajk had been liquidated, Rákosi paid tribute to Stalin's guidance and the shining example of the Soviet party's great purges of the 1930s: "It was not easy to work out the way, and I must confess to you that it cost me many a sleepless night until the plan of action finally crystalized. . . . We made the deduction from the Rajk trial that the touchstone of every communist leader is his relationship with the Soviet Union."[33] He would soon have to eat his words and admit that the Rajk purge had been a gigantic fabrication, for as a biographical profile of Rajk concluded twenty years later, "there was not one ounce of truth in the accusations at the trial."[34]

At the time the exposure, by the party's full propaganda network, of dastardly Titoist and imperialist plots fell on a stunned but credulous public. Within the party the possibility of fabrication was hardly entertained even in private by most members. They, as one recalled in 1969, "believed and rationalized the charge."[35] Given the history of the communist movement, it did not seem implausible that, as Révai thundered in a front-page editorial in *Szabad Nép* on 25 September, the "Tito and Rajk gang [had] continued the work of Trotsky and Bukharin."

**The Permanent Purge.** The 1949 show trials were only the opening salvo in a devastating series of high-level purges and low-level expulsions that crowned the general application of terror beyond the party itself. The more important cases were handled by Soviet as well as AVH officers, and the most bestial forms of torture were applied in the course of the interrogations. In the words of the official party history: "The serious and responsible task of political vigilance turned into hysteria and into the tool of irresponsible and careerist interests. Suspicion fell primarily on preliberation party members, many among whom were slandered with accusations that they owed their survival in illegality to treason."[36] In early 1950 the purge hit over four thousand former social democrats, including such prominent fellow travelers as Szakasits, Marosán, and Ries. It was during a dinner party in May with Rákosi, Gerő, and Farkas that Szakasits, then president of the republic, was handed a confession admitting he had been a Gestapo and British spy. "If you sign it," said Rákosi, "your fate will be that of Zoltán Tildy. If you refuse, it will be that of Rajk."[37] (Tildy was under house arrest.) Szakasits was thereupon taken away by Gábor Péter and tortured until he signed. A few months later most of the army's communist officer corps, including Generals László Sólyom and Gusztáv Illy, were also purged.

Finally, in the spring of 1951, the bulk of the prewar generation of home communists fell under Rákosi's axe. Kádár, their most prominent member, was arrested in April on the usual charges of treason and espionage; the dissolution of the party during the war was now cited as proof of his duplicity. Kádár was tortured chiefly by Péter's deputy and Farkas's half-Russian son, Vladimir; he is reported to have reflected later that "prison under Horthy and the Gestapo were bad enough, but they were nothing compared to what one suffered in Rákosi's jails."[38] The leading members of the prewar Debrecen group, Kállai (then foreign minister), Donáth (at one time head of Rákosi's own secretariat), Losonczy (a secretary of state in Révai's culture ministry), and Szilárd Ujhelyi were swept up on similar charges. Eventually all confessed. The death sentences on Kállai and Losonczy were commuted; Kádár received four years, Donáth two. Another Debrecen veteran and Kádár's successor in the interior ministry, Sándor Zöld, reacted to intimations of his imminent demise by killing his family and committing suicide. As the news spread, recalls Nógrádi, "no one would discuss this tragedy. People withdrew into themselves; everyone was left alone with his doubts."[39]

Rákosi thus eliminated from his party the preliberation generation of home communists, the "nineteeners," the "Westerners," the Spanish Civil War vet-

erans, and the social democrats. They were regarded as being variously susceptible to nationalism, Western influences, and non-Stalinist variants of communism. Even old Muscovites were not beyond suspicion. In May 1950 Rákosi
summoned Nógrádi to inform him of allegations that he was an American spy.
The evidence was the recent arrest of a number of Nógrádi's friends on the
same preposterous charge. Nógrádi was saved, probably, by his good Soviet
connections, but Rákosi's purge mania was such that even in 1954, at the
height of the New Course, he would raise new accusations against his Muscovite comrade.[40] In another instance, when advised by telephone in 1951 of the
arrest of his brother-in-law László Gács (a home communist and former deputy
secretary-general of the Trade Union Council), a stunned Révai reportedly protested: "That was close, that was close, you are striking dangerously near."[41]
There is, to be sure, little honor among thieves, but Rákosi's purges seemed to
be extraordinarily free from the restraints of friendship or comradeship, let
alone morality.

The Central Committee was never apprised of the extent of the purges. Few,
indeed, apart from Rákosi, Farkas, Gerő, and Péter (with the other leading
AVH thugs) were fully aware of the dimensions of this campaign of terror.
Most convinced communists had long ago sacrificed any concept of individual
human rights on the altar of revolutionary social justice, and their fragmented
perception of the purges seemed to confirm the leadership's warning that the
threat of imperialism and of its renegade agent, Tito, required greater vigilance.
Over time, the disappearances did induce a pervasive sense of insecurity within
the party, and eventually the thousands of imprisoned comrades came to realize
that they were all victims of the same fraud. As for the perpetrators of this
macabre drama, they lived in a world of soulless cynicism. When György
Faludy, a poet who had come back from exile to serve as the literary editor of
*Népszava,* was arrested in 1950 for refusing to eulogize Rákosi, Gábor Péter
reportedly mocked him: "You silly fool, returning from America to this
filth!"[42] The party's prize-winning young writer Tamás Aczél recalled in 1960:
"Never had an executioner hanged so many Communists, not even in the days
of the bloodiest 'white terror' of the Horthy era. The regime had hanged its best
Party workers, its most talented public servants."[43]

The reign of terror ensured fearful obedience from the mass of members who
had joined out of careerism and self-preservation. However, many of the party
veterans who had retained some ideological convictions and the radical intellectuals who had been seduced by utopian visions were now compelled, often
in a prison cell, to take stock of the monster they had unleashed. The full
reckoning was yet to come. In later years the Hungarian party, like its Soviet
parent, would have a difficult time indeed in persuading its members and the
population at large that murder and terror were a Stalinist aberration and not an
integral part of the political system fathered by Lenin.

Stalin's final paranoiac outburst was the anti-Semitic "doctors' plot" purge in early 1953. The fact that Rákosi, along with his principal lieutenants, was Jewish did not make his conduct of the pogrom any milder. The Hungarian scapegoats, arrested in January and February, included such experts in the arts of torture and perversion of justice as Gábor Péter and justice minister Gyula Décsi. Rákosi's suspicions against Péter had been fueled for some time by evidence that the latter had intrigued against him with Beria.[44] Also arrested were István Szirmai, lately director of Hungarian radio, and Lajos Stöckler, leader of the Jewish community in Hungary. Stalin's death aborted the pogrom and was reportedly greeted with great relief by the leading foursome, who were themselves secretly terrified at their patron's anti-Semitic rampage.[45]

Several thousand upper- and middle-level party functionaries were thus executed or imprisoned. Meanwhile the party at large underwent a congruent process of purification. The purges and more routine expulsions hit more than 350,000 members of the HWP from 1948 to 1956.[46]

The proportion of white-collar employees who were members of the HWP had already been swelled by the transfer to it of the bulk of social democrats. Following the 1948 merger an influx of new recruits seeking the apparent security of membership had increased the proportion still further. On 2 September 1948 the Politburo imposed a six-month moratorium on new candidacies and ordered a massive screening of the existing membership. The screening committees, manned by some 60,000 activists, proceeded to examine the records of over 1 million party members. Individual cases occasionally prompted violent debate at local membership meetings, and the entire operation was conducted in an atmosphere of fear and arbitrariness. The thrust of the purge was less to rid the party of inactive elements than to restore a "proper" social balance in the membership. In practice this meant the expulsion primarily of white-collar and lower-middle-class members. Half the 178,850 expellees were former social democrats. Some 130,000 other members did not even bother to submit to formal screening. As a result, overall membership fell by more than 300,000. Officially the purified membership in 1949 stood at 880,717 full or candidate members, a number that was in reality reduced by the refusal of over 30,000 people to pick up their party cards.

The purge, however, did not result in a major transformation of the party's social profile, the new proportions being 49.3 percent industrial and agricultural workers, 13.4 percent peasants, 4 percent intelligentsia, and 33.3 percent employees and others.[47] The moratorium on admission to full membership was therefore extended to 1 November 1949 and an aggressive recruitment campaign launched to increase the proportion of workers and collectivized peasants. The peasantry's reluctance to join its persecutors was so strong, however, that in 1950 the Central Committee decided to offer admission to tens of thousands of hitherto undesirable but influential middle peasants. This tactic, too, failed miserably. Worried by the poor response of the most desirable social strata, Rákosi also proposed in early 1950 that carefully screened middle-class elements be admitted. Kádár reportedly opposed this lowering of standards and had to exercise self-criticism at the subsequent party congress.[48] A new wave of screenings and expulsions in 1952/53 reduced party membership by another 240,000, most of them former social democrats and adherents of the premerger period. Despite the concurrent recruitment drive, then, after reaching a peak of 945,606 in early 1952 party membership in mid-1953 stood at 885,197, or 9.4 percent of the population.

**The Price of Upward Mobility.** The influx of workers into administrative jobs was reflected in the frequent discrepancy between a party member's current employment and his or her original occupation. Thirty-eight percent were active industrial and agricultural workers and 38.8 percent white-collar workers, whereas by original occupation the proportions were, respectively, 59.2 percent and 13.2 percent. The proportion of active workers thus declined in the party between 1950 and 1953, as did the proportion of industrial workers who were members of the HWP.[49] Yet by 1953 over 227,000 former workers belonging to the party were exercising administrative functions. In sum, while the bulk of the proletariat remained estranged from its vanguard, the party had managed to draw the politically most susceptible or ambitious industrial workers with the lure of bureaucratic jobs and authority.

Expected to man the vastly expanded party and state apparatus of the new totalitarian system, these cadres came equipped with no technical expertise and little ideological preparation. The party imposed heavy demands in discipline and amorality on its new functionaries, but it also offered tangible rewards. It held out to the selected young intellectual and unskilled worker the prospect of extraordinarily rapid upward mobility, of prestige and a semblance of power, as well as relative affluence. That the intellectual lacked creative gifts, or that the worker had no managerial talents, mattered little compared with his suitably modest social origins and submissiveness to iron discipline. As Rákosi observed to a returning Muscovite, the challenge was to turn cobblers into diplomats.[50] The party was in too much of a hurry to create an authentically meritocratic system of social mobility, and the dogmatic stress on social origins excluded most talented people from serving either the revolutionary cause or the nation's secular interests.

**The Abuses of Ideology.** On its road to power the party had played down Marxism-Leninism, with the result that when it achieved monopoly power its membership was ill prepared for the educational function of justifying its position ideologically. The Horthy regime had isolated the masses from the Soviet Union, reflected Rákosi: "Thus, the great majority of party members are not familiar with Stalin's latest elaboration of Marxism-Leninism. He has truly enriched it and deepened it day by day over the last twenty-five years; consequently our action program should not be pure Marxism or Leninism but Marxism-Leninism in its Stalinist form.''[51] Within the party the "nineteeners"—those veterans who had not emigrated—were especially urged to recognize the exclusive and universal validity of the Stalinist orthodoxy. Their own heritage was rewritten by Rákosi to denigrate his predecessors at the helm of the party and, not incidentally, to inflate his own historical role. In Rákosi's Stalinist account of the Commune, "Kun did not represent Lenin and Bolshevik principles but promoted on the decisive questions the hostile and treacherous views of Bukharin and Trotsky, and thus caused irreparable harm to the Hungarian proletarian revolution.''[52] The handful of surviving nineteeners were swept away in the purges, and thus presented no real danger. On the ideological front, however, such reiteration of alleged past errors and betrayals served the obsessive vigilance campaign against the enemy within and confirmed the historical supremacy of Stalinism.

A graduated political education program was instituted; it extended from the seminar through party school and Party High School to the Party Academy. Depending on their employment, party members were required to take more or less extensive courses in Hungarian and Soviet party history and ideology. Their basic texts, such as the Stalinist Soviet party history, were translations of Russian school materials. Ordinary members were expected to complete three levels of the party seminar in four years. Middle-level functionaries and members of the intellectual professions had to graduate from the Party High School. The most important party and state posts required completion of the four-year Party Academy course, while the select few acquired the invaluable cachet of further training in the Soviet Union.

Ideology served the regime in many ways. On an abstract level, it represented of course the Stalinist version of a historically preordained value system. As such, it was designed to be absorbed into every individual's consciousness. More practically, ideology provided the authoritative justification for the party's possession and daily exercise of power. It provided criteria for the most minute aspects of political, economic, social, and cultural life. It excluded all competing values, especially individualism and spontaneity. And it served as the symbolic vehicle for popular expression of support. Its terminology, parroted by the humble as well as the powerful, debased the language and numbed the intellect but created a synthetic consensus and uniformity.

## THE EXERCISE OF TYRANNY

Ideology had its uses, but terror was the essential tool of enforcement within both the party and the population at large. "Dammit, let them feel that there is a dictatorship of the proletariat," Rákosi would say.[53] In December 1949 the AVO was renamed AVH and made independent of the interior ministry. Now formally answerable only to the council of ministers, it served, much as before, as the personal instrument of the party leaders. The AVH was officially described as the "most important organ of the dictatorship of the proletariat."[54] At the same time, it was fully integrated into the Soviet security network, and over two thousand Russian experts worked in its various divisions.

Under Gábor Péter's direction the AVH had expanded into a monstrous organization with powers of surveillance, investigation, and detention in all spheres of organized and private activity. These functions, exercised through the operational division's 16 departments, were also served by a stable of some 300,000 informers, many of them party members, others complying in self-preservation. The AVH's file system ultimately included dossiers on 1 million citizens, over 10 percent of the entire population. The agency also encompassed the paramilitary internal security and frontier guard detachments, whose members were specially picked, trained, and armed. The former was the regime's first line of defense against internal disturbance and administered all jails and internment camps as well as special industrial development projects. The elite frontier guard manned the elaborate border installations sealing off Hungary from the outside world. The arbitrariness and brutality of the AVH's reign of terror has been recounted by too many victims to need retelling. There existed no clearer indication of the communist leaders' insecurity and cynical contempt for their comrades and subjects than their reliance on this well-honed instrument of terror.

The construction of a totalitarian state begun in 1948 required that all autonomous social activity, communist inspired or not, be extirpated. The works committees and the national committees, designed originally to serve the battle from below, had outlived their usefulness. The former, as was noted earlier, were absorbed by the communist-run trade unions. The national committees were formally dissolved on 1 February 1949.[55] The people's college movement was disbanded. There remained a few vestigial noncommunist parties and, of greater consequence, the churches.

**The Churches Are Crushed.** By mid-1948 active political opposition had been effectively reduced to Barankovics's party and the Roman Catholic church. The latter, led in Hungary by Cardinal Mindszenty, fought its final battle on the issue of education, where together with the Protestant churches it administered some two-thirds of primary and secondary schools. The communists had launched their offensive in May by mobilizing the lay teachers' union and organizing a petition campaign, with duress and intimidation, in favor of secularization. The party then responded to these "spontaneous" demands with a draft law that was promulgated amidst widespread popular protest on 16 June.

The Protestant churches assented, and some of the Catholic clergy favored compromise, but Mindszenty remained adamant and fought bitterly to obstruct implementation. In November the HWP instigated a new petition campaign now demanding that Mindszenty be removed from office and prosecuted. Even the famous composer Zoltán Kodály and the historian Gyula Szekfű were driven to sign the petition, and indeed Mindszenty's opposition to secularization was not endorsed by all Hungarians. Nevertheless, his courageous stand against communist coercion aroused virtually unanimous respect and admiration.[56]

The communists predictably resorted to the well-tried "antistate conspiracy" tactic to crush the church, and on 23 December 1948 Mindszenty was arrested. "Here the police decide what is confessed, not the defendant," he was told.[57] Humiliated, beaten, drugged into a state of terror, the prelate finally signed a statement; the subsequently reproduced handwritten confession of espionage, conspiracy, and currency speculation was, however, a forgery. At the show trial that opened on 3 February 1949 the shadow of a man mechanically confessed to such crimes as "illegal" contacts with the U.S. ambassador. Mindszenty was sentenced to life imprisonment. Meanwhile, Barankovics fled abroad and his Democratic People's Party was dissolved. At the time of the 1956 revolution the Nagy regime issued a superfluous rectification: "The government of Hungary solemnly declares that the charges made in 1948 against Primate József Mindszenty lacked all legal foundation."[58]

When, with the nationalization of all schools, religious instruction was made optional, most parents ostentatiously requested it. The stunned regime had to resort to all its powers of persuasion and intimidation to repress this symbolic gesture of defiance. In June 1950 the communists stepped up their harassment with mass arrests of priests and the closing down of monasteries and convents. On 30 August, after two months of negotiation, the Catholic episcopate finally signed a concordat to save what remained of the church. The government undertook to guarantee freedom of religion and to provide a subsidy that would decline as the church was expected to decline. The clergy was required to publicly endorse the government's policies, such as collectivization, and to tolerate a "Clerical Peace Movement," created by the regime, that consisted of docile "peace priests." When the episcopate resisted the forced expansion of this subversive group, Mindszenty's interim successor, Archbishop József Grősz, was given the show trial treatment in June 1951. Other leading churchmen, including the Lutheran bishop Lajos Ordass and the Presbyterian bishop László Ravasz suffered a similar fate. A State Office of Church Affairs, directed by the AVH and staffed by renegade peace priests and secret police officers, assumed full control over what remained of overt religious activity.

The destruction of clerical resistance was accompanied by the uncovering of other "conspiracies," notably that of a group in the agriculture ministry known as the "extraparty bloc" and another involving alleged cases of sabotage at the U.S.-owned MAORT oil fields (which, along with other foreign property, were soon expropriated by the state).* The mounting police terror served to suppress all potential opposition and to isolate the country from the slightest contact with the West. Formal pluralistic activity was reduced to the drafting of a program for a people's front by the HWP, SHP, NPP, and trade union representatives in the fall of 1948. Delegates of these organizations and of poor peasant associations met on 1 February 1949 to proclaim the Hungarian People's Independence Front. They elected a provisional national council that included twenty-seven communists, nine smallholders, and six NPP representatives. Three weeks later the remaining two opposition fragments, István Balogh's Independent Hungarian Democratic Party and the Hungarian Radical Party, associated themselves with the front. In January the Nationwide National Committee had announced the abolition of all national committees and the assumption of their responsibilities by the front.

**The Liquidation of Allies.**   In the midst of this consolidation of all political activity, Rákosi reported to the Central Committee on 27 November 1948 that the party's strategy was complex: "We are in alliance, and at the same time must move to liquidate our allies. . . . One does one thing, and simultaneously the opposite." By the meeting of the Central Committee on 5 March 1949 the prevailing view was that the very existence of allied parties could serve hostile interests. Such fears were a product of the proletarian dictatorship dogma and were not based on any real threat, since the SHP and the NPP, reduced to their crypto-communist rumps, were hardly likely to challenge the HWP. Nevertheless, one function of the front in the forthcoming elections, said Rákosi, was to "decrease the significance of the bourgeois parties and hasten their decline, their liquidation."[59]

At the May 1949 general elections the People's Independence Front was the sole contender, with a single program and list of candidates. Dissent could only be expressed by way of a negative ballot, a form of protest that was encouraged by the clergy in particular and that in some districts accounted for over one-quarter of the vote. Of the eligible voters, 94 percent (5.7 million out of 6.1 million) dutifully marched to the polls, and 95.5 percent endorsed the single list. (Later, as the vigilance campaign intensified, Rákosi would charge that nonvoters were a priori enemies: "Those who are not with us are against us.") In the new parliament, 43 percent of deputies were of working-class origin, 28 percent from the lower peasantry, and 23 percent from the intelligentsia; 71 percent were HWP members.

---

*MAORT stands for "Magyar-Amerikai Olajipari Részvénytársaság" (Hungarian-American Oil Company). Its fields were in Transdanubia.

Creation of the HWP in spring 1948 had changed the alignment of political forces, and the government had been reshuffled accordingly. Already, in December that year, the fellow traveler Dobi had been named prime minister in place of Dinnyés, and retained the post after the 1949 elections. Rákosi continued to hold the title of deputy prime minister until August 1952 when, following Soviet practice, he replaced Dobi as head of government. In the eighteen-member cabinet three were nominal smallholders (Dobi himself, Ortutay in religion and education, and József Bognár in commerce) and two (Darvas in construction and Erdei in agriculture) from the NPP. Kádár retained the interior ministry, where he had succeeded Rajk in August 1948, while Rajk, who had been shifted to foreign affairs, was already under arrest, leaving his portfolio momentarily vacant until Kállai was assigned to it.

**Constitutional Dictatorship.** Since the new order required ceremonial codification, one of the first acts of the parliament was to ratify the constitution of the Hungarian People's Republic. It came into effect on 20 August 1949, intentionally coinciding with the traditional St. Stephen's Day, renamed Constitution Day. A delegation had visited Moscow in January 1949 to study the Soviet constitutional model, the Russians supplied a draft for Hungary, and the HWP published the result on 15 March. In imitation of Soviet practice at the time of the Stalin constitution of 1936, public debates were staged on the draft, and six of the sixty-seven proposed amendments (which were anything but spontaneous) were incorporated.[60] Party activists were instructed to popularize the new charter by stressing that it followed the example of the Soviet constitution, the world's most progressive, and differed fundamentally from its capitalist counterparts, which entrenched the rule of exploiters. The HWP and comrade Rákosi were to be hailed jointly as creators of the workers' first constitution.[61]

The new constitution was at once a formal recognition of the recent transformation and an action program.[62] After paying fulsome tribute to the Soviet liberators, it stated that Hungary had begun to lay the foundations of socialism and was progressing on the road of people's democracy toward full socialism. The notable departure from the Soviet model was omission of the latter's conclusion that antagonistic social classes had been eliminated. The Hungarian People's Republic was a "state of workers and working peasants"; citizens not belonging to the category of "working people" were denied full political rights.

Civil rights in the new totalitarian state owed less to constitutional safeguards, which were laudably explicit, than to the practice of the ruling party. This consisted of a blend of prohibition and compulsion that virtually excluded individual discretion, for instance in the choice of employment or degree of political participation. The judiciary was instructed by the constitution to "punish the enemies of the working people; safeguard the state, the social and economic order, the institutions of the people's democracy, and the rights of the workers; and educate working people to observe the rules governing the life of a socialist commonwealth." Socialist justice demanded that the courts apply class criteria in judging the accused. The principles of equality before the law and presumption of innocence were thus expunged from Hungarian legal practice. Throughout Rákosi's reign the judiciary (some of whose leading figures, such as the presiding judge at Rajk's trial, Vilmos Olti, were former Nazis) was a servant of the party leader and an adjunct of the secret police.[63]

The constitution provided for a presidential council in lieu of head of state, a council of ministers as the chief executive organ, and a unicameral parliament. It avoided delineating their rule-making function for the good reason that they were destined to serve as a facade for party rule. The national assembly would meet for a few days each year to ceremonially ratify a few bills, but most rules took the form of presidential or ministerial decrees. "This is the way the Soviet comrades are doing it" was the answer to party members' questions regarding the inactivity of parliament.[64] Article 56 of the constitution in effect enshrined the dominant position of the HWP. Replication of the Soviet model allowed no concession to national sensibilities: a new Soviet-style coat of arms replaced the traditional Kossuth emblem.

A council system of local government was prescribed by the constitution, and the first single-list elections at the local level were held in October 1950. One-third of the 220,000 elected councilors belonged to the HWP. Far from providing for a devolution of authority, the local councils served merely as the instruments of central state control. As for the People's Independence Front, after 1949 it retained the periodic formal function of organizing elections, but the vestigial "allied" parties within it withered away.

The public service was also reduced to a shadow of its former self. A systematic purge removed what was left of the old complement after the new constitution had taken effect. It also removed many postwar recruits, mainly social democrats. In 8 ministries surveyed by the Central Statistical Office in 1954, out of 6,788 officials 2,600 were of worker and 739 of peasant origin, the proportion of both being highest in the upper echelons.[65] This massive influx of inept recruits had a predictably disastrous effect on administrative efficiency—an effect that mirrored the politicization and debilitation of enterprise management.

## ECONOMIC STALINISM

The HWP's second congress, held from 25 February to 2 March 1951, came at the height of the purges and of Rákosi's dictatorial powers. The 754 hand-picked voting delegates went through the motions of electing the party's executive bodies (the 71-member Central Committee, 17-member Politburo, and 8-member Secretariat) and of approving the leadership's recommendations. In his keynote speech, Rákosi began by overestimating the results of the three-year plan and exaggerating the initial performance of the five-year plan. He went on to stress the gathering threat of war. Finally, he reached the point: a huge increase would be required in the current plan's economic targets. He also called for accentuation of the class struggle, greater vigilance, and "communist iron discipline."

With the party in undisputed power, an army of Russian experts descended on Hungary to supervise the reorganization of the economic mechanism along Soviet lines. Their intervention extended from the People's Economic Council and State Planning Office down to the sectoral directive organs. Bureaucratic centralization became an end in itself. Soviet labor techniques (such as the Stakhanovite and shock-worker movements) and production methods were similarly replicated with Procrustean zeal at a time when Stalinist dogma required recognition of Soviet superiority in every sphere. State control over industry and commerce was essentially completed in December 1949 with the expropriation of all enterprises employing ten or more workers.

**Forced Industrialization.** The overriding objective of the first five-year plan, which ran from 1950 to 1954, was, in the words of its chief domestic architect Gerő, to turn Hungary into a country of iron and steel.[66] This was required by the imperatives of the Soviet autarkic model and by Stalin's new "war economy." The sudden impact of Stalin's war hysteria was such that the 1949 defense budget was quadrupled within a few weeks of its initial formulation in September 1948. The five-year plan's original target, already illusory, of raising heavy industry's output by 204 percent was increased to a fantastic 380 percent at the time of the second party congress.

Rapid industrialization required careful planning: the central planners therefore busily issued quantitative quota directives and, when all else failed, fabricated suitable statistics. It required managerial talent: managers there were, in the form of 60,000 workers selected by the party's cadre department in late 1948. It urgently required skilled workers: they could be trained—inadequately, it turned out, so that major problems resulted. It required investment: this was generated from forced savings (including the hated "voluntary" peace loans) and by concentrating on the heavy industrial sector at the expense of consumer goods. It required raw materials: most of the coking coal and iron ore for the new metallurgical complex at Sztalinváros near Budapest had to be imported—uneconomically—from the Soviet Union. With political considerations invariably taking precedence over economic rationality, the modernization of Hungary's industrial sector was undermined by unproductive investments, inadequate maintenance, and the stockpiling of inferior products.

A cooperative labor force was also an essential prerequisite to industrialization. The traditional functions of the trade unions were denigrated, notably in a resolution of the Politburo on 24 July 1950; this was coupled with a campaign against the industrial workers' old leaders, the social democrats. Even their left-wingers were denounced by the party as a fifth column which "at the critical moment [might] move in strength against the people's democracy."[67] Trade union initiatives to advance labor's interests were branded as disloyal, and promises to improve the standard of living were supplanted by Rákosi's call for a "self-sacrificing Spartan spirit." The regime meanwhile systematically falsified statistics in order to demonstrate improvement in the standard of living. In December 1951 a 20 percent wage raise was accompanied by increases from 50 to 100 percent in the prices of consumer goods; in fact, the per capita real income of workers and employees fell by 18 percent between 1949 and 1952.[68] In addition to this general decline, a policy of wage equalization lowered skilled workers' wages and the salaries of engineers and technicians.[69] Between 1949 and 1952, some 370,000 workers were transferred from agriculture and light industry to the heavy industrial and mining sector. The already critical housing shortage in urban areas was thereby increased, although some relief was obtained from the summary deportation of expendable "class enemies."

Productivity was spurred by labor competitions, "voluntary" overtime, and a discipline imposed from above that surpassed the darkest episodes in capitalist industrialization. Although even the increased norms did not match Western levels of labor productivity, the industrial proletariat was understandably reluctant to work harder for no tangible reward. Their alienation was only accentuated by the blatant incompetence of their new managers and of communist officialdom in general. But Rákosi's dogmatic pursuit of industrialization could not, in view of the basic weakness of the economy, allow for adequate positive incentives for labor, and the regime had no choice but to resort to compulsion. As Imre Nagy ruefully observed, in the mushrooming prison population the majority had come from the ranks of the working class.[70]

Although the targets of the five-year plan were not met, the regime could claim a dramatic expansion of the industrial sector, an apparently favorable rate of growth in national income, and a state of full employment. Among the negative corollaries were a severe distortion in Hungary's economic structure in terms of the country's natural endowments, an unfavorable balance of trade in 1949 and 1952, and a decline in real wages and private consumption. Moreover, the new industries were technologically obsolete from the start, while the quota system and worker disaffection led to a deterioration in product quality.[71] The economic cost of Soviet exploitation will be noted below. Politically, the most dangerous consequence of these economic policies was the alienation of the party's chosen class, the industrial proletariat.

The artisans and small producers who remained outside the socialist sector were regarded by the party as potential capitalist backsliders and were used as a labor reserve for industrialization. Their numbers (not counting employees) declined from 180,087 in 1949 to 46,199 in 1953. Small merchants suffered a similar fate. The resulting distortion was only partly alleviated by the growth of small manufacturing cooperatives and the creation of state-run retail shops.

**The Collectivization of Agriculture.** In the agricultural sector dogmatism was even more clearly antithetical to rational economic and social alternatives. Despite the ordinary peasant's attachment to his private plot, a policy of positive incentives might have induced a certain natural growth of large-scale farming. The 1945 redistribution of land, however, had not inspired sympathy for socialism among the peasantry. In fact, wrote a party historian in 1966, "the conversion of the agrarian proletariat and poor peasants into 'proprietors' strengthened the possessive, petit bourgeois instincts of this peasant category, in consequence of which some of them regarded with mistrust the socialist strivings of the working class."[72] The kulaks were always regarded by the party as class enemies, but smaller-scale private farming was defended as late as the unification congress of the HWP. It was then considered that even without compulsion the collective farms would "remove the middle peasant from the kulak's influence . . . and put him on the side of the working class."[73]

The dogma, issuing from the 1948 Cominform crisis, that the class struggle should be sharpened altered all the Hungarian leaders' former preconceptions, although Rákosi initially argued that the Cominform's call for the socialist transformation of agriculture did not mean that all the communist parties would have to "put the collectivization of the villages on the current year's agenda."[74] At its meeting of 13 July 1948, however, the Politburo did decide to undermine at all costs the kulaks' dominant role in the villages, and a series of restrictive measures followed. Rákosi told the Central Committee on 27 November: "We can only deal with [the kulaks] fundamentally by taking away their land, houses, machines, and what we do with them I don't know yet. . . ." The bait of kulak lands would, he anticipated, give a "giant push" to other peasants to join the collective farms.[75]

In the event, some 70,000 peasants were included on the notorious "kulak lists," but at least half of them were no more than middle peasants, and instead of inciting the latter against the wealthier farmers the measures united all peasant proprietors in abhorrence of the regime. The peasantry was only further alienated by the concurrent decision to raise independent farmers' taxes and by unrealistically high compulsory delivery quotas, severe penalties, and petty persecution. Moreover, the regime's inability to provide adequate guidance and machinery for the existing collective farms, whose members were drawn largely from the less competent landless peasantry, hardly turned these farms into attractive alternatives for the outsiders. An ill-conceived "patronage" system was instituted in 1950 to send "volunteer" worker-activists from the factories to collective farms to offer advice and demonstrate the worker-peasant alliance. "The patronage work must be launched in such a way that the producers' cooperatives themselves ask for the help of the designated factory," instructed the Secretariat.[76]

The intractability of the peasantry was well illustrated by the party's attempt to resort to mass mobilization. On 18 December 1948 the two former radical peasant organizations, the FEKOSZ and UFOSZ, were merged into the National Federation of Working Peasants and Agricultural Workers (Dolgozó Parasztok és Földmunkások Országos Szövetsége, or DEFOSZ), which was given the task of winning over the middle peasants to socialism. Elections for local DEFOSZ leaders in early 1949 resulted in 48.3 percent support for the HWP, 17.1 percent for the NPP, 15.5 percent for the SHP, and 19.1 for nonparty candidates. A dissatisfied party leadership demanded better HWP representation and the dissolution of DEFOSZ units "penetrated by the class enemy." The brutal measures that ensued improved the HWP's position by a mere 1.9 percent while creating an atmosphere of terror in the countryside. Rákosi qualified the DEFOSZ as "one of our biggest mistakes in four years." The dogmatic leadership of the organization, including Imre Dögei, was driven to conduct recurrent and essentially counterproductive purges and persecution among the peasantry. Admitted Rákosi to the Central Committee on 27 October 1950: "It must be said, comrades, clearly and openly, that in village after village our party organizations have regressed, weakened over the last two years." In fact, the proportion of peasants in the HWP fell from 18 percent in 1948 to 13 percent in 1950. The programmed HWP majority in the local DEFOSZ leaderships was finally achieved by the simple recourse of reducing their complement. Far from fulfilling its original function of defending peasant interests, the DEFOSZ had been used by the party as an agent of collectivization, and as such it proved unequal to the task. It was liquidated in January 1952 and replaced by a simple trade union of agricultural workers.[77]

To return to the history of collectivization, by early 1949 any inclination toward gradualism had been dispelled by Stalin's warning that the discrepancy between socialized industry and private farming was intolerable. The Hungarian leadership responded with conditioned zeal. Gerő's young understudy, András Hegedüs, was assigned to supervise the collectivization campaign in his capacity as head of the Central Committee's agricultural department. The destruction of the kulak class could only be accomplished in the Soviet fashion, said Gerő.[78] Collectivization, declared Rákosi, was the road that Soviet peasants were following with great success, and it was "the road that the masses of private farmers in the people's democracies must also follow."[79]

One dissenting voice was that of Imre Nagy, who in late 1947 had argued that small private farms were not essentially capitalist and could coexist with collective farms during the transition to socialism. Rákosi cautioned him in September 1948: "In no circumstances should you tie the party to any peasant private property, better keep silent on this question."[80] But Nagy accused Rákosi of excessive leftism and persisted in advocating a constructive alliance with the middle peasants. Needless to say, Moscow's dictate overrode such marginal reservations. At a Central Committee meeting on 3 September 1949 Nagy's views were branded as "right wing" and he was compelled to confess to "opportunism."[81] In the party's 1949 harvest campaign local secretaries were instructed to be watchful for kulak resistance and to take measures against a few as a warning to the others. However, they were also warned against persecuting all persons branded by local activists as kulaks, since many of them might turn out to be middle and poor peasants.[82]

From 1949 onwards the party progressively intensified its battle against the kulaks and for the creation of collective farms, and the second congress set even higher targets for agricultural production and collectivization. Amidst increasingly brutal repression, Rákosi would insist (at the Politburo meeting of 19 November 1950) that "the peasant must be forced to sacrifice more for the building of socialism."[83] The sacrifice, for the beleaguered peasantry, was a heavy one to bear. While the price paid for compulsory deliveries hardly increased between 1949 and 1953, that of goods consumed by the peasants nearly doubled. Managed by transplanted industrial workers or ignorant laborers, the collective farms held little attraction for the more successful farmers, who had to be threatened with being placed on the kulak lists if they did not join. Not surprisingly, party reports warned of an emerging hostile "peasant unity," and in fact, despite all the regime's efforts, the progress of collectivization proved to be painfully slow. In 1953 the 3,768 agricultural producers' cooperatives accounted for only 20.3 percent of arable land and 19.1 percent of working peasants.[84]

Shortages of competent managers, machinery, fertilizers, and an apathetic and undisciplined labor force contributed to a decline in production to well below prewar levels, converting Hungary from an exporter to a net importer of grain. The Soviet-inspired machine-tractor stations were notoriously inefficient. Concurrently, hundreds of thousands of peasants abandoned the land for industrial jobs, and some 10 percent of arable land was left fallow. The program of rural electrification, which benefited a thousand additional villages by 1952, was a rare positive aspect of this generally dismal conjuncture.

## THE MANIPULATION OF CULTURE AND SOCIETY

In education and culture the party's rule imposed rigid ideological orthodoxy and cultural russification. The creation of a socialist society demanded elimination of the historical culture and its replacement by "communist culture," for which there was only one paradigm, namely, the Soviet Union. The educational system was converted to the Soviet model down to the smallest detail, such as the grading scale for students. The teaching of religion was effectively obstructed and replaced by pervasive ideological indoctrination. Youth organizations from the Young Pioneers (Uttörők) to the Federation of Working Youth (Dolgozó Ifjúság Szövetsége, or DISZ) were dedicated to the creation of new generations of convinced communists free from precommunist parental influence. While the offspring of the lower classes flooded into educational institutions, often at the price of lower entrance standards, the door to higher education was barred to all children of class enemies regardless of their ability.

Mass organizations for all ages and occupations, the Soviet–Hungarian Friendship Society, party-directed libraries, and houses of culture all served to propagate the party's values and approved culture. Loudspeakers in factories and villages allowed no escape from the regime's message. All communications media were under tight party control. *Szabad Nép,* the Hungarian *Pravda,* was edited until 1951 by Révai and the home communist Horváth, then by Oszkár Betlen, a Slovakian acolyte of Farkas. The paper's huge editorial staff, including several AVH agents, were dutiful hacks, but some of the recent recruits (together with a holdover from the postliberation period, Miklós Gimes) would eventually undergo a crisis of conscience and follow the revisionist road to revolution.

Literature, theater, the cinema, and even music could only exist as the didactic agents of the party line and socialist realism. Their task was to glorify Rákosi and Stalin, the Soviet Union and communism; to denigrate the imperialist enemy and the bourgeois past, national and Western cultural traditions; and to project an idealized image of socialist man. In 1952, for instance, 162 out of 277 "important publications" were translations of Soviet works.[85] The public, in turn, had little opportunity beyond passive withdrawal to show its contempt for oppressive russification and indoctrination, as well as for the abysmally banal and adulatory style pervading the arts.

A few representatives of the urbanist and Populist variants of prewar progressivism accepted the party's cultural constraints, as did a new generation of young intellectuals, and this small cadre of housebroken literati received extravagant official praise and privileges. But most of the literary luminaries left in Hungary, even such progressive figures as Gyula Illyés, preferred silence to surrender of their self-respect. With vastly expanded staffs, Révai's culture ministry and Horváth's agitprop department policed the cultural scene. The new Writers' Association was a creature of the party, and its chief organ, *Irodalmi Ujság* (Literary Journal; founded in November 1950 as the Hungarian equivalent of *Literaturnaya Gazeta*) was the authoritative voice of orthodoxy under the editorship of the Muscovite writer Béla Illés. Révai told a congress of Hungarian writers in 1951 that literature's task was to defend the working class and the "peace camp" with the weapons of socialist realism and dialectical materialism. The rare intellectual demurral at the regime's excesses he dismissed as "petty-bourgeois moralizing."[86]

Any hint of deviation was swiftly repressed. In 1949 Lukács came under attack, first from László Rudas (who had returned from Moscow to head the Party High School and then became rector of the economics university), and then from Révai, for underestimating Soviet literature and for a Western orientation. His unorthodoxy was traced back to the controversial Blum theses of 1928.[87] Lukács, in fact, had merely exhibited a remnant of intellectual integrity in the face of the regime's obsessive idolatry of all things Soviet, but he was compelled to go through a perfunctory self-criticism and withdrew into silence. In another demonstration case, the talented young novelist Tibor Déry was savagely censured in 1952 for not depicting with sufficient Manichaean clarity the party's stereotypes of good and evil.[88] The party's writers rationalized their sycophancy with a naive idealism that was soon dispelled by the inescapable contradictions of Stalinism. In their disillusionment many of them would turn with righteous wrath against the Machiavellian tempters who had exploited their youthful enthusiasm and ambitions.

**Social Upheaval.** The country's social structure was drastically altered under Rákosi's rule. According to a Hungarian historian's estimate, between 1945 and 1953 some 350,000 to 400,000 families belonging to the former upper and middle classes were obliged to seek new places in society.[89] Their homes confiscated, dismissed from their old occupations, humiliated and persecuted, prevented even from choosing exile, over a million men, women, and children were thus subjected to the punishing hand of historical justice, the same inhuman imperative used by the Nazis to justify their own pogroms. The deportation of masses of class enemies to the countryside, where they were allowed a bare subsistence, served to disperse potential opponents, to provide superior accommodation for the new party elite, and to make room in the overcrowded cities for the expanded industrial labor force.

The intelligentsia was the stratum most severely affected by the party's vigilance campaign. Recapitulated the Central Committee in the summer of 1956: "Indoctrination on the leading role of the working class and on the worker-peasant alliance was in practice occasionally distorted and interpreted as if the civil rights guaranteed in the constitution of our people's republic did not apply to the intelligentsia."[90] The latter were readily identified by the party as bearers of bourgeois values and therefore hostile to the working class. Those who remained in white-collar and middle-class occupations fearfully withdrew into an apolitical shell. Others who were forcibly declassed contributed to what a party historian termed a "temporary strengthening" of bourgeois or petit bourgeois ideology among the workers.[91]

The new intelligentsia were identified by occupational more than by educational status. They generally came from modest social backgrounds, and rationalized their careerism in terms of the egalitarian myth preached by the party. The latter rewarded believer and opportunist alike with prestige, relative affluence, and unprecedented upward mobility. There was room for such mobility, for the totalitarian state had created a bureaucratic monster. Between 1949 and 1954 the state apparatus expanded by 80 percent. In industry, there were 35.9 white-collar employees for every 100 workers in 1954, compared to 20 in 1938. At the same time the training of professionals in the officially favored disciplines underwent rapid expansion, so that, for example, the number of engineers was 612 percent greater in 1953 than in 1938. Accelerated industrialization meanwhile inflated the industrial working class by 460,000 between 1949 and 1954, largely at the expense of the agricultural sector and the old middle classes.[92]

Hungarian society thus became a laboratory case in revolutionary social engineering. In some respects, such as the reorientation of the educational system away from traditional and oversupplied fields like law and toward more technical disciplines, the exercise promised to serve the needs of a modernizing society. But in its mistreatment of the old middle classes, and in the creation of a gigantic and incompetent bureaucracy, the party perpetrated a gross injustice as well as a tragic waste and misallocation of human resources.

Of equal consequence was the general degradation of public and private morality. Few could ignore the fraudulence of a system that propelled the uneducated and inexperienced to positions of power and rewarded only blind loyalty; that tolerated the tyranny and arbitrariness of its servants high and low; that preached human liberation, equality, and social justice while delivering subjection, discrimination, and economic distress. The party's perversion of moral standards induced widespread alienation and antisocial behavior such as petty theft and sabotage. Its reign of terror, far from creating social cohesion and responsibility, only atomized the society into lonely and fearful submissiveness. Political participation, manipulated by the regime's various mobilizing agents, was reduced to a compulsory and ritualistic charade of chanted slogans.

Hungary's defeat in the war and the disintegration of the old regime had created a tabula rasa propitious for a new start on social and economic modernization. The beginnings of genuine pluralistic democracy, in which Hungarians were admittedly untutored, and the already established pattern of a mixed economy could, with foreign aid, have provided the impetus for such a modernizing process. A truly national communist party— if that were not a contradiction in terms—might have played a constructive role in that process. In the event, the drive for hegemony by a Soviet-directed communist leadership precluded orderly, rational, and popular modernization. What communist historians call the "distortions" of the 1949-55 period were part and parcel of the Bolshevik tradition. Those few convinced communists who were both rational in their reformism and sincere in their patriotism may have felt uncomfortable with the excesses of Stalinism, but they questioned tactics rather than the inherent dynamics of Marxism-Leninism. Nevertheless, Imre Nagy's devastating summation stands the test of evidence:

> The "left-wing" deviationists, primarily Rákosi and Gerő, in the years 1949 to 1953 brought the socialist reorganization of agriculture to a dead end, bankrupted agricultural production, destroyed the worker-peasant alliance, undermined the power of the People's Democracy, trampled upon the rule of law, debased the people's living standards, established a rift between the masses and the Party and government—in other words, swept the country toward catastrophe.[93]

## THE MAKING OF A SATELLITE

This brief account of the party's exercise of totalitarian control must not obscure the dominant part played by Soviet rule; indeed, Hungary became the colonial appendage of an imperial power. Stalin's *Gleichschaltung* of his East European domain after 1948 resulted not only in the de facto surrender of Hungary's sovereignty but also in the penetration of Soviet influence into the innermost reaches of the nation's life. The Soviet embassy was only the most obvious and official channel of command. Rákosi and his lieutenants sinned by excess in fulfilling or anticipating Stalin's wishes, which were conveyed through a multitude of channels. The most direct source of authority was the Soviet Politburo member bearing special responsibility for the Hungarian party, beginning with Voroshilov in the early postwar years and later including Suslov and Mikoyan.[94] Ideology and culture were the special preserve of Zhdanov, then Suslov, while Kaganovich dealt with economics. The party's central apparatus was advised and controlled by its counterparts, Soviet specialists in Budapest and Moscow.[95] The most continuous and intimate supervision was exercised by Beria over the secret police. There, and in other key sectors, notably economic planning, an army of Soviet advisers provided daily guidance. Some of these experts acquired dual citizenship and masqueraded as Hungarians. A notable example was Leo Konduktorov, a Russian assigned by Molotov to serve first as secretary of state in the Hungarian foreign ministry, then, under the alias of Péter Kós, to represent Hungary at the United Nations.

The Hungarian satellite moved in perfect orbit because at all levels the Soviet official's word was command. The head of the Hungarian news agency MTI (Magyar Távirati Iroda, or Hungarian Telegraphic Office) would seek instructions by telephone from Moscow. The *Pravda* correspondent's displeasure was sufficient to stop performance of one of the classics of Hungarian theater, Imre Madách's *Tragedy of Man*.[96] Indeed, seldom in European history had one nation-state been so thoroughly absorbed by another.

The duality of Soviet and HCP control was most striking in the military sphere. The initial postwar policy had been to purge and reduce the armed forces at the expense of other communist-dominated security agencies; the vestigial army was controlled by Soviet military attachés. When Farkas became defense minister in September 1948 he began, with the aid of a Soviet military advisory mission, to sovietize the armed forces, notably by introducing political officers. In late 1949 the Soviet function was expanded, so that Russian advisers operated even at the regimental level, while political officers from the HWP reached down to the company level. The top posts in the military were assigned to old Muscovite communists such as Nógrádi and, eventually, to more recent Hungarian graduates of Soviet military schools; the former cadre of communist officers, including Pálffy, was liquidated. When in late 1949 three senior Soviet military advisers casually asked what manner of man was General László Sólyom, the Hungarian communist chief of staff, Rákosi replied: "English spy." (Farkas later said Sólyom was a French spy. . . .) The visitors were visibly embarrassed by this absurd allegation, but Sólyom was soon thrown in jail and replaced by the even less competent István Bata.[97]

In 1951/52 the Hungarian armed forces, adapted in the smallest detail to the Soviet model, numbered over 210,000 men, three times the limit set by the Paris treaty, and this figure did not include the AVH's paramilitary forces and the frontier guard. By that time over 80 percent of the officer corps was newly appointed and came from politically acceptable social backgrounds. The criterion of professional competence was overshadowed, of course, by the requisite of political reliability. The contemporary task alloted Hungary's armed forces by Soviet strategic planners was that of front-line offense against Yugoslavia and northern Italy.[98]

Hungary's integration into the Soviet sphere rested on the ruling party's subordination to Moscow rather than on legal covenants. The formal linkages were bilateral, in keeping with Stalin's mistrustful rejection of various postwar proposals for Danubian and Balkan cooperation. A series of bilateral treaties were signed by Hungary and the Soviet Union (18 February 1948), Romania (24 January 1948), Poland (18 June 1948), Bulgaria (16 July 1948), Czechoslovakia (16 April 1949), and the German Democratic Republic (26 June 1950). They were precursors of the 1955 Warsaw treaty in their stress on common defense against German revanchism and Western imperialism. The Soviet pact legitimized the continued presence of Russian forces in Hungary. Other clauses in this and all the pacts enjoined respect for each other's sovereignty and called for cultural and economic cooperation.

The contentious issue of Hungarian minorities in Czechoslovakia and Romania were submerged in the process. The population exchange with Czechoslovakia was terminated in June 1948, as was the internal exile imposed on the Magyar minority. The latter remained the object of harassment, discrimination, and cultural assimilation programs, although a marginal improvement in its circumstances slowly materialized after the trial of Husak and other "Slovakian bourgeois nationalists" in April 1954.[99] As for the more numerous Hungarians of Transylvania, they momentarily benefited from a certain regional autonomy and cultural concessions. With regard to both minorities the Hungarian government remained an uninterested and impotent observer, for Stalin was as determined to isolate his satellites from each other as to sever their ties with the West.

The Hungarians actively participated in the Cominform's propaganda campaigns; Zoltán Biró, for instance, served on the editorial committee of *For a Lasting Peace, for a People's Democracy* in Bucharest. Rákosi, Gerő, Kádár, and Révai attended the fourth Cominform conference, held in late November 1949 in Hungary, which confirmed the "peace movement" strategy, denounced Tito's "fascism," and, in anticipation of the purges, called for vigilance against enemies within the ruling parties. The Cominform's utility to Stalin had diminished by the time of the fifth, Bucharest meeting in 1950; concurrently, Biró returned home and was replaced by Dezső Nemes.[100] The organization was formally dissolved in April 1956.

The Stalin-Tito split had important negative economic consequences, for Yugoslavia had been one of Hungary's major trading partners. A bilateral treaty had been concluded by the two countries in 1947, but subsequently all formal relations were broken off and the border sealed. In 1948 the Soviet Union took up the slack in Hungarian trade and, in addition, reduced the outstanding balance of reparations and extended the schedule of payment to eight years. In 1952, sixty-nine Soviet-owned enterprises were transferred to Hungarian state ownership, and two years later the Soviet shares in the joint-stock companies were sold back. (Hungary's uranium mines remained, however, under direct Soviet management.) These well-publicized measures were designed to enhance the prestige of the Soviet Union and of the Rákosi regime, but they did not alleviate Hungary's economic problems.

An agency for regional economic coordination, the Council for Mutual Economic Assistance (commonly known as Comecon), had been established in January 1949, but it remained largely inactive during Stalin's reign. In practice trade was conducted bilaterally, on terms set by the Soviet Union. Soviet interests determined development policy, and seldom were local advantages in the factors of production taken into account. A rare exception was Hungary's specialization in communications equipment in response to the regional coordination of military production during the Korean War. The generally exploitative character of Soviet-Hungarian trade produced some glaring anomalies. In key commodities, such as bauxite, production costs far exceeded the predetermined selling price to the Soviet Union.[101] By 1950 the Soviet bloc accounted for 56.3 percent of Hungary's imports and 64.7 percent of her exports. The Soviet Union, for whom the corresponding figures were 24.5 percent and 18.9 percent, became Hungary's dominant trading partner (taking, for example, 90 percent of bauxite exports), whereas in 1938 her share of Hungarian trade had been an infinitesimal 0.1 percent. The costs of Soviet hegemony in inflated reparations, unequal terms of trade, irrational development policies, the maintenance of "visiting" forces, and other exploitative measures defy precise calculation, but there can be no doubt that their willing assumption by the communist regime severely retarded the country's reconstruction and economic modernization.

In sum, the Stalinist phase saw the Hungarian party fritter away what little popularity it had managed to acquire in the immediate postwar period. Historically, Hungarians had been singularly unreceptive to ideologies lacking a national foundation, and the 1919 Commune had served as a further inoculation. The imposition of an alien and atheistic dogma by the Russians and by Soviet-trained communists was therefore bound to be poorly received. Nevertheless, given the general desire for modernization, a genuine improvement in the living standard of industrial workers and peasants might have induced a modicum of respect for the regime. Instead, harsh oppression and material hardship alienated the very masses whose vanguard the party claimed to be. The absence of legitimate outlets for popular discontent produced a pent-up resentment and loathing for the system and widespread hope for some war of liberation, an expectation that was implicitly encouraged both by Stalin's war hysteria and by the exhortations of U.S. propaganda.[102] Moreover, the tyranny and dogmatism of the communist leaders destroyed the party's inner credibility. Whatever the objective imperatives of domestic circumstances, the signals for change had invariably come from the Kremlin. The next signal began a process of decompression whose climax would be the collapse of communist power.

# 11. The New Course, 1953–1955

Stalin died on 5 March 1953. The funeral in Moscow was attended by his faithful disciple Rákosi, whose position now appeared to be impregnable. His name was extolled by the regime's propaganda machinery the length and breadth of the nation, and the party trumpeted its success in launching the building of socialism. General elections on 17 May returned the obligatory vote of support (98.2 percent) for the single list of candidates.

The appearance of stability was somewhat deceptive. Economic distress had become so acute as to cause dismay and disagreements even within the party. Wildcat strikes as well as the occasional spontaneous peasant demonstration were the most visible signs of popular discontent. None of this presented an immediate threat to the party's rule, but the chaotic state of the economy must have impressed the Soviet delegation that arrived in April to survey the situation. In Moscow, while grappling with the problem of succession, Stalin's lieutenants had assessed the acute tensions in the dead dictator's domain and moved to take remedial measures. Their sense of urgency was only heightened by the riots in Pilsen, Czechoslovakia, and by the outbreak of open revolt in East Germany on 17 June.

## IMRE NAGY AND THE JUNE RESOLUTIONS

In keeping with the new orthodoxy of separating the leadership of party and government, the Kremlin had instructed Rákosi in May to appoint a new prime minister. He procrastinated, however, while searching for a candidate both docile and acceptable to the Russians. A week after the eruption of the East German uprising Rákosi was ordered to present himself in Moscow and to bring along not only his acolytes Farkas and Gerő but also, ominously, Imre Nagy (then nominally a deputy premier and powerless) and Dobi, the puppet president.

The Hungarians were confronted by the assembled Soviet party presidium, whose members took turns acrimoniously berating Rákosi for his mismanagement. Unless the criminal mistakes of the leading foursome were remedied, warned Khrushchev, they would be "booted out summarily" by the Hungarian people. Rákosi's cult of personality, his recourse to terror, and the disastrous economic consequences of forced collectivization all came under censure.[1] Beria (whose arrest was only a few days away) mocked Rákosi for trying to become the "Jewish king" of Hungary.[2] The Soviet leaders (Nagy cites Khrushchev, Malenkov, and Molotov) then ordered Rákosi to relinquish the premiership to Imre Nagy, to reconstruct the party leadership, and to draft a new political and economic program.[3] A plausible explanation of their choice of Nagy rests on his Muscovite background, his moderation in contrast to Rákosi, and perhaps on the fact that he was not Jewish. Rákosi, however, would never reconcile himself to the sharing of power with the independent-minded Nagy, and the two men became bitter rivals.

The delegation returned to Budapest and called a meeting of the Central Committee for 27 and 28 June. The Central Committee members listened in stunned silence as Rákosi delivered the prescribed self-critical speech.[4] He admitted to being the object of an unpardonable cult of personality, to placing himself above the party and repressing all advice and criticism. He spoke of three or four leaders enjoying a "special position," the doubtful fourth being Révai, who was marginally less equal than Rákosi, Gerő, and Farkas, and who was probably not fully initiated in the purges. "I directed the AVH," confessed Rákosi. "In this connection I involved myself in the disposition of cases, I intervened in determining who should be arrested."[5] His three lieutenants dutifully followed suit. Gerő acknowledged that his economic policies had lowered the standard of living, Révai confessed to errors in ideology, while Farkas spoke in evasive generalities. The revolutionary discipline of these old Comintern hands was sorely tested by this command performance, and they stopped short of admitting that the purges had been a wholesale fabrication. Other members then rose to the occasion with critical and self-critical statements.

A series of recommendations based on the Soviet leaders' advice had already been drafted, principally by Nagy himself, and were now unanimously adopted by the Central Committee; they came to be known as the "June resolutions." The resolutions must have dealt a hard blow to Rákosi's pride, since they attributed the sectarian mistakes to the absence of collective leadership and to the cult of personality propagated by the leading foursome. These mistakes had had "an unfavorable effect on the standard of living of the population, not least of the working class; had loosened the links between the party and working class, generally harmed relations between the party, state, and working masses, and caused serious difficulties in the people's economy.'' The resolutions went on to denounce as unsuitable and adventurist the regime's attempts at industrial autarky and criticized the supplanting of political education with "administrative practices.''[6] They recommended a deceleration of industrialization, greater emphasis on light industry, improvement in the standard of living, a lower rate of capital investment except in agriculture, a reduction in the peasants' taxes and compulsory deliveries, aid for small farming as well as for collective farms, a slower rate of collectivization, with permission granted for peasants to withdraw from the producers' cooperatives and retrieve their land, and support for artisans and small merchants.

The resolutions called for the restoration of collective leadership and nominated Nagy for the premiership while leaving Rákosi as first secretary of the party (a change from his former title of secretary-general, to fit the new Soviet practice). The flouting of socialist legality demanded a sacrifice, and Farkas was momentarily dropped from the Politburo along with Révai and four others. The truncated Politburo now included Rákosi, Gerő, Nagy, Apró, Hegedüs, and four other members. Only three secretaries were appointed: Rákosi and two of his minor creatures, Lajos Ács and Béla Vég.[7]

**The Struggle for Power Begins.**  For the first time since 1948 the Hungarian political system had two competing centers of power, around Rákosi and Nagy. Each continued to vie with the other because the unanimous endorsement of the June resolutions was only a formalistic acquiescence to Soviet wishes and did not reflect domestic political reality. The Politburo remained Rákosi's domain, and he retained the allegiance of most of the party apparat. Already while drafting the report to the Central Committee, Nagy had met with an uncooperative attitude among party and state officials fearful of exposing the misdeeds of the past. Rákosi managed not only to steer the Central Committee away from a review of the purges but also to block publication of the resolutions.[8]

The newly elected national assembly convened on 4 July to elect Nagy chairman of the council of ministers and to hear his "New Course" program.[9] This followed the outlines of the June resolutions with the notable omission of the latter's denunciation of the party leadership. The program concentrated on economic reforms, promising that the government would "permit the winding up of cooperative farms where the majority of members wishes it.'' In addition, Nagy noted that in the past the authorities had "often disregarded the provisions of the Constitution which safeguard the rights, liberties, securities of the citizen.'' He undertook to "consolidate legality" by abolishing internment camps, granting amnesty to minor offenders, reviewing the sentences of "people who have been wronged,'' and to show greater religious tolerance.

The basic thrust of the New Course departed radically from Rákosi's practice, but it was a statement of intentions rather than a carefully developed program of political and economic reform. In the prevailing milieu of political intrigue and sabotage its implementation turned out to be haphazard and perfunctory. The dual leadership degenerated into a tug-of-war that could be arbitrated only by the Kremlin. Of the two protagonists, Nagy felt that he had received a mandate from the Soviet leaders, especially Malenkov, to carry out his reforms, while Rákosi perceived the fragility of the consensus around Malenkov and chose to temporize. Fearing above all exposure of his purges, he and his supporters would at times support Nagy to try to limit the damage. The demoted Farkas calculatedly courted Nagy, got the Soviet ambassador to intervene on his behalf, and was soon reinstated to the Secretariat and the Politburo.[10] Rákosi and Gerő even pretended to endorse Nagy's charges of "leftist opposition" against those who protested, and with some justice, that the abrupt abandonment of major industrial projects was wasteful.[11] But such accommodations were purely tactical, for Rákosi saw that his own power and hold over the party would be undermined if the New Course was left to run unchecked.

Encouraged by the liquidation of Beria, whom he regarded as his principal enemy, Rákosi gave a speech before a meeting of Budapest party activists on 11 July that was full of veiled warnings against overestimating the reform program. He reminded his listeners that the source of government proposals was the party, whose basic policies remained unchanged. He denounced the kulaks (Nagy had abolished the notorious kulak lists), and warned peasants to remain in the collective farms at least until the end of the harvest.[12] Nagy later commented that this speech "left the party inclined to feel that there was no need for great changes in Party life, leadership, and policy; that actually the old policy could be continued."[13] And Rákosi had the means to subvert Nagy's efforts, for the latter could not command the party's support; he was outnumbered in the Politburo and was not in the Secretariat. Gerő not only remained in charge of the party's economic policy committee but had also acquired the interior portfolio in the new government, while Rákosi himself chaired the party's rehabilitation committee. Béla Szalai, a Rákosi man and alternate member of the Politburo, headed the National Planning Office.

Nagy's recourse, based on his interpretation of Soviet advice and on the June resolutions, was to strengthen the role of the state. He would subsequently argue that the party's proper role of directing the state organs had been perverted into an outright expropriation of the government's functions, and that this represented a "swing toward degeneration of the dictatorship of the proletariat." Rákosi, however, would make the ideologically damning allegation that Nagy was attempting to force the party into the background.[14] In practice, the months following the June resolutions were marked by a bureaucratic battle between Nagy's supporters, who were found mainly in the state administration, and the central party apparat. As a result, the implementation of policy was virtually paralyzed. By August Rákosi was pressing the Politburo to blunt the edge of the negative reappraisals. This aroused criticism at the Central Committee's meeting of 31 October, when the Politburo and the government were instructed to pursue the reforms.[15]

In the meantime, the Politburo's resolution of 9 September calling for an investigation into the problems of the working class had led to the creation of a five-man committee from the ranks of the Central Committee. Within a month this working group had visited thirty factories, mines, and construction projects. It concluded that the various initiatives being taken to implement the New Course were regarded by many workers as hasty and arbitrary, and that a fully developed government program was essential to prevent further erosion of the party's credibility. In the event, the reassertion of Rákosi's line in late 1954 prevented the elaboration of comprehensive guidelines on working class policy anticipated in the Central Committee's investigation.[16]

A frustrated Nagy traveled to Moscow in January 1954 to complain to Khrushchev and Malenkov about Rákosi's obstructionism. As a result, it appears, the latter was instructed to show greater cooperation.[17] The rivalry between the two men was nevertheless unconcealed. At a Politburo meeting in February at which Nagy succeeded in winning approval for new cultural guidelines, Rákosi expanded on the "tremendous achievements of the Party in the last eight years." Nagy interjected: "There were plenty of mistakes in these eight years." "But there were also achievements," insisted Rákosi, and the other retorted: "Let's not argue. . . . I know what I know."[18] Profoundly humiliated by his sudden fall from grace in Moscow and the resulting curtailment of his dictatorial powers, Rákosi refused to accept the judgment of the June resolutions. István Kovács, the Budapest party secretary, had sent a letter to the leadership professing alarm at the disharmony between government and party. It is quite likely that he had been prompted to do so by Rákosi himself. In any case, Rákosi seized on the letter and extracted from the Politburo and the Central Committee resolutions that indirectly indicted the momentarily absent and ailing Nagy.[19] With the party immersed in debate in preparation for its forthcoming congress, Rákosi asked for an audience with the Soviet leadership. To his dismay the latter insisted that he be accompanied by Nagy, whose illness delayed the trip, and the date of the congress was put back from 18 April to 24 May.

**The New Course Confirmed.**  The May visit to Moscow dashed Rákosi's hopes for a quick exoneration and return to undivided power. The Soviet leaders persisted in urging that he correct past mistakes (including "Führerism"!) and maintain collective leadership. The debate on the Kovács letter, they charged, "lacked Bolshevik frankness." Khrushchev dismissed Rákosi's claim that he was merely a victim of Beria's treachery. Thus the spirit of the June resolutions received Soviet confirmation, and upon his return to Budapest Rákosi had to suffer the ignominy of moving resolutions in the Politburo and the Central Committee that contradicted his earlier measures.[20] He probably perceived more clearly than Nagy that the collective leadership in the Kremlin, with Malenkov and Khrushchev momentarily preeminent, was only an interregnum. Behind that facade a struggle for supremacy was under way whose outcome, he calculated, would not benefit Nagy's principal champion, Malenkov. But Rákosi had jumped the gun, while Nagy, whose mind was of a less Machiavellian cast, felt vindicated.

For all these setbacks Rákosi remained the undisputed head of the HWP. At its third congress, held from 24 to 30 May 1954, he delivered the principal address, speaking for five hours. While paying lip service to the June resolutions he intimated that the mistakes of the past had already been remedied, and alluded to the harmful effect of the reforms on peasant and worker discipline. He presented the Central Committee's draft guidelines for the next five-year plan, which called for a shift in emphasis from capital to consumer goods, and for large-scale agricultural development in both the collective and private sectors. The political turmoil of the preceding twelve months had prevented comprehensive development of a new five-year plan. The Central Committee therefore recommended that the starting date be postponed to 1956 in order to allow for adequate preparation. In his address to the congress, the head of the Soviet delegation, Marshal Voroshilov (at that time titular head of state as well as a member of the Politburo), essentially endorsed the principle of collective leadership and the orientation of the New Course.

The congress elected a Central Committee of seventy members, twenty-three of them new; a nine-member Politburo (compared with seventeen in 1951) consisting of Apró, Ács, Farkas, Gerő, Hegedüs, István Hidas, Nagy, Rákosi, and Szalai, along with alternative members Bata and József Mékis; and a five-member Secretariat (compared with seven in 1951) that included Farkas and Rákosi as well as three minor figures, Ács, János Matolcsi, and Vég. These changes did not alter the political profile of the leading bodies, where Rákosi's supporters, whether sincere or opportunistic, remained predominant. Apart from Nagy, the Politburo members were all in Rákosi's thrall. Also elected were a Central Control Committee, chaired as before by that doctrinaire nonentity Károly Kiss, and a new Central Review Committee.

The party statutes endorsed by the congress reflected the stress laid on collective leadership and democratization in the June resolutions. The latter had recommended in part:

> Criticism and self-criticism must be boldly encouraged in the party from top to bottom and be made an integral part of daily party work. Apart from correcting the errors in economic policy and curtailing violent administrative official

methods, [this policy] must play a decisive role in ensuring that the party's members, organizations, and leadership take prompt notice of the signals coming from the workers and recognize errors, so that the latter are not allowed to worsen but can be corrected before they cause more serious damage.[21]

Among the early corrective measures were the abolition of the Organizational Committee and the reorientation of the Secretariat from a policy-making role to one of supervising implementation by the apparat. (This directive led to the personnel changes in the Secretariat effected at the congress.) The party elections in the months preceding the congress were conducted by secret ballot, even in the basic units, in accordance with the Central Committee's denunciation of the former practice of imposing leaders from above. Only 55.1 percent of the leaders were reelected. Incompetence was held to be the reason for the demotion of at least half of those who were not reelected.[22]

Rákosi tried to paint a rosy picture of the party's unity and reserved criticism for the alleged mounting threat from the right. The congress nevertheless reiterated the undesirability of excessive centralization, of bureaucratic methods, and of an inward-looking style of party work, and it recommended a quantitative reduction in party directives. The new statutes provided for a Central Review Committee to monitor the administrative and budgetary efficiency of the central apparat; for a triennial party congress; and for election of the Central Control Committee, the party's disciplinary body, by the Central Committee instead of by the congress. The secret ballot in all party elections was made mandatory, and the ceiling on the number of coopted members in elected bodies was lowered.[23] All these reforms were designed to enhance intraparty democracy. Its chances, however, depended in large measure on the inclination of the leadership to break with authoritarian practice, and Rákosi and his army of emulators proved unwilling to do more than pay lip service to the new line.

The membership, accustomed to the simplicity of blind obedience and the exercise of petty tyranny, could not readily adapt to a more participatory style of party life. It became increasingly demoralized and confused as the Rákosi-Nagy struggle ran its course. Party strength fell from 945,606 full and candidate members in January 1952 to 862,603 two years later, and stabilized at that level until the revolution. Recruitment declined, and some 40,000 members were expelled between 1954 and 1956.[24] Membership status offered little indication of loyalty, since there was no provision for voluntary withdrawal, and few members would willingly seek expulsion and the consequent risk to employment and privilege.

**The Patriotic People's Front.**   The party's low prestige among the masses, the apparent Soviet endorsement of a new duality of state and party, and—not least—his own need for a more secure power base all impelled Nagy to propose that the political system be revitalized by a certain decentralization of authority. His plan, presented to the Politburo before the congress, was to improve the work of local councils by making them less bureaucratic and more representative. He also proposed to revive the People's Independence Front under the name of Patriotic People's Front, and to include in it both individual members and mass organizations. But the Politburo, evidently fearing a potential competitor, preferred the format of a mass movement with only organizational membership. This was the version that was submitted and gained the approval of the Soviet party leaders.[25]

The congressional agenda precluded debate on the Patriotic People's Front proposal. Nagy had introduced it in the context of administrative schemes for decentralization; it would be, he argued, a means to restore the links between the party and all strata of the population:

> Intellectual, petty bourgeois and non-proletarian strata have a part in the building of Socialism and are active participants. Thus Socialism cannot be built without their cooperation. . . . The mere formal existence of the [People's Independence Front] with its activities limited to occasional action did not at all correspond to the important mission which it would have had if it had been included into our People's Democratic system by creating the broadest popular unity and expanding the democratic basis of the proletarian dictatorship. . . . The new People's Front must be broader and more democratic than it has ever been in the past . . . a mass movement comprehending the broadest layers of the workers and popular committees in which there is a place for the trade unions, the DISZ, the MNDSZ, social organizations working in the field of science, culture, and sociology, the National Peace Council and its committees, leading personalities of the government, church, and social life, representatives from the intelligentsia, and so forth.[26]

Implementation of the congressional resolution on the Patriotic People's Front began in August with a conference attended by a number of nonparty notables; a nine-man committee that included Rákosi was charged with drafting the statutes. It was decided not to revive the old coalition parties within the reorganized front but to adopt the model of a broad, sociopolitical mass movement in which the HWP's leading role would not depend on a numerical preponderance of party members.

The Central Committee resolution of 13 October on the structure of the front struck a fine balance between party control and mass appeal:

> 1. The chairmen of the county people's front committees should be generally extraparty people who are well known in the county, popular, and accept the leadership of the party. If such an extraparty person is not available, a well-known party member may be elected chairman of the county people's front, but this comrade must not come from the party apparatus.
>
> 2. The secretaries of the county people's front committees must be party members. . . .

3. The secretary heads the permanent office. . . .

4. The county people's front office should number from five to seven persons with an appropriate number of nonparty members.[27]

As for the political content of the front, a party historian related that the stress was on patriotism and national traditions; socialism was played down to placate the masses. National unity, he continued, was to be fostered through nationalism and the illusion of class peace. All this prompted the impression that the front's purpose was to balance the party's radical socialism with a more liberal orientation.[28] Imre Nagy's address to the inaugural congress of the front on 24 October was in the same spirit. He asked for support for his New Course policies and intimated that the obstacles lay within the party.[29] The congress elected the Politburo's nominee for general secretary of the front, Ferenc Jánosi, a onetime Calvinist seminarian and Imre Nagy's son-in-law. While Nagy proceeded to staff the fledgling front with his supporters, the movement's nationalist and Populist flair began to arouse popular enthusiasm. Rákosi, in turn, immediately recognized a potential rival to his disciplined party in Nagy's brainchild and moved to obstruct its development while plotting the downfall of Nagy himself.

## REFORM AND OBSTRUCTION

The central objectives of the June resolutions had been the realization of collective leadership and the reform of economic management. The former turned into a struggle for power between Rákosi and Nagy. The latter, however, produced immediate effects. True, the implementation of the economic program approved at the Central Committee meeting of October 1953 was uneven and uncoordinated; the party leadership, notably Gerő and István Friss, retained ultimate directing authority, and was inclined to sabotage the reforms in order to discredit Nagy. Nevertheless, the New Course reversed virtually every trend that had characterized the Stalinist model.

The most striking change occurred in agriculture. Hardly had the new permissive policy been made public than a massive exodus from the collective farms got under way. The party sent not only hundreds of agitators but also the army's own political officers into the countryside to persuade peasants to remain in the collective farms and to promise them state aid, but the rout could not be halted. Within one year the agricultural producers' cooperatives' share of arable land fell from 26 to 18 percent and their share of agricultural manpower from 19.1 to 13.1 percent. Concurrently the number of private farms grew by 200,000 and that of collective farms fell by 500. Recently abandoned land was once again tilled, and it was reported that the private peasants' inclination to produce had "significantly improved." Occasional complaints of neglect from the remaining collectives were persistently exploited by Rákosi, who grumbled at the meeting of the Politburo on 10 February 1955: "We praise these private peasants so much that willy-nilly the collective farm is driven into the background."[30] In fact, various government measures to reduce taxation and compulsory deliveries and to improve the leadership and equipment of the collective farms had a positive influence on the productivity of both private and collective farms and on the real income of peasants. If the living standard of private farmers improved more markedly than that of collective farm employees, this was because the latter had lower incentives and were generally less skilled and less productive.[31]

In the industrial sector the New Course aimed at mitigating the Stalinist command economy's single-minded concentration on the quantitative, forced development of the iron and steel industry. Investments in heavy industry were 41.1 percent lower in 1954 than they had been in 1953, while the proportion of investments in light and consumer industries (and agriculture) was increased.[32] Moreover, the decline in the handicraft industries, which had led to a serious shortage in essential goods and services in the preceding period, was halted; by the end of 1954 there were twice as many artisans as before the New Course.

Nagy tried to satisfy consumer demands by augmenting the supply of goods, by reducing prices, and by granting special wage increases, all of which raised the standard of living of industrial workers by some 15 percent in 1954. However, the concurrent relaxation of Rákosi's harsh labor policies took its toll in productivity, which in 1954 did not meet even the reduced targets of the plan's last year. In contrast, the output of cooperative industry increased by 30 percent over the previous year, and that of private small industry doubled.

**Economic Difficulties.**  While the initial measures of the New Course brought about an improvement in the standard of living, they were also inflationary and had a disruptive impact on the economy at a time when Hungary was already suffering from an accumulated debt in foreign trade. That debt had been generated not only by the resource requirements of heavy industry and the exploitative terms of trade with the Soviet Union, but also by the heavy investments in military materiel prescribed by, and imported from, the Soviet Union. According to Nagy, these excesses were criticized in the June resolutions. He also records that "foreign trade was not under my direction but under the supervision and direction of Ernő Gerő. . . . Furthermore, since Rákosi considered foreign trade his special field, he kept it under his immediate direction."[33]

The New Course objective of transforming the product profile of the industrial sector could not be achieved without new capital goods, which in turn required credits. But the balance of trade rapidly deteriorated towards the end of 1954, at which time the Soviet Union unexpectedly announced that its raw material deliveries would be halved for the following year. The measure was probably prompted by the state of flux of Soviet economic policies. Whatever the reason, it combined with a similar retrenchment in the other satellites to sharply reduce the availability of credits at Hungary's moment of need. Meanwhile, Nagy's proposal to consolidate debts in the Western trade sector was blocked by the Politburo.[34]

The Rákosi clique soon began to accuse Nagy of profligacy and sounded the alarm about the slackening of labor discipline and productivity. Raising the specter of inflation, Gerő's economic policy committee developed in mid-1954 a proposal for major cuts in state expenditure, including social benefits, and for higher taxation. This drastic deflationary program was then approved by the Politburo in the absence of Nagy, who was on vacation in the Soviet Union. Recalls Nagy: "All these measures were so timed that their implementation would have occurred at a time when the local councils were holding elections and Patriotic People's Front committees were being set up. In this way the 'left-wing' opposition would have succeeded in turning all sectors of the population against the Party, the People's Democracy, and mainly the government."[35]

Still confident of the Kremlin's backing, Nagy returned ready to repel this latest challenge to his reforms. In the event, his program was confirmed at the October plenum of the Central Committee. The resulting recapitulation, drafted by Nagy, paid tribute to the earlier achievements but reiterated the shortcomings of Rákosi's economic management. It confirmed that "the main thrust of our policy is to raise the workers' standard of living." The slow pace of conversion to a more consumer oriented industry was attributed to the "indecisive, uncoordinated implementation of the New Course policy."

The fundamental factor in the regime's economic difficulties, according to the Central Committee, was, first, hesitation in implementing the New Course policy; and second, a resistance to that policy that showed itself in covert forms. "This resistance," the committee continued, "is fed by theoretically unfounded, erroneous conceptions that aim to resolve the economic problems by a 'withdrawal of purchasing power'—therefore by a reduction in the standard of living—and to develop agriculture without improving the welfare of the peasantry." This (according to Nagy) conflicted with the Marxist-Leninist principle of maximizing the workers' material and cultural welfare. It was impossible to raise agricultural production without improving the peasants' standard of living. Since currently private farming predominated, peasants had therefore to be allowed to sell most of their output on the free market. The new industrial policy aimed not to abandon industrialization but to correct earlier biases that had caused the nation's real needs and resources to be overlooked. A number of immediate problems were identified: the incorrect, permissive, and liberal interpretation of the New Course, which had promoted a serious slackening of labor and plan discipline; ingrained habits of wastefulness and low productivity; and bureaucratization, which served to conceal the leadership's impotence and isolation.

The Politburo was criticized for still neglecting to draw the Central Committee into decision making and for making Central Committee members fearful of voicing their opinions. Rákosi insisted that the Politburo was totally united. (His saying so, recalls a participant, made most of his audience disbelieve it.) The Central Committee thus reaffirmed its earlier prescriptions. It instructed the Politburo to remove uncooperative cadres from posts in economic administration, to work out a detailed economic program for 1955, and to mobilize the hitherto passive party apparatus into active support for the New Course.[36]

Much to the amazement and disgust of the party rank and file, Gerő, whose economic edifice was being destroyed, declared in a speech at Szolnok that the opponents of Nagy's program would be "swept away with an iron hand."[37] Even the appearance of success can act as a magnet, especially in a totalitarian system where the cult of personality had induced a fine sensitivity to changes in personal power. Nagy's open denunciation of "leftist" and "sectarian" opposition to the New Course and the Central Committee's positive response coincided with a surge of influential support for Nagy. Much of this was tactical, as in the case of István Kovács and Andor Berei (who had replaced Béla Szalai at the National Planning Office). More genuine sympathy for Nagy materialized among journalists and intellectuals and among ordinary party members.

**Centralism Challenged.**   At *Szabad Nép* a veritable palace revolt erupted when the editor refused to print an article exposing the manipulation of elections. The purges and other misdeeds of the Rákosi regime were brought up during a three-day debate in which the majority of the editorial staff favored what one speaker called a "purifying storm." The party's watchdog over the newspaper, Farkas, dropped his conciliatory mask and thundered: "We are not a debating Party. We are not Social Democrats. Here, the Party leadership decides what would be done!"[38] The most rebellious journalists were thereupon purged from the staff, but the tyranny had been openly challenged by its former servants.

Among those who shook off the shackles of party discipline were older home communists and graduates of the people's colleges. Some of them penetrated the culture ministry, where Révai had been replaced by the former NPP leader József Darvas, momentarily a Nagy supporter, and they proceeded to exploit ideology in service of the reform movement. Even village exploring, that phenomenon of the 1930s, enjoyed a certain revival as Populist writers and journalists sounded the depths of dissent and despair engendered by Rákosi's rule.[39] Without necessarily abandoning Marxism, these intellectual dissenters sought a more humane formula than the one offered by Stalin and his satraps.

Much ink has been spilled in attempts to attribute Nagy's ultimate failure to certain personal traits and deficiencies. He was a man of solitary and reflective disposition, ill suited to the demands of leadership and the intrigue of communist politics. In the words of an émigré historian, he was unaware that "the large masses of Hungarians were ready to ascribe intentions and characteristics to him which he was far from possessing. He had felt neither a dedication nor a vocation to redeem his country from the Soviet-Communist yoke; he was only ready to fight for his ideals, Communist-Socialist ideals interwoven with streaks of humanitarianism and a sense of democracy.''[40] As a convinced communist, he thought that the new Soviet leadership fully shared his views, and assumed that in time the Hungarian party elite would follow suit. Studious of avoiding the sin of factionalism, he misread the opportunistic support of former Rákosiites. Despite his attempts to construct a new people's front, he did not seek to organize his dispersed supporters, and few among the latter occupied positions of power. In contrast, Rákosi never relented in his determination to discredit Nagy within Hungary and in Moscow, and he devoted much of his time to preserving his power base in the party and plotting against his rival.[41] But the fact that Nagy was no match for Rákosi in the art of political manipulation was overshadowed by the location of ultimate authority in the Kremlin.

**The Problem of Rehabilitation.** An essential element in Rákosi's exercise of power had been the massive and calculatedly unpredictable application of terror. By 1953 the vast network of prisons and internment and labor camps held some 150,000 prisoners. Most heavily represented were the old upper and middle classes, the rural gentry, the clergy, and the kulaks; they were joined by the social democrat and communist victims of the party purges. Many were detained without trial; others had passed through perfunctory trials in which guilt was assumed and class origin served as damning evidence. The political police and the communist judiciary were the managers of this macabre travesty of justice. There is a surfeit of evidence that the entire population, up to the highest levels of officialdom, lived in dread of the AVH's nighttime appearance. Those visited often disappeared without trace, while torture or harsh treatment and detention without appeal awaited those who escaped execution.

Such was the state of socialist legality when Nagy assumed the premiership. Delving into the files of the purges, he reportedly discovered that he himself had at one time been selected for the role ultimately assigned to Rajk.[42] Nagy undertook to restore some credibility to the legal system, but there were too many skeletons in Rákosi's closet for the latter to allow open investigation and rehabilitation. The internment and labor camps were closed by the late summer of 1953, but most of the inmates were summarily retried by people's courts and transferred to ordinary jails. On 26 July amnesty was proclaimed for those on short sentences, but few political prisoners were affected.

Within the party, a rehabilitation committee consisting of Nagy, Rákosi, and Gerő (then interior minister) was created to consider the problem of the purges. But to correct past perversions of justice, especially against communists, would have amounted to a devastating indictment of the Rákosi clique. Rákosi pursued a dilatory tactic, and Nagy finally resigned from the committee. The announcement on 13 March 1954 that former AVH chief Gábor Péter, under arrest since December 1952, had been sentenced by a military tribunal to life imprisonment, with two of his deputies receiving shorter terms, was probably calculated by Rákosi to deflect the pressures for full exposure.

The risks of rehabilitation were also recognized by the Soviet leadership. At the May 1954 meeting in Moscow, Khrushchev (as reported by Nagy) wrestled with the problem: "Rákosi is responsible for the arrests. Therefore he does not want to release these people. He knows that he is guilty and will compromise himself. . . . the rehabilitations should be carried out so as not to destroy Rákosi's authority. We will protect Rákosi's authority only in so far as it is not prejudicial to Party authority." To increase that authority, he concluded, "what happened must be told."[43] As a result, between one and two hundred communists were released by October 1954, and Nagy made brief mention of the "liberation of unjustly sentenced comrades" in *Szabad Nép* on 20 October.[44]

Most of the liberated communists returned to the party. Some, like Losonczy and Donáth, were soon drawn to Nagy's reformism, while others avoided taking sides in the debate that they found outside prison walls. One such dutiful activist was Kádár, who was released in July 1954. Rákosi greeted him effusively and professed dismay that all but the last of Kádár's letters protesting his innocence had been intercepted by Péter. Asked by Rákosi what his plans were, Kádár volunteered to return to party work or to his original trade of machinist. Assigned the job of secretary of the party committee in Budapest's thirteenth district, he quietly adopted a middle line between Rákosi and Nagy.[45] For the vast majority of noncommunist political prisoners, however, the New Course brought at best some relief to the hardships of detention.

## RÁKOSI RESURGENT

The Central Committee resolutions of October 1954 proved to be a Pyrrhic victory for Nagy. Such tactical concessions by the Rákosi clique did not prevent them from promoting a whispering campaign among the party faithful that a "hostile right-wing wave was sweeping the country."[46] There were allegations that the Patriotic People's Front, with its strategic role in the forthcoming local council elections, was designed by Nagy to dilute the party's hegemony—allegations that received unwitting reinforcement from an intensive propaganda campaign launched by Radio Free Europe on 1 October. This "Operation FOCUS" exhorted Hungarians to exploit the possibilities of the New Course. Balloons dropped millions of leaflets carrying the letters NEM (for Nemzeti Ellenállási Mozgalom, or National Resistance Movement) or the number 12 (indicating the movement's twelve demands), as well as Liberty

Bell medals bearing the inscription "Hungarians for freedom—all the free world for the Hungarians," while RFE's broadcasting schedule was expanded to elaborate on these themes.[47] After the Central Committee meeting Rákosi repaired to the Soviet Union to nurse his wounds and court favor with the Soviet leadership, notably Kaganovich.[48] These discussions must have been encouraging, for upon his return to Hungary in December the attacks on Nagy's alleged deviation intensified. Farkas, a reliable barometer of shifts in power, now taunted Nagy: "There is no New Course . . . it is rightist to pursue it."[49]

In fact, by December a new coalition led by Khrushchev had emerged at Malenkov's expense in the Soviet party presidium. Rákosi's incriminating dossier on Nagy could now be put to use. When a Hungarian delegation presented itself in January 1955, Malenkov was compelled to take the lead in berating Nagy for pursuing the very policies he had earlier advocated. Nagy was blamed for the economic problems encountered by the New Course, for encouraging factionalism and popular opposition, for denigrating the leading role of the party, and even for chauvinism (this for having paraphrased in public a patriotic verse by Petőfi). Nagy put up a spirited defense but was reportedly shouted down and instructed to reverse his industrial policy and restore order in Hungary.[50] Shortly after this confrontation Khrushchev denounced the post-Stalin reversal in industrialization, and on 8 February Malenkov resigned as prime minister.

While Nagy lay ill with a serious heart condition and composed letters protesting the accusations and calling for an open debate, Rákosi proceeded to engineer his downfall. The Central Committee, passively submitting once again to Rákosi's rule, met from 2 to 4 March and unanimously passed a resolution confirming the new Soviet line. Without totally denying the validity of the June resolutions, the committee concentrated on the mistakes of implementation, which were attributed to "rightist opportunist deviation." It cited the excessive retreat from heavy industry, the abandonment of collectivization, the insufficient fulfillment of production targets (which meant that the "rise in the standard of living did not rest on a solid, permanent foundation"), the efforts to reduce the party's leading role in the Patriotic People's Front, and the inclination of the press to ignore the positive achievements of the earlier phase. The resolution placed the blame squarely on the shoulders of Imre Nagy, who had "supported such anti-Marxist views in his writings and speeches."[51]

Nagy, however, refused to recant or resign, insisting that he be given the opportunity to present his case to the Central Committee. Rákosi would not test his strength against Nagy's popularity. In early April the Kremlin dispatched Suslov to settle the matter. After failing to persuade Nagy to withdraw voluntarily from the premiership, Suslov supervised the preparation of a final prosecution brief against him. He was charged with factionalism, with trying to put himself above the party by seeking the presidency of the Patriotic People's

Front (the Politburo had only allowed him to assume the vice-presidency), and with clericalism and nepotism (arising from Jánosi's appointment). At its meeting of 14 April the Central Committee acted on these charges by expelling Nagy from its ranks and other party offices: "Comrade Nagy, in the interest of realizing his rightist, opportunist policies, resorted to un-Party-like, anti-Party and even factional methods, which are completely incompatible with the unity, the discipline, of the Marxist-Leninist Party."[52] For good measure, the Central Committee also expelled Mihály Farkas from the Politburo and the Secretariat, ostensibly for having lent support to Nagy. Perhaps Farkas had shown too much opportunism even for Rákosi's taste. Moreover, the less dogmatic elements in the party were likely to welcome his sacrifice in view of his role in the purges and that of his son Vladimir, who as Péter's deputy had tortured less fortunate comrades with visible relish. Four days later the national assembly endorsed Dobi's motion to remove Nagy from the premiership for having failed to properly carry out his duties. He was also relieved of his vice-presidency of the Patriotic People's Front, of his status as a parliamentary deputy, and of his university teaching post.

Assessed objectively, the censure of Nagy was patently unjust. Whatever his differences with Rákosi, he had remained loyal to the party and to the Soviet Union throughout his premiership. The New Course he regarded as wholly compatible with Leninism, as a correction, endorsed by the Soviet leadership, of Rákosi's ideologically aberrant excesses. As such, he believed that it would serve to both legitimize and economically underpin the socialist system. Only in disgrace would he indulge in a more fundamental reappraisal of socialism under Soviet tutelage and veer toward so-called national communism. But clearly his fortunes had been governed by Moscow. For a time he had benefited from the ascendancy of Malenkov and the latter's economic reformism, but even then he had not been allowed to entirely supplant Rákosi. As Khrushchev's star rose, the Kremlin became more wary of the potentially disintegrative tendencies of the New Course and called for retrenchment. Khrushchev reportedly explained: "I have to keep Rákosi in Hungary, because in Hungary the whole structure will collapse if he goes."[53] Had Nagy been allowed to prevail, it is more likely that the New Course would have stabilized the system without inducing mass support for communist rule. In the event, neither the Soviet nor the Hungarian party leaders fully anticipated the psychological impact of curtailing the New Course. The wave of optimistic expectancy was stifled by Nagy's fall from grace, but within the party the dominion of Rákosi's Stalinism had been irreparably undermined. Little by little, the masses came to perceive the inner weakness of the monolith.

**New Constraints on Tyranny.**  Rákosi's return to undivided dictatorial power did not bring the immediate reimposition of the status quo as it had existed before the New Course. An external limitation was the new Khrushchevian orthodoxy, a blend of economic neo-Stalinism, modest political relaxation and decentralization, and "peaceful coexistence" with Tito and the West. Only the first of these elements suited Rákosi, who had earned his spurs outdoing Stalin in autocracy and terror, not to mention vilification of Tito and the imperialist foe. Elaboration of the second five-year plan had once again been delayed by the political turmoil. Meanwhile, one immediate consequence of Rákosi's triumph was a partial return to the development of heavy industry, mainly through the revival of investment projects suspended under Nagy. Ironically, labor discipline and productivity improved in the new atmosphere of threatened duress, and industrial production rose at a significantly higher annual rate (9.6 percent) in 1955 than in the preceding year.

The peasantry, which had benefited most directly from the New Course, foresaw another round of collectivization and promptly lost its will to produce. Food shortages ensued. At its meeting of 7–8 June 1955, the Central Committee reiterated the goal of collectivization, which it linked with such fanciful objectives as raising production by 25 percent, strengthening the worker-peasant alliance, isolating the kulaks, and converting the middle peasants into firm allies. The committee's obsessive concern with the latter two peasant strata was not justified by reality, for over the preceding few years the peasantry had been largely homogenized both in terms of the size of holdings and in their hostility to state intervention. By August this animosity impelled Rákosi to tell the Politburo that if collectivization could only be achieved by administrative methods, i.e., compulsion, that would be a "lesser evil." He called for the "most Draconian" measures against peasants who failed to fulfill the new delivery quotas and other obligations.[54] The anguished peasantry once again became the object of harassment, confiscation, and impossible demands. It resorted to passive resistance. In the second half of 1955 the number of collective farms increased by 450, and by the following year the agricultural cooperative sector accounted for 22.2 percent of arable land and 15.4 percent of working peasants. Even these modest results were achieved at a disastrous cost in productivity and alienation.[55]

In the political sphere, the limited reforms of Nagy's New Course were stalled. Organization of the Patriotic People's Front was abandoned, as was the barely begun process of rehabilitating political prisoners. For the time being Rákosi abstained from launching another purge and from raising the AVH's level of activity to its earlier heights. Vigilance against enemies of the state was not relaxed, however, and the discovery in early 1955 of an alleged anti-state conspiracy led to executions and imprisonment.

Khrushchev's mitigation of Stalinist terror thus imposed limits on Rákosi's freedom to seek revenge, and the shift in Soviet foreign policy proved equally irksome to him. In word and deed Rákosi had been an enthusiastic participant in the Cominform campaign against Tito. Now, like Molotov in Moscow, he found himself in a minority position in advising against a compromise that would allow for "several roads to socialism." The reconciliation was sealed with the visit of Khrushchev and Bulganin to Belgrade in May and June 1955, but Rákosi dragged his feet in responding to the new orthodoxy. He feebly blamed Péter, who was already in prison, for the anti-Tito hate campaign of years past (imitating Khrushchev, who had blamed Beria at Belgrade), while delaying the release of hundreds of interned Yugoslavs.[56] A grudging concession was the release in July of Rajk's wife. Tito repaid him with a bitter denunciation of hostile Hungarians who had their hands "soaked in blood" and had "sentenced innocent men to death," specifically Rajk.[57] The Soviet leaders soon had to face the fact that reconciliation between the two parties would not be complete without some drastic resolution of the deep personal enmity between Rákosi and Tito.

The Soviet proclamation of peaceful coexistence with the capitalist enemy was also difficult for Rákosi to swallow, for he had never ceased to warn that the cold war would be intensified. The state treaty of 15 May 1955 that neutralized Austria and ended allied occupation also removed the admittedly superfluous legal pretext that allowed the Soviet Union to maintain troops in Hungary and Romania, namely, in order to protect its lines of communication to the occupied zone. A day earlier the Soviet Union and its satellites signed a treaty in Warsaw that specified a joint (i.e., Soviet) command for the region's military forces and implicitly legitimized the continued maintenance of Soviet troops in Hungary. Such reassurances were evidently invited by Rákosi and the other East European party leaders, whose chronic feelings of insecurity were only accentuated by the prospect of the East-West summit conference at Geneva in July.

The Soviet Union wished to overcome the Western powers' obstruction of United Nations membership for Hungary, Bulgaria, and Romania (officially, because they had not fulfilled the human rights clauses in the Paris peace treaties), and it instructed Rákosi to make some symbolic concession. As a consequence, in July Cardinal Mindszenty was transferred to house arrest, and in October, shortly before Hungary's admission to the UN, Archbishop Grősz and other priests were set free. The "spirit of Geneva" was a will-o'-the-wisp, but the winds of change were not blowing favorably for Mátyás Rákosi either in Moscow, where Khrushchev was about to deliver his stunning denunciation of Stalin, or in Hungary, where disaffection even within the ranks of the party was spreading inexorably.

★ ★ ★ ★ ★

# *Power Lost and Regained*

# PART FIVE

*The progressive disaffection within party circles and the more gradual articulation of popular discontent have been termed respectively the elite and mass process in the genesis of the 1956 revolution.*[1] *The mass process materialized only in the summer of 1956, when the repercussions of the intraparty debates and of the twentieth Soviet party congress, with the Hungarian party's perceptible paralysis, began to activize a broader public. The malaise at the top, on the other hand, spread much earlier, for the New Course had planted seeds of doubt and discord, particularly among the party's intellectual cohorts. Caught in the ideological crosscurrents, the confused leadership sought desperately to recapture a sense of certitude and authority as the party's monolithic facade crumbled.*

*After his expulsion from the party, Imre Nagy devoted himself to composing an ideological defense of the New Course. He condemned the oppressive dogmatism of his rivals and suggested that the Soviet-Yugoslav reconciliation allowed for a more nationally based version of communism. He drew support from the party intelligentsia and university students, but Rákosi held fast and blocked the rehabilitation of the victims of his purges.*

*Khrushchev's anti-Stalin speech in February 1956 precipitated Rákosi's downfall. Attacked in the party press and at student forums and abandoned by his associates, he was replaced in July on the Kremlin's orders by Gerő. The new leadership tried to adopt a marginally more liberal line but was left behind by the momentum of dissent. The "revisionism" of the intellectuals and students progressed to demands for independence from Soviet rule. The rehabilitation of Rajk and the readmission of Nagy to the party, both reluctantly sanctioned by the leadership, and the revolutionary wave in Poland only emboldened the dissenters and aroused the population.*

*While Gerő tried to reach an accommodation with Tito, demonstrations in Budapest on 23 October sparked off a spontaneous national uprising. A limited Soviet intervention ended inconclusively, Gerő was replaced by Kádár, and Imre Nagy assumed the premiership. With only the remnants of the secret police to defend its rule, the party rapidly disintegrated. While impromptu revolutionary councils pressed for independence and democratic reform, the Soviet Union temporized and dispatched reinforcements. When the Nagy government restored the multiparty system and, on 1 November, proclaimed Hungary's neutrality and withdrawal from the Warsaw Pact, the die was cast. Kádár, who had initially endorsed Nagy, was spirited out of the country to form a countergovernment. Three days later the revolution was crushed. Above all the Hungarians had fought for independence, but the revolution's general objectives encompassed a pluralistic democracy, some form of mixed economy, and the guarantee of basic human rights. Without Soviet intervention, the discredited communist party would have been relegated to a minor political role.*

*Kádár's restoration regime tried to reconcile the nation to the inevitability of communist and Soviet rule, but when resistance, notably on the part of workers' councils, persisted, harsh repression became the order of the day. The renamed Hungarian Socialist Workers' Party was painstakingly rebuilt while Kádár struggled with both dogmatist and revisionist critics. At Soviet instigation, Nagy was executed in 1958. The final collectivization of agriculture was launched in 1959. Economic reform was considered, then dismissed as politically premature. Cultural life stagnated.*

*The circumstances of his elevation brought Kádár opprobrium at home and abroad. The restoration of power had indeed been painful, but from the start Kádár had professed a two-front battle against the excesses of Stalinism and the heresy of national communism. Over time the worst offenders of the Rákosi era were dismissed, and at the party's eighth congress in 1962 Kádár's "alliance policy" received confirmation. That policy rested on the assumption that with the conclusion of collectivization domestic class conflicts had been essentially resolved. Accordingly, it invited nonparty members to participate in the economic modernization of Hungary. Imprisoned revolutionaries were amnestied, class discrimination in education eased, and persuasion rather than terror became the preferred tactic of the Kádár regime. Not all party veterans were comfortable with this conciliatory pragmatism, and most Hungarians still regarded Kádár as the Kremlin's satrap, but a workable compromise between rulers and ruled was in the making.*

# 12. *From Decompression to Revolution*

The leading force in intraparty revisionism was that uncommon Muscovite Imre Nagy. His role, however, was more ideological and self-justifying than power-seeking or conspiratorial. In the late summer of 1955, after being ousted from party and state office, Nagy had withdrawn to prepare a formal explanation of his actions for the Central Committee. Protesting his unwavering faith in Marxism-Leninism, he aimed to demonstrate that the New Course program had been closer to the essence of that ideology than the version propagated by Rákosi. Only after the Central Control Committee, acting on Rákosi's direct orders, had, in November 1955, expelled him from the party, did an embittered Nagy indulge in harsh condemnation of the prevailing orthodoxy and even some cautious criticism of the Soviet Union's pervasive interference in Hungarian political life. Encouraged by the Soviet-Yugoslav reconciliation, he called for the "application of Marxism-Leninism to specific Hungarian situations." Denouncing Rákosi's "Führerism," Nagy diagnosed the party's sorry state and proclaimed the need for its moral and political regeneration:

> As a result of the degeneration of power, individuals whose actions went counter to the morals of socialist society and to existing laws acquired positions in important fields of public life. It is not compatible to have in positions of leadership the directors and organizers of mass trials, those responsible for torturing and killing innocent men, organizers of international provocations, and economic saboteurs or squanderers of public property who, through the abuse of power, either have committed serious acts against the people or are forcing others to commit these acts.[1]

The party, he wrote, "is not a den of criminals, whose unity must be preserved by hiding their crimes." He warned that public opinion was condemning both party and government and would repudiate them unless rapid remedial action were taken.[2]

Nagy's later writings were also distinguished by a patriotic sentiment that had been notably absent from the public statements of the Rákosi clique. He revived Kossuth's vision of "close cooperation with neighboring peoples within the framework of free and independent nations." Seizing on the five principles of international relations proclaimed at the 1955 Bandung Conference of nonaligned nations (and endorsed by Moscow as an anti-imperialist charter), he insisted on their applicability within the socialist camp. He accused those in power of accepting "dependence, subordination, humiliating slavery"—a scarcely veiled allusion to Soviet hegemony—and urged that Hungary remain neutral in the contest of great powers: "The inner tension of Hungary, which is chiefly political, is caused by the fact that the leadership is opposing the ideals of national independence, sovereignty, and equality, as well as Hungarian national feeling and progressive traditions."[3]

In sum, Nagy was advancing a model of national communism analogous to that practiced by Tito, lately with formal Soviet acquiescence. Although his reconsiderations bordered dangerously close to heresy, he took the precaution of submitting a copy to the Soviet leadership; otherwise, only a small circle of friends was privy to the piecemeal elaboration of his views. The shifts in ideological orthodoxy, however, had the effect of unsettling the hitherto sycophantic intellectual establishment. Numerically small and composed of a few older Populists as well as younger recruits, this official intelligentsia had been motivated by opportunism as well as idealism in its service of Rákosi's Stalinist rule. The slightest display of nonconformism had brought swift retribution, the most notable case being that of Tibor Déry in 1952. But the perturbations and revelations of the New Course induced in many of them a profound soul-searching that turned adulation into bitter resentment against their former masters. The party would subsequently argue that 70 percent of the broadly defined intelligentsia had been a product of the precommunist period and therefore tainted with bourgeois values.[4]

The ghastly testimony of recently released victims of the purges played no small part in the alienation of the intelligentsia. These walking wounded of the Rákosi era were a living testimony to the system's irrationality and inhumanity, and their moral outrage could not readily be suppressed.

After his triumph over Nagy, Rákosi had quickly moved to purge *Szabad Nép* and *Irodalmi Ujság* of his rival's more exposed sympathizers. As a result, a few journalists who pressed for Rajk's rehabilitation were expelled from the party. The confiscation of the September 1955 issue of *Irodalmi Ujság* for a critical piece on the minister of culture galvanized the disaffected intellectuals. The presidium of the Writers' Association resigned in protest, and a "writers' memorandum" signed by fifty intellectuals and artists was delivered in early November to the Central Committee. Deploring censorship, the banning of certain noncommunist works, and the recent purges, the memorandum found the "despotic, antidemocratic methods of leadership in the cultural field more and more intolerable." Although Nagy had not been privy to the memorandum, Rákosi seized the excuse to accuse him of being a "rallying point of the enemies of socialism" and force his expulsion from the party.[5] The promoters of the memorandum were denounced in a Central Committee resolution as rightist opportunists, and most of them were prudent enough to comply with the order to withdraw their signatures.

Rákosi's retaliation against dissent was entirely in character and just as entirely counterproductive. His harsh treatment of Nagy and the intellectuals prompted the public to take notice of their quarrel with him and to follow it at first with detached curiosity and later with passionate interest. As Nógrádi, who had been asked by Gerő to take over the party's agitprop department in December, records in his memoirs: "Control of the press began to slip from the hands of the party leadership. Even *Szabad Nép* was no longer as servile as Rákosi would have wished. Ideological debates began among university youth. Those young intellectuals who had been nurtured in the people's colleges, who had personal contacts with László Rajk and held him in high esteem, began to emerge with notable combativeness." During a visit to a communist student meeting, Nógrádi dismissed some nationalist accusations against Hungary's communist neighbors but found it "much more difficult to answer why foreign travel was impossible, or why correspondence with relatives in the West had to be feared; why the deportations and internments had been necessary; why László Rajk and other communists had been executed; who was personally responsible for the illegalities. . . . These young people sought the truth!"[6]

Taking their cues from the intraparty debate and often adopting the ideological tactic of attacking Stalinism with Leninism, ever wider circles of the population gradually became infected with the spirit of dissent. An ideological void separated those few critics who were true believers from the masses of subterranean anticommunists, a few of whom—war veterans, religious youth—sustained some illicit organization. Momentarily they had a common enemy, and once again the final push would come from the Kremlin.

## THE IMPACT OF DESTALINIZATION

Nikita Khrushchev's struggle for preeminence in the Soviet leadership culminated at the Soviet party's twentieth congress, which opened on 14 February 1956. The Hungarian delegates—Rákosi, István Kovács, Béla Szalai—were not present at the closed night session of 24 and 25 February, when Khrushchev delivered his famous speech denouncing the sins of Stalin. The address was designed to discredit Khrushchev's more overtly Stalinist colleagues, notably Molotov; it concerned Stalin's domestic atrocities and his mishandling of Soviet-Yugoslav relations, but made no reference to Stalinism in the East European satellites.[7] The latter's leaders would have to draw their own conclusions from what they learned of this attack on Stalin and from the general thrust of the congress.

Rákosi was determined to limit as far as possible the impact of Khrushchev's bombshell, which thanks to American intelligence soon became public knowledge. In his report to the Central Committee meeting of 12 to 13 March he allowed that a revolutionary must not be afraid of admitting mistakes. He insisted, however, that the June 1953 resolutions had been "essentially implemented" and that the Soviet congress had led him to conclude that the Hungarian party's main policy line was "correct in all areas" and that the party itself was "strong and unified." "Our people's democracy," he concluded, "rests on a healthy foundation." Apart from some questions regarding Farkas's culpability and the delays in rehabilitation, the Central Committee accepted Rákosi's reassuring assessment and his disingenuous recommendation that the Politburo consider how to "place socialist legality on an even firmer basis." The resolution affirmed the desirability of collective leadership and intraparty democracy, better economic planning, more relaxed cultural guidelines, and a reinvigoration of the Patriotic People's Front.[8]

As news of the secret speech spread, in Rákosi's expurgated version and in fuller versions by word of mouth and Radio Free Europe's broadcasts and leaflets, a mood of expectancy arose in party and nation. "People breathed freely after the twentieth congress," reads an internal report on county party-activ conferences. Party and government were besieged with demands that the new line be implemented, that the Central Committee "speak with the workers as adults," and with complaints that the regime was forcing people to rely on foreign news media for this momentous news. Protests at economic hardship and bureaucratic oppression multiplied. A report to the leadership on 17 March observed that "the great expectations that materialized after the CPSU's twentieth congress and before the Central Committee meeting were not entirely fulfilled by the resolution and the report. They expected more. . . ."[9]

Rákosi chose an audience of party activists in the provincial town of Eger to offer, on 27 March, a carefully circumscribed account of the party's compliance with the new Kremlin line. Finally giving up his obfuscation of the Rajk case, he admitted that the trial had been based on "provocation," but he suggested that responsibility lay with the "imperialist agent" Beria and "Gábor Péter's gang." He continued: "Therefore the Supreme Court, in accordance with the Central Committee's June resolution, has rehabilitated comrade László Rajk and other comrades. Other cases have similarly been reviewed: the innocently condemned have been rehabilitated, others have been pardoned."[10] The attribution of guilt did not endear Rákosi to the secret police; when he addressed a meeting of senior AVH officers in June he was reportedly booed.[11] Moreover, he failed in his plan to stage a show trial at which Péter would assume the blame for Rajk's purge, thereby exonerating Rákosi in the eyes of the party and of that most important observer, Tito. When, in the summer of 1956, Péter was interviewed in prison by a commission established by the Central Committee to investigate the purges, he laid all blame on Farkas. Even under torture Péter refused to confess, as long as Rákosi was in power. But the moment he learned, by the prison grapevine, of Rákosi's dismissal, he pleaded for another interview and insisted that Rákosi was the chief culprit.[12] The precise extent of the rehabilitations is not known, although Gerő once referred to 474 cases that had been reviewed.[13] Few of those rehabilitated would show much gratitude to the Rákosi clique in the months ahead. Beginning that summer, moreover, even noncommunist political prisoners were gradually released to join the growing army of the regime's active enemies.

By the spring of 1956 the beleaguered Rákosi was visibly losing his grip. The party press was reporting instances of overt dissent; at a communist writers' meeting Rákosi was denounced as a Judas.[14] On 18 May he conceded that by tolerating, even supporting, the cult of personality he had indirectly allowed the purges to occur.[15] By then such circumscribed confessions struck most Hungarians as irrelevant and ridiculous. In June the Central Committee received reports of openly expressed views that "the communists have lost the game."[16] The party itself was in turmoil. An article in its organizational monthly admitted that "undoubtedly the cult of personality affected all spheres of life and induced harmful, inappropriate work styles among the mass of functionaries."[17]

Even the leadership was in disarray. Rákosi became progressively isolated as his closest lieutenants began to maneuver to save the system and enhance their own power. The recently released, more left-wing anti-Stalinists, Kádár, Kállai, and Marosán foremost among them, were potentially susceptible to overtures from the old guard. In anticipation of Rákosi's eclipse an offer of alliance was reportedly made by Gerő to Kádár, but the latter temporized. When, at a Central Committee meeting, Kádár spoke up demanding exposure of the chief villains in the Rajk affair, Rákosi was armed for battle. He produced a secret tape recording of Kádár's conversation with Rajk in prison. Kádár was no doubt embarrassed by this incriminating evidence, but the ploy backfired when Erik Molnár asked for a replay of the tape. It began with a passage purposely skipped by Rákosi: "Dear Laci, I come on behalf of Comrade Rákosi," said Kádár's voice.[18] The emperor had no clothes, and his servants were no longer prepared to turn the blind eye.

**Decompression Breeds Dissent.** Rákosi's grudging concessions to the spirit of liberalization proved to be counterproductive. The state of the national economy had improved marginally in 1955, and a draft of the second five-year plan was released for public comment.[19] The step was without precedent, but it reflected the wishes of the Central Committee, which ruled on 7 May: "It is not permissible to conceal our economic difficulties, and the methods for overcoming them must be openly displayed."[20] But the response of the public, and in particular the economists, to Rákosi's and Gerő's plan was harshly critical. Concurrently, strikes broke out at several factories in protest against low wages, and reports reaching party headquarters on 12 July assessing public reaction to the Poznan riots indicated that in Hungary too the ground was fertile for such "provocation."[21]

Decompression in the cultural sphere turned out to have an even more debilitating impact on the regime's legitimacy. On 17 March the party authorized the creation of a debating club, the Petőfi Circle, under the aegis of the DISZ. Intended, presumably, to serve as a safety valve for restive students and writers, the Petőfi Circle became instead the crucible of open revolt.

The twentieth CPSU congress had sparked off a public debate that rapidly acquired the dimension of a national campaign for destalinization. The journalists of *Szabad Nép*, the writers around *Irodalmi Ujság*, intellectuals of all colors spearheaded this ostensibly ideological offensive. Wrote the old Muscovite writer Gyula Háy in May: "The cult of personality has contaminated all our literature."[22] The writers' demands for cultural freedom and for a realistic appraisal of the plight of the masses suggested a painful but definite emancipation from the bonds of ideology, although in practice few among them aimed further than the replacement of Rákosi by Nagy. The dearth of channels for the articulation of popular demands at first limited revisionism to these debates within the elite. The writers did look for support to the workers, but the latter were intensely suspicious of any appeals that were couched in ideological jargon and came from the establishment.[23]

Instead, the main response was from university students. The policy of the Rákosi regime in higher education had been to increase the proportion of working-class and peasant youth at the expense of "class enemies." Nevertheless, heavy-handed indoctrination could not prevent the students from perceiving the sharp contrast between theory and reality, and this perception in turn induced a cynicism that was only partially compensated for by remnants of religious faith.[24] Nor had the prestige of the new order been enhanced among lower-class youth by the abrupt closure of the people's colleges. Now an opportunity was presenting itself to abandon cynicism for passionate idealism.

The Petőfi Circle was designed to serve as the forum for discussion of certain topical questions: student organization, the economy, historiography, pedagogy, philosophy, the judiciary, and finally, on 27 June, the press. The debates, as the organizers intended, turned into more and more embarrassing manifestations of disenchantment with the regime. When representatives from party headquarters protested at the violent denunciations, they were shouted down with cries of "we are the party, we are the masses, not you!" More than a thousand people heard György Lukács acknowledge the bankruptcy of Marxist-Leninist philosophy among Hungarian youth and call for freedom of philosophical enquiry. The high point of the debate on socialist legality was the dramatic adjuration of Julia Rajk: "The communist word can never be pure in Hungary while murderers of my husband sit in ministerial seats!" By the last meeting the mood was no longer one of debate but of virtual revolt. Declared Tibor Déry: "The real trouble is not the personality cult, dogmatism, or the lack of democracy; it is the lack of freedom." Finally, Géza Losonczy, who had been reluctantly elevated by the party to the editorial board of the Patriotic People's Front newspaper *Magyar Nemzet,* called for Nagy's readmission to the party. He was met with the thunderous applause of thousands.[25]

Although Nagy, like his supporters, had drawn great encouragement from Khrushchev's speech, he refrained from organizing a formal opposition faction and awaited his readmission to the party. His obdurate loyalty to the party frustrated many of his friends, but the latter continued to pursue by various means, and for various political goals, the destruction of Rákosi. They participated in the Petőfi Circle debates, and a few even sought out former noncommunist politicians such as the social democrat Anna Kéthly. Meanwhile, Rákosi was further isolated by the dissolution of the Cominform in May and the Soviet-Yugoslav declaration of friendship. His belated attempts to court Tito's favor were rebuffed. Indeed, the latter pointedly avoided Hungary and took a circuitous rail route to reach Moscow, where he tried to persuade the Soviet leadership that Rákosi should be dismissed. The Russians demurred, arguing that they had no one else in Hungary they could rely on.[26]

On 30 June, armed with the recent evidence of the Poznan riots, Rákosi prevailed on the Central Committee to retaliate against the mounting opposition. The Petőfi Circle, identified as the center of antiparty attacks, was ordered temporarily suspended. The resolution charged that certain persons had gone so far as to "deny the leading role of the party of the working class, and advocated bourgeois and counterrevolutionary views." It further alleged that "a group which formed around the person of Imre Nagy" had organized an offensive concealed behind allusions to the Soviet congress, and that the press had issued "misleading, unprincipled laudatory reports" which created confusion within the party.[27] In view of the gravity of the charges, the sanctions were extraordinarily mild. The doctrinaire head of Hungarian radio, Valéria Benke, came away from the meeting with premonitions of disaster. She saw the leadership divided by personal antagonism, indecisive and apparently unaware that power was slipping from the party's hands.[28]

**Rákosi Departs.**   Imre Nagy wrote a letter on 1 July denying the charges and arguing that he was simply using Leninist weapons to combat Stalinism.[29] But Rákosi was preparing to play his last card. On 16 July, having assembled a massive dossier, he put before the Politburo a scheme for drastic reprisals. It envisaged the arrest and trial on charges of conspiracy against the party of Imre Nagy and some four to five hundred other communists, dissolution of the Writers' Association and the Petőfi Circle, and the suspension of *Irodalmi Ujság*. The stunned Politburo adjourned, and word was passed to the Soviet ambassador, Yuri Andropov. When the Politburo reconvened the following day, it was joined by Mikoyan, a Soviet party presidium member who had flown straight from Moscow for the meeting. Mikoyan indicated that Rákosi would have to step down and be replaced by Gerő as first secretary. Clinging desperately to power, Rákosi pleaded for party unity, to which Kádár was reportedly inspired to respond: "There are mountains of corpses between us." Finally, Rákosi insisted on confirming Mikoyan's ukase by telephoning Khrushchev. "If I go, everything collapses," he began, but the other retorted "Nothing will collapse. You must resign." (Later, with the dubious wisdom of hindsight, Khrushchev would claim that the revolution would not have happened if the regime had simply shot ten writers!)[30] Rákosi's reign had come to an end.

The deposed leader delivered his abject farewell at the Central Committee plenum that opened on 18 July. He was in ill health, he explained. Moreover, since the Soviet party congress it had become clear to him that the harm done to the party by his mistakes had been more serious than he had previously believed. He was thereupon flown to the Soviet Union, never to return. The Central Committee duly elected Gerő first secretary and Kádár secretary; Kádár, Kiss, Marosán, and Révai were added to the Politburo. In his inaugural address Gerő called for a "clean slate" and a "two-front battle" against both left-wing sectarian and right-wing deviationist views—the line presumably recommended by Moscow. One resolution acknowledged that, in 1955, the party's leadership had repeated some of its earlier mistakes. Others endorsed the two-front battle, approved the five-year plan, and called for the democratization of state organs and mass organizations, for a certain decentralization of economic guidance, and for a strengthening of the collectivized sector in agriculture.[31] Three days later the Central Committee met again in order to strip Farkas of his party offices.

The tactical reorientation adopted at the June plenum was, in its bare essentials, similar to that followed by the party in later years. In the interval, however, the choice of Rákosi's successor and the dynamics of decompression would precipitate a bloody revolution. Rákosi's ouster came only when the Soviet leadership had become persuaded that retaining him would be counterproductive. From their point of view the intrinsically doctrinaire but disciplined Gerő was the best available alternative. Nagy, though obviously popular both within and outside the party, was surrounded by overly independent advisers and was becoming too nationalistic and liberal to serve as a reliable and prudent viceroy. The Kremlin also wished to propitiate Tito, but the latter was unenthusiastic about the appointment of Gerő. He later claimed that the Soviet leaders "made it a condition that Rákosi would go only if Gerő remained. And this was a mistake because Gerő differed in no way from Rákosi."[32] Indeed, the choice of another old Stalinist was a dangerous gamble, for the classic symptoms of a prerevolutionary period were already in evidence: the alienation of the intellectuals, disorganization within the ruling circles, and widespread social unrest.

The change in leadership scarcely improved party morale, although Kádár would later claim that all members understood the July plenum to represent a turn toward the rectification of past errors. Some activists apparently hoped that the mantle of succession would fall on the prudent centrist Kádár, an expectation that was later inflated in party histories to lend a proper pedigree to Kádár's eventual assumption of the leadership. In the event, the once-disciplined party could not withstand the unaccustomed stresses. The apparat had undergone repeated purges and changes in personnel under Rákosi and had acquired a bureaucratic and authoritarian style of work that isolated it from ordinary members. The protracted revisionist-dogmatist debates had undermined party discipline and paralyzed the apparat. One retrospective report from Budapest's seventh district noted that "the middle and lower functionaries were impotent, the ordinary party members were confused, but everyone felt that there was something fateful in the air."[33]

**Concessions and New Challenges.** Gerő began his tenure by preaching unity and a safe middle course between right and left deviations. He apparently made unsuccessful attempts to coopt some of his opponents with offers of high office. He also authorized a few symbolic concessions.[34] A Politburo resolution on 1 September prohibited the naming of streets and institutions after living Hungarian citizens, prompting the removal of Rákosi's name from hundreds of locations. On 16 September the sanctions against some of the rebellious writers were lifted, and the Politburo announced that the people's college network would be revived. The Soviet Union lent a helping hand on 4 October by granting Hungary ruble and hard currency credits.

The intellectual ferment only intensified after Rákosi's fall. In August the Central Committee had passed a resolution on "party policy toward the intelligentsia." Various problems were noted, including inadequate education, political apathy, and the low proportion of functionaries with higher education (only 4.3 percent in the Secretariat). Among the various measures designed to draw the intelligentsia back to the party was discontinuance of the compilation of "confidential cadre material," i.e., files on their political reliability.[35] The discussions on this resolution generated no support for the leadership. At the annual general meeting of the Writers' Association on 15 September, complete creative freedom and punishment for their erstwhile censors was demanded by the speakers. Warnings were voiced against the threat of a "Stalinist and Rákosiite restoration."[36] In the election (by secret ballot) for the new executive committee, the party's official candidates, including Illés and Culture Minister Darvas, were defeated. Two-thirds of the new members were noncommunists representing the Populist and other moderate left-wing orientations. The totality of party control had been broken. On 28 September came the turn of the National Council of Trade Unions to press for change with a resolution demanding more autonomy and welfare for workers.

The public at large was kept abreast of such extraordinary events by a press only nominally under party control. Vilification of the regime became a consuming activity spurred to new heights by the apparently irrepressible revisionist intellectuals. An article by Gyula Háy, "Why Don't I Like Comrade Kucsera?" mocked the typical party bureaucrat's stupidity, immorality, and cruelty: "Kucsera is the know-nothing by conviction and passion, who looks down on us from the pedestal of his ignorance and clings fanatically to the fallacious principle of the permanent sharpening of the class struggle because it allows him to go on playing the part of political reliability personified with rarity value."[37] Within days the mythical Kucsera became famous across the land. The powerful weapon of ridicule was undermining a party whose rule had rested on silent fear.

In the midst of these disintegrative trends a critical hiatus occurred at the top. Gerő departed on 8 September for his annual holiday in the Soviet Union, and a delegation led by Kádár left the following day to attend the eighth congress of the Chinese party. Gerő met Khrushchev and Tito in the Crimea on 30 September, and was joined by the Kádár group for discussions with Mikoyan and Suslov on 6 October. But until their return on 7 October the leadership was effectively in the hands of the two secretaries Ács and István Kovács and Prime Minister András Hegedüs, men of little consequence whose exercise of authority, notes a party history, was the "embodiment of uncertainty and impotence."[38]

For some time Rajk's real and professed friends had been demanding his ceremonial reburial as a symbolic gesture of atonement by the party. The Central Committee had apparently resolved to comply in early September, but had been deterred by fears and divisions among the party elite. In the face of mounting pressure, the committee finally authorized the public ceremony for 6 October, at the same time mobilizing security forces against a possible outburst. The bodies of Rajk and his associates were retrieved from a secret AVH burial ground and reinterred in Budapest amidst a huge silent demonstration organized by the opposition. Eulogies on behalf of the party were delivered by Münnich and Apró, the latter asserting unconvincingly that "the guarantee that similar violations of law [would] not recur" was the party itself.[39] A week later it was the turn of Pálffy, Sólyom, and other officers to receive such posthumous honors. In the interval the regime had decided to make a not undeserved example of Mihály and Vladimir Farkas, who were placed under arrest. The public demands for an open trial had little chance of being fulfilled, however, in view of the elder Farkas's threats to expose his former acolytes and even the Russians.[40] The public impact of Rajk's reburial was devastating. One county party committee reported to the Politburo that the speeches had induced a "profound crisis of conscience" among functionaries and activists.[41]

**The Eve of Revolution.** In the meantime sporadic negotiations took place between party headquarters and Imre Nagy. Gerő spoke of "alliance," but Nagy steadfastly refused to exercise self-criticism, which remained the precondition for his being readmitted.[42] In July Mikoyan had reportedly convinced him that the Russians had had nothing to do with his mistreatment by Rákosi, and indeed the Kremlin became more sympathetic to his case if only in the interest of pacifying Tito. Khrushchev had arranged for Gerő and Tito to meet in the Crimea, and Gerő rose to the occasion with apologies and a plea for support. Tito relented and invited the Hungarians to send a party delegation to Belgrade; as he later observed, "we hoped that by not isolating the Hungarian Party we could more easily influence that country's proper internal development."[43] There was, apparently, one condition: readmit Nagy. The latter made only a small concession in formally asking to be readmitted for the sake of party unity, but on 13 October the Politburo agreed to reinstate his membership. The resolution blamed Rákosi for the unjustified expulsion and invited the Central Committee to "clarify the ideological questions" in the case, but it also confirmed that Nagy had been "guilty of political errors."[44] The compromise was timed to coincide with the departure for Belgrade of the delegation consisting of Gerő, Kádár, Apró, and Hegedüs.

Gerő's quest for an eleventh-hour accommodation with Tito bore fruit in a signed declaration of friendship and cooperation between the two parties. In Hungary, however, it had little impact. To the denouement of the Rajk affair was now added news of the successful stand taken by Gomulka against Soviet interference. For the opposition, both organized and popular, this was fuel to the flames. The reactivated Petőfi Circle organized new debates, and on 17 October the former smallholder Zoltán Tildy was invited to one dealing with agriculture. University students across the country stepped up their agitation for everything from reduced indoctrination to better dormitories. Without openly attacking the communist system, the tone of the opposition became increasingly nationalistic and anti-Soviet. At a debate in Győr on 16 October the impossible finally occurred: an open demand that "Soviet forces must leave our homeland." Disconcerted local party secretaries met to criticize the leadership's inopportune travels and to ask, "Who today is the political guide, the writers or the Central Committee?"[45]

Suddenly, manifestoes were the order of the day. On 20 October university students at Szeged decided to abandon the DISZ and found an association better suited to their needs, the Federation of Hungarian University and College Associations (Magyar Egyetemi és Főiskolai Egyesületek Szövetsége, or MEFESZ). That same day *Irodalmi Ujság* published a resolution of the party group within the Writers' Association calling for an early party congress on the grounds that "only a new, democratically elected party leadership" was capable of developing a forward-looking policy—an unprecedented arrogation of initiative by a local party body. The litany of discontent lengthened. A mass meeting at the Budapest Technological University on 22 October adopted a manifesto that made sixteen demands: evacuation of Soviet forces; new, secret party elections; reinstatement of Nagy to the premiership; public trial for Farkas and his accomplices; multiparty general elections; equality in Soviet-Hungarian relations; economic reorganization by experts; publication of foreign trade agreements, including those concerning the Soviet exploitation of Hungarian uranium; a review of industrial production norms; a similar review of the agricultural delivery system; release of political prisoners; freedom of expression and of the press; removal of Stalin's gigantic statue in Budapest; restoration of the Kossuth coat of arms; solidarity with Poland; and the convocation of a youth parliament.[46] Concurrently the Petőfi Circle issued a set of ten rather more moderate and gradualist demands. By now the students and other extraparty elements were outpacing the revisionist writers in the onslaught against the regime.

The security police, according to one source, warned on two occasions of an impending outburst, but the leaders left behind in Budapest professed unconcern. On 22 October, at a party-activ meeting at the Csepel iron works, Károly Kiss dismissed these fears: "We can liquidate such a manifestation in thirty minutes." A state of alert in the armed forces ordered on 20 October had been called off the following evening.[47] Although there are indications that as early as August Gerő was toying with the idea of provoking a confrontation that would serve as a pretext for crushing the opposition, it appears that the eventual outbreak of insurrection caught him unprepared.[48] Certainly neither the party leadership nor the security forces would react in a fashion suggesting a prearranged plan.

## THE DYNAMICS OF REVOLUTION

The mass process that gave rise to the revolution became truly manifest only in the week preceding it. More than a century earlier, Tocqueville had described the phenomenon of decompression: evils that are endured with patience as long as they are inevitable suddenly seem intolerable as soon as hope can be entertained of escaping them. Such was now the case in Hungary. The monolithic image of a party armed with an unimpeachable ideology had been shattered by the revisionist surge. The consequent division within the party elite proved to be the major catalytic factor in the collapse of the entire system. The momentary alliance between previously irreconcilable elements—the alienated masses and the now increasingly revisionist intelligentsia—and the concurrent atrophy and paralysis of the system's regulative organs left the orthodox leadership powerless at the critical moment of open revolt.

Few historical events have been as exhaustively described and analyzed as the Hungarian Revolution. What follows, then, is a brief account, principally of those aspects that relate directly to the communist party. In a period of thirteen days the revolution passed through several distinct phases. The first phase extended from the limited Soviet intervention to Gerő's fall and Nagy's accession to effective power. The second phase was one of consolidation; it saw the Nagy government evolve under popular pressure toward a multiparty coalition while the communist party totally disintegrated. The third phase began with the declaration of Hungarian neutrality and ended with the forcible removal of the revolutionary regime on 4 November. In less than two weeks the gamut had been run from an eroded totalitarianism to an embryonic pluralistic democracy and back to Soviet hegemony and communist dictatorship. In the interval, however, there had been created in the communist bloc a breach that placed the Soviet Union as well as the Western powers in a unique dilemma.

**The Party Loses Control.** The essential spontaneity of the revolution was underscored by its obvious absence of leadership. There were nevertheless attempts at manipulation. Some members of Nagy's circle did suggest to the students on 20 October that a mass meeting be held at the statue of General Bem (a hero of the Polish revolution of 1830 and of the Hungarian revolution of 1848) to both show support for the Polish resistance and protest against the Hungarian Stalinists. Late on 22 October the Petőfi Circle leaders met with student delegations to organize this peaceful demonstration, which was set for the following afternoon.

That night Gerő's delegation returned from Yugoslavia to a capital in turmoil. The issue of *Szabad Nép* on the morning of 23 October carried the Petőfi Circle's demands. The lead editorial noted that the students were not bourgeois reactionaries but "firm believers in socialism"; though previously repressed, they were now showing "serious political maturity." After cautioning against counterrevolutionary manifestations it closed with a few lines from a poem by Endre Ady that spoke of a happy transformation. In the district and works party committees confusion reigned regarding the upcoming demonstration. The committee in Budapest's eleventh district even decided to join the movement by composing its own demands to the Central Committee and having them debated at factory meetings. But in the absence of central directives many local units chose to condemn the demonstration. Revisionist sympathies prevailed in some central party institutions, notably the Party Academy, and delegations descended on the headquarters to protest against any prohibition of the demonstration.[49]

When some journalists from *Szabad Nép* visited the party headquarters to assess the leadership's mood they found a state of near-panic.[50] They encountered Gerő, Kádár, Marosán, and Révai, the last two voicing a hard line that Kádár endorsed with apparent reluctance. At 12:53 P.M. the radio announced that the planned demonstration had been prohibited, but 1½ hours later the order was rescinded. Even the interior ministry was divided on the question, and evidently Gerő had decided to have a showdown with his tormentors. A writers' delegation that had come to urge the leadership to regain some prestige by endorsing the demonstration found Gerő "aged, his eyes sick . . . shivering"—and obdurate.[51] In the meantime Imre Nagy, recently returned from a brief holiday, was meeting with Losonczy and other close advisers. Professing to fear a provocation, he chose to remain passive, but even his friends were not of one mind and were far from plotting a coup.

A huge crowd of students and other citizens, many of them party members, gathered before Bem's statue, and soon similar demonstrations materialized at other points in the capital. Demands for Imre Nagy proliferated along with anti-Soviet slogans. Eventually Nagy's advisers persuaded him to make what turned out to be an inconsequential and largely inaudible address to a crowd gathered before the parliament building (his use of the term "comrades" was not well received), and he retired to party headquarters. A speech by Gerő, broadcast at 8:00 P.M., only inflamed popular passions. The demonstrators, he declared, were chauvinist enemies of the working class who were slandering the Soviet Union; the choice ahead lay between socialist and bourgeois democracy. These abrasive remarks, utterly lacking in sensitivity to the mood of the moment, were hardly calculated to appease.[52]

Earlier in the day Kádár had visited the Budapest radio headquarters. Benke had assured him that the radio would do its duty by party and government, but many of its workers had chosen to join the demonstrations. That evening Benke rejected a delegation's request to have the students' sixteen points broadcast, and a threatening crowd gathered in front of the building even before Gerő's address.[53] A panicky security police detachment assigned to defend the station fired the first shots of the revolution into the unarmed assembly. Army units dispatched to the scene not only refused to attack the demonstrators but handed over their weapons. During the night insurgent groups penetrated the radio station as well as the *Szabad Nép* buildings and some local party and police offices, military depots, warehouses, and factories, securing arms in the process. One group toppled the hated statue of Stalin. Of the regime's security forces—army, frontier guards, police, and workers' militia—only the AVH managed to survive as an organized opponent of the rebels until 31 October. Budapest's chief of police, Sándor Kopácsi, was soon persuaded to side with the revolution, while the bulk of the military either remained inactive or joined the insurgents.

A Central Committee meeting had originally been scheduled for 31 October, but it was hurriedly convened during the night of 23 to 24 October for a protracted and heated session. It was informed that the leadership, in light of the potential unreliability of the armed forces, had called Soviet troops to the rescue. The Russians would have preferred a political solution, and Mikoyan later reportedly chided Gerő for this rash decision.[54] Russian military intervention certainly exacerbated public hostility. Since it turned out to be limited in scope and effect, it also gave the rebels the illusion of victory. There is little doubt that in its absence they would have in short order invested the remaining bastions of the regime.

Gerő was confirmed as first secretary, but the Central Committee approved a partial changing of the guard. Nagy, Donáth, Losonczy, Lukács, and Münnich were added to the committee. Nagy, Kállai, and three apparent Nagy supporters, Sándor Gáspár, József Köböl, and Zoltán Szántó joined Apró, Gerő, Hegedüs, Kádár, Kiss, and Marosán in the Politburo; six hardliners, including István Kovács and Révai, had been dropped from the latter body, while Losonczy and Rónai were named alternate members. Donáth was also named to the Secretariat. The changes were far from revolutionary, and some of the new additions would subsequently serve the restoration. Imre Nagy was "recommended" for the premiership, from which Hegedüs stepped down to become first deputy premier. Finally, the Central Committee called for the proclamation of martial law. Until 26 October Nagy remained in some isolation at party headquarters, overwhelmed by the events but apparently hoping to work out some compromise.[55] During the same interval his more forceful associates Donáth and Losonczy refused to assume the party offices to which they had been named in absentia.

Party headquarters reacted to the spread of anarchy with an uncertainty that bordered on panic. Activists who gathered at local party offices on the morning of the twenty-fourth were instructed first to go home, then to "go among the masses to agitate." Most functionaries were too demoralized and too overdisciplined to rise to the challenge. An AVH detachment was dispatched to guard the headquarters of the Budapest party committee, which functioned as a focal point for attempts to coordinate the armed defense of the district party offices. There was much talk of arming trustworthy workers, and in the tenth district several hundred activists were in fact equipped with weapons and held the local headquarters until 30 October.[56] But the popular mood was so hostile to the communists that most of the party buildings were easily occupied by insurgent groups. The bulk of the membership thereupon deserted, leaving discarded party cards in the streets. The attempts of the remaining core of activists to organize armed resistance and to retain some initiative within the proliferating national and workers' committees were soon swallowed up by the revolutionary maelstrom.

**Nagy and Kádár Take Over.**   Meanwhile, on 24 October, Nagy broadcast a prime ministerial address. He called on the insurgents to lay down their arms and promised them amnesty and "systematic democratization." The Central Committee, which remained in almost continuous session during the first few days of revolution, concurrently issued a more denunciatory communiqué that already had the ring of impotence. Soviet armored forces, recently reinforced and on alert since 20 October, had engaged the insurgents at various points in Budapest and had thrown a cordon around the government buildings and the central party headquarters. This first intervention caused some casualties on both sides and the destruction of much Soviet armor. It was met with some remarkable acts of heroism on the part of the poorly armed rebels, but it was limited in scope and soon receded to an essentially defensive deployment. After the initial engagement only sporadic clashes occurred in the capital area. In the countryside local communist officials handed over power with scarcely any resistance or Soviet involvement. A tragic exception was the town of Moson-magyaróvár, where some eighty people were massacred by a security police detachment. The bloodiest encounter occurred on 25 October in Budapest, before the parliament buildings, where a crowd of demonstrators was waiting for Nagy and fraternizing with visibly embarrassed and demoralized Russian tank crews. Security police stationed on surrounding rooftops apparently opened fire on the crowd below, some Russians were hit, and the ensuing melee caused over one hundred casualties. In the nearby party headquarters, Gerő was about to lose his job.

The Kremlin's troubleshooters, Mikoyan and Suslov, had arrived on 24 October. They found that despite the reconstitution of the party's leading bodies Gerő remained in command, but that his effective authority hardly extended beyond a few government and party strongholds. After protracted discussions they ruled that Gerő had to go and be replaced by Kádár. Gerő, like his predecessor, fought his dismissal but was spirited out of the country on the twenty-sixth. The Russian authorities organized the evacuation of other leading figures of the discredited regime, including Hegedüs, Defense Minister Bata, Interior Minister László Piros, and Berei, and of Soviet advisers.

The news of Kádár's appointment was broadcast shortly after noon on the twenty-fifth. Kádár himself then addressed the nation. Blowing hot and cold, he referred on the one hand to antidemocratic and counterrevolutionary elements but promised on the other that once order was restored negotiations would follow with the Soviet Union "in the spirit of complete equality." Nagy's concurrent public appeals for order were couched in more conciliatory terms and stressed prospective reforms and the negotiated withdrawal of Soviet forces. Consultations between Mikoyan and Suslov and the Hungarians on the degree of reform necessary to stabilize the situation produced a declaration by the Central Committee—"led by comrade Imre Nagy"—on the afternoon of the twenty-sixth.[57] Although presented as a final offer, the declaration was notably conciliatory and free from jargon. It invited the Patriotic People's Front to recommend the election of a new government on the "broadest national foundations." This government would create a "free country of prosperity, independence, and socialist democracy," make good the "crimes of the past," and conduct negotiations on the Polish model with the Soviet Union. The preservation of socialism could not be put in question, but the formation of workers' councils was endorsed. The declaration reflected the ineffectiveness of earlier appeals in repeating the call for cease-fire and the promise of amnesty. That evening Nagy finally made the move from party headquarters to parliament, symbolically severing his dependence on the party.

Meanwhile, in city, town, and village the hated symbols of communist rule disappeared. Red stars were removed from public buildings, the communist coat of arms was torn from flags, and there was the occasional bonfire of party publications. Public readings of traditional patriotic verse were delivered to emotional crowds as a wave of euphoria swept the land. Revolutionary committees sprung up at all levels, and some regional councils, notably those located in the northern cities of Győr and Miskolc, became essentially autonomous revolutionary centers.

It was against this background of spontaneous revolutionary activity that Imre Nagy formed his new "people's patriotic government" on the twenty-seventh. In its composition the government represented an only moderate dilution of communist monopoly. The three deputy premiers, Apró, Bognár (an adroit former smallholder), and Erdei would eventually serve the restoration. Among the communist ministers were Stalinists like Kossa, centrists like Kádár, and outright revisionists like Lukács. The two exceptions to the communist rule were Zoltán Tildy and Béla Kovács. The latter had retired to his home town of Pécs after returning from Soviet imprisonment and did not physically join the new government. The radios of the provincial revolutionary councils did not tarry in denouncing the communists' predominance in the unwieldy twenty-six-member government.

While domestic reform was one of the insurgents' chief aims, they were most adamant on the question of Soviet withdrawal. The ensuing war of words proceeded in a vicious circle. Moscow was willing to tolerate a reformist regime as long as the party's supremacy was maintained—necessarily by the presence of Soviet armed force. The revolutionaries, in turn, rejected any government that did not guarantee immediate evacuation. Clearly Nagy did not have Moscow's mandate to make such a promise, although he would reiterate that negotiations were in progress. He was, moreover, a somewhat indecisive man who lacked the charismatic quality that might have rallied support for a national communist compromise. Nor was he helped at this stage by such external critics as Radio Free Europe, which in the first days of revolution branded his appointment a Trojan horse tactic and broadcast military and political instructions to the insurgents. While the revisionist intellectuals in Budapest offered cautionary advice and faded into the background, the programmatic initiative passed to the provinces, where "national councils" were formed to coordinate local revolutionary and workers' councils and to press the Nagy government for more and more radical reforms.

With power slipping from their hands and the party well on the way to disintegration, some of the communist diehards prepared for a final show of force. On 24 October the Central Committee had established a military committee to muster armed defense. This committee devised a plan for a concerted offensive with Soviet assistance at dawn on the twenty-eighth against the principal insurgent strongholds in the capital. Half an hour before the scheduled attack Imre Nagy called to threaten resignation if the operation were not aborted.[58] He would not countenance bloodshed, he said, and in a broadcast later that day rendered the ideologically fundamental judgment that the uprising was not a counterrevolution. He undertook to dissolve the AVH, to restore national emblems, to review wages, production norms, and welfare benefits, and to aid both private and collective farms. Nagy also announced that agreement had been reached for Russian military withdrawal from Budapest.[59] The government ordered its security forces to cease fire and indicated that a new national army would be created.

Also on the twenty-eighth, the Central Committee announced its abdication: "In view of the exceptional situation which has emerged, the Central Committee transfers its mandate to lead the party, which it received from the third congress, to a six-member party presidium whose chairman is comrade János Kádár and whose membership includes Antal Apró, Károly Kiss, Ferenc Münnich, Imre Nagy, and Zoltán Szántó."[60] But this caretaker presidium was a leader without troops, while the Nagy regime functioned less as a government than as the target of nationwide pressures for more rapid change. The country was already in the grips of a general strike in support of radical reforms. On 30 October the cabinet, including a reluctant Nagy, felt compelled to accept Tildy's conclusion that nothing short of a return to a multiparty system could save what remained of socialism and central authority from total collapse. Every member of the party presidium, declared Kádár, was "in agreement with the decision reached by the Council of Ministers today."[61] Nagy thereupon announced by radio that the cabinet was abolishing the one-party system and placing the country's government "on the basis of democratic cooperation between the coalition parties reborn in 1945." The government, he promised, would set up an "inner cabinet" composed of Nagy, Tildy, Béla Kovács, Erdei, Kádár, Losonczy, and a nominee of the SDP.[62] The old parties promptly began to reorganize their long-dispersed forces.

**The Illusion of Victory.** At this critical juncture the Kremlin still appeared hesitant. According to Khrushchev the Soviet party presidium was divided on the advisability of intervention; the Chinese initially opposed, and some satellites, notably Romania (where unrest was spreading among the Hungarian minority) urged military measures.[63] Mikoyan and Suslov paid a second visit to Budapest on the twenty-seventh and yet another three days later. In the interval the Kremlin issued a remarkable policy statement upholding peaceful coexistence between the Soviet Union and the other socialist states "on the principles of complete equality, of respect for territorial integrity, state independence and sovereignty, and of noninterference in one another's internal affairs." Noting that the Warsaw treaty stipulated the consent of the host country, the declaration voiced willingness to negotiate—specifically with the Hungarian government—on the stationing of Soviet forces. It ended with a cautionary expression of "confidence that the peoples of the socialist countries [would] not permit foreign and domestic reactionary forces to shake the foundations of the people's democratic system."[64]

Mikoyan came ostensibly prepared to negotiate on the basis of this declaration. On 31 October he met Tildy to discuss four specific points: the immediate recall of Soviet forces, Hungary's withdrawal from the Warsaw Pact, the restoration of a multiparty system, and preparations for free elections. Reported Tildy after the meeting: "I raised all the problems and he agreed with everything."[65] In fact, the mood in the Kremlin must have been anything but conciliatory once the Hungarians' intent had been conveyed back by Mikoyan. The withdrawal of Soviet troops to a cordon around Budapest may well have been a tactical redeployment, for a few hours later fresh military units began to move into Hungarian territory.

What advice Mikoyan concurrently relayed to the isolated and helpless party presidium is not known, but Kádár's pronouncements suggest that it favored cooperation and reconstruction. If the ultimate violent repression of the revolution was deemed inevitable by the Soviet envoys, Kádár gave no public indication of it. On 30 October he endorsed the cabinet's decision to restore the multiparty system and acknowledged that his own party had suffered attrition: "The ranks of the party will shake . . . but I am sure that no honest, sincere communist will leave the party. Those who joined for selfish personal reasons will be the ones to leave."[66] That same day the party would be dealt the most brutal reminder of its unpopularity.

Apart from the Central Committee headquarters, the Budapest party committee building on Republic Square was one of the few offices that survived the first revolutionary wave. Notable among the small band of functionaries who tried against all odds to rally the loyalist forces were Imre Mező, a secretary of the Budapest party committee, and Béla Biszku, secretary of the thirteenth district committee. The fifty-one-year-old Mező came from a poor peasant background. Seeking employment, he turned up in Belgium and joined the local communist party in 1929. He subsequently served in an international brigade in Spain, then in the communist underground in occupied Paris, and returned to Hungary in June 1945. He rose in the Hungarian party to the post of second secretary of the Budapest party committee until, on 1 August 1953, he was dismissed in the purge of "Westerners." He had shown some sensitivity to the growing alienation of industrial workers, and after his reinstatement in 1954 he adopted a moderately critical line against the excesses of the Rákosi leadership.[67]

With the outbreak of revolution Mező proved indefatigable in his efforts to preserve the party. When an insurgent group occupied the offices of *Szabad Nép*, Mező arranged for another existing newspaper, *Esti Budapest* (Evening Budapest), to be edited at his headquarters, and one issue did appear, on 29 October, although most of the copies were burned by the hostile populace.[68] *Szabad Nép* had meanwhile turned into an extreme revisionist mouthpiece. Its editorial of 29 October, *Hajnalodik* ("It Is Dawning"), welcomed the rapid democratization of the political system and induced even greater uncertainty in the thinning ranks of the party. Having failed to persuade the Budapest police chief to take action against the insurgent groups, Mező prevailed upon the military committee, entrenched at the defense ministry, to dispatch trustworthy officers to aid in the mobilization of a workers' militia. Mező was not alone. A political and military counteroffensive to stem the advance of counterrevolution was imperative, said Dezső Nemes, rector of the Party Academy, to the Republic Square leaders on 29 October. That evening Kádár himself paid a visit to Mező, after which the latter reported to his comrades: "The Central Committee, as a body, no longer exists. There are only individual leaders. It is left up to us to do what we can. . . . Comrade Kádár brought us no directives." Kádár had lamely suggested that the Budapest party committee gather evidence of counterrevolutionary excesses and organize discussions of these in the factories.[69]

The party functionaries and AVH men at the Republic Square headquarters had more immediate problems than the launching of a counteroffensive, for they correctly suspected that the nationalist rebels would not long tolerate their communist bastion. Upon news of the government's dissolution of the AVH, the guards were prudently supplied with ordinary police uniforms. On the afternoon of 29 October, as part of the general redeployment, the Soviet armored detachment assigned to protect the building departed. Debate was raging among the assembled comrades over Imre Nagy's intentions. The Budapest Committee's first secretary, the Stalinist István Kovács, was considered an embarrassment and, partly for his own safety, was spirited out of the building the following night.[70]

Shortly after 10:00 A.M. on 30 October bands of insurgents began the siege of the party building. Mező and Nemes appealed for help to the party headquarters, the police, and the army, and tried to reach Imre Nagy—all to no avail. When a Hungarian armored unit dispatched to the scene joined the attackers and began to shell the building, the occupants surrendered. Among some of the insurgents the spirit of revenge gained the upper hand. Mező was fatally wounded as he emerged. A number of his associates and AVH men were executed on the spot, and a few were lynched.[71] The various insurgent bands that ruled scattered enclaves in Budapest had perhaps inevitably attracted some wilder elements; the Republic Square executions were nevertheless a departure from the generally judicious behavior of the revolutionaries. A party history claims that in the first week of the revolution nearly 300 communists were killed. The figure is plausible, but most of these casualties were in fact agents or hapless soldiers of the universally detested AVH.[72]

The fall of the Budapest party headquarters struck terror in the hearts of the remaining loyalists. Their worst fears of a punitive counterrevolution seemed to be realized. Most went into hiding, while a few tried to regroup in the capital's outskirts. Such rearguard actions could scarcely conceal the disastrous collapse of the HWP. In the wake of this final blow a shaken Kádár was interviewed by an Italian journalist. He professed to anticipate a new Hungarian national communism, a "third line" that would not be "inspired by the USSR [or] by other types of Communism. . . ." "There will be an opposition and no dictatorship," he continued. "This opposition will be heard because it will have the national interests of Hungary at heart and not those of international Communism." He expressed approval of Tito and invited Western economic aid.[73] In another interview, Lukács gave an even more sober (and perhaps more sincere) appraisal:

> Communism in Hungary has been totally disgraced. Collected around the Party will probably be small groups of progressive intellectuals, writers and a few young people. The working class will prefer to follow the Social Democrats. In free elections the Communists will obtain five percent of the vote, ten percent at the most. It is possible that they won't be in the government, that they will go into opposition.[74]

Such prospects, especially when anticipated by communists, could not have been palatable to the Kremlin.

**The Die Is Cast.** On the morning of 1 November Yuri Andropov, the Soviet ambassador, met with Nagy to confirm that the withdrawal was under way. But when Nagy confronted him with information that new armored divisions were streaming into Hungary, he could offer no explanation beyond vague reassurances. Nagy thereupon consulted leading communists and secured their concurrence that in the circumstances there was no alternative but to withdraw from the Warsaw Pact and to declare Hungary's neutrality. Kádár was present, but only Lukács and Szántó voiced reservations. When later that afternoon Nagy convoked Andropov to convey this ultimatum, Kádár reportedly shouted at the ambassador, "I am a Hungarian and I will fight your tanks with my bare hands if necessary."[75] Following this meeting Nagy notified UN Secretary-General Dag Hammarskjöld of his protests at the Soviet troop movements and of Hungary's formal abrogation of membership in the Warsaw Pact, asking the "four Great Powers" for recognition and protection of Hungary's neutrality. In a radio address to the nation, he observed: "Today our people are as united in this decision as perhaps never before in their history."[76] But the four Great Powers were now embroiled in the Suez crisis, and in the West the Hungarian Revolution was observed with sympathetic but impotent fascination.[77]

## DEMOCRATIZATION AND DEFEAT

That same day the Hungarian party underwent another, stillborn, transformation. Kádár's announcement, probably prerecorded, was broadcast at 10:00 P.M. A renamed Hungarian Socialist Workers' Party (Magyar Szocialista Munkáspárt, or HSWP) would be formed, said Kádár, "in accordance with the wishes of many true patriots and socialists who fought against the despotism of Rákosi." It would be a rejuvenated party, smaller but qualitatively superior to its predecessor, cleansed of the "crimes of the past." A provisional organizing committee consisting of Kádár, Donáth, Kopácsi, Losonczy, Lukács, Nagy, and Szántó would plan the rebuilding of the party. (It is noteworthy that this committee, unlike the caretaker presidium, included only one figure who would serve the restoration: Kádár.) While endorsing national independence and Soviet withdrawal, Kádár made no reference to the decision on neutrality. Recalling the "tragic fate of Korea," he urged a consolidation to "overcome the danger of a menacing counterrevolution and intervention from abroad."[78]

With these ominous words Kádár parted company with the revolution. As he was driven away from the parliament with Münnich the latter apparently conveyed a persuasive message from the Kremlin, for they proceeded to the Soviet embassy and were flown by military aircraft that same night to Uzhgorod, a city in the Carpatho-Ukraine (known as Ungvár when it was part of pre-1919 Hungary) near the Hungarian frontier. Apprised the next day of Kádár's flight, a few other leading communists, including Marosán, Apró, Kiss, and Nógrádi, followed suit.[79]

Were Kádár's actions governed throughout these dramatic days by the tactical shifts of the Soviet leadership? Did he only gradually come to acknowledge the utter hopelessness of the party's position? Did the bloody seizure of the Republic Square headquarters and the fatal shooting of his friend Mező embitter Kádár? Did he truly fear, as he later claimed, that Nagy would lose control and give way to a "White terror" similar to the aftermath of the 1919 Commune? Or did he calculate that if Soviet restoration of communist rule was inevitable, he might as well play his part and perhaps retrieve some of the less contentious goals of the revolution? Only Kádár knows the full story behind his apparent volte-face. In all likelihood, however, the decisive factor was the imperative final message from the Soviet leadership.

After the revolution had been crushed, Kádár would explain to parliament on 11 May 1957 that the party leadership had divided into two wings. The first, including himself, was devoted to the implementation of the July 1956 resolutions, and under its guidance "the mistakes could have been resolved within a year without much damage or human sacrifice." This wing was confused by the outbreak of revolution and uncertain as to its tasks. They had not fully understood the other wing, Nagy's group. He would never deny, said Kádár, that he had voted for Nagy's elevation to the premiership in the belief that despite his errors Nagy was an honest man who stood on the side of the working class. When this impression was gradually dispelled, "we realized we could no longer follow this road."[80]

The days between the proclamation of neutrality and the second Soviet intervention saw a further democratization of the government; a pluralistic system, it appeared, was about to be consolidated. The coalition cabinet was reconstructed on 3 November under the continuing premiership of Imre Nagy, who also assumed the foreign affairs portfolio. It now included only two other communists, Losonczy and (in name only) Kádár, three smallholders, three social democrats, and two representatives of the Petőfi (formerly National Peasant) Party. The extraparty defense minister, General Pál Maléter, was an armored unit commander who had won fame in the skillful defense of the Kilián barracks against a Soviet onslaught. He and the military commander of Budapest, Béla Király, began to merge various military units and armed groups into a National Guard. The workers' councils meanwhile came to terms with the government and agreed that work would be resumed on 5 November.

Subsequent party histories have emphasized the role of underground clerical youth and veteran's organizations as well as of lumpenproletariat elements in the revolution, and have weighed these elements against the loyalty or merely misguided disaffection of the genuine working classes. While excoriating Western propaganda, they have also conceded that the few returning émigrés exerted a negligible influence.[81] The truth is that the profoundly nationalistic spirit of the uprising aroused a responsive chord in all socioeconomic groups. One survey showed that the proportion of active insurgents among professionals was 14 percent, among white-collar workers 2 percent, among industrial workers 13 percent, among peasants 6 percent, and among students and others 20 percent.[82] The youthfulness of the freedom fighters is indicated by some official casualty figures, which show that of the approximately 3,000 fatalities, 20 percent were under 20 years of age, and 28 percent between 20 and 29 years.[83]

**Parties and Interests.** In the immediate prerevolutionary stage the revisionist intelligentsia acted as the vanguard, while the first phase of revolution saw students and other young people play the most active role. At first the old dispossessed classes and those of their erstwhile political leaders who were still in Hungary showed great reluctance to become involved, partly out of mistrust and partly because they recognized that their participation might be counterproductive. The formation of revolutionary and workers' councils, and of autonomous insurgent bands such as that led by József Dudás, an anti-Moscow communist who had been jailed from 1947 to 1954, brought into play a wider cross section of society ranging from opportunistic adventurers to released political prisoners. The peasantry, far from the centers of revolutionary activity, reacted to the upheavals by abandoning collective farms and voluntarily supplying food to the urban combatants.[84]

The collapse of one-party rule allowed the reemergence of a relatively heterogeneous belief system. Although up to 23 October the revisionists remained preeminent by virtue of their access to the media, thereafter the immense disillusionment of the masses and the general revolutionary momentum relegated them to a supporting role. To the extent that Nagy was one of them, he too performed more as follower than guide in this essentially leaderless revolution. The multitude of economic and other grievances was overshadowed by the dominant aspiration to national independence. The noncommunist parties reappeared because the monolithic communist system had lost all legitimacy. The popular consensus clearly favored a pluralistic system. The core of these parties necessarily consisted of the remnants of their postwar elites, and a variety of socioeconomic models found advocates, but there is little evidence that return to an unqualified capitalistic system was generally considered desirable or imminent.

The communists had tried to keep Cardinal Mindszenty isolated from the revolution (he was under house arrest, outside Budapest), but on 31 October he was liberated by a military escort and returned to the capital amidst emotional acclaim. In a radio address on 3 November the conservative prelate could not bring himself to give his unequivocal blessing to the Nagy government. Rather, he cautioned his listeners against vengefulness and called for the formation of a

Christian democratic party. In conclusion, he looked forward to a pluralistic system based on private ownership "rightly and justly limited by social interests."[85]

The programmatic contribution of the revived postwar parties and other new factions was cut short by the Soviet intervention. It can be said, however, that by 3 November there had emerged the outlines of a pluralistic political system encompassing common as well as conflicting interests. The most forceful demands for political reform and neutrality came from the provincial national councils, most notably the Transdanubian Council at Győr led by Attila Szigeti, and from groups such as that led by Dudás. The last-named, in direct competition with the Nagy regime, created a short-lived National Council and was temporarily put under arrest on Nagy's orders. The workers' councils that materialized in factories and other industrial concerns did not evince a distinctive ideology apart from general opposition to the reinstatement of unqualified capitalism. Various Catholic groupings had coalesced by 3 November, evidently attracting the more clerical and conservative elements, and could have been the harbingers of a powerful Christian democratic movement. Old Populists such as Áron Tamási, István Bibó, and László Németh formed the core of the Petőfi Party.

The subsequent communist party line, that most of the authentic working class stood by, weaponless and impotent, while extreme right-wing elements usurped power in their name, was an inevitable but false rationalization of the party's collapse.[86] Certainly, individuals who from the communist perspective were reactionary—declassed officers and other middle-class survivors—eventually became active in various spheres, even in the workers' councils. But their role was neither reactionary nor divisive, and it remained submerged in the remarkable display of patriotic solidarity that was the glory of the revolution. Although some of the more undisciplined insurgents indulged in the occasional reprisals it is noteworthy that despite the chaos and destruction in the streets of Budapest there was no incidence of looting until the second Soviet intervention.

The overall ideology of the revolution, dominated though it was by the goal of national independence, embodied fairly consistent and generalized demands for political and economic reform. It was formulated in its most comprehensive form by Bibó himself, who became a minister of state in the last Nagy cabinet. He took up a theme expounded by some Populists and social democrats in the early postwar period, that of a "third road" lying between the capitalist and Soviet communist archetypes, a road that would combine the more positive and relevant aspects of socialism and capitalism to produce a mixed economy, allow the development of a multiparty system consistent with the preservation of certain socialist achievements, and turn Hungary into a neutral actor in the international system. This essentially national, neutralist, non-Marxist yet "progressive" ideology would probably have predominated in the value system of an independent postrevolutionary Hungary.[87]

And what of the communist party? The majority of lower party units, writes a party historian, "were paralyzed by the revisionist attacks and the counter-revolutionary armed groups. Their paralysis was induced by the fact that over the years the bureaucratism in party life had accustomed them to total dependence, and in a complex situation they became impotent with the disappearance of higher authority."[88] Many of the rank and file, whether from relief or in fear of persecution, burned or discarded their party cards. With most of their local party buildings requisitioned by insurgent groups, the hard core of communist veterans and fanatics made some attempts to regroup and organize armed resistance in the industrial suburbs of Budapest and in a few provincial mining centers. Until the second Soviet intervention got under way, however, these were rearguard actions of little consequence.[89]

Abandoned by Kádár and other less sanguine leaders, the vestigial party remained, under the nominal direction of the revisionists, a supporter of the revolution. The Stalinist István Kovács was replaced as Budapest party secretary by a follower of Nagy, József Köböl, on 30 October (the day that the Republic Square headquarters fell to the insurgents). On 3 November the renamed *Népszabadság* (People's Freedom) carried an editorial entitled "Purified" that reiterated the party's renunciation of its Stalinist past and the need to rebuild its strength from below on a more modest scale. Losonczy spoke for his communist colleagues Nagy and Donáth at a press conference that evening when he proclaimed the devotion of party and government to national independence and friendship with East and West. Socialism, he insisted, would not be abandoned: "The land belongs to the peasants, the factories to the workers!"[90] By then the decision had been taken beyond Hungary's borders that a very different communist party should be recreated.

**The Politics of Intervention.** The report brought back by Mikoyan and Suslov after their last meetings with Hungarian leaders on 31 October must have confronted the Soviet party presidium with the imperative of choice. According to Khrushchev, some of his colleagues were reluctant to sanction repression, for which the military preparations were well under way. Most of the Soviet Union's allies were recommending intervention. By the end of October the Bulgarian, Czechoslovakian, East German, and Romanian regimes had all become acutely apprehensive about the events in Hungary.

The reaction of the Romanian and Czechoslovak authorities was partly inspired by their fear of Hungarian irredentism and its effect among their Magyar minorities. Irredentism did not receive much play in Hungary during the revolution, but the fate of the minorities and the hoary palliative of a Danubian federation was discussed in the liberated press. Many Magyars in Slovakia and Transylvania did respond to the call of the motherland and crossed into Hungary to join the insurgents. In Transylvania there was widespread unrest and even demonstrations that had to be quelled by force; a number of "separatist plotters" were executed or imprisoned. The Prague and Bucharest regimes resorted to displays of military power in their minority districts as well as to urgent appeals for unity. After the defeat of the revolution, both regimes played up its allegedly chauvinistic and irredentist character.[91] For ideological as well as national reasons, Hungary's orthodox neighbors felt imperiled by the uprising.

Poland, in the midst of a less radical political transformation, had reacted more positively. The Polish press reported on developments in Hungary with remarkable objectivity, and the historical ties between the two nations added to the sympathy felt by most Poles. Gomulka, however, could ill afford to further antagonize the Soviet Union and thereby jeopardize his own momentary gains. Accordingly, official opinion finally fell into line and condemned the "forces of reaction pushing Hungary towards disaster."[92] As for the Chinese, whose word still weighed heavily in Moscow, they soon reversed their original favorable construction of the Hungarian events. Nearly seven years later, the Peking *People's Daily* recalled: "At the critical moment, when the Hungarian counter-revolutionaries had occupied Budapest, for a time [the Soviet leaders] intended to adopt a policy of capitulation and abandon socialist Hungary. . . . We insisted on the taking of all necessary measures to smash the counter-revolutionaries."[93]

The rapid pace of revolution had caught the communist world off balance. While the Kremlin and its allies might well have accommodated themselves to a reformed communist party under Nagy that still enjoyed monopoly power— perhaps along with a semblance of pluralism through a communist-dominated Patriotic People's Front—the prospect of genuine neutrality and multiparty democracy could only be regarded, on both ideological and strategic grounds, as intolerable counterrevolution. The concurrent involvement of the Western powers in the Suez imbroglio and the adjournment of debate at the United Nations on the Hungarian question must have confirmed the Soviet leadership's view that no effective external obstacle, apart from the inevitable propaganda losses, lay in the path of military intervention.

The forces for change in Hungary had been unleashed by Khrushchev's destalinization and the attendant reconciliation with Tito, and the latter was in a sense the godfather of the revolution. He had been the decisive factor in Rákosi's dismissal, and had looked favorably on Nagy's accession to power, anticipating the entrenchment of a moderate national-communist regime. In a letter to the Hungarian party on 28 October, he hailed the initial thrust of the revolution while warning against its exploitation by reactionaries.[94] The Soviet declaration of 30 October and its implications for Hungary were also well received in Yugoslavia. Communications between Nagy's circle and Yugoslav representatives were frequent and cordial throughout the revolution, although Tito must have observed with alarm how the revolutionary momentum swept Nagy far beyond the political limits of the Yugoslav model.

Tito deplored the radical turn of the revolution and feared the side effects on Yugoslavia of a possible Soviet intervention. In his widely reported speech at Pula on 11 November he would insist: "We have never advised [the Russians] to go ahead and use the army."[95] He had, however, been consulted. On the evening of 2 November Khrushchev and Malenkov arrived in great secrecy to confer with Tito at his Brioni retreat. According to Yugoslav accounts, Khrushchev indicated at the outset that the other East European leaders and the Chinese concurred in the necessity of intervention; the West would do no more than protest for it was "mired deep in the mud of Egypt," as the Soviet Union was in Hungary. Khrushchev cursed Rákosi and Gerő for having brought on the disaster: "All events in Hungary are turning into a counterrevolution. They are killing communists. Some want to restore capitalism. We cannot permit this. The capitalists would then reach the very frontiers of the Soviet Union." When he told Tito that he was considering military intervention, Tito demurred: "I am not sure whether this would be good. . . . One should look for other solutions, rely on the workers, on the workers' councils, get them to start armed action." But Khrushchev was more realistic: "We cannot wait for the working class to take action. One should act quickly." The Russians proposed to have Münnich appointed as prime minister, but their interlocutors expressed a strong preference for Kádár, who had been tortured in Rákosi's prisons while Münnich was ambassador to Moscow and would be more acceptable to the workers. The Soviet leaders claimed to have come to Yugoslavia seeking not approval of intervention but to be understood. They did not reveal the timing of the intervention and, as Tito reported to a closed session of his Central Committee, "left very satisfied."[96]

Upon their arrival in Uzhgorod on 2 November, Kádár and his small retinue engaged in discussions with the Kremlin's representatives on the modalities of restoration. Apart from Kádár and Münnich, the principal defectors were Marosán, Apró, Kossa, Dögei, Rónai, and Imre Horváth (the latter changing course for Uzhgorod while on his way to the United Nations when Nagy took over his foreign affairs portfolio).[97] Upon the return of the Soviet delegation from Brioni on 3 November the final decision was made in favor of Kádár for the leadership of both party and government. According to Kádár, Münnich himself had withdrawn from the contest with the argument that "he had been away for a long time and people were less familiar with his views and actions."[98] Thus came into being, on Soviet soil, the "Hungarian Revolutionary Worker-Peasant Government."

While this countergovernment was secretly assembled and Soviet forces were preparing for the assault, a final deception was being played out in Budapest. Official Soviet-Hungarian contact had been reduced to negotiation between the Nagy government and Ambassador Andropov on Russian evacuation. On 3 November the military delegations of the two sides met in the parliament building. There was a semblance of progress on the terms of withdrawal, and the meeting adjourned—to reconvene that night at the Soviet military headquarters at Tököl, outside Budapest. The Hungarian negotiators, led by Defense Minister Maléter, walked into a trap, for they were summarily arrested by the head of the KGB, General Ivan Serov, who would subsequently oversee the roundup of freedom fighters.

Concurrently, a massive land and air attack was launched against all points of resistance by Soviet forces. (Unlike the forces in the first Russian intervention, which had been stationed in Hungary and were not easily persuaded that the revolution was a fascist, Western-directed attack on the workers' power, the fresh troops from Central Asia were told that they were fighting imperialists and took the Danube for the Suez canal. . . . ) The government had no contact with its military delegation, but a warning from the Yugoslav embassy of the impending offensive (and an offer of asylum from the same source for Nagy and his entourage) was soon followed by the sound of heavy gunfire. At dawn Nagy broadcast to the nation: "This is Imre Nagy speaking, the President of the Council of Ministers of the Hungarian People's Republic. Today at daybreak Soviet troops attacked our capital with the obvious intention of overthrowing the legal Hungarian democratic government. Our troops are in combat. The Government is at its post. I notify the people of our country and the entire world of this fact."[99] There followed radio appeals for the return of the military delegation, for the Russian "friends" not to shoot, and, by the Writers' Association, for Western assistance.

In fact, Nagy, recognizing perhaps the futility of resistance, had not given the order to fight. In any case, the reorganization of the army had barely been started and was being sabotaged by a group of senior Hungarian officers (and in particular by a former partisan, General Gyula Uszta) who had returned from a Soviet military academy on 1 November ostensibly to serve the new government.[100] There was nevertheless fierce scattered armed resistance in Budapest, and sporadic guerrilla actions, mainly in Transdanubia, persisted for nearly ten days. Some two hundred thousand refugees fled westward, first across open borders and later at the risk of their lives. Cardinal Mindszenty found refuge in the U.S. legation. Before seeking asylum in the Yugoslav embassy, Imre Nagy dictated a final statement in which he warned that Soviet imperialism would not stop at Hungary.[101] The revolution had run its course.

The restoration regime introduced itself early that same tragic morning in a radio broadcast by Ferenc Münnich. This "Open Letter to the Hungarian Working People'' proclaimed that the undersigned, Apró, Kádár, Kossa, and Münnich, had broken with the Nagy government on 1 November to fight against "reaction, the threat of fascism, and their murderous bands.'' It called on the socialist faithful to support the liberating struggle of the Hungarian Revolutionary Worker-Peasant Government.[102] Brute force had crushed the revolution, but the restoration of communist power would require a protracted struggle both against the alienated populace and within the party itself. For the third time since 1919, the party had imposed itself on the Hungarian people, and with more violence than ever before.

# 13. From Restoration to Consolidation

Seldom has a government assumed office in less propitious circumstances than did that of János Kádár. With his small retinue he returned to Budapest by Soviet armored car at dawn on 7 November and ensconced himself in the parliament building. Radio was the only safe means of communicating with the bitterly hostile population. The party's first newssheet was issued in the east-central city of Szolnok; the offices of *Népszabadság* were reoccupied only by force. The immediate popular verdict was devastating: Kádár had betrayed his country.

Until early 1957 much of the effective administration was in the hands of the Soviet military commanders, and the government itself was surrounded by Russian advisers.[1] Although the regime would claim that the restoration of order had been accomplished with Soviet "assistance," in fact it had little other organized support in the initial period. Moscow's determination to impose its will at any cost was reflected in the brutally candid comment of a certain General Grebennik that "Soviet troops will leave the territory of Hungary only when crayfish whistle and fishes sing."[2]

## GOVERNMENT AND OPPOSITION

From the first, Soviet commanders issued directives to the population, and the Soviet secret police, aided by its gradually reconstructed Hungarian counterpart, conducted arrests and interrogations. Former AVH agents formed the core of the hurriedly assembled security force regiments *(karhatalom)*, and summary proceedings were instituted to deal with the seized opponents of the regime. Nagy's dissolution of the AVH was confirmed by decree on 3 December, but a renamed variant, the State Security Department of the State Police, continued to perform its functions within the interior ministry. The workers' guard units, which had operated in factories since the creation of workers' councils during the revolution (and subsequently served the organs of worker resistance to the regime), were finally disbanded in February 1957. Their place was taken by a Workers' Militia under the direction of former AVH officers, old party activists, and former partisans. The armed forces were progressively purged and reintegrated. The government dissolved the military revolutionary committees and demanded from officers an oath of loyalty that denounced both the "old mistakes" and the Nagy line, and explicitly recognized the necessity of Soviet intervention.[3] The elite Frontier Guards were also purged. By mid-1957 they were ready to take over border control from the Soviet military, a function in which they were aided by the restoration of the physical barriers—mine fields and electrified barbed wire—that had been eliminated in early 1956.

The judiciary had to be forcefully prodded to deal harshly with alleged enemies of the state. At a judicial conference in February 1957, acting Justice Minister Ferenc Nezvál warned: "The most important task of the court is to defend and strengthen the People's Democratic State order, to pass sentence in the spirit of the struggle . . . against subversive counter-revolutionary elements."[4] A subsequent purge disbarred 45 percent of the practicing lawyers in Budapest. It is estimated that in the year following the crushing of the revolution some 20,000 persons were arrested, 2,000 executed, and many thousands more deported to the Soviet Union.[5]

The regime's reliance on Soviet forces for coercion and control would have been reduced if it could have counted on a mass of activists, but the party's strength had largely dissipated by the end of the revolution. The new ruling circle itself was small and of dubious quality. Apart from Kádár, the government included Apró (minister of industry), Imre Horváth (foreign affairs), Kossa (finance), Marosán (minister of state), Münnich (deputy prime minister, armed forces and public security), and Rónai (commerce). Kádár's wish to dissociate himself from the Rákosi regime was circumscribed by the limited talent available, for most of his interim cabinet (excepting Marosán and Münnich) was heavily tainted with Stalinism.

**Reconstructing the Party.** A similar problem prevailed in the party at large. On 6 November the provisional Central Committee, consisting initially of Kádár, Apró, Kossa, and Münnich but gradually expanded with coopted members, issued an appeal to all former party members to join forces against the counter-revolutionary attack that aimed to restore capitalism. In much altered circumstances, it reiterated the battle on two fronts. "We must decisively break;" it declared, "with the harmful policies and culpable methods of the Rákosi clique, which shattered the faith in our party of the broad working masses and undermined the party's strength." Equally culpable, however, was the Nagy-Losonczy group, "which surrendered the leading position of the working class and the people's power, opened the way to counterrevolutionary forces by its nationalist-chauvinist character, and thereby effectively betrayed the cause of socialism." To symbolize its break with the past, the party assumed (in fact, retained) the name of Hungarian Socialist Workers' Party. "Drawing on all its healthy elements," the committee proclaimed, "we will restore and revive the party's organizations." Reminding communists that love of country was inseparable from proletarian internationalism, the committee ended by calling for support for the new government's task of normalization: "Let every party member who is ready to fight for the power of the working people present himself without delay at our party organizations and begin work." The situation was difficult, but far from hopeless: "If we unite and marshal our ranks, our strength will suffice!"[6]

The reconstruction of the party was a painstaking process. Many of the early volunteers—mainly functionaries from the interior ministry—were redirected to the security force regiments, whose activities had greater priority than party building. Popular hatred for the communists, accentuated by the Soviet invasion, made overt party organization a perilous task, and in the early weeks of restoration the few renascent party groups functioned in secrecy and quasi-illegality. Slogan-painting and poster-sticking teams had to be sent out under the cover of darkness and with armed escorts. Distribution of *Népszabadság* was similarly surreptitious, and most copies were burned by irate citizens.

The retrospective appraisal of a Budapest district party group speaks of "incredibly difficult circumstances," including the reemergence, within a few days of the invasion, of violent anti-communism, nationalism, and anti-Soviet feelings: "The police is not yet purged, the counter-revolutionaries are still in various key economic and even political positions together with those who switched sides. They were reinforced by certain former HWP members who had dropped their mask. They were aided in many places by weak, cowardly managers and supervisors." The report continues: "In more than one place attempts were made to keep workers away from the party with outright terror and intimidation. We had to simultaneously wage a sharp political struggle against the counter-revolutionary forces, fight for the party's purity, and expose the revisionist views designed to mislead the workers."[7] Indeed, in the plants and factories where the revolutionary workers' councils held sway, known communists were forcefully silenced or expelled, and many local union leaders displayed their independence by refusing to rejoin the party.[8]

In such unfavorable circumstances it is not surprising that the bulk of reactivated members were the more doctrinaire preliberation and 1945 veterans, along with a sprinkling of early adherents to Kádár's "centrist" line. The new leaders, notably Biszku in Budapest, faced formidable odds in their effort to revive the party. The overwhelming majority of the prerevolution membership was profoundly mistrustful of the restoration regime, and it confronted the

Kádár group with unanswerable, critical questions regarding the party's past and future. Many insisted that economic tasks should take precedence over party building. Until the end of November the revisionists remained entrenched at *Népszabadság* and the radio, and propagated a line at variance with that of the leadership. They spoke of a "national revolution" rather than of counterrevolution, criticized the Soviet intervention, and trained their fire on the old HWP, denying that it was truly Marxist-Leninist and demanding the expulsion of its "Rákosiite-Stalinist" members. Party records indicate 37,818 members on 1 December and the reactivation of 11,980 cells and organizations (9.1 percent of the HWP level). By the end of the year the membership rose to 101,806, 11.9 percent of the HWP's strength, with Budapest well behind the national average.[9]

Party life in this early phase of reconstruction consisted largely of internal disputes and self-justification. Violent arguments arose regarding the behavior of members during the revolution. Many had burned their party cards more or less voluntarily and were now compelled to explain this symbolic betrayal. The AVH, which had earlier been denounced as a tool for Rákosi's rampages but had served as the party's last and now first line of defense, also prompted much debate. The official branding of the recent events as a counterrevolution was not readily accepted by all members, while the kidnapping of Imre Nagy and his entourage (see pp. 322–323, below) only reinforced the doubts of those who had some sympathy for the revisionists. Many felt that the revolution's initial thrust had been positive; although they endorsed the new government, they anticipated an early Soviet withdrawal. Kádár had to emphasize on 11 November that whoever demanded withdrawal helped the counterrevolution. There was also discord over the future role of the workers' councils and even over the question of sanctioning other parties. The more dogmatic veterans, on the other hand, regarded the revolution as proof of the dangers of tolerance. They demanded a return to the forceful administrative methods of the past, and accused the new party leaders of making concessions of principle, notably in their conciliatory approach to the workers' councils.[10]

The Kádár leadership's two-front battle manifested itself, first, against the Rákosi legacy. A resolution of 14 November banished from party and state office a representative group of the old elite. Twelve prominent former Politburo or Central Committee members were "directed back to their original occupations": Gerő, Ács, Bata, Berei and his wife Erzsébet Andics, Hidas, Hegedüs, István Kovács, Szalai, Piros, György Non (a former chief prosecutor), and Vég. At the same time, new guidelines were issued on admission or readmission to the party. Preference was given to working-class and former HWP members; those who had abused power or participated in the counterrevolution were excluded. The necessarily loose and arbitrary application of these criteria could not eradicate ideological uncertainty and discord. At the national party-activ meeting on 27 November, Károly Kiss stressed the immediate imperative of reconstructing the party's organization, especially in industrial plants, and for "revolutionary agitation"; these difficult tasks took precedence over the even more problematical creation of ideological unity.[11]

**The Liquidation of Revisionism.** Indeed, the leadership had more pressing problems than the cleavages within the renascent party, for most of its attention was drawn to the forces opposing it in the society at large. These were of two kinds: a persistent core of active resisters, and a much larger number of passive ones. The government's initial program, broadcast by Kádár on 4 November, was, in the circumstances, remarkably conciliatory. It resembled Nagy's platform in its emphasis on national independence, economic reform, and the grave mistakes of the past. Many honest workers and the majority of youth had been misled by reactionaries abetted by the revisionists, said Kádár, but this "fratricidal struggle" had to be ended and socialism and the workers' power secured, for without the latter there could be no national independence.[12]

The program did not confront the question of a multiparty system, but Kádár initially made attempts to coopt some opposition politicians and nonparty men into his government. He held talks with Tildy, Bibó, and a social democrat, and he voiced willingness to negotiate with Imre Nagy. In a radio address on 11 November, Kádár spoke of the need to involve men of other parties and world outlooks and even made the surprising claim that "neither Nagy nor his political group [had] willingly supported the counter-revolution."[13] (According to one report, Kádár also raised the possibility of other parties' existence in discussions with the leaders of the Central Workers' Council of Greater Budapest on 14 November.)[14] He invited Nagy and Losonczy to leave the Yugoslav embassy for negotiations and denied that they had anything to fear from the government or the Soviet occupier; they could either admit to their errors and collaborate with the new government, or find asylum in another socialist country.

At the Yugoslav embassy the Nagy group, which included Donáth, Lukács, Zoltán Vas, and Julia Rajk, maintained contact with their supporters at large. They allegedly styled themselves the party's provisional executive committee and reissued their revolutionary program, now stressing the role of the workers' councils.[15] Meanwhile, the revisionist journalists—notably Gimes—and intellectuals and the opposition politicians still at liberty formed themselves into a "Hungarian Democratic Independence Movement." In leaflets and an illegal newspaper they propagated the movement's "ten commandments," one of which designated the revolutionary committees and workers' councils as the government's only legitimate basis. Their newssheet, called *October 23,* appeared as late as December, faithfully reiterating the revolution's basic demands. The MEFESZ student groups and the Writers' Association also remained active, the latter issuing a manifesto on 12 November. Another initiative of the opposition was the creation on 20 November of the Revolutionary Council of Hungarian Intelligentsia under the titular presidency of the composer Zoltán Kodály, but this was a symbolic gesture of little practical consequence.[16]

These initiatives were due chiefly to the revisionist communist intellectuals, who thus returned to the forefront of opposition after their eclipse in the later phase of the revolution. Their goals were the restoration of the Nagy government, independence and neutrality, the withdrawal of Soviet forces, and assistance from the United Nations. Their identification with Nagy, and the latter's presence in the Yugoslav embassy, were becoming an embarrassment to Tito. In his speech at Pula on 11 November the latter had endorsed Kádár and his program while blaming Stalinism for the temporary collapse of communist power in Hungary. This was an essentially defensive tactic and was prompted by charges (voiced notably in *Pravda* on 8 November by the Albanian leader Enver Hoxha) that Tito's national communism had promoted disintegration in the communist bloc. The Yugoslavs did not totally abandon the Hungarian revisionists, but they momentarily entertained the hope that Kádár was both free and willing to forge a broad coalition. Thus in a speech on 7 December Edvard Kardelj reproached the Kádár regime for its repression of the workers' councils.

Kádár, however, was in no position to exercise free choice: a new Soviet campaign against Titoism was in the making. On Moscow's orders his overtures to the opposition politicians were curtailed, but there remained the problem of Nagy. Tito sent his deputy foreign minister, Dobrivoje Vidic, to Budapest to seek some compromise. On 21 November Kádár wrote to Tito guaranteeing Nagy's safety and asking that his asylum be withdrawn, while Vidic persuaded the reluctant Nagy to accept the offer. In the early evening of 22 November Nagy and his party boarded a bus sent by the government to take them home. A Soviet military escort promptly appeared, ejected the protesting Yugoslav diplomats, and redirected the bus to a military academy. The following day, while the Yugoslavs delivered a sharp protest, Radio Budapest reported that the group had voluntarily gone to Romania.

In fact, the group had been detained at a military academy in Budapest. There they were visited by Münnich, who reportedly made a final futile attempt to win Nagy's collaboration. Five days later, on the twenty-seventh, Nagy and his friends were flown to Romania. Explained Kádár in an interview with Swedish journalists: "For a certain period I consider it more expedient that they do not reside in this country—not for ever, but until the situation is more normal."[17] In all likelihood Kádár had been the helpless partner in a Soviet scheme to eliminate Nagy. By early December most of the leading revisionists, including Gimes, had been arrested. Their organizations fell apart. But there remained another and even less tractable challenge to Kádár's legitimacy.

**The Workers' Councils to the Fore.** Even before the kidnapping of Nagy, the opposition groups had begun to emphasize the role of the workers' councils, notably in the 12 November manifesto of the Writers' Association, which was endorsed by eleven other intellectual, professional, and student organizations.[18] Young writers took to visiting factories and urging the councils to take up the revolutionary initiative and form an organized opposition to the regime. Despite the obvious risks, such an opposition did emerge. On 14 November the Central Workers' Council of Greater Budapest held its founding meeting in the industrial suburb of Ujpest; it forthwith adopted a program prepared by István Bibó. The program affirmed that the total disgrace of the communist party left only one respectable communist leader: Imre Nagy. It called for his reinstatement, for a multiparty system, and for the retention of an essentially socialist economy; it also guaranteed the safety of communists (!).[19] The underlying assumption was that organized passive resistance might persuade the Kremlin to agree to some compromise on Hungary's autonomy and neutrality.

Claiming to speak for the industrial workers of the Budapest area, this ad hoc council demanded Nagy's return to office, amnesty for freedom fighters, Soviet withdrawal, free elections with the participation of noncommunist parties, and the "withdrawal of all political parties from the factories"; it also protested the return of former AVH agents to the new security forces. Until these demands were answered, said their resolution, only essential services would be provided by the workers.[20] The Central Council's leaders thereupon delivered their brief to the government. Almost instantly district and provincial councils materialized on Budapest's model, and by the following day Sándor Rácz, who was to become the council's chairman, was proposing a National Workers' Council that might serve as a countergovernment. Predictably, Kádár refused to countenance such a competitor; he called for a return to work and tried to revive the party in the factories. Undeterred, the council called for a meeting of nationwide delegates to found the national body. When, on 21 November, this was aborted by the government, it responded with a forty-eight-hour strike.

Four days later a meeting of the two sides in the parliament building was addressed by Kádár, Apró, and Marosán, who invited the delegates to assist the consolidation by resuming production. But the deadlock remained, and was only aggravated by the kidnapping of Nagy.[21] On 28 November the council met to reiterate its opposition to the regime's attempt to regain control over the trade unions through the National Council of Trade Unions led by Sándor Gáspár. Momentarily the Central Council enjoyed notable success. By controlling factory funds it could ease the workers' financial hardship; it effectively prevented the party from organizing in the plants and expelled the more undesirable communists and police informers; it aided the organization of similar councils in the provinces; it issued its own illegal newssheet, while some provincial councils controlled the local press; it formed workers' guard units; it launched the formation of independent trade unions with the active collaboration of former social democratic functionaries; and it wielded the effective weapon of the strike.[22]

Kádár could not long tolerate the paradox of workers' councils challenging the reimposition of the dictatorship of the proletariat. A decree on 22 November granted the workers' councils extensive responsibility in enterprise management and labor matters but specified that the existing bodies would have to be replaced through more democratic elections conducted with the help of the official trade unions.[23] The measure clearly aimed at eliminating the councils' political autonomy and was accordingly rejected by the Central Council, which proceeded to organize its own elections. In the provinces the workers' councils endorsed the Central Council's policies and in some localities surpassed the parent body by assuming general governing and administrative functions. Party historians would later brand the council leaders as mainly "petit bourgeois anarchists" and estimate that some 20 percent of the members were declassed remnants of the precommunist elite; while conceding that the majority of members were authentic workers, they claimed that other elements had the decisive voice.[24] Such rationalizations could not explain, however, why the mass of industrial workers sided with the councils against the regime.

By the beginning of December the Central Council was the focal point of all resistance. Western journalists maintained regular contact with this virtual countergovernment, and the councils would repeatedly appeal for UN observation and peacekeeping forces. On 1 December the Central Council issued a call for a boycott of newspapers until the government restored freedom of the press. Concurrently it prepared drafts of organizational statutes and of a general program. The latter encompassed political, economic, and cultural objectives. It called for a provisional "worker assembly" to serve as a parallel and equal government pending general, multiparty elections on 23 October 1957 and for the immediate prosecution of former AVH agents. In the economic sphere the platform envisaged maintaining state ownership of heavy industry, returning light industry to private management, and converting uneconomic collective and state farms to private farming on long leases from the state.[25]

On 4 December the Central Council and other opposition groups organized a massive demonstration by women in Budapest's Heroes' Square. The government had meanwhile tried to whittle away at the workers' councils by arrests, intimidation, and sporadic negotiations. When, on 8 December, a meeting of the Central Council, attended by provincial delegates, called for another forty-eight-hour general strike, the axe fell. All remaining revolutionary committees and workers' councils above the local level were ordered dissolved, their leaders were arrested, martial law was proclaimed, and all public gatherings not officially sanctioned were forbidden for one month. The strike's effectiveness was thereby reduced, and although for a time the Csepel Central Workers'

Council persevered in attempts to coordinate the opposition, many workers' councils now chose to disband rather than serve the regime.[26] The old Central Council never met again.

Recognizing that the majority of workers remained alienated, the party tried to salvage the workers' councils by converting them into organs of enterprise democracy. In early 1957 the government and the National Council of Trade Unions created a preparatory committee for this purpose, but it met with a defiance that was only exacerbated by the vengeful activity of the renascent party groups in the factories. A decree on 15 January made incitement to strike a criminal offence. Finally, in November 1957, the few remaining workers' councils were ordered dissolved and replaced by factory committees, two-thirds of whose membership was elected by the party-controlled trade unions. Thus was the industrial working class forcibly reintegrated by its self-designated vanguard. Addressing a restive assembly of miners in April 1958, an irritated Khrushchev delivered his verdict: "Your demonstration is in vain. You have to swallow the fact: What is to be will be."[27]

## CONCILIATION AND REPRESSION

The repatriated Kádár regime found not only widespread defiance but also a state of administrative and economic anarchy. It appointed special state commissioners to oversee the operation of the county councils and invited those civil servants and administrators who had held appointment on 1 October to return to their posts. It also decreed a 10 percent wage increase for 1 January 1957 and the abolition of compulsory deliveries. With the collapse of the revolution the exodus from the collective farms only accelerated, so that by the end of January 1957 only 9 percent of arable land was held by producers' cooperatives. For the moment the regime accommodated itself to this decline. Domestic production and the balance of trade had suffered from the protracted work stoppages. The Soviet Union and its allies therefore came to Kádár's assistance with goods and credits amounting to some $275 million.[28] Kádár also made some symbolic concessions to national pride: among other measures, the Kossuth coat of arms was retained (with the addition, however, of a red star), more traditional military uniforms were introduced, and compulsory Russian language instruction in the schools was abolished.

Whether it was sincere or merely tactical, Kádár's initial policy of conciliation was soon undermined by his failure to generate support and by the Kremlin's instruction to abandon such crypto-revisionist initiatives. The provisional Central Committee met from 2 to 5 December to pass a resolution that offered a relatively balanced interpretation of the roots of the revolution: first, the Rákosi-Gerő clique's departure from the principles of Marxism-Leninism at the end of 1948; second, the intraparty opposition led by Nagy and Losonczy;

third, the activity of the former capitalist-landowner elite (in illegality in Hungary, openly in West Germany); and fourth, the decisive role of international imperialism. The resolution called for struggle against the counterrevolutionary peril with persuasion and, if necessary, armed force; for the development, with the aid of the best economic experts, of an appropriate economic policy; and for the constant strengthening of the worker-peasant alliance.

The party's manifesto exhibited a certain moderation, not only in its stress on the "mistakes" of Nagy in the early phase of the revolution, but also in its assertion that "the majority of the masses who participated in the events was composed of good patriots and honest workers and not counterrevolutionaries, and was faithful to the Hungarian People's Republic." The workers' councils were still described as "important organs of the working class" and the unions were to be assisted to become "true defenders and effective representatives of the workers' interests." The manifesto anticipated freedom of discussion in scientific affairs, the "maintenance of our national traditions," and "development of all progressive tendencies" in literature and the arts.

The party thus sought to provide a palliative response to the popular demands for change, but it also insisted on its own unity and monopoly. The Central Committee declared that the historic merger in 1948 of the two working-class parties could not be undone. Marxism-Leninism had to be applied in accordance with national peculiarities and current historical requirements, but there could be no compromise on internationalism, and those adopting a nationalist position could not be admitted to membership. Party organizations were instructed to maintain "understanding, friendly, comradely contacts" with former HWP members.[29]

On 6 December, prior to publication of the resolution, the party mounted a series of mass meetings and parades in Budapest, its first organized appearance in the streets since before the revolution. Even then, a month after the invasion, there were violent clashes that led the party to cut these demonstrations short. The resolution itself did not reach many Hungarians, and impressed few of those it did reach.[30]

**Dictatorship Reimposed.** Indeed, passions were too high for compromise, while the dominant political tendency within the Soviet bloc was one of retrenchment. Kádár's centrism, which had him fighting on two fronts, could not in the short run conjure up a broad consensus on the terms of his regime's legitimacy. Meanwhile, the hard-line faction in the Kremlin and the like-minded parties of Bulgaria and Czechoslovakia were intent on isolating the Yugoslavs and limiting the Titoist deviation in Poland. For Hungary this meant the rapid erosion of Kádár's policy.

Between 1 and 4 January, Khrushchev (together with his resurgent rival Malenkov) and the leaders of the Bulgarian, Czechoslovak, and Romanian parties conferred in Budapest with the Hungarians and impressed on Kádár the necessity for a forceful and definitive reimposition of the party's monopoly rule. Two weeks later it was the turn of Chinese premier Chou En-lai to visit Budapest and endorse the Kádár regime. By 12 February *Népszabadság* was repeating *Pravda*'s undifferentiated denunciation of the uprising as a counter-revolution essentially from the start (when the counterrevolutionaries were still "disguised"), while the Rákosi factor received progressively less emphasis. The Hungarian-Soviet declaration of 28 March 1957 blamed the revolution on a conspiracy of reactionary imperialists and émigrés and on treason by Nagy. Despite Kádár's initial promises, it indicated that the existence of NATO required the "provisional" presence of Soviet forces in Hungary. On 27 May an agreement was signed in Budapest by the two governments' representatives on the "legal status of Soviet forces temporarily stationed" in Hungary. It stressed that Hungarian sovereignty was in no way affected and that the forces would not interfere in Hungary's internal affairs.[31]

Through December and January increasingly severe steps were taken to stamp out all organized resistance. As was noted earlier, the regime forcibly disbanded the various revolutionary committees and regional workers' councils and provided by decree for summary trials, restriction of public assembly, and (on 19 January) for the creation of a Workers' Militia. Recurring acts of overt resistance in various provincial centers and in Budapest were quelled by force of arms, culminating in the repression of the demonstration at Csepel on 11 January. Two insurgent leaders, József Dudás and János Szabó, were executed on 19 January. These harsh measures and reprisals, together with the government's confirmation on 5 January that the proletarian dictatorship remained in force and excluded any pluralistic alternative, did not enhance the regime's popular appeal, but they gave a much-needed boost to the activists' confidence in their party's monopoly power and permanence.[32]

Concurrently, for both economic and political reasons, the regime moved to reduce the public service rolls by 40–45 percent. At the radio, for instance, 100 out of 500 "political workers" were dismissed. The purges momentarily cut both ways, however, for in some offices dominated by hostile elements the communists were the first to go. The battle for legitimacy was particularly acute in the schools, where teachers and pupils took to wearing black armbands in mourning for the lost revolution. Here, police intervention could restore only a semblance of order and loyalty.[33]

The liquidation of the workers' councils was accompanied by similar measures against the revisionist intelligentsia. In the first few weeks after the revolution journalists and writers had continued to enjoy a certain latitude, but when they refused to condone Soviet imposition of Kádár by force, constructive communication between them and the regime became impossible. After a number of arrests and the reimposition of strict censorship in December they retaliated with a strike. A final secret session of the Writers' Association denounced the regime and the "historic mistake" of Soviet intervention. On 17 January the writers' and journalists' associations were suspended (they would later be dissolved for "assaulting the socialist system"), and the more revisionist writers, including Gyula Háy, were placed under arrest. In July two revisionist journalists, József Gáli and Gyula Obersovszky, were first sentenced to death and then reprieved following international pressure; four months later Háy, Tibor Déry, and two other writers, Zoltán Zelk and Tibor Tárdos, received prison sentences. The outspoken István Bibó had been arrested in May and was later sentenced to life imprisonment. Intellectual dissent was thus crushed, but it was a Carthaginian peace that further undermined the credibility of Kádár's centrism. Most of the writers who escaped imprisonment chose internal emigration, the financially hard road of silent protest.

Kádár's problem had now become how to exercise repression in the name of moderation. This he did by evoking the memory of Stalinism. Both sides of the proletarian dictatorship had been deficient during the old regime, declared Kádár before a conference of county and district party secretaries on 1 February. Stronger dictatorship needed to be exercised against the class enemy and stronger democracy for the working class.[34] In the circumstances, the vilification of the enemy gained first priority. At its plenum on 26 February the provisional Central Committee expanded on the treason of the "Nagy-Losonczy group." The latter was now characterized as the counterrevolution's advance guard prior to 23 October and its rear guard after 4 November. Within the party the total extirpation of revisionism was identified as the immediate task. The Central Committee was enlarged from twenty-three to thirty-seven members, and a Secretariat was named consisting of Kádár, Jenő Fock (secretary of the National Council of Trade Unions before the revolution), Kállai, Kiss, and Marosán. The deadline for the reactivation of individual memberships had been 1 May and this was now confirmed; thereafter, even former HWP members would be treated as new applicants. The Central Committee also urged the intensification of party activity, of local conferences and party days, the resumption of lecture programs and of the publication of *Társadalmi Szemle,* and the reopening of the one-year central party school (which for lack of available cadres was delayed until 1 September).[35]

**The Dogmatist Counterattack.** The gap between the desirable and the practicable remained wide. Within party ranks the Central Committee's stress on the revisionist enemy fed the dogmatic old guard's sense of grievance and self-sufficiency. They regarded late joiners and all nonworkers with suspicious resentment and dreamed of an ideologically pure workers' militia that would teach a hard lesson to their multitudinous foes. Intraparty debates became even more acrimonious than before. One Budapest district group reported that the shock of defeat in the revolution had induced a polarization of right and left in the ranks: "Some comrades are mesmerized by the Yugoslav model . . . personal and clique battles are intense." Opportunistic members "avoid confronting the enemy and adopt a critical view of the leadership. They are afraid to join the party. If they join, they conceal their membership." Some demanded that dissenting members not be bound by party decisions and even that the central leadership be chosen by direct elections. The greatest danger, many felt, was a restoration of the hateful "Rákosi system."[36]

The lingering fear and insecurity of most party members was accentuated by the revolution's final twitch, the "MUK" campaign (for *márciusban ujra kezdjük,* "we will start again in March"). The slogan, which spread like wildfire especially among young people, hinted that 15 March, the old national holiday, would be a fateful day of reckoning for their communist tormentors. The threat of revolution, real or fancied, was again in the air, and the apprehensive regime paraded all its armed strength—army, border guards, police, and workers' militia—to forestall a new conflagration.

After this display of raw power had confirmed the immutability of communist rule, the party's ranks began to swell with recruits anxious to ensure their future. By 1 April the HSWP counted 227,420 members, 26.5 percent of the HWP peak. Some 9 to 10 percent were new adherents. The proportion of active industrial workers, and particularly of the older socialist skilled workers, had declined from 36.2 to 29.8 percent, with a reverse shift in the proportion of white-collar workers and security force members.[37] By this time the cadre system, which required that all important administrative posts be filled by communists, was again in force, and by natural selection most of these posts, particularly in economic management, were manned by the more doctrinaire veterans. The latter were incensed at the influx into the party of white-collar workers and mistrusted former social democrats and recent recruits, particularly those who joined after the MUK scare. Their nostalgia for a simpler, purer exercise of proletarian dictatorship received its greatest boost from the reappearance of the old ideological warrior Révai.

Despite the rejection of Stalinism implicit in the two-front struggle, the numerical weakness of the new leadership and Kádár's notable lack of personal vengefulness prevented him from repudiating all members of the old guard. Gerő and Rákosi were safely remote in Soviet exile, and in April 1957 the universally despised Farkas and his son were sentenced to sixteen years of imprisonment. However, in January Révai had returned from the Soviet Union to lead a dogmatist counterattack that drew some strength from the Soviet bloc's retrenchment in the face of Titoism. To propagate his neo-Stalinist views Révai promptly founded an ideological debating society, the Táncsics Circle, within the Partisan Federation, as well as the weekly *Magyarország* (Hungary). An article by him published in *Népszabadság* on 7 March had a stunning impact within the party, for it was a frontal attack on the centrist orientation of Kádár and his friends. Révai denounced the "concessions," in the Central Committee's December resolution, to the positive aspects of Nagy's revisionism: "It is high time to liquidate this myth. Imre Nagy should be condemned without reservation or appeal." Rákosi and Gerő, on the other hand, had at least "never betrayed the dictatorship of the proletariat by allying themselves with the counterrevolution." The "balance sheet of the last twelve years was largely positive," maintained Révai. He even took Kádár to task for changing the name of the party's publishing house from Szikra (Spark, after Lenin's newspaper) to Kossuth. An article in *Népszabadság* on 29 January by Kádár's favorite journalist, Lajos Mesterházi, had suggested a conciliation of national sentiment by linking the revolutionary tradition of the 1919 Commune, the Kossuth revolution, and the sixteenth-century peasant rebellion led by György Dózsa, with the more peaceful reformist precedents of János Zápolya, Széchenyi, and Ferenc Deák.* Retorted Révai: "[To] try to prove the national character of the party by isolating it from proletarian internationalism is to adopt reactionary views." Any national policy had to be based on loyalty to the Soviet Union. The party should direct everything, and in the two-front battle the "struggle against dogmatism should in no case involve concessions to revisionism." Révai went so far as to take exception to the "campaign of calumnies" against Stalin, claiming that "anti-Stalinism was only the mask of anticommunism, an alibi for revisionism." This dogmatism suggested that Révai had reached a certain identity of views with the hard-line faction of Molotov, Malenkov, and Kaganovich in the Kremlin.[38]

Révai's broadside struck a responsive chord among veteran activists, who had suffered unaccustomed humiliation in the past months and were yearning for restoration of the party's iron rule. He encouraged the latent view in certain party organizations that Kádár's conciliatory approach was culpably opportunistic.[39] These internal attacks and the struggle within the Soviet leadership impelled Kádár to shift his course a few degrees. He now conceded that the Rákosi regime, in contrast to Nagy's outright treason, had ultimately worked for socialism and close relations with the Soviet Union. But Khrushchev's victory over the "antiparty group" in June strengthened his resolve to pursue an essentially centrist line. Although the dogmatists within the party were not disarmed, the star of the ailing Révai rapidly waned. His magazine and the Táncsics Circle ceased operation in January 1958; the following year he died. His career had been punctuated by ideological miscalculations from which, until this final outburst, he had recovered with agility. The revolution had turned him into an

---

*Zápolya was the sixteenth-century ruler of Transylvania who reached an accommodation with the Ottoman court; Count István Széchenyi was a moderate, liberal reformer and modernizer of Hungary in the first half of the nineteenth century; and Deák was the architect of the 1867 Compromise with Austria.

embittered dogmatist whose railings were out of tune with the dominant mood in the Soviet and Hungarian parties.

**The Party Conference.** The HSWP's first national conference, held from 27 to 29 June 1957, served to celebrate the party's revival and the progressive consolidation of its rule. The economic and political problems it faced were formidable. Industrial production was nearing the prerevolution level, but the overall economic picture was grim. Although the party had succeeded in stifling its opponents, popular hostility and internal divisions persisted. At preparatory party meetings conflicting views were aired on the merits of the old and new leaderships and styles of party democracy. Some old HWP functionaries did not conceal their opinion that the Kádár group and its policies were merely transitory or even irrelevant to the country's needs. Such overconfidence and dogmatism were more than balanced by contrary demands for greater intraparty democracy. There were arguments over procedure, which ended in a decision to avoid preliminary debate on the draft theses and hold the conference in closed session; and arguments on the selection of delegates, as a result of which the provisional Central Committee gave up its intention to appoint them and agreed to have them elected by the county and Budapest district organizations.[40]

Finally, 348 delegates and 211 invited participants heard Kádár's report and Marosán's presentation of the new party statutes. The conference unanimously adopted a resolution stating that the creation of a worker-peasant government to defend the (communist) revolution had been a historical necessity, and that the government had acted in the interest of the nation's freedom, of socialism, and of peace in calling for Soviet assistance. Party resolutions antedating 4 November were summarily declared invalid. The resolution reinforced the Central Committee's December analysis of the revolution's origins and noted that although all hostile forces had not yet been annihilated, workers who had been misled ought not to be regarded as counterrevolutionaries. An ideological battle had to be waged against revisionism and its exponents banished from the party. Dogmatism had "loosened the ties between the party and the masses," and there were many party members who retained dogmatic and sectarian views and who now underestimated the "political task to be carried out among the masses." Democratic centralism, which had been perverted by the Rákosi clique, had to be implemented in intraparty relations. The stress was on centralism and party discipline: the resolution instructed the Central Committee to employ the strongest measures—to dissolve dissenting party organizations, if necessary—in order to prevent the enemy from once again destroying the party's unity from within.

In his speech Kádár recalled the party's darkest days during the revolution, when it seemed that the whole nation was united against it: "Why did we have to destroy this unity? Because it was born on a reactionary platform. . . . We do not want this kind of unity.'' Révai once again advanced his view that revisionism was the main enemy, whose defeat would be impeded by criticism of earlier mistakes: "One must differentiate between counterrevolutionary treason and mistakes committed in the building of socialism.'' The actions of the restoration regime, he charged, had been misguided. The reaction of the delegates to Révai's critique was harshly negative, and Kádár himself observed that it had "diverged on essential questions" from the views of the other speakers.[41]

The conference confirmed that the discredited workers' councils would have to be supplanted by a strengthened trade union movement. It also anticipated Kádár's eventual "alliance policy", first, in calling for the cooperation of non-party members (in the restored single-party system, this was to be ensured through the Patriotic People's Front); and second, in affirming the controversial principle that nonmembers with the requisite skills could fill all nonparty posts. Only in this way could the party reserve membership for the ideologically convinced.

In what was to become a congressional ritual, the new party statutes prescribed the improvement of both aspects of democratic centralism, and provision was made for more orderly disciplinary and complaint procedures. Although at many preparatory meetings the name Hungarian Communist Party had been favored, the conference endorsed the provisional Central Committee's motion to retain the new name, which did not alter the party's communist identity but would theoretically ease the qualms of former social democrats.

The conference elected a fifty-three-member Central Committee that bore relatively little resemblance to its prerevolution predecessors. Fifteen had also served as full or alternate members in the Central Committee elected at the 1954 congress, and eighteen in that chosen in 1951. The ten members who had served on both of the earlier Central Committees included such adept survivors as Apró, Friss, Gáspár, Kiss, Kossa, Nógrádi, Révai, and Rónai. The eleven-member Politburo consisted of Apró, Biszku, Fehér, Fock, Kádár, Kállai, Kiss, Marosán, Münnich, Rónai, and Miklós Somogyi. Kiss turned out to be an inveterate dogmatist. Fehér was a former Latin teacher and wartime partisan who had acquired expertise in agriculture and had been a follower and defender of Nagy since 1954. He had resigned from Népszabadság upon hearing of Nagy's kidnapping but was soon persuaded to join Kádár's team.[42] Münnich and the former social democrat Marosán had little love for Rákosi, although Marosán's demagogy and personal ambition, both very much in Rákosi's style, would lead to his downfall. Some of the new leaders, like Marosán and Rónai, were mere opportunists, but others, like Biszku, Fehér, Fock, Kállai, and Somogyi, who were all veterans of the days of illegality, would adopt Kádár's reformist pragmatism with some conviction and dedication. Two alternate members were also named, Nemes (one of Rákosi's ideologists), and Zoltán Komócsin, former head of the party's agitprop department. The Secretariat consisted of Kádár as first secretary, Fock, Kállai, Kiss, and Marosán. A noteworthy change from earlier regimes was the dominant position of indigenous communists, for only Nemes and Münnich could be described as authentic Muscovites. A further change that did not pass unnoticed among a population whose historical anti-Semitism had been aroused by the heavily Jewish character of the party elite in Rákosi's time was the small number of Jews in Kádár's entourage. Initially this was the incidental consequence of the demotion of much of the Muscovite old guard, but subsequently Kádár would, apparently by design, maintain a certain "de-Judaization" of the party's leading bodies.[43]

## THE TACTICS OF CONSOLIDATION

The conference thus endorsed the basic principles of the centrist line, to which Kádár seemed genuinely committed. He had suffered humiliation and torture under Rákosi, and one analyst suggests that one of his "deepest motives has been and will be to prove that he, a simple man, despised by the 'great intellectuals,' will be more successful than the brilliant Rákosi."[44] In any case, it is evident that the unimaginative and disciplined party man in Kádár abhorred the divisive factionalism of the Nagy revisionists. The supremacy of the party and its historic task, to which Kádár was blindly devoted, could not therefore tolerate either form of deviation. At the time, neither the Hungarian public nor the world at large paid much heed to such ideological convolutions, and indeed Kádár himself was too absorbed in the immediate task of government to implement significant reforms. Only years later did a certain continuity of purpose become apparent, a purpose with a blend of ideological and pragmatic values.

**The New Party.** By the time of the national conference party membership approached 350,000. Most of the prerevolution party organizations had been revived, including those based on territorial units and on machine-tractor stations, but in the industrial plants only 55.2 percent of the HWP level was reached and in the collective farms only 30.2 percent. In the factories the workers' councils had made way for the rule of dogmatic veterans, but Marosán had cause to complain that in heavy industry the party was "very weak" and had "not yet won the battle there."[45] Perhaps half the reactivated members were party functionaries or state and security agency employees; among the working class and the intelligentsia there endured a strong reluctance to join the party. Moreover, Kádár reported to the conference that relatively few former social democrats had rallied to the HSWP.[46]

Although the June conference rejected Révai's theses and confirmed that the two-front struggle was also aimed against left-wing deviation, a sizable part of the membership remained unsympathetic to Kádár's centrist moderation. The leadership would reiterate that "to use coercion without mass political information work is a crime," and Kádár was repeatedly driven to defend the opening of important offices to nonmembers. At the ceremonial inauguration of the Party High School on 2 September he referred to unrest in the ranks concerning this principle and warned: "If by an unwritten law only party members could hold public office, it would be the same as if we had voted to make our party the association of all those who aspired to public office in Hungary. In that case, however, we should not call ourselves a Marxist party."[47] The less adaptable members also resented the relative tolerance shown for private artisans and cooperatives and for the private farmers. The induction into the party elite of unlettered journeymen in the Rákosi years was an inheritance that would be a heavy burden for the HSWP in its drive for modernization.

Doctrinaire dissent would rear its head time and again within the new party, but it would be kept in check by Kádár's prudent leadership as well as by the party's expansion, which after the rapid recovery in 1957 settled down to a fairly steady rate of 5 to 6 percent a year. The December 1957 party card exchange was made necessary by the limited validity of the cards originally issued, but it raised the hard-liners' hopes for a general purge. In the event, the exchange brought about the exclusion of only 3,141 members and the resignation of a further 1,668. The concurrent reconstruction of the party organization did occasion a certain changing of the guard, for only 47.3 percent of the former HWP officeholders were reelected. The initial drive to drastically reduce the size of the apparat was reversed in early 1957. By the end of that year it had reached roughly half of the HWP level, with 67 percent of full-time paid functionaries being holdovers from the HWP apparat. Nearly half the elected officials and permanent functionaries came from the ranks of those who had joined the party either before liberation or in the remaining months of 1945. In mid-1957 former HWP members made up 85.2 percent of the entire membership, and the proportion of veterans among them was higher than before the revolution.[48] This reliance on the old soldiers of the movement was momentarily unavoidable, but the price of political reliability and experience was an unhealthy degree of continuity from the Rákosi era.

The youth of Hungary had been swept up by the nationalistic spirit of the revolution. Reintegrating it into an ideologically sound organization was therefore a task to which the party gave high priority. The dissident MEFESZ survived the revolution, and the communists had launched various organizations of young workers, students, and peasants in the early days of restoration to combat the opposition movements with a pluralistic facade. Their success was only marginal. Therefore, on the recommendation of the provisional Central Committee, the Federation of Communist Youth (Kommunista Ifjusági Szövetség, or KISZ) came into being on 21 March 1957. It gradually absorbed the earlier groups, while the MEFESZ was harassed into disintegration. The party exerted itself to develop the KISZ into a mass movement for political indoctrination. At the federation's first national conference Kádár indicated that children of the old middle classes were welcome to its ranks even though their parents were excluded from the party.[49] Party veterans, however, had little sympathy for youth and even less for university students. Kádár had to argue unconvincingly that some of the latter could only be accused of token participation in the revolution.[50] Within three months the membership of KISZ reached 120,000; eventually, political and class discrimination in higher education would swell its ranks with young people in need of proper credentials. But in the KISZ, even more than in the parent party, the cleavage between an ideologically committed (and often doctrinaire) minority and those who joined by force of circumstance would undermine the political significance of bare membership statistics.

**Party and Government.**  A semblance of constitutional propriety had been preserved when Dobi, still chairman of the presidential council, administered the oath of office to the repatriated Revolutionary Worker-Peasant Government. (He had performed the same service for the successive Nagy governments.) The national assembly, reduced by twenty-eight members who had resigned or escaped, was convened in May 1957 to mechanically endorse the reports of Kádár and Dobi and to postpone the scheduled general elections so as not to impede the task of reconstruction.[51] The cabinet underwent periodic changes, and in January 1958 Kádár ceded the premiership to Münnich. At that time the more important party leaders holding ministerial portfolios were Apró (deputy premier), Kádár and Kállai (ministers of state), Biszku (interior), Dögei (agriculture), Révész (defense), Kossa (transportation and communication), and Benke (culture).

The party's June conference had anticipated reorganization of the Patriotic People's Front as a framework for cooperation between communists and nonparty members, under the leadership of the HSWP. This was to be an important component of Kádár's embryonic alliance policy, which was designed to secure the practical collaboration if not ideological commitment of the mass of Hungarians (particularly those whose expertise could remedy the party's own weaknesses). The new front was described as a mass movement distinct from, but resting on, the various mass organizations. There was to be no return to the New Course orientation, toward a mass organization with individual memberships and potential autonomy. In the course of elections for the local front committees in January 1958 it was made clear that the Patriotic People's Front could not become a "forum for hostile views."[52] Gyula Kállai, one of Kádár's intimates, assumed the presidency of the front.

Through its national council and local committees, the front would eventually come to serve as the occasional mobilizing agent for various national and local policy objectives. Its primary function, however, remained the same as in the Rákosi era, namely, the organization of parliamentary and council elections. Simultaneous elections for these two levels of government were held in November 1958 on the basis of a single list presented by the front. An unofficial campaign, encouraged by Western propaganda, materialized to urge citizens that they register their protest by abstaining from the vote. But the regime's counterpressures prevailed. According to official statistics, 98.4 percent of eligible voters cast their ballots, with 99.6 percent of these endorsing the single list; the invalid and negative notes numbered a little over 60,000. Of the 338 deputies elected, 139 were party functionaries and 53 members of the Central Committee. A notable if nominal deputy was the former smallholder leader Béla Kovács, who enjoyed widespread prestige and had shown extreme prudence during the revolution. Persuasion bordering on compulsion drove Kovács to an ambivalent endorsement of the regime, but he was already seriously ill and died in 1959.[53] This charade of an election could not conceal that parliament was merely a servile tool of the party leadership. The assembly would meet for only a few days each year and perfunctorily ratify the regime's measures, most of which were in any case promulgated in the form of decrees.

**Titoism and the Execution of Nagy.**   With Titoism again in disrepute and its opponents still powerful within the Soviet leadership, Kádár had to pursue a balancing act finely attuned to the subtle shifts in Soviet orthodoxy. At the conference of twelve communist parties held in Moscow from 14 to 16 November 1957, the Yugoslav delegates refused to endorse a declaration that condemned revisionism as well as sectarian dogmatism. *Pravda*, in its issue of 23 November, thereupon denounced the Yugoslav party for its deviation from proletarian internationalism. The Hungarian and Yugoslav delegations did agree to a meeting between Kádár and Tito, and this took place at Karadjordjevo, just across the Hungarian border, on 27 and 28 March 1958. The official communiqué referred to a friendly atmosphere; other sources suggest that the discussions encompassed the case of Imre Nagy and were less than cordial.[54] The anti-Tito campaign had received new impetus from the draft program of the League of Yugoslav Communists, published on 13 March, and the Hungarian party press dutifully followed suit.[55] While Kádár probably favored closer economic and political relations with Yugoslavia, he was hardly in a position to swim against the tide.

Kádár returned from his inconclusive meeting with Tito to greet Khrushchev in Budapest. Khrushchev's personal prestige was heavily dependent on the success of communist restoration in Hungary after the debacle precipitated by his destalinization campaign. He heaped fulsome praise on his protégé—"the magnificent qualities of a warrior and leader"—and on the new party, whose policies he was confident would avoid a repetition of past mistakes. The joint statement at the end of Khrushchev's visit evenhandedly denounced dogmatism, revisionism, and nationalism.[56] But for the moment revisionism and its most despicable symbol, Imre Nagy, held center stage.

Partly in response to pressure from the Chinese and other Soviet bloc hard-liners, the treason of Nagy received new prominence in the Soviet press as the Soviet-Yugoslav dispute heated up. Since early 1957 various Hungarian party leaders had alluded to an eventual trial for Nagy and his associates, and in January 1958 Münnich confirmed this prospect at a press conference.[57] The party's ideological monthly *Társadalmi Szemle* meanwhile heaped abuse on Nagy for betraying the dictatorship of the proletariat, for seeking to establish state capitalism and a nationalistic bourgeois regime, and for plotting with the maverick Yugoslav communist Milovan Djilas to create an anti-Soviet federation of Hungary, Yugoslavia, and Austria.[58]

The preferable outcome from the point of view of both Kádár and the Kremlin would have been public self-criticism by Nagy. Reportedly, two of his original companions in Romanian internment, Zoltán Szántó and Vas, tried on their behalf to coax him into it.[59] But Nagy refused to recant, and while Kádár's visit to Tito may have delayed the outcome, the breakdown in Soviet-Yugoslav relations after the Yugoslav League's congress in April probably opened the way for his elimination. The official notice came in communiqués from Moscow and Budapest on 16 June 1958: "The Hungarian legal authorities have concluded the proceedings in the case of the leading group of those persons who on 23 October 1956 started a counterrevolutionary armed uprising." Nagy, Maléter, Gimes, and József Szilágyi (an early follower of Nagy) had been sentenced to death and executed. Kopácsi, Tildy, Donáth, Jánosi, and the journalist Miklós Vásárhelyi received prison sentences.[60] Losonczy, Nagy's closest adviser, had died in prison. The nature of the judicial proceedings remains unclear, for the published account is a propagandistic piece riddled with legal contradictions. On the basis of some of the contrived charges, Kádár's initial association with the Nagy government was equally culpable.[61] Kádár later claimed that the trial had been conducted in Budapest: "The proceedings were legal in every way . . . only Hungarians took part. . . . they were sentenced because they had broken Hungarian laws. . . . In no way were we inspired by feelings of revenge."[62] The liquidation of Nagy was clearly ordered by the Kremlin, and the so-called trial could only have been a sordid political charade. A few days after the announcement Kádár reportedly told a reception committee: "Comrades, because we entered on this course on November 4, it was necessary to go to the very end." As an émigré analyst observed, these were "disenchanted words, more sad than triumphant."[63]

Of Nagy's other companions in exile, Vas, Szántó, and Lukács were repatriated in the spring of 1957, and Julia Rajk and her son in October 1958. Szántó presumably owed his freedom to his willingness to act as prosecution witness at Nagy's trial. Vas was reportedly invited to assume an economic post but declined, was barred from the party, and withdrew from public life to write his memoirs. He seems to have owed his freedom to his attempt to coax Nagy into self-criticism (until he followed the latter into the Yugoslav embassy, his adherence to the revolution was in any case barely noticeable). Lukács, as will be related below, would become embroiled once again in sharp ideological controversy.

As the campaign against Titoist revisionism gathered strength in 1958, Kádár had to respond with a series of measures that appeared to strengthen the more dogmatic wing of his party. In February the Central Committee gave permission for most of the leading former Stalinists, including István Kovács, Bata, Hegedüs, László Piros (the new head of the AVH), Olti, and Gyula Alapi (Rákosi's chief prosecutor) to return to Hungary and to the party, although assurances were given that they would not be restored to public office. Some Central Committee members apparently even championed the return of Rákosi and Gerő, but the latter's case remained in suspension.[64] At the same time, it was reported that "several thousand army and police officers" and former government officials were expelled from the party for their alleged revisionism and nationalism.[65] And in November 1959, on the eve of the first congress of the reconstituted party, the Central Committee announced the expulsion of another eleven prominent members on similar charges of prorevisionist views and activities during the revolution, and the exercise of self-criticism by twenty others.[66] The party's initial recruitment drive had evidently precluded effective screening of all revisionist sympathizers, and the changing ideological climate required a certain purification of the ranks. Upon his return in March 1959 from the Soviet party's twenty-first congress, Kádár noted that many people "wrongfully pushed aside" had been reinstated.[67]

**The Seventh Congress.** The Soviet-inspired resurgence of a certain dogmatism was evident in the Central Committee's resolution of 6 March 1959, which confirmed the relaunching of agricultural collectivization and of the old system of work competition in industry.[68] These elements in the task of laying the foundations of socialism received formal approval at the HSWP's gathering from 30 November to 5 December, officially designated the seventh congress to stress the continuity from the HCP and the HWP, which had held three congresses each.* In his opening address to the 669 voting delegates and other observers, Kádár reiterated the party's commitment to the two-front battle against revisionism and dogmatism. Revisionism was identified as the principal domestic and international threat, and Kádár noted that there was no contact between the Hungarian and Yugoslav parties while asserting that state relations were normal.[69] Khrushchev, in his greeting to the congress, nevertheless endorsed centrism when he attributed much blame for the revolution to the Rákosi leadership, which had presumed to "disregard objective conditions and the

---

*Not counting the HCP's brief fourth congress, which immediately preceded the unification congress on 12 June 1948.

views of the working people," and when he praised the "correct guidance of your party, of its Central Committee led by comrade János Kádár, a true son of the Hungarian people."[70]

With regard to internal party affairs, Kádár reported that the departure of the prerevolution careerists and antiparty elements and the return of true revolutionary communists had strengthened the party's unity, if not its numbers. Members would now be judged by their behavior in 1956 and not on their earlier record. Of the 402,456 full members (distributed among 16,805 basic organizations), 60 percent were workers and 14 percent working peasants by original occupation, the proportions being 56 percent and 19 percent respectively for the 35,500 candidate members. Membership in the KISZ had reached 380,000. The party apparat was now 40 percent smaller than it had been before the revolution, said Kádár, and it relied on the aid of the party-activ.[71] Amendments to the party's organizational statutes, reported by Marosán, were once again designed to improve the application of both facets of democratic centralism. Central decisions had to be implemented, but contrary opinions should not be suppressed. Provision was made for voluntary surrender of membership. Another amendment allowed the participation of nonparty experts in the development of certain party policies.

The congress elected a seventy-one-member Central Committee (as well as twenty-three alternate members) and elevated Dezső Nemes to full membership in the now twelve-man Politburo, naming Gáspár and Szirmai as alternates in addition to Komócsin. Kállai was dropped from the Secretariat, and Fehér and Szirmai were added to Fock, Kádár, Kiss, and Marosán. Szirmai had been a victim of Rákosi's purges in 1953; at the time of his promotion he was serving as head of the Central Committee's agitprop department.

Kádár emerged from the congress fortified by Khrushchev's praise of his leadership and of his carefully balanced policies. Under the latter, the most repressive measures of the early restoration period, with some unpopular features of the Rákosi phase, would gradually be eliminated; political life would become less subject to ideology; and the economy would be modernized. The major structural concession to Soviet orthodoxy would be the collectivization of agriculture. In January 1960 Kádár retrieved the premiership from Münnich and appointed Gyula Kállai as vice-premier. Subsequently he would have to contend on a number of occasions with a resurgence of dogmatic opposition within the party, but by the judicious application of sanctions and by marginal policy adjustments he would preserve his leadership and the integrity of his basic policies.

**Economic Measures.** The revolution and its aftermath had cost Hungary one-fifth of its gross national product, and the government, faced with economic disarray, toyed for a moment with the idea of major structural reform. In December 1956 a team of 200 economists headed by the former smallholder István Varga was commissioned to study the economic system and recommend improvements. Their report, published the following winter, included a standard critique of the Rákosi command model and advanced general proposals for a more rational and decentralized planning system.

In the context of the antirevisionist campaign it is not surprising that the party rejected the committee's recommendations. The development of collective farms could not be left to spontaneity. The economists' stress on Hungary's natural endowments was countered with the availability of Soviet aid. Decentralization would run counter to the essence of a socialist planned economy. Instead, minor changes were instituted, including the permanent abolition of compulsory agricultural deliveries, incentives for technological innovation, a profit-sharing system in industry, a more rational system for the calculation of producer prices, restraint in the issuing of central planning indices, mergers of related enterprises, and a limited devolution of authority from ministries to so-called industrial trusts.[72]

Economic recovery was aided by a reduction in the rate of investment, three years of good harvests, the temporary relief provided by Soviet and other credits, and a very low level of defense spending. By mid-1957 industrial production had reached its prerevolution level. Despite rapid price inflation, however, the government decided in August to rescind its January wage hike, and the standard of living showed no real improvement that year. In what was left of the private sector, the number of artisans grew to 120,000 in 1957 but declined thereafter with the introduction of discriminatory fiscal and other measures. After the initial recovery, production stagnated. In December 1958 the regime accordingly introduced the Soviet-inspired "socialist brigade movement" as the latest form of work competition. With the active involvement of party organizations the movement became institutionalized, and by 1960 some 40,000 brigades were in existence. It is hazardous to estimate the impact of the socialist brigades on labor productivity; in a period of wage restraint they served both economic and political functions. Hungary became an enthusiastic proponent of Comecon integration when that organization was invigorated in 1958, and while according to some calculations the bloc's trade price system favored the Soviet Union, Comecon did provide Hungary with a protected market and access to essential raw materials.

**Collectivization Again.** The principal socioeconomic transformation in the period of consolidation was the final collectivization of agriculture. From the beginning its implementation was fraught with controversy not only among the peasantry but also within the party. The flight from the collective farms had turned into a rout following the defeat of the revolution. From mid-1956 to mid-1957 the proportion of collective farm members in the agricultural labor force fell from 14.7 percent (294,536) to 6.1 percent (122,456). In that same period the number of collective farms declined by one-third, while the number of private farms grew by 15 percent, from 1,445,000 to 1,662,700, to reach the 1949 level.[73] There was no return to large private holdings; the average acreage was smaller than in the immediate postwar period, indicating a certain leveling of the peasantry.

Initially the regime tolerated this ideologically regressive phenomenon. Kádár later reflected that "at a historic moment the decisive problem was the problem of power. It was the struggle for power that determined the agricultural policy of the party."[74] Evidently, in the difficult days of restoration the party could not risk the total alienation of the peasantry. With the abolition of compulsory deliveries and of certain fiscal and insurance burdens the peasants' real income increased, as did their willingness to invest and produce. The party did not abandon for all that its ultimate objective of socialization. The agrarian theses adopted at the Central Committee's July 1957 meeting affirmed that the socialist transformation of the countryside would rest on the agricultural producers' cooperatives. The modernization of agriculture would require large-scale farming and heavy state investment.[75] Contrary to the expectation of more doctrinaire communists, however, this general goal was not translated into action. For another year private farming would continue to predominate in agriculture, while the remaining collective farms exercised no attraction for the liberated peasantry.

In the course of 1958 the acceleration of socialist economic development emerged as a common political objective in the communist world, coinciding with the Chinese "great leap forward." For Hungary, whose socialist sector in agriculture was the smallest in the bloc after Poland's, the message was clear. The decisive Central Committee resolution of 7 December 1958 underscored that "international experiences and particularly those closest to our circumstances, the Czech and Bulgarian" were to be emulated.[76] By then the socialist sector accounted for 92 percent of arable land in Bulgaria, and 75 percent in Czechoslovakia, where a collectivization campaign was in full swing. Responding to the recent Soviet party congress, the Central Committee declared on 6 March 1959 that economic growth at home and economic cooperation abroad were "making it possible for us to overcome more rapidly the relative backwardness" in the country's socialist development that had been caused by "the old mistakes and the counterrevolution."[77]

Obviously, the impetus for collectivization had come more from Moscow than from domestic economic or political imperatives. Since early 1958 the HSWP had been grappling with the development of appropriate targets and techniques. The debate on rates of progress and methods was by all accounts heated and brought a polarization of opinion. On one side were those, including economic experts, who either opposed collectivization or preferred a slow and gradual process, a sort of free competition in which the enhanced drawing power of strengthened collective farms would induce spontaneous expansion of that sector without undermining once again the peasants' will to produce. Rejecting spontaneity and gradualism, the more dogmatic elements, including Agriculture Minister Dögei (a notorious promoter of the 1949 campaign) and many middle-rank members of the apparat, agitated for a forced pace of collectivization, with heavy taxation and administrative compulsion, even at the expense of a transitory decline in agricultural output.[78]

In April 1958 the Central Committee had requested preparation of a detailed plan for socialist reorganization, observing that it could not be left to natural evolution. Within two months its agricultural department completed a draft.[79] Earlier in 1958 a fifteen-year schedule had been envisaged, but the draft anticipated that by 1965 some 60 to 65 percent of arable land could be brought into the collective sector. The debates continued. Kádár, in his usual centrist style, would warn against sectarianism as well as against a "compromising, permissive (right-wing) passivity."[80] The dogmatists appeared to weigh more heavily in the balance, and successive drafts reduced the carrot of projected state support for agriculture and adumbrated stronger sticks in the form of unfavorable price and tax treatment of private producers. (In fact, taxes had already been raised in 1958, and the peasantry was suffering from the new agrarian scissors effect of inflated industrial consumer goods prices.) But a consensus on pace and methods could not be reached in time for the Central Committee meeting in September, and the Politburo had to appoint a special preparatory committee in order to resolve "certain matters in dispute regarding the HSWP agrarian policy."[81]

Finally, on 7 December 1958, the Central Committee passed with ostensible unanimity a resolution on the acceleration of the collective movement. It criticized the prevalence in state and party of incorrect views departing from the party's line and demanded unwavering and unambiguous implementation of its resolution. The resolution recognized that the majority of private farmers did not desire change and called for massive utilization of coopted activists and experts in the forthcoming campaign. The resolution was notably cautious in reserving judgment on the feasibility of a "sudden, great revolution" and avoided specifying either a firm timetable or the extent of state support.[82]

The remaining uncertainty was dispelled upon Kádár's return from Moscow in late January 1959, when he announced that the necessity for Hungary to overcome her lag in collectivization must be their "great lesson" from the Soviet party congress.[83] Earlier that month he had told a mass meeting of activists that this third launching of collectivization would be a torment for the peasantry. Evoking the peasant's complaint—"I wish the state would just order me to join and stop persecuting me"—Kádár insisted that the party exert itself to ease the process by relying on agitation and local persuasion instead of coercion. "We should step a little more quickly now, but we should not leap," he said.[84] The Central Committee's party and mass organization department proceeded to transfer several hundred party functionaries and "politically conscious" agronomists to rural councils and party organizations and to the collective farms.

The pace of collectivization surpassed most party and public expectations. The outside agitators began their rural door-to-door campaign in midwinter, impressing on peasants the imperative necessity of collectivization. There were inducements, such as cancellation of certain debts, the provision of household plots, and other concessions to new recruits to the collective farms. And there were threats of "unpaid holidays" for family members in industry, of expulsion of children from high school or college, and other forms of harassment and intimidation, all of which prompted the Central Committee to censure "administrative methods" in its October 1959 review.[85] On 6 March the committee ordered a temporary halt to the first wave of collectivization in the interest of undisturbed production and the consolidation of the new collective farms. By then close to 350,000 new members had been recruited, and Kádár remarked that progress had been more rapid than anticipated.[86] In October 1959 the Central Committee reaffirmed that collectivization and growth in production should go hand in hand, and called for a "new and significant step" over the coming winter. There were already signs of disarray: the new collective farm members were reluctant to start work and private farmers were neglecting their land. That winter a further 400,000 peasants were driven into the collective farms, while nearly 100 party activists were disciplined and 23 others prosecuted for their excessive zeal.[87]

If the first wave had swept along the least reluctant peasants, this second phase required greater coercion. Again, hundreds of activists and experts were thrown into battle, and the "patronage movement" was resuscitated, with urban party organizations sending some five hundred teams to assist the new collective farms. There were reported instances of counterreprisals and crop burnings. In January 1960 Dögei, the leading instigator of the forced pace of collectivization, was dismissed as minister of agriculture and replaced by Pál Losonczi, a former farm laborer who had become a competent collective farm manager and a member of the Central Committee. Perhaps even the Soviet leaders were taken aback by the excesses and attendant political risks of the Hungarian collectivization drive, for upon Kádár's return from an agricultural conference in Moscow in February the Central Committee hurriedly suspended the campaign. In an attempt to boost the party's local strength, it was also decided to waive the probationary requirement for party membership in the case of deserving new collective farm recruits. As a result, between 1959 and 1961 membership in rural party organizations rose from 110,000 to a still modest 140,000.[88]

The final phase of collectivization was launched more discreetly and largely without coercion in winter 1960/61. Fehér, the Central Committee's agrarian expert and an early advocate of moderation and gradualism, had earlier in the year adumbrated the peasants' realization that international conditions, meaning the tacit Western acceptance of Soviet hegemony in East-Central Europe, and the regime's determination to prevail left them with no alternative.[89] Indeed, the remaining private farmers submitted with little active resistance. Officially terminating the campaign, the Central Committee declared on 17 February 1961: "We have reached a milestone in the transformation of Hungarian agriculture: after industry, socialist conditions of production have become dominant in agriculture."[90] By 1962 the collectivized sector in agriculture accounted for 75 percent of working peasants; 6.5 percent still worked private farms, while the remainder were employed on state farms.

The political objective of bringing Hungary into line with Soviet orthodoxy had been achieved. So, too, had the ostensible consolidation of the ideologically prescribed "worker-peasant alliance." The modernization of agriculture, however, remained a task for the future. Production stagnated, not even reaching the 1934–38 average level in plant cultivation, and the 1961 drought only added to the problem. Hundreds of farms had been established in areas unsuitable for efficient collective production, as even the party was compelled to recognize. The family income of collective farm members declined steadily, and a wide gap separated agricultural income from that of other workers. State investment per acre of collective land also declined. Thousands of disappointed members chose to take advantage of the right to withdraw. Others concentrated on their private plots and avoided collective work, or called for an eight-hour work day. Many younger peasants escaped to industry. Friction developed between old members and new recruits who were usually better qualified for managerial functions.[91] The decision over the admission of former kulaks was officially left by the party to collective farm members, and those admitted were excluded from elected office for the first two years. Many dogmatic party cadres would continue to resent the admission of former wealthy peasants (many of whom were eventually elected to leading positions) and to fight the regime's "opportunistic" flexibility, notably in using differential incentives to stimulate production and permitting the retention of household plots. Only after many years of heavy state support would the collective farms become reasonably productive and viable.

**Cultural Orthodoxy.**  In the cultural sphere, the key role played by the revisionist intelligentsia in the genesis of the revolution impelled the Kádár leadership to first seek compromise and then reimpose strict orthodoxy. The magazine *Élet és Irodalom* (Life and Literature) was revived in the spring of 1957 under the editorship of the dogmatist György Bölöni, and in its August issue it invited the writers to propose some modus vivendi. As Culture Minister Gyula Kállai admitted, "unfortunately communist intellectuals on whom the government could rely were not very numerous."[92] Indeed, most respectable writers had opted for a moratorium on creating works with any political message, let alone one endorsing the ideological dogma of restoration. The regime, on the other hand, was acutely aware of the necessity for such literary support in a nation whose novelists, essayists, and poets had traditionally served an essential political function. A tentative compromise was hammered out at a meeting on 20 August between some leading figures of the defunct Writers' Association and Kádár's team, led by Mesterházi, who was soon to become the new editor of *Élet és Irodalom*. Apparent agreement was reached that neither side had desired the revolution, in which the "tendency" had become counter-revolutionary, and both sides rejected the capitalist alternative. The writers also agreed to sign a protest against the report of the United Nations Special Committee on Hungary.[93] Two new literary reviews, *Kortárs* (Contemporary) and *Új Hang* (New Voice), were launched, and writers were encouraged to create "according to their own artistic concepts and literary taste."[94]

The reinvigoration of the area-wide antirevisionist campaign that autumn soon put an end to these early moves toward accommodation. As noted earlier, Déry, Háy, Zelk, and Tárdos received long prison sentences. The Populist writers were denounced by Kádár as "opposed to the leading role of the working class," and eventually all varieties of intellectual opposition were commonly branded as revisionist.[95] University students and faculty were excoriated for their attachment to nationalistic, bourgeois-democratic, or national-communist "third road" illusions. A special party study on the Populist tradition singled out Gyula Illyés, László Németh, and Áron Tamási (all leading literary figures) and the peasant writer Péter Veres, a former president of the Writers' Association, for having joined the enemy and for refusing to admit their errors. Party and state could not "permit the Populist writers to organize themselves into a political unit or literary clique," but they were invited as individuals to assist in the construction of socialism.[96]

That the regime's attitude toward the intellectuals had stiffened was evident from the new cultural guidelines approved by the Central Committee in July 1958. Recognizing that "the reshaping of man's way of thinking is the most protracted of all the fundamental social processes," the guidelines asserted that socialist culture could develop "only through a purposefully and tenaciously led class struggle, through the more efficient dissemination of the Marxist-Leninist world view and the defeat and displacement of bourgeois views." The HWP's cultural policy had neglected the cultural traditions of the workers' movement, notably the "legacy of the Republic of Councils," and had been intolerant of the nation's broader cultural heritage. The revisionists, on the other hand, had opened the door to bourgeois traditions alien to democratic culture. Only part of the intelligentsia now accepted Marxism-Leninism, the foundation of Hungary's social life, although the non-Marxist majority was loyal to the system. Therefore the state and party would condone nonsocialist works and attitudes that were "well intentioned and loyal to the people's democracy," but they would resort to all necessary measures to repress "all those endeavors openly or covertly directed against our people's democratic order." Rejecting the "individualistic, bourgeois" interpretation of artistic freedom, the party refused to allow the "inferior, formalistic products of bourgeois decadence" to infest popular cultural tastes. It would support, on the other hand, realistic styles that could evolve into socialist realism.[97]

More educators had to be converted to Marxism-Leninism, ruled the party, in order to ensure that young people would be exposed to proper ideological and moral values. A further elaboration of the party's literary-political objectives called for application of the Leninist principle of "party-mindedness," meaning the use of literary tools to support the battle for socialism with a socialist realist style that depicted the "victory of the arising new over the dying old."[98]

Another party document, released in September 1959, focused on the struggle against nationalism and for the propagation of socialist patriotism. It noted that bourgeois nationalism had served a positive function in the historic battle against feudalism and foreign oppression, but that it had turned into a tool of the exclusively Western-oriented (and even pro-Hitler), chauvinistic ruling classes. The petit bourgeois, "third road" version of nationalism differed in some respects from the former but shared its fundamental hostility to Marxism and the Soviet Union. The counterrevolutionaries had exploited these forms of nationalism, which remained the principal enemy on the ideological battlefront. These phenomena were not limited to an intellectual faction, for, as the seventh congress had concluded, "remnants of capitalistic attitudes, nationalism, and small proprietor mentality among the peasantry, the urban middle class, and part of the intelligentsia" were major obstacles to progress. "Petit bourgeois views, individualism, and indifference to social interests," the document concluded, "even affect the more backward strata of the working class."[99]

The Writers' Association was reorganized with a cooperative but undistinguished leadership in September 1959. At the December congress Kádár observed with disappointment: "The revolution on the cultural front is to some extent lagging behind the results achieved in the political and economic spheres."[100] The Populists, with their progressive national, clearly nonbourgeois, and at best quasi-marxist orientation, represented an enduring challenge to the party's ideological monopoly. Official disapprobation only enhanced their popularity, and new young writers would follow in the Populist tradition. Such was Erzsébet Galgóczi, who at the height of the collectivization campaign would write a scarcely veiled criticism of the peasantry's persecution.[101] Dialogue between party and Populists was revived in 1960, when the latter pleaded for the liberation of István Bibó. Eventually, the regime's growing flexibility in the application of guidelines, coupled with the writers' economic needs and a certain resignation on their part, facilitated a revival of literary activity. Prevented from criticizing the regime, let alone Soviet hegemony, the best writers reverted to largely apolitical novels and essays of cautious social comment. But Kádár never succeeded in converting their free creative spirit to ideological orthodoxy.

That orthodoxy was also threatened in the spheres of philosophy and historiography by the post-Stalin decompression and the legacy of the revolution. Lukács, in particular, continued to enjoy a certain popularity among communist intellectuals and students, and the party also had to contend with his international renown. However, when he refused to publicly recant his philosophical defense of the revolution's progressive democratic thrust, the party felt compelled to stage a formal criticism at a meeting of the Academy of Sciences in October 1958. The HSWP's spokesman, Béla Fogarasi, dismissed Lukács's ideological work as idealistic, anti-Marxist, and revisionist, and charged that he had persisted in his "erroneous ideas" on the nature of the counterrevolution.[102] The old philosopher withdrew into scholarly seclusion and was not allowed to publish in Hungary until 1964. He was readmitted to the party in 1967 but remained sharply critical of the Soviet bloc's applied version of Marxism-Leninism.

Another prominent party veteran and scholar, the former Rákosiite Erik Molnár, found himself at the center of controversy following the publication in 1959 of a work questioning some Stalinist tenets concerning the inevitable collapse of capitalism. The Central Committee's philosophical study group charged that Molnár had transgressed the limits of destalinization and invited him to reconsider.[103] To these accusations of revisionism Molnár retorted that dogmatism was the greater impediment to the development of the social sciences. His defense was fortuitously reinforced shortly thereafter by the new wave of destalinization inaugurated at the Soviet party's twenty-second congress, and Molnár remained the leading establishment historian until his death in 1966.

As in the Stalinist era, religion was the only competing value system possessed of an institutional structure. During the revolution the churches had quickly cleared their ranks of collaborationist clergymen and peace priests. For a few short days, Cardinal Mindszenty had recovered his office of primate of the Hungarian Catholic Church. At first Kádár tried to be conciliatory, formally dissolving the already inactive Office of Church Affairs on 29 December 1956. Tolerance did have its limits, however, and in January a group of priests received prison sentences for their takeover of that same office during the revolution. By the spring of 1957 the party's stance had stiffened, and both the peace priest movement and the old restrictions on religious education were revived. The episcopate, like the writers, agreed to sign the August protest against the United Nations report in the hope of forging a modus vivendi with the regime;

in another tactical concession, it founded a Catholic National Peace Commission, the Opus Pacis, which included the peace priests.

Two years later, when the regime had grown more self-confident and Soviet pressures for greater orthodoxy had increased, the churches' already tenuous autonomy was curtailed still further. After threatening to reduce subsidies, the government in June 1959 revived the Office of Church Affairs and secret police supervision of church administration, demanded public oaths of allegiance from bishops and priests, and launched a systematic drive to discourage religious practice. A deadlock with the Vatican over the status of Cardinal Mindszenty, who remained in the U.S. legation, and over the authority to make ecclesiastical appointments, was not resolved until the early 1970s. By reimposing direct state control, however, the regime intended to make sure that, in any eventual negotiations with the Vatican, the voice of the Hungarian church would be properly submissive.[104]

**Foreign Relations.** Kádár's foreign policy in the period of restoration was marked by two equally disagreeable realities: in the West, by the lingering stigma of a regime that had been imposed on the Hungarian people; and within the Soviet bloc, by his own dependence on Soviet support. In the latter sphere the centrality of friendly Soviet-Hungarian relations was reaffirmed with monotonous regularity, as if to exorcise the ghost of armed intervention. The presence of Soviet troops in Hungary was the symbol of national subjection most deeply resented by the population. In vain would the party's media deplore popular obsession with their withdrawal.[105] Khrushchev's maladroit allusion, during a visit to Hungary, to the role played by the tsar's armies in the crushing of the 1848–49 revolution required tortured explanations, notably by Mesterházi, to differentiate the positive function of the 1956 intervention from its unfortunate precedent.[106] Kádár could only insist that a progressive man was by definition loyal to the Soviet Union, and that international tensions demanded the temporary maintenance of Soviet forces in Hungary.[107] When, in March 1958 (just before Khrushchev's visit), some 17,000 Soviet troops were withdrawn from the much larger occupation force, the authorities felt compelled to issue a stern warning:

> There are—here at home as well as abroad—counterrevolutionary elements who nurse high hopes in connection with the withdrawal of Soviet troops. They believe that the time has again come when their reactionary dreams shall come true. We wish to state that they are mistaken in hoping for a weakening of the democratic regime. . . . Our faithful allies, the remaining Soviet units, will stand at our side in the future also.[108]

The presence of Soviet forces was the most tangible guarantee of the Kádár regime's survival. The latter's compatibility with Soviet interests was further ensured by a supervisory network that ranged from frequent top-level contacts to intimate linkages between the central organizations of the two parties. The visibility of Soviet advisers attached to the party and the key state agencies receded with the process of restoration. But the overlapping Soviet diplomatic, party, and secret police services never ceased their covert intervention in the Hungarian political system. This intervention was and is aided by the presence of many Muscovites and naturalized Russians in the administrative and security areas.[109] Accordingly, although the most oppressive manifestations of Stalinism were gradually abandoned, the fundamental subordination of the Hungarian party and state to the Kremlin did not change.

The regime's tenuous domestic legitimacy and Kádár's relative distaste for polemics conspired to mute Hungarian participation in the revived anti-Tito campaign and in the verbal skirmishes of the emerging Sino-Soviet dispute. Kádár had paid his respects in Peking in October 1957, and until late 1959 the Hungarian press gave favorable attention to Chinese developments.[110] The Hungarians, like the Chinese, were present in Moscow for the meeting of eighty-one communist parties in November 1960. Here the peaceful coexistence of different social systems was reaffirmed, but the Chinese were already turning critical of what they construed as Soviet liberalism. After the twenty-second Soviet party congress, which condemned the dogmatism exhibited by the Albanian party leadership (and, implicitly, by the Chinese), *Társadalmi Szemle* dutifully parroted the new line. The general tone of the HSWP in interparty debates continued to be one of unconditional but somewhat perfunctory solidarity with the Soviet position.[111]

Consolidation of the Kádár regime depended not only on domestic measures but also on visible endorsement by the other East European socialist states. The cordiality and unanimity required by Moscow were duly displayed in a series of meetings between party dignitaries. Gomulka, in a visit to Budapest in May 1958, was the last to bestow his unqualified blessing on Kádár. When after 1958 the Romanian regime began to implement a nationalistic policy of brutal cultural repression, assimilation, and dispersal against the Magyar minority in Transylvania—a minority over 1.5 million strong—Hungarian public opinion was outraged. Kádár, however, lacked the freedom and the will to protest at these measures in an officially friendly socialist state. Apart from other restraints he feared the outburst of domestic nationalism that an official protest might unleash.

The United Nations, after serving as the forum for dilatory debates during the revolution, sent out a special committee that reported in June 1957 on the Hungarian question. The report characterized the revolution as a "spontaneous national uprising" and the Kádár regime as one "imposed on the Hungarian people by the armed intervention of the Union of Soviet Socialist Republics."[112] Thereafter, and until 1962, an annual resolution was voted in the

General Assembly condemning the Soviet and Hungarian governments for their refusal to comply with the UN's earlier demands for withdrawal of Soviet troops and the restoration of human rights. Western ostracism of the Kádár regime gradually made way for more normal relations, but the United States in particular was adamant that it would not allow full recognition of the Hungarian delegates' credentials by the UN (where they enjoyed only observer status) until the government at least amnestied its political prisoners. Kádár was acutely embarrassed by such constant reminders of his government's illegitimate origins, and insisted on normalization of relations and the dropping of the Hungarian question from the UN's agenda as preconditions to any consideration of a full amnesty. After protracted negotiations, in the course of 1963 the amnesty was promulgated, Hungary was restored to full UN membership, and the perennial debate on the Hungarian question was abandoned. Secretary-General U Thant paid his respects in Budapest in July.[113] Kádár had finally been released from diplomatic purgatory.

## THE ALLIANCE POLICY

As the regime gradually emerged from international isolation, it consolidated its ideological-political status at home. The Central Committee proclaimed in March 1962 that with collectivization the laying of the foundations of socialism had been completed; this represented a giant step toward the integration of "the working class, the collectivized peasantry, and the intelligentsia into a unified, socialist society."[114] Encouraged by the anti-Stalinist thrust of the Soviet party's twenty-second congress, Kádár began to implement his alliance policy with a program of controlled liberalization. He ushered in the new thaw with words that would be quoted long thereafter: "Whereas the Rákosiites used to say that those who are not with us are against us, we say those who are not against us are with us."[115]

**Stalinism Exorcised.** At the same time, certain political and personnel issues left over from the Rákosi era were finally settled. The Central Committee established an investigatory commission in 1961 and twice sent a delegation, composed of Nógrádi and György Aczél (a veteran home communist, purged from 1949 to 1955), to hold discussions in the Soviet Union with Rákosi. The latter, reports Nógrádi, was "blinded by hate". He would not recognize the enormity of his reign of terror; revolutions have no laws, Rákosi would intimate. Moreover, he would charge that a "social democratic revival" had occurred in Hungary since 1956.[116] Rákosi, stated the eventual Central Committee resolution, "refuses to weigh his responsibility, shows no contriteness, opposes the party's line and pursues factional activities."[117] He was not invited to return. Gerő, who had reportedly demanded rehabilitation from Kádár, lectured for a time at Moscow University, then returned to Hungary in December 1960.[118] Like Imre Nagy, both Rákosi and Gerő refused to make a public confession. Of the other members of the original foursome, Révai had died in 1959, while Farkas was released together with his son in March 1960 and given a quiet sinecure. Gábor Péter was also released, to work as a librarian.

While the new investigation of the purge trials was proceeding, a more recent villain bit the dust: in April 1962 the party announced the expulsion of Imre Dögei. In May 1960, following his dismissal from the agriculture ministry at the height of the collectivization drive, Dögei had been quietly dropped from the Central Committee (of which he had been a member since 1948) for having pursued "sectarian and pseudoleftist activities." When he persisted with radical agitation among party cadres during unofficial provincial tours, Kádár had no choice but to expel him. At the same time Iván Altomare was also expelled from the party for bribery and corruption while holding the office of minister of food industry from 1952 to 1956.

At its meeting of 14 to 16 August 1962 the Central Committee passed a resolution designed to close the books on the "unlawful trials of the years of the cult of personality."[119] It noted that the rehabilitation measures after 1953 had been impeded by the presence of individuals who exercised a "decisive influence in minimizing their own responsibility and obstructing the full uncovering of the facts and discovery of the truth." The resolution proceeded to enumerate the circumstances that produced the purges: departure from the fundamentals of Marxism-Leninism in favor of dogmatism in theory and sectarianism in political practice; deification of personality and underestimation of the history-making role of the masses; the Stalinist dogmas that the class struggle intensified with the advance of socialist construction and that the class enemy had to be sought within the ranks of the party; the abandonment of Leninist norms of collective leadership and the "administrative" resolution of intraparty disagreements; and the flouting of socialist legality by the state.

The resolution charged that "the members of the Rákosi clique had already decided before liberation to seize the party's leadership." After 1948 their goal had been to extend their personal power, and by taking the road of political adventurism they severed their links with the party membership and with the masses. The then-members of the Central Committee were not responsible for the purges, for Rákosi had misinformed them; they were guilty, however, of not standing up for Leninist norms of party leadership because of their "blind faith in Rákosi." The Central Control Committee, on the other hand, had to bear responsibility for having enforced Rákosi's persecutive measures. Rákosi himself had gone so far as to denounce leaders and members of sister parties. Gerő was responsible along with Rákosi and Farkas for the fabricated charges and the purges and, as interior minister after June 1953, for the delays in rehabilitation. The resolution also condemned the "leaders and many officers of the AVH and the highest officials of the judiciary.'' The Central Committee therefore undertook to aid the families of the purge victims and to rehabilitate another 190 who had earlier been set free. Rákosi, Gerő, and István Kovács were expelled from the party along with Alapi, Olti, and fourteen former AVH officers. Six other party members were expelled for ''faction mongering,'' a charge that implied more recent opposition to Kádár.

Most of the other participants in the purges, the resolution continued, had been dismissed from the judiciary and the security forces. Others had atoned for their mistakes and were barred from these spheres and from disciplinary functions in the party. With these measures, the Central Committee insisted, the party had definitively atoned for its past sins: ''Legality and socialist order have been consolidated. All law-abiding citizens of the Hungarian People's Republic can live and work in tranquillity in our socialist homeland.''

Inevitably, the resolution had swept under the carpet the role played in the purges by the Russians and by hundreds of other leading or minor party figures, including such men as Apró and Kádár himself. Even this limited though final purge did not pass without protest. Károly Kiss, who had been chairman of the Central Control Committee from 1945 to 1956, was removed from the Politburo, reportedly at the Central Committee's own initiative, for being ''still unable to see clearly the wrong practice of the Central Control Committee prior to 1956 and to recognize his own responsibility in it.'' Of the leading culprits, Rákosi requested in 1971 that he be allowed to die in Hungary, but Kádár refused, and the former dictator, having died that year in the Soviet Union, was ultimately reburied in Hungary without ceremony. Mihály Farkas died in 1965. The nearly blind Gerő has been allowed to live out his days in quiet obscurity in Budapest.

**A Landmark Congress.**   As the time of the eighth congress drew near, Kádár could draw satisfaction from having formally fulfilled his promise to dissociate the party from its Stalinist antecedents. Not all of the party apparat, however, showed readiness to espouse the tolerance of his alliance policy. In addition to the expulsion of Dögei, Kádár had to impose sanctions on rural party functionaries who were sabotaging the more lenient prescriptions of collectivization, notably the admission of kulaks and the allowance of household plots. He also had to contend with the dogmatic cadres' opposition to the projected abolition of class discrimination in education and to the access permitted nonparty experts to high administrative offices. In his remarks to the congress on the necessity for continuing the two-front struggle, Kádár stressed that the fight against dogmatism required greater attention. The party underscored that it would ''never place the advancement of any member of the party above the interest of the socialist community. . . .'' Rather, it would ''endeavor to create a situation in which the apparats of industry, of agriculture, of the state administration, and of culture are staffed with competent individuals.'' One party analyst observed that ''if we persist in naming only party members to responsible posts the consequence will be to attract careerists to the party.''[120] Over time, career considerations and a persisting premium on symbolic displays of ideological loyalty would swell the ranks of the party with ambitious administrators and managers. Nevertheless, Kádár's invitation to nonbelievers, first adumbrated in June 1957, was still a significantly liberal gesture that aroused much apprehension among the older and less qualified cadres.

The liberalization of criteria for admission to higher education came at a time when the children of active or former workers and peasants accounted for a relatively low 47.1 percent of postsecondary students. The reform was nevertheless required by the unpopularity, particularly among the urban intelligentsia, of the existing discriminatory provisions, and by the alliance policy's stress on secular expertise and the essential conclusion of the class struggle.[121] Although the reform prompted violent debate within the party—Kádár reported that ''there are certain comrades who do not find this proposal correct or comprehensible''—the congressional resolution confirmed that candidates would be judged by attitude and ability. The wrong class origin would no longer automatically disqualify a student, although demonstrated political loyalty remained a factor in access to higher education.

In the days before the congress Kádár had to deal with one challenge that was apparently more personal than ideological. Marosán, the crude and ambitious former social democrat, had sent a memorandum to the Central Committee alleging the existence of an unrepresentative clique around Kádár. Apparently the maneuver arose from Marosán's pique at being excluded from the center of decision making and aimed to rally the dogmatist opposition to Kádár. On 12 October the Central Committee relieved him of his party offices; three years later he resigned from the HSWP.

Six hundred and fourteen voting delegates gathered in Budapest from 20 to 24 November 1962, for the eighth congress of the HSWP.[122] In his report, Kádár reiterated the Central Committee's message that the foundations of socialism had been laid and that Hungary had entered the era of the full construction of socialism. The new tasks were largely economic: ''The boosting of productivity, the raising of profitability, the expansion of production are today the principal battlefronts.'' To this end the economic system had to be improved and modernized. Cooperation within Comecon had not developed sufficiently and had to be expanded to win the economic contest with capitalism. In this task of socialist construction the party rejected the ''false thesis of the constant and absolute intensification of the class struggle'' and invited the cooperation of those who in earlier times stood in opposition to party rule. There could be no ideological coexistence with the enemies of communism, but the nation could be united through ''political alliance and ideological debate.'' Socialist legality had been consolidated to prevent a repetition of earlier transgressions, and the battle of ideas would be waged by means of ideological education to expand the socialist consciousness of the masses. All this was consonant with the "general line elaborated at the twentieth congress of the Soviet party," which had been "elevated by the declarations of the communist parties of 1957 and 1960 into the general line of the whole international communist movement."

The congress noted that the majority of party members were free of harmful sectarian and revisionist attitudes, although these still existed, and it adopted a revised set of party statutes that included some noteworthy changes from the 1957 version. Much of the new document replicated the 1961 Soviet party statutes and reflected an emphasis on the democratic side of democratic centralism. In keeping with the consolidation of a "united peasant class" the qualification of "working" peasant was expunged from the statutes, as were the exclusion from membership of former "exploiters" and the specific call for vigilance against class enemies in the party. Factionalism, however, had to be rooted out.

The party, proclaimed the statutes, "does not aim at a large-scale increase in its membership." Two-thirds of the members of an applicant's party organization had to approve his candidacy and membership (instead of the former provision for a simple majority). The same qualified majority could recall an unsatisfactory leader. Party members had to loyally implement resolutions, but they could present their dissenting views not only to the higher bodies but also in their own organization (which was more than the Soviet statutes allowed). Suppression of criticism and persecution of critics were made subject to penalties. As a safeguard against unjustified disciplinary procedures, penalties had to be approved by a two-thirds majority of the affected member's basic organization (in the Soviet statutes, expulsion was the only penalty so approved). The statutes also provided for censure from below: disciplinary proceedings against a member holding higher party office could now be "suggested" by the membership of the basic organization to which he belonged.

Party elections were to be by secret ballot, the officials' term being four years in the leading bodies and two years for leaders of the basic organizations. Collective leadership, asserted the statutes, was not only essential within the party but also the "indispensable condition of the further democratization of life in state and society." The Central Control Committee was given greater autonomy—ostensibly to prevent it being manipulated, as happened under Rákosi—by the provision that it should be elected by the congress rather than by the Central Committee and by the prohibition of dual membership on the two leading bodies. Party committees were now expressly charged with the task of applying higher resolutions to local conditions. The statutes also provided for the creation of such committees in city districts, villages, and places of work that had as a rule more than 200 party members (compared with 300 in the 1957 statutes). Communists in nonparty state and social organizations were instructed to resort to persuasion to implement the party line.

In sum, the new statutes represented an attempt to enhance the party's democratic image and set an example in keeping with Kádár's professed desire to expand "socialist democracy." However, approving the revised statutes in principle was easier than altering ingrained modes of party life, and the democratization of the party would remain a perennial concern of its leaders.

The changes in leadership effected by the eighth congress showed how entrenched Kádár's centrist line had become. Gáspár, Komócsin, and Szirmai were raised to full membership in the Politburo, which had earlier lost Kiss and Marosán. The new Secretariat consisted of Kádár, Biszku, Nemes, Rezső Nyers (a former printer who had risen from the party ranks to become finance minister), Szirmai, and Károly Németh, the first secretary of the Budapest party committee. The congress also elected an 81-member Central Committee, a 13-member Central Control Committee (whose chairman since 1959 had been Sándor Nógrádi), and a 15-member Central Auditing Committee. Party membership on 31 August 1962 stood at 511,965, including candidate members.[123] Kádár had noted at the preceding congress the numerical decline of the apparat, but the profile of delegates to the eighth congress indicated that it remained in firm control of party policy: 41 percent of the delegates belonged to the party apparat, and 27 percent to state, military, and mass organization apparats.[124] This preponderance of full-time activists indicated that party congresses, much as before, were ritualistic gatherings rather than exercises in democratic policy making.

**Amnesty and Compromise.** Effective application of the alliance policy required that the repressive legacy of the restoration period be laid to rest. The two-front struggle did not allow for ideological concessions to those who had virtually destroyed the party during the revolution, and Kádár warned as much after the twenty-second Soviet party congress had confirmed the principles of destalinization:

There are people among us who think now that Stalin's coffin has been removed from the mausoleum, a new spring will arise for the right. I have heard voices saying that one should rehabilitate in our country those who knocked down Stalin's statue. But here is what I answer them: If this statue were still in place, then we would adopt a resolution to remove it next December or January. But those who knocked the statue down in our country did not do it because Stalin committed errors but because they did not like communism. We will therefore never rehabilitate them.[125]

Hungary's prisons and internment camps had been filled with "counter-revolutionaries" in the early years of restoration. In February 1958 Prime Minister Münnich announced that the prosecution of the rebels had been concluded, but more than a year later members of the defunct workers' council of Ujpest were brought to trial, and eight were executed.[126] The first partial amnesty was promulgated on 12 April 1959, and on 31 March 1960 a few more political prisoners were amnestied or pardoned, including the writers Tibor Déry and Gyula Háy as well as Donáth, Jánosi, Tildy, and Vásárhelyi. Concurrently the dissolution of the internment camps was decreed and a new criminal code was drawn up eliminating summary proceedings.

The final amnesty, in March 1963, returned to freedom most of the remaining political prisoners, including István Bibó. These measures, together with the insistence on socialist legality and the lower profile adopted by the secret police, allowed Kádár to claim that peace had been made and the illegalities of the Rákosi era eradicated. The occasional arrest for antistate activity would still occur, but the regime generally resorted to less forceful methods of persuasion to achieve an order consonant with the possibilities and limitations of the alliance policy.

The implementation of that policy represented a remarkable triumph for the man who had been propelled to power by Soviet military might. The Soviet Union imposed the party's monopoly and rejected, with varying emphasis, the claims of left and right deviation. Within those confines, however, Kádár enjoyed a certain discretion in domestic policy. The collectivization of agriculture in East-Central Europe (with the enduring exception of Poland) was preordained by Soviet orthodoxy, but it also allowed Kádár to proclaim the essential conclusion of the class struggle and cleared the way for an ostensibly more consensual construction of socialism. The discredited patriotic unity of Imre Nagy's interregnum had been based on premises of national independence and voluntarism that were now excluded from the realm of the possible. Given the constraints of Soviet hegemony, the Hungarian party postulated a vaguely defined "socialist national unity." This rested on Kádár's pragmatic calculation, encouraged by his patron Khrushchev, that he could generate genuine support for economic modernization.

Kádár thus appealed to the realism of the Hungarian people, who had learned a bitter lesson from the revolution. He, unlike the Rákosi clique, was possessed of a sincere concern for the welfare of the masses and understood that the methods of his predecessors had profoundly alienated the nation from the party. The party was his life, and he firmly believed that the purified vanguard was predestined to lead the country to a higher state of socialism. But he was also enough of a realist to recognize that popular legitimacy could not be secured at the party's command. The alternative was ostensibly to remove the exercise of political power somewhat from the realm of ideology and to enlist the largely apolitical middle classes in the pursuit of practical objectives. The management of economic modernization and the attendant token democratization was not without risks—the revolutionary outcome of decompression in 1956 was sufficient evidence of that—but Kádár's party and the Hungarian people had entered into a historic compromise.

★ ★ ★ ★ ★ ★

# The Modernization of Power

# PART SIX

Celebrating his sixtieth birthday in May 1972, a mellow János Kádár reflected on the crisis that had brought him to power:

> In 1956, a very serious and critical situation presented itself, a situation that is called, scientifically, the counterrevolution. We are aware that this is the scientific definition of what took place in 1956. But there is also another concept we might all accept: it was a national tragedy. A tragedy for the party, for the working class, for the people, and for the individual. We lost our way, and the result was tragedy. And if we have overcome this now—which we can state with confidence—this is a very big thing.

With time and tolerance, he continued, "we will find ways and means for believers and nonbelievers to work together for the common socialist goal."[1]

Three years later, in the days leading up to the party's eleventh congress, popular apprehensions revolved around the possibility that the avuncular Kádár might be replaced and the party led toward a more rigid and dictatorial line. At the conclusion of the congress Kádár referred to such fearful speculations in an extemporaneous address. The dictatorship of the proletariat would remain in force, he said, but eighteen years' experience had shown that "it was not such a bad dictatorship after all. One can live under it, create freely, and gain honor." There were no longer any antagonistic classes, only class allies, and the remaining differences were not over the desirability of socialism but on the rate of progress of the socialist revolution. The role of the party was to lead and to persuade.[2]

There was an equal measure of realism and wishful thinking in these assertions, reflecting the accommodation reached by Kádár and his subjects. The regime frequently reiterates the historical significance and future demands of *that compromise. In a typical retrospective article written in 1977, the then editor of Népszabadság, István Katona, invited the party, and particularly the 70 percent of its members who had joined since 1956, to reflect on their inheritance. The HSWP was heir to the struggle that began in November 1918 on behalf of the working class and the working people of Hungary. The party rejected both the personality cult distortions of the Rákosi era and the revolution's deceptive slogan of "national communism." Instead, it consistently followed the guiding principles elaborated at the provisional Central Committee's meeting of December 1956 and at the June 1957 national party conference. The party sustained the two-front struggle, consolidated the worker-peasant alliance, and preserved its leading role while modernizing the economy and acquiring the support of all social strata. At the same time, in its alliance with the Soviet Union, it remained true to the principle of proletarian internationalism. If the lessons of 1956 were not forgotten, anticipated Katona, the second twenty years would see a continuation of the balanced and vigorous construction of socialism.[3]*

*The scope and limitations of this political strategy had been succinctly outlined by Politburo member Zoltán Komócsin some nine years earlier:*

> There has never been, nor is there likely to be for a long time to come a Communist Party that could on a class basis attract to its side every citizen of a country without exception. But the Party and its leadership should always be able to attract —chiefly through persuasion—the majority of the working people. And the main method of winning the working people for socialism is action that accords with their interests and aspirations. Of course, we should debate with our political enemies, too. But in a country committed to the building of socialism we cannot, in our view, renounce the use of the instruments of power in relation to those who actively oppose socialism and the socialist system.[4]

*He emphasized further that the abstract concepts of democracy, sovereignty, and humanism were necessarily subordinated to the class perspective and to "internationalism," for only the two last named could lead to a proper understanding of sociopolitical life.[5]*

*In fact, the alliance policy, whose complex implementation has dominated the Hungarian scene since 1962, has served the dual purpose of legitimization and modernization to some effect, producing what is currently the most humane polity in the Soviet sphere of dominance. The later Kádár era has been subjected to numerous exhaustive and generally judicious Western analyses.[6] This final part aims, therefore, at a mere overview of the evolution of the party and its policies and of the salient features of contemporary Hungarian society.*

*The central problem of a single-party system is how to reconcile the task of government with that of representation. The party must be simultaneously policy maker and executive branch as well as the responsive and responsible aggregator and arbiter of national and group interests. In the Hungarian context, it must also satisfy the requisites of Soviet hegemony. And it must do all this without testing the legitimacy of its power through democratic competition for popular support.*

*From the early 1960s onwards, Kádár sought legitimacy by partially accommodating this multiplicity of often conflicting demands. Without compromising the HSWP's monopolistic position, he lowered the profile of the party in the routine tasks of government and enhanced the secular, managerial role of state administration. Central and local government were allowed a certain latitude and charged to exhibit greater responsiveness to public opinion. New emphasis was laid on popular participation in the development and execution of policy through the Patriotic People's Front, the various elected bodies, and organized interest groups. Finally, the party itself was exhorted to expand democracy in its own ranks and increase its links with the population.*

*These reforms, subsumed under the conciliatory alliance policy, diverged radically from Rákosi's practice of Stalinism in two major respects: their relative decentralization of authority, and their appeal for nonideological collaboration. They rested on the recognition that legitimacy could not be won by a frontal, doctrinal assault on the Hungarian people's historical reservations about communist rule. The nation would have to be gradually seduced by the demonstration of administrative competence in meeting its daily needs. The eventual political outcome was a degree of openness and quasi-pluralism that continues to distinguish the Hungarian polity from its East European neighbors.*

*If the alliance policy is the political framework of Kádárism, economic modernization has been its most tangible accomplishment. The two, it has often been stated, are inseparable, for the former facilitates popular commitment to the latter. The test of applied socialism is no longer ideological unanimity but rather balanced economic development. The New Economic Mechanism serves as the vehicle of modernization, and it has indeed fostered commendable improvement in both the agricultural and industrial sectors of the Hungarian economy. The synthesis of ideology and economic rationality has, more than any other factor, contributed to the current degree of popular confidence in the regime.*

*These results were not achieved by international brinkmanship. The circumstances under which Kádár was imposed on the Hungarian people and the enduring fact of Soviet hegemony ruled out any attempt by the leadership to seek legitimacy in the realm of high politics. Kádár would assiduously avoid the perilous posturings on the theme of national independence practiced by his Romanian counterpart Ceausescu. From the start, his overriding goal was to win the confidence and tolerance of the Soviet leaders. At the same time, he both pursued cordial relations with the other East European parties and attempted to normalize diplomatic and commercial relations with the West. Over time, his subjects came to the grudging conclusion that the stratagem of a low profile in foreign relations was a wise one, obeisance to the immovable hegemonic power being a price worth paying for domestic liberalization.*

*The application of Kádárism did not proceed without many political, social, and economic stresses. The more conservative veterans of the movement floundered like fish out of water amidst the complex accommodations of the alliance policy. Economic modernization brought with it a certain restratification and embourgeoisement of Hungarian society, which in turn induced friction between the new middle class, the industrial workers, and the peasantry. Moreover, as rapid economic growth was superseded by the retrenchment of the mid-1970s, it became apparent that stagnation, even at a higher level of affluence, sharpened competing demands. Liberalization in the realm of culture made definition of the ideologically permissible more elusive. The secularized practice of the arts of government served both Kádár's prestige and the interests of administrative efficiency, but it made the party's preordained monopoly of political wisdom even less credible and had a negative impact on ideological certitude among the membership. Finally, as the reforms of yesterday turned into the orthodoxy of today, the population became sensitized to any hint of regression from liberalism, imposing on Kádár and his eventual successor the unenviably delicate task of preserving the revolution-turned-evolution from both Soviet displeasure and domestic disaffection.*

# 14. The Governors: Party and State

Following confirmation of Kádár's centrist alliance policy at the HSWP's eighth congress, the party leadership began the long and contentious process of developing a new economic policy. The basic tasks requiring attention, reported Nyers to the Central Committee in May 1963, were improvement in the rate of growth of national income, in the balance of payments with the West, in the standard of living, and in enterprise management. He adumbrated desirable structural changes in the direction of more efficient central planning and greater enterprise autonomy. He would subsequently lay stress on the need for technological modernization, which had been neglected under the dogmatic preconceptions of Rákosiite economic orthodoxy.[1]

At its December 1963 plenum the Central Committee passed a resolution calling for a study of economic reform. Nyers then organized a major research effort by party and outside experts. Their report was endorsed in principle by the Central Committee in November 1965. Nyers's experts were thus able to proceed to the next stage, that of developing the basic directives. Finally, at its May 1966 meeting, the Central Committee approved the directives and opened the way for the extensive preparations needed to launch the New Economic Mechanism (NEM) on 1 January 1968.

The distinctive features of this radical transformation of the system of economic management will be sketched below. Its genesis was by no means as smooth and uneventful as the foregoing schedule might suggest.

## THE POLITICS OF REFORM

Midway through the planning process a conjuncture of events placed the incipient reform in jeopardy. A serious deceleration in economic growth brought about such emergency measures as the raising of production norms in 1965 and of consumer prices in 1966. The result was widespread popular discontent. The party's more dogmatic elements were already resentful of other liberal measures such as the abandonment of the class struggle among the peasantry, the reform of admission criteria for higher education, and the gradual influx of nonparty experts to higher office. They seized on popular resentment at the austerity measures to denigrate Kádár's alliance policy in general and the proposed economic reform in particular. There followed a tug-of-war between the party leader and his reformist colleagues on one side and the dogmatists on the other. The latter, charged Kádár, stood to the left of the party on the issue of socialist construction and were only happy when they could "start a brawl."[2]

The fall from power on 14 October 1964 of Kádár's patron, Khrushchev, only emboldened the dogmatist wing. Kádár cut short a visit to Warsaw and upon his return paid tribute to the deposed leader while pointedly confirming that the "political attitude of the Hungarian Socialist Workers' Party and the government of the Hungarian People's Republic [had] not changed one iota and [would] not change either."[3] Past experience with shifts in the Soviet leadership understandably induced uncertainty among the general public and raised the hopes of Kádár's detractors in the party. Addressing the national assembly in February 1965, Kádár admitted that the "unexpected personnel changes" in the Kremlin had prompted the expectation among dogmatists that a new HSWP leadership would emerge and follow a "militant, strong-handed" policy. Then he lost his temper and, defending his economic policies, he shouted: "It is good! It's the implementation that is bad! Where? Everywhere—at the bottom, at the middle, and at the top! Even at the ministerial level it's bad!"[4] The solution, he intimated, lay in the recruitment of competent administrators regardless of their political status.

Kádár lost no time in securing the endorsement of Khrushchev's successors; he and Brezhnev met seven times during the latter's first year in office. Dogmatist pressure and the relatively more conservative inclination of Brezhnev impelled a certain hardening in official attitudes, and over the next two years arrests for "antistate activities" and personnel shifts in the cultural sphere occurred with greater frequency. But Kádár remained determined to override the opposition of those who, he said, "remembered the early 1950s with nostalgia, who felt that we were stronger then."[5] This opposition was manifest not only among middle-level and rural cadres but also at the party's apex, for at its May 1966 plenum the Central Committee reportedly endorsed the final reform plan by only a narrow margin.[6] Asserting the necessary linkage between economics and politics, the resolution stated that it was a "political goal of the reform" to speed the development of socialist democracy. "The management of economic affairs," it continued, "must be based on the expertise, wide authority, and personal responsibility of managers, and in addition sufficient scope must be given at every level to the supervising function of democratically elected bodies and of the general public."[7]

Despite this victory, Kádár could not afford a purge of the party dogmatists. He chose instead to pacify and persuade. In a departure from previous practice, the guidelines of the ninth congress of November–December 1966 were not published in order to preclude extraparty debate. In another concession to the vanity of party cadres, the congress amended the party statutes to enhance their local authority. But the practical implications of the alliance policy received congressional approval, and there followed a series of reforms affecting the electoral process, the trade unions, and the agricultural producers' cooperatives.

**The Tenth Congress.** The desirability of implementing the noneconomic aspects of the alliance policy was confirmed at the March 1969 plenum of the Central Committee. On that occasion, seven commissions were established to study and recommend further changes in the electoral law, the constitution, the councils, the judiciary, and other spheres of state administration. The legislated outcome of these party initiatives will be noted below. But the HSWP was still far from unanimous in its appraisal of the NEM and the reforms deriving from it. The leftist dogmatists provoked an intense debate in the months leading up to the tenth congress in November 1970. Their basic complaint was that the party had seriously undermined its own leading role and the supremacy of the industrial proletariat by the attenuation of ideology and by the decentralizing impact of the alliance policy, as well as by a degree of income differentiation, derived from the NEM, that worked to the detriment of the proletariat.

Indeed, the industrial workers were acutely aware that the peasantry and the growing middle stratum of managers, bureaucrats, and artisans were deriving relatively greater economic benefits from the NEM. Their trade union representatives concurred with the party dogmatists in arguing that the Marxist class basis of the system was being diluted in favor of creeping petit bourgeois liberalism. The report of the National Council of Trade Unions on the congressional guidelines reminded the party that a true working-class spirit was a more precious commodity than easily acquired secular expertise. The depth of the controversy was indicated by the complaint in *Népszabadság* that the recent outburst by the editor of its trade union sister, *Népszava*, fueled the flames of leftist intolerance.[8]

Kádár had to defend his reforms at the congress against open criticism.[9] "The reform ensures better than before," he insisted, "that the interests of individuals, of groups, and of the entire nation are all appropriately represented." Denigration of the entire system because of "temporarily unresolved" problems, he charged, betrayed ignorance or, at worst, represented "hostile slander." Moreover, it was an "erroneous belief that the leading role of the working class is asserted only when the workers are physically present and in a majority." This might be indispensable in the Central Committee and the national assembly, he granted, but "numerical proportion [was] not the essence of the matter."[10] Árpád Pullai, a party secretary, argued that, contrary to leftist critiques, by perfecting the planned economy they could create more favorable conditions for the suppression of bourgeois materialism and egotism; "pseudoradical demagogy," he added, was an equally anti-Marxist phenomenon.[11] Delivering the crucial blessing, Brezhnev endorsed the "principled approach" of the HSWP in its economic reforms, the two-front struggle, and the development of socialist democracy, all of which met with the "full understanding and high appreciation of the Communists of the Soviet Union."[12]

Nevertheless, the debate on the undesirable social consequences of the NEM did not subside, while the economy itself ran into trouble. At an extraordinary conference of top party, government, and enterprise economic activists on 22 October 1971, Prime Minister Fock gave a frank report on the shortcomings. These included deficiencies in investments (unfinished projects accounted for 80 percent of annual investments), in manpower management (i.e., a high rate of labor turnover), and foreign trade (the trade deficit that year was already the highest in Hungarian history).[13] A stabilization program was thereupon introduced to alleviate these problems. The socioeconomic anomalies debated at the congress had been corrected, said Kádár at a meeting of the Budapest party committee in February 1972, "to better coordinate group and social interests, abolish certain wage anomalies, ensure greater moral and material appreciation of people working decently and well, regulate secondary and part-time jobs, levy heavier taxes on socially unjustified high incomes, and prevent building plot speculation; we have increased the severity of the penal code as well."[14]

At least one calculation underlying these corrective measures was revealed in a comment made by the secretary-general of the Academy of Sciences in 1972: "Leftist tendencies of a kind able to influence important strata would strengthen if the fight against right-wing bourgeois and petty-bourgeois phenomena were slackened."[15] In a lecture at the party's political academy, Béla Biszku, Kádár's de facto deputy, observed: "We have currently reached a phase of social development in which we are decentralizing." This development, he continued, had led some people to fear for the leading role of the party, but there was "no indication so far of the failure of party management to assert itself in making some significant decisions."[16]

The Central Committee's November 1972 plenum responded to criticism of the reform with both carrot and stick. It approved a special wage hike for 1.3 million workers in large state industries and construction, and passed a resolution censuring "certain party organizations" for allowing open dissent. Such disrespect for centralism would invite expulsion, said the Central Committee; instead of disputing party decisions, members should work unanimously for their implementation. Kádár acknowledged the intensity of the ongoing debate but ruled that "the main line of the tenth party congress, including domestic and foreign policy, economic policy, social and cultural policy, and the resolutions, [had] proven correct." Inadequate implementation of the resolutions had caused problems and would be met by a restructuring of the top planning bodies. A new tax on movable property and real estate would be added to earlier measures in order to combat excessive incomes. The principle, added Kádár, was that "he who has more goods should bear a larger part of the common burden," but there was no "new class" in Hungary (a reference to the Djilas thesis on the embourgeoisement of communist elites).[17] Following the plenum an intensive propaganda campaign was launched in the party organizations and in newly created political debating circles to "discuss" the Central Committee resolutions. The latter, declared Biszku, were final, and further argument would be incompatible with Leninist norms of party life.[18]

The party attached great importance to the November 1972 resolutions, and a year later, on 28 November 1973, the Central Committee took additional steps to improve the quality of state administration. It also remedied certain grievances (the remedy took the form of another "special" wage increase for other groups of industrial as well as white-collar workers). The more far-reaching resolution on cadre policy aimed to upgrade the qualifications for leading positions—political reliability, professional competence, and leadership ability—outlined in a 1967 Politburo directive. It called for better political preparation, noting that 80.5 percent of the party apparat, 42 percent of the state apparat, 51 percent of economic leaders, and 42 percent of cooperative leaders had already benefited from political education. General education was also stressed. Here only 58 percent of the party apparat, but nearly 88 percent of the central apparat, had postsecondary credentials, compared to 89 percent in state administration, 65 percent in state industrial management, and 28 percent in cooperative management.

The resolution went on to deplore negative tendencies in all spheres of leadership, such as neglect of political and social duties, indifference to the views of the workers, failure to combat bourgeois and Western trends, the pursuit of material gain and of narrow group interests, and the abuse of power. The eligibility of nonmembers for all nonparty offices was reaffirmed, but this was accompanied by a directive to improve the education of physical workers and their access to positions of leadership. The resolution also recommended that the party's cadre lists (i.e., its authority to appoint) be reviewed and, if necessary, reduced.[19] In sum, the party confirmed the decentralization of authority and division of labor inherent in the new version of socialist democracy while stressing the need to upgrade political and professional standards and to extirpate abuses.

The HSWP was becoming increasingly concerned with the ideological and political necessity of reaffirming the leading role of the working class and restoring its confidence in the party and the NEM. This concern was given full expression at the important enlarged plenum of the Central Committee on 19 and 20 March 1974. The resolution issuing from the meeting called for improvement in the ratio of workers in party membership and leadership and for more workers "experienced in public life to assume systematically more leading posts in our society"; for the development of shop-floor democracy; for a "deliberate effort to develop the most competent workers into public figures whose word carries weight"; and for a rise in the workers' standard of living and education.[20]

**The Eleventh Congress.**  Confirmation of the working class' preeminence was not only a response to domestic pressures but also a corollary of the general ideological retrenchment in the Soviet bloc during the era of professed East-West detente. These themes, and the new economic crisis induced by worldwide inflation and an unfavorable alteration in the terms of trade with the Soviet Union, dominated the eleventh congress of the HSWP, held from 17 to 22 March 1975.[21] The congress was attended by 843 HSWP delegates; the foreign visitors included Brezhnev and the leaders of the Bulgarian, Czechoslovak, East German, and Polish parties. In his general report at the opening session, Kádár appealed for greater ideological unity of all citizens in the construction of socialism; in particular, he stressed the role of enterprise democracy and the need for greater worker involvement in decision making. The NEM had proven itself, he said, but the state had to provide central direction and supervision; group and individual interests were useful incentives but had to remain subordinated to the national interest. Hungary had to exert the utmost effort to cope with the effects of external inflation by raising productivity and adjusting its price system. Kádár anticipated an exchange of party membership cards to heighten ideological and functional unity. He warned that in the social sciences and the cultural and educational spheres more positive action had to be taken against non-Marxist views and in favor of "socialist consciousness." The following day, Brezhnev delivered an address full of unstinting praise for Kádár and his party and calling for even closer ideological, cultural, scientific, and economic cooperation between Hungary and the Soviet Union.

The economic difficulties inspired Prime Minister Fock to exercise a self-criticism that foreshadowed his fall: "In the eight years that I have been premier we have not made any great headway in getting everyone to realize his responsibility for the economy as a whole." The party secretary in charge of economic policy, Károly Németh, lamented that "the intent of central guidance [was] not effectively translated into practice at all levels and in every respect." The application of democratic centralism to economic affairs meant the strengthening of both central direction and local independence. Németh accordingly underscored the persistent weaknesses in phasing out unprofitable production, as well as in technological modernization, manpower management, and labor discipline.

Among the final acts of the congress were the unanimous approval of a program declaration, an anodyne statement of the general tasks for the transformation of socialism into communism over the next fifteen to twenty years, and a resolution setting out the more specific tasks for the next five years. Confirming the alliance policy, the resolution stated that in the building of socialism "social cooperation, which embraces all progressive and creative forces of the Hungarian population, party members and nonparty people alike, the various nationalities and generations, atheists and believers, is being permeated with a socialist content." It also designated enterprise democracy as a major party objective—a "fundamental part of socialist democracy" that provided for worker participation in management, for a greater sense of responsibility on the part of the workers, and for improved productivity. "The enterprise party organizations are responsible for consistently enforcing enterprise democracy, a task in which their main support is the trade union." The task was to be achieved by the inclusion of physical workers in managerial councils and committees, by internal systems of management that better informed workers of the enterprise's operation, and by the discussion of essential matters in workers' assemblies. Enterprise democracy, warned the union leader and Politburo member Sándor Gáspár, was not a formality or periodic consultation but daily contact with the workers.

The various organizational, economic, and cultural aspects of the eleventh congress will be examined below. Árpád Pullai, a former Rákosiite who had been first secretary of the KISZ, said of the resolution: "Fundamentally, it merely calls for more consistent pursuit of past political practice." The congress, however, did indicate a certain shift in emphasis toward a less liberal orthodoxy.[22] This was noticeable in the demands for tighter central control of economic management, for stronger leadership by the party and greater worker participation, and for vigilance against deviations in ideology and culture. The reasons were a mixture of economic necessity and Soviet-inspired ideological consolidation. During the congress Kádár took the unusual initiative of meeting informally with a group of scientists and other intellectuals, including nonparty members, who were attending as delegates or guests. To these he reassuringly expressed his gratitude for their political understanding and cooperation. For the Hungarian public, however, the most important outcome of the congress was the retention at the helm of Kádár, who was reportedly in poor health and considering resignation.

To sum up this broad outline of the evolution of party policy since 1962: the dual objectives of economic modernization and "socialist democracy" were pursued with remarkable consistency by the Kádár leadership, but the context was an external policy of faithful concurrence with the Soviet Union's positions in international and interparty relations. Economic decentralization had engendered positive results as well as new inefficiencies and inequities. These shortcomings invited continuous tinkering with the NEM. Together with the negative external economic developments, they imposed a certain recentralization of control during 1974/75. However, as the economic crisis worsened, the

Central Committee passed resolutions in October 1977 and April 1978 that indicated the regime's steadfast commitment to the basic principles of the NEM.

Manipulation of the NEM was inspired in part by ideological reconsiderations of its impact on the welfare and political status of the industrial working class. The enhancement of socialist democracy consisted of a variety of devolutionary measures and of a certain flexibility in cultural policy. The limitations imposed on this liberalization by the party's monopolistic position, by the integrity of the dominant ideology, and by the ideological retrenchment of the Soviet bloc became more palpable in the mid-1970s. Kádár's original assumption, that once the orthodox step of collectivizing agriculture had been taken, innovation in the economic structure to improve productivity would have Moscow's blessing, remained valid. However, the Soviet Union would not entertain significant alteration in the ideological and political spheres, and the secularizing impact of the NEM inspired misgivings in Moscow as well as among the more orthodox elements in the HSWP.[23]

Kádár himself has remained true to a pragmatic centrist orientation that derived as much from his own political career as from the domestic and external milieu of the postrevolution period. He had been both persecutor and victim in Rákosi's purges. The latter experience, after the harsh repression of the restoration phase, probably inspired him to avoid Rákosi's terroristic methods. Kádár's experience in the days of illegality of collaboration with other leftist and Populist elements, his limited capacity for, and interest in theoretical abstractions, and an ingrained simplicity of habit and demeanor all facilitated his pursuit of a modus vivendi with the noncommunist majority of Hungarian society.[24] As he matured at the helm of the party, he developed an aptitude for trimming his sails to the prevailing Soviet and domestic winds without losing the bearings of his reform program.

## PARTY LEADERSHIP AND ORGANIZATION

Although there has been a high degree of continuity in personnel at the apex of the party, the shifts in emphasis from rapid reform to retrenchment and consolidation have been reflected in a number of changes in leadership.

At the ninth congress in 1965, Apró, Biszku, Fehér, Fock, Gáspár, Kádár, Kállai, Komócsin, Nemes, Nyers, and Szirmai were elected to the Politburo, and Biszku, Lajos Cseterki, Kádár, Komócsin, Nyers, and Pullai to the Secretariat. In April 1967, as the NEM was about to be launched, Fock, who had been one of its most fervent and experienced advocates, was appointed to the premiership in place of the genial but lazy Kállai. With the reform in full swing, the tenth congress in 1970 saw the demotion of the aging Szirmai back to his old agitprop job, and the addition of Aczél, Benke, and Károly Németh to the Politburo. Aczél had already been appointed to the Secretariat in 1967, where he was joined by Miklós Óvári, a veteran of the Central Committee's agitprop department. Aczél, a graduate of the illegal movement and a victim of Rákosi's purges, had served as deputy minister of culture and became identified with the new, more flexible cultural policy.

As the economic and social shortcomings of the NEM began to materialize, the Central Committee announced a personnel shuffle at its November 1973 meeting. Nyers was dismissed from the Secretariat and demoted to director of the Institute of Economics of the Academy of Sciences. The move was due as much to his proprietary and enthusiastic advocacy of the NEM as to official dissatisfaction with any major aspect of the system. Aczél, whose identification in the West with cultural liberalism had become an embarrassment, was also removed from the Secretariat, but he retained much of his influence over culture and ideology in his new post of deputy premier. Both men remained members of the Politburo. Newly appointed to the Secretariat were Németh and Imre Győri. The former, a peasant's son and onetime butcher's apprentice, had joined the party in 1945, was elected to the Central Committee in 1957, and became first secretary of the Budapest party committee in 1965. In 1970 he rose to the Politburo and with his new promotion took over Nyers's supervision of economic policy. Gyori had been first secretary of the Csongrád County party committee.

Following the Central Committee plenum, the party launched a major propaganda effort to dispel speculation, notably in the Western press, that these personnel changes and the concurrent stress on the leading role of the industrial working class indicated a shift away from economic and cultural liberalization. Komócsin wrote in *Népszabadság* that the main lines of the party's policy remained unchanged, but he warned against a dogmatic adherence to established practice: "It is precisely to safeguard our correct principles and system of economic management that we must improve our practical work without delay." He praised the other economic management systems in the Soviet sphere —their results, he said, "do not lag in any way behind our successes"—and deplored undue pride in the superiority of the NEM.[25]

At the eleventh congress four new members—György Lázár, László Maróthy, István Sarlós, and Óvári—were elected to the Politburo to fill the vacancies created by the death of Komócsin and the dismissal of Nyers, Fehér, and Kállai. Nyers was thus totally excluded from the political arena. Fehér had been closely identified with the modernization of agriculture, but he was in ill health and had earlier resigned as deputy premier. Kállai remained in the largely ceremonial job of president of the Patriotic People's Front. Among the new Politburo members, Sarlós was slated to represent the Patriotic People's Front, of which he was secretary-general, at a time when the party's alliance policy required that the front be reinvigorated. Originally a skilled worker and a social democrat, Sarlós became a literature professor and, in 1970, editor in chief of *Népszabadság* and a member of the Central Committee. The elevation of the thirty-three-year-old Maróthy, who had become first secretary of the KISZ and a Central Committee member only two years earlier, reflected the party's concern with the political mobilization of youth. Lázár, who joined the party in 1945, was a technocrat who had recently become deputy premier, chairman of the State Planning Committee, chairman of the National Planning Office, and permanent representative to Comecon in 1973. Also at the time of the Congress, the Secretariat gained an additional member in András Gyenes, a onetime people's college administrator who was also a former ambassador to East Germany and deputy foreign minister and had served as an assistant to Imre Nagy. He would soon assume Komócsin's responsibilities for foreign and interparty affairs.

Following Fock's self-criticism at the eleventh congress, the Central Committee on 15 May 1975, approved his replacement as prime minister by György Lázár. Then, on 2 July, the Central Committee's enlarged plenum took the unusual step of changing the Politburo's membership between congresses by adding István Huszár, a deputy premier, and Losonczi to the roster; the latter was the first head of state since 1952 to sit on the Politburo. In October 1976 the Central Committee dismissed the authoritarian but otherwise inconsequential Pullai from the Secretariat and replaced him with Sándor Borbély, a graduate of the Soviet party academy.

The reshuffle effected at the Central Committee's April 1978 plenum caused a sensation, for it included the dismissal of Biszku from the Secretariat. A major figure in the reconstruction of the party after the revolution, the relatively young Biszku (he was fifty-seven to Kádár's sixty-six) had acquired wide powers, being responsible for both the party apparat and the military and security forces. Generally regarded as Kádár's deputy, he was an unpopular leader with a reputation for authoritarianism and for an increasingly critical view of the economic reform. These flaws, and a possible ambition to succeed Kádár, contributed to his eclipse. In the redistribution of powers, Németh was given responsibility for the apparat, while two new secretaries, Ferenc Havasi (a reformist technocrat and former deputy premier) and Mihály Korom (formerly minister of interior) were given, respectively, economic policy and the armed forces.

The party leadership in mid-1978 was therefore a heterodox collection of party veterans and postwar adherents, of conservative ideologues and younger reformers. The Politburo had fifteen members, with an average age of 58: Kádár, Aczél, Apró, Benke, Biszku, Fock, Gáspár, Huszár, Lázár, Losonczi, Maróthy, Nemes, Németh, Óvári, and Sarlós. Seven of them (Kádár, Aczél, Apró, Benke, Biszku, Gáspár, and Nemes) had joined the party in illegality. The Secretariat included Kádár as first secretary, Németh as his apparently like-minded deputy, and Óvári, as well as Borbély, Gyenes, Győri, Havasi, and Korom. Calculations of power can only be speculative, but the distribution of other responsibilities offered a certain indication of spheres of authority. Óvári was chairman of the agitprop committee and of the working collective for cultural policy. Of the other Politburo members, Benke was editor of *Társadalmi Szemle* and exerted a conservative influence on ideological and cultural affairs, while Gáspár, in his capacity as president of the National Council of Trade Unions, was a forceful advocate of the industrial working class's political and economic interests. Sarlós and Maróthy represented two other mass organizations, the Patriotic People's Front and the KISZ. Premier Lázár and Deputy Premier Huszár were reform-minded economic experts. The chairman of the presidential council, Losonczi, was also a remote link with agrarian interests. The veterans Apró and Nemes were, respectively, president of the national assembly (a largely ceremonial position) and editor in chief of *Népszabadság*.

Since the revolution, no cohesive factional opposition had emerged within the leadership against Kádár's line. He had shown consummate skill in disarming both reformers and conservatives with a combination of persuasion and apparent concessions to both tendencies; at the same time, he had deftly removed from the leadership embarrassing critics and power-seekers at both extremes. By these tactics Kádár had succeeded in preserving his centrist policies, but he had failed to groom an obvious successor as he approached the ineluctable end of his tenure. With Biszku's unexpected demotion, speculation focused on Németh as well as some dark horses like Gáspár and Korom. It seemed clear that whoever inherited Kádár's mantle would inevitably lack his established domestic and international prestige and therefore would likely be even more susceptible to Soviet influence.

**The Structure of Authority.** Although the top leadership appeared to be more collegial than in Rákosi's day, its recruitment and deliberations were cloaked in secrecy. Changes in personnel as well as in policy remained, it is safe to assume, subject to the approval of the Kremlin. The Politburo generally met twice a month and was the supreme executive organ of the party. A partly overlapping circle of power encompassed the eight secretaries who were the key executive officers of the HSWP, in charge of the Secretariat's permanent staff. Located in the "white house," the party headquarters near the parliament building, the Secretariat's departments covered all major areas, including the administration of the party and mass organizations; agitprop; science, education, and culture; foreign and interparty affairs; economic policy; industry, agriculture, and transportation; and state administration. They were responsible for both policy formulation and implementation, and many of the Secretariat's officers held related government posts. The Secretariat performed the critical liaison function with respect to the party and state authorities of the Soviet Union. The degree of party control varied with the sphere of state activity, being at its highest in security and foreign policy. As a former senior diplomat recalls of the early 1960s: "Even on less important questions decisions were not made in the Foreign Ministry. The party headquarters was the center of decision-making, and [foreign minister János] Péter would be invited there only as a guest or as an adviser."[26] Such intimate links are of course inevitable in a one-party system whatever the official claims of a division of labor.

At the base of the party's pyramidal structure reposed, in 1977, 24,450 primary organizations, of which 7,066 were active in industry and construction, 4,215 in agriculture, 1,473 in transportation, and 1,216 in commerce. At the next level there were 97 district party committees and 104 city and Budapest district party committees. County party committees, together with the Budapest party committee, numbered 24. The committee and secretary (or secretaries) were elected at each level. Lower units elected delegates to the next higher level, and conferences of county delegates elected participants in the quinquennial party congress, which was the ultimate legislative body. The 843 delegates to the eleventh party congress elected the 125-member Central Committee and the 25-member Central Control Committee. The Central Committee, in turn, elected the Politburo, the secretaries, and the Secretariat department heads. It also elected its own committees for economic policy, agitprop, and youth, the first two being important organs in the development and implementation of guidelines. Also under the authority of the Central Committee were the political academy, the social science institute, the institute of party history, and the principal publications: Népszabadság, the official party newspaper, with a circulation of 750,000; the ideological monthly Társadalmi Szemle, circulation 40,700; and the organizational monthly Pártélet (Party Life), circulation 130,000. In the real world of intraparty democracy, elections for the leading organs generally took the form of ratification of Politburo nominations.

The Central Committee met at least four times a year, normally for two days. It was charged with monitoring the implementation of congressional resolutions and seldom presented a challenge to the policies of the leadership. It routinely heard reports on international affairs and on two or three other current policy issues, and its resolutions were reported in the media. A preponderant number of Central Committee members held key positions of power elsewhere, including thirty-nine in government and in state and local administration, seventeen in central party organizations, and fourteen in trade union and other mass organizations; also included were a few token full-time workers and intellectuals.[27]

Both the alliance policy's goal of socialist democracy and the decentralizing thrust of the NEM led to a certain devolution of authority from the party to state and local administration, to sectoral organizations, and to enterprises, with a consequent penetration of nonparty talent into positions of responsibility. Nevertheless, direct and indirect party control continued to pervade the Hungarian political system. Senior party members held all significant posts in government and in mass organizations. Moreover, as reported by Pullai in November 1973, the party retained full cadre authority (also known as *nomenklatura*) over 90,000 posts and an advisory right, which was generally respected, over a further 350,000 leading positions.[28] In the 1971–75 national assembly, 71 percent of deputies were party members; so were 46.9 percent of local and municipal council members, 90 percent of commissioned police officers, and 81 percent of the participants in the paramilitary Workers' Militia. In the People's Control Commissions 70 percent of the salaried commissioners are HSWP members.

**Party Life.** Bare statistics like those just quoted offer no assurance of the ideological commitment and political activity of party members, and indeed these qualitative issues have perennially exercised the leadership. Over the years, alterations in the party statutes and other internal measures have aimed to democratize party life with two objects in mind: to guarantee that the Rákosi style of leadership will not reoccur; and to sustain the unity and dedication of party members at a time when Kádár's reforms were inducing a certain sense of remoteness and irrelevance. The Central Control Commission, the party's internal watchdog, was made independent of the Central Committee at the eighth congress, and at the ninth congress, in 1966, it acquired additional responsibilities by assuming the functions of the Central Review Committee. Other changes effected at the latter congress served both to enhance democracy and to partially alleviate party functionaries' apprehensions at the growing number and authority of nonparty officials. Not only the principal secretary but all party leaders at all levels were henceforth to be elected by secret ballot; nominating committees were to be elected in advance, and were to accept all suggestions for candidacy from the rank and file. Officials of state, cooperative, and mass organizations were required to deliver performance reports to their local party organ, which also retained an advisory right over important appointments.

In general, party members have been exhorted to improve their expertise and political education; to become intimately involved in local affairs; to provide realistic appraisals of local conditions to higher levels; to limit their interference to persuasion; and, above all, to set a high moral and ideological example. They are constantly urged to exploit the democratic possibilities of party life, to canvass widely for the best candidates for party posts and take into account local public opinion in the process, and to formulate alternative policy proposals. In 1970 membership meetings without a fixed agenda were introduced and local party secretaries were instructed to engage in consultations in preparing their reports to the membership and to report in concrete terms rather than in generalities. The tenth congress again amended the statutes so that party leaders were required to reply to questions at the forum at which they were raised, and to provide further protection to members against discrimination and retaliation for criticism.[29] The congresses are the ultimate demonstration of intraparty democracy, and in the elaborate party-wide preparations for the eleventh congress the draft guidelines and revised statutes were reportedly debated by some 200,000 party members at meetings of primary organizations. Of the 4,000 proposals for modification that reached the Central Committee, more than 100 were incorporated in the final drafts. Whatever real influence ordinary party members may have acquired through the much-touted democratization of life, the congresses remain essentially ritualistic displays of unanimity.

Recurring central appeals for activization of the party's rank and file indicate the difficulty in overcoming both the Rákosi legacy of centralism without democracy and the new sense of alienation in lower party bodies. The original objective of democratization was not only to invigorate the mass membership into active support for the reforms (and, not incidentally, to reduce the power of the many dogmatic old functionaries), but also to display the party's permanent commitment to the alliance policy. Said Béla Biszku in a lecture at the party's political academy in March 1969:

> The question is posed whether, under a one-party system, there are institutional guarantees of the continuous development of democracy in our social life and the prevention of abuses of power. Although we have done a great deal in this area during the past decade, our tasks will be even greater in the future. Nevertheless, I believe that the supreme guarantee has already been given—namely, the Party itself, which has never forgotten the lessons of 1956 and which, in its inner life, incessantly fosters democracy. We are doing everything to prevent any group from ever again monopolizing the Party and the socialist system and abusing power.[30]

The various economic and political reforms have affected the party's army of functionaries in two ways. Veterans of the movement, often ill-educated and jealous of the new secular elite's expertise and authority, have retreated into doctrinaire hostility to such ostensibly liberal measures as the official endorsement of private plots. At the same time, many members have succumbed to the general embourgeoisement induced by the economic reforms and have indulged in the corrupt practices of "money-grubbing" and influence-peddling that are so regularly denounced.

The chairman of the Central Control Committee, János Brutyó, reported to the eleventh congress that since the previous congress 3.9 percent of the membership (29,181) had been disciplined and 7,133 expelled. (In addition, 7,478 had resigned their membership and another 15,474 memberships had been canceled.) He singled out cases of abuse of power and laxity, and deplored the incidence of retaliation for justified criticism. He also called for an improvement in supervision at all party levels to protect members from the deplorable views and habits that seeped in from the society at large and that, he said, members ought to be fighting to eradicate in the first place. In addition to the existing provisions for resignation, cancellation for nonpayment of dues, and expulsion, the amended party statutes allowed for release of a member on the initiative of the primary organization. This innovation aimed to facilitate the removal of unenthusiastic party members.[31]

The diffusion of authority and the stress on secular expertise have evidently induced a measure of alienation and apathy. As one party analyst has observed: "The decline in the political content of party life, . . . the ebbing of the critical spirit, the fading away of responsibility hinder the operation of democratic centralism, the basic rule of party life. Inevitably this gives rise to liberalism and arbitrary interpretations in the implementation of party decisions."[32] Religious practice, an unpardonable deviation for purveyors of an atheistic dogma, has also come under censure for compromising the purity of socialist commitment and setting a bad example. A survey in Tolna County showed that families of party members—frequently at the instigation of grandparents—were in the habit of participating in religious ceremonies such as baptism, confirmation, weddings, and funerals. Activists were therefore instructed to combat such temptation and to advise the party if participation was unavoidable.[33]

The party offers its members a variety of programs in political education, ranging from brief introductory courses to one- and two-year courses administered by the political college. The latter provides a more sophisticated ideological preparation for positions of leadership. Before 1968 students were selected by district party committees, but since then they have been free to apply individually for admission.[34] The most promising candidates are sent to Soviet party schools for further training. Both members and nonmembers are given incentives to take advantage of the evening programs offered by the University of Marxism-Leninism, and in 1974 an Evening College of Marxism-Leninism was established for the benefit of workers who lacked the educational credentials for normal postsecondary education.[35] As the Kádár regime became consolidated, growing numbers of not only industrial workers but also middle-class technocrats were drawn to membership. Since the proportion of ideological communists in the population is at most 2 percent, it is safe to assume that most new members were motivated more by social pressure, a realistic calculation of career advancement (despite the alliance policy's relative de-emphasis of party membership), and the lure of participation in policy making, than by philosophical conviction.[36] Of course, more than lip service to Marxism-Leninism is expected of those who aspire to higher party office, but for the rest of the population and of the party membership ideology is an inconsequential and expendable commodity.

It was precisely this creeping ideological relativism and sense of irrelevance that prompted the party-card exchange anticipated by the eleventh congress. Introduced cautiously as merely an opportunity for "sincere conversations and comradely exchanges of views," the card exchange was the first major cleansing operation since the early restoration period.[37] Approved by the Central Committee in October 1975, it was implemented during 1976, with an interim report presented by Pullai shortly before his removal from the Secretariat. The final statistics indicated that 20,760 members, 2.7 percent of the total membership, were released from the party, with 40 percent of the basic organizations being affected. More than half resigned their membership voluntarily, and allegedly only 34 of these did so for political reasons. Of those who were expelled, 64 appealed the ruling. An additional 1 percent of the membership was put on probation for 6 to 12 months, and this led to additional expulsions and resignations.

The party took pains to stress that departure from its ranks carried no further negative consequences. In his report to the Central Committee, Borbély affirmed that the card exchange had in no way transgressed the authority of party organizations or the rights of individual members. Some 150,000 activists had conducted "comradely interviews" with the entire membership, and the process had served not only to weed out unsuitable elements but also to survey opinion within the party. Among the issues raised were the need to make leaders answerable for their actions. Borbély recognized that more suitable positions would have to be found for incompetent leaders, while the dictatorial and corrupt would have to be disciplined. He claimed that the card exchange had both strengthened party unity and confirmed the existence of collective leadership and intraparty democracy. It had also reflected a spirit of democratic debate that was healthy as long as members recognized they were bound to accept and implement the ultimate decision of the majority, i.e., follow the Leninist principle of democratic centralism. The survey confirmed the wisdom of making the party's rulings applicable not to the mass organizations as such, but only to party members serving within the latter. The growing responsibility of membership was illustrated by the fact that 85 percent of members were charged with accountable party tasks.

Borbély reported that two-thirds of the departed members were physical workers, that a majority were members of some seniority, and that many had joined the party as early as 1945. In its recruitment the party had to follow the prescription of the eleventh congress for an increase in the proportion of physical workers, particularly from the large industrial plants. However, observed Borbély, in order to preserve the distinction between the vanguard party and the working masses, the emphasis had to be on quality and not on massive recruitment. It was not sufficient for candidates to be in general agreement with party policy; they had to be exemplary in their ideological conviction and in their public and private life. Casual and careerist members were not acceptable, and for this reason the party adhered to the principle that competent nonmembers could hold all offices outside of the party itself.

Dealing with other suggestions and complaints, Borbély dismissed the view, advanced by the party committees of Budapest and two counties, that members elected to party bodies did not receive adequate moral and material reward. Another recommendation endorsed by all the county party committees called for greater recognition of those veterans who had joined in 1944/45. Borbély admitted that pre-1944 members did receive special benefits, but he argued that this was warranted by their struggles under conditions of illegality; to similarly favor the 10 percent of members who joined immediately upon liberation and worked in less difficult circumstances would be inappropriate. He received more favorably the complaint that intellectuals and white-collar workers were often the subject of discrimination and urged that mechanical application of the recruitment guidelines against these groups be avoided.[38]

The Central Committee resolution on the lessons of the card exchange recommended inter alia that party members be given more opportunities to air their views and that the basic organizations devote greater attention to matters of immediate public concern. A subsequent round-table discussion on admission policy organized by *Népszabadság* produced confirmation of the undesirability of "quotas" favoring industrial workers. It also indicated that, at least in student circles, candidates for party membership were regarded by others as careerists.[39] The party daily had concluded earlier that the exchange did not constitute a purge, and indeed the operation was a pale reflection of the pogroms of the Rákosi era. It did testify, however, to the leadership's concern with the ideological homogeneity and political vigor of the rank and file at a time when the distinction between vanguard party and state administration was becoming blurred in the pursuit of modernization. Reporting to the Central Committee in October 1976 on ideology and education in the HSWP, Győri stressed the dangers of both right and left distortions and invited further study of the "nature of state power," on the one hand, and of proletarian internationalism, on the other. The latter stood in contradistinction to anticommunism and "all varieties of anti-Sovietism."[40] (For the debate on Eurocommunism, see below.) In short, the Hungarian party, like its sisters, remained essentially a conveyor-belt for information up and orders down. Evidently it was proving difficult to adjust this traditional model to the requisites of modernization and socialist democracy while retaining internal discipline and revolutionary commitment.

## PARTY AND SOCIETY

Statistics published on the occasion of the eleventh congress gave the generational, occupational, and educational profile of Kádár's party, whose membership on 1 January 1975 stood at 754,353 out of a population of 10,509,000.

(Candidate membership had been abolished at the ninth congress in 1966.) In the 4.5 years between the tenth and eleventh congresses the membership had grown by 91,956, or 13.9 percent. The number of veterans was dwindling inexorably: only 8,212 dated their adherence to before the country's liberation in April 1945, and 67 percent had become members after the 1956 revolution. By current occupation the membership was composed of 45.5 percent physical workers (including collective farmers), 6.1 percent "immediate supervisors of production," 40 percent intellectual workers, and 8.4 percent dependents and others. By original occupation 59.2 percent were workers, 13 percent peasants, 8.9 percent intellectual workers, 16.3 percent white-collar employees, and 2.6 percent others. The latter distribution corresponds fairly closely to the social profile of the population at large but is a rather meaningless categorization, since even Kádár is identified as a onetime worker.

In fact, the leadership has professed alarm at the low proportion of industrial workers, women (now 26.5 percent), and especially peasants in the membership. In the early years of the reform, between 1967 and 1971, the courting of middle-class talent resulted in a 4.5 percent decline in the proportion of physical workers. There followed a corrective policy inspired by ideologically motivated criticism of the relative weakening of working-class power. Accordingly, of the recruits since the tenth congress, 54.2 percent were physical workers, 33.5 percent intellectual workers, and 12.3 percent in other categories; 32 percent were women. Of the 1975 membership, 55.4 percent had up to 8 years of schooling, 33.8 percent possessed secondary school diplomas, and 10.8 percent had some postsecondary credentials. The expulsions and resignations resulting from the 1976 card exchange were largely balanced by the intake of 27,620 new members, with the result that the overall membership at year's end stood at 765,566.[41]

**The Communist Youth League.**  The party has devoted great energy to secure the ideological loyalty and active cooperation of the younger generations through its mass organization, the KISZ. In the mid-1970s the KISZ had over 800,000 members in 25,600 basic organizations. Membership was limited to the 14–28 age group, although the KISZ was also responsible for the Úttörok (Young Pioneers), which included children under 14 years of age. Hungarian surveys have shown remarkable passive resistance among young people to indoctrination, and the apparent ineffectiveness of the KISZ has prompted a series of remedial measures.[42] A Politburo resolution in November 1973 criticized the inadequacy of ideological education among young persons as reflected in the persistence of patriotic, Western-oriented, and religious sentiments at the expense of appreciation for the achievements of socialism and friendship for other socialist states. Party organizations were therefore instructed to assign better qualified activists to work with the KISZ. At the April 1974 meeting of the KISZ Central Committee it was resolved to increase the activity and discipline of the basic organizations with two devices: a test of political and practical knowledge before admission, and an annual exchange of membership cards to weed out undesirable members.[43]

The KISZ was also charged with the organization of "youth parliaments" during 1974/75 in places of work and educational institutions. These meetings were intended to be a forum for discussions on the implementation of the 1971 Youth Law and on the problems and responsibilities of young people. The outcome did not suggest that they were a particularly effective mobilizing technique. The popularity of rock music and the proliferation of independent youth clubs (deplored by the authorities as uncontrolled purveyors of Western fads and attitudes) prompted official measures to impose central direction and political indoctrination.[44] The media meanwhile voiced recurring criticism of the opulent way of life of the children of the "new class." Another KISZ function was to administer voluntary summer labor camps. During 1975 these had over 25,000 young people working on agricultural, industrial, and construction projects. The implicit political criteria for future educational opportunities are, it seems, a powerful incentive to volunteer.

The ninth KISZ congress, convened from 8 to 11 May 1976, was attended by 907 delegates. In his keynote address, Maróthy called for more participation of youth in socialist work competition and stressed the need for better ideological and educational work. At the same time, he recognized that it was impossible to "inoculate our youth against the petty-bourgeois and bourgeois ideologies and an idealistic world outlook," and identified a fundamental task of the KISZ as the preparation of members for admission to the HSWP.* Kádár also addressed the congress, expounding on general economic problems, in the context of which he noted that while more intensive and rational use of manpower was imperative, this was not tantamount to a return to the days of "sheer brute force." He disagreed, moreover, with suggestions that religious youths and those involved with private plot farming ought to be barred from the KISZ.[45] It is clear from such statements that the party faces a dilemma in wishing both to open wide the doors of the KISZ and to strengthen the organization's political function. While only a minority of working youths bother to join the KISZ, most postsecondary students are members. The membership profile thus suggests that belonging to the KISZ is an asset for access to higher education and the more desirable careers. Most young people, however, join for the nonpolitical activities, and remain largely indifferent to political indoctrination.[46]

---

*At that time 7.5 percent of KISZ members also belonged to the party, where the minimum age was eighteen.

**Socialist Democracy.** In a political system where a single party reigns unchallenged, the formal institutions of state administration are necessarily its intimate servants. Where accountability and alternative policies are not left to the free contestation of pluralistic politics, the task of reconciling central direction with popular participation falls upon the one party, which is thereby placed in the difficult position of having to seek legitimacy without putting its supremacy to the test of popular choice.

The Kádár regime's panacea has been to effect a certain delineation of the implementing functions of party and state, reserving for the former the power of initiating policy, and to try to enhance the responsiveness and accountability of both party and government. Kádár recognized early that the task of economic modernization could not be assumed by the party alone, but would require a division of labor and the activation of broad social strata. Socialist democracy, he told the ninth congress in November 1966, meant the "better allocation of spheres of authority." On the same occasion he observed that for "historical reasons" the multiparty system had disappeared forever from the Hungarian scene.[47] The party would concentrate on developing the basic principles and general policies, but would not seek to duplicate the elaborating and implementing work of the state institutions. In practice, the promotion of Kádár's socialist democracy and the requisites of efficient administration have resulted in significant modifications in the sphere of state authority. The main thrust has been to give greater scope to elected bodies, and to recruit expert talent into the administrative service regardless of party membership. In recent times, however, the political education of cadres has received renewed emphasis.

When the constitution was amended in 1972, the revision was presented as less a political program (the case with the 1949 version) than a reflection of achievements.[48] The final version must await the day when Hungary can be proclaimed a "socialist republic"; the 1972 constitution states that Hungary is only a people's republic. The new preamble still pays tribute to the Soviet liberators but also takes a longer historical perspective in referring to a millennium of the people's struggle. The earlier discrimination between "working people" and other citizens is abandoned; all are now entitled to participate in public affairs. The "Marxist-Leninist party of the working class is the leading force in society," and the role of mass movements and trade unions in the building of socialism also receives formal recognition. The equal ranking of state and cooperative ownership is asserted, and private producers are recognized though they "must not violate collective interests."

**Parliamentary Government.** Hungary has a unicameral system of government. The constitution describes the national assembly as the "supreme organ of the representation of the people" and the "guarantor of the constitutional order of society." A clear definition of the distinct spheres of legislative authority of the Presidential Council (21 members), the Council of Ministers (23 members), and the national assembly (352 deputies) is still lacking. Budget approval and basic rules on citizens' rights and obligations are formally the prerogative of parliament, and all three bodies have the right to initiate legislation. In practice, however, most rules take the form of presidential or ministerial decrees, and all legislative proposals issue from the same sources.

The assembly meets at least twice a year, for some ten days in all. Its standing committees have become more active in the preparation of certain draft bills, and there is occasional debate in plenary session on matters of detail, but parliament remains essentially a rubber stamp for party policy. It has been difficult to inspire public confidence in deputies whose tasks are so perfunctory. In October 1972 the council of ministers issued directives enjoining members of parliament to keep in contact with their constituents and to investigate their complaints; at the same time, it ordered the state administration to respond promptly to the deputies' enquiries.[49] On the other hand, the regime has taken pains to canvass opinion and generate support for its policies. For instance, two ministerial directives in late 1975, one imposing a freeze on white-collar hiring, and another proposing that schoolchildren once again be classified by social origin, aroused a great deal of public debate, and the latter measure was prudently withdrawn. A government agency conducts public opinion surveys (on sensitive issues the results are not published), and the public is usually prepared well in advance for the implementation of potentially unpopular measures such as price increases.

Since 1966 the electoral law has provided for single-member parliamentary constituencies; it has also permitted multiple candidacies. In practice, the party controls the electoral process through the Patriotic People's Front. Despite a 1971 law that suspended the front's exclusive screening authority, candidacies opposed to the common program are unthinkable, and voters are reminded that they are choosing not between policies but between the personal qualities of candidates. The handful of multiple candidacies that have materialized in the last three general elections (nine in 1967, forty-nine in 1971, and thirty-four in 1975) hardly represent a pluralistic revolution. A few of these were indeed spontaneous, but behind the facade of the Patriotic People's Front the party organizations are in fact responsible for making the proper nominations and for ensuring that party members attend the nomination meetings and make the right choice.[50] The party has cautioned the public against assuming that multiple candidacies are intrinsically desirable, and the risks of spontaneity will foreseeably limit the extension or even sustained application of this modest experiment in political competition.

Recent elections consequently exhibit the same artificial image of unanimity that characterized the discredited Rákosi system. In the 1975 general elections 0.4 percent of valid votes were cast against the Patriotic People's Front, and

299 candidates received over 99 percent of the votes. The party and state apparats accounted for 99 seats, with the rest broadly distributed across the occupational spectrum.[51] (In 1975 a constitutional amendment extended the parliamentary term from 4 to 5 years to make it coincide with the five-year plans and the quinquennial party congresses.) In a 1963 speech before the national assembly Kádár allowed: "In realistically considering the results of the elections, we should admit that a number of electors who voted for the people's front candidates did not have complete confidence in us and voted for the official lists only to avoid the worst."[52] While Kádár's popularity undoubtedly grew over the years, the elections by their very nature could offer neither proof nor refutation.

The leadership of party and government was split in 1958 (Prime Minister Münnich), reunited in 1961, and separated again since 1965 (prime ministers Kállai, Fock, and Lázár), with each premier being also a member of the Politburo. The initiative for appointment and dismissal of government leaders, formally vested in the presidential council, lies with the party. Of the 1975 cabinet three were Politburo members, nineteen were in the Central Committee, and only seven were elected members of parliament.

**The Patriotic People's Front.**   The alliance policy's principal institutional symbol is the Patriotic People's Front, which in the mid-1970s possessed a network of some 4,000 committees with 112,400 members. The front's tasks are to organize elections, to raise public consciousness of certain problems, e.g., the need for environmental protection, and to mobilize individual and group action in support of state and council measures by such devices as unpaid "social work." A related agency is the National Peace Council, which purports to be a broadly representative exponent of the party's line on international issues.

Preparations for the front's sixth congress in 1976 began with the election of local committees and the selection of delegates. This process provided for the airing of local problems, notably the difficulties of private plot farming and the inadequacy of facilities and services in the smaller villages. Concurrently, special national minority conferences were held to demonstrate the HSWP's policy of exemplary treatment of these groups. Official statistics showed 175,000 persons (1.8 percent of the population in 1960) belonging to minority groups, the largest being the southern Slavs, the Germans, and the Slovaks.[53]

The congress, held from 18 to 19 September 1976, was attended by 776 delegates as well as 200 other guests and numerous foreign delegations. The report of the national council, presented by Secretary-General Sarlós, adopted the resolutions of the HSWP's eleventh congress as a national program: "An indispensable criterion of our social system is the expansion of socialist democracy in every sphere of life. It is our task to strengthen this process. An essential element and method of socialist democracy is that the population participates in the elaboration of important enactments, in the preparation and the formulation of laws." "Politically," Sarlós averred, "our people are unified. Of course, we cannot fail to recognize that this is still not a perfect unity, for there are citizens who hold views different from ours, but the actual picture of the whole country is formed by the overwhelming majority that approved our program at the time of elections." He endorsed the role of the private sector, the ancillary activities of agricultural cooperatives, and the importance of garden and household plots. The national minorities, he noted, were "freely cultivating their national traditfons, mother tongues, and customs." The activity of the churches had been "developing favorably." Sarlós called for support for economic and cultural tasks, for labor discipline and more voluntary work: "The People's Front not only inspires every worker at every level to fulfill national or local plans, but also seeks to bring to the surface the criticisms and proposals of the masses and to represent them in state and political organizations." He also stressed the virtues of socialist patriotism, which he defined as an amalgam of patriotism and internationalism. The latter demanded "commitment to the Soviet Union, to the socialist community, and to the cause of international progress."[54]

The front thus serves to endow the policies of the vanguard party with an aura of consensus. As the programmatic statement approved by the congress put it, the Patriotic People's Front is

> the most comprehensive framework of the alliance policy of the Hungarian Socialist Workers' Party. The conscious cooperation of Hungarian social strata is embodied in it. The policy of alliance plays a conclusively determining role in the historical stage of the building of socialism as one of the basic prerequisites of our progress. It is our task to urge, in the name of this policy, the gathering together of our country's creative forces—party members and nonmembers, materialists and religious believers, people following different ideologies—and their conscious cooperation in the shaping and execution of this policy.[55]

As a bridge between the party and the masses, the front thus performs a useful mobilizing function, and its all-inclusiveness provides a rationale for the absence of organized political contestation in the Hungarian model of socialist democracy.

**Public Administration.** The process of devolution and decentralization also affected the local councils, which prior to 1967 were simple agents of the central government. With the introduction of the NEM official emphasis shifted to the transformation of local councils into more autonomous organs of self-government. Little by little, they were granted budgetary and economic planning authority, greater local generation of revenue, and responsibility for a wide range of local economic, welfare, and cultural tasks. The 1970 electoral law provided for the indirect election of the Budapest city and county councils by the lower councils, a majority of the members having to be councilors at the lower level; the Patriotic Front supervised the nomination process. The Local Council Law of 1971 had two main goals: to delineate more precisely the spheres of responsibility and thus to enhance the initiative and efficiency of the councils; and to reduce the role of the central government to general guidance and partial, long-term financial support. Certain council revenues were linked to the performance of enterprises under local jurisdiction. The law required the councils to meet at least four times a year, continuity being assured by an elected executive committee. In practice the councils tend to be dominated by these committees, are often not presented with real alternatives, and routinely rubber stamp the decisions of the apparatus. However, the law does provide some protection against executive domination in specifying a list of powers that cannot be delegated by the council plenum. In balance, the council reforms certainly represent a step in the direction of greater popular participation in the resolution of local problems.[56]

Another modification in state administration affected the people's control commissions, a network of supervisory agencies that had become notorious for oppressive and high-handed interference in defense of the economic interests of the state. The commissioners had indefinite terms of office and frequently behaved as autonomous, petty local tyrants. In 1968 the system was reformed to lay greater stress on the protection of consumer interests. The commissioners' term was set at four years, while a new nominating and election process placed the Central People's Control Commission under the direct supervision of the council of ministers and the regional control commissions under that of the central body and of the county councils. In 1971 some 70 percent of the indirectly elected commissioners were party members and the old style of arbitrary interference has not disappeared, but the investigative and advisory function of the revamped system had been improved by its new accountability and by greater reliance on volunteer experts.[57]

Like other communist state organs, the Hungarian judiciary has traditionally been a servant of the ruling party's political goals. It reached a nadir of subjection and arbitrariness in the purge trials and legalized class discrimination of the Rákosi era. After the revolution the pursuit of "counterrevolutionary" dissidents required the revival of police and judicial terror. Although the domestic class struggle was declared essentially concluded and some of the more vicious perpetrators of that terror were dismissed in 1962, the recurring abuse and imprisonment of priests and other suspect elements indicated that the party would not shrink from using the law and the secret police to impose its will.

Finally, at the November 1969 plenum of the Central Committee, Interior Minister András Benkei delivered a report that ushered in a review of his ministry's activities. Benkei recognized the disintegrative threat inherent in a policy of peaceful coexistence, but he criticized the sectarian and dogmatic mistakes of the past and asserted that the interior ministry would henceforth demonstrate its respect for socialist legality. His staff would be trained to distinguish between outright political crimes and "pardonable ideological-political errors." The latter would be left to the corrective influence of ideological persuasion.[58] Since then, greater administrative constraints have been imposed on the secret police and its old practice of summary justice has been largely eliminated. Although its fearsome prominence in the lives of ordinary citizens has been reduced, its basic function of monitoring and suppressing politically deviant behavior remains in force. But it is exercised with greater prudence and reliance on warnings to desist. Official reports have deprecated the incidence of antistate activity, which in 1975 accounted for 0.5 percent of all crimes; in that year 214 adults and 28 juveniles were sentenced, mostly for "minor incitement." In 1976 "offenses against the state, peace, or humanity" reportedly accounted for 0.2 percent of crimes.[59] The will and power of the state to curb political deviance remain unaltered, and the low frequency of prosecution for political crimes can be attributed to public resignation in face of this deterrence as well as to the positive socializing impact of Kádár's reforms.

In sum, the Kádár regime has taken pains to supplant administrative terror with a more consensually based rule of law. While it has inevitably remained a defender of the established order, socialist legality has been reformulated into a more impartial code of law. In 1972 a procedural and jurisdictional reorganization of the judicial system was implemented to serve this end.[60] By the mid-1960s the regime had closed down the internment and forced labor camps, ended the expensive jamming of Western radio broadcasts, and relaxed the restrictions on travel to the West. The granting of passports remains the prerogative of the interior ministry, and is still marked by unexplained delays and the occasional punitive withholding of the privilege. However, the official obstacles to travel arise more commonly from foreign exchange regulations than from outright political discrimination. In the late 1970s, the most recent in a series of amnesty laws allowed persons who left illegally to return to Hungary by 31 December 1976. Some 500 individuals reportedly availed themselves of the offer, while 8 percent of the applications were rejected. In March 1977 parliament enacted a law inviting citizens to submit reports on matters of public interest as well as suggestions and complaints. Designed to enhance socialist democracy by ensuring the security of social property and the purity of public life, the new law provided a comprehensive framework for dealing with the numerous collective and individual grievances through official channels.[61]

Within the limitations of Soviet dominance and single-party rule, the requisites of economic modernization and socialist democracy have led to the transformation of the Hungarian political system from the authoritarian and dogmatic model of the early 1950s into a more open, pragmatic and responsive style of government. Hungary is now a complex industrial society. The activation of organized interest groups (to be surveyed below), the willingness of state officials to debate practical (if not fundamental) policy issues, and the innovative use of the social and managerial sciences all serve its needs. While the contemporary Hungarian system is far from being a model of participatory, let alone pluralistic democracy, the Kádár regime can take credit for having devised a symbiotic compromise between ideology and modernization.

# 15. The Policies: Reforms and Reconsiderations

With the party's reassertion of monopoly power the objectives of economic growth and modernization received early attention. Rejecting the Varga committee's proposals as altogether too sweeping and ideologically perilous, the leadership opted for only minor tinkering with the command model. The marginal adjustments proved to be futile if not counterproductive. In the absence of other structural changes, the reduction in central directives only added to the difficulties of enterprise management, and explicit orders were soon reintroduced. The partial producer price reform of 1959 failed to generate a rational cost-based price system, and growing state subsidies continued to insulate that system from economic reality. The sectoral consolidation of industries and the selective development of preferred branches did not overcome the problems of low productivity and low product quality.

This was the generally dismal economic conjuncture when, in 1963, the party began to develop plans that ultimately led to the new economic mechanism (NEM). (Concurrently, and not by coincidence, specialist scholars received the green light to publish devastating critiques of the command economy as it had operated in the early 1950s.)[1] The new model that emerged from this laborious exercise differed radically from its predecessor. The national economic plan prescribed global targets and desirable trends, but it was no longer to be broken down into detailed and binding directives. Instead, indirect regulators were introduced to induce appropriate performance, and enterprises and cooperatives were invited to draw up their own production plans in accordance with their perception of local market conditions. The enhanced role of the market required a more flexible price structure. Accordingly, a multitier price system was introduced providing for fixed, maximum, limited-range, and free-floating prices for different categories of goods. It was anticipated that the new phase of intensive growth would require a more flexible investment and credit policy, one oriented toward profitability and technological innovation. Since the demographic curve did not point to significant net additions to the labor force, productivity could be improved only through more efficient use of labor and through new technologies. The success of the NEM clearly depended in large measure on the ability of enterprises to exploit the devolved responsibilities and incentives.[2]

The economic reform brought an important modification in the ideological status of the producers' cooperatives, which were mainly agricultural. Hitherto they had been considered an inferior and transitional form of economic organization destined to evolve into ideologically preordained state farms and industries. Recognition that this orthodoxy dampened the cooperatives' incentive to produce led to reassurances that "even in the long term, [cooperatives] are irreplaceable institutions of socialism."[3] One immediate consequence of this revision was the ninth congress's decision, enacted in the 1967 land law, to permit the gradual acquisition by cooperatives of their land, which was normally rented from individual owners or from the state. Dogmatic opposition within the party to the new principle that collective and state ownership of the means of production were equally socialist was denounced as anachronistic. Thus the way was opened for the secure and ultimately productive development of collectivized agriculture.[4] The relaxation of central control anticipated in the NEM was introduced in the agricultural sector as early as 1965. In that year, the leadership took a series of measures to enhance the collective farms' production and marketing authority. Other measures were designed to raise the peasantry's standard of living and thereby slow down the migration of young peasants to industry.

## THE NEW ECONOMIC MECHANISM

The NEM was introduced on 1 January 1968, fortuitously at a time when the economy had already begun to recover from the slump of 1964/65. In its first three years of operation the results were on the whole positive. The introduction of market forces produced a notable improvement in the supply and variety of consumer goods and in the standard of living. Agricultural production boomed, and (in 1969) even the foreign trade balance turned positive. The view prevailing in official circles was the optimistic one that, in the words of Lajos Fehér, even without central directives "planned development can be guaranteed—in fact, more effectively guaranteed—by economic regulators."[5]

As was noted earlier, by 1971 there had emerged a number of economic and social shortcomings linked to the NEM. The most negative economic aspects were the drastic deterioration in the balance of trade, caused mainly by the rapid growth in the import of Western technology and consumer goods, and the heavy burden of uncompleted investments. These were generally attributed to lack of good management at the enterprise level, where there also occurred instances of what was officially termed excessive profit seeking. Among the social problems were the unpopularity of the wage differentiation and bonus systems. These were intended to spur productivity but were seen by some workers as favoring the managerial strata.

Meanwhile, the labor code's guarantee of freedom of employment, together with the competition for labor in an economy that was becoming increasingly market oriented and poor in manpower, led to an annual industrial labor turnover of over 30 percent. This was met in 1970 by the "temporary" introduction of compulsory labor exchanges for specified categories of workers. It must be noted that in practice the ideologically required full employment tends to produce underemployment, which in a capitalist system would be denounced as featherbedding. Moreover, productivity in Hungary is on the average scarcely more than half the level prevailing in the Western industrial economies. The regime's complaints about the manpower shortage must therefore be taken with a grain of salt. The problem is less one of unfavorable demographic trends than of a reluctance on the part of much of the labor force to work hard for the basic wage. Apart from some self-motivated professionals, merchants, and private farmers, most Hungarians reserve their energies for their household plots, for moonlighting, and for special inducements such as tips or bribes.

The regime took pains to dispel speculation that the remedial measures amounted to drastic curtailment of the NEM. Addressing a national agitprop conference in February 1972, Nyers declared the reform to be a success. Equal distribution was "not practicable during the building of socialism because the volume of production [was] not enough for a truly communist distribution. This would result only in an equality of poverty, would slow down development, and would fail to make the people either contented or happy." The growth rate, he insisted later, had been a little better since the inception of the NEM, and economic development was better balanced than before. He ruled out any evolution toward a Yugoslav-style management by works councils or the breakup of state property into enterprise property. While defending the development of the cooperative sector, Nyers noted that it was necessary "to establish a socially acceptable limit on the acquisition of property, to set up a system which [would] regularly siphon off excess income."[6]

With regard to production efficiency, favorable trends were identified at the macrostructural level, with improvements in agricultural productivity and in the favored industrial sectors. At the enterprise level, however, modernization was too slow, the resources being used instead to increase capacity. At the same time, the application of a new basic wage decree, which aimed at a higher wage floor as well as greater differentiation of wage rates, ran into trouble, for many enterprises lacked the financial means to implement it. The problem of fostering enterprise autonomy after a long period of tight central planning was made clear in a report on the five-year projections produced by individual enterprises. In the aggregate, these plans proved to be far more optimistic than the national plan in estimating the sources of investment, and they overrated the possibilities of growth in projecting a 38 percent increase in industrial labor productivity over the next five-year period.[7] The managers thus became convenient scapegoats for the teething troubles of the NEM. At the same time, charges were heard almost daily that the NEM's stress on efficiency was leading to technocracy. These the party rejected with the argument that the specialists needed to run a complex economy were also committed to socialism and and were not alienated from the workers.[8]

The manpower shortage, about which more will be said below, has prompted the government to introduce some palliatives. One remedy has been the provision of incentives in early 1972 for men and women of pensionable age (60 and 55 years respectively) to keep on working. Another has been to reassert the value of work competition, particularly through the "socialist brigades" that include some 30 percent of industrial workers. In December 1971 the Central Committee passed a resolution criticizing the past shortcomings of such competition, noting that it was often unrelated to economic targets, that the results were inadequately evaluated, that it was regarded by economic leaders as merely a political campaign, and that it was overly bureaucratized.[9] Another measure in 1971 placed restrictions on the diversification of agricultural producers' cooperatives into ancillary industrial activities, a tactic that had enticed scarce labor away from state industry.

**Energy and Other Problems.**  Hungary's long-term needs for imported raw materials, the role of the Soviet Union as principal supplier, and the Kremlin's possible displeasure with the NEM were the subjects of much domestic and international speculation in the course of 1972. An article in *Pravda* preceding an unofficial visit by Kádár made reference to nationalistic tendencies, social problems, and petty-bourgeois symptoms in Hungary. Then, at the end of March, Prime Minister Fock returned from negotiations in Moscow to report that the Hungarians had been "unable to get a definite answer at present from the Soviet comrades" regarding their commitment to supply raw materials: "We had to rack our brains as to what proposals would not only be good for the Soviet Union, but also useful and necessary for Hungary."[10] Official sources denied the existence of a serious rift while admitting to routine and friendly disagreements. Fock wrote in *Pravda* to denounce as hostile rumors the Western allegations of Soviet displeasure with the NEM and to stress that Hungary had to be cooperative in order to secure essential raw materials.[11] Suggestions that Soviet-Hungarian trade was not conducted on the most equitable terms surfaced once again; a principal target was the agreement whereby aluminous earth is exported to the Soviet Union, turned into aluminum with relatively cheap power, and paid for by some of the end product. In the course of a question-and-answer program on television on 15 September, Deputy Premier Péter Vályi had to remind his listeners that it was Hungary's "international duty" to ship uranium to the Russians; it would not be possible, he claimed, to make a better deal elsewhere. In July, at the twenty-sixth session, in Moscow, of the Comecon council, Fock endorsed the complex integration program adopted the previous year and indicated that coordination of long-term economic policies, product specialization, and cooperative ventures were all imperative if a small country like Hungary was to solve its raw material problems.[12] The Hungarians have consistently argued, however, in favor of maintaining noncompulsory coordination rather than central direction within Comecon by some joint planning board, and of expanding use of the convertible ruble or even adopting full convertibility. When, in late November, Brezhnev paid a visit to Budapest he praised Hungary's progress and "political maturity," but Hungary's economic problems were not thereby resolved.

At its November 1972 plenum the Central Committee passed a resolution that tightened the economic planning process, notably by imposing more intensive supervision, through the branch ministries, on 51 major enterprises. Taken together, these enterprises accounted for 55 percent of gross industrial production, 66 percent of industrial exports, and 50 percent of the labor force. In addition, 6 enterprises were singled out for major transformation of their production structure at the expense of uneconomical lines. These changes, reported Prime Minister Fock to parliament, would ensure a more regular flow of information to the branch ministries; he did not rule out economic incentives and central intervention if these proved necessary to improve efficiency.[13] The plenum also recommended the establishment of a state planning commission to coordinate the work of the Planning Office and the economic ministries, make proposals to the government on plans and regulators, and act as a general economic watchdog.

The balance of trade turned positive again in 1972 and 1973, but only thanks to the accumulation of a ruble surplus that was inconvertible and therefore of limited value. A major shock came with the Hungarian-Soviet trade agreement signed in Moscow on 31 January 1975 but reported by Foreign Trade Minister József Biró on 21 February.[14] The Soviets had decided to gradually bring energy and raw material prices into line with world market conditions by means of a three-year moving average. The decision carried grave implications for a country as poor in energy and primary resources as Hungary. Biró stressed that, at least initially, the new prices would be more advantageous than those prevailing on the open market, but in fact the average price of raw materials and sources of energy rose by 52 percent, while the export prices of Hungarian machinery and agricultural produce were increased by 15 and 28 percent respectively. The net result of the Comecon price changes was a deterioration in the terms of trade with Poland, Czechoslovakia, and, most seriously, with the

Soviet Union. Meanwhile, Hungary's trade balance with the West continued to worsen due to the aforementioned factors and to the European Economic Community's protectionist embargo on Hungarian beef.

The eleventh congress's resolution called for improved efficiency in economic regulation and state management along with the preservation of enterprise independence: "Control over plan implementation and observance of economic discipline must be made more effective on every level." This, said Károly Németh, "is not in conflict with our desire to increase the independence of enterprises and cooperatives in conformity with national economic interests." The resolution warned that the permanent changes in world market prices would probably have an impact on domestic producer prices and demand even greater managerial efficiency; consumer prices would also be affected. In their addresses Kádár and Biszku reaffirmed the right, within limits, of artisans and shopkeepers to private property and the acquisition of wealth—limits that had to be enforced to fight "nonsocialist tendencies." The resolution instructed trade unions to invigorate their activities in political, professional, moral, and cultural education, in the "application of the principles of democracy in their internal operations," and in increasing productivity.[15] In general, 1975 was a time of economic soul-searching.[16]

Private retail trade has grown steadily under the NEM. The increased competition stimulated by this sector is officially sanctioned, although the government encourages private retail outlets chiefly in areas where state or cooperative shops have proved unprofitable. There has been criticism of the excessive profits earned by private retailers as well as by the managers of certain cooperative businesses, mainly in catering, and the government has imposed stricter controls to limit such opportunities for self-enrichment. The number of private artisans, who are badly needed particularly in the consumer service sector, has been declining steadily over the past fifteen years due to deterrents that include complex regulations, high taxation, erratic supply of materials, and inadequate social benefits. Official endorsement is tempered by a certain fear of entrepreneurial excess, but limited tax concessions were instituted in 1977 to stimulate activity in the areas of greatest need, and the number of artisans promptly began to rise. The regime is evidently torn between ideological disapprobation of private enterprise and recognition that latent entrepreneurial talents can be stimulated to great economic advantage.

**Responses to the Economic Crisis.**  The gravity of Hungary's economic dilemma was confirmed by an unprecedentedly unfavorable trade balance in both the socialist and Western sectors in 1975. Official statements emphasized the difficulties in the Western sector. "It is one of the typical features of our production structure," noted Finance Minister Lajos Faluvégi, "that nonprofitable export—which we shall sell to acquire foreign exchange and not because of the advantages of the international division of labor—is comparatively high."[17] It was already probable, however, that the Comecon price changes would require the allocation of a much greater proportion of Hungarian production to payment for expensive Soviet raw materials. Probability became reality in the agreement on the coordination of Hungarian and Soviet national economic plans for the 1976–80 period. This projected a 40 percent increase (by value) in trade over the preceding five-year period, including a 60 percent increase in Soviet raw material and energy deliveries. Much of the latter increase was made contingent on Hungarian participation in Soviet resource development projects such as the Kiembaev asbestos factory, the Kingisepp ammonia phosphate project, the Orenburg natural gas pipeline, and a long-distance electric power transmission line. Among the continuing difficulties in Soviet-Hungarian trade are delays in the fulfillment of these investment commitments; insufficient market research by Hungarian exporters at a time of aggressive Western sales promotion in the Soviet Union; and the frequently inadequate quality of Hungarian exports. The general marketing practice in Hungary has been to reserve the best quality for Western markets, medium quality for the socialist bloc, and the lowest quality for the domestic market. The government has launched a drive for the production of single-quality, "convertible" goods that are competitive on the Western market, and in 1976 the director of a large enterprise was dismissed for producing substandard goods and thereby losing the firm's most important customer, the Soviet Union.

At the fall session of the national assembly György Lázár, who had become premier in 1975, unveiled a series of measures to cope with the crisis; in prospect were restraints on consumption, rises in the prices of basic consumer goods, and a slower increase in the standard of living in the years ahead. Most significant was his confirmation that a new system of economic regulators, representing a major and complex modification of the NEM, would be introduced on 1 January 1976. The stated purpose of the regulators was to reduce the discrepancies between domestic and world market prices and thereby to improve managerial efficiency and competitiveness. Enterprise independence, the profit motive, and the use of economic (as distinct from administrative) methods of control would remain unaltered. The new regulators, however, would serve to reduce retained profits through taxation and to lower direct state subsidies for producer and consumer prices. At the same time, investments left to the enterprises' discretion would be funded no longer from subsidies but by state and bank loans. Finally, the regime decided to expand the sectors covered by the centrally regulated wage system and to impose strongly progressive taxes in order to discourage inflationary increases.[18]

This avalanche of corrective measures sparked widespread debate on the future course of the NEM. In GNP per capita Hungary ranks fifth among socialist countries and thirty-sixth in the world, and the ratio of highest to lowest personal income is five to one. Reflected the government's semiofficial daily: "We reject what used to be called 'barracks communism,' but the capitalist road of a consumer society is of course not our ideal either. So let us seek a future socialist way of life. The question is urgent, as the high-income brackets of our society have by now reached, if not surpassed, the relative limits of their requirements."[19] On the changing economic situation József Bognár, a leading Hungarian economist, observed ruefully: "The NEM was a model for a good period, not for an emergency situation. Now we cannot keep up so consistently the whole system as we did before the changes in the world economy. If we want to defend our economy against the world crisis, it has to happen in a more centralized way."[20]

Global recession, the increase in energy costs, Hungary's desire to modernize her industries with Western technology, the limited competitiveness of her industrial products on Western market, and EEC restrictions on agricultural imports have all had a debilitating effect on the country's trading strength. The aggregate of Hungary's trade deficit with the West and of her gross credits (excluding repayments) raised on Western money markets has been estimated at $2.2 billion for the 1970–76 period. The new imbalance in the terms of trade within Comecon prompted Nyers, the NEM's demoted architect, to hazard a rare criticism. His particular concern was over the "national economic effects" of Hungary's contribution to joint Comecon investments (equivalent to over 10 percent of Hungarian industrial investments) in developing Soviet natural resources. Their impact, he argued, could not be accurately measured due to the inadequacies of Comecon's systems of price, foreign exchange, and credit; national and international interests needed to be harmonized in determining the limits of such investments, but the Comecon mechanism was inadequate for this purpose.[21]

Foreign trade is vitally important to Hungary's economy; indeed, it accounts for 40–45 percent of the national income. In recent years, trade with the Soviet Union has expanded to over 36 percent of total trade, with the rest of Comecon slipping to 28 percent. Trade with the West has risen to 23 percent, West Germany and Austria being the most important partners. Energy and raw materials account for 55–60 percent of imports, and finished products for 65–70 percent of exports. Hungary is a member of GATT, and the government has encouraged various forms of industrial cooperation with foreign firms; of these West German concerns take the lion's share. Of all the socialist states, Budapest claims to have the largest number (but not value) of cooperative ventures with Western partners. Cooperation has generally taken the form of licensing or commission deals. In 1977, however, a finance ministry decree allowed for joint enterprises with foreign partners in production as well as in trade and services; with ministerial permission, the foreign partner could exercise majority control, though only in financial and service activities. Another decree specified the terms under which foreign banks could open branches in Hungary to serve cooperative ventures and export-import financing. By 1978, three Western banks had established offices in Budapest.[22] The government was also seeking alternative sources of oil to be delivered through the "Adria" pipeline, a Yugoslav-Hungarian-Czechoslovak venture slated to be operational in 1978.

As the balance of trade continued to worsen through 1976/77, the regime redoubled its efforts to dampen popular expectations of sustained growth. Addressing a national conference on economic propaganda in March 1977, Győri observed that the changes in the world economy had caught Hungary unprepared; her system of economic regulators was proving less than adequate in stimulating the appropriate responses from Hungarian enterprises. At the same time, he reflected, public opinion surveys were showing that most Hungarians were dissatisfied with the standard of living and believed that improvement was feasible. The regime's task was therefore to explain that while the socialist state "regulates price changes by systematic and purposeful planning . . . our party and state authorities have no absolute freedom in the shaping of prices." Győri concluded that the need was for better quality rather than greater quantity of economic information for the population.[23] This public relations campaign was dictated by a series of price increases designed to gradually align the economy with the world market. Despite such remedial actions, price supports and other subsidies still accounted for 32.6 percent of the 1977 state budget, and the servicing and repayment of foreign debts for 7.2 percent.[24]

Although the economic guidelines approved by the Central Committee at its October 1977 meeting did not depart significantly from previous official pronouncements, they imparted a sense of heightened urgency. The communiqué confirmed that the terms of trade had deteriorated and that qualitative standards in both socialist and capitalist markets had risen. The guidelines called for transforming and simplifying the state's subsidy and profit-regulating system by curtailing unjustified subsidies, among other measures; for better harmony between the domestic price system and world market prices; for greater differentiation of enterprise and personal income according to performance; and for the selective development of industrial branches. In April 1978 a Central Committee resolution confirmed the viability of the NEM as well as the need to phase out subsidies. The resolution was all the more significant in view of the concurrent changes in leadership noted in the preceding chapter.[25] Whether these measures would promote a reinvigoration of the more competitive, market-oriented aspects of the NEM and restore a healthier economic balance remained to be seen. The Kádár regime's stability depended in large measure on the outcome.

**The Modernization of Agriculture.** The most remarkable facet of Hungary's economic growth has been the revival in agriculture, where by the end of 1973 production reached the level planned for the conclusion of the fourth five-year plan in 1975. A major contributing factor has been the introduction, with the aid of Western technology and know-how, of integrated, closed-production systems. As a result, Hungary has once again become a grain-exporting country. At the same time, the weight of agriculture in the national economy has shifted markedly, for in 1975 it accounted for 23 percent of the labor force and 15 percent of the national income, down from 39 percent and 29 percent respectively in 1960. Agriculture nevertheless remains a key sector not only in terms of domestic consumption but also because food and livestock account for over one-fifth of all exports, and for more than half of the exports to the West.

In imitation of the Soviet example, a policy of consolidating agricultural production by mergers of cooperative farms was pursued for many years. From a peak of 4,500, the number of agricultural producers' cooperatives fell to under 1,500 in 1976, covering 67 percent of arable land and with a membership of 1 million (42 percent of them pensioners). By 1975 it was realized that this precipitous consolidation had not always been in tune with economic rationality. Indeed, many of the earlier mergers, encompassing several villages, were attributable to the zeal of local party and state officials and did not produce real economies of scale. Moreover, it has been alleged that the large merged cooperatives induced alienation between management and members and between the membership and production. Instead of more mergers, the party therefore came to favor the formation of agroindustrial complexes linking cooperative and state farms and food industry enterprises.

This shift in emphasis was confirmed at the third national congress of agricultural cooperatives, held from 14 to 15 December 1976, and attended by Kádár and Németh. Kádár noted with satisfaction that the socialist brigade movement was spreading in agriculture and that 10 percent of cooperative members belonged to the HSWP. He reiterated the party's endorsement of private plots and ancillary farms; its opposition to diversifying the cooperatives into ancillary nonagricultural activities, a phenomenon of the early years of the NEM; and the promotion of agroindustrial complexes as the new stage in the development of socialist agriculture.[26] Subsequently the 1967 law on agricultural cooperatives was amended to accommodate changes in their scale and style of work. The amendments regularized the status of private plot farming; provided for new levels of self-management, with delegate meetings and working collectives in addition to the annual membership meeting; relaxed rules for entry to and departure from the cooperatives and abolished arbitrary exclusion; and expanded the role of regional associations of cooperatives, in part to "assert the national economic interest."[27] Since 1976 the over 130,000 employees of the cooperatives have been allowed to join the agricultural and forestry workers' union, but the cooperatives, in order to preserve their own form of self-management, tend to prefer that employees become members.

In addition to the agricultural producers' cooperatives, there were, in 1977, 134 state farms encompassing 12.6 percent of arable land and accounting for 14 percent of gross agricultural output. They benefit from heavy subsidies that allow for a higher level of specialist and manual labor and technical aid than that enjoyed by the cooperatives. Western, and particularly American, technology and know-how have had significant application in Hungarian agriculture, including the aforementioned closed-production systems, high-yield seeds, and the manufacture under license of heavy machinery. All this has prompted some political reservations. In January 1977 the responsible minister, Pál Romány, felt compelled to issue the reassurance that "no enterprise should fear for Hungary's socialist integrity just because it has relations with an enterprise in one of the capitalist states."[28]

Agricultural cooperative managers as well as the more dogmatic party members have shown persistent hostility toward private plot farming, but the regime has assessed as vitally important the latter's contribution to the domestic market. The Central Committee's plenum of 1 December 1976 confirmed that "support of the private plot and ancillary farms must continue in order to exploit their production potential."[29] By 1978, small-scale producers accounted for 18 percent of arable land (including 800,000 private plots within the cooperatives) and provided a far higher proportion of net agricultural output, including approximately half of horticultural and livestock production. Over 1.5 million families were involved in some minor agricultural activity, mostly on a part-time basis, and three-quarters of them were not professional farmers. To stimulate this sector, the state had recently provided new tax concessions, subsidies, and technical assistance.

Rural society has undergone a drastic transformation since the communist takeover. In 1949, 40 percent of the peasants were small-scale farmers. Now even among the village dwellers more than half do not pursue farming as their principal occupation. Many work in industry, and only half of all cooperative members are engaged in peasant activities; the rest fill white-collar or auxiliary jobs generated by larger collectives, by mechanization, and by product diversification. The standard of living of cooperative members has in recent years reached and even surpassed that of urban industrial workers.[30] These dramatic changes in a society long dominated by a romantic vision of the numerically vast peasant class are attributable to both secular trends and to the manipulation of successive communist administrations. While the modernization of agriculture could well have been achieved by less painful methods, it was an economically imperative task that the Kádár regime has pursued with some success.

**Demography and Manpower.** The impact of demographic trends on economic growth has exercised central planners since the early years of communist rule. In the 1950s the Rákosi regime banned abortions and restricted the sale of contraceptives. In 1954, the rate of natural increase reached a high of 12 per thousand. After the revolution the pendulum swung in the opposite direction. Thanks to freely available abortions and birth control devices, the rate plunged to 2.1 (with a live birth rate of 10.8) in 1962. Faced with an aging population and a declining active labor force, the government adopted a new demographic policy in 1974. This aimed to reduce the earlier reliance on induced abortions as the principal method of family planning and, together with increased family and child welfare allowances and maternity grants, to bring the birth rate up to the level considered necessary to stabilize the demographic curve. As a result, by 1976 the birth rate had risen to 18 per thousand, alleviating not only economic concerns but also the apocalyptic visions of some patriotic writers, notably Gyula Illyés, of the decline and disappearance of the Magyar people.

Nevertheless, the effects of past demographic declines and the current problems of slack labor discipline and misallocation have impelled the regime to intervene in the sphere of manpower management. In the 1966–70 period Hungary's labor force increased by 345,000, and in the following five-year period by 100,000; in contrast, the estimated increase for the 1976–80 period is no more than 50,000–60,000. In December 1975 the ministries of labor and finance issued a decree imposing a total or partial freeze on the hiring of white-collar workers, whose number had been rapidly expanding amidst acute labor shortages in other areas. A lively public debate ensued on the controversial measure, but Kádár confirmed that the "really urgent need is to put a stop to the avalanche-like increase in administrative staffs." He described a positive instance: "They had the guts in the Győr Wagon and Machine Works to transfer 450 office workers to the workshops. At the time these people showed their annoyance, but in a couple of months they were gladly accepting their new circumstances and were even earning more."[31] The widespread practice of moonlighting brought down a decree restricting the freedom to take ancillary or secondary jobs; said an official, "The objective is to restore the prestige of the primary job."[32] These measures, along with others tightening "sick pay discipline" and offering incentives to mothers and pensioners to remain employed, responded to genuine needs and inefficiencies, but they also limited the freedom of both employers and job seekers. Meanwhile, unpaid "social work" (including the extra shift known as "communist Saturdays") remains an important contributor to the economy.

**Social Measures.**   In the later Kádár era the standard of living improved markedly, with consumption rising by 30 percent between 1968 and 1975. The regime, as befits its socialist principles, has also distinguished itself in the provision of universal welfare and social services. Health care was fully subsidized, as was education, and there was fierce competition for admission to the universities. The announcement by the ministries of labor and education in December 1975, that all schoolchildren would henceforth be classified by social origin in a yearly census aroused fears that the alliance policy's abandonment of class discrimination was being reversed; even party officials voiced belated reservations. What was proposed, explained Kádár, was "nothing but a simple instrument for assembling statistical data. In the ministry they wanted to know the percentage of workers' children in the primary and grammar schools. Statistics do have their uses, but the introduction of the form was clumsily handled and gave the impression that it presaged a return to a discarded practice."[33] Nevertheless, the regime's concern for social restratification has led to a covert bias against the admission of too many middle-class children to academic high schools and to universities.

Pensioners account for 17.6 percent of the population, a proportion that has been rising steadily over recent years. The retirement age for workers and employees is 60 for men and 55 for women; it is being gradually lowered for agricultural workers to reach the same level by 1980. All this places a heavy burden on the economy, although there are wide discrepancies in pension income and the majority of pensioners live at a bare subsistence level.[34] The acute housing shortage that resulted from wartime destruction and rapid urbanization has been gradually alleviated, the number of people per 100 rooms having fallen from 236 in 1960 to 157 in 1976. But demand, particularly in Budapest, still far outstrips new construction, and the shortages have contributed in no small measure to a high abortion rate and to such symptoms of social stress as alcoholism, divorce, and suicide, in all of which Hungary outpaces most other countries. In recent years the government has encouraged private construction and, to reduce the burden of maintenance, has permitted tenants to purchase their state-owned apartments. State subsidies also facilitate wide access to cultural and sports events.[35]

## CULTURE AND IDEOLOGY

The tension between culture and science, on the one hand, and ideology, on the other, has never yet been successfully resolved by a communist regime. The cultural dogmatism and russification of the Rákosi era proved so devastatingly unpopular and counterproductive, and the alienation of creative intellectuals from the restoration regime became so profound, that well into the 1960s Kádár's party was still searching for some compromise formula while tacitly tolerating a degree of cultural pluralism. The writings of such Russians as Yevgeny Yevtushenko and Andrey Voznesensky during the revival of destalinization aroused much interest among young Hungarian writers and were echoed in their review *Új Irás* (New Writing), but they contained no novelty for those who had witnessed the far bolder literary outbursts of 1956. The publication of derogatory accounts of the Rákosi regime, notably by Nógrádi, served the purposes of Kádár's two-front struggle. The appearance in 1963 of an account by József Lengyel exposing the horrors of Stalin's forced labor camps (which he had witnessed in 1937) touched on more sensitive nerves.[36] Although this Hungarian Solzhenitsyn had been awarded the high accolade of a

Kossuth Prize for his literary work, his semiautobiographical accounts of party life under Stalinist terror soon earned him official disfavor. It was one thing to vilify Rákosi, and another to expose the darker side of Soviet rule. Meanwhile, old Populist writers like László Németh and Péter Veres made their peace with Kádár and along with younger colleagues began once again to publish essentially apolitical works.

**Cultural Liberalization.** The shift to greater cultural tolerance was foreshadowed by the guidelines of the eighth congress in November 1962. There was lengthy debate within the party on the adaptability of socialist realism to changing conditions. At last, in 1966, the Central Committee's cultural study group issued a policy statement sanctioning works that were "ideologically debatable and more or less in opposition to Marxism or socialist realism, as long as they [possessed] humanistic value and [were] not politically hostile." Artistic work was categorized as party-minded, supportive of socialism, decadent (inviting persuasion), and hostile (requiring suppression).[37] Upon the inauguration of the NEM two years later, the secretary responsible for cultural affairs, György Aczél, elaborated the ideological rationale behind the new permissiveness. The old policy of imposing the monopoly of Marxism, he said, had been premature and had led to the overpoliticization of culture; it had fostered domineering and exclusive cliques who had repressed divergent orientations and thereby impoverished the arts and sciences. The assumption of Marxist monopoly was unrealistic in view of the survival of religious and other non-Marxist views among the public. The party's task was therefore to assert the hegemony of Marxism, its preeminence rather than its exclusivity. Even artists representing a "bourgeois-humanistic" outlook could serve socialist society. It was not liberalism, Aczél later observed, that made the party tolerate art of this kind, but "the alliance policy of the working class and the international workers' movement in its domestic and international sense, which makes it necessary to link ourselves in the cultural field with other anti-imperialist and humanist forces in the interest of socialism and the working class."[38]

The cultural guidelines of 1966 became generally known as the "three Ts," short for *támogatott, türt,* and *tiltott* (Hungarian for "supported," "tolerated," and "prohibited"). Works of ideological or general political importance fall into the first, subsidized category. Classics with wide popular appeal require no price support and fall between the first and second categories. A range of profitable best-sellers of mixed literary merit is tolerated. Subsidies come from a cultural fund that is financed in part by a levy on less meritorious but profitable publications. As a last recourse, authors also have the option of paying the cost of printing their works as long as they are not seditious.

The line of prohibition is difficult to ascertain. Apart from a few causes célèbres noted below, there have been instances when works already published have been withdrawn from circulation or not reprinted on the party's orders.

Such sensitive themes range from the trials of émigré life in Moscow during Stalin's purges (related by the veteran communist Endre Sik, a Central Committee member and Kádár's foreign minister from 1958 to 1961) to corruption and mismanagement in Hungary's major sport, soccer.[39] For diplomatic reasons the regime is wary of exposés of the Stalinist era in Russia and of details of the Rákosi party's Soviet connections. The more vivid memoirs (such as those of Zoltán Vas) remain in their authors' desk drawers or see print in an expurgated version.

Within these vague and somewhat unpredictably applied limitations, the creative arts enjoyed a renaissance in Hungary in the late 1960s. Even the leadership of the reconstituted Writers' Association came to reflect a degree of stylistic and political pluralism. It played an initiating role in the "discovery of Hungary" series of sociographic investigations and defended the first project, describing dismal conditions in a remote village, against the outraged protests of local officials.[40] Another politically significant aspect of the literary revival was that the writers were allowed to show their concern for the cultural survival of the neighboring Magyar minorities (privately, of course, they had always been concerned). This was an explosive issue that the regime studiously ignored until the mid-1970s.

In the same period, theater and the cinema also gained in quality and occasionally ventured into political criticism. The Rákosi era, the revolution, and contemporary disharmonies received cautious attention in a few productions. The internationally acclaimed films of Miklós Jancsó and the satirical plays of István Örkény reflect the regime's stylistic tolerance. A 1977 film portrait of the prematurely retired Olympic pentathlon champion András Balczó, in which the latter criticized the administration of sports and affirmed his religious convictions, was a huge popular success and strained the party's permissiveness. A further notable safety valve was the political satire staged by two theater groups, which went so far as to present gentle parodies of Kádár.

**Ideological Tensions.** The constraints of ideology have been more visible in the spheres of the social sciences and philosophy. The party's experimental liberalization was a response to the complexities of implementing and assessing the economic reform. The reform, as was noted earlier, soon generated tensions between its technocratic proponents and the more conservative apparat. In 1963 a sociological research group was set up within the Academy of Sciences under Hegedüs, now repented of his Rákosiite past. Three years later the party established its own Institute of Social Sciences; henceforth, its functionaries were to be equipped with the proper blend of ideology and expertise to cope with the NEM.

In 1966, after some procrastination, the party allowed the publication of an analysis of social stratification in contemporary Hungary.[41] Hegedüs, for his part, acquired a reputation for iconoclasm with his insistence that Marxism be updated with the findings of modern sociology. In an analysis of the structure of socialist society he observed that the destruction of the old class system had not produced a leveled community; occupation remained the key determinant of social stratification and induced attitudes that impeded social mobility. This, he noted, undermined earlier "subjective-voluntaristic" illusions regarding the effectiveness of agitprop and education, and imposed the necessity of recognizing various social groupings. Socialist society was threatened not by particularism as such but by the claims of particular interests to represent the common interest.[42]

By the late 1960s the party had become apprehensive at such transgressions of orthodoxy in the social sciences. When Hegedüs criticized the 1968 invasion of Czechoslovakia, he was dismissed from his post and replaced by the academically better qualified Kálmán Kulcsár. But the spirit of free inquiry had spread. When a group of academics and university students began to exhibit some of the "New Left" radicalism popular in similar Western circles, the party responded with a denunciation of their ostensibly Marxist "pluralism" and "relativism."[43] The numerically insignificant New Left phenomenon, with other ideologically incompatible manifestations released by the decompression of the alliance policy and the NEM, continued to exercise the party through the 1970s. With the coincidence of East-West detente and its attendant risks, official cultural policy turned more restrictive.

In the summer of 1972 Aczél told a group of visiting Soviet youth representatives that "there cannot be freedom for 'art' that preaches alien ideological views, appeals to base instincts, and is antihumane and the result of 'anticulture'." He observed that young people envied the "romance" of the older generation's revolutionary struggles while being at the same time particularly susceptible to bourgeois ideology, against which the Hungarian party was waging "an implacable struggle."[44] According to the guidelines released that October by the Central Committee's cultural collective, the spectrum of criticism had widened to the extent that Marxist critics were threatened by a wave of bourgeois and ideologically neutral literary and artistic views; critics, editors, and other creative intellectuals were therefore enjoined to return to Marxist cultural principles.[45] In the wake of a Central Committee resolution calling for improvement in the ideological basis of education, an article in the party's theoretical monthly acknowledged tendencies among the young toward a romantic nationalism tinged with anti-Sovietism. Historians, it urged, should stress the primacy of the class struggle.[46]

The impact of the region-wide campaign to counter the subversive effects of detente was manifest at the Central Committee's national agitprop conference in January 1973. In a meeting that saw open and sharp discussion, Aczél delivered a broadside attack on "negative symptoms" in the social sciences. Intellectual renegades, he charged, had questioned the leading role and very existence of the working class, denied that it was a true revolutionary force, and claimed to find authentic revolutionary spirit in the radical left movements in the West. By elaborating a theory of "pluralist Marxism," he continued, they were attempting to ideologize their abandonment of the working class and genuine Marxism. The Secretariat thereupon launched an investigation of three dissenting intellectuals, Hegedüs and the philosophers János Kis and Mihály Vajda. A cultural policy team analyzed the writings of the three and invited them to participate in the debate, but they declined, reportedly demanding a public forum.

Elaborating Aczél's charges, the team reported that the writings contained "traditional right-wing revisionist views mixed with the so-called New Left attitudes fashionable in contemporary anti-Marxist literature." While the party defended freedom of research in the social sciences, without prohibited subjects or prescribed conclusions, it categorically opposed the pluralization of Marxism-Leninism, which could lead to political pluralism and, ultimately, to the denial of the leading role of party and working class. The intellectuals under investigation were said to have failed to exercise the necessary self-control. The writings of Hegedüs and of his associate Mária Márkus on modernization in the socialist states postulated a "state management" model, dominated by a self-serving bureaucratic apparatus, and a market model (i.e., Hungary) which attempted to foster development by quasi-capitalist methods. The first they viewed as not sufficiently dynamic, the second as leading to a profit-oriented society. The masses would therefore have to turn toward a third, humanized and economically efficient model which would require a major structural transformation of the prevailing system. Mihály Vajda, reported the investigators, denied the existence of a single and authentic Marxism and of laws determining the course of history. A related deplorable tendency, found in the work of the philosopher Ágnes Heller, was the advocacy of a pseudosocialist New Left alternative modeled on "petty-bourgeois utopianisms about communities intended to secure individual self-realization and free self-expression." By such efforts to pluralize Marxism these scholars had "overstepped the boundaries of our ideological public life." Since some of the accused had been disciples of Lukács, the team took it upon itself to insist that the latter had explicitly rejected any pluralization of Marxism. The report also called to account officials in the cultural sphere for allowing such dangerous heresies to be published. Young people, it observed, were readily deceived by "attractive sham-theoretical, sham-revolutionary platitudes and unscientific political manipulations."[47]

The investigation established that Hegedüs and Mihály Vajda had been repeatedly cautioned against political errors, and that they and Kis had grossly violated party rules and refused to make amends. By a resolution of the Secretariat on 14 May the three were expelled from the party. Like Heller and Mária Márkus who, with Márkus's husband György, had been expelled earlier, they lost their professional positions and were forbidden to publish. The punishment was mild by Soviet standards, but the party was evidently determined to demarcate more clearly the bounds of the permissible in social science research. Sociology was seen as having gone through stages of acceptance and proliferation into trivial statistical surveys; it would now have to be reoriented to make Marxist sociology and Marxist social theory complementary.[48]

More recent cases have served to demonstrate the limits of tolerance. One was that of the ultraleftist writer Miklós Haraszti. Already under close police surveillance because of his radical critiques and alleged affiliation with a Maoist group, Haraszti gained first-hand experience in a tractor factory to write an exposé of the inequities of the wage system and of the harsh working conditions. When he circulated his manuscript, entitled *Darabbér* (Piecework), he was charged with "grave incitement" and, in January 1974, was fined and received a suspended sentence. In October of that year the police briefly detained the sociographer György Konrád, his sociologist collaborator Iván Szelényi, and the avant-garde poet Tamás Szentjóby on charges of antisocialist agitation. The first two were charged with illegally disseminating more than the prescribed number of copies of Konrád's manuscript *A városalapitó* (The City Founder), a study of alienation in an urbanized society. A quiet compromise was worked out: Szelényi and Szentjóby left the country, while Konrád's contentious book was published with excisions two years later.[49]

At the eleventh party congress in 1975 the deficiencies in ideology and culture came under attack from Benke. Quantitative indicators were not enough to measure the progress of socialism, she said; it was also essential to collectively evaluate attitudes and behavior. Nationalism, the "most dangerous of bourgeois ideas," persisted in the social sciences; certain individuals had "drifted into the troubled waters of revisionism and ultraleftist or other turbid streams." Open debate was essential, but there could be no compromise on certain fundamentals: socialist patriotism; proletarian internationalism and Hungarian-Soviet friendship; the leading role of the working class and of the party; and the worker-peasant alliance.[50] Nevertheless, cultural policy in Hungary remains liberal by East European standards, which is to say that most of the censorship is self-imposed. Culture Minister Imre Pozsgay affirmed in an interview in 1977 that his ministry relied on ideological and intellectual persuasion rather than on "administrative methods" to apply the official guidelines; sometimes, he noted, this led to sharp arguments with the leaders of cultural organizations.[51] In a country where writers have traditionally served as the vanguard of political protest, creative freedom and ideological orthodoxy can only coexist in a state of perpetual and acute tension.

These frictions at the borderline of ideological tolerance exercise only a narrow stratum of the Hungarian public, whose cultural tastes, since the abandonment of russification, are satisfied by the classical works of Hungarian and foreign literature and by contemporary nonpolitical best-sellers. This largely apolitical mass culture is also served by the now ubiquitous television, which carries some Western programs. All communications media remain of course under party and state control and therefore serve as agents of political socialization—with little success, as will be seen. By Western standards the press is excessively didactic and exhortatory and is remarkably uninformative regarding the backstage of political decision making. Only seldom is any divergence on matters of substance perceptible among the major newspapers of party (*Népszabadság*), government (*Magyar Hirlap*), the Patriotic People's Front (*Magyar Nemzet*), and the National Council of Trade Unions (*Népszava*). In contrast to the modest degree of cultural pluralism, freedom of the press is unknown in Hungary. Western newspapers and periodicals are not generally available outside a few tourist hotels, but Western radio broadcasts (and, in Transdanubia, Austrian television) enjoy a wide audience.

**The Compromise with Religion.** In its application to organized religion the alliance policy has produced a modus vivendi with the Vatican and the local clergy; the latter it attempts to enlist in the task of building socialism. The tension between the immediate necessity of compromise and the long-term objective of demonstrating the superiority of atheistic socialism remains in evidence, but the Kádár regime has come to the conclusion that frontal attack on the churches only reinforces their appeal. Acknowledging the persistence of religious belief, the party has concentrated its efforts on eradicating religious practice within its ranks, notably by mounting courses on the criticism of religion, and on low-key counterpropaganda. In fact, religious practice is still widespread, and the demand for baptism and religious weddings has not declined despite official promotion of "family institutes" providing free civil ceremonies. The chairman of the Office of Church Affairs, Imre Miklós, has judged this situation to be "essentially satisfactory," claiming that "sober-minded and far-sighted church leaders are able effectively to overcome obstructionist churchmen and church groups bent on forcing on the churches a political line at variance with the socialist state and society."[52] The state continues to furnish a "provisional" subsidy to the churches and has assisted in the renovation of historic buildings such as the cathedral at Esztergom (it is safe to assume, more in the interest of tourism than that of the church). Budapest has the only rabbinical seminary in the Soviet bloc.

Accord with the Vatican, initiated in a preliminary agreement in 1964, was facilitated when, in 1971, Cardinal Mindszenty left the U.S. embassy and went into exile. Kádár subsequently remarked: "Those who claim that it was under our pressure that Pope Paul VI relieved Mindszenty of the archiepiscopal seat of Esztergom overestimate our means and underestimate the Vatican."[53] Mindszenty remained outspokenly hostile to the regime and to the Vatican's policy of accommodation, and only after his death in Vienna in 1975 was a successor, László Lékai, named as his successor in the archbishopric of Esztergom. Following the conclusion of the Helsinki Accord, the HSWP intensified its efforts to demonstrate to the world its tolerance of organized religion. Said Kádár in February 1976: "Without exception the churches are loyal to our system. . . . Is it possible that by doing this the churches may be prolonging their existence? It may be so. . . . It could be said that this is a compromise. . . . But we learn from Lenin that any compromise which advances our revolutionary course is acceptable."[54] It would be a mistake, wrote Miklós, "to minimize the role played by religious belief in the private life of the individual, in interpersonal relations, and in the service of moral norms." The churches and their adherents could help to attain national goals by offering "constructive criticism" through the Patriotic People's Front.[55] Kádár's audience with Pope Paul during a state visit to Italy in June 1977 served to symbolize the normalization of state-church relations. The HSWP leader asserted afterwards that in Hungary the state did not interfere in the life of religious organizations or with the free practice of religion.[56] Hungary's chief rabbi, speaking for an active Jewish community of some 100,000, was also impelled to proclaim that Hungarians enjoyed complete religious freedom. Billy Graham's visit to Budapest in September 1977, in the course of which he addressed an open-air gathering of Hungarian Baptists, was an unprecedented display of official tolerance that was presumably aimed at both the Belgrade review of the Helsinki Final Act and the normalization of Hungarian-American relations.

Although the churches survive, their difficulties and the limits of tolerance receive less airing. Party members and their families are of course forbidden to practice or show ideological tolerance for religion, and KISZ members are similarly discouraged from religious practice and receive instruction in atheism. A more general discrimination prevails against religious adherents in education and employment, and they are excluded from high office. Eight Catholic church-administered high schools remain in existence, but most of the religious orders have been proscribed since 1950, and the teaching of catechism is limited to a restricted number of children, in the churches, twice a week. Although state-church negotiations are proceeding on minor issues, Miklós has taken pains to dampen speculation that such amelioration in state-church relations might amount to a "historic change"; ideological convergence was impossible, he insisted, and secularization was in the ascendant.[57]

## FOREIGN RELATIONS

The Kádár regime's foreign policy stands in sharp contrast to the domestic liberalization of the last fifteen years. This has invited comparison with the Romanian alternative of oppressive orthodoxy in internal affairs and independent posturing in foreign policy, a comparison suggesting the rather facile conclusion that the Soviet Union will allow a certain particularism in only one of the two spheres. Whatever the degree of conscious choice exercised in Moscow, Budapest, and Bucharest, the fact remains that in interparty and general external relations Kádár has pursued a line of steadfast if low-keyed loyalty to the Soviet Union.

**Communist China.** The Kádár regime endorsed Moscow's open letter to the Chinese in March 1963, but did not initially repeat the Soviet call for an all-party conference to debate the issue. There was no doubt, however, about Hungary's allegiance. That November, on the occasion of the anniversary of the Bolshevik Revolution, the Hungarian party affirmed that "the attitude toward the Soviet Union remains the only criterion for what communist and internationalist means." This was only one in an unbroken series of statements of solidarity.[58] Nor did Kádár show any overt sympathy for the momentary polycentrist tendencies in Eastern Europe. In the Romanian-integrationist debate Hungary refrained from open condemnation of the Bucharest regime but adapted herself readily to the ensuing decentralization within Comecon and to the stress on coordination instead of a supranationally determined division of labor. The regime would meanwhile warn against any interpretation of the Sino-Soviet schism as offering opportunities for a "third road" for Hungary.[59]

Trade with China dwindled after the split; a mutual expulsion of students occurred in 1966; and when, the following year, mobs attacked the Hungarian ambassador's car in Peking, the regime denounced Mao's cultural revolution in no uncertain terms. Over the next decade Hungary dutifully echoed the Kremlin's annoyance at the estranged Chinese. A party observer commented in 1975: "The Peking leadership is approaching imperialist countries under the banner of anti-Sovietism, antisocialism, and nationalism, and there is not a single international sphere in which it is prepared to cooperate, or at least pursue a parallel policy with the Soviet Union and other like-minded socialist countries."[60] The HSWP expressed regret that, since the death of Mao Tse-tung, China had continued to pursue great power and nationalistic policies that impeded detente, and to prepare for war against the Soviet Union despite the willingness of the socialist countries to improve relations.

**The Czechoslovakian Crisis.** Kádár's general inclination has been to moderate interparty conflicts. In February 1968, a consultative meeting convened in Budapest to plan for a world communist conference. When it broke up after the Romanian delegation's walkout (the issue was the criticism of individual parties), the Hungarians remained true to Moscow's line. However, when the reform movement in Czechoslovakia gathered momentum that spring, Kádár was thrust into a mediating role that was apparently inspired by his own apprehensions as well as those of the Kremlin. The Hungarians had anticipated that the reforms adumbrated by the Czech economist Ota Šik would bolster the newly introduced NEM; indeed, their original position was that the Czechs were fighting the same two-front battle against sectarianism and revisionism that they had faced in 1956 and that the Czechs would be well advised to learn from that precedent. The Hungarian regime took exception to a criticism of Nagy's trial and execution that appeared in the Czech literary review *Literární listy* in June, but Dubček's general reformist orientation was favorably construed by Kádár as well as by the Hungarian public.[61]

Meeting with Dubček on at least three occasions (before the Warsaw conference of the eventual invaders, before the Soviet-Czech confrontation at Cierna, and just before the invasion), Kádár acted as a concerned intermediary who realized that suppression of the Czech experiment—inevitable unless the pace of liberalization could be checked—might endanger his own reforms. At the Warsaw summit on 14 July, Kádár, accompanied by Fock, reported on his discussions with Dubček. According to one account, Kádár warned in a quiet tone against anything more forceful than a cautionary letter to the Czech party. At this East Germany's Walter Ulbricht retorted furiously: "If you think, Comrade Kádár, that you are helping the cause of socialism with your objections and reservations then you are making a big mistake. And you have no idea what will happen next. Once the American-West German imperialists have got Czechoslovakia in their control then you will be next to go, Comrade Kádár. But that is something you can't or won't understand!" The Russian participants, led by Brezhnev, stopped short of demanding immediate intervention, to the evident relief of the Hungarians, who were reportedly shunned like lepers by the other delegates during the recesses.[62] After the Warsaw conference a *Népszabadság* editorial did warn the Czech comrades to "not let the same things happen which led to open counterrevolution in Hungary." But the HSWP continued to profess confidence that the Czech reformers would avoid the pitfalls of heresy, and the Bratislava declaration was hailed in this spirit.[63]

Ultimately Dubček failed to satisfy the Kremlin, and the latter launched a massive police operation at dawn on 21 August. The invasion and Hungary's participation in it induced widespread dismay among not only the public but also the military. Two Hungarian divisions were sent into southern Slovakia, where they maintained a low profile, for even the Magyar minority was less than enthusiastic in its welcome (the troops were withdrawn at the end of October). Conversely, the Dubček regime reserved for Hungary's action an understanding that it did not extend to the other invaders.

Public sympathy for the Prague spring and apprehension over the invasion produced little overt dissent in Hungary, where the pervasive but unstated concern was for the survival of Kádár's reforms. There was some debate in party and intellectual circles, and four scholars (the philosophers Zádor Tordai and

György Márkus and the sociologists Vilmos Sós and Ágnes Heller) attending a conference at Korcula in Yugoslavia signed a declaration denouncing the invasion.[64] Significantly, these dissenters were merely reprimanded, and ultimately Premier Fock offered an embarrassed rationale for the intervention:

> We could not take a popular vote on the event of August 20. This would not have been proper, because it was not our affair alone. We were confident that the workers in Hungary would understand why we had to do this and that it was our international duty. We acted as we did on August 20 together with the other socialist countries in this belief.[65]

Kádár himself was evidently distressed at the turn of events, and he disappeared from public view for over two months. Thereafter he combined apologetics for the invasion—"unavoidable and necessary because of the danger of counterrevolution"—with assurances that the Hungarian economic reform was a proper adaptation of Marxism-Leninism to local conditions and would be sustained.[66]

When, some eight years later, the impending review of the Helsinki Final Act impelled Czech dissidents to issue their famous Charter 77, thirty-four Hungarian intellectuals responded with a statement of support. The message, sent to dissident leader Pavel Kohout on 9 January 1977, read in part: "We declare our solidarity with the signers of Charter 77 and we condemn the repressive measures used against them. We are convinced that the defense of human and civil rights is a common concern of all of Eastern Europe." The signatories included not only inveterate dissenters such as György Márkus, Kis, Mihály Vajda, Heller, Sós, and Haraszti, but also the popular writers Sándor Csoóri and Miklós Mészöly and the communist veteran and Nagy supporter Ferenc Donáth. In a Radio Vienna interview on 20 January one of the signatories, the philosopher Ferenc Fehér, pointed out that the letter was a simple act of solidarity that did not represent an organized movement and had no bearing on the situation in Hungary. Nevertheless, by the end of the year four of the troublesome intellectuals, György and Mária Márkus with Ferenc Fehér and his wife Ágnes Heller were induced to leave the country for an indeterminate period.

**The World Communist Movement.** The HSWP maintained a relatively low profile in the interparty controversies that marked preparations for the conference of European communist and workers' parties in East Berlin on 29 and 30 June 1976. At that conference, Kádár observed: "Today, when the communist world movement does not have a center or a leading party, when the fraternal parties determine their tactics and strategy independently, the safeguarding of the purity of Marxist-Leninist theory is of special significance, together with the theoretical application of experience gained in practice and the

enforcement of the principle of proletarian internationalism."[67] Translated into
the vernacular, what Kádár advocated was the voluntary endorsement by all
communist parties of the Soviet line. The issue of Eurocommunism subsequently sparked a dispute between Dezső Nemes and the French Politburo
member Jean Kanapa. When the latter criticized the Soviet and East European
model for having banned all political opposition, Nemes denounced Western
communists who professed a preference for socialist-pluralist democracy over
proletarian dictatorship. "[The] failure of the counter-revolution," he noted
defensively, "marked the end of attempts to revive the multi-party system. In
1956 it was strongly discredited in our country as a weapon of the enemies of
working-class power, of the agents of Western imperialism."[68]

The Kádár regime pursued a line of finely calculated moderation and balance
in the developing Eurocommunist dispute. In the course of a visit to Vienna in
December 1976, Kádár disagreed with the Bulgarian leader Todor Zhivkov's
equation of Eurocommunism with anti-Sovietism. In a contemporary article,
Kádár underscored the "special significance" of the Soviet party's theoretical
and practical experience, but denied the necessity of its "mechanical application" or of the curtailment of a sister party's independence. Socialism, he observed, could conceivably be developed by way of a multiparty system. In the
Hungarian single-party model, the party had to give consideration to various
group and individual interests; it could not build a socialist society alone but
had to seek allies and appeal to the masses.[69] What mattered, said Kádár at a
press conference during his Italian visit, was the achievement of socialism,
"with or without the dictatorship of the proletariat, with pluralistic socialism
or any other kind of socialism."[70] According to one report on a conference of
East European party secretaries held at Sofia in March 1977, the Hungarians
voiced reservations in face of the urgings, notably by the Bulgarians, that the
Eurocommunist deviation be publicly condemned. The HSWP delegation, led
by Óvári and including Gyenes and Győri, brought back the message that the
ideological struggle between capitalism and socialism had become accentuated;
Eurocommunism was an imperialist fabrication requiring an intensification of
communist counterpropaganda.[71] In his meetings in late 1977 with the other
communist leaders, notably the Italian party's Enrico Berlinguer and France's
Georges Marchais, Kádár avoided taking extreme positions; he invoked the
1976 East Berlin agreement, and laid nuanced emphasis on its provisions for
party autonomy and proletarian internationalism (i.e., the minimum degree of
conformity palatable to Moscow). But as the schismatic debate dragged on it
began to arouse uncertainty within the ranks of the HSWP, and the very term
Eurocommunism was expunged from official statements. While Kádár probably
genuinely favored a degree of permissive pluralism within the communist
movement, he could not allow his party's monopolistic position to be put in
question. He continued to profess unstinting loyalty to the Soviet Union and
was rewarded in 1977.with the Lenin Peace Prize.

Kádár, who in the mid-1970s emerged as the doyen of East European communist leaders, has nurtured generally cordial relations with his counterparts. His domestic economic and cultural reforms did arouse some misgivings, particularly on the part of the East Germans, and Hungarian officials have been pressing fruitlessly for years within Comecon for changes in the exchange system and other procedures to facilitate a common market more compatible with the spirit of the NEM. The regime endorsed the "complex integration program" unveiled at the Comecon council's twenty-fifth session in Bucharest in May 1971; periodically, it has tried to reassure the public regarding the benefits of membership. The road of socialist economic integration, said Deputy Prime Minister Gyula Szekér in 1976, "corresponds to the interests of our nation and of the whole socialist community." It has also been stressed, notably by Deputy Premier Huszár, that Comecon's "institutional and decision-making system guarantees that expanding reciprocal relations will not lead to the violation of the national economic interests of any individual country."[72] In fact, given the limited competitiveness of Hungarian industry on the world market and the country's lack of major sources of energy, a degree of economic integration may be not only politically inescapable but also of some material benefit.

**Magyar Minorities.** Regional integration has not resolved the problem of Hungarian minorities, which has plagued relations among the states of the Danubian basin since World War I. The over half-million-strong Magyar minority in Slovakia (constituting a local majority in several hundred villages) won a largely nominal recognition as a separate national group in the 1960 constitution, but it continued to suffer from less-than-equal educational and cultural facilities and from low socioeconomic status. During the Prague spring this minority's organization, Csemadok, issued a declaration calling for a variety of cultural rights plus national self-administration. In October, concurrently with the federalization of the Czechoslovak republic, a nationalities law was enacted confirming the rights of the Hungarian and other minority groups. Although the tension between Slovakian and Magyar nationalism remains unresolved, the Hungarian minority is no longer the subject of systematic official discrimination. It enjoys some cultural intercourse with the mother country, and its status does not seem to have had a negative effect on relations between the two ruling parties.[73]

In Romania, on the other hand, the minority problem is more acute and has led to perceptibly cool interparty relations. The 1952 constitution had created an autonomous province for the linguistically indistinguishable Magyars and Székelys of Transylvania. After 1958, however, the opportunistic nationalism of the Romanian party leadership ushered in a period of harsh repression that has endured. The Hungarians lost their ancient independent university at Kolozsvár (Cluj), other educational and cultural facilities were restricted, and the county system was gerrymandered in order to fragment the minority. The

Bucharest regime has resorted to a variety of tactics to disperse and assimilate the around 2 million Magyars who live in Romania (while manipulating census data to underestimate their numbers, now officially some 1.7 million). Moreover, it has promoted a nationalist version of the region's history that deprecates the historic role of the Magyars and other minorities. The repressiveness of the Ceausescu regime has affected all Romanian citizens, but the elaboration of a nationalistic myth in aid of the system's legitimacy has necessarily taken its toll of ethnic tolerance.

Since Marxist theory views nationalism as an aberration intimately linked with bourgeois imperialism, and since the victory of communism by definition eradicated national oppression, the Hungarian regime has had little latitude to rise to the defense of Magyar minorities. The fate of the latter, and particularly of the oppressed Magyars of Transylvania, remains an issue of passionate concern to most Hungarians, and Kádár has had to exercise restraint to avoid fanning the flames of domestic (and minority) nationalism. Party leaders have at times made veiled references to the problem, generally within the context of the Soviet denigration of Romanian nationalism. Arguing in 1972 that "no permanent success can be attained by professing sovereignty charged with nationalism," the HSWP's onetime foreign policy expert, Zoltán Komócsin, concluded pointedly: "We Hungarian communists do not consider a comradely exchange of opinions or sincere criticism in connection with our problems to be interference in our domestic affairs."[74] The minority issue has been allowed occasional airing in intellectual circles, beginning with a speech by the Writers' Association's secretary-general, Imre Dobozy, at a conference at Eger in October 1967. Solidarity with the Hungarian minorities and responsibility for their fate could not be considered nationalistic, he said: "The more open and active our good relations with our neighbors, the more naturally they will accept the fact that we still consider the minority of our people living in their country as Hungarians."[75]

Since that unprecedented declaration, Hungarian intellectuals have regularly returned to the theme of cultural freedom for the Magyar minorities and their importance for the preservation of the Hungarian heritage. The occasional article has reflected on the difficulty of solving nationality problems even under socialism. The Romanian historians who praise the Versailles peace settlement have been criticized for neglecting to note its anti-Bolshevik character and the ensuing oppression of minorities by the bourgeois-nationalist regime. Most recently, Gyula Illyés has written a powerful·piece observing that Europe's largest national minority is Hungarian and denouncing its oppression as a "violation of elementary human rights."[76]

The publication of commentaries on such an explosive issue is of course closely controlled by the regime, which appears to have come to the conclusion that pent-up domestic resentment necessitated, and Romania's unpopularity in Moscow allowed, a measure of protest. Ceausescu was the only Soviet-bloc party leader absent from the HSWP's eleventh congress, and the infrequent high-level bilateral meetings are noticeably free from the fulsome cordiality that marks relations with other parties. Kádár's meeting with Ceausescu at Debrecen, Hungary, and Oradea, Romania on 15 and 16 June 1977 produced an official communiqué that noted: "The just solution in the spirit of Marxism-Leninism of the ethnic minorities issue, and securing equal rights and many-sided development of the ethnic minorities, are a minor element of socialist construction in the two countries, and of deepening Hungarian-Romanian friendly relations." It referred to international norms for the protection of minority rights, although the latter were the exclusive responsibility of each country, and stressed that the ethnic minorities should serve as a link in Hungarian-Romanian rapprochement.[77] With such cautious probes the Kádár regime was finally responding to a national interest that carries grave implications for the future of regional relations.

In the meantime, Budapest has treated with notable liberalism Hungary's own Romanian, Slovakian, southern Slav, and German minorities. The party's nationality policy aims to provide cultural and educational facilities and to integrate the minorities into social and political life without necessarily assimilating them—a policy that, it is pointedly argued by the party's spokesman, also serves to "beat down Hungarian nationalism and the nationalist symptoms that have appeared lately in some neighboring countries."[78] There is frequent reiteration of the distinction between antisocialist nationalism, allegedly a symptom of the 1956 counterrevolution, and socialist patriotism, inseparable from proletarian internationalism, which is the policy of the HSWP.

**Regional Cooperation.** The strains in Hungarian-Yugoslav relations created by the Nagy affair took many years to dissipate, but a new entente was sealed with Tito's visit to Budapest in 1964. The invasion of Czechoslovakia led to a temporary relapse, and in 1974 the Yugoslavs, having uncovered a "Stalinist" plot against the Tito regime, alleged that seditious material had been printed in Hungary—all, presumably, part of a Soviet-directed subversive operation. On the whole, however, relations between the two countries have remained cordial. Commercial exchanges have been aided by the similarities in their systems of economic management. Trade is cleared in convertible currency, direct contact between enterprises is permitted, and a variety of joint projects have been initiated, such as the Adria pipeline. Harmony also prevails over the question of minorities (over 500,000 Magyars live in the Voivodina, an affluent district in northern Yugoslavia), which are regularly hailed as bridges between the two neighbors.

For a time in the mid-1960s the Hungarian regime laid emphasis on Danubian cooperation. On more than one occasion Kádár observed that while membership in the socialist camp predetermined Hungary's relations with other states, geographical concepts retained a certain validity.[79] The possible Soviet interest in this orientation was suggested by Foreign Minister Péter's argument (consonant with the Gaullist view) that Western Europe had to turn to the East to reduce its economic dependence on the United States: "Cooperation among the Danubian countries," he added, "especially those situated along the line dividing the two social systems, may become a factor of considerable value in furthering the development of a European organization of peace and security." Reflecting on the minority problem, he lamented: "Even today international reaction is trying to exploit the Treaty of Trianon, dictated to Hungary by the imperialist powers, in order to stir up trouble among the peoples of the Danubian basin."[80] Concurrently a prominent publicist averred that Czechoslovakia, Hungary, Yugoslavia, and Austria formed a promising nucleus for regionalism, since among the first three there existed a trend toward "still greater cooperation and the gradual reduction in the importance of national frontiers"; moreover, the relationship between them and Austria was the "keystone of peaceful coexistence in the Danube Valley."[81] These regionalist hopes were soon dampened by the invasion of Czechoslovakia, then superseded by the campaign for a European security conference, but Hungary has in fact pursued close relations with Austria in trade, joint industrial ventures, and the exchange of electric power. She has also promoted trade and energy projects with Czechoslovakia and Yugoslavia.

**Security and Detente.** Danubian cooperation may well be in Hungary's objective economic and political interests. Unfortunately, the limits of westward initiatives are set by Soviet policy, by the security structure of the Warsaw Pact and of the twenty-year treaties of friendship, cooperation, and mutual assistance that were renewed with the other Soviet-bloc states. Brezhnev's assertion that the Warsaw Treaty Organization "has served and continues to serve as the principal coordinating center for the members' foreign policy" overstates the pact's politically integrative function compared to other channels, but it does indicate the last line of defense of the "socialist commonwealth."[82] Hungary is host to the headquarters of the Warsaw Pact's southern group, and to four Soviet divisions and a tactical air force; her own armed strength consists of a small army and air force (103,000), the frontier guard (20,000), and the workers' militia (60,000).

Most Hungarians construed as a diplomatic defeat for Kádár the Soviet Union's insistence that Hungary be excluded from direct participation in the Vienna talks on mutual force reductions. Hungary's status had been the principal stumbling bloc to the start of negotiations, but the Soviet stand, that Hun-

gary and Italy participate on an equal footing or not at all, was officially described as "rational" since the exclusion of Italy would have left some U.S.
forces out of the bargaining and led to "unbalanced" reductions.[83] When the
Western side refused to reconsider letting Italy participate, Hungary was relegated to the status of an observer. The compromise left out of negotiation Hungary's national and Soviet forces, although the dilatory pace of the ensuing
talks made the exclusion of little immediate consequence. The "temporary"
presence of Soviet troops in Hungary, uninterrupted since 1944, may owe more
to Moscow's military strategy than to considerations of domestic stability, for
memories of the 1956 and 1968 armed interventions are probably a sufficient
deterrent to Hungarian secessionists. All the same, the scarcely visible Russian
soldiers remain a painful, symbolic reminder of hegemonic constraints. When
questioned on the matter at a press conference in Vienna in December 1976,
Kádár allowed that Soviet forces would remain in Hungary until the general
situation of world politics changed.

The HSWP has consistently followed the Soviet line on the significance of
detente and European security. This line was, to parody von Clausewitz, a
continuation of the cold war by other means. A European security system based
on the status quo was feasible, but it was anticipated that detente would only
intensify the ideological struggle. Contact with the capitalist world in the guise
of peaceful coexistence was still class warfare, for there were irreconcilable
differences, and Marxist-Leninist principles allowed no compromise in the
sphere of ideology. Neighborly relations and the exchange of "ideas serving
progress" were acceptable. As the concept of detente gained currency, the regime stepped up its denunciation of Western propaganda for its message of
inevitable convergence, for using the lure of apparent objectivity in accounts
of life in the West, and of popular music to undermine the leading role of the
party by seducing ill-informed young people and exploiting their natural rebel-
liousness. The KISZ was instructed to "expose the intentions of the enemy,"
and Western visitors were also identified as a subversive influence against
which young people in particular had to be indoctrinated.[84]

At the preliminary talks before the security conference Hungary sided with
the Soviet Union in opposing a Romanian proposal to underscore the equality
of states without regard for their alliance membership. Kádár's address at the
Helsinki summit (July–August 1975) was notable for its reference to Hungary's
historical role in the Danubian Basin and its territorial truncation in 1919, but
his remarks suggested that nothing in the Final Act would require substantial
change in his policies. The official Hungarian position on the review of the
Helsinki Accord has been to minimize opposition in Eastern Europe and to
claim that the socialist countries have a better record on the "free flow of
people and ideas" than Western ones. At the same time, it has been emphasized that differences in their respective social systems mean that it would

take decades to fully implement the accord.[85] To demonstrate Hungary's openness to debate, three television programs were aired during 1976/77 in which
panels of communist and Western journalists engaged in fairly unrestricted discussions on aspects of East-West relations. President Carter's human rights
campaign, on the other hand, has been sharply condemned for creating an atmosphere unpropitious for the successful conduct of the talks on strategic arms
limitation and on force reductions in Europe.[86] At the opening session of the
Belgrade review conference, the Hungarian delegate retaliated against the
American stress on human rights by complaining of trade discrimination and
visa restrictions on the part of the West.[87] On the whole, however, the Kádár
regime could take comfort from the relative benevolence with which it was
viewed from both East and West.

On all contentious East-West issues, such as Vietnam, the Middle East,
Angola, and Chile, the HSWP has routinely echoed the Soviet position. Hungary provided aid to the North Vietnamese, and in consequence of the Paris
agreement was invited to participate in the International Commission of Control
and Supervision. While fulfilling these obligations to the Soviet Union, however, the Kádár regime has earnestly sought to normalize commercial and diplomatic relations with the West. In the case of the German Federal Republic,
the settlement of German-Czechoslovak differences delayed full diplomatic
recognition until December 1973, but West Germany soon became Hungary's
principal Western trading partner. With the United States, the key objective has
been to win most-favored-nation tariff status. For symbolic rather than tangible
reasons, however, Budapest has refused to condone the strictures of the
Jackson amendment, which made trade concessions conditioned on the relaxation of constraints on emigration. Permission for the visit of Billy Graham was
a finely calculated gesture designed to demonstrate the regime's tolerance of
religious freedom. The Carter administration indicated a few months later that
in light of "substantial improvement" in U.S.-Hungarian relations the 977-
year-old crown of Saint Stephen and other royal jewels, in U.S. safekeeping
since the end of World War II, would be finally returned to Hungary. That
symbolic gesture, in the same year that Kádár received the Lenin Peace Prize,
marked the distance that he had come since the dark days of 1956. Apart from
his unhappy appearance at the United Nations accompanying Khrushchev in
1960 and his attendance at the Helsinki summit, Kádár avoided travel to Western countries for the next twenty years. In 1976/77, however, he spearheaded a
flurry of diplomatic activity that raised Hungary's profile in the West, beginning with a visit to Austria in December 1976 and continuing with trips to Italy
and West Germany the following year. As the leader of the least oppressive
regime in Eastern Europe, Kádár served as a relatively persuasive spokesman
for the Soviet bloc in the context of detente, and he acquitted himself of that
political task in a relaxed manner while seeking commercial benefits for his
economically troubled country.

Finally, it is worth noting that the regime has embarked on an active campaign of reconciliation with the over 1.5-million-strong Hungarian diaspora. Political calculations have played their part in the activities of the "World Federation of Hungarians" and the amnesties for illegal emigrants, but the cultural and linguistic thrust of the programs have struck a responsive chord in many émigré hearts without alleviating political differences.

The final impression left by the Kádár administration is that it is inclined to devote its energies to domestic problems and avoid as much as possible embroilment in the complicated world of international and interparty politics. Hungary is a minor power, and one that has suffered greatly from its exposed position in the heart of Europe and the crosscurrents of great-power conflicts. In advocating peaceful coexistence the regime is therefore not simply parroting the Soviet line but also reflecting the wish of the weak to be left alone, an objective that currently translates into the unimpeded consolidation of Kádár's centrist rule. The two dimensions of this conciliatory orientation were succinctly described by Kádár in a speech in 1974. The first pillar was unswerving political loyalty to the ruling power. "In foreign policy, we have always openly sided with the Soviet Union even in the most difficult of times," said Kádár, clearly alluding to the Czechoslovakian crisis. The other dimension was normal relations, particularly in the commercial realm, with the West. "Our capitalist partners know," he added, "that the Hungarian People's Republic is a reliable partner."[88] In this way the Kádár regime hopes to assure its permanence as well as the economic modernization of Hungary.

# 16. The Governed: Social Change and Political Legitimacy

As long as the Manichaean myth pitting the phalanx of working people and their vanguard party against class enemies prevailed in Hungarian communist dogma, the question of social stratification and plural interests did not arise. With the completion of collectivization, and the gradual conversion of the alliance policy from theory to practice, the party leadership could claim that the domestic class struggle was essentially concluded and thus invite the entire population to collaborate in the building of socialism.

As the momentum of reform, primarily in the economic sphere, gained strength in the late 1960s, so too did the idea that distinct group interests were intrinsic to social life and that the planning and administering institutions should adapt to this reality. The recognition that an undifferentiated society was little more than an eschatological concept was a notable manifestation of the new realism. Kádár himself acknowledged this when he told the Central Committee in November 1967 that the dichotomic view of society and individual had to be amended to allow for the collective interests of certain socioeconomic units. Moreover, it was anticipated that the NEM would reveal the existence of a variety of social strata distinguished in their interests by occupation and income.[1]

Perception of emerging patterns of social differentiation and stratification had to be reconciled on the ideological plane with the basic tenet of a classless society. The explanation was offered that the "differences between us and capitalist societies resides not in their structure being hierarchical and ours not, but rather in the qualitative differences that characterize their class-based society."[2] Debate on the significance of these concepts ran the gamut. At one extreme, radicals argued that since socialist society remained differentiated both in structure and interests, the party's proper function was that of an ultimate but rather remote arbiter. At the other, orthodox thinkers rejected such revisionism as being inconsistent with the party's preordained task of gaining and consolidating the allegiance of the whole of society.

## SOCIAL STRUCTURE

Underlying these ideological debates was the transformation in the social structure that had come about over the last fifteen years.[3] While the size of the ruling elite of party, government, military, and security officials had remained relatively constant at 3 percent of the population, a new middle stratum had emerged to radically alter the atomized and diffuse social structure of the Rákosi period. The proportion of this predominantly technocratic middle class, composed of professionals, managers, intellectuals, and other white-collar workers, rose from 15 to 24 percent between 1965 and 1975. Although in the early 1960s two-thirds of this stratum could claim working-class or peasant origins, its expansion confronted the regime with the predictable problems of vested interest and self-perpetuation.[4] As a Hungarian historian observed, "upward mobility, at least in terms of its proportion, was a unique phenomenon during this period"—a period of rapid modernization.[5] To the extent that education replaced politics as the criterion for advancement, the growing over-representation and better performance of the new middle class in postsecondary education promised to entrench its status. Concurrently, urbanization and the modernization of agriculture led to further expansion of the industrial working class (from 51 to 55 percent) and to decline in the proportion of agricultural manual workers (from 29 to 15 percent); the proportion of independent producers increased from 2 to 3 percent in the same period.

**The Middle Class.** The rise of an autonomous middle class possessed of its own secular value system and offering the party a loyalty that is essentially opportunistic has placed the regime in a dilemma. The privileges of the new class are not only symbolic but also material. The range of income distribution (though not, of course, the real levels) in Hungarian society approximates that in developed Western countries, and while this may be the inevitable characteristic of a modernizing meritocracy, it has also induced ideologically powerful counter-pressures in favor of egalitarianism.[6]

If in its immediate origins the Hungarian middle class differs from its Western counterparts, in its behavior it exhibits universal tendencies. The stratum consists of a few early middle-class adherents to the communist movement, of offspring of the old discredited bourgeoisie who managed to overcome political discrimination and regain a status analogous to that of their parents, and, in the majority, of former workers and peasants who benefited from the regime's preferential treatment. The class as a whole is achievement and property oriented, devoted to career advancement and to the transfer of their status to their offspring. It exploits the opportunities for power and affluence while ignoring or deriding the ruling party's ideological convolutions. Its members adhere to the party when necessary, but many professionals and middle-level officials and managers prosper without taking that step. It has a more highly developed sense of social justice than its predecessors, but remains covertly contemptuous of the proletariat from which many of its members rose. It rejoices in such manifestations of affluence as private cars, weekend cottages, and foreign travel, but fears the possible political repercussions of overly conspicuous consumption. It takes pride in being the prime purveyor and consumer of culture and in its awareness and imitation of Western intellectual and material innovations. The new middle class, in sum, owes much to Kádárism but also senses that the latter depends on its cooperation and therefore on the security of its status.

**Workers and Their Unions.**   The impact of modernization on the industrial working class has been to induce both fervid consumerism and resentment at the more rapid material advancement of the peasantry and the expanding middle classes. As a class, the proletariat remains largely indifferent to the theory and practice of communist politics, a passivity demonstrated by the party's own surveys.[7] Its egalitarian tendencies have, however, been invigorated by the income differentiation and social restratification of the last fifteen years, and worker criticism of the more privileged strata has visibly embarrassed a regime that officially claims to represent the interest of the proletariat. As noted earlier, the leadership's dilemma was only accentuated by the espousal of the egalitarian line by party dogmatists and the New Left fringe groups.

The self-assertion of the industrial working class came at a time when the logic of the alliance policy was leading the regime to legitimize a degree of pluralistic interest group activity. Close to four million workers now belong to trade unions, which are organized along sectoral rather than craft lines and are coordinated by the National Council of Trade Unions. Their original function as a downward transmission belt has been expanded to include servicing the "legitimate interests of a smaller community." The party leadership has pursued a dual and sometimes contradictory policy of urging more vigorous union activity at the enterprise level while preserving labor discipline and the decentralization of economic management.[8] The necessity for reinvigorating the unions was explained as follows by the national council's secretary-general, Sándor Gáspár: "The new management system allows factories much greater independence—they can draw up their own plans, with due regard to local potential and resources, and determine the funds necessary to implement the plans. This means that basic union organizations must enjoy wider jurisdiction, which, moreover, has to be precisely defined to avoid overlapping." Since hitherto trade unions (and managers) had served in effect as extensions of the party-state apparatus, having an only illusory independence, their newly acquired latitude represented an alteration of the ideological concept of an indivisible public interest. According to the new orthodoxy, "there can be a certain divergence of interests, certain contradictions which the unions make it their job to disclose and resolve." The 1967 labor code granted unions the right of advice and veto over working conditions, and of advice regarding plant operation and the appointment and dismissal of managers. Unresolved management-labor disputes were to be settled by "higher bodies," presumably the relevant ministry, although Gáspár asserted that if necessary the unions could submit differences between state and union bodies to the "judgment of the public."[9]

The right to strike is purposely omitted from the labor code, and while the occasional brief work stoppage has occurred, this ultimate weapon of organized labor is proscribed. Worker participation in management along the lines of the Yugoslav model has also been ruled out by the HSWP as unrealistic. On certain policy matters the workers are said to have no professional expertise; on other, procedural and environmental questions, they are invited to express opinions, but surveys show that even here they lack the necessary information.[10] In fact, the unions have not taken full advantage of their right to be consulted by management, nor followed up consistently management's handling of their advice. A survey conducted by the National Council of Trade Unions found that the unions resorted only infrequently to their right of veto, apparently because of the timidity and incompetence of local union leaders and the absence of clear precedents. Thus, instead of trying to implement enterprise democracy, the officials resort to informal compromises.[11]

The party's efforts to enhance the status of the workers through enterprise democracy have been spurred by accusations that the managers misuse their authority, disregard the workers' opinions, and retaliate against justifiable criticism. According to a party resolution: "Despite repeated warnings by the party's leading organs, tolerance of such phenomena is still encountered." While the party concedes that the veto as a "political instrument of last resort" is appropriate in cases of flagrant mismanagement, the official attitude is one of ambivalence.[12] The managers, said Nyers in 1973, "should be resolute and firm and yet combine this with democratic prodecures."[13] Another concern of organized labor has been the protection of craft interests and the inadequacy of the existing branch unions. The restructuring that took place in 1948, replacing craft unions with industrial unions, was dictated by political expediency. Pressures have since been mounting for more direct representation of the interests of workers in individual enterprises and crafts, for recognition of the principle of "one plant—many interests."[14]

When the NEM's capacity to accommodate the stresses of the economic crisis of the mid-1970s came into question, the party issued reassurances that the attendant policy of democratization would not be reversed.

"Not less, but more democracy is required, so that the masses can be brought to consider as their own the nation's struggle, to realize its aims, and to overcome its difficulties. It is true that discipline is not possible without disciplined work, but socialist democracy and socialist discipline are not contradictory terms. . . . Socialist work discipline requires that leaders and political activists make their decisions only after consulting the workers and asking for their advice. . . . There are still a large number of people who try to sidestep this question.[15]

Party leaders, indeed, particularly Sándor Gáspár, have tirelessly reiterated the theme espoused by the eleventh congress, that the trade union movement must "exploit the potential for enterprise democracy." The exercise of "direct democracy" by conferences of shop stewards was introduced on an experimental basis in fifty enterprises in late 1975 and subsequently recommended for the rest of industry. In the new system, the allocation of retained profits, hitherto determined by management, the party organization, and trade union bodies, also comes before the shop stewards for consideration and discussion with the workers.[16] In April 1977 the council of ministers and the National Council of Trade Unions passed a resolution providing for joint meetings of each enterprise's trade union council and shop stewards' committee, with concurring and advisory rights over the collective contract and over distribution of certain funds, wage rates, and enterprise plans. The party's principal hope is that this extension of enterprise democracy will stimulate productivity. At the same time, managers are exhorted to overcome their bureaucratic caution and show greater willingness to take risks.[17]

All socialist regimes face the problem of assuring full employment while achieving high productivity, and the NEM's decentralization has only added to the complexity of the task. According to the party daily,

> it is the task of the state, not of the enterprise, to provide full employment, to check and eliminate social disproportions. Enterprise production can be carried out only on the basis of the principle of rational employment and economic efficiency, even if this must result in a regrouping of the labor force and the closing down of some factories. . . . So far as the factory goes, good wages can be determined only by efficient performance.[18]

But the optimal mechanism for manipulating the educational system to fit the manpower needs of a modernizing and complex economy remains elusive. Between 1970 and 1976 the number of pupils entering vocational and technical schools declined by 25 percent. As a result, there was a shortage of skilled workers while white-collar employment soared. The hiring freeze on administrative employees noted earlier was designed to steer young job-seekers to less desirable blue-collar jobs. While it was economically rational, the measure aroused the apprehensions of a population accustomed to identifying upward mobility with white-collar employment.

Apart from the trade unions, enterprise management and agricultural cooperatives have also benefited from the decentralizing impact of the NEM. Such organizations as the Hungarian Chamber of Commerce and the National Council of Agricultural Cooperatives have come to act as the advocates of sectoral interests.[19] Thus in the spirit of the alliance policy various mass organizations and officially recognized interest groups have emerged as recognized intermediaries and aggregators of opinion. Their mandate, however, is bounded by their technical competence, narrowly interpreted, and by the societal objective of building socialism. This, clearly, cannot be characterized as political pluralism. Nevertheless, the latest activities of these groups represent a significant advance over their erstwhile ritualistic and transmission-belt functions.

## THE POLITICAL CULTURE

Recognition that an officially classless society could in its structure still be highly stratified and in need of interest-group expression was accompanied by acknowledgment that the official ideology lacked consensual support. Wrote Gyula Kállai in 1976:

> We must take into account that a significant part of the masses . . . is still not unified in its world outlook. This is linked to the fact that there remain traces of the old system's ideology, and indeed in certain political and economic circumstances this harmful legacy may and does reemerge. We must confront calmly but determinedly the fact that the philosophy of individualism and egoism is, under the ostensible veneer of socialism, spreading through not negligible strata of our society.[20]

Indeed, as an analyst of the contemporary Hungarian polity has concluded, "the Party leadership and some members of the Party accept the ideology of Marxism-Leninism, but the general population only accepts some of the basic values of the system, rejecting the applicability of the entire ideology to their daily lives."[21]

In the wake of the resounding rejection it suffered at the hands of its constituents in 1956, Kádár's party took the pragmatic path of modernizing the economic system by forging a largely apolitical alliance with the mass of nonbelievers. The brutal imposition of ideological conformity in the Rákosi era had generated the illusion of popular consensus but proved in fact to have been a disastrously alienating exercise. Kádár wisely opted for the alternate approach of socialization by persuasion, a tolerant tactic which in the event enhanced his popularity but demonstrated scarcely greater effectiveness in converting the masses to the communist faith.

In its socialization policies the regime has stressed the virtues of its theory and practice in contrast to a variety of unacceptable alternatives: the Rákosi era's distortions, the values of the bourgeois past, current Western alternatives, and the values of organized religion.[22] It has tried to instill loyalty to the idealized goals of "socialist construction," "socialist patriotism" and the "socialist commonwealth." Since in the popular view socialist construction, shorn of its millenarian perspective, is identified with the secular task of economic modernization, it meets with little resistance apart from egalitarian reservations. Socialist morality remains an amorphous concept despite the attempts of the party to differentiate it in some tangible way from traditional moral and ethical codes. To the extent that it connotes civic responsibility and high personal ethics, it is noticeable by its absence in contemporary Hungarian society, where social mores are no better and in some respects (such as bribery and influence peddling) inferior to those found in the West. The regime and its media regularly excoriate such petty bourgeois sins as individualism, materialism, egotism, and corruption, but the socialist superman appears to be even more elusive than the Christian saint. The regime has taken pains to absolve the new middle class from special responsibility for these deplorable traits. As the journalist Lajos Mesterházi explained, the enemy was not necessarily the petty bourgeois, who might well be an honest citizen, but rather the pervasive spirit of "petty-minded bourgeoisism," self-centered, acquisitive, and lacking in social consciousness. The worker who viewed his main job as incidental to his material well-being was as culpable as the manager who catered to enterprise interest at the expense of the public interest.[23]

Socialist patriotism is the party's alternative to traditional nationalism and to Rákosi's insulting denigration of national sentiments. By allowing for a degree of patriotic pride and cultural self-respect, the concept has served the legitimacy of the regime. Its attendant strictures against hostility toward the Soviet Union and some of the neighboring states, notably Romania (where Magyar minorities have been suffering from a different version of socialist patriotism), have constrained only the more overt expression of profound nationalistic emotions.

**Intractable Youth.** Recognizing the difficulty of overcoming the ingrained prejudices of the older generation, which in any case remembers worse times and is acutely conscious of the external restraints, the Kádár regime has concentrated on the socialization of the presumably more malleable youth. The hope that the younger generation was the core of a future, genuinely socialist polity was dashed by the experience of the 1956 revolution, then revived under Kádár, but the regime has been once again confronted with evidence of youthful alienation and apathy. A study conducted by a primary school teacher in the late 1960s testified not only to widespread anti-Russian sentiments among her students, but also to a marked preference for the great figures of Hungarian history over the much-touted heroes of the "workers' movement." Another local survey among older adolescents and youths disclosed that over half adhered to a traditional value system, one-third also admitted to religious faith, and only 14 percent appeared to espouse Marxist values. A broader survey carried out by the KISZ among its members found that 83 percent of the respondents considered patriotism to be a desirable value.[24]

The regime has tried to remedy these deficiencies, notably by mounting new courses on "Fundamentals of Our World Outlook" (introduced at the secondary level in 1972) and on civics, but the competing influences of family, religion, and information regarding the West inevitably reduce the impact of indoctrination. The KISZ has received its share of the blame for the inadequacies of political socialization. According to one party analysis undertaken in 1973, a small group of ultraleftists viewed the KISZ as an obstacle to revolution, while young people in general yearned for a more creative and romantic outlet for their energies than that provided by the KISZ and the system as a whole. Young people were unimpressed by comparisons with the (to them) unknown "bad old days of capitalism"; instances of discrimination against non-KISZ members only aroused hostility; the KISZ leadership elections were frequently stage-managed; the leadership was too old, bureaucratized, conservative, and often of lower intellectual caliber than the rank and file.[25] A mixture of youthful frustration, patriotism, and New Left ideology inspired minor spontaneous demonstrations during the 15 March national holiday celebrations in both 1972 and 1973. On the latter occasion forty-one were arrested, and the authorities denounced the protesters as "irresponsible nationalists," although many of the slogans were of the New Left variety, such as "All power to the workers' councils" and "Down with the bureaucrats." Such isolated outbursts are less significant, however, than the general political apathy predominating among the youth of Hungary.

The problem of integrating the young without resorting to regimentation remains one of the regime's most painful dilemmas. Their cult of Western fads, ranging from denim clothes to rock music, and their occasional antisocial behavior are but the surface manifestations of a more deeply rooted sense of impotence and futility. Kádár's pragmatism has yet to offer a credible answer to youth's implicit demands for participation and self-realization. The KISZ and the "youth parliaments" have failed to meet the challenge, and the regime's attempts to control the thousands of youth clubs and use them for political indoctrination have alienated most members, who seek only entertainment. The majority of young people dutifully pursue the material rewards offered by the system, but their pursuit is largely devoid of ideological content or appreciation for the regime. As a Western observer has noted regarding East Europe in general, "the Party's successes in modernizing the region have turned its young only further westwards." On the other hand, economic and technological backwardness is widely attributed to the inefficiencies of communist and Soviet rule.[26]

Uninhibited by their past, the young can also ask embarrassing questions. Aging servants of the Rákosi regime are occasionally the butt of ostensibly innocent interrogation at youth meetings. Why is it, they are asked for instance, that Rákosi himself had been able to turn his trial into a propaganda victory against his Horthyite persecutors, whereas they in the Stalinist period cowered in mute submission? The hapless veterans, inclined to rebuff such provocative inquisition, are urged by the party to be candid about past mistakes. Even officially encouraged candor has its limits, however. The line is drawn at public admission that the Soviet Union was ultimately responsible for the horrors euphemistically ascribed to the "cult of personality" and that single-party rule of any political shade facilitates such abuses. The youthful syndrome of impatient searching and idealism is universal, but accommodating it is clearly more of a problem in an intolerant and authoritarian political system.

**Values and Behavior.**    The overall political profile of the general public is marked by apathy and cynicism.[27] Lip service to popular participation notwithstanding, the Kádár regime has exploited this depoliticization. The unspoken but universally understood fact that all change in Hungary is subject to Soviet restraint, and general appreciation that within these limits Kádár has skillfully served Hungarian interests, indicate the nature of the regime's legitimacy: it is built on the satisfaction of material needs. Kádár's pragmatism is thus rewarded by an ideologically neutral public acceptance that is equally pragmatic. Public recognition that the standard of living has improved is only partly qualified by evidence of greater affluence in the developed Western democracies. The nationalistic abhorrence of Soviet hegemony is largely neutralized by the obvious lack of alternatives and by the regime's demonstrated commitment to a national model of domestic reform.

Beneath this tacit political compact between rulers and ruled, in the words of a Hungarian historian, "traditional ways of living, habits, and prejudices are still very much alive."[28] Popular prejudices against gypsies, Jews, and the Romanian oppressors of the Transylvanian Hungarians remain in evidence. Although the traditional preponderance of Jews in the party leadership was reduced partly by circumstance and partly by calculation in the restoration period, their presence in the state and economic administration and in certain spheres of culture and the media still inspires anti-Semitic sentiments. Of more general consequence is the petty and authoritarian bureaucratism, inherited from earlier times but aggravated by party norms and the expansion of the party-state administrative network. The habits acquired under a succession of authoritarian regimes are difficult to amend. Consider this heartfelt plea by a young writer:

> It's true, we can't expect to have democracy until international alignments change. But meanwhile, how about changing what we have inside the country, and in people's minds? So we can have democracy when the chance arises. What we have at the moment is more or less a socialist reproduction of what there was before the war. Instead of feudal capitalism, we have feudal socialism. And inside people's heads too, a feudal mentality, of either ordering others about or waiting to be ordered about. If there is going to be change, that's where it'll have to start.[29]

It is doubtful that behavioral change can precede political reform in the direction of authentic pluralism, a prospect which is equally remote. Shortly before his death in 1971, György Lukács expressed deep pessimism regarding the attainment of genuine socialist democracy within the bureaucratic-authoritarian systems of the Soviet bloc. "A true economic reform can be achieved only through a democratization of the daily life of the workers," he said, and went on to observe that "a system that is based on having us sit on bayonets is not a solid system."[30] Lukács's ideal of democracy may not be analogous to Western versions, but in Hungary it is just as unrealizable. Thus Kádár's quest for popular legitimacy is limited by the nonnegotiable premises of single-party monopoly and ideological conformity. Dilution of either premise, while undoubtedly desired by the majority of constituents, would incur the intolerable risk of Soviet intervention.

In sum, the more prevalent popular values in Hungary are the pursuit of material wealth and a profound patriotism. These are conditioned by pragmatic acknowledgment of the inescapable fact of communist rule and by a certain acceptance of socialist-collectivist principles. Soviet hegemony, the secrecy of political decision making and leadership selection, pervasive propaganda and limited cultural freedom, bureaucratic authoritarianism, a standard of living that despite improvement remains well behind that of the affluent West—all are perceived as negative features of the system. On the other hand, central economic planning, state ownership of at least the larger industries, industrial-scale agriculture, assured employment, cradle-to-grave social services, and subsidized culture are elements of the system that few Hungarians would willingly exchange for the uncertainties of a fully market-driven model. But then, the latter's advocates have become a minority even in the West.

## THE DECEPTIVE COMPROMISE

The key hypothetical question about Hungary's political structure—how could all these positive and negative interests best be served?—cannot of course be put there. Some very tentative answers are provided by the series of surveys conducted by independent public opinion research institutes on behalf of Radio Free Europe among sociologically representative samples of Hungarian travelers in Western Europe. The political profile presented by these soundings shows remarkable consistency over the last decade. The response in 1969 to questions regarding political concepts indicated a relatively negative attitude toward communism, socialism, people's democracy, and imperialism; ambivalence regarding capitalism; and a very favorable disposition toward pluralistic democracy. Attitudes toward religion ranged from ambivalent to positive. The survey found no striking variance by age or education.[31] A contemporary study of national images found a generally positive stereotyping of the Hungarians themselves and of Americans, a mixed image of the Germans, and a negative stereotyping of the Russians and particularly of the Romanians.[32] Surveys conducted in 1976 indicated that a majority of those expressing an opinion assessed the basic idea of communism as bad or more bad than good. Fifty percent thought that socialism worked badly in Hungary, compared to 38 percent who thought it worked well; in contrast, 59 percent believed that democracy in the West worked well, and 13 percent that it worked badly.[33] A study in late 1971 of Hungarian attitudes regarding domestic issues revealed a relatively high recognition of the regime's efforts to use experts in economic administration, general economic management, and the provision of community services. Its distribution of income and pensions, however, was appraised negatively, as was its handling of such political issues as constitutional rights, the national interest, and impartial justice.[34]

The choice of parties in hypothetical free elections has been periodically put before such Hungarian samples. The 1976 survey suggested that 5 percent would vote for a communist party, 42 percent for a democratic-socialist party, 27 percent for a Christian democratic party, 17 percent for a peasant party, and 6 percent for a conservative party. A similar sounding four years earlier had given the communist party 10 percent; the subsequent decline may be attributable to the deterioration in the economic climate. The procommunist minority was above average among the technical intelligentsia, the industrial workers, and the younger age groups, and lowest among the farmers. Similarly, the younger and better-educated respondents were relatively better disposed to democratic socialism than to the Christian democratic alternative.[35] A certain "third road" tendency was discernible in the respondents' hopes for the future of East-West relations: 74 percent wished for genuine rapprochement, 24 percent for greater Western influence, and 2 percent for greater Eastern influence.[36] On the other hand, a later survey aggregating the response of Czechs, Hungarians, and Poles indicated that 87 percent favored association with the European Economic Community and 83 percent membership in a politically united Europe.[37]

The circumstances of such extraterritorial soundings impose a wide margin of error, but the results corroborate other, more impressionistic appraisals of the Hungarian political culture. These indicate that, despite the proclaimed democratization of party life and the decompression of the alliance policy, the vast majority of Hungarians would ideally prefer a pluralistic political system, within which only a small fraction would freely vote for a communist party. On the other hand, they accurately perceive the merits and weaknesses of the regime's domestic policies and entertain reservations regarding the capitalist alternative. Of equal significance is the low intensity of popular hostility toward the regime. Despite an inbred predisposition to criticize government and bureaucracy, most Hungarians say they find life tolerable under Kádár's version of socialism without volunteering active endorsement of communist rule. For

Kádár himself they reserve an admiration bordering on grudging affection, recognizing that this unpretentious man has skillfully served their interests within the limitations of one-party rule and Soviet hegemony. He has been successful in satisfying the minimal material and cultural needs of the Hungarian people; they, in turn, have understood external constraints to which he is subject. Or so it can be inferred from the absence of overt challenges to the regime (apart from the ultraleftist syndrome) and from the low level (by East European standards) of illegal emigration; each year only a few hundred Hungarians choose not to return from trips to the West. Thus have Kádár and his people reached a transitional historic compromise.

Within the party itself, the revolutionary zeal of earlier times has been largely swept under by the tide of secular values intrinsic to modernization. The veterans of the movement are fading away amidst displays of nostalgia for the days of militant struggle in illegality and in the postwar era and of resentment at the redundancy of their simple talents. Despite the material achievements claimed by the party, even its most devoted activists must be disheartened by the evident failure of thirty years of indoctrination. For the new breed of functionaries, the immediate concerns are those of career and the system's efficacy in delivering material benefits. For most party members, the creation of an authentic communist man and communist society is conveniently relegated to the twilight of pious hope. Roughly one in ten Hungarians belongs to the party, but for the vast majority membership is a pragmatic choice rather than an act of faith. The population at large, and particularly the intelligentsia, accept the party as an inevitable political fixture but regard its messianic revolutionary essence as increasingly anachronistic in the technocratic age. The small band of true believers suffers from this popular contempt and divides along predictable lines of theory and practice. This alienated group includes veterans whose dogmatic, aggressively proletarian orientation is sharply at odds with the attenuation of dictatorial rule and with the stratification and embourgeoisement of Hungarian society. The two last-named phenomena also irritate the ultraleftist intellectuals and youthful idealists who dream of unadulterated egalitarianism and direct democracy. These disparate tendencies have occasionally converged in opposition to the official centrist line which, it must be assumed, has its own ideological believers as distinct from its pragmatic proponents. Kádár himself and some of his associates are presumably sincere in their belief that the persuasive tactics of the alliance policy are no more than concessions to a political reality that must inevitably evolve into a communist utopia. Although similar theoretical and tactical divergences may obtain with the Soviet party, there remains a critical and ineradicable difference: that party has succeeded in welding Marxism-Leninism, oriental despotism, nationalism, and national interest into an organic whole which for historical reasons the Hungarian and other deriva-

tive communist movements can never hope to replicate. Hungary is too close
to the Soviet Union and the HSWP too subordinate to the Kremlin for Hungarian communism ever to be popularly accepted as a creed in harmony with
indigenous cultural traditions and national interests.

With his alliance policy and economic reforms Kádár did achieve the remarkable feat of overshadowing the brutal imposition of his rule by a foreign
power. Just as remarkably, he succeeded in forging a modus vivendi that, without according with the Western concept of legitimacy, has fostered a political
stability more consensually based than any found in other East European
socialist states. The Hungarian people have willingly taken up the challenge of
participating in the modernization of their country, and they take no small pride
in the achievements of the last decade. The party claims the credit, but aside
from Kádár receives little of it. Meanwhile, the answer to the hoary political question, Who governs the governors? lies largely beyond the confines
of Hungary.

# A Reckoning

# EPILOGUE

*History offers only too many instances of the power of great simplicities, such as egalitarianism and its myriad Marxist derivatives, to seduce the intellectual and exploit the unlettered. The promise of escape from the confines of personal and collective limitations appeals equally to the humble and the proud. Such visions make the momentary sacrifice of self and others seem rational and noble. In the realm of practical politics, however, utopian purpose quickly degenerates into the expedient manipulation of the present by the few. An assessment of the dynamics, performance, and distinctiveness of communism in Hungary must therefore initially confront the question of the degree to which ideology has predetermined political practice.*

*The Marxist vision is of course one of an international society that is classless, unified, and egalitarian. The predestination of the industrial working class to lead this revolution is an act of faith couched in the pseudoscientific terms of the dialectics of economic determinism and ineluctable class conflict. Lenin, in adapting this messianic paradigm to the requisites of time and place, developed a model for the seizure and retention of power whose applicability was claimed to be universal. Power was to be the exclusive property of those initiated to the mysteries of an abstract model of society, of the self-anointed interpreters of the faith. Marxism-Leninism had the uncommon advantage of satisfying both elitist and egalitarian aspirations. It armed the proud practitioner with the purported secret of historical change; it also provided the comforting corollary that at all times the application of these scientific revelations served the interests of the common man. The latter's salvation deserved every sacrifice, certainly that of political freedom when it threatened the rule of the vanguard and the prescribed leveling of society. Revolutionaries, in Chamfort's succinct comment on the French Revolution, readily make the one impossible demand: Be my brother or I will kill you. The Marxist vision was thus transformed into the practice of a tyranny as soulless and brutal as any that had preceded it. Nevertheless, its egalitarian essence retained a capacity to excite the imagination of successive generations and their willingness to condone or, at best, deny the inevitability of repression on the road to utopia.*

*Béla Kun and his Hungarian comrades were impelled to revolutionary action by this egalitarian faith, by the plan of action devised and implemented by their Russian mentors, as well as by their alienation from a conservative and nationalistic ethos and their thirst for personal power. They thrust themselves into the power vacuum that occurred in Hungary in 1918/19 with a radical alternative to the old order, failed to make it either credible or palatable, and were crushed by the weight of external and domestic hostility. In the process, they succeeded in discrediting in the eyes of many of their countrymen not only Bolshevism but also social democracy and, indirectly, even liberal democracy.*

*In the inimical milieu of interwar Hungary, the party was reduced to a tiny conspiratorial movement that exercised a negligible influence on the political culture. It attracted a handful of disaffected workers and intellectuals seeking social revolution, but the mass of Hungarians remained immune to the lure of an ideology that they perceived as alien to individual and national interests. Even the absurdities of racist-fascist radicalism proved more attractive to those estranged from the conservative and authoritarian political ethos than the emanations of Stalinist Bolshevism. If the interwar governments made the occasional concession to the welfare requirements of an industrializing society, they did so in pragmatic accommodation of obvious needs and secular trends, not in response to the scarcely heard protestations of a minuscule communist party.*

*When, with the inestimable weight of Soviet sponsorship behind it, the party emerged once again on the political scene at the end of World War II, it encountered a mood of innovation and pluralism. The old order had hardly been the unmitigated tyranny depicted by the communists and other detractors; indeed, at war's end most Hungarians were far from yearning for revolution. But amidst the rubble of defeat the nation was ready for spiritual renewal and the adoption of a more egalitarian and pluralistic style of politics. The communist party, armed with an explicit program of reform and with the support of the occupying power, exploited this mood of change but failed to overcome mistrust of its strategic designs and the fear induced by its aggressive tactics. Above all, the party failed to convince the nation that it placed the interests of Hungary before those of the Soviet Union. Its acquisition of monopoly power aborted*

*Hungary's brief experiment with pluralistic democracy and confirmed suspicions of the party's tyrannical thrust and subservience to Stalin.*

*Of the people of Hungary, even the industrial working class has shown a persistent reluctance to live up to the expectations of the champions of communism. In 1919 it had readily abandoned its revolutionary vanguard in favor of the social democrats. In 1945 again the majority of workers expressed clear preference for less radical routes to social and economic reform. In 1956, it overwhelmingly rejected the Stalinist style of political rule. At these moments of confrontation and choice most Hungarians judged the communist party to be a corrupt and false defender of economic welfare, individual freedoms, and national sovereignty. The party promised an equality of relative affluence, and delivered an equality of poverty; it promised political emancipation for the working people, and delivered arbitrary terror. Hungarians had little historical experience of liberal democracy, but they took an extravagant pride in constitutionalism and legal propriety, both of which were blatantly flouted by the communists in the name of people's democracy. As before, and since, communist rule meant dictatorship by a small elite, with the rest of the party, opportunists and believers alike, serving as instruments of the tyranny instead of as aggregators of the popular will. Finally, the party promised national revival, and delivered cultural russification and subjugation to the Soviet Union.*

*The gap between promise, which relatively few believed (or believed to be realistic), and performance, which virtually all regarded as detestable, was therefore immense. Once Soviet might had crushed the 1956 revolution, Kádár labored mightily to win credibility and legitimacy by narrowing that gap, by promising less and delivering more, and by relying on quiet persuasion more than on violent coercion. But if the party finally managed to dispense a more humane form of socialism than that imposed by its earlier incarnation, it was powerless to erase its fatal flaw: service of the interests of the Soviet Union. While, arguably, Hungary's national survival demands a degree of compatibility with its neighboring superpower, the model of accommodating neutrality exemplified by Finland strikes most Hungarians as infinitely preferable to the constraints of communist rule and of integration in the Soviet bloc.*

*The communists' ideological nemesis has been, first and foremost, nationalism, the manifestation of man's ethnocentric predisposition. Nurtured in the historic national rivalries and imperial contests of Eastern Europe, the Hungarian psyche is marked by a sense of cultural distinctiveness and perilous isolation that manifests itself in pervasive nationalism. The communist party's*

*theoretical alternatives of supranational class solidarity and of "socialist pa-
triotism" defined as loyalty to the Soviet Union are therefore seen by Hungarians as an inescapable but superficial deception. The instrumental antithesis of
dictatorship, institutionalized political pluralism, has been another enduring
challenge to the legitimacy of communist rule. The party has denied the permanent necessity of an open contest of interests, proclaiming that its victory had
resolved socioeconomic cleavages. The quest for some minimal consensual support did drive Kádár to permit constructive as well as ritualistic popular participation in the affairs of state, but this compromise with pluralism was clearly
limited by the unchallengeable principle of single-party rule.*

*Economic imperatives and the party's professions of national alliance
played their part in this modest and cautious process of devolution and decompression. Economic modernization does not invariably foster pluralistic modes
of political behavior, and indeed authoritarian systems may well enjoy a short-
term advantage in this respect, but it does engender two phenomena that imperil the party's ideological supremacy. The first is the reemergence of a competitive, acquisitive individualism that may be deplored by Marxist purists but
which at least in Western civilization appears to be ineradicable. The second is
a diffusion and atrophy of the revolutionary impulse nurtured in the less complex and more exploitative phases of early industrialization. The party has thus
moved from fervent belief to disillusionment to a pragmatism that remains
necessarily shrouded in the rituals of an increasingly anachronistic faith.*

*Marxism, like Christianity, invites belief in ultimate salvation. But while the
religion offers deliverance to all who seek it in the afterlife, the ideology promises an existential reward whose demonstrable elusiveness makes the call to
sacrifice ring hollow. The test of performance therefore imposes a heavy dose
of rationalization. The material benefits of the applied ideology can be hailed
as evidence of its superiority only with the aid of the most selective of comparisons. The party has proven its ability to redistribute existing wealth, but it has
yet to show a capacity for creating new wealth as effectively as the pluralistic
welfare states, which offer comparable social security without the constraints of
ideological exclusiveness and authoritarian rule. While most Hungarians can
draw satisfaction from the improvement in material and cultural welfare since
the Stalinist nadir of communist rule, they attribute this to the party's pragmatism rather than to the validity of its basic ideology. Decades of energetic
propagation of the faith have thus produced dismal results that can only have a
dispiriting effect on the communist functionaries and induce a profound cynicism in them and in the society generally. The few zealots may be able to
rationalize all setbacks and disappointments, but the failure to inculcate com-*

*munist ideology into the masses by force or by cajolery has produced a
dichotomous and almost surrealistic political culture in which the sincere supporters of the official and ubiquitous dogma account for a negligible fraction of
the population.*

*The generally perceived irrelevance of communist ideology has not reduced
the party's capacity to rule. It has, however, imposed the choice between degrees of coercion and of accommodation to secular demands. To its credit,
Kádár's party has been inclined to mitigate repression and to pursue economic
and cultural policies that the majority of Hungarians regard as tolerable if not
optimal. The answer to the question, whether communism has ever had a dis-
tinctively Hungarian variant, depends on the degree of voluntarism one can
attribute to the party's leaders. The party was truly independent only during
Imre Nagy's brief revolutionary interregnum, and in those circumstances it was
rapidly reduced to a marginal political force professing a dedication to
pluralism and national independence as well as to socialism. Such a theoretical
compromise has never yet stood the test of the acquisition of power, an outcome that would have been highly improbable in a democratic Hungary. Béla
Kun, as was seen, was the archetypical revolutionary zealot, but his frenetic
radicalism owed nothing to the circumstances and needs of the country he had
once ruled. The dogmatism of Stalin's sinister satrap, Mátyás Rákosi, was no
more than the enthusiastic imitation of his master's tyrannical style; it possessed no originality in either theory or practice, and it varied from the rule of
the other East European party leaders only to the limited extent that Stalin's
policies allowed for some calculated differentiation.*

*Kádár's communism, in contrast, has acquired a more humane face than
that of his Soviet-bloc comrades. In the mid-1970s the Hungarian model of
political decompression, economic eclecticism, and cultural tolerance was ap-
proximated only in Poland, where the social stresses were nevertheless far
more explosive. The East German party managed its economy with efficiency
but remained highly repressive; dogmatists led the Czech and Bulgarian parties; in Romania Ceausescu had created a peculiar amalgam of personal despotism, domestic orthodoxy, and voluntaristic posturing in foreign policy.
Hungarian communism had thus become the envy of the other East European
peoples as well as the version least repellent to Western democrats. Kádár's
political acumen, the capacity of the Hungarian people to exploit the opportunities inherent in his policies, and the willingness of the Kremlin to accommodate a degree of distinctive liberalism in its once most volatile dependency
have all played a part in this transformation of communism from Procrustean
savagery to the art of the possible.*

*The broad outlines of the history of Hungary's communist party are clear enough, but many questions of substance and detail remain unanswered, if only because the clues are locked in the archives of Moscow and Budapest and in the memory of the surviving actors. This account is therefore not the end but a beginning, and communism has not yet run its course in Hungary. Its future, dependent as it is less on the will of the Hungarian people than on the force majeure of international politics, lies beyond this writer's powers of prophecy.*

# APPENDIXES

# 1. Organizational Statutes of the Hungarian Socialist Workers' Party

The Hungarian Socialist Workers' Party is a communist party, the revolutionary vanguard of the working class, and part of the international communist and workers' movement; it is guided in its activities by Marxism-Leninism and proletarian internationalism.

The Hungarian Socialist Workers' Party is a voluntary, militant association; it assembles in its ranks the most progressive forces of the Hungarian people, those who assume the socialist ideals and goals of the working class and fight for their realization. It organizes and leads the people's struggle for the construction of a socialist society, for the prosperity of the Hungarian People's Republic, for the nation's progress. The party's ultimate goal is the construction of a communist society.

## I. THE PARTY MEMBER, HIS DUTIES AND RIGHTS

1. Membership in the Hungarian Socialist Workers' Party is open to those who are at least 18 years of age; who appropriate Marxist-Leninist ideals, accept the policies, guidelines, and organizational rules of the party and fight selflessly for their realization; are politically and morally above reproach; live in a socialist fashion and are respected for their work, their conduct, and their social activity; participate regularly in the work of one of the party's basic organizations and pay their party dues.

2. The party member's duties:

   *a)* To master the fundamentals of Marxism-Leninism, systematically expand his theoretical and political knowledge, and enrich his education; to strengthen and protect the party's ideological, political, organizational, and operational unity, to fight against factionalism and the remnants of bourgeois ideology and morality; to demonstrate revolutionary vigilance against all antisocialist phenomena;

From Magyar Szocialista Munkáspárt, *A Magyar Szocialista Munkáspárt XI. kongresszusa, 1975. március 17–22* (Budapest: Kossuth, 1975), pp. 224–35.

*b)* To consistently serve socialism and to fight in all circumstances for the defense and interests of socialist society; to set the example at work in the pursuit of his vocation;

*c)* To consistently observe the rules of party discipline, to execute the decisions of the party and the laws and decrees of the state;

*d)* To be sincere and honorable; to expose shortcomings without regard for personal considerations, to fight against the suppression of criticism and against complacency;

*e)* To strengthen and expand the party's links with the masses, to propagate the party's ideals and policies, to participate actively in political and social life.

3. The party member's rights:

*a)* To participate in the discussion of the party's theoretical, political and organizational issues at party meetings and in the adoption of resolutions. If he holds a dissenting opinion, the member may express this at the membership meeting or before a higher party organ, but he is obligated to represent and execute the resolution even if he disagrees with it;

*b)* To criticize in a party-like manner at party meetings the work of a party member or organization. To present a request, recommendation, or submission to his basic organization, to higher party organs up to the congress; to receive a valid response to his observations and submissions;

*c)* To receive at the same level an answer to the comments made at a membership meeting or at a session of the elected party organ;

*d)* To request the intervention of the membership meeting or of the elected party organ if his critical comments or the exposure of mistakes result in personal distress. The appropriate party organ is obliged to initiate proceedings against suppressors of criticism;

*e)* To participate in the election of the party's leading organs as both voter and candidate; to stand for election as secretary of the party organization or as member of the party organ after three years of membership; in special cases the appropriate party committee may waive this requirement;

*f)* Before taking a decision regarding a member and his work, the appropriate party organ must seek his opinion.

## II. THE ADMISSION OF PARTY MEMBERS, THE TERMINATION OF MEMBERSHIP, THE TRANSFER OF PARTY MEMBERS, DISCIPLINARY PROCEDURES

4. Entry into the party is voluntary. Admission takes place on the basis of individual evaluation. The candidate must request admission in writing. His request must be accompanied by the recommendation of two members who have been in the party for three years and who know him through common activity. The recommenders are responsible for their opinions. If a KISZ member is admitted to the party, one of the recommenders may be the membership meeting of the KISZ basic organization. The membership meeting rules on admission. The decision is implemented upon the assent of the appropriate party committee. The membership is dated from the decision of the membership meeting.

5. Every party member is a member of the responsible party organization at his place of work, or, if he is not employed, at his domicile. The party member who changes employment or domicile must register within thirty days with his new party organization.

6. The party member may leave the party on his own initiative or on that of the basic organization as long as there are no disciplinary proceedings against him at the time. He must convey in writing to the leadership of the basic party organization his intention to withdraw and the reasons therefor. His withdrawal must be announced at the membership meeting.

7. The membership meeting must strike off the rolls those who despite warnings have for three months failed to participate in the work of the basic organization without excuse, or have not paid their membership dues. Those struck from the rolls may appeal to the higher party organs within thirty days of the delivery of the ruling.

8. Party members who violate the organizational statutes will incur party punishment following disciplinary investigation by the membership meeting of the basic organization, by the higher party organ, or by the Central Control Committee.

    Depending on the gravity of the case, the party punishment may be reprimand, censure, severe censure, severe censure with final warning, and expulsion from the party.

    The party member may be suspended for a specified period of time from his party office or recalled from public office where he represents the party.

    The party member must be notified at the beginning of the disciplinary investigation and must be interviewed during the investigation. He must be invited to the hearings on his case. If he willingly fails to attend the hearings, a ruling can still be made in his case. The ruling must be communicated in writing.

    The party punishment comes into force with the initial ruling. The expelled member's membership book must be retrieved.

    Both the interested individual and the responsible party organ may appeal to the higher party organ within thirty days of the ruling. The higher party organ must rule on the appeal within sixty days of its receipt. Both the interested individual and the party organ may appeal the ruling of the higher party organ. A disciplinary ruling may be made public with the permission of the Budapest or county party committee or of the Central Control Committee.

9. Cancellations of membership and expulsions approved by the membership meeting of the basic organization must be confirmed by the appropriate higher party organ.

10. Disciplinary proceedings against the member of a higher elected party organ can be conducted, and a decision made, by the body of which he is a member or by its superior organ.

    Disciplinary proceedings can also be initiated by the basic party organization.

    At the meeting of the higher party organ, the standpoint of the membership meeting of the lower party organization must be made known before a ruling is made.

    The membership meeting of the responsible basic party organization must be informed of the disciplinary ruling.

11. Cancellation of the party punishment may be requested by the responsible party

organization after one year, and by the affected party member after two years. After three years the party leadership must investigate whether further application of the party punishment is warranted, or whether it can be cancelled. Its conclusion must be communicated to the party organization or party organ that made the original disciplinary ruling.

## III. THE PARTY'S ORGANIZATIONAL STRUCTURE AND OPERATIONAL PRINCIPLE

12. The Hungarian Socialist Workers' Party is built on the principle of democratic centralism:

   *a)* All leading organs of the party and their members are elected democratically and by secret ballot.

   The rules of election are set by the Central Committee.

   Vacancies on the Central Committee, the Central Control Committee, and the party committees may in justified cases be filled by invitation. The proportion of invited to elected members may not be more than 20 percent.

   The principles of collective leadership and individual responsibility prevail in the party. Members of elected bodies have equal rights. Any member of the leading organs may be suspended if for whatever reason he is unable to fulfill his assumed responsibilities; if he proves to be unsuitable for his party office, he may be recalled; if he proves unworthy of his office, he may be excluded from the body's membership. The suspension can be initiated by the affected individual or by the responsible party organ or basic organization.

   *b)* The lower party organs and organizations are subordinated to the higher party organs. The resolutions of the higher organs are binding on the lower organs. The party organizations may take independent decisions on local issues, but these decisions must not be contrary to the party line and the decisions of the higher party organs. It is the right and duty of the higher party organs to amend or repeal decisions of the basic party organizations and lower party organs if they are not consonant with the party line or are contrary to the decisions of the higher party organs. The higher party organs must justify their measures to the affected lower party organ. Party organs and organizations may direct proposals and submissions to the higher party organs up to the congress, and they must receive a response.

   *c)* The leading organs must regularly report on their activities to their party organizations and to the higher organs.

   *d)* Meetings of the party membership and of leading organs may only pass resolutions if at least two-thirds of the members are present. Passage of resolutions requires a simple majority.

13. The party's organizational structure follows the territorial-works principle. Departure from this principle may be authorized by the Central Committee or the Budapest or county party committees.

14. If any party organization or party committee operates at variance with the organizational statutes, it may be dissolved by the Central Committee.

## IV. THE PARTY'S HIGHEST ORGANS

15. The highest organ of the Hungarian Socialist Workers' Party is the congress, which is convened by the Central Committee every five years. At least three months' public notice must be given of the calling of a congress.

Delegates to the party congress are elected at the Budapest and county party conferences, at party conferences with county rights, and at large-industry party conferences which have the required membership to elect congressional delegates. The principle of representation of the party membership is determined by the Central Committee.

Members of the Central Committee and of the Central Control Committee possess voting rights at the congress.

The congress:

a) debates the reports of the Central Committee and of the Central Control Committee;

b) determines the general guidelines of party policy and indicates the most immediate and important tasks of socialist construction and international relations;

c) approves the party's organizational statutes;

d) elects the Central Committee and the Central Control Committee;

e) rules on the proposals and appeals put before the congress.

16. Between congresses all of the party's organs and organizations are directed by the Central Committee; the latter acts on behalf of the party with respect to state and social organs and in international relations.

The Central Committee meets as necessary, but at least every three months. Members of the Central Committee must be informed on all important issues.

Between congresses the party's Central Committee may call a national party conference.

The Central Committee makes special rules for the representation of party organizations at the national party conference.

17. The Central Committee elects from among its members:

a) The Politburo, which directs party activity between the meetings of the Central Committee;

b) The first secretary of the Central Committee and the members of the Secretariat. The Secretariat ensures and supervises the implementation of the decisions of the leading party organs and directs the apparatus of the Central Committee.

18. The Central Committee:

a) elects the Central Committee's working committees and their leaders;

b) appoints the department heads of the Central Committee;

c) directs the party's central institutions, its newspaper and periodicals, and appoints their leaders.

19. The Central Control Committee works to assist the strengthening of the party's ideological, political, and organizational unity, and the instruction of the party membership; keeps watch over the political behavior, party loyalty, and moral purity of the party membership; fights consistently against all forms of antiparty factional activity.

Within its sphere of authority it examines appeals against the disciplinary rulings of the lower organs; if necessary, it calls to account those who transgress principles binding on all party members; it supervises the financial affairs of the Central Committee; it reports on its work to the congress.

From among its members the Central Control Committee elects its chairman, its secretary, and the members of its Secretariat.

## V. THE PARTY COMMITTEES

20. Party committees must be elected in the capital and its districts, in the counties, districts, and cities.

    A party committee to direct the area's party organizations must be elected in every community, factory, enterprise, office, institution, and military and armed unit where the number of party members is over 200. In justified cases the Budapest or county party committee may authorize the creation of a party committee even in areas where the party membership does not reach 200.

21. The party committee's higher organ is the party conference, which the party committee convenes every five years. The members of the party committee participate in the party conference with voting rights. The party conference assesses the report of the party committee, elects the members of the party committee, and elects the delegates to the higher party conference (Budapest or county party conference, congress).

    The party committee meets as necessary, but at least every three months. The calling of party conferences is specially regulated by the Central Committee.

22. Party committees with authority equivalent to that of the Budapest and county party committees operate in the People's Army and the Frontier Guard. Party committees with authority equivalent to district party committees operate in the latter's higher units and comparable organs; at the company level and in institutes there operate party committees, party leaderships, and basic organizations.

23. The party committees elect from among their members an executive committee and the party committee's first secretary and secretaries. They elect permanent working committees to aid in their guiding task.

    Between party committee meetings the executive committee directs the work of the party organizations and of the apparatus and supervises the implementation of resolutions.

24. The Budapest, county, district, city, and Budapest district party committees, as well as those party committees having the right to approve new members and disciplinary authority, elect a disciplinary committee.

    Except for the chairman, the disciplinary committee may include party members who do not belong to the party committee. The disciplinary committee investigates matters of party discipline and appeals and makes recommendations to the party executive committee.

25. In those production, office, institutional, or administrative units where several basic organizations operate, but where there is no party committee, a party leadership is elected every five years at a general membership meeting or conference of delegates; this leadership directs and coordinates the work of the basic organizations; it takes a stand and rules on the most important issues affecting the entire area under its supervision. The party leadership must report on its work at least once a year to a general membership meeting or conference of delegates.

## VI. THE PARTY'S BASIC ORGANIZATIONS

26. With the approval of the higher party organ, a basic organization can be created in every production, office, or residential unit where there are at least three party members.

    The highest organ of the basic organization is the membership meeting, which must be called at least every two months.

27. The membership meeting of the basic organization elects a leadership every five years to direct party work and perform administrative functions.

    In those basic organizations where the membership is less than ten, the membership meeting elects a secretary and a deputy secretary.

28. The leadership must call an annual reporting membership meeting at which the party membership can assess the activity of the leadership and of the entire party organization during that year as well as the work of party members and the fulfillment of party tasks on the basis of the leadership's report.

29. Depending on numbers, party groups must be created within the basic organizations. The party groups regularly assess the work and behavior of their members and the fulfillment of party tasks. The work of the party groups is directed by stewards elected at a group meeting and confirmed by a membership meeting.

30. The party organization has the right and duty within its sphere of activity to enforce party policy, to provide overall supervision of work, to exercise its authority in personal and cadre matters, and to call to account state and economic leaders.

## VII. THE PARTY'S DIRECTING WORK IN STATE AND MASS ORGANIZATIONS

31. With its ideological and political direction the party ensures that the goals of the working class are realized through the activities of the socialist state and its organs.

    The party enforces its policies and resolutions through its members working in state organs; these members are responsible to both party and state organs for their professional activity and for the execution of laws and decrees.

    Their guidance and supervision is provided by the relevant party and state organs.

32. Party members and party organizations serving and operating in the armed forces and armed bodies, whose task is to preserve the workers' power and the lawful order, sovereignty, and territorial integrity of the socialist state, act effectively to ensure that in all circumstances the armed forces and armed bodies fulfill their duties to the fullest extent.

33. The party gives ideological and political direction to the mass organizations and mass movements through the party members who work within the latter. The party organs and organizations in the mass organizations and mass movements pass resolutions binding on the communists working within the latter.

    Communists carrying out their party work in trade unions and other mass organizations and mass movements are responsible for the implementation of party policy by persuasion among the masses, and by the utilization of experience gained among the masses, all with respect to the intended purpose of the organ.

34. The party organs may establish communist groups to assist unified action by communists working in the National Assembly, the councils, the mass organizations, and mass movements.

35. The Hungarian Communist Youth Federation [KISZ] is the youth organization of the party as well as the mass organization of Hungarian youth. The party's resolutions are of a binding character on the Communist Youth Federation and its organizations. The KISZ organs and organizations accomplish their work with the support and guidance of the party organs and organizations.

## VIII. PARTY MEMBERSHIP DUES

36. Party members pay their membership dues as follows. . . .

The Organizational Statutes of the Hungarian Socialist Workers' Party are the party's constitution and the law for every party member and party organization.

# 2. Hungary: Communist Party Membership, 1919–1976

| | | | |
|---|---|---|---|
| January 1919 | 10,000 | January 1954 | 862,603 |
| November 1924 | 120 | January 1956 | 859,037 |
| December 1929 | 1,000 | August 1956 | 871,497 |
| February 1945 | 30,000 | 1 December 1956 | 37,818 |
| July 1945 | 226,577 | 14 January 1957 | 125,088 |
| January 1946 | 608,728 | 8 December 1957 | 394,910 |
| December 1947 | 660,000 | 31 December 1958 | 416,646 |
| July 1948 (HCP) | 887,472 | 31 December 1961 | 498,644 |
| July 1948 (HWP) | 1,128,130 | 31 December 1967 | 601,917 |
| January 1950 | 828,695 | November 1970 | 662,000 |
| January 1952 | 945,606 | 1 January 1975 | 754,353 |
| January 1953 | 906,087 | 31 December 1976 | 765,566 |

SOURCES: Tibor Erényi and Sándor Rákosi, eds., *Legyőzhetetlen erő*, 2d ed. (Budapest: Kossuth, 1974), pp. 22, 63, 82, 162, 169, 175, 185, 193, 204, 224, 236, 250, 257, 285; the revised estimate for December 1947 is by Miklós Habuda and Sándor Rákosi, "A Magyar Kommunista Párt és a Szociáldemokrata Párt munkásösszetételének alakulása 1945–1948-ban," *PK* 22, no. 3 (September 1976): 45; Magyar Szocialista Munkáspárt, *A Magyar Szocialista Munkáspárt X. kongresszusának jegyzőkönyve* (Budapest: Kossuth, 1971), p. 102; idem, *A Magyar Szocialista Munkáspárt XI. kongresszusa, 1975. március 17–22* (Budapest: Kossuth, 1975), p. 6; *Pártélet*, July 1977, p. 7. Figures in this table include candidate members until the abolition of that category at the ninth congress in 1965. The estimates for 1924 and 1929 do not include party members outside of Hungary.

# 3. Principal Party Conferences, 1918–1975

24 March 1918 ......... Founding conference of the Hungarian Section of the Russian Communist Party (Bolshevik), Moscow

24 November 1918 ....... Founding conference of the Communist Party of Hungary (CPH), Budapest

12–13 June 1919 ....... Congress of the Hungarian Party of Socialist-Communist Workers, Budapest

18–21 August 1925 ...... First (reorganizing) congress of the CPH, Vienna

25 February—
15 March 1930 ........ Second congress of the CPH, Aprilovka, USSR.

20–21 May 1945 ........ National conference of the Hungarian Communist Party (HCP), Budapest

28 September—
1 October 1946 ....... Third congress of the HCP, Budapest

12–14 June 1948 ....... Unification congress of the HCP and SDP (first congress of the Hungarian Workers' Party or HWP), Budapest

25 February—
2 March 1951 ......... Second congress of the HWP, Budapest

24–30 May 1954 ........ Third congress of the HWP, Budapest

27–29 June 1957 ....... National conference of the Hungarian Socialist Workers' Party (HSWP), Budapest

30 November—
5 December 1959 ...... Seventh congress of the HSWP, Budapest

20–24 November 1962 .... Eighth congress of the HSWP, Budapest

28 November—
3 December 1965 ...... Ninth congress of the HSWP, Budapest

23–28 November 1970 .... Tenth congress of the HSWP, Budapest

17–22 March 1975 ....... Eleventh congress of the HSWP, Budapest

# 4. Key Economic Indicators, 1938–1975

| | 1938 | 1950 | 1955 | 1960 | 1965 | 1966 |
|---|---|---|---|---|---|---|
| Population number (at the beginning of the year), thousands | 9,138 | 9,293 | 9,767 | 9,961 | 10,140 | 10,166 |
| Natural increase Per 1,000 population | 5.7 | 9.5 | 11.4 | 4.5 | 2.4 | 3.6 |
| Percentage distribution of active earners | | | | | | |
| State sector | . . . . | 34.7 | 54.9 | 57.5 | 66.4 | 66.6 |
| Cooperative sector | . . . . | 2.1 | 9.5 | 17.9 | 27.8 | 27.6 |
| Private sector | . . . . | 63.2 | 35.6 | 24.6 | 5.8 | 5.8 |
| Index of the national income, 1950 = 100 | 80 | 100 | 132 | 177 | 216 | 233 |
| National income by origin, percentage | | | | | | |
| Industry | 20 | 26 | 33 | 36 | 42 | 42 |
| Construction | 5 | 9 | 9 | 11 | 11 | 10 |
| Agriculture | 58 | 48 | 42 | 29 | 23 | 24 |
| Other | 17 | 17 | 16 | 24 | 24 | 24 |
| *Industry* | | | | | | |
| Index of production, 1950 = 100 | 63 | 100 | 186 | 267 | 386 | 412 |
| Percentage distribution of persons employed | | | | | | |
| State industry | 55.4 | 80.2 | 82.5 | 82.6 | 84.8 | 84.5 |
| Cooperative industry | . . . . | 1.6 | 9.9 | 11.5 | 11.3 | 11.6 |
| Private craftsmanship | 44.6 | 18.2 | 7.6 | 5.9 | 3.9 | 3.9 |
| *Agriculture* | | | | | | |
| Index of gross production, 1950 = 100 | 113 | 100 | 118 | 120 | 127 | 139 |
| Percentage distribution of arable land | | | | | | |
| State sector | . . . . | 5.2 | 14.4 | 13.8 | 14.3 | 14.2 |
| Cooperative sector | . . . . | 4.4 | 17.9 | 60.4 | 80.2 | 80.3 |
| Private and auxiliary farms | . . . . | 90.4 | 67.7 | 25.8 | 5.5 | 5.5 |
| *External Trade* | | | | | | |
| Index of external trade, 1960 = 100 | . . . . | 35 | 62 | 100 | 164 | 171 |
| *Income and Consumption* | | | | | | |
| Index of real wages per wage earner, 1950 = 100 | . . . . | 100 | 105 | 154 | 168 | 172 |
| Per capita consumption of the population, 1950 = 100 | 93 | 100 | 115 | 152 | 176 | 184 |

SOURCE: Hungary, Central Statistical Office, *Statistical Yearbook 1975* (Budapest, 1977).

| 1967 | 1968 | 1969 | 1970 | 1971 | 1972 | 1973 | 1974 | 1975 |
|---|---|---|---|---|---|---|---|---|
| 10,203 | 10,244 | 10,284 | 10,322 | 10,354 | 10,381 | 10,416 | 10,448 | 10,509 |
| 3.9 | 3.9 | 3.6 | 3.1 | 2.6 | 3.3 | 3.2 | 5.8 | 6.0 |
| 66.6 | 66.5 | 67.1 | 67.7 | 68.0 | 68.5 | 68.8 | 69.9 | 70.3 |
| 27.9 | 28.4 | 28.3 | 27.7 | 27.5 | 27.0 | 26.6 | 25.5 | 25.3 |
| 5.5 | 5.1 | 4.6 | 4.6 | 4.5 | 4.5 | 4.6 | 4.6 | 4.4 |
| 252 | 265 | 286 | 300 | 320 | 336 | 361 | 386 | 407 |
| 42 | 43 | 41 | 43 | 42 | 43 | 44 | 44 | 45 |
| 11 | 11 | 11 | 12 | 12 | 12 | 11 | 11 | 12 |
| 22 | 21 | 22 | 17 | 17 | 17 | 17 | 16 | 15 |
| 25 | 25 | 26 | 28 | 29 | 28 | 28 | 29 | 28 |
| 448 | 470 | 481 | 523 | 558 | 587 | 628 | 680 | 712 |
| 83.6 | 83.8 | 83.9 | 83.3 | 83.2 | 83.7 | 83.9 | 84.0 | 84.0 |
| 12.7 | 12.7 | 12.8 | 13.3 | 13.5 | 13.2 | 13.1 | 13.3 | 13.4 |
| 3.7 | 3.5 | 3.3 | 3.4 | 3.3 | 3.1 | 3.0 | 2.7 | 2.6 |
| 144 | 145 | 155 | 146 | 160 | 164 | 175 | 181 | 185 |
| 14.2 | 14.1 | 14.1 | 14.2 | 14.3 | 14.3 | 14.3 | 14.2 | 14.0 |
| 80.4 | 80.5 | 80.3 | 80.1 | 80.2 | 80.2 | 80.3 | 80.4 | 80.7 |
| 5.4 | 5.5 | 5.6 | 5.7 | 5.5 | 5.5 | 5.4 | 5.4 | 5.3 |
| 188 | 194 | 217 | 261 | 297 | 321 | 365 | 451 | 524 |
| 178 | 182 | 190 | 199 | 204 | 208 | 214 | 226 | 235 |
| 195 | 203 | 213 | 228 | 240 | 247 | 259 | 275 | 285 |

# Notes

Publication data have been omitted for those books included in the bibliography. The few items from the archives of the Institute of Party History ("Party Archives") are cited according to a system that assigns a unique number to each document. In Hungarian usage the surname precedes the given name, but the more familiar English order has been adopted here.

## PART ONE

### 1. The Socialist Prelude

1. See Magyar Munkásmozgalmi Intézet, *A magyar munkásmozgalom történetének válogatott dokumentumai*, vol. 1, pp. 73–75 (hereafter cited as *MMTVD*).

2. See Edit S. Vincze, *A Magyarországi Szociáldemokrata Párt megalakulása és tevékenységének első évei, 1890–1896*.

3. *MMTVD*, vol. 3, p. 67.

4. László Réti, *Lenin és a magyar munkásmozgalom*, pp. 36–38.

5. See Zoltán Horváth, *Magyar századforduló: A második reformnemzedék története, 1896–1914*.

6. See Andrew C. Janos, "The Decline of Oligarchy: Bureaucratic and Mass Politics in the Age of Dualism (1867–1918)," in Andrew C. Janos and William B. Slottman, eds., *Revolution in Perspective*, pp. 1–60.

7. Márta Tömöri, *Új vizeken járok: A Galilei kör története*, pp. 105–14, 253–54; and V. Urashov, "Az orosz forradalmárok segitenek," in Borbála Szerémi, ed., *Nagy idők tanui emlékeznek*, pp. 35–37.

8. Dezső Nemes et al., *A magyar forradalmi munkásmozgalom története*, p. 101.

9. *Népszava*, 8 and 15 October 1918.

10. For detailed accounts of the Károlyi revolution, see Tibor Hajdu, *Az 1918-as magyarországi polgári demokratikus forradalom*; Sándor Juhász-Nagy, *A magyar októberi forradalom története*; Gusztáv Grátz, *A forradalmak kora*; Oszkár Jászi, *Revolution and Counter-revolution in Hungary*; and Mihály Károlyi, *Memoirs: Faith without Illusion*.

11. Réti, *Lenin*, p. 75.

## 2. The Communist Party

1. For Kun's Tomsk writings, see György Milei, "Kun Béla 1917–1918-ban Tomszkban megjelent irásai: Dokumentumok," *Párttörténeti Közlemények* 8, no. 1 (March 1962): 110–30 (hereafter cited as *PK*). See also Ferenc Münnich, *Viharos út*, pp. 34ff.

2. See Rudolf L. Tőkés, *Béla Kun and the Hungarian Soviet Republic*, pp. 56–61.

3. Béla Kun, *Válogatott irások és beszédek*, vol. 1, p. 247.

4. Harold Nicolson, *Peacemaking 1919*, p. 298.

5. See György Milei, "Dokumentumok az OK(b)P magyar csoportjának történetéből, 1918–1919," *PK* 4, no. 1 (March 1958): 168, 173–74.

6. Kun, *Válogatott*, vol. 2, p. 237.

7. Tőkés, *Kun*, pp. 71–72.

8. See Antal Józsa and György Milei, *A rendithetetlen százezer*.

9. Tőkés, *Kun*, pp. 74–79.

10. Réti, *Lenin*, p. 82.

11. *Társadalmi Szemle*, November 1958, pp. 92–93.

12. Kun, *Válogatott*, vol. 1, p. 180.

13. See György Milei, "Az OK(b)P magyar csoportja a KMP megalakulásáért, 1918 október–november: Dokumentumok," *PK* 10, no. 2 (June 1964): 160–71; and Hajdu, *1918-as forradalom*, pp. 197–98.

14. Márta B. Szinkovich, "Két dokumentum a Tanácsköztársaság előzményeiről," *PK* 5, no. 1 (March 1959): 197.

15. György Milei, "A Kommunisták Magyarországi Pártja megalakulásának történetéhez," *PK* 4, no. 4 (December 1958): 57–58.

16. Béla Kun, "Összehivjuk az alakuló ülést," *Társadalmi Szemle*, November 1958, pp. 96–98.

17. Kun, *Válogatott*, vol. 1, p. 104.

18. On the debate concerning the date of this meeting, see György Milei, "Mikor alakult meg a KMP?" *PK* 11, no. 3 (September 1965): 124–41.

19. See Hajdu, *1918-as forradalom*, pp. 202–3.

20. Kun, *Válogatott*, vol. 2, pp. 99, 226.

21. Réti, *Lenin*, p. 111.

22. Hajdu, *1918-as forradalom*, pp. 213–15.

23. Kun, *Válogatott*, vol. 2, pp. 73, 33. See also Mrs. Sándor Gábor, "A Kommunisták Magyarországi Pártjának megalakulása. Az egyesült munkáspárt," in Tibor Erényi and Sándor Rákosi, eds., *Legyőzhetetlen erő*, 2d ed. pp. 10–23.

24. Hajdu, *1918-as forradalom*, pp. 212–13: and Tőkés, *Kun*, p. 102 and appendix F.

25. Mrs. Gábor, "A Kommunisták Magyarországi Pártjának megalakulása," pp. 16, 22.

26. See János Kende, "A szakszervezetek szerepe a Tanácsköztársaság államában," *PK* 20, no. 4 (December 1974): 67–71.

27. Szerémi, *Nagy idők*, p. 13. For more detailed accounts, see Tőkés, *Kun*, pp. 103–12; and Hajdu, *1918-as forradalom*, pp. 216–22.

28. Hajdu, *1918-as forradalom,* p. 249.
29. Ibid., pp. 249–51.
30. Kun, *Válogatott,* vol. 1, pp. 188–89.
31. *MMTVD,* vol. 5, pp. 453–54.
32. Hajdu, *1918-as forradalom,* p. 283. See also Kun, *Válogatott,* vol. 2, pp. 74–75.
33. Kun, *Válogatott,* vol. 1, p. 189.
34. *MMTVD,* vol. 5, p. 548.
35. Ibid., p. 569.
36. Hajdu, *1918-as forradalom,* pp. 313–19, 348.
37. Ibid., p. 187.
38. See Ferenc Rákos, "A Kommunisták Magyarországi Pártja második (illegális) Központi Bizottságának munkájárol," *Társadalmi Szemle,* February 1959, pp. 94–99; and Gyula Hevesi, *Egy mérnök a forradalomban,* pp. 211–15.
39. Kun, *Válogatott,* vol. 1, p. 190.
40. Hajdu, *1918-as forradalom,* p. 344.
41. Tibor Hajdu, "Adatok a Tanácsköztársaság kikiáltásának történetéhez," *PK* 18, no. 3 (September 1972): 138.
42. Tibor Hajdu, *A Magyarországi Tanácsköztársaság,* pp. 21–22.
43. See Hajdu, *Magyarországi Tanácsköztársaság,* pp. 23–25. On Hungary and the Paris Peace Conference, see Francis Deak, *Hungary at the Paris Peace Conference;* Alfred D. Low, *The Soviet Hungarian Republic and the Paris Peace Conference;* Zsuzsa L. Nagy, *A párizsi békekonferencia és Magyarország, 1918–1919;* and Arno J. Mayer, *Politics and Diplomacy of Peacemaking.*
44. Paul Ignotus, *Hungary,* p. 148.
45. Hajdu, *Magyarországi Tanácsköztársaság,* pp. 26–29.

## 3. The Republic of Councils

1. For details of this busy day's negotiations, see Hajdu, *Magyarországi Tanácsköztársaság,* pp. 31–34.
2. Kun, *Válogatott,* vol. 2, p. 75.
3. *MMTVD,* vol. 5, pp. 688–89.
4. Hajdu, *Magyarországi Tanácsköztársaság,* p. 34.
5. Kun, *Válogatott,* vol. 2, pp. 253–54; *MMTVD,* vol. 6a, pp. 13, 41, 62; Hajdu, *Magyarországi Tanácsköztársaság,* p. 34; and György Lukács, *Történelem és osztálytudat,* p. 62.
6. Béla Szántó, "Emlékezés a magyar Tanácsköztársaságra," *PK* 5, no. 1 (March 1959): 132. See also Tőkés, *Kun,* pp. 148–50.
7. Hajdu, *Magyarországi Tanácsköztársaság,* p. 45.
8. Hajdu, "Adatok a Tanácsköztársaság, pp. 150–52.
9. *MMTVD,* vol. 6a, p. 7.
10. See, for instance, Kun, *Válogatott,* vol. 1, p. 242.
11. Réti, *Lenin,* pp. 122–31.
12. Hajdu, *Magyarországi Tanácsköztársaság,* p. 79.

13. For an analysis of the minority policies of the Commune, see Eva S. Balogh, "Nationality Problems of the Hungarian Soviet Republic," in Ivan Völgyes, ed., *Hungary in Revolution, 1918–19: Nine Essays*, pp. 89–120.

14. *MMTVD*, vol. 6a, p. 60.

15. Hajdu, *Magyarországi Tanácsköztársaság*, p. 57.

16. Tőkés, *Kun*, p. 166.

17. See Hajdu, *Magyarországi Tanácsköztársaság*, p. 250.

18. Tőkés, *Kun*, pp. 168–70.

19. See László Svéd, *Utat tör az ifjú sereg*, pp. 216–29 and passim.

20. Kun, *Válogatott*, vol. 2, p. 131.

21. Hajdu, *Magyarországi Tanácsköztársaság*, pp. 98–105.

22. Ibid., pp. 214–16; George Bárány, " 'Magyar Jew or Jewish Magyar?' Reflections on the Question of Assimilation," in Béla Vágó and George L. Mosse, eds., *Jews and Non-Jews in Eastern Europe, 1918–1945*, pp. 51–90; and Richard V. Burks, *The Dynamics of Communism in Eastern Europe*, p. 162.

23. Mrs. Sándor Gábor, "Dokumentumok Szovjet-Oroszország és a magyar Tanácsköztársaság kapcsolatairól," *PK* 7, no. 1 (March 1961): 219.

24. Tőkés, *Kun*, pp. 138–41.

25. For information and analysis going beyond the following synopsis, see Frank Eckelt, "The Internal Policies of the Hungarian Soviet Republic," in Völgyes, *Hungary in Revolution*, pp. 61–88; and Jenő Pongrácz, ed., *A Forradalmi Kormányzótanács és a népbiztosságok rendeletei*.

26. On the economic policies of the Commune, see Hajdu, *Magyarországi Tanácsköztársaság*, pp. 360–98; Iván T. Berend and Miklós Szuhay, *A tőkés gazdaság története Magyarországon, 1848–1944*, pp. 178–92; Gyula Hevesi, *Szociális termelés: A magyar Tanácsköztársaság iparpolitikája*; and Jenő Varga, *Die wirtschaftpolitischen Probleme der proletarischen Diktatur*.

27. See Hajdu, *Magyarországi Tanácsköztársaság*, pp. 114, 376; and Tőkés, *Kun*, p. 157n.

28. See Katalin Petrák, *Az első magyar munkáshatalom szociálpolitikája, 1919*; and Katalin Petrák and György Milei, eds., *A Magyar Tanácsköztársaság szociálpolitikája*.

29. See Tőkés, *Kun*, pp. 185–88, and Hajdu, *Magyarországi Tanácsköztársaság*, pp. 377–87. Cf. Jenő Varga, *Die Agrarfrage in der ungarischen proletarischen Revolution*.

30. *MMTVD*, vol. 6a, p. 48.

31. Ibid., p. 520.

32. See Andrew C. Janos, "The Agrarian Opposition at the National Congress of Councils," in Janos and Slottman, *Revolution in Perspective*, pp. 85–108.

33. See Farkas József, *Rohanunk a forradalomba: A magyar irodalom eszmélése, 1914–1919*, 2d ed., pp. 216–51.

34. See László Svéd, "Kassák Lajos és a Tanácsköztársaság ifjúsági mozgalma," *PK* 20, no. 1 (March 1974): 163–83; and Lajos Kassák, *Egy ember élete*, vol. 8.

35. See Hajdu, *Magyarországi Tanácsköztársaság*, pp. 398–405.

36. See Grátz, *Forradalmak*, pp. 156–68.

37. *MMTVD*, vol. 6a, p. 100.

38. Tőkés, *Kun*, pp. 160–61.

39. This detachment was commanded by the young fanatic Imre Dögei, who upon the party's return to power would gain notoriety for his brutal conduct of the collectivization campaigns.

40. Hajdu, *Magyarországi Tanácsköztársaság*, pp. 126–28.

41. See Tőkés, *Kun*, p. 163.

42. See Hajdu, *Magyarországi Tanácsköztársaság*, pp. 129–32.

43. József Lengyel gives an inside account of this terroristic elite in his novel *Prenn Ferenc hányatott élete*.

44. See Ferenc Stein, "A nép nevében," in Szerémi, *Nagy idők*, pp. 45–47.

45. See Ervin Liptai, ed., *A magyar Vörös hadsereg*.

46. Hajdu, *Magyarországi Tanácsköztársaság*, pp. 95–98.

47. W. K. Hancock and Jean van der Poel, eds., *Selections from the Smuts Papers*, vol. 4, pp. 103–5.

48. Hajdu, *Magyarországi Tanácsköztársaság*, p. 166.

49. Hajdu, *Magyarországi Tanácsköztársaság*, p. 153.

50. See György Lukács, *Taktika és ethika*.

51. Hajdu, *Magyarországi Tanácsköztársaság*, p. 155.

52. *MMTVD*, vol. 6a, p. 326; and Hajdu, *Magyarországi Tanácsköztársaság*, pp. 167–68.

53. Hajdu, *Magyarországi Tanácsköztársaság*, pp. 172–73.

54. Hajdu, *Magyarországi Tanácsköztársaság*, pp. 178–83; and *MMTVD*, vol. 6a, pp. 386–405.

55. See Hajdu, *Magyarországi Tanácsköztársaság*, pp. 241, 273.

56. To dispel rumors that he was absconding to Moscow with requisitioned jewels, Szamuely had himself searched before takeoff (ibid., p. 211).

57. *MMTVD*, vol. 6a, pp. 567, 575–78; see also Réti, *Lenin*, pp. 154–61.

58. See Hajdu, *Magyarországi Tanácsköztársaság*, pp. 299–30, and Réti, *Lenin*, pp. 161–63.

59. Hajdu, *Magyarországi Tanácsköztársaság*, pp. 240–41.

60. Ibid., p. 250.

61. Kende, "Szakszervezetek szerepe," pp. 82–84.

62. *MMTVD*, vol. 6a, pp. 518, 541–42, 480, 462.

63. *MMTVD*, vol. 6b, pp. 49–53; see also Hajdu, *Magyarországi Tanácsköztársaság*, pp. 259–68, and Tőkés, *Kun*, pp. 177–84.

64. Hajdu, *Magyarországi Tanácsköztársaság*, p. 252; and Tőkés, *Kun*, pp. 179–81.

65. See *MMTVD*, vol. 6b, p. 22.

66. *Népszava*, 15 June 1919, quoted in Tőkés, *Kun*, p. 183. See also *MMTVD*, vol. 6b, pp. 44–49, 53–58.

67. Hajdu, *Magyarországi Tanácsköztársaság*, pp. 257–58.

68. *MMTVD*, vol. 6a, p. 696; see also Mrs. Sándor Gábor, *Ausztria és a magyarországi Tanácsköztársaság*, pp. 154–68.

69. See *MMTVD*, vol. 6b, pp. 242, 245; and Hajdu, *Magyarországi Tanácsköztársaság*, p. 174.

70. *MMTVD*, vol. 6a, p. 697.

71. See Peter A. Toma, "The Slovak Soviet Republic of 1919," *American Slavic and East European Review* 17 (April 1958): 203–15; and Hajdu, *Magyarországi Tanácsköztársaság*, pp. 277–79.

72. *MMTVD*, vol. 6b, p. 274.

73. Hajdu, *Magyarországi Tanácsköztársaság*, pp. 283–89.

74. See Márton Sarlós, ed., *A Magyar Tanácsköztársaság állama és joga*.

75. Hajdu, *Magyarországi Tanácsköztársaság*, pp. 290–92.

76. *MMTVD*, vol. 6b, p. 330.

77. See Tőkés, *Kun*, pp. 197–99.

78. *MMTVD*, vol. 6b, p. 370.

79. Mihály Károlyi, *Az új Magyarországért: Válogatott irások és beszédek, 1908–1919*, p. 318.

80. Vilmos Böhm, *Két forradalom tüzében*, pp. 438–40.

81. See *MMTVD*, vol. 6b, pp. 426, 432, 444; Low, *Soviet Hungarian Republic*, pp. 77–79; Z. Nagy, *Párizsi békekonferencia*, pp. 183–200.

82. *MMTVD*, vol. 6b, pp. 486, 508.

83. Ibid., pp. 545–46, 552.

84. On the Vienna negotiations, see Böhm, *Két forradalom*, pp. 442–48; and Eva S. Balogh, "The Hungarian Social Democratic Centre and the Fall of Béla Kun," *Canadian Slavonic Papers* 18, no. 1 (March 1976): 27–35.

85. Hajdu, *Magyarországi Tanácsköztársaság*, p. 351.

86. Vladimir I. Lenin, *A Magyar Tanácsköztársaságról*, p. 112.

87. Hajdu, *Magyarországi Tanácsköztársaság*, pp. 412, 254.

88. Grigory Zinoviev, "Two Dates," *The Communist International* 1, no. 5 (August 1919): 13, quoted in Tőkés, *Kun*, p. 219; Leon Trotsky, *The First Five Years of the Communist International*, vol. 2, pp. 28–29.

89. See Tőkés, *Kun*, pp. 209–11, and idem, "Béla Kun: The Man and the Revolutionary," in Vőlgyes, *Hungary in Revolution*, pp. 170–207.

90. Hajdu, *Magyarországi Tanácsköztársaság*, p. 249.

91. Ibid., pp. 382–83.

92. Ibid., p. 443; Kun, *Válogatott*, vol. 2, p. 258.

93. Hajdu, *Magyarországi Tanácsköztársaság*, p. 94.

# PART TWO

## 4. Exile and Factionalism, 1919–1924

1. See Béla Kirschner, *A "szakszervezeti kormány" hat napja (1919)*, chaps. 3–5.

2. See Eva S. Balogh, "István Friedrich and the Hungarian Coup d'État of 1919: A Reevaluation," *Slavic Review* 35, no. 2 (June 1976): 269–86.

3. Váry, *Vörösuralom*, pp. 2ff.

4. Ágnes Szabó, *A Kommunisták Magyarországi Pártjának ujjászervezése, 1919–1925*, p. 15 (hereafter cited as *KMP ujjászervezése*).

5. The Karlstein group included Kun, Landler, Hamburger, Vágó, Varga, Gyula Lengyel, László Rudas, Pogány, Pór, Seidler, Bettelheim, and Rákosi (A. Szabó, *KMP ujjászervezése*, p. 221).

6. Münnich, *Viharos út*, p. 80.

7. Ágnes Szabó, "A KMP ujjászervezése," in Erényi and Rákosi, *Legyőzhetetlen erő*, p. 45.

8. Originally published under the pseudonym of Balázs Kolozsváry, *Forradalomról forradalomra*; also in Kun, *Válogatott*, vol. 2. See A. Szabó, *KMP ujjászervezése*, pp. 44–53.

9. Béla Kirschner, "A nemzetközi forradalom lehetőségének megítélése és a magyar forradalom kérdése a KMP-ben 1919 augusztusa és 1921 tavasza között," *PK* 21, no. 1 (March 1975): 95; Kun, *Válogatott*, vol. 2, p. 26.

10. Réti, *Lenin*, pp. 227–29.

11. Ibid., pp. 231–32.

12. See Robert A. Goldwin, ed., *Readings in Russian Foreign Policy*, pp. 349–55. For Rákosi's report, see Communist International, *Le mouvement communiste international: Rapports, adresses au deuxième congrés de l'Internationale Communiste, 1920*, pp. 35–39.

13. See, for instance, Béla Kun, "Néhány megjegyzés jóhiszemüek számára: utóhang," in Grigory Zinoviev and Karl Radek, eds., *Mit mond a III. Internacionálé a magyarországi proletárforradalomról*, pp. 25–48.

14. See Kirschner, "Nemzetközi forradalom," pp. 104–123.

15. A. Szabó, *KMP ujjászervezése*, pp. 56–57; see Lukács, *Történelem és osztálytudat*.

16. Mrs. Mátyás Imre et al., eds., *Dokumentumok a magyar forradalmi munkásmozgalom történetéből, 1919–1929*, pp. 105–10.

17. A. Szabó, *KMP ujjászervezése*, pp. 89–90.

18. A. Szabó, "KMP ujjászervezése," in Erényi and Rákosi, *Legyőzhetetlen erő*, pp. 52–53.

19. See Béla Kovrig, *Magyar szociálpolitika, (1920–1945)*.

20. See Erika Rév, *A népbiztosok pere;* and József Gábor, "A szovjet kormány akciója a magyarországi fehérterror üldözöttjeinek megmentésére," *PK* 10, no. 4 (December 1964): 93–111.

21. A. Szabó, *KMP ujjászervezése*, pp. 95–96.

22. Ibid., pp. 96–97.

23. Ibid., pp. 97–99.

24. György Lukács, "Marxista fejlődésem: 1918–1930," *Magyar Filozófiai Szemle* 13 (1969): 1187.

25. See, for instance, László Rudas, *Abenteuer- und Liquidatorentum; die Politik Béla Kuns und die Krise der K.P.U.*

26. A. Szabó, *KMP ujjászervezése*, pp. 99–103.

27. Victor Serge, *Memoirs of a Revolutionary, 1901–1941*, p. 140.

28. Réti, *Lenin*, p. 238. On Kun's role in the March action, see Werner T. Angress, *Stillborn Revolution: The Communist Bid for Power in Germany, 1921–1923*, pp. 120–96.

29. Serge, *Memoirs*, p. 140.

30. See Franz Borkenau, *European Communism*, pp. 211–13.

31. Aino Kuusinen, *Before and After Stalin*, pp. 61, 64–65.

32. A. Szabó, *KMP ujjászervezése*, pp. 107–11.

33. Ibid., pp. 112–13.

34. Ibid., pp. 120–21.

35. Ibid., pp. 239n, 121–28.

36. Borkenau, *European Communism*, pp. 221–34.

37. A. Szabó, *KMP ujjászervezése*, pp. 129–34; Imre, *Dokumentumok*, pp. 141–44.

38. A. Szabó, *KMP ujjászervezése*, pp. 137–40.

39. Ibid., pp. 143–44.

40. A. Szabó, "KMP ujjászervezése," in Erényi and Rákosi, *Legyőzhetetlen erő*, p. 57.

41. See Mrs. Ervin Liptai, *A Magyarországi Szocialista Munkáspárt, 1925–1928*, pp. 30–34 (hereafter cited as *MSZMP*).

42. Borkenau, *European Communism*, pp. 176–80, 419.

## 5. The Search for Relevance, 1924–1932

1. A. Szabó, "KMP ujjászervezése," in Erényi and Rákosi, *Legyőzhetetlen erő*, p. 63.

2. A. Szabó, *KMP ujjászervezése*, p. 182.

3. Ibid., pp. 182–83; and idem, *A KMP első kongresszusa*, pp. 13–20.

4. Agnes Szabó and Magda Imre, eds., *A KMP első kongresszusa*, p. 65.

5. Imre, *Dokumentumok*, pp. 228–30.

6. Günther Nollau, *International Communism and World Revolution*, pp. 86–88.

7. A. Szabó, *KMP ujjászervezése*, pp. 186–87, Mrs. Liptai, *MSZMP*, pp. 39–40.

8. Mrs. Liptai, *MSZMP*, pp. 43–48.

9. Ibid., pp. 60–62.

10. Ibid., pp. 68–84.

11. Ibid., pp. 81–82, 102; and A. Szabó, *KMP ujjászervezése*, p. 192.

12. Károly Kiss, *Nincs megállás*, pp. 5–22.

13. A. Szabó and Imre, *KMP első kongresszusa*, pp. 47–61.

14. On the congress, see A. Szabó and Imre, *KMP első kongresszusa*; A. Szabó, *KMP ujjászervezése*, pp. 192–215; A. Szabó, *KMP első kongresszusa*, pp. 27–63; Mrs. Liptai, *MSZMP*, pp. 84–95. For an analysis of the party's agrarian policies, see Kálmán Szakács, *A Kommunista Párt agrárpolitikája, 1920–1930*.

15. See Tibor Hajdu, "Károlyi Mihály és a KMP kapcsolatáról a huszas években," *PK* 21, no. 2 (June 1975): 145–58. On the émigrés in France, see Irén Komját and Anna Pécsi, *A szabadság vándorai*.

16. See Mrs. Liptai, *MSZMP*, pp. 130–41; and Magyar Munkásmozgalmi Intézet, *A Rákosi-per*.

17. Béla S. Szász, *Volunteers for the Gallows: Anatomy of a Show Trial*, pp. 157–58.

18. Mrs. Liptai, *MSZMP,* pp. 145, 136.

19. A. Szabó, "KMP ujjászervezése," in Erényi and Rákosi, *Legyőzhetetlen erő,* pp. 70–71.

20. Mrs. Liptai, *MSZMP,* p. 159.

21. Ibid., pp. 164–67.

22. Ibid., p. 171.

23. Ibid., pp. 198–99.

24. Ibid., p. 215.

25. A. Szabó, "KMP ujjászervezése," in Erényi and Rákosi, *Legyőzhetetlen erő,* p. 72.

26. Mrs. Liptai, *MSZMP,* pp. 217–20.

27. Ibid., pp. 223–24.

28. Kiss, *Nincs megállás,* p. 82; and Mrs. Liptai, *MSZMP,* p. 236.

29. György Borsányi, "Kun Béla 1928-as bécsi letartóztatása," *PK* 21, no. 2 (June 1975): 159–78.

30. See Béla Kirschner, "A Kommunisták Magyarországi Pártjának 1928 júliusi plénuma," *PK* 7, no. 1 (March 1961).

31. Dezső Nemes et al., *A magyar forradalmi munkásmozgalom története,* p. 262 (hereafter cited as *Magyar munkásmozgalom*).

32. Kiss, *Nincs megállás,* pp. 86–88.

33. Jane Degras, ed., *The Communist International, 1919–1943: Documents,* vol. 3, pp. 456–61.

34. Sándor Szerényi, "Megjegyzések Lackó Miklós tanulmányához," *PK* 21, no. 4 (December 1975): 147–48.

35. Serge, *Memoirs,* p. 187.

36. "Dokumentumok: A Blum-tézisek," *PK* 21, no. 4 (December 1975): pp. 154–206.

37. Cf. Iván T. Berend and György Ránki, *Magyarország gazdasága az első világháború után, 1919–1929.*

38. Oszkár Betlen, "A KMP II. kongresszusa politikájának nemzetközi vonásairól és a párt stratégiájáról," *PK* 9, no. 3 (September 1963): 119–20.

39. Lukács, "Marxista fejlődésem," p. 1198.

40. Szerényi, "Megjegyzések," especially pp. 148–49. See also "Vita a Blum-tézisről," *PK* 2, no. 3–4 (October 1956): 96–127; Miklós Lackó, "A Blum-tézisek," *Történelmi Szemle* 17 (1974): 360–71; and Mrs. Liptai, *MSZMP,* pp. 198–99, 217–18.

41. See Mrs. Zoltán Horváth, *A KMP második kongresszusa,* pp. 26–35.

42. László Kővágó, "A Magyar Kommunista Párt nemzetiségpolitikája a Tanácsköztársaság megdöntésétől a felszabadulásig," *PK* 23, no. 2 (June 1977): 78–84 (hereafter cited as "MKP nemzetiségpolitikája").

43. György Borsányi, "Kommunista szervezkedés a gazdasági világválság és a fasizmus előretörése idején", in Erényi and Rákosi, *Legyőzhetetlen erő,* pp. 79–82 (hereafter cited as "Kommunista szervezkedés").

44. Mrs. Horváth, *KMP második kongresszusa,* pp. 40–63.

45. György Borsányi, *"Munkát! Kenyeret!" A proletariátus tömegmozgalmai Magyarországon a gazdasági válság éveiben (1929–1933),* pp. 70–71.

46. Sándor Szerényi, "Révai József 1930-as hazatérésének körülményeiről," *PK* 23, no. 1 (March 1977): 184.

47. Lukács, "Marxista fejlődésem," p. 1199.

48. Borsányi, *"Munkát! Kenyeret!"*, pp. 71, 232–33.

49. Sallai was a former clerk and revolutionary socialist who adhered early to the CPH and was a prominent figure in the Commune's political investigation agencies. He subsequently worked at the Moscow Marx-Engels-Lenin Institute, in Hungary on the illegal communist press, and again in the Soviet Union for the Soviet party. Fürst, also a former clerk, was the leader of an SDP communist cell, having joined the CPH in 1926; he had already served a prison term in 1929/31. Poll had joined the CPH in 1918, served in the Red Army, was a founding member of the SWPH in 1925, became a member of the CPH Central Committee, was jailed 1927/30, then became a CPH representative on the Comintern's Executive Committee. Kilián was a locksmith who in 1929 joined the KIMSZ, studied in Moscow in 1930/31, then was repatriated to head the KIMSZ.

50. Borsányi, *"Munkát! Kenyeret!"*, pp. 235–54. See also József Domokos, ". . . emlékezz, proletár!" Sallai Imre és Fürst Sándor pere.

51. Borsányi, *"Munkát! Kenyeret!"*, pp. 78–79.

52. Ibid., pp. 80–89.

53. Ibid., pp. 102–4, 116.

54. Nemes, *Magyar munkásmozgalom*, p. 280; Borsányi, *"Munkát! Kenyeret!"*, pp. 128, 135.

55. Borsányi, *"Munkát! Kenyeret!"* pp. 136–38.

56. Ibid., pp. 175–76.

57. Ibid., pp. 193–95.

58. See Piroska Ördögh, *A szakszervezetek antifasiszta tevékenysége a Gömbös-kormány idején*, pp. 100–10 (hereafter cited as *Szakszervezetek*).

59. Borsányi, *"Munkát! Kenyeret!"*, pp. 262–65.

60. Nemes, *Magyar munkásmozgalom*, pp. 287–89.

61. Borsányi, *"Munkát! Kenyeret!"*, pp. 255–56. On the party's organizing efforts in rural areas, see Kálmán Szakács, "A KMP falusi szervezeti tevékenységéről a II. kongresszustol 1933 májusáig," *PK* 14, no. 3 (August 1968): 78–108.

62. Kiss, *Nincs megállás*, pp. 149, 153, 160.

63. Magda K. Nagy, "Viták, vélemények az irodalom és a politika kapcsolatáról, a szocialista irodalom elvi követelményeiről (1929–1933)," *PK* 22, no. 4 (December 1976): 44–89.

64. See György Lukács, *Művészet és irodalom.*

65. See György Vértes, *József Attila és az illegális Kommunista Párt.*

66. Gyula Schöpflin, "Az illegális Kommunista Párt Magyarországon," *Látóhatár*, 5, no. 1 (January 1959): 39.

67. Miklós Lackó, *Válságok—választások*, pp. 75–76.

## 6. Popular Front, Hungarian Front, 1932–1944

1. Borsányi, "Kommunista szervezkedés," in Erényi and Rákosi, *Legyőzhetetlen erő*, pp. 94–96.

2. Nemes, *Magyar munkásmozgalom*, pp. 298–99.

3. Ibid., p. 308; Ördögh, *Szakszervezetek*, pp. 112–37.

4. See Ördögh, *Szakszervezetek*, pp. 218–31.

5. Nemes, *Magyar munkásmozgalom*, p. 327.

6. See Hugh Thomas, *The Spanish Civil War*, pp. 578–79; Robert Conquest, *The Great Terror*, p. 439; and Imre Gergely, *Magyarok a spanyol néppel, 1936–1939.*

7. See Kermit E. McKenzie, *Comintern and World Revolution, 1928–1943*, chap. 6.

8. Bálint Szabó, *Népi demokrácia és forradalomelmélet*, p. 38.

9. B. Szabó, *Népi demokrácia*, p. 37.

10. Ibid., pp. 46–48; and Ágnes Ságvári, *Népfront és koalició Magyarországon, 1936–1948*, pp. 34–35, 50. For Kun's amended arguments, see Kun, *Válogatott*, vol. 2, p. 366.

11. *PK* 10, no. 1 (March 1964): 168.

12. B. Szabó, *Népi demokrácia*, p. 48.

13. István Pintér, "A KMP az 1936–1944-es években," in Erényi and Rákosi, *Legyőzhetetlen erő*, pp. 106–10.

14. See B. Szabó, *Népi demokrácia*, p. 49; Nemes, *Magyar munkásmozgalom*, pp. 329–30; and István Pintér and László Svéd, eds., *Dokumentumok a magyar forradalmi munkásmozgalom történetéből, 1935–1945*, pp. 61–64.

15. Pintér, "A KMP," in Erényi and Rákosi, *Legyőzhetetlen erő*, pp. 112–14.

16. B. Szabó, *Népi demokrácia*, p. 53.

17. József Révai, *Marxizmus, népiesség, magyarság*, 4th ed., p. 326.

18. See Ferenc Pölöskei and Kálmán Szakács, eds., *Földmunkás- és szegényparaszt-mozgalmak Magyarországon, 1848–1948*, vol. 2, pp. 632–35.

19. Gyula Szekfű, *Három nemzedék, és ami utána következik*, 5th ed., pp. 422–71.

20. György Oláh, *Három millió koldus* (Miskolc, 1928); and Dezső Szabó, *Az egész látóhatár*, 3 vols. (Budapest: Magyar Élet, 1939).

21. László Németh, *A minőség forradalma*, 2 vols. (Budapest: Magyar Élet, 1940).

22. Gyula Illyés, *Puszták népe* (Budapest: Nyugat, 1936).

23. See István Pintér, "A KMP és a Márciusi Front," *PK* 22, no. 4 (December 1976): 3–43 (hereafter cited as "Márciusi Front"); and Gyula Borbándi, *Der Ungarische Populismus*, pp. 156–71.

24. Pintér, "Márciusi Front," p. 29.

25. Ibid., p. 39.

26. *Új Hang*, May–June 1940, quoted in Pintér, "Márciusi Front," p. 43n.

27. Henrik Vass et al., eds., *Munkásmozgalomtörténeti Lexikon.*

28. Anton Ciliga, *The Russian Enigma*, p. 253.

29. Mrs. Béla Kun, *Kun Béla*, pp. 415–16.

30. Ibid., p. 418.

31. This account is given by Arvo Tuominen, a former secretary-general of the Finnish party, in *Uusi Kuvalehti*, 10/13, 1956.

32. Mrs. Kun, *Kun Béla*, p. 419.

33. R. V. Ivanov-Razumnik, *The Memoirs of Ivanov-Razumnik*, p. 315.

34. Endre Sik, *Vihar a levelet . . .,* pp. 78, 136. For other accounts, see Gyula Kékesdi, *A forradalom katedráján: Lengyel Gyula élete,* pp. 170–73; and Sándor Nógrádi, *Történelmi lecke,* pp. 362–78.

35. Sik, *Vihar,* p. 273.

36. Ignotus, *Hungary,* p. 185.

37. Winston S. Churchill, *The Grand Alliance,* p. 168.

38. Pintér, "A KMP," in Erényi and Rákosi, *Legyőzhetetlen erő,* pp. 117–18.

39. Mrs. Éva Nemes Berán and Ervin Hollós, eds., *Megfigyelés alatt . . . Dokumentumok a Horthysta titkosrendőrség működéséből (1920–1944),* pp. 311–12.

40. Szász, *Volunteers for the Gallows,* p. 158.

41. Sik, *Vihar,* pp. 205, 209–10.

42. Szász, *Volunteers,* p. 158.

43. Sik, *Vihar,* pp. 238–39.

44. Ibid., p. 377.

45. Ibid., p. 410–12.

46. Nógrádi, *Történelmi lecke,* pp. 388–90.

47. Kővágó, "MKP nemzetiségpolitikaja," p. 90.

48. Pintér and Svéd, *Dokumentumok,* pp. 241–42; "A Kommunista Internacionálé Végrehajtó Bizottságának a Kommunisták Magyarországi Pártja feladatairól 1939-ben és 1940-ben hozott határozatai," *PK* 8, no. 2 (March 1962): 163–90. See also Lóránt Tilkovszky, *Revízió és nemzetiségpolitika Magyarországon, 1938–1941.*

49. B. Szabó, *Népi demokrácia,* pp. 57, 61. See also Pintér, "A KMP," in Erényi and Rákosi, *Legyőzhetetlen erő,* pp. 119–30.

50. The mystery of the bombings remains unresolved. Various hypotheses have been advanced blaming the Russians, the Germans, prowar Hungarians, and vengeful Czechs. See N. F. Dreisziger, "New Twist to an Old Riddle: The Bombing of Kassa (Košice), June 26, 1941," *Journal of Modern History* 44, no. 2 (June 1972): 232–42.

51. Ernő Zágoni, *A magyar kommunisták a munkásegységért, 1939–1942,* pp. 151–56. On the activities of former Romanian party members in reannexed Transylvania, see Dániel Csatári, *Forgószélben; magyar-román viszony 1940–1945.*

52. István Pintér, *Magyar antifasizmus és ellenállás,* pp. 28–34.

53. Pintér, *Magyar antifasizmus,* p. 35.

54. Zágoni, *Magyar kommunisták,* pp. 169–71.

55. Ibid., pp. 180–83.

56. Pintér, " A KMP," in Erényi and Rákosi, *Legyőzhetetlen erő,* p. 135n.

57. Pintér, *Magyar antifasizmus,* p. 47–49.

58. Ibid., pp. 62–78.

59. Ibid., pp. 85–87.

60. See William Shawcross, *Crime and Compromise: Janos Kadar and the Politics of Hungary since Revolution,* pp. 20–44.

61. Tonhauser returned to the Czechoslovak party after the war.

62. Pintér, *Magyar antifasizmus,* p. 116.

63. Ibid., pp. 117–18.

64. See Pintér, "A KMP," in Erényi and Rákosi, *Legyőzhetetlen erő,* pp. 140–43.

65. István Dobi, *Vallomás és történelem,* vol. 2, pp. 174–84.

66. Pintér, *Magyar antifasizmus,* pp. 182–83.

67. Pintér and Svéd, *Dokumentumok,* pp. 394–97.

68. Pintér, *Magyar antifasizmus,* pp. 192–96.

69. For a survey of the anti-Nazi political opposition movement, see C. A. Macartney, *October Fifteenth: A History of Modern Hungary, 1929–1945,* vol. 2, chap. 19.

70. See Borbándi, *Ungarische Populismus,* pp. 222–29; Gábor Havas et al., "A 43-as szárszói találkozó előzményeihez," *Valóság* 8 (1973): 43–55: *Szárszó* (Budapest, 1943).

71. See Révai, *Marxizmus, népiesség, magyarság;* and László Illés, "Az Új Hang kritikai munkássága," in Miklós Szabolcsi and László Illés, eds., *Jöjj el, szabadság: Tanulmányok a magyar szocialista irodalom történetéből,* pp. 409–41.

72. Pintér, *Magyar antifasizmus,* pp. 286–87, 291–94.

73. Ibid., pp. 177–78, 304–5.

74. Ibid., pp. 360–61.

75. Lajos Fehér, *Harcunk Budapestért,* 2d rev. ed. Rather inflated accounts of the participation of Hungarian communists in partisan activities in Hungary and elsewhere can be found in János Harsányi, ed., *Magyar szabadságharcosok a fasizmus ellen,* 2d ed.; József Gazsi and István Pintér, eds., *Fegyverrel a fasizmus ellen;* Katalin Petrák and Ernő Vágó, eds., *Harcok, emlékek;* Mihály Fekete, *Ellenállók az Avas alján;* József Fábry, *A szabadságért harcoltunk;* Sándor Futó Galambos, *Három nehéz esztendő;* and Ágnes Godó, *Magyarok a jugoszláv népfelszabadító háborúban.*

76. Pintér, *Magyar antifasizmus,* pp. 369–75.

77. Magyar Szocialista Munkáspárt, *A Magyar Kommunista Párt és a Szociáldemokrata Párt határozatai, 1944–1948,* p. 28 (hereafter cited as "MKP és SDP határozatai"). See Pintér, *Magyar antifasizmus,* pp. 379–80.

78. Pintér, *Magyar antifasizmus,* p. 382.

79. Ibid., pp. 393, 395, 407–8.

80. Ibid., p. 420.

81. Ibid., pp. 437–38.

82. Ibid., pp. 432–37.

## PART THREE

## 7. The Party as Liberator, 1944–1945

1. See Adam B. Ulam, *Expansion and Coexistence: Soviet Foreign Policy, 1917–73,* 2d ed., chap. 7; and Bennett Kovrig, *The Myth of Liberation: East-Central Europe in U.S. Diplomacy and Politics since 1941,* chap. 1.

2. Milovan Djilas, *Conversations with Stalin,* p. 114.

3. Anthony Eden, *The Reckoning,* p. 483; United States, Department of State, *Foreign Relations of the United States, 1945: The Conference at Malta and Yalta,* pp. 242–45; and Philip E. Mosely, *Face to Face with Russia,* p. 23.

4. The following account is based on B. Szabó, *Népi demokrácia,* pp. 77–106.

5. Ibid., p. 106.

6. Zoltán Vas, "Moszkvától Budapestig," *Magyar Nemzet*, 7, 8, and 14 January 1975.

7. Ernő Gerő, *Lesz magyar ujjászületés*.

8. Mihály Korom, "Az Ideiglenes Nemzetgyűlés és kormány létrehozásának előkészitése," *PK* 20, no. 4 (December 1974): 105, 107–8 (hereafter cited as "Ideiglenes Nemzetgyűlés"). Overtures were also made to the retired Bethlen, who was under Soviet guard, but he declined to participate.

9. B. Szabó, *Népi demokrácia*, pp. 90–96, 101n.

10. Vas, *Magyar Nemzet*, 19 January 1975.

11. See Béla Balázs, *Népmozgalom és nemzeti bizottságok*, pp. 72ff.

12. Korom, "Ideiglenes Nemzetgyűlés," pp. 116–20.

13. Ibid., pp. 121–22.

14. Ibid., pp. 122–23.

15. Ibid., p. 132. Cf. Péter Gosztonyi, "Az Ideiglenes Nemzeti Kormány megalakulásának előtörténetéhez," *Új Látóhatár* no. 3 (1972), pp. 228–32.

16. Dezső Sulyok, *A Magyar Tragédia*, p. 560.

17. Nógrádi, *Történelmi lecke*, pp. 263, 267.

18. Béla Rácz, "A Belügyminisztérium ujjászervezése," *Levéltári Közlemények* 40, no. 1 (1970): 91 (hereafter cited as "Belügyminisztérium").

19. United States, House of Representatives, *Fifth Interim Report on Hungary*, pp. 264–66.

20. Nemes, *Magyar munkásmozgalom*, p. 437. See also Ságvári, *Népfront és koalició Magyarországon, 1936–1948*, p. 106.

21. József Suli, *Hidfő*, p. 147.

22. Vince Nagy, *Októbertől—októberig*, p. 293.

23. For details of the land reform, see Ferenc Donáth, *Demokratikus földreform Magyarországon, 1945–1947;* and Sándor Orbán, *Két agrárforradalom Magyarországon*, pp. 22–45.

24. See Ferenc Nagy, *The Struggle behind the Iron Curtain*, pp. 109–10.

25. Nógrádi, *Történelmi lecke*, pp. 281–83.

26. See Tamás Földi and György Ránki, "A Szovjetunió gazdasági segitsége az ujjáépülő Magyarországnak (1945–1948)," in Miklós Lackó, ed., *Tanulmányok a magyar népi demokrácia történetéből*, pp. 377–78.

27. Antal Bán, "Hungary," in Denis Healey, ed., *The Curtain Falls: The Story of the Socialists in Eastern Europe*, p. 72.

28. Nógrádi, *Történelmi lecke*, pp. 267–74.

29. Zoltán Vas, *Magyar Nemzet*, 17 and 29 January 1975; and Vas, "1945—az első napok Budapesten," *Élet és Irodalom* 14, no. 12 (1970): 3–4.

30. Ságvári, *Népfront*, p. 95n.

31. Kiss, *Nincs megállás*, p. 365.

32. See Tamás Aczél and Tibor Méray, *The Revolt of the Mind*, pp. 8–9.

33. Miklós Molnár and László Nagy, *Imre Nagy: Réformateur ou révolutionnaire?*, p. 20.

34. Erzsébet Strassenreiter and Péter Sipos, "Rajk László (1909–1949)," *PK* 15, no. 1 (March 1969): 173. See also Béla Kirschner and Béla Rácz, "Adalékok a felszabadult Csepel WM első nagy hónapjának," *PK* 7, no. 3 (August 1961): 124–33.

35. Ságvári, *Népfront*, p. 97n.

36. Miklós Habuda and Sándor Rákosi, "A Magyar Kommunista Párt és a Szociáldemokrata Párt munkásösszetételének alakulása 1945–1948-ban," *PK* 22, no. 3 (September 1976): 42–44, 51 (hereafter cited as "MKP és SDP"). See also Éva Szabó, "A Magyar Kommunista Párt," in Erényi and Rákosi, *Legyőzhetetlen erő*, pp. 155–69.

37. Nógrádi, *Történelmi lecke*, pp. 296–97.

38. Endre Sik, *Egy diplomata feljegyzései*, 2d ed., p. 12.

39. Ernő Gerő, *A Magyar Kommunista Párt*, pp. 4–5, 18.

40. *Szabad Nép*, 28 March 1946.

41. See Eugene Duschinsky, "Hungary," in Peter Meyer et al., eds., *The Jews in the Soviet Satellites*, pp. 391–450.

42. B. Szabó, *Népi demokrácia*, pp. 110–17.

43. Mátyás Rákosi, *A magyar jövőért*, pp. 322–23.

44. B. Szabó, *Népi demokrácia*, pp. 119–22.

45. Ibid., pp. 125–28.

46. Rácz, "Belügyminisztérium," pp. 93–108.

47. See Ságvári, *Népfront*, pp. 114–17; and B. Szabó, *Népi demokrácia*, pp. 130–34.

48. B. Szabó, *Népi demokrácia*, pp. 132–34.

49. See Andor Csizmadia, *A nemzeti bizottságok-állami tevékenysége (1944–1949)*, pp. 148–57.

50. See János Rácz, *Az üzemi bizottságok a magyar népi demokratikus átalakulásban*, pp. 24–38.

51. Rácz, *Üzemi bizottságok*, p. 53.

52. Ibid., pp. 53, 56.

53. See István Tóth, *A Nemzeti Parasztpárt története, 1944–1948*, pp. 7–91.

54. Bán, "Hungary," in Healey, *The Curtain Falls*, p. 72.

55. Erzsébet Strassenreiter, "A két munkáspárt együttműködése a felszabadulás után," *PK* 19, no. 2 (June 1973): pp. 56, 70 (hereafter cited as "Két munkáspárt"). See also György Marosán, *Tüzes kemence*, pp. 779–92; idem, *Az úton végig kell menni* (hereafter cited as *Az úton*); and Árpád Szakasits, "Hajnalhasadás," in Mrs. Ernő Lányi et al., eds., *A szabadság hajnalán*, 184–200.

56. Rácz, *Üzemi bizottságok*, 136n, 146n. See also Miklós Habuda, ed., *A magyar szakszervezetek a népi demokratikus forradalomban, 1944–1948;* and Robert Gabor, *The Bolshevization of the Hungarian Trade Unions, 1945–1951*.

57. Ságvári, *Népfront*, p. 120.

58. See Magyar Kommunista Párt, *Harc az ujjáépitésért: A Magyar Kommunista Párt 1945 május 20-an és 21-én tartott országos értekezletének jegyzőkönyve*.

59. B. Szabó, *Népi demokrácia*, pp. 138–39; and Nógrádi, *Történelmi lecke*, pp. 298–99.

60. B. Szabó, *Népi demokrácia*, p. 140; and I. T. Zamercev, *Emlékek, arcok, Budapest . . .* , p. 102.

61. Sándor Balogh, *Parlamenti és pártharcok Magyarországon, 1945–1947*, pp. 38–39.

62. Dobi, *Vallomás és történelem*, vol. 2, p. 426.

63. See Sulyok, *Magyar Tragédia*, pp. 559–62.

64. Balogh, *Parlamenti*, pp. 40–41.

65. B. Szabó, *Népi demokrácia*, pp. 153–58. See "Vita demokráciánk válságáról," *Valóság*, January–February 1946, pp. 86–103.

66. See Gyula Szekfű, *Forradalom után*.

67. Strassenreiter, "Két munkáspárt," pp. 74–76. On the background of the various parties, see Balogh, *Parlamenti*, pp. 16–36.

68. See Balogh, *Parlamenti*, pp. 56–62.

69. Magyar Kommunista Párt, *Nemzeti kérdés és magyar demokratikus külpolitika*. On the other parties' electoral platforms, see Balogh, *Parlamenti*, pp. 62–76.

70. Nicholas Nyárádi, *My Ringside Seat in Moscow*, p. 10.

71. Balogh, *Parlamenti*, p. 90.

72. Nyárádi, *My Ringside Seat*, p. 10; Balogh, *Parlamenti*, pp. 91–94.

73. Magyar Kommunista Párt, *Hadifogoly zsebkönyv*.

74. *Magyar Hiradó*, 6 September 1947. *Magyar Hiradó* is an internal bulletin of the foreign ministry cited in Paul A. Hámori, "Soviet Influences on the Establishment and Character of the Hungarian People's Republic (1944–1954)", p. 54 (hereafter cited as "Soviet Influences").

75. An alternative hypothesis assesses the leading parties' orientation in terms of "bourgeois-democratic," "populist-agrarian," and "communist-industrial" models of development, and concludes that the last two taken together enjoyed a narrow majority of support, which was however overshadowed by an anticommunist, anti-Soviet consensus. See Charles Gati, "Hungary: The Dynamics of Revolutionary Transformation," in idem, ed., *The Politics of Modernization in Eastern Europe*, pp. 78–83.

76. Ságvári, *Népfront*, p. 124.

77. F. Nagy, *The Struggle behind The Iron Curtain*, p. 154.

78. F. Nagy, *Struggle*, pp. 159–64; Sulyok, *Magyar Tragédia*, pp. 559–60; and Imre Kovács, *Im Schatten der Sowiets*, pp. 235–36.

79. András Kis, *A Magyar Köszösségtől a Földalatti Fővezérségig*, p. 77.

80. Nógrádi, *Történelmi lecke*, p. 307.

81. József Révai, "A választások és a magyar demokrácia néhány főkérdése," *Társadalmi Szemle*, January 1946, pp. 5–13.

82. Mátyás Rákosi, *A magyar demokráciáért*, p. 140.

## 8. The Tactics of Attrition, 1945–1947

1. Mátyás Rákosi, *A népi demokrácia*, pp. 4–6, 9, 12, 14, 18, 15.

2. B. Szabó, *Népi demokrácia*, p. 178.

3. Ibid., pp. 182–83.

4. József Révai, *Élni tudunk a szabadsággal*, pp. 180, 512.

5. Mátyás Rákosi, *A békéért és a szocializmus épitéséért*, p. 222.

6. *Szabad Nép*, 29 November 1948.

7. Bán, "Hungary," in Healey, *The Curtain Falls*, p. 67.

8. B. Szabó, *Népi demokrácia*, pp. 183–85.

9. *Szabad Nép*, 7 February 1946; see Ságvári, *Népfront*, pp. 136–37.

10. E. Szabó, "A Magyar Kommunista Párt,' in Erényi and Rákosi, *Legyőzhetetlen erő,* pp. 170–73.

11. See Rácz, *Üzemi bizottságok,* pp. 97–98.

12. Marosán, *Az úton,* pp. 162–88.

13. Balogh, *Parlamenti,* pp. 227–28.

14. See János Molnár, "Irányzatok harca a Szociáldemokrata Pártban 1946–1947-ben," *PK* 23, no. 1 (March 1977): 12–22.

15. Balogh, *Parlamenti,* p. 124.

16. Rácz, "Belügyminisztérium," p. 111.

17. András Kis, "A jobboldali erők veresége a hadseregben (1946)," *Hadtörténelmi Közlemények* 1969, no. 3, pp. 507–9; Károly Munk, "A nevelőtisztek szerepe a Magyar Kommunista Pártnak a hadsereggel kapcsolatos célkitűzései megvalósitásáért folytatott harcban," *PK* 8, no. 2 (June 1962): 133–48. For a general account of the reorganization of the armed forces, see Sándor Mucs, *A magyar néphadsereg megszervezése és fejlődése, 1945–1948.*

18. Ságvári, *Népfront,* p. 144n.

19. See Sándor Balogh, "A politikai pártok és a szövetkezetek kérdése Magyarországon 1945–1946-ban," *PK* 21, no. 4 (December 1975): 51–82.

20. See Balogh, *Parlamenti,* pp. 157–65; and V. Nagy, *Októbertől—októberig,* pp. 271–72.

21. Balogh, *Parlamenti,* pp. 177–82.

22. Ibid., p. 182.

23. Ibid., pp. 190, 222.

24. Ibid., pp. 222–23.

25. Ibid., pp. 222, 224.

26. Ibid., pp. 232–33.

27. Sándor Balogh, "A baloldali erők küzdelme a közigazgatás demokratizálásáért. A 1946. évi bélista végrehajtása és reviziója," *PK* 20, no. 2 (June 1974): 55 (hereafter cited as "Baloldali erők").

28. Nemes, *Magyar munkásmozgalom,* p. 474.

29. The B-list operation is described in Balogh, "Baloldali erők," pp. 55–86; Rácz, "Belügyminisztérium," pp. 111–18; and Balogh, *Parlamenti,* pp. 106–16.

30. Balogh, *Parlamenti,* pp. 559, 572–73.

31. Magyar Kommunista Párt, *A népi demokrácia útja: A Magyar Kommunista Párt III. kongresszusának jegyzőkönyve,* p. 168.

32. Balogh, *Parlamenti,* pp. 235–37.

33. See István Vida, "A 'demokratikus államrend és a köztársaság büntetőjogi védelméről' szóló törvényjavaslat megszületése és parlamenti vitája," *Történelmi Szemle* 7 (1965): 245–47.

34. Magyar Szocialista Munkáspárt, *MKP és SDP határozatai,* p. 626.

35. Balogh, *Parlamenti,* pp. 243–44.

36. Ibid., pp. 245–46; Strassenreiter and Sipos, "Rajk László, (1909–1949)," p. 176.

37. The Soviet Union's exploitation is generally glossed over by Hungarian historians. For fragmentary evidence, see Iván T. Berend, *Ujjáépités és a nagytőke elleni*

*harc Magyarországon, 1945–1948,* p. 29; and Ferenc Gáspár et al., eds., *A munkásság az üzemekért, a termelésért, 1944–1945: Dokumentgyüjtemény,* pp. 230–31, 258–59, 267–70, 294–95.

38. See Berend, *Ujjáépités,* p. 46; and Nicholas Spulber, *The Economics of Communist Eastern Europe* (New York: Wiley, 1970), p. 170.

39. András B. Göllner, "Foundations of Soviet Domination and Communist Political Power in Hungary: 1945–1950," *Canadian-American Review of Hungarian Studies* 3, no. 2 (Fall 1976): 84.

40. See F. Nagy, *Struggle,* pp. 136–38.

41. Ibid., p. 134.

42. Schoenfeld voiced this opinion in a report of 2 May 1946. See United States, Department of State, *Foreign Relations of the United States: Diplomatic Papers, 1946* vol. 6 (Washington, D.C.: U.S. Government Printing Office, 1969), p. 293.

43. On Western policies regarding Hungary, see Bennett Kovrig, *Myth of Liberation,* pp. 64–66.

44. Balogh, *Parlamenti,* p. 138.

45. Ibid., pp. 138–40; Berend, *Ujjáépités,* p. 41.

46. Balogh, *Parlamenti,* p. 202.

47. Ibid., pp. 252–68.

48. Ságvári, *Népfront,* p. 145.

49. See István Molnár, "Adalékok a 'Munkások a tudományért—tudósok a munkásokért' akció történetéhez," *PK* 9, no. 4 (December 1963): 148–64.

50. Robert R. King, *Minorities under Communism,* pp. 54–55.

51. See Balogh, *Parlamenti,* pp. 268–94.

52. Balogh, *Parlamenti,* p. 274.

53. United States, Department of State, *Foreign Relations of the United States: Diplomatic Papers, 1946,* vol. 6, pp. 272–73.

54. See Bennett Kovrig, *Myth of Liberation,* pp. 66–67.

55. Balogh, *Parlamenti,* p. 290.

56. See Bennett Kovrig, *Myth of Liberation,* pp. 68–72; and Balogh, *Parlamenti,* pp. 297–306.

57. *Szabad Nép,* 24 November 1946.

58. Ságvári, *Népfront,* p. 146.

59. See Stephen Kertész, "The Expulsion of Germans from Hungary: A Study of Postwar Diplomacy," *Review of Politics* 15, no. 2 (April 1953): 179–208.

60. Magyar Szocialista Munkáspárt, *MKP és SDP határozatai,* p. 256.

61. Balogh, *Parlamenti,* pp. 310, 323.

62. *Szabad Nép,* 3 August 1946.

63. Balogh, *Parlamenti,* p. 332.

64. *Szabad Nép,* 22 September 1946.

65. Magyar Kommunista Párt, *Népi demokrácia útja,* p. 169. On the congress, see also János Blaskovits and Lajos Labádi, *A Magyar Kommunista Párt III. kongresszusa.*

66. Magyar Kommunista Párt, *Népi demokrácia útja,* pp. 138, 23, 184, 89. See also B. Szabó, *Népi demokrácia,* pp. 187–97.

67. *Szabad Nép,* 22 September 1946.

68. Magyar Kommunista Párt, *Népi demokrácia útja,* pp. 65, 346.

69. Magyar Szocialista Munkáspárt, *MKP és SDP határozatai,* p. 268.

70. E. Szabó, "Magyar Kommunista Párt," in Erényi and Rákosi, *Legyőzhetetlen erő,* pp. 175–76.

71. *Kis Ujság,* 22 September 1946.

72. See József Kővágó, "Kovács Béla emlékezete," *Nemzetőr* (Vienna), 1–15 July 1961; and Balogh, *Parlamenti,* pp. 366–68.

73. Ságvári, *Népfront,* pp. 169–70; Balogh, *Parlamenti,* pp. 356–57.

74. Ságvári, *Népfront,* pp. 170–71; and Tóth, *A Nemzeti Parasztpárt története, 1944–1948,* pp. 198–99.

75. Molnár, "Irányzatok harca a Szociáldemokrata Pártban," pp. 23–28.

76. See Balogh, *Parlamenti,* pp. 373–75; Rácz, *Üzemi bizottságok,* pp. 103–17; and Habuda, *A magyar szakszervezetek a népi demokratikus forradalomban, 1944–1948,* pp. 177–79.

77. Szabó, *Népi demokrácia,* p. 200.

78. The communist version of the conspiracy can be found in Kis, *A Magyar Közösségtől a Földalatti Fövezérségig;* and István Vida, "A Független Kisgazdapárt és a Magyar Közösség," *Történelmi Szemle* 13 (1970): 169–80.

79. See Balogh, *Parlamenti,* p. 366; Gábor Nagy, "Pálffy György," *PK* 10, no. 4 (December 1964): 165; F. Nagy, *Struggle,* p. 314.

80. Balogh, *Parlamenti,* p. 377.

81. F. Nagy, *Struggle,* p. 357, Balogh, *Parlamenti,* p. 383.

82. Sulyok, *Magyar Tragédia,* pp. 592–94.

83. Ferenc Z. Nagy, *Ahogy én láttam . . . ,* p. 251.

84. Bennett Kovrig, *Myth of Liberation,* p. 75. See Balogh, *Parlamenti,* pp. 405–7.

85. Balogh, *Parlamenti,* pp. 426–27; and Magyar Szocialista Munkáspárt, *MKP és SDP határozatai,* p. 467.

86. Balogh, *Parlamenti,* pp. 453–62.

87. Balogh, *Parlamenti,* p. 413. One indirect consequence of this was the resumption of Hungarian-Czechoslovak negotiations, which led to an exchange of population beginning in April.

88. F. Nagy, *Struggle,* p. 387.

89. Balogh, *Parlamenti,* p. 464.

90. F. Nagy, *Struggle,* pp. 422–23; and Balogh, *Parlamenti,* p. 466.

91. Hungary, Tájékoztatásügyi Minisztérium, *Fehér Könyv. A magyar köztársaság és a demokrácia elleni összeesküvés.* See Bennett Kovrig, *Myth of Liberation,* pp. 75–76.

92. Balogh, *Parlamenti,* p. 469.

93. Ibid.

## 9. The Party Triumphant, 1947–1948

1. József Révai, *A magyar népi demokrácia jellege és fejlődése,* p. 17.

2. B. Szabó, *Népi demokrácia,* p. 200.

3. Ibid., pp. 201–2.

4. Ibid., pp. 202, 204–5.

5. Ságvári, *Népfront*, p. 209.

6. Ibid., p. 203.

7. Balogh, *Parlamenti*, p. 479.

8. Hugh Seton-Watson, *The East European Revolution*, p. 200.

9. Ságvári, *Népfront*, p. 228n.

10. Balogh, *Parlamenti*, p. 485.

11. Ibid., p. 508.

12. *Magyar Hiradó*, 6 September 1947, cited in Hámori, "Soviet Influences," p. 114. Cf. Balogh, *Parlamenti*, p. 511.

13. Ságvári, *Népfront*, p. 211.

14. Révai, *Élni tudunk a szabadsággal* p. 123; see Balogh, *Parlamenti*, pp. 506–7.

15. Mátyás Rákosi, *A fordulat éve*, pp. 132–33.

16. Magyar Socialista Munkáspárt, *MKP és SDP határozatai*, pp. 495–97.

17. Endre Arató, *A magyar-csehszlovák viszony ötven éve; történeti áttekintés*, p. 77.

18. Révai, *Élni tudunk*, p. 121.

19. Idem, *A magyar értelmiség útja*.

20. Balogh, *Parlamenti*, p. 517.

21. Ibid., p. 518.

22. Marosán, *Az úton*, pp. 304–13; see also Nógrádi, *Történelmi lecke*, pp. 341–43.

23. Rákosi, *A fordulat éve*, p. 82.

24. Balogh, *Parlamenti*, p. 524.

25. Desiderius Sulyok, *Zwei Nǎchte ohne Tag*, p. 415; Bán, "Hungary," in Healey, *The Curtain Falls*, p. 73; J. Molnár, "Irányzatok harca a Szociáldemokrata Pártban," p. 45; and Balogh, *Parlamenti*, pp. 532, 601–602.

26. U.S. House of Representatives, *Fifth Interim Report on Hungary*, p. 148; Sulyok, *Zwei Nǎchte ohne Tag*, p. 415; and Bán, "Hungary," in Healey, *The Curtain Falls*, p. 73.

27. Orbán, *Két agrárforradalom Magyarországon*, p. 63.

28. B. Szabó, *Népi demokrácia*, p. 212.

29. Eugenio Reale, *Avec Jacques Duclos. Au Banc des Accusés à la Réunion Constitutive du Kominform à Szklarska Poreba (22–27 Septembre 1947)*, pp. 118–29.

30. Reale, *Avec Jacques Duclos*, p. 166.

31. Ibid., pp. 138–40; see also Ágnes Ságvári, "Népfront és proletárdiktatúra," *Történelmi Szemle* 9 (1966): 216.

32. Reale, *Avec Jacques Duclos*, p. 181. Although the Soviet-Yugoslav line prevailed, during the conference both Gomulka and Slansky had raised the possibility of maintaining purified multiparty coalitions.

33. B. Szabó, *Népi demokrácia*, pp. 219–22.

34. Ibid., pp. 220–21.

35. Ibid., pp. 222–28. For the economic and agricultural guidelines, see Magyar Szocialista Munkáspárt, *MKP és SDP határozatai*, pp. 537–47, 564–76.

36. B. Szabó, *Népi demokrácia*, pp. 231–34.

37. Berend, *Ujjáépités*, p. 376.

38. Ibid., p. 373. The "Czechoslovakian event" was the communist coup in Prague.

39. Rákosi, *A fordulat éve*, pp. 390, 411, 427–29.

40. Rácz, *Üzemi bizottságok*, pp. 126–27.

41. Marosán, *Az úton*, pp. 323–38.

42. F. Nagy, *Struggle*, p. 438; and J. Molnár, "Irányzatok harca," pp. 44–50.

43. Nemes, *Magyar munkásmozgalom*, p. 513.

44. Ságvári, *Népfront*, p. 238.

45. Mátyás Rákosi, *Tiéd az ország, magadnak épited*, p. 34.

46. Strassenreiter and Sipos, "Rajk László (1909–1949), pp. 178–79. See also Rácz, "Belügyminisztérium," pp. 121–28.

47. Imre Vajda, *Van e harmadik út?*, pp. 14–15.

48. Marosán, *Az úton*, pp. 388–417, 424.

49. Habuda and Rákosi, "MKP és SDP," pp. 44, 60, 63–64; E. Szabó, "A Magyar Kommunista Párt," in Erényi and Rákosi, *Legyőzhetetlen erő*, pp. 183, 185–86; and Sándor Rákosi, "A Magyar Dolgozók Pártja," in ibid., pp. 193–94.

50. E. Szabó, "A Magyar Kommunista Párt," in Erényi and Rákosi, *Legyőzhetetlen erő*, pp. 184–86.

51. Ilona Sánta, *A két munkáspárt egyesülése 1948-ban*, pp. 100–101.

52. Magyar Szocialista Munkáspárt, *MKP és SDP határozatai*, pp. 587–605.

53. B. Szabó, *Népi demokrácia*, p. 236.

54. Ibid., pp. 237–38.

55. Révai, *A magyar népi demokrácia*, p. 19.

56. Ibid., p. 26.

57. Ibid., p. 20.

## PART FOUR

## 10. The Totalitarian State, 1948–1953

1. Lilly Marcou, *Le Kominform*, pp. 203, 215n.

2. B. Szabó, *Népi demokrácia*, pp. 240–44.

3. Ibid., p. 245.

4. Ibid., p. 247.

5. Ibid., pp. 248–49.

6. *Szabad Nép*, 16 January 1949.

7. B. Szabó, *Népi demokrácia*, p. 253.

8. Révai, *Élni tudunk*, p. 516.

9. Dobi, *Vallomás és történelem*, vol. 2, p. 431.

10. Révai, *A magyar népi demokrácia*, pp. 17–18.

11. Ernő Gerő, *Harcban a szocialista népgazdaságért,* p. 82.
12. Nógrádi, *Történelmi lecke,* p. 400.
13. Aczél and Méray, *Revolt of the Mind,* p. 31.
14. Nógrádi, *Történelmi lecke,* p. 423.
15. Imre Nagy, *On Communism: In Defence of the New Course,* p. 279.
16. Nógrádi, *Történelmi lecke,* p. 410.
17. Julius Háy, *Born 1900: Memoirs,* p. 291.
18. Rákosi, "A Magyar Dolgozók Pártja," in Erényi and Rákosi, *Legyőzhetetlen erő,* p. 214.
19. See Vera Szemere, "A NÉKOSZ történetéhez," *PK* 21, no. 4 (December 1975): 3–50; and Borbándi, *Ungarische Populismus,* pp. 273–76. Apart from the Szemere article, the official rediscovery of the people's college movement led to publication, in 1976, of Gábor Tánczos, *A népi kollegisták útja 1939–1971,* and, in 1977, of Ferenc Rottler, ed., *Sej, a mi lobogónkat fényes szelek fújják . . . Népi kollégiumok 1939–1949.*
20. *Szabad Nép,* 8 September 1946.
21. Szemere, "A NÉKOSZ történetéhez," pp. 41–42, 48.
22. Dezső Nemes, *A népiesség hatása a magyar trockistákra* (Budapest: Szikra, 1951), p. 40, cited in Hámori, "Soviet Influences," p. 21.
23. Paul Ignotus, *Political Prisoner,* p. 47.
24. Shawcross, *Crime and Compromise,* p. 58.
25. Nógrádi, *Történelmi lecke,* p. 426.
26. Strassenreiter and Sipos, "Rajk László (1909–1949)," p. 181.
27. Sik, *Egy diplomata feljegyzései,* p. 224. Cf. László Rajk, *A magyar külpolitika útja,* pp. 13, 18.
28. Nógrádi, *Történelmi lecke,* p. 403.
29. *Nowa Kultura,* November 1956, quoted in Shawcross, *Crime and Compromise,* pp. 66–67.
30. Paul E. Zinner, *Revolution in Hungary,* p. 148.
31. Hungary, Népbíróság [People's Court], *László Rajk and His Accomplices before the People's Court* (Budapest, 1949).
32. Gerő, *Harcban,* p. 115.
33. Rákosi, *A békéért,* pp. 166–72.
34. Strassenreiter and Sipos, "Rajk László (1909–1949)," p. 181.
35. Aladár Mód, quoted in Shawcross, *Crime and Compromise,* p. 63.
36. Nemes, *Magyar munkásmozgalom,* pp. 545–46.
37. György Pálóczi-Horváth, *The Undefeated,* pp. 238–39.
38. Shawcross, *Crime and Compromise,* p. 72.
39. Nógrádi, *Történelmi lecke,* p. 430.
40. Ibid., pp. 404–6.
41. Zinner, *Revolution,* p. 135.
42. Pálóczi-Horváth, *The Undefeated,* p. 231.
43. Aczél and Méray, *Revolt of the Mind,* p. 253.
44. Ferenc A. Váli, *Rift and Revolt in Hungary,* p. 68.

45. András Hegedüs in *Le Quotidien de Paris*, 27–28 October 1976, quoted in *Radio Free Europe Research: Situation Report, Hungary, 9 November 1976*, mimeo. (Munich: RFE, 1976).

46. Rákosi, "A Magyar Dolgozók Pártja," in Erényi and Rákosi, *Legyőzhetetlen erő*, p. 224n.

47. Ibid., pp. 194–99.

48. Zinner, *Revolution*, pp. 137–38.

49. Rákosi, "A Magyar Dolgozók Pártja," in Erényi and Rákosi, *Legyőzhetetlen erő*, p. 205.

50. Sik, *Egy diplomata*, p. 337.

51. Mátyás Rákosi, *Válogatott beszédek*, vol. 1, p. 464.

52. Mátyás Rákosi, *A Kommunisták Magyarországi Pártjának megalakulása és harca a proletárforradalom győzelméért*, p. 18.

53. Nógrádi, *Történelmi lecke*, p. 411.

54. János Beér and Imre Szabó, *Az új magyar alkotmány és magyarázatai*, p. 76.

55. Csizmadia, *A nemzeti bizottságok állami tevékenysége*, p. 398.

56. Reportedly, Szekfű was coerced to collaborate with imported medicine essential to his survival (György Faludy, *My Happy Days in Hell*, p. 245).

57. József Cardinal Mindszenty, *Memoirs*, p. 96.

58. Ibid., p. 137. Cf. Hungary, *Documents on the Mindszenty Case*. For the party's version of the evolution of state-church relations, see Sándor Orbán, *Egyház és állam: A katolikus egyház és az állam viszonyának rendezése, 1945–1950*.

59. András Zsilák, "A magyar társadalom osztályszerkezetének alakulása a szocializmus épitésének kezdeti időszakában és a MDP szövetségi politikájának főbb vonásai (1949–1956)," in Henrik Vass, ed., *A kommunista párt szövetségi politikája, 1936–1962*, p. 202.

60. János Beér and István Kovács, *A Magyar Népköztársaság alkotmánya*, pp. 13–18.

61. Institute of Party History, Archives (hereafter cited as Party Archives), 276–10.K/33, Tájékoztató a Sz.B. 1949 aug. 1–i üléséről.

62. A translation of the constitution can be found in Jan F. Triska, ed., *Constitutions of the Communist Party-States*, pp. 182–94. See also Beér and I. Szabó, *Az új magyar alkotmány*.

63. See László Varga, *Human Rights in Hungary*, pp. 16–91.

64. Váli, *Rift and Revolt*, p. 41n.

65. Zsilák, "Magyar társadalom," in Vass, *Kommunista párt*, pp. 151–52.

66. See Iván T. Berend, *Gazdasági politika az első ötéves terv meginditásakor (1948–1950)*.

67. Zsilák, "Magyar társadalom," in Vass, *Kommunista párt*, p. 153.

68. Béla A. Balassa, *The Hungarian Experience in Economic Planning*, p. 34.

69. Zsilák, "Magyar társadalom," in Vass, *Kommunista párt*, pp. 154–62.

70. I. Nagy, *On Communism*, p. 54.

71. See Iván T. Berend, *A szocialista gazdaság fejlődése Magyarországon, 1945–1968*, pp. 86–93; Berend, *Gazdasági politika*; and János Kornai, *Overcentralization in Economic Administration*.

72. Zsilák, "Magyar társadalom," in Vass, *Kommunista párt*, p. 147.

73. Orbán, *Két agrárforradalom Magyarországon*, p. 70.

74. *Hungarian Bulletin*, 8 July 1948.

75. Zsilák, "Magyar társadalom," in Vass, *Kommunista párt*, p. 197; and Orbán, *Agrárforradalom*, pp. 72–73.

76. Party Archives, 276-10.K/161, A Titkárság határozata ipari üzemek patronázs-munkájáról, a termelőszövetkezeti csoportokban, 1950.nov.6.

77. Kálmán Szakács, "A középparaszt-kérdés és a DÉFOSZ 1949-ben," *PK* 18, no. 4 (December 1972): 82–109.

78. Gerő, *Harcban*, p. 411.

79. Rákosi, *A békéért*, p. 510.

80. Orbán, *Agrárforradalom*, p. 72n.

81. Zsilák, "Magyar társadalom," in Vass, *Kommunista párt*, p. 173.

82. Party Archives, 176-10.K/24, Szervező Bizottság, A pártszervezetek feladatai a cséplési ellenőrzési és termény-begyüjtési kampány megszervezésében (9 June 1949).

83. Orbán, *Agrárforradalom*, p. 98.

84. Ibid., pp. 99, 102, 113. Vivid reminiscences of the persecution of real and alleged kulaks can be found in a sociographic study of a small district in Western Hungary, György Moldova, *Az Őrség panasza*, published in 1974.

85. Aczél and Méray, *Revolt of the Mind*, pp. 119–43.

86. József Révai, "A magyar irodalom feladatai," *Társadalmi Szemle*, May 1951, pp. 345–59; and Váli, *Rift and Revolt*, p. 56.

87. József Révai, "Megjegyzések irodalmunk néhány kérdéséhez," *Társadalmi Szemle*, March–April 1950, p. 196.

88. See Aczél and Méray, *Revolt of the Mind*, pp. 57–80, 94–118.

89. György Ránki, "Has Modernity Made a Difference?" in Gati, *The Politics of Modernization in Eastern Europe*, p. 317.

90. Zsilák, "Magyar társadalom," in Vass, *Kommunista párt*, p. 193.

91. Ibid., p. 150.

92. Jenő Rédei, *A magyar társadalom strukturájának átalakulása a statisztikai adatok tükrében*, pp. 24, 23, 6.

93. I. Nagy, *On Communism*, p. 144.

94. See Hámori, "Soviet Influences," pp. 211–12.

95. See I. Nagy, *On Communism*, pp. 106–7, 180–84.

96. Váli, *Rift and Revolt*, pp. 52, 54.

97. Nógrádi, *Történelmi lecke*, pp. 401–3, 429.

98. See Ithiel de Sola Pool, *Satellite Generals*, pp. 120ff.; and Váli, *Rift and Revolt*, chap. 5.

99. Arató, *Magyar-csehszlovák viszony*, pp. 77–81.

100. Marcou, *Le Kominform*, pp. 75–76, 99–111.

101. See Kazimierz Grzybowski, *The Socialist Commonwealth of Nations*, pp. 57–70; Howard J. Hilton, *Hungary: A Case History of Soviet Economic Imperialism*; and I. Nagy, *On Communism*, p. 191.

102. See S. Kracauer and P. L. Berkman, *Satellite Mentality*; and Bennett Kovrig, *Myth of Liberation*, chap. 3.

## 11. The New Course, 1953–1955

1. I. Nagy, *On Communism*, p. 66.
2. Váli, *Rift and Revolt*, p. 5.
3. I. Nagy, *On Communism*, p. 252.
4. Nógrádi, *Történelmi lecke*, pp. 433–35.
5. *Népszabadság*, 19 August 1962.
6. Zsilák, "Magyar társadalom," in Vass, *Kommunista párt*, pp. 162–63.
7. Nógrádi, *Történelmi lecke*, p. 453; see also Váli, *Rift and Revolt*, pp. 92–94; and Nemes, *Magyar munkásmozgalom*, pp. 551–53.
8. I. Nagy, *On Communism*, p. 73.
9. *Szabad Nép*, 5 July 1953.
10. See Aczél and Méray, *Revolt of the Mind*, pp. 213–15.
11. Nemes, *Magyar munkásmozgalom*, pp. 554–55.
12. *Szabad Nép*, 12 July 1953; and Nógrádi, *Történelmi lecke*, pp. 437–38.
13. I. Nagy, *On Communism*, p. 283.
14. Ibid., pp. 251–52.
15. Ibid., pp. 283, 176.
16. Zsilák, "Magyar társadalom," in Vass, *Kommunista párt*, pp. 164–67.
17. I. Nagy, *On Communism*, p. 271.
18. Aczél and Méray, *Revolt of the Mind*, p. 229.
19. Váli, *Rift and Revolt*, p. 111; I. Nagy, *On Communism*, p. 282.
20. I. Nagy, *On Communism*, pp. 281–82, 143.
21. Rákosi, "Magyar Dolgozók Pártja," in Erényi and Rákosi, *Legyőzhetetlen erő*, p. 217.
22. Ibid., pp. 216–18.
23. Ibid., pp. 218–19.
24. Ibid., p. 224.
25. I. Nagy, *On Communism*, pp. 207–8.
26. Váli, *Rift and Revolt*, pp. 125–26.
27. Party Archives, 276–10.K/463, Határozat a népfrontirodák megszervezésére, 1954 okt. 13.
28. Zsilák, "Magyar társadalom," in Vass, *Kommunista párt*, pp. 209–10.
29. *Szabad Nép*, 25 October 1954.
30. Orbán, *Agrárforradalom*, p. 136.
31. Ibid., pp. 131–45.
32. Balassa, *Hungarian Experience*, p. 36.
33. I. Nagy, *On Communism*, pp. 191–93.
34. Ibid., pp. 191–92.
35. Ibid., p. 273.
36. Party Archives, 276–10.K/464, Tervezet, A Magyar Dolgozók Pártja Központi Vezetőségének határozata népgazdaságunk helyzetéről és gazdaságpolitikai feladatainkról, 1954 okt. 18; see also Nógrádi, *Történelmi lecke*, pp. 441–42.
37. Aczél and Méray, *Revolt of the Mind*, p. 282.

38. Ibid., pp. 282, 284.

39. See, for instance, Péter Kuczka, "Nyirségi napló," *Irodalmi Ujság*, 7 November 1953.

40. Váli, *Rift and Revolt*, p. 137.

41. See Tibor Méray, *Thirteen Days that Shook the Kremlin*, p. 22.

42. M. Molnár and L. Nagy, *Imre Nagy*, p. 28.

43. I. Nagy, *On Communism*, p. 296.

44. The estimate is by Váli, *Rift and Revolt*, p. 149.

45. Szász, *Volunteers for the Gallows*, p. 217.

46. I. Nagy, *On Communism*, p. 275.

47. Robert T. Holt, *Radio Free Europe*, p. 162; on the underlying American liberation policy, see Bennett Kovrig, *Myth of Liberation*, chaps. 3 and 4. Reference to the general impact of the campaign and to certain underground opposition groups can be found in János Berecz, *Ellenforradalom tollal és fegyverrel*, pp. 22–47.

48. See Méray, *Thirteen Days*, pp. 24–25.

49. Váli, *Rift and Revolt*, p. 155.

50. Méray, *Thirteen Days*, pp. 25–28.

51. *Szabad Nép*, 9 March 1955; and Nemes, *Magyar munkásmozgalom*, pp. 557–58.

52. Méray, *Thirteen Days*, p. 30; *Szabad Nép*, 18 April 1955; and I. Nagy, *On Communism*, pp. xliii–xliv.

53. George Mikes, *The Hungarian Revolution*, p. 61.

54. Orbán, *Agrárforradalom*, p. 148.

55. Ibid., pp. 147–55, 131.

56. *Szabad Nép*, 9 August 1955.

57. Royal Institute of International Affairs, *Documents on International Affairs, 1955*, p. 271.

## PART FIVE

1. See Paul Kecskeméti, *The Unexpected Revolution*. The following account of the antecedents and course of the revolution is an elaboration of the summary in Bennett Kovrig, *The Hungarian People's Republic*, pp. 104–24.

## 12. From Decompression to Revolution

1. I. Nagy, *On Communism*, p. 55.

2. Ibid., pp. 57, 15.

3. Ibid., pp. 22–24, 33–34, 40.

4. *Népszava*, 8 June 1958.

5. Aczél and Méray, *Revolt of the Mind*, pp. 343–50; Méray, *Thirteen Days*, p. 40.

6. Nógrádi, *Történelmi lecke*, pp. 447–48.

7. The text of the speech can be found in Russian Institute, Columbia University, *The Anti-Stalin Campaign and International Communism*, pp. 1–89.

8. *Szabad Nép*, 14 and 15 March 1956. See also Nógrádi, *Történelmi lecke*, pp. 452–53.

9. Berecz, *Ellenforradalom*, pp. 49–51.

10. *Szabad Nép*, 29 March 1956. A concurrent symbolic rehabilitation was that of Béla Kun. One 21 February *Pravda* had carried a laudatory article by one of his original accusers, Jenő Varga. Then, on 22 March, *Szabad Nép* reported that "recent research" had revealed that the accusations against Kun had been without foundation. Finally, in May 1964, the Soviet ambassador visited Mrs. Kun to deliver a document attesting to his rehabilitation.

11. Kecskeméti, *Unexpected Revolution*, p. 75.

12. Nógrádi, *Történelmi lecke*, p. 425.

13. Paul E. Zinner, ed., *National Communism and Popular Revolt in Eastern Europe*, p. 351.

14. *Szabad Nép*, 1 April 1956.

15. Ibid., 19 May 1956.

16. Berecz, *Ellenforradalom*, p. 64.

17. Sándor Lakos, "Gondolatok a személyi kultuszról és funkcionáriusaink munkastílusáról," *Pártélet*, May 1956, p. 45.

18. See Pálóczi-Horváth, *The Undefeated*, pp. 259–62, and Szász, *Volunteers*, p. 146.

19. *Szabad Nép*, 17 April 1956.

20. Party Archives, 276–10.K/628, Határozat a második ötéves terv irányelveinek agitációs és propaganda feladatairól, 1956. május 7.

21. Berecz, *Ellenforradalom*, p. 65.

22. *Irodalmi Ujság*, 5 May 1956.

23. Kecskeméti, *Unexpected Revolution*, p. 79.

24. See Elinor Murray, "Higher Education in Communist Hungary, 1948–1956," *American Slavic and East European Review* 19 (1960): 395–413.

25. See Aczél and Méray, *Revolt of the Mind*, pp. 399–412.

26. See Tito's speech at Pula, 11 November 1956, in Zinner, *National Communism*, pp. 520–24.

27. Zinner, *National Communism*, p. 329.

28. Vera Horváth, "A Rádio ostroma," in Eta Nagy and Katalin Petrák, eds., *Szabadság, te szülj nekem rendet!*, p. 217 (hereafter cited as *Szabadság*).

29. Berecz, *Ellenforradalom*, p. 66.

30. Aczél and Méray, *Revolt of the Mind*, pp. 412–19; Kecskeméti, *Unexpected Revolution*, p. 76; Ignotus, *Hungary*, p. 234; and *The Economist*, 27 November 1976, p. 12.

31. *Szabad Nép*, 19 July 1956.

32. Zinner, *National Communism*, p. 524.

33. Iván Szenes, *A Kommunista Párt ujjászervezése Magyarországon, 1956–1957*, pp. 35, 19 (hereafter cited as *KP ujjászervezése*).

34. Kecskeméti, *Unexpected Revolution*, pp. 76–77.

35. *Társadalmi Szemle*, August 1956, pp. 19–41.

36. *Irodalmi Ujság,* 22 September 1956.

37. Ibid., 6 October 1956.

38. Nemes, *Magyar munkásmozgalom,* p. 567.

39. *Szabad Nép,* 7 October 1956.

40. Váli, *Rift and Revolt,* p. 249.

41. Berecz, *Ellenforradalom,* p. 77.

42. Ibid., pp. 68–69; and Váli, *Rift and Revolt,* pp. 249–60.

43. Zinner, *National Communism,* p. 525.

44. *Szabad Nép,* 14 October 1956.

45. Berecz, *Ellenforradalom,* pp. 78–79.

46. Váli, *Rift and Revolt,* p. 266.

47. Berecz, *Ellenforradalom,* p. 80.

48. See Váli, *Rift and Revolt,* pp. 254–57, 273; and Zinner, *Revolution,* p. 254.

49. János Molnár, *Ellenforradalom Magyarországon 1956-ban; a polgári magyarázatok bírálata,* pp. 46–47.

50. Zinner, *Revolution,* pp. 245–46.

51. Háy, *Born 1900,* p. 310.

52. Zinner, *National Communism,* pp. 402–7.

53. Horváth, "Rádio ostroma," in E. Nagy and Petrák, *Szabadság,* pp. 217–19.

54. Zinner, *Revolution,* p. 258.

55. See Váli, *Rift and Revolt,* pp. 282–83.

56. Berecz, *Ellenforradalom,* pp. 97–98, 107; and Szenes, *KP ujjászervezése,* pp.
28–29.

57. Zinner, *National Communism,* pp. 419–20.

58. Ervin Hollós and Vera Lajtai, *Köztársaság tér 1956,* p. 57.

59. Zinner, *National Communism,* pp. 428–32.

60. Ibid., p. 432.

61. Ibid., pp. 455–56.

62. Ibid., pp. 453–54.

63. See the distorted account of the uprising in Nikita Khrushchev, *Krushchev Remembers,* ed. by Strobe Talbott, pp. 416–29. Another, and even more questionable
source claims that the Soviet general staff also argued against intervention (Oleg Penkovskiy, *The Penkovskiy Papers,* p. 212). Cf. Giuseppe Boffa, *Inside the Khrushchev
Era,* p. 105.

64. Zinner, *National Communism,* pp. 487–89.

65. U.S. House of Representatives, Committee on Un-American Activities, *International Communism (Revolt in the Satellites),* p. 24. See also Méray, *Thirteen Days,*
pp. 164–65.

66. Zinner, *National Communism,* pp. 455–56.

67. See Irén Komját, *Mező Imre.*

68. Hollós and Lajtai, *Köztársaság tér 1956,* p. 56.

69. Miklós Szántó, "Köztársaság tér 1956," in E. Nagy and Petrák, *Szabadság,*
p. 231.

70. Hollós and Lajtai, *Köztársaság tér 1956,* pp. 66–73.

71. Ibid., pp. 13–36, 120–72. The attackers were partly impelled by rumors that the building was held by a much larger AVH detachment guarding prisoners in deep underground cells. After the building was invested excavations were begun in the square but no secret cells were ever uncovered.

72. Nemes, *Magyar munkásmozgalom*, p. 576.

73. *Il Giornale d'Italia*, 2 November 1956, quoted in Shawcross, *Crime and Compromise*, pp. 83–84.

74. *Nowa Kultura*, 2 December 1956, quoted in Melvin J. Lasky, ed., *The Hungarian Revolution: A White Book*, p. 159.

75. Shawcross, *Crime and Compromise*, p. 15.

76. Zinner, *National Communism*, pp. 462–64.

77. See Bennett Kovrig, *Myth of Liberation*, chap. 5.

78. Zinner, *National Communism*, pp. 464–67.

79. Shawcross, *Crime and Compromise*, p. 85; and Nógrádi, *Történelmi lecke*, p. 457. Nógrádi alleges that insurgent bands were planning a "night of long knives" massacre of communists for 6 November.

80. János Kádár, *Szilárd népi hatalom: független Magyarország*, pp. 134–35. See also Shawcross, *Crime and Compromise*, p. 89.

81. J. Molnár, *Ellenforradalom*, pp. 39–40, 57–58, 167.

82. Radio Free Europe analysis, quoted in Kecskeméti, *Unexpected Revolution*, p. 109.

83. Berecz, *Ellenforradalom*, p. 89.

84. A party historian's account of the activities of revisionist groups, workers' councils, and armed groups can be found in J. Molnár, *Ellenforradalom*, chaps. 4–6.

85. Mindszenty, *Memoirs*, pp. 331–33. For the communist view of the other parties, see J. Molnár, *Ellenforradalom*, pp. 198–218.

86. See J. Molnár, *Ellenforradalom*, pp. 64–75.

87. István Bibó, *A harmadik út*. See Gyula Borbándi, "István Bibó: Hungary's Political Philosopher," *East Europe* 13, no. 10 (October 1964): 2–7. See also Edmund O. Stillman, *The Ideology of Revolution*.

88. J. Molnár, *Ellenforradalom*, p. 223.

89. Ibid., pp. 225–27.

90. Váli, *Rift and Revolt*, p. 339.

91. See King, *Minorities under Communism*, chap. 4.

92. Zinner, *National Communism*, p. 282.

93. *People's Daily* (Peking), 5 September 1963.

94. Zinner, *National Communism*, pp. 446–48.

95. Ibid., p. 530.

96. *Vjesnik*, 27 April 1976, cited in *Radio Free Europe Research, Background Report (Yugoslavia), 27 April 1976*, mimeo. (Munich: RFE, 1976); and Veljko Micunovic, *Moskovske godine 1956–1958* (Belgrade, 1977), excerpted in *Radio Free Europe Research, Background Report (Yugoslavia), 21 December 1977*, mimeo. (Munich: RFE, 1977).

97. Váli, *Rift and Revolt*, p. 372. A party history also refers to the participation of Béla Biszku, Lajos Fehér, Gyula Kállai, and Károly Kiss in the "new revolutionary center established November 1–2 under the leadership of János Kádár" (Nemes,

*Magyar munkásmozgalom,* p. 581). It is not clear whether any of them (apart from Kiss) left to join Kádár, or indeed at what point they learned of Kádár's departure and the impending formation of a countergovernment.

98. *Népszabadság,* 29 January 1958.

99. Váli, *Rift and Revolt,* p. 375.

100. See Béla K. Király, "The First War between Socialist States: Military Aspects of the Hungarian Revolution," *Canadian-American Review of Hungarian Studies* 3, no. 2 (fall 1976): 121–23; Váli, *Rift and Revolt,* pp. 318, 360; and Árpád Szabó, *A Magyar Forradalmi Honvéd Karhatalom (1956. november–1957. június),* p. 22 (hereafter cited as *Karhatalom*).

101. Váli, *Rift and Revolt,* p. 376.

102. Nemes, *Magyar munkásmozgalom,* p. 583.

## 13. From Restoration to Consolidation

1. See Váli, *Rift and Revolt,* pp. 384–86.

2. United Nations, General Assembly, *Report of the Special Committee on the Problem of Hungary,* p. 57.

3. János Molnár, *A Nagybudapesti Központi Munkástanács,* p. 40 (hereafter cited as *Munkástanács*).

4. Váli, *Rift and Revolt,* p. 398.

5. Ibid., pp. 439–40.

6. *Szabad Nép* (Szolnok), 7 November 1956.

7. Árpád Szabó, *Karhatalom,* pp. 33–40.

8. J. Molnár, *Munkástanács,* pp. 67, 74–78, 80; and Szenes, *KP ujjászervezése,* p. 53.

9. Szenes, *KP ujjászervezése,* pp. 40–41, 50–51, 54–55.

10. J. Molnár, *Munkástanács,* pp. 107–12.

11. Ibid., p. 114.

12. Zinner, ed., *National Communism,* pp. 474–78.

13. Shawcross, *Crime and Compromise,* p. 239.

14. J. Molnár, *Munkástanács,* p. 31n.

15. Hungary, Minisztertanács [Council of Ministers], *The Counterrevolutionary Conspiracy of Imre Nagy and His Accomplices,* p. 151.

16. J. Molnár, *Munkástanács,* pp. 27–33.

17. *Dagens Nyheter,* 2 December 1956, quoted in Shawcross, *Crime and Compromise,* pp. 243–44.

18. J. Molnár, *Munkástanács,* pp. 52–53.

19. Bibó, *Harmadik út,* p. 357; cf. J. Molnár, *Munkástanács,* pp. 54–58.

20. J. Molnár, *Munkástanács,* pp. 58–59.

21. Ibid., pp. 64–67.

22. Ibid., pp. 70–88.

23. *Népszabadság,* 22 November 1956.

24. J. Molnár, *Munkástanács,* pp. 70, 103–5.

25. Ibid., pp. 118–24.

26. Ibid., pp. 129–40.

27. *Népszabadság,* 10 April 1958.

28. J. Molnár, *Munkástanács,* p. 11.

29. Magyar Szocialista Munkáspárt, *A Magyar Szocialista Munkáspárt határozatai és dokumentumai, 1956–1962,* pp. 13–24 (hereafter cited as *MSZMP határozatai 1956–1962*).

30. Szenes, *KP ujjászervezése,* p. 70.

31. *Népakarat,* 29 May 1957.

32. Szenes, *KP ujjászervezése,* pp. 84–95.

33. Ibid., pp. 99, 104–5.

34. Ibid., p. 107.

35. Ibid., pp. 110–18.

36. Ibid., pp. 126, 143.

37. Ibid., pp. 128–31.

38. François Fejtő, "Hungarian Communism," in William E. Griffith, ed., *Communism in Europe,* vol. 1, pp. 230–31.

39. J. Molnár, *Munkástanács,* p. 110.

40. Szenes, *KP ujjászervezése,* pp. 154–58.

41. See Magyar Szocialista Munkáspárt, *A Magyar Szocialista Munkáspárt országos értekezletének jegyzőkönyve, 1957. június 27–29,* pp. 142–45, 213, and passim (hereafter cited as *Országos értekezlet*).

42. Fejtő, "Hungarian Communism," in Griffith, ed., *Communism in Europe,* vol. 1, p. 206.

43. Ibid., pp. 185–87.

44. Ibid., p. 209.

45. Szenes, *KP ujjászervezése,* pp. 151–52.

46. Magyar Szocialista Munkáspárt, *Országos értekezlet,* pp. 46–47.

47. Szenes, *KP ujjászervezése,* pp. 179–81.

48. Ibid., pp. 205, 208–10, 218.

49. *Népszabadság,* 26 October 1957.

50. Szenes, *KP ujjászervezése,* p. 121.

51. See Hungary, *Speeches of István Dobi, President of the Presidential Council, and János Kádár, Chairman of the Council of Ministers, Delivered to the Parliament of the Hungarian People's Republic at the Session of May 9–11, 1957.*

52. *Magyar Nemzet,* 11 January 1958.

53. Váli, *Rift and Revolt,* pp. 417–18.

54. See Fejtő, "Hungarian Communism," in Griffith, *Communism in Europe,* vol. 1, p. 239; and Váli, *Rift and Revolt,* p. 475.

55. See *Társadalmi Szemle,* May 1958.

56. *Népszabadság,* 6 and 10 April 1958.

57. Fejtő, "Hungarian Communism," in Griffith, *Communism in Europe,* vol. 1, pp. 250–52; and Váli, *Rift and Revolt,* pp. 443–44.

58. *Társadalmi Szemle,* January 1958, quoted in Váli, *Rift and Revolt,* p. 444.

59. *New York Times*, 18 September 1957, cited in Váli, *Rift and Revolt*, p. 443.

60. *Népszabadság*, 17 June 1957.

61. See Hungary, Minisztertanács, *Counterrevolutionary Conspiracy of Imre Nagy*; and *The Truth about the Nagy Affair*, parts 1 and 2.

62. *Le Monde*, 19 February 1964, quoted in Shawcross, *Crime and Compromise*, pp. 246–47.

63. Fejtő, "Hungarian Communism," in Griffith, *Communism in Europe*, vol. 1, p. 252.

64. *Magyar Nemzet*, 5 March 1958. See Váli, *Rift and Revolt*, p. 408.

65. The same interior ministry report estimated that at least 700,000 "class enemies" stood ready to strike at the regime (*Társadalmi Szemle*, April 1958, quoted in Váli, *Rift and Revolt*, p. 412).

66. *Népszabadság*, 21 November 1959.

67. Ibid., 14 March 1959.

68. Ibid., 8 March 1959.

69. Magyar Szocialista Munkáspárt, *A Magyar Szocialista Munkáspárt VII. kongresszusának jegyzőkönyve, 1959. november 30–december 5*, pp. 70–72 (hereafter cited as *VII. kongresszus*).

70. *Népszabadság*, 2 December 1959.

71. Magyar Szocialista Munkáspárt, *VII. kongresszus*, pp. 73–76.

72. The economists' proposals and the party's rebuttal can be found in *Közgazdasági Szemle* 4, no. 10 (October 1957): 997–1009; ibid. 4, no. 12 (December 1957): 1231–47; and ibid. 5, no. 7 (July 1958): 688–95.

73. Orbán, *Két agrárforradalom Magyarországon*, pp. 162, 179.

74. *Társadalmi Szemle*, May 1962, p. 2.

75. Magyar Szocialista Munkáspárt, *MSZMP határozatai 1956–1962*, pp. 106–8.

76. Ibid., p. 176.

77. Ibid., p. 321.

78. Orbán, *Agrárforradalom*, pp. 211–12; and Péter Simon, "A mezőgazdaság szocialista átszervezésének meggyorsulása 1959 elején," *PK* 18, no. 3 (September 1972): 43–44.

79. Magyar Szocialista Munkáspárt, *MSZMP határozatai 1956–1962*, pp. 188–89.

80. Orbán, *Agrárforradalom*, pp. 212–14.

81. Ibid., p. 215.

82. Magyar Szocialista Munkáspárt, *MSZMP határozatai 1956–1962*, pp. 267–77.

83. *Népszabadság*, 29 January 1959.

84. Simon, "Mezőgazdaság," pp. 44–46; Orbán, *Agrárforradalom*, p. 219.

85. Magyar Szocialista Munkáspárt, *MSZMP határozatai 1956–1962*, pp. 353–54; Orbán, *Agrárforradalom*, pp. 221–22.

86. Orbán, *Agrárforradalom*, pp. 218–19.

87. Ibid., pp. 225–28.

88. Nemes, *Magyar munkásmozgalom*, p. 623.

89. *Népszabadság*, 17 January 1960.

90. Magyar Szocialista Munkáspárt, *MSZMP határozatai 1956–1962*, p. 474.

91. Orbán, *Agrárforradalom*, pp. 225–43, 255.

92. *Népszabadság,* 6 August 1957.

93. *Élet és Irodalom,* 13 September 1957.

94. Ibid., 11 October 1957.

95. *Népszabadság,* 28 January and 16 July 1958.

96. "A 'népi' irókrol," *Társadalmi Szemle,* June 1958, pp. 38–69. See also Paul Ignotus, "Hungarian Intellectuals under Fire," *Problems of Communism* 8, no. 3 (May–June 1959): 16–21.

97. Nemes, *Magyar munkásmozgalom,* pp. 633–35.

98. *Társadalmi Szemle,* February 1959, pp. 46–72.

99. Nemes, *Magyar munkásmozgalom,* pp. 636–37.

100. *Népszabadság,* 1 December 1959.

101. *Élet és Irodalom,* 13 March 1959.

102. *Népszabadság,* 23 October 1958.

103. See Róbert Pogány, "Az elméleti munkaközösség vitája Molnár Erik könyvéről," *Magyar Filozófiai Szemle* 5, no. 4 (July 1961): 553–96; and Erik Molnár, *A jelenkori kapitalizmus néhány gazdasági problémája.*

104. See Mindszenty, *Memoirs,* pp. 221ff.

105. See *Népszabadság,* 21 January 1958.

106. *Magyar Nemzet,* 23 April 1958.

107. *Népszabadság,* 29 January 1958.

108. *Magyar Nemzet,* 16 March 1958, quoted in Sándor Kiss, "Soviet Troops in Hungary," *East Europe* 13, no. 10 (October 1964): 13.

109. See Váli, *Rift and Revolt,* pp. 428–31. Yuri Andropov, the Soviet ambassador during the revolution, eventually became head of the KGB.

110. See Fejtő, "Hungarian Communism," in Griffith, *Communism in Europe,* vol. 1, pp. 247–48, 288–92.

111. *Társadalmi Szemle,* April 1962, pp. 20–33.

112. See UN General Assembly, *Report of the Special Committee.*

113. See Bennett Kovrig, *Myth of Liberation,* pp. 205–10, 244–45; and János Radványi, *Hungary and the Superpowers.*

114. Nemes, *Magyar munkásmozgalom,* pp. 631–32.

115. *Népszabadság,* 21 January 1962.

116. Nógrádi, *Történelmi lecke,* pp. 398, 411.

117. *Népszabadság,* 19 August 1962.

118. *New York Times,* 7 April 1957.

119. *Népszabadság,* 19 August 1962.

120. Ibid., 3 June 1962; and *Társadalmi Szemle,* June 1961, p. 39, quoted in Fejtő, "Hungarian Communism," in Griffith, *Communism in Europe,* vol. 1, pp. 268 and 270.

121. See *Társadalmi Szemle,* February 1963, pp. 7–8.

122. Magyar Szocialista Munkáspárt, *A Magyar Szocialista Munkáspárt VIII. kongresszusának jegyzőkönyve, 1962. november 20–24.*

123. Vera Lajtai, "A párt szervezeti fejlődése a VIII. pártkongresszus után," in Erényi and Rákosi, *Legyőzhetetlen erő,* p. 267.

124. *Népszabadság,* 23 November 1962.

125. *Népszabadság,* 3 December 1961, quoted in Fejtő, "Hungarian Communism," in Griffith, *Communism in Europe,* vol. 1, p. 209.

126. See Váli, *Rift and Revolt,* pp. 440–42.

## PART SIX

1. *Társadalmi Szemle,* June 1972, p. 9.

2. *Radio Free Europe Research, Situation Report, 22 March 1975* (mimeo.).

3. István Katona, "Pártunk fő irányvonalának húszéves alapelvei," *Társadalmi Szemle,* June 1977, pp. 3–13.

4. Zoltán Komócsin, "The Class Approach and Internationalism," *World Marxist Review* (Prague) 11, no. 10/11 (October–November 1968): 9.

5. Ibid.

6. See especially William F. Robinson, *The Pattern of Reform in Hungary;* and Peter A. Toma and Ivan Völgyes, *Politics in Hungary.*

## 14. The Governors: Party and State

1. See Rezső Nyers, *Gazdaságpolitikánk és a gazdasági mechanizmus reformja.*

2. *Népszabadság,* 12 February 1964.

3. Magyar Távirati Iroda (MTI), 18 October 1964.

4. *Népszabadság,* 12 February 1965; and Robinson, *Pattern of Reform,* p. 85.

5. See *Társadalmi Szemle,* July–August 1966, pp. 17–28.

6. Robinson, *Pattern of Reform,* pp. 89–90.

7. Ibid., p. 197.

8. *Népszava,* 6 October 1970; and *Népszabadság,* 11 October 1970.

9. See Magyar Szocialista Munkáspárt, *A Magyar Szocialista Munkáspárt X. kongresszusának jegyzőkönyve, 1970. november 23–28.*

10. *Népszabadság,* 24 November 1970.

11. Ibid., 27 November 1970.

12. Ibid., 25 November 1970.

13. Ibid., 23 October 1971.

14. Ibid., 13 February 1972.

15. Béla Köpeczi, "A Controversy on the New Left," *New Hungarian Quarterly* 13, no. 45 (spring 1972): 119.

16. *Népszabadság,* 2 March 1972.

17. Ibid., 17 November 1972; and *Pártélet,* December 1972, pp. 8–30.

18. *Népszabadság,* 24 December 1972.

19. *Pártélet,* January 1974, pp. 23–31.

20. *Népszabadság,* 22 March 1974.

21. See *Népszabadság,* 18–23 March 1975; and Magyar Szocialista Munkáspárt, *A Magyar Szocialista Munkáspárt XI. kongresszusa, 1975. március 17–22* (hereafter cited as *XI. kongresszus*).

22. *Pártélet,* May 1975.

23. See *Pravda,* 3 February 1972.

24. See Charles Gati, "The Kádár Mystique," *Problems of Communism* 23, no. 3 (May–June 1974): 23–27.

25. *Népszabadság,* 23 March 1974.

26. Radványi, *Hungary and the Superpowers,* p. 91.

27. See Toma and Völgyes, *Politics in Hungary,* pp. 24–25, 28, 65.

28. Árpád Pullai, "Összhangban politikánk elveivel," *Pártélet,* January 1974, p. 16.

29. See Robinson, *Pattern of Reform,* pp. 203–6, 264–66.

30. Ibid., pp. 263–64.

31. Magyar Szocialista Munkáspárt, *XI. kongresszus,* p. 226.

32. László Rózsa, "Aktivitás, kiállás, demokrácia," *Társadalmi Szemle,* May 1976, p. 29.

33. *Pártélet,* December 1973, pp. 29–35.

34. *Pártélet,* February 1968, pp. 9–12. For statistics on participation in the various courses, see Magyar Szocialista Munkáspárt, *XI. kongresszus,* pp. 8–10.

35. See Toma and Völgyes, *Politics in Hungary,* pp. 95–96.

36. Ibid., pp. 21, 142.

37. *Népszabadság,* 24 October 1975.

38. *Pártélet,* July 1977, pp. 8–19.

39. *Népszabadság,* 27 August 1977.

40. Ibid., 28 October 1976.

41. Magyar Szocialista Munkáspárt, *XI. kongresszus,* pp. 6–7; and *Pártélet,* July 1977, p. 7.

42. For one such survey, see *Magyar Nemzet,* 17 May 1964.

43. *Pártélet,* January 1974, pp. 32–36; and *Népszabadság,* 18 April 1974.

44. *Magyar Ifjuság,* 29 March 1974.

45. *Népszabadság,* 11 May 1976.

46. See Toma and Völgyes, *Politics in Hungary,* pp. 95–96.

47. *Népszabadság,* 29 November 1966.

48. Hungary, *A magyar népköztársaság alkotmánya.*

49. *Magyar Hirlap,* 21 October 1972.

50. See Robinson, *Pattern of Reform,* pp. 106–12.

51. A more elaborate analysis of the composition of the assembly can be found in Toma and Völgyes, *Politics in Hungary,* pp. 57–62.

52. Fejtő, "Hungarian Communism," in Griffith, *Communism in Europe,* vol. 1, p. 276n.

53. See King, *Minorities under Communism,* pp. 264–65.

54. MTI, 18 September 1976.

55. *Népszabadság,* 20 September 1976.

56. See Robinson, *Pattern of Reform,* pp. 245–52.

57. Ibid., pp. 212–15.

58. *Pártélet,* January 1970, pp. 18–28.

59. *Magyar Nemzet*, 26 February 1977.

60. See Toma and Völgyes, *Politics in Hungary*, pp. 74–82.

61. *Magyar Közlöny*, 30 March 1977.

## 15. The Policies: Reforms and Reconsiderations

1. See György Ránki, *Magyarország gazdasága az első 3 éves terv időszakában;* and Berend, *Gazdasági politika.*

2. An analysis of the mechanism can be found in Robinson, *Pattern of Reform,* chaps. 3, 5, and 6.

3. Ferenc Erdei, "A szövetkezetek elméleti kérdései," *Társadalmi Szemle,* February 1968, p. 31.

4. See Imre Tar, "A földtulajdon továbbfejlesztésének útján," *Társadalmi Szemle,* January 1967, pp. 25–31.

5. Robinson, *Pattern of Reform,* p. 101.

6. *Népszabadság,* 6 February 1972; and *Társadalmi Szemle,* June 1972, pp. 12–27.

7. *Népszabadság,* 22 June and 27 August, 1972.

8. Ibid., 23 December 1971.

9. *Pártélet,* January 1972, pp. 15–19.

10. *Pravda,* 3 February 1972; Radio Budapest, 29 March 1972.

11. *Pravda,* 13 May 1972.

12. *Népszabadság,* 13 July 1972.

13. Ibid., 22 March 1973.

14. Radio Budapest, 21 February 1975.

15. Magyar Szocialista Munkáspárt, *XI. kongresszus,* pp. 173–76, 163.

16. See *Magyar Nemzet,* 3 July 1975; and *Társadalmi Szemle,* July 1975, pp. 3–13.

17. *Magyar Hirlap,* 18 June 1975.

18. *Népszabadság,* 26 September 1975.

19. *Magyar Hirlap,* 8 August 1976.

20. *New York Times,* 12 June 1975.

21. *Gazdasági Szemle,* April 1977.

22. *Magyar Közlöny,* 6 May and 24 January 1977.

23. *Társadalmi Szemle,* May 1977, pp. 3–16.

24. *Magyar Hirlap,* 17 December 1976.

25. *Népszabadság,* 22 October 1977; ibid., 23 April 1978.

26. Ibid., 15 December 1976.

27. *Magyar Közlöny,* 12 March 1977.

28. *Magyar Hirlap,* 7 January 1977.

29. *Népszabadság,* 3 December 1976.

30. *Magyar Nemzet,* 9 February 1974. On the transformation of Hungarian agriculture, see Lewis A. Fischer and Philip E. Uren, *The New Hungarian Agriculture;* and Jenő F. Bangó, *Das neue ungarische Dorf.*

31. *Társadalmi Szemle*, March 1976, p. 15.

32. *Magyar Hirlap*, 6 February 1976.

33. *Társadalmi Szemle*, March 1976, pp. 15–16.

34. *Magyar Hirlap*, 27 February 1977.

35. See Toma and Völgyes, *Politics in Hungary*, chap. 10.

36. *Új Irás*, February 1963.

37. *Társadalmi Szemle*, July–August 1966, pp. 29–58.

38. *Népszabadság*, 27 April 1968; and *Társadalmi Szemle*, November 1970, p. 24.

39. Sik, *Vihar a levelet* . . . ; Antal Végh, *Miért beteg a magyar futball?* (Budapest: Magvető, 1974).

40. See Antal Végh, "Állóviz," *Valóság*, April 1968, pp. 41–53.

41. See Zsuzsa Ferge, *Társadalmunk rétegződése*, 2d ed.

42. András Hegedüs, *A szocialista társadalom strukturájáról*, pp. 63–77, 115–16. See also "Documents: Hegedüs, His Views and His Critics," *Studies in Comparative Communism* 2, no. 2 (April 1969): pp. 121–52.

43. *Pártélet*, December 1968, pp. 36–38.

44. *Komsomolskaya Pravda*, 1 July 1972.

45. *Társadalmi Szemle*, October 1972, pp. 26–39.

46. Ibid., pp. 16–25.

47. *Magyar Filozófial Szemle*, 17 (1973): 159–69.

48. *Pártélet*, June 1973, p. 44; and *Valóság*, April 1973.

49. Translated editions of the two works are Miklós Haraszti, *A Worker in a Worker's State* (Harmondsworth [England]: Penguin, 1977), which includes an account of the author's trial; and George Konrad, *The City Builder* (New York: Harcourt Brace Jovanovich, 1977).

50. *Népszabadság*, 20 March 1975.

51. *Valóság*, August 1977.

52. *Magyar Hirlap*, 19 August 1974.

53. *Népszabadság*, 30 March 1974. See also Mindszenty, *Memoirs*, p. 246.

54. *Társadalmi Szemle*, March 1976, p. 18.

55. *Világosság*, no. 1, 1977.

56. *Népszabadság*, 10 June 1977.

57. *Magyar Hirlap*, 20 August 1977.

58. *Népszabadság*, 16 July 1963; ibid., 8 November.

59. *Népszabadság*, 25 June 1964.

60. *Társadalmi Szemle*, November 1975, p. 89.

61. *Népszabadság*, 27 June 1968.

62. Erwin Weit, *Eyewitness*, pp. 201, 211.

63. *Népszabadság*, 25 July 1968. See also H. Gordon Skilling, *Czechoslovakia's Interrupted Revolution*, pp. 688–95.

64. See George Gömöri, "Hungarian and Polish Attitudes on Czechoslovakia, 1968," in E. J. Czerwinski and Jaroslav Piekalkiewicz, eds., *The Soviet Invasion of Czechoslovakia: Its Effects on Eastern Europe*, pp. 107–13; and Rudolf L. Tőkés, "Hungarian Intellectuals' Reaction to the Invasion of Czechoslovakia," in ibid., pp. 139–53.

65. Radio Budapest, 1 January 1969, quoted in *East Europe* 18, no. 2 (1969): 46.

66. *Magyar Hirlap*, 26 October 1968.

67. *Népszabadság*, 1 July 1976.

68. *World Marxist Review*, September 1976, pp. 11–14.

69. *Béke és Szocializmus*, January 1977, pp. 6–15.

70. *Népszabadság*, 10 June 1977.

71. *Il Giornale*, 12 April 1977; and *Pártélet*, April 1977, pp. 3–10.

72. *Népszabadság*, 10 July 1976; ibid., 10 June 1976.

73. See King, *Minorities under Communism*, chap. 6; and Skilling, *Czechoslovakia's Interrupted Revolution*, pp. 606–10, 875–77.

74. *Társadalmi Szemle*, July–August 1972, p. 29.

75. Robinson, *Pattern of Reform*, pp. 298–99.

76. *Magyar Hirlap*, 31 October 1976; *Élet és Irodalom*, 6 November 1976; *Magyar Nemzet*, 25 December 1977; ibid., 1 January 1978. See also King, *Minorities*, chaps. 8 and 9; and the protest by a former member of the Romanian party's Central Committee, Károly Király, in the *New York Times*, 1 February 1978.

77. MTI, 17 June 1977.

78. *Pártélet*, August 1973, pp. 33–37.

79. *Népszabadság*, 12 February 1965; ibid., 23 February 1966.

80. János Péter, "Hungary and Europe," *New Hungarian Quarterly* 8, no. 25 (spring 1967): 14–19.

81. Tibor Pethő, "Modern Forms of Cooperation in the Danube Valley," *New Hungarian Quarterly*, 8, no. 27 (autumn 1967): 10–16.

82. *Pravda*, 31 March 1971.

83. *Magyarország*, 6 May 1973.

84. *Ifjú Kommunista*, July–August 1973.

85. *Népszabadság*, 18 February 1977.

86. *Népszabadság*, 20 March 1977.

87. Reuters, 8 October 1977.

88. *Népszabadság*, 30 March 1974.

## 16. The Governed: Social Change and Political Legitimacy

1. *Társadalmi Szemle*, December 1967, p. 25: ibid., March 1968, pp. 7–21.

2. Ibid., May 1967, pp. 15–33.

3. See Toma and Völgyes, *Politics in Hungary*, pp. 45–46.

4. See Ferge, *Társadalmunk rétegződése*, 2d ed.

5. Ránki, "Modernization," in Gati, *The Politics of Modernization in Eastern Europe*, p. 317.

6. See Toma and Völgyes, *Politics in Hungary*, pp. 132–33.

7. See for instance *Pártélet*, April 1972, pp. 41–44; and Ferenc Kovács, *A munkásosztály politikai-ideológiai műveltségéről és aktivitásáról*.

8. *Népszabadság*, 16 January 1971.

9. Sándor Gáspár, "Trade Union Problems in Hungary," *World Marxist Review*, June 1968, pp. 9–10.

10. *Figyelő,* 3 January 1973.

11. *Magyarország,* 9 September 1973.

12. *Pártélet,* January 1974, p. 25; ibid., January 1973, pp. 32–36.

13. Television interview, 8 June 1973.

14. *Népszava,* 27 May 1973; and *Társadalmi Szemle,* February 1974, pp. 58–65.

15. *Társadalmi Szemle,* April 1977, pp. 7–8.

16. *Népszava,* 28 November 1976.

17. Ibid., 1 May 1977; and *Népszabadság,* 4 March 1977.

18. *Népszabadság,* 21 January 1973.

19. See Robinson, *Pattern of Reform,* pp. 132–34, 236–38; and Toma and Völgyes, *Politics in Hungary,* pp. 69–70.

20. *Népszabadság,* 27 June 1976.

21. Toma and Völgyes, *Politics in Hungary,* p. 92.

22. Ibid., pp. 90–100, 117–20.

23. *Új Irás,* February 1973.

24. *Társadalmi Szemle,* March 1967, pp. 97–111; *Kortárs,* November 1968; and Radio Szülőföldünk, 7 June 1969.

25. *Társadalmi Szemle,* May 1973, pp. 54–68.

26. Paul Neuburg, *The Hero's Children: The Post-War Generation in Eastern Europe,* p. 340.

27. See László Molnár et al., *Ipari munkások politikai aktivitása;* and Toma and Völgyes, *Politics in Hungary,* chap. 11.

28. Ránki, "Modernization," in Gati, *Politics of Modernization,* p. 321.

29. Neuburg, *Hero's Children,* p. 321.

30. See the interview with Yvon Bourdet, *L'homme et la société,* April–June 1971, pp. 3–12.

31. Radio Free Europe [RFE] Audience and Public Opinion Research Department, *Attitudes Toward Key Political Concepts in East Europe* (Munich: RFE, December 1969), pp. 33–37, 40–49, 51, 104.

32. Radio Free Europe, *The Hungarian Self-Image and the Hungarian Image of Americans, Russians, Germans, Rumanians and Chinese* (Munich: RFE, February 1970).

33. Radio Free Europe, *Eastern Socialism, Western Democracy, and RFE's Coverage of the Two Systems* (Munich: RFE, December 1976); idem, *Approval and Rejection of the "Basic Idea of Communism"* (Munich: RFE, February 1977).

34. Radio Free Europe, *Major Domestic Issues as Ranked by Hungarian Respondents* (Munich: RFE, January 1972).

35. Radio Free Europe, *Political Orientation and Listening to Western Radio in East Europe* (Munich: RFE, July 1977), p. 6; idem, *Attitudes Toward Communism and Party Preferences in East Europe* (Munich: RFE, January 1973), pp. 13–19.

36. Radio Free Europe, *Hungarian Views on East-West Relations in the 1970s* (Munich: RFE, February 1972).

37. Radio Free Europe, *Radio Free Europe in the 1970s* (Munich: RFE, 1974). This survey indicated that 70 percent of the respondents listened to Western broadcasts; domestic radio was regarded as the more reliable reporter of home events by 23 percent, and of foreign affairs by 9 percent.

# Bibliography

The literature relating to the sixty-year-long history of Hungarian communism and its environment is immense, and this bibliography represents only a small proportion of it. It includes most of the major monographs and published documentary collections consulted in the preparation of this study. Newspaper and periodical articles and archival items can be found in the reference notes. The most comprehensive specialized bibliography, A magyar munkásmozgalom történetének válogatott bibliográfiája, 1945–1971, was edited by Mrs. László Kálmán and published under the auspices of the Institute of Party History in 1973; it is not, however, widely available. The most useful English bibliographies are those of Bakó, Halász de Béky, and László, cited below.

Aczél, Tamás, and Méray, Tibor. The Revolt of the Mind. New York: Praeger, 1960.

Aczél, Tamás, ed. Ten Years After. London: Macgibbon and Kee, 1966.

Ákos, Károly, ed. Új haza, új hadsereg: Visszaemlékezések az 1945–1947-es évekre. Budapest: Zrinyi, 1970.

Alton, Thad Paul, et al. Hungarian National Income and Product in 1955. New York: Columbia University Press, 1963.

American Friends of the Captive Nations. Hungary Under Soviet Rule. Vol. 5. New York, 1961.

Angress, Werner T. Stillborn Revolution: The Communist Bid for Power in Germany, 1921–1923. Princeton, N. J.: Princeton University Press, 1963.

Apró, Antal. A szocializmus épitésének útján. Budapest: Kossuth, 1975.

Aranyosi, Magda. Frankel Leo. Budapest: Akadémiai, 1974.

Aranyossy, Georges. Ils ont tué ma foi: Un itinéraire communiste. Paris: Laffont, 1971.

Arató, Endre. A magyar-csehszlovák viszony ötven éve: Történeti áttekintés. Budapest: Kossuth, 1969.

Auer, Pál. Fél évszázad; események, emberek. Washington, D.C.: Occidental, 1971.

Bakó, Elemér, comp. Guide to Hungarian Studies. Stanford, Calif.: Hoover Institution Press, 1973.

Balassa, Béla A. The Hungarian Experience in Economic Planning. New Haven, Conn.: Yale University Press, 1959.

Balázs, Béla. A középrétegek szerepe társadalmunk fejlődésében: Egy évszázad magyar történelmének néhány sajátosságáról, 1849–1945. Budapest: Kossuth, 1958.

———. Népmozgalom és nemzeti bizottságok. Budapest: Kossuth, 1961.

Bálint, József. *A gazdasági reform kibontakozásának kérdései.* Budapest: Kossuth, 1969.

Balogh, Sándor. *Parlamenti és pártharcok Magyarországon, 1945–1947.* Budapest: Kossuth, 1975.

Bangó, Jenő F. *Das neue ungarische Dorf.* Bern: SOI, 1974.

Barabás, Tibor. *Egy nép nevelői: Arcképek és tanulmányok.* 5th ed. Budapest: Magvető, 1966.

Barber, Noel. *A Handful of Ashes: A Personal Testament of the Battle of Budapest.* London: Wingate, 1957.

Beér, János, and Kovács, István. *A Magyar Népköztársaság alkotmánya.* Budapest: Közgazdasági és Jogi, 1959.

Beér, János, and Szabó, Imre. *Az új magyar alkotmány és magyarázatai.* Budapest: Szikra, 1950.

Berán, Mrs. Éva Nemes, and Hollós, Ervin. *Megfigyelés alatt . . . Dokumentumok a Horthysta titkosrendőrség működéséből (1920–1944).* Budapest: Akadémiai, 1977.

Berecz, János. *Ellenforradalom tollal és fegyverrel.* Budapest: Kossuth, 1969.

Berend, Iván T. *Gazdasági politika az első ötéves terv megindításakor (1948–1950).* Budapest: Közgazdasági és Jogi, 1964.

————. *A szocialista gazdaság fejlődése Magyarországon, 1945–1968.* Budapest: Kossuth, 1974.

————. *Ujjáépités és a nagytőke elleni harc Magyarországon, 1945–1948.* Budapest: Közgazdasági és Jogi, 1962.

Berend, Iván T., and Ránki, György. *A magyar gazdaság száz éve.* Budapest: Kossuth, 1972.

————. *Magyarország gazdasága az első világháború után, 1919–1929.* Budapest: Akadémiai, 1966.

Berend, Iván T., and Szuhay, Miklós. *A tőkés gazdaság története Magyarországon, 1848–1944.* Budapest: Kossuth, 1973.

Betlen, Oszkár. *Párizs, Madrid, Bécs: A Komintern egységpolitikája, 1933–1937.* Budapest: Kossuth, 1968.

Bibó, István. *A harmadik út.* London: Magyar Könyves Céh, 1960.

Bihari, Ottó. *Az államhatalmi-képviseleti szervek elmélete.* Budapest: Akadémiai, 1963.

————. *Socialist Representative Institutions.* Budapest: Akadémiai, 1970.

————. *A szocialista államszervezet alkotmányos modelljei.* Budapest: Közgazdasági és Jogi, 1969.

Biszku, Béla. *A párt és az állam a nép szolgálatában.* Budapest: Kossuth, 1972.

————. *A párt vezető szerepének néhány időszerű kérdése.* Budapest: Kossuth, 1969.

Blaskovits, János, and Kiss, György. *Gondolatok az első negyedszázadról, 1944–1969.* Budapest: Gondolat, 1970.

Blaskovits, János, and Labádi, Lajos. *A Magyar Kommunista Párt III. kongresszusa.* Budapest: Kossuth, 1968.

Blaskovits, János, and Zsilák, András, eds. *A népi Magyarország negyedszázada; nemzetközi tudományos ülésszak Magyarország felszabadulásának 25. évfordulóján, 1970 március 16–17.* Budapest: Akadémiai, 1972.

Blumenfeld, Yorick. *Seesaw: Cultural Life in Eastern Europe.* New York: Harcourt Brace & World, 1968.

Boffa, Giuseppe. *Inside the Khrushchev Era*. New York: Marzani & Munsell, 1959.

Böhm, Vilmos. *Két forradalom tüzében: Októberi forradalom, proletárdiktatúra, ellenforradalom*. Munich: Verlag für Kulturpolitik, 1923.

Bolgár, Elek. *Válogatott tanulmányok*. Budapest: Kossuth, 1958.

Borbándi, Gyula. *Der Ungarische Populismus*. Mainz: Hase & Koehler, 1976.

Borkenau, Franz. *European Communism*. New York: Harper, 1953.

Boros, Ferenc. *Magyar-csehszlovák kapcsolatok 1918–1921-ben*. Budapest: Akadémiai, 1970.

Borsányi, György. *Kun Béla*. Budapest: Akadémiai, 1974.

———. *"Munkát! Kenyeret!" A proletariátus tömegmozgalmai Magyarországon a gazdasági válság éveiben (1929–1933)*. Budapest: Kossuth, 1971.

Borsányi, György, and Friss, Mrs. István, eds. *Dokumentumok a magyar forradalmi munkásmozgalom történetéből, 1929–1935*. Budapest: Kossuth, 1964.

Brown, Archie, and Gray, Jack, eds. *Political Culture and Political Change in Communist States*. London: Macmillan, 1977.

Brugère-Trélat, Vincent. *Budapest*. Paris: La Table Ronde, 1966.

Brzezinski, Zbigniew K. *The Soviet Bloc: Unity and Conflict*. Rev. ed. New York: Praeger, 1961.

Buchinger, Manó. *Küzdelem a szocializmusért; emlékek és élmények*. 2 vols. Budapest: Népszava, 1946–47.

Budapest. Fővárosi Szabó Ervin Könyvtár [Ervin Szabó Library, Budapest]. *Budapest munkásmozgalmának válogatott irodalma, 1919–1945*. Budapest, 1965.

Burks, Richard V. *The Dynamics of Communism in Eastern Europe*. Princeton, N.J.: Princeton University Press, 1961.

Churchill, Winston S. *The Grand Alliance*. Boston: Houghton Mifflin, 1950.

Ciliga, Anton. *The Russian Enigma*. London: Labour Book Service, 1940.

Claudin, Fernando. *The Communist Movement: From Comintern to Cominform*. Harmondsworth, England: Penguin, 1975.

Communist International. *Le mouvement communiste international: Rapports, adresses au deuxième congrès de l'Internationale Communiste, 1920*. Petrograd: n.p., 1921.

Conquest, Robert. *The Great Terror*. New York: Macmillan, 1968.

Crozier, Brian. *Since Stalin: An Assessment of Communist Power*. New York: Coward-McCann, 1970.

Csatári, Dániel. *Forgószélben; magyar-román viszony, 1940–1945*. Budapest: Akadémiai, 1968.

Csépányi, Dezső. *Az ellenforradalmi rendszer munkásellenes politikája, 1935–39*. Budapest: Akadémiai, 1972.

Cserei, Pál, and Varga, Tibor. *Ködös napok*. Békéscsaba: Békés Megyei Lapkiadó Vállalat, 1958.

Csikós Nagy, Béla. *Magyar gazdaságpolitika*. Budapest: Kossuth, 1971.

Csizmadia, Andor. *A nemzeti bizottságok állami tevékenysége (1944–1949)*. Budapest: Közgazdasági és Jogi, 1968.

Csizmadia, Ernő; Nagy, Sándor; and Zsarnóczai, Sándor. *Az egységes szocialista szövetkezeti parasztosztály kialakulása*. Budapest: Kossuth, 1966.

Czerwinski, E. J., and Piekalkiewicz, Jaroslav, eds. *The Soviet Invasion of Czechoslovakia: Its Effects on Eastern Europe*. New York: Praeger, 1972.

Daim, Wilfried. *The Vatican and Eastern Europe.* New York: Ungar, 1970.

Dallin, Alexander, and Breslauer, George W. *Political Terror in Communist Systems.* Stanford: Stanford University Press, 1970.

Deak, Francis. *Hungary at the Paris Peace Conference.* New York: Columbia University Press, 1942.

Degras, Jane, ed. *The Communist International, 1919–1943: Documents.* 3 vols. London: Oxford University Press, 1956–1965.

Djilas, Milovan. *Conversations with Stalin.* New York: Harcourt Brace & World, 1962.

Dobi, István. *Vallomás és történelem.* 2 vols. Budapest: Kossuth, 1962.

Domokos, József. *". . . emlékezz, proletár!" Sallai Imre és Fürst Sándor pere.* Budapest: Kossuth, 1962.

Donáth, Ferenc. *Demokratikus földreform Magyarországon, 1945–1947.* Budapest: Akadémiai, 1969.

Dózsa, Mrs. Rudolf. *A MOVE, egy jellegzetes magyar fasiszta szervezet, 1918–1944.* Budapest: Akadémiai, 1972.

Drachkovitch, Milorad M., and Lazitch, Branko, eds. *The Comintern: Historical Highlights.* New York: Praeger, 1966.

Eden, Anthony. *The Reckoning.* London: Cassell, 1965.

Égető, Lajos. *A szervezeti szabályzat—a párt alkotmánya.* Budapest: Kossuth, 1974.

Eisele, Hans. *Bilder aus dem kommunistischen Ungarn.* Innsbruck: Tyrolia, 1920.

Erdei, Ferenc. *Futóhomok: A Duna-Tiszaköz földje és népe.* Budapest: Atheneum, 1957.

Erényi, Tibor. *Kunfi Zsigmond.* Budapest: Akadémiai, 1974.

Erényi, Tibor, and Rákosi, Sándor, eds. *Legyőzhetetlen erő: A magyar kommunista mozgalom szervezeti fejlődésének 50 éve.* 2d ed. Budapest: Kossuth, 1974.

Fábry, József. *A szabadságért harcoltunk.* Budapest: Zrinyi, 1973.

Faludy, György. *My Happy Days in Hell.* New York: Morrow, 1963.

Farrell, Barry, ed. *Political Leadership in Eastern Europe and the Soviet Union.* Chicago: Aldine, 1970.

Fehér, István. *Politikai küzdelmek a Dél-Dunántúlon 1944–1946 között.* Budapest: Akadémiai, 1972.

Fehér, Lajos. *Harcunk Budapestért.* 2d rev. ed. Budapest: Zrinyi, 1969.

Fejtő, François. *Budapest 1956.* Paris: Julliard, 1966.

Fekete, Mihály. *Ellenállók az Avas alján.* Budapest: Kossuth, 1974.

Felix, Christopher [pseud.]. *A Short Course in the Secret War.* New York: Dutton, 1963.

Fenyő, István. *Haza és tudomány.* Budapest: Szépirodalmi, 1969.

Ferge, Zsuzsa. *Társadalmunk rétegződése: Elvek és tények.* 2d ed. Budapest: Közgazdasági és Jogi, 1973.

Fischer, Lewis A., and Uren, Philip E. *The New Hungarian Agriculture.* Montreal: McGill-Queen's University Press, 1973.

Fock, Jenő. *A szocializmus épitésének gazdaságpolitikája: Beszédek és cikkek, 1963–1972.* Budapest: Kossuth, 1972.

Földes, István. *Választási zsebkönyv: Tények és adatok.* Budapest: Kossuth, 1967.

Földes, Péter. *Drámai küldetés: Szamuely Tibor életregénye.* Budapest: Kossuth, 1962.

Free Europe Committee. *The Revolt in Hungary: A Documentary Chronology of Events Based Exclusively on Internal Broadcasts by Central and Provincial Radios, October 23, 1956–November 4, 1956.* New York: Free Europe, 1956.

Friss, István, ed. *Reform of the Economic Mechanism in Hungary: Nine Essays.* Budapest: Akadémiai, 1969.

Gábor, Róbert. *The Bolshevization of the Hungarian Trade Unions, 1945–1951.* New York: Hungarian Research and Information Center, 1952.

————. *Organization and Strategy of the Hungarian Workers' (Communist) Party.* New York: Free Europe, 1952.

Gábor, Sándor, and Mucsi, Ferenc, eds. *A Magyarországi Tanácsköztársaság 50. évfordulója: Nemzetkőzi tudományos ülésszak, Budapest, 1969. március 17–19.* Budapest: Akadémiai, 1970.

Gábor, Mrs. Sándor. *Ausztria és a magyarországi Tanácsköztársaság.* Budapest: Akadémiai, 1969.

————. *Szamuely Tibor.* Budapest: Akadémiai, 1974.

Gadó, Ottó, ed. *Reform of the Economic Mechanism in Hungary: Development, 1968–71.* Budapest: Akadémiai, 1972.

Gál, Lajos, ed. *Egységbe ifjuság! Válogatott iratok a magyar ifjusági mozgalom történetéből, 1944 október–1948 március.* Budapest: Kossuth, 1973.

Galambos, Sándor Futó. *Három nehéz esztendő.* Budapest: Zrinyi, 1973.

Gáspár, Ferenc; Jenei, Károly; and Szilágyi, Gábor, eds. *A munkásság az üzemekért, a termelésért, 1944–1945: Dokumentgyüjtemény.* Budapest: Táncsics, 1970.

Gati, Charles G., "The Populist Current in Hungarian Politics, 1935–1944." Ph.D. dissertation, Indiana University, 1965.

————, ed. *The Politics of Modernization in Eastern Europe.* New York: Praeger, 1974.

Gazsi, József, and Pintér, István, eds. *Fegyverrel a fasizmus ellen.* Budapest: Zrinyi, 1968.

Gergely, Imre. *Magyarok a spanyol néppel, 1936–1939.* Budapest: Kossuth, 1977.

Gerő, Ernő. *Harcban a szocialista népgazdaságért.* Budapest: Szikra, 1950.

————. *Lesz magyar ujjászületés.* Pécs: Új Dunántúl, 1944.

————. *A Magyar Kommunista Párt.* Budapest: MKP, 1945.

Godó, Ágnes. *Magyarok a jugoszláv népfelszabaditó háborúban.* Budapest: Zrinyi, 1972.'

Goldwin, Robert A., ed. *Readings in Russian Foreign Policy.* New York: Oxford University Press, 1959.

Gondos, Ernő, ed. *Tájak, gondok, emberek: Irók a magyar valóságról.* Budapest: Kossuth, 1965.

Gosztony, Péter, ed. *Der ungarische Volksaufstand in Augenzeugenberichten.* Düsseldorf: Rauch, 1966.

Grátz, Gusztáv. *A forradalmak kora.* Budapest: Magyar Szemle, 1935.

Griffith, William E., ed. *Communism in Europe.* Vol. 1. Cambridge, Mass.: MIT Press, 1964.

Grzybowski, Kazimierz. *The Socialist Commonwealth of Nations.* New Haven, Conn.: Yale University Press, 1964.

Gyenis, János, and Söptei, János. *Új falu, új emberek.* Budapest: Kossuth, 1970.

György, Andrew. *Governments of Danubian Europe.* New York: Rinehart, 1949.

György, Ervin. *Ich Kämpfte für den Frieden: Erinnerungen eines Funktionärs aus dem Ostblock.* Bern: SOI, 1972.

Habuda, Miklós, ed. *A magyar szakszervezetek a népi demokratikus forradalomban, 1944–1948.* Budapest: Táncsics, 1971.

Hajdu, Tibor. *Az 1918-as magyarországi polgári demokratikus forradalom.* Budapest: Kossuth, 1968.

————. *A Magyarországi Tanácsköztársaság.* Budapest: Kossuth, 1969.

Halász, Zoltán. *Cultural Life in Hungary.* Budapest: Pannonia, 1966.

Halász de Béky, I. L., comp. *A Bibliography of the Hungarian Revolution 1956.* Toronto: University of Toronto Press, 1963.

Halmos, Paul, ed. *Hungarian Sociological Studies.* Keele, England: University of Keele, 1972.

Hámori, Paul A. "Soviet Influences on the Establishment and Character of the Hungarian People's Republic (1944—1954)." Ph.D. dissertation, University of Michigan, 1964.

Hancock, W. K., and van der Poel, Jean, eds. *Selections from the Smuts Papers.* Vol. 4. Cambridge, England: Cambridge University Press, 1966.

Harrer, Ferenc. *Egy magyar polgár élete.* Budapest: Gondolat, 1968.

Harsányi, János, ed. *Magyar szabadságharcosok a fasizmus ellen: Dokumentumok a magyar antifasiszta ellenállási mozgalom történetéből, 1941–1945.* 2d ed. Budapest: Zrinyi, 1969.

Hautmann, Hans. *Die verlorene Räterepublik.* Vienna: Europe, 1971.

Háy, Julius. *Born 1900: Memoirs.* London: Hutchinson, 1974.

Healey, Denis, ed. *The Curtain Falls: The Story of the Socialists in Eastern Europe.* London: Lincolns-Prager, 1951.

Hegedüs, András. *A szocialista társadalom strukturájáról.* Budapest: Akadémiai, 1971.

Hegedüs, Miklós. *Az ipar és a mezőgazdaság kapcsolatainak néhány kérdése.* Budapest: Akadémiai, 1972.

Helmreich, Ernst C., ed. *Hungary.* New York: Praeger, 1957.

Herczeg, Károly. *A választott pártszervek és az agitációt irányitó apparátus munkamegosztása, munkamódszere.* Budapest: Kossuth, 1974.

Hetés, Tibor. *A magyarországi forradalmak krónikája, 1918–1919.* Budapest: Kossuth, 1969.

Hevesi, Gyula. *Egy mérnök a forradalomban.* Budapest: Europa, 1959.

————. *Szociális termelés: A magyar Tanácsköztársaság iparpolitikája.* Budapest: Közgazdasági és Jogi, 1959.

i..iton, Howard J. *Hungary: A Case History of Soviet Economic Imperialism.* Washington, D.C.: U.S. Department of State, 1951.

Hollós, Ervin. *Kik voltak, mit akartak?* 2d rev. ed. Budapest: Kossuth, 1967.

————. *Rendőrség, csendőrség, VKF 2.* Budapest: Kossuth, 1971.

Hollós, Ervin, and Lajtai, Vera. *Köztársaság tér 1956.* Budapest: Kossuth, 1974.

Holt, Robert T. *Radio Free Europe.* Minneapolis: University of Minnesota Press, 1958.

Horthy, Miklós. *Horthy Miklós titkos iratai.* Budapest: Kossuth, 1963.

————. *Memoirs.* London: Hutchinson, 1956.

Horváth, Zoltán. *Magyar századforduló: A második reformnemzedék története, 1896–1914.* Budapest: Gondolat, 1961.

Horváth, Mrs. Zoltán. *A KMP második kongresszusa.* Budapest: Kossuth, 1964.

Hungary. *Documents on the Mindszenty Case.* Budapest: Atheneum, 1949.

————. *Speeches of István Dobi, President of the Presidential Council, and János Kádár, Chairman of the Council of Ministers, Delivered to the Parliament of the Hungarian People's Republic at the Session of May 9–11, 1957.* Budapest: n.p., 1957.

————, *A magyar népköztársaság alkotmánya.* Budapest: Kossuth, 1977.

————, Büntető Törvényszék [Criminal Court], Budapest. *I. Geiger, R. Vogeler, E. Sanders and Their Accomplices before the Criminal Court.* Budapest, 1950.

————. Központi Statisztikai Hivatal [Central Statistical Office], *Mezőgazdaságunk a szocialista átszervezés idején, 1958–1962.* Budapest, 1963.

————, Külügyminisztérium [Foreign Ministry]. *Documents on the Hostile Activity of the United States Government against the Hungarian People's Republic.* Budapest, 1951.

————, ————. *La Hongrie et la Conférence de Paris.* Vols. 1, 2, and 4. Budapest, 1947.

————, ————. *The Hungarian Peace Negotiations (1920).* Budapest, 1921–1922.

————, ————. *Le problème de la minorité hongroise de Slovaquie.* Budapest, 1946.

————, ————. *Le problème hongrois par rapport à la Roumanie.* Budapest, 1946.

————, ————. *Le problème hongrois par rapport à la Tchécoslovaquie.* Budapest, 1946.

————, Megyei Biróság [County Court], Budapest. *Strafprozess Tito–faschistischer Menschenräuber, Budapest, 15–17 November 1952.* Budapest, 1952.

————, Minisztertanács [Council of Ministers]. *The Counter-revolutionary Conspiracy of Imre Nagy and His Accomplices.* Budapest, 1958.

————, ————. *The Counter-revolutionary Forces in the October Events in Hungary.* Budapest, n.d.

————, Népbiróság [People's Court], Budapest. *László Rajk and His Accomplices before the People's Court.* Budapest, 1949.

————, Tájékoztatásügyi Minisztérium [Information Ministry]. *Fehér Könyv. A magyar köztársaság és a demokrácia elleni összeesküvés.* Budapest, 1947.

Huszár, István. *Tudományos-műszaki forradalom—társadalmi struktura és gazdaság.* Budapest: Kossuth, 1969.

Ignotus, Paul. *Hungary.* London: Benn, 1972.

————. *Political Prisoner.* London: Macmillan, 1960.

Imre, Mrs. Mátyás; Mándi, Magda S.; and Szabó, Ágnes, eds. *Dokumentumok a magyar forradalmi munkásmozgalom történetéből, 1919–1929.* Budapest: Kossuth, 1964.

International Commission of Jurists. *The Hungarian Situation and the Rule of Law.* The Hague: n.p., 1957.

Ivanov-Razumnik, R. V. *The Memoirs of Ivanov-Razumnik.* London: Oxford University Press, 1965.

Jackson, George D. *Comintern and Peasant in East Europe, 1919–1930.* New York: Columbia University Press, 1966.

Janos, Andrew C., and Slottman, William B., eds. *Revolution in Perspective: Essays on the Hungarian Soviet Republic of 1919*. Berkeley: University of California Press, 1971.

Jász, Dezső. *Budapesttöl Budapestig*. Budapest: Magvető, 1971.

———. *Tanácsmagyarországtól a Pireneusig*. Budapest: Magvető, 1969.

Jászi, Oszkár. *Revolution and Counter-revolution in Hungary*. London: King, 1924.

Józsa, Antal, and Milei, György. *A rendithetetlen százezer: Magyarok a nagy októberi forradalomban és a polgárháborúban*. Budapest: Kossuth, 1968.

József, Farkas. *Rohanunk a forradalomba: A magyar irodalom eszmélése, 1914–1919*. 2d ed. Budapest: Gondolat, 1969.

Juhász, Gyula. *Magyarország külpolitikája*. Budapest: Kossuth, 1969.

Juhász, William. *The Hungarian Revolution: The People's Demands*. New York: Free Europe Press, 1957.

Juhász-Nagy, Sándor. *A magyar októberi forradalom története*. Budapest: Cserépfalvi, 1945.

Kabos, Ernő, ed. *Tanulmányok a magyar szakszervezeti mozgalom történetéből*. Budapest: Táncsics, 1969.

Kádár, János. *Hazafiság és internacionalizmus*. Budapest: Kossuth, 1968.

———. *Híven a forradalomért*. Budapest: Kossuth, 1972.

———. *Szilárd népi hatalom: Független Magyarország*. Budapest: Kossuth, 1958.

———. *A szocialista Magyarországért: Beszédek és cikkek, 1968–1972*. Budapest: Kossuth, 1972.

———. *Válogatott beszédek és cikkek, 1957–1974*. 2d ed. Budapest: Kossuth, 1975.

Kállai, Gyula. *A magyar függetlenségi mozgalom, 1936–1945*. 5th rev. ed. Budapest: Kossuth, 1965.

———. *Szocializmus, népfront, demokrácia*. Budapest: Kossuth, 1971.

Kállay, Miklós. *Hungarian Premier*. New York: Columbia University Press, 1954.

Kálmán, Lajos. *The Lawyer in Communism: Memoirs of a Lawyer behind the Iron Curtain*. Boston: St. Paul, 1960.

Kardos, László. *Egyház és vallásos élet egy mai faluban: Bakonycsernye—1965*. Budapest: Kossuth, 1969.

Károlyi, Mihály. *Memoirs: Faith without Illusion*. London: Cape, 1956.

———. *Az új Magyarországért: Válogatott irások és beszédek, 1908–1919*. Budapest: Magvető, 1968.

Károlyi, Mrs. Mihály. *Együtt a forradalomban*. Budapest: Europa, 1973.

Karsai, Elek, and Somlyai, Magda, eds. *Sorsforduló: Iratok Magyarország felszabadulásának történetéhez, 1944 szept.–1945 ápr.* 2 vols. Budapest: n.p., 1970.

Kassák, Lajos. *Egy ember élete*. Budapest: Magvető, 1966.

Kecskeméti, Paul. *The Unexpected Revolution: Social Forces in the Hungarian Uprising*. Stanford, Calif.: Stanford University Press, 1961.

Kékesdi, Gyula. *A forradalom katedráján: Lengyel Gyula élete*. Budapest: Kossuth, 1973.

Kende, János. *Szakszervezeti vita a Tanácsköztársaságban*. Budapest: Táncsics, 1970.

Keresztes, Mihály. *Az első lépések*. Budapest: Kossuth, 1971.

Kertész, Stephen D. *Diplomacy in a Whirlpool*. Notre Dame, Ind.: University of Notre Dame Press, 1953.

Khrushchev, Nikita. *Krushchev Remembers*. Ed. by Strobe Talbott. Boston: Little, Brown, 1970.

King, Robert R. *Minorities under Communism: Nationalities as a Source of Tension among Balkan Communist States*. Cambridge, Mass.: Harvard University Press, 1973.

Kirschner, Béla. *A "szakszervezeti kormány" hat napja (1919)*. Budapest: Kossuth, 1968.

Kis, András. *A Magyar Közösségtől a Földalatti Fővezérségig*. Budapest: Zrinyi, 1969.

Kiss, Károly. *Nincs megállás*. Budapest: Kossuth, 1974.

Komját, Irén. *Mező Imre*. Budapest: Kossuth, 1968.

Komját, Irén, and Pécsi, Anna. *A szabadság vándorai*. Budapest: Kossuth, 1973.

Komócsin, Zoltán. *Válogatott beszédek és cikkek*. Budapest: Kossuth, 1975.

Konkoly, Kálmán. *Das Geheimnis des Mátyás Rákosi: Eine Fibel des Weltkommunizmus*. Vienna: Wancura, 1962.

Kornai, János. *Overcentralization in Economic Administration*. London: Oxford University Press, 1959.

Kóródi, József. *Változások Magyarország gazdasági térképén*. Budapest: Kossuth, 1970.

Kovács, Endre. *Népek országútján*. Budapest: Magvető, 1972.

Kovács, Ferenc. *A munkásosztály politikai-ideológiai műveltségéről és aktivitásáról*. Budapest: Kossuth, 1976.

Kovács, Imre. *Im Schatten der Sowiets*. Zürich: Thomas, 1948.

———, ed. *Facts about Hungary*. Rev. ed. New York: Hungarian Committee, 1966.

Kovács, István. *New Elements in the Evolution of Socialist Constitution*. Budapest: Akadémiai, 1968.

Kővágó, József. *You Are All Alone*. New York: Praeger, 1959.

Kovrig, Béla. *Magyar szociálpolitika (1920–1945)*. New York: Hungarian National Council, 1954.

Kovrig, Bennett. *The Hungarian People's Republic*. Baltimore: The Johns Hopkins Press, 1970.

———. *The Myth of Liberation: East-Central Europe in U.S. Diplomacy and Politics since 1941*. Baltimore: The Johns Hopkins Press, 1973.

Kracauer, S., and Berkman, P. L. *Satellite Mentality*. New York: Praeger, 1956.

Kreybig, Karl. *Die Entstehung der Räterepublik Ungarn*. Berlin: "Der Arbeiter-Rat," 1919.

Kriegel, Annie. *Les grands procés dans les systèmes communistes*. Paris: Gallimard, 1972.

Krivitsky, Walter G. *In Stalin's Secret Service*. New York: Harper, 1939.

Kulcsár, Viktor. *Falusi település és életszinvonal*. Budapest: Kossuth, 1971.

Kun, Béla [Kolozsváry, Balázs]. *Forradalomról forradalomra*. Vienna: A Kommunisták Németausztriai Pártja, 1920.

———. *Válogatott irások és beszédek*. 2 vols. Budapest: Kossuth, 1966.

Kun, Mrs. Béla. *Kun Béla*. Budapest: Magvető, 1966.

Kuusinen, Aino. *Before and After Stalin.* London: Michael Joseph, 1974.

Lackó, Miklós. *Válságok—választások.* Budapest: Gondolat, 1975.

———, ed. *Tanulmányok a magyar népi demokrácia történetéből.* Budapest: Magyar Tudományos Akadémia, 1955.

Lackó, Miklós, and Szabó, Bálint, eds. *Húsz év: Tanulmányok a szocialista Magyarország történetéből.* Budapest: Kossuth, 1964.

Lányi, Mrs. Ernő; Nagy, Eta; and Petrák, Katalin, eds. *A szabadság hajnalán.* Budapest: Kossuth, 1965.

Lasky, Melvin J., ed. *The Hungarian Revolution: A White Book.* New York: Praeger, 1957.

László, Ervin. *The Communist Ideology in Hungary: Handbook for Basic Research.* Dordrecht: Reidel, 1966.

Lauter, Géza P. *The Manager and Economic Reform in Hungary.* New York: Praeger, 1972.

Lazitch, Branko, and Drachkovitch, Milorad M. *Biographical Dictionary of the Comintern.* Stanford: Hoover Institution Press, 1973.

Lederer, Emma. *A magyar polgári történetirás rövid története.* Budapest: Kossuth, 1969.

Lengyel, József. *Prenn Ferenc hányatott élete.* Budapest: Szépirodalmi, 1958.

———. *Visegrádi utca.* Budapest: Magvető, 1972.

Lenin, Vladimir I. *A Magyar Tanácsköztársaságról.* Budapest: Kossuth, 1969.

Leonhard, Wolfgang. *Child of the Revolution.* London: Collins, 1957.

Liptai, Ervin. *A Magyar Tanácsköztársaság.* 2d ed. Budapest: Kossuth, 1968.

Liptai, Ervin, ed. *A magyar Vörös hadsereg.* Budapest: Kossuth, 1957.

Liptai, Mrs. Ervin. *A Magyarországi Szocialista Munkáspárt, 1925–1928.* Budapest: Kossuth, 1971.

Litván, György. *Szabó Ervin.* Budapest: Akadémiai, 1974.

———, ed. *Magyar munkásszociográfiák, 1888–1945.* Budapest: Kossuth, 1974.

Litván, György, and Remete, László, comps. *A magyar szociológiai irodalom bibliográfiája.* Budapest: Magyar Tudományos Akadémia Szociológiai Kutatócsoport, 1970.

Low, Alfred D. *The Soviet Hungarian Republic and the Paris Peace Conference.* Philadelphia: American Philosophical Society, 1963.

Lukács, György. *Művészet és irodalom.* Budapest: Gondolat, 1968.

———. *Political Writings, 1919–1929.* London: NLB, 1972.

———. *Történelem és osztálytudat.* Budapest: Magvető, 1971.

———. *Taktika és ethika.* Budapest: Közoktatási népbiztosság, 1919.

Macartney, C. A. *Hungary: A Short History.* Edinburgh: Edinburgh University Press, 1962.

———. *October Fifteenth: A History of Modern Hungary, 1929–1945.* 2 vols. Edinburgh: Edinburgh University Press, 1956–57.

Magyar Kommunista Párt. *Hadifogoly zsebkönyv.* Budapest, 1945.

———. *Harc az ujjáépitésért: A Magyar Kommunista Párt 1945 május 20-an és 21-én tartott országos értekezletének jegyzőkönyve.* Budapest: Szikra, 1945.

————. *Nemzeti kérdés és magyar demokratikus külpolitika*. Budapest, 1945.

————. *A népi demokrácia útja: A Magyar Kommunista Párt III. kongresszusának jegyzőkönyve*. Budapest: Szikra, 1946.

————. *A pártbizalmi*. Budapest: Szikra, 1948.

Magyar Munkásmozgalmi Intézet and Párttörténeti Intézet. *A magyar munkásmozgalom történetének válogatott dokumentumai*. Budapest, 1951–1960. Vol. 1, *1848–1890*, Szikra 1951; vol. 2, *1890–1900*, Szikra 1954; vol. 3, *1900–1907*, Szikra 1955; vol. 5, *1917–1919*, Szikra 1956; vol. 4a, *1907–1914*, Kossuth 1966; vol. 4b, *1914–1918*, Kossuth, 1969; vol. 6a, *1919 március 21–június 11*, Kossuth 1959; vol. 6b, *1919 június 11–augusztus 1*, Kossuth 1960.

Magyar Munkásmozgalmi Intézet. *A Rákosi-per*. Budapest: Szikra, 1950.

Magyar Szocialista Munkáspárt. *Békés egymás mellet élés—ideológiai harc*. Budapest: Kossuth, 1974.

————. *Érdekviszonyok a szocializmusban*. Budapest: Kossuth, 1973.

————. *Ifjuságpolitika a megvalósitás útján*. Budapest: Kossuth, 1974.

————. *A Kommunista Internacionálé válogatott dokumentumai*. Budapest: Kossuth, 1975.

————. *A Magyar Kommunista Párt és a Szociáldemokrata Párt határozatai, 1944–1948*. Budapest: Kossuth, 1967.

————. *A Magyar Szocialista Munkáspárt határozatai és dokumentumai, 1956–1962*. Budapest: Kossuth, 1964.

————. *A Magyar Szocialista Munkáspárt határozatai és dokumentumai, 1963–1966*. Budapest: Kossuth, 1968.

————. *A MSZMP Központi Bizottságának tudománypolitikai irányelvei*. Budapest: Kossuth, 1969.

————. *A Magyar Szocialista Munkáspárt országos értekezletének jegyzőkönyve, 1957. június 27–29*. Budapest: Kossuth, 1957.

————. *A Magyar Szocialista Munkáspárt VII. kongresszusának jegyzőkönyve, 1959. november 30–december 5*. Budapest: Kossuth, 1960.

————. *A Magyar Szocialista Munkáspárt VIII. kongresszusának jegyzőkönyve, 1962. november 20–24*. Budapest: Kossuth, 1963.

————. *A Magyar Szocialista Munkáspárt IX. kongresszusa, 1966. november 28–december 3*. Budapest: Kossuth, 1966.

————. *A Magyar Szocialista Munkáspárt X. kongresszusa, 1970. november 23–28*. Budapest: Kossuth, 1970.

————. *A Magyar Szocialista Munkáspárt X. kongresszusának jegyzőkönyve, 1970. november 23–28*. Budapest: Kossuth, 1971.

————. *A Magyar Szocialista Munkáspárt XI. kongresszusa, 1975. március 17–22*. Budapest: Kossuth, 1975.

————. *A pártélet és a pártmunka időszerű kérdései*. Budapest: Kossuth, 1973.

————. *Pártépités: a párt- és tömegszervezeti munka kérdései*. Budapest: Kossuth, 1971.

————. *Pártmunkások kézikönyve, 1971*. Budapest: Kossuth, 1971.

————. *A szocialista hazafiság és a proletár internacionalizmus időszerű kérdései*. Budapest: Kossuth, 1975.

————. *Pártépitési kisszótár*. Budapest: Kossuth, 1973.

Magyar Tudományos Akadémia. Történettudományi Intézet. *A magyar történettudomány válogatott bibliográfiája, 1945–1968*. Budapest: Akadémiai, 1971.

Mályusz, Elemér. *The Fugitive Bolsheviks*. London: Richards, 1931.

Marcou, Lilly. *Le Kominform*. Paris: Presses de la Fondation Nationale des Sciences Politiques, 1977.

Markovits, Györgyi, and Tobiás, Áron, eds. *A cenzura árnyékában*. Budapest: Magvető, 1966.

Márkus, László. *A Károlyi Gyula kormány bel- és külpolitikája*. Budapest: Akadémiai, 1968.

Marosán, György. *Tüzes kemence*. Budapest: Magvető, 1968.

————. *Az úton végig kell menni*. Budapest: Magvető, 1972.

Márton, Endre. *The Forbidden Sky*. Boston: Little, Brown, 1971.

Máté, György. *Vörös jelek a hadak útján: Krónika*. Budapest: Táncsics, 1969.

Matolcsy, Mátyás. *Új élet magyar földön*. Budapest: Cserépfalvi, 1938.

Mayer, Arno J. *Politics and Diplomacy of Peacemaking: Containment and Counterrevolution at Versailles, 1918–1919*. New York: Random House, 1967.

McCagg, William O., Jr. "Communism and Hungary, 1944–1946." Ph.D. dissertation, Columbia University, 1965.

McKenzie, Kermit E. *Comintern and World Revolution, 1928–1943*. New York: Columbia University Press, 1964.

Méray, Tibor. *That Day in Budapest, October 23, 1956*. New York: Funk & Wagnalls, 1969.

————. *Thirteen Days That Shook the Kremlin*. London: Thames and Hudson, 1958.

Mérei, Gyula. *A magyar októberi forradalom és a polgári pártok*. Budapest: Akadémiai, 1969.

Mészáros, István. *A szent, a várt szélvész: Tanulmányok a Tanácsköztársaság közoktatásügyéről*. Budapest: Akadémiai, 1970.

Meyer, Peter; Weinryb, B. D.; and Duschinsky, E. *The Jews in the Soviet Satellites*. Syracuse, N.Y.: Syracuse University Press, 1953.

Mieczkowski, Bogdan. *Personal and Social Consumption in Eastern Europe: Poland, Czechoslovakia, Hungary, and East Germany*. New York: Praeger, 1975.

Mikes, George. *The Hungarian Revolution*. London: Deutsch, 1957.

————. *A Study in Infamy: The Operations of the Hungarian Secret Police*. London: Deutsch, 1959.

Milei, György. *A Kommunisták Magyarországi Pártjának megalakitásáról*. Budapest: Kossuth, 1962.

Mindszenty, József Cardinal. *Memoirs*. New York: Macmillan, 1974.

Mocsár, Gábor. *Nálunk vidéken*. Budapest: Kossuth, 1967.

Mód, Aladár. *400 év küzdelem az önálló Magyarországért*. 7th rev. ed. Budapest: Szikra, 1954.

————. *Válaszutak, 1918–1919*. Budapest: Magvető, 1970.

Moldova, György. *Az Őrség panasza*. Budapest: Magvető, 1974.

Molnár, Erik. *A jelenkori kapitalizmus néhány gazdasági problémája*. Budapest: Kossuth, 1959.

Molnár János. *Ellenforradalom Magyarországon 1956-ban: A polgári magyarázatok birálata*. Budapest: Akadémiai, 1967.

————. *A Nagybudapesti Központi Munkástanács*. Budapest: Akadémiai, 1969.

Molnár, László; Nemes, Ferenc; and Szalai, Mrs. Béla. *Ipari munkások politikai aktivitása*. Budapest: Kossuth, 1970.

Molnár, Miklós. *Budapest 1956: A History of the Hungarian Revolution*. London: Allen and Unwin, 1971.

Molnár, Miklós, and Nagy, László. *Imre Nagy: Réformateur ou révolutionnaire?* Geneva: Droz, 1959.

Montgomery, John F. *Hungary, the Unwilling Satellite*. New York: Devin-Adair, 1947.

Mosely, Philip E. *Face to Face with Russia*. Washington, D.C.: Foreign Policy Association, 1948.

Mucs, Sándor. *A magyar néphadsereg megszervezése és fejlődése, 1945–1958*. Budapest: Zrinyi, 1963.

————. *A magyar néphadsereg története, 1945–1959*. Budapest: Zrinyi, 1974.

Münnich, Ferenc. *A Magyar Tanácsköztársaság*. Budapest: Kossuth, 1969.

————. *Viharos út*. Budapest: Szépirodalmi, 1966.

Nagy, Eta, and Petrák, Katalin, eds. *Szabadság, te szülj nekem rendet!* Budapest: Kossuth, 1970.

————. *Tanúságtevők*. Budapest: Kossuth, 1975.

Nagy, Ferenc. *The Struggle behind the Iron Curtain*. New York: Macmillan, 1948.

Nagy, Ferenc Z. *Ahogy én láttam . . .* Budapest: Gondolat, 1965.

Nagy, Imre. *Egy évtized: Válogatott beszédek és irások*. 2 vols. Budapest: Szikra, 1954.

————. *On Communism: In Defence of the New Course*. London: Thames and Hudson, 1957.

Nagy, Vince. *Októbertől—októberig*. New York: Pro Arte, 1962.

Nagy, Zsuzsa L. *A budapesti liberális ellenzék, 1919–1944*. Budapest: Akadémiai, 1972.

————. *A párizsi békekonferencia és Magyarország, 1918–1919*. Budapest: Kossuth, 1965.

Nagy, Zsuzsa L., and Zsilák, András, eds. *Ötven év: A nagy október és a magyarországi forradalmak. Tanulmányok*. Budapest: Akadémiai, 1967.

Nagy-Talavera, Nicholas M. *The Green Shirts and the Others: A History of Fascism in Hungary and Rumania*. Stanford: Hoover Institution Press, 1970.

Nemes, Dezső. *Az ellenforradalom története Magyarországon, 1919–1921*. Budapest: Akadémiai, 1962.

————. *Magyarország felszabadulása*. Budapest: Kossuth, 1960.

Nemes, Dezső, et al. *A magyar forradalmi munkásmozgalom története*. Three volumes in one. Budapest: Kossuth, 1974. Volume 3 was also published as *History of the Revolutionary Workers Movement in Hungary, 1944–1962*. Budapest: Corvina, 1973.

Nemeskürti, István. *Requiem egy hadseregért*. Budapest: Gondolat, 1968.

Neuburg, Paul. *The Hero's Children: The Post-War Generation in Eastern Europe*. London: Constable, 1972.

Nicolson, Harold. *Peacemaking 1919*. London: Constable, 1933.

Nógrádi, Sándor. *Történelmi lecke.* Budapest: Kossuth, 1970.

Nollau, Günther. *International Communism and World Revolution.* London: Hollis & Carter, 1961.

Nyárádi, Nicholas. *My Ringside Seat in Moscow.* New York: Cromwell, 1952.

Nyers, Rezső. *Gazdaságpolitikánk és a gazdasági mechanizmus reformja.* Budapest: Kossuth, 1968.

———. *Népgazdaságunk a szocializmus épitésének útján.* Budapest: Kossuth, 1973.

———. *A szocialista gazdasági integráció elvi és gyakorlati kérdései.* Budapest: Kossuth, 1966.

Nyitrai, Mrs. Ferenc. *A magyar ipar fejlődése és távlatai.* Budapest: Kossuth, 1971.

Orbán, Sándor. *Egyház és állam: A katolikus egyház és az állam viszonyának rendezése, 1945–1950.* Budapest: Kossuth, 1962.

———. *Két agrárforradalom Magyarországon (Demokratikus és szocialista agrárátalakulás 1945–1961).* Budapest: Akadémiai, 1972.

Ördögh, Piroska. *A szakszervezetek antifasiszta tevékenysége a Gömbös-kormány idején.* Budapest: Akadémiai 1977.

Pálóczi-Horváth, György. *The Undefeated.* London: Secker & Warburg, 1959.

Pándi, Ilona. *Osztályok és pártok a Bethlen-konszolidáció időszakában.* Budapest: Kossuth, 1966.

Pándi, Pál. *"Kisértetjárás" Magyarországon: Az utópista szocialista és kommunista eszmék jelentkezése a reformkorban.* Budapest: Magvető, 1972.

Penkovskiy, Oleg. *The Penkovskiy Papers.* Garden City, N.Y.: Doubleday, 1965.

Petrák, Katalin. *Az első magyar munkáshatalom szociálpolitikája, 1919.* Budapest: Táncsics, 1969.

Petrák, Katalin, and Milei, György, eds. *A Magyar Tanácsköztársaság szociálpolitikája.* Budapest: Gondolat, 1959.

Petrák, Katalin, and Vágó, Ernő, eds. *Harcok, emlékek.* Budapest: Zrinyi, 1969.

Pintér, István. *Igy lett végre rend!* Budapest: Táncsics, 1974.

———. *Magyar antifasizmus és ellenállás.* Budapest: Kossuth, 1975.

———. *A magyar front és az ellenállás (1944. március 19.–1945. április 4).* Budapest: Kossuth, 1970.

———. *Magyarok amerikai koszton.* Budapest: Táncsics, 1972.

Pintér, István, and Svéd, László, eds. *Dokumentumok a magyar forradalmi munkásmozgalom történetéből, 1935–1945.* Budapest: Kossuth, 1964.

Pintér, István, and Szabó, László, eds. *Criminals at Large.* Budapest: Pannonia, 1961.

Pölöskei, Ferenc, and Szakács, Kálmán, eds. *Földmunkás- és szegényparaszt-mozgalmak Magyarországon, 1848–1948.* 2 vols. Budapest: Táncsics, 1962.

Pongrácz, Jenő, ed. *A Forradalmi Kormányzótanács és a népbiztosságok rendeletei.* 3 vols. Budapest: Franklin, 1919.

Pool, Ithiel de Sola. *Satellite Generals.* Stanford: Stanford University Press, 1955.

Puja, Frigyes. *Egység és vita a nemzetközi kommunista mozgalomban.* Budapest: Kossuth, 1969.

———. *Szocialista külpolitika.* Budapest: Kossuth, 1973.

Rácz, János. *Az üzemi bizottságok a magyar népi demokratikus átalakulásban.* Budapest: Akadémiai, 1971.

Radványi, János. *Hungary and the Superpowers: The 1956 Revolution and Realpolitik.* Stanford: Hoover Institution Press, 1972.

Rajk, László. *A magyar külpolitika útja.* Budapest: Szikra, 1949.

Rákosi, Mátyás. *A békéért és a szocializmus épitéséért.* Budapest: Szikra, 1951.

———. *A fordulat éve.* Budapest: Szikra, 1948.

———. *A Kommunisták Magyarországi Pártjának megalakulása és harca a proletárforradalom győzelméért.* Budapest: Szikra, 1954.

———. *A magyar demokráciáért.* Budapest: Szikra, 1948.

———. *A magyar jövőért.* Budapest: Szikra, 1945.

———. *A népi demokrácia.* Budapest: Szikra, 1946.

———. *The Road of Our People's Democracy.* London: Hungarian News and Information Service, 1952.

———. *A szocialista Magyarországért.* Budapest: Szikra, 1952.

———. *Tiéd az ország, magadnak épited.* Budapest: Szikra, 1948.

———. *Válogatott beszédek.* 2 vols. Budapest: Szikra, 1950.

Ránki, György. *Magyarország gazdasága az első 3 éves terv időszakában.* Budapest: Közgazdasági és Jogi, 1963.

Reale, Eugenio. *Avec Jacques Duclos: Au banc des accusés à la réunion constitutive du Kominform à Szklarska Poreba (22–27 septembre 1947).* Paris: Plon, 1958.

Rédei, Jenő. *A magyar társadalom strukturájának átalakulása a statisztikai adatok tükrében.* Budapest: Társadalom- és Természettudományi Ismeretterjesztő Társulat, 1955.

Remete, László. *Barikádok Budapest utcáin, 1912.* Budapest: Kossuth, 1972.

Rényi, Péter. *A vita folytatása.* Budapest: Szépirodalmi, 1972.

Réti, László. *A Bethlen-Peyer paktum.* Budapest, 1951.

———. *Igy látta az ellenség: Adalékok a Magyar Tanácsköztársaság történetéhez a TAGYOB anyagából.* Budapest: Gondolat, 1969.

———. *Lenin és a magyar munkásmozgalom.* Budapest: Kossuth, 1970.

———. *A Magyar Tanácsköztársaság központi szervei és pecsétjeik.* Budapest: Akadémiai, 1970.

Rév, Erika. *A népbiztosok pere.* Budapest: Kossuth, 1969.

Révai, József. *Élni tudunk a szabadsággal.* Budapest: Szikra, 1949.

———. *A magyar értelmiség útja.* Budapest: Szikra, 1947.

———. *A magyar népi demokrácia jellege és fejlődése.* Budapest: Szikra, 1950.

———. *Marxizmus, népiesség, magyarság.* 4th ed. Budapest: Szikra, 1955.

———. *Válogatott történelmi irások.* 2 vols. Budapest: Kossuth, 1966.

Révész, László. *Der Liquidierung der Sozialdemokratie in Osteuropa.* Bern: SOI, 1971.

Ritter, Dr. Tibor. *A politikai agitácios munka különböző szintű irányitásának módszertani kérdései.* Budapest: Kossuth, 1974.

Robinson, William F. *The Pattern of Reform in Hungary: A Political, Economic, and Cultural Analysis.* New York: Praeger, 1973.

Rottler, Ferenc, ed. *Sej, a mi lobogónkat fényes szelek fújják . . . Népi kollégiumok 1939–1949.* Budapest: Akadémiai, 1977.

Royal Institute of International Affairs. *Documents on International Affairs, 1955.* London: Oxford University Press, 1958.

Rudas, László. *Abenteuer- und Liquidatorentum; die Politik Béla Kuns und die Krise der K.P.U.* Vienna: Vörös Ujság, 1922.

Russian Institute, Columbia University. *The Anti-Stalin Campaign and International Communism.* New York: Columbia University Press, 1956.

Ságvári, Ágnes. *Népfront és koalició Magyarországon, 1936–1948.* Budapest: Kossuth, 1967.

————. *Tömegmozgalmak és politikai küzdelmek Budapesten, 1945–1947.* Budapest: Kossuth, 1964.

Sánta, Ilona. *A két munkáspárt egyesülése 1948-ban.* Budapest: Kossuth, 1962.

Sarlós, Béla. *A Tanácsköztársaság forradalmi törvényszékei.* Budapest: Közgazdasági és Jogi, 1961.

Sarlós, Márton, ed. *A Magyar Tanácsköztársaság állama és joga.* Budapest: Akadémiai, 1959.

Schoenwald, Pál. *A Magyarországi 1918–19-es polgári demokratikus forradalom állam- és jogtörténeti kérdései.* Budapest: Akadémiai, 1969.

Serge, Victor. *Memoirs of a Revolutionary, 1901–1941.* London: Oxford University Press, 1963.

Seton-Watson, Hugh. *The East European Revolution.* New York: Praeger, 1956.

Shawcross, William. *Crime and Compromise: Janos Kadar and the Politics of Hungary since Revolution.* New York: Dutton, 1974.

Sik, Endre. *Bem rakparti évek.* Budapest: Kossuth, 1970.

————. *Egy diplomata feljegyzései,* 2d ed. Budapest: Kossuth, 1967.

————. *Vihar a levelet . . .* Budapest: Zrinyi, 1970.

Skilling, H. Gordon. *Czechoslovakia's Interrupted Revolution.* Princeton, N.J.: Princeton University Press, 1976.

Somlyai, Magda. *Nagy csaták után: Az új élet kezdete Magyarországon, 1944–1945.* Budapest: Kossuth, 1975.

Stillman, Edmund O. *The Ideology of Revolution.* New York: Free Europe Press, 1957.

————, ed. *Bitter Harvest: The Intellectual Revolt Behind the Iron Curtain.* London: Thames and Hudson, 1959.

Strassenreiter, Erzsébet, and Sipos, Péter. *Rajk László.* Budapest: Akadémiai, 1974.

Suli, József. *Hidfő.* Munich: Ledermüller, 1960.

Sulyok, Dezső. *A Magyar Tragédia.* Newark, N.J., 1954.

————. *Zwei Nächte ohne Tag.* Zürich: Thomas, 1948.

Svéd, László. *Utat tör az ifjú sereg.* Budapest: Kossuth, 1962.

Szabó, Ágnes. *A KMP első kongresszusa.* Budapest: Kossuth, 1963.

————. *A Kommunisták Magyarországi Pártjának ujjászervezése, 1919–1925.* Budapest: Kossuth, 1970.

————. *Landler Jenő.* Budapest: Akadémiai, 1974.

Szabó, Ágnes, and Imre, Magda, eds. *A KMP első kongresszusa.* Budapest: Kossuth, 1975.

Szabó, Ágnes, and Vértes, Róbert, eds. *Negyedszázados harc.* Budapest: Akadémiai, 1975.

Szabó Árpád. *A Magyar Forradalmi Honvéd Karhatalom (1956. november–1957. június).* Budapest: Zrinyi, 1977.

Szabó, Bálint. *Felszabadulás és forradalom.* Budapest: Akadémiai, 1975.

————. *Népi demokrácia és forradalomelmélet: A marxista forradalomelmélet fejlődésének néhány kérdése Magyarországon, 1935–1949.* Budapest: Kossuth, 1970.

Szabó, Bálint, ed. *A szocializmus útján:_ A felszabadulást követő negyedszázad kronológiája.* Budapest: Akadémiai, 1970.

Szabó, Imre. *A népköztársaság alkotmánya.* Budapest: Szikra, 1949.

Szabó, Miklós. *Professional Émigrés.* Budapest: Pannonia, 1959.

Szabolcs, Ottó. *Köztisztviselők az ellenforradalmi rendszer társadalmi bázisában, 1920–1926.* Budapest: Akadémiai, 1965.

Szabolcsi, Miklós, and Illés, László, eds. *Jöjj el, szabadság: Tanulmányok a magyar szocialista irodalom történetéből.* Budapest: Akadémiai, 1962.

Szakács, Kálmán. *A Kommunista Párt agrárpolitikája, 1920–1930.* Budapest: Kossuth, 1961.

Szamuely, Tibor. *Riadó.* Budapest: Kossuth, 1957.

————. *Válogatott cikkek, 1908–1915.* Budapest: Tankönyvkiadó, 1969.

————. *A Kommunisták Magyarországi Pártjának megalakulása és harca a proletárdiktatúráért.* Budapest: Kossuth, 1964.

Szamuely, Mrs. Tibor. *Emlékeim.* Budapest: Zrinyi, 1966.

Szántó, Miklós. *Magyarok a nagyvilágban.* Budapest: Kossuth, 1970.

Szász, Béla S. *Volunteers for the Gallows: Anatomy of a Show Trial.* London: Chatto & Windus, 1971.

Szekér, Nándor. *Föld alatt és föld felett.* Budapest: Kossuth, 1968.

Szekfű, Gyula. *Forradalom után.* Budapest: Cserépfalvi, 1947.

————. *Három nemzedék, és ami utána következik.* 5th ed. Budapest: KMEN, 1938.

————, ed. *Mi a magyar?* Budapest: Magyar Szemle, 1939.

Szenes, Iván. *A Kommunista Párt ujjászervezése Magyarországon, 1956–1957.* Budapest: Kossuth, 1976.

Szerémi, Borbála, ed. *Nagy idők tanui emlékeznek.* Budapest: Kossuth, 1959.

Tamás, Aladár. *A 100% története.* Budapest: Magvető, 1973.

Tánczos, Gábor. *A népi kollegisták útja 1939–1971.* Budapest: Statisztikai, 1976.

Thomas, Hugh. *The Spanish Civil War.* Harmondsworth, England: Penguin, 1965. Revised U.S. edition published in New York in 1977 by Harper & Row.

Tilkovszky, Lóránt. *Revizió és nemzetiségpolitika Magyarországon, 1938–1941.* Budapest: Akadémiai, 1967.

Timár, Mátyás. *Reflections on the Economic Development of Hungary, 1967–1973.* Leyden: Sijthoff, 1976.

Timmer, József. *Beszélő mult.* Budapest: Táncsics, 1969.

Tőkés, Rudolf L. *Béla Kun and the Hungarian Soviet Republic.* New York: Praeger, 1967.

Toma, Peter A., and Völgyes, Iván. *Politics in Hungary.* San Francisco: Freeman, 1977.

Tömöri, Márta. *Új vizeken járok: A Galilei kör története*. Budapest: Gondolat, 1960.

Török, Lajos. *Az állami ellenőrzés szocialista rendszere*. Budapest: Közgazdasági és Jogi, 1971.

Tóth, István. *A Nemzeti Parasztpárt története, 1944–1948*. Budapest: Kossuth, 1972.

Triska, Jan F. *Constitutions of the Communist Party-States*. Stanford: Hoover Institution Press, 1968.

Trotsky, Leon. *The First Five Years of the Communist International*. 2 vols. New York: Pioneer, 1945.

*The Truth about the Nagy Affair: Facts, Documents, Comments*. London: Secker & Warburg, 1959.

Turóczi, Károly. *Az Imrédy-kormány belpolitikája*. Budapest: Zrinyi, 1970.

Ulam, Adam B. *Expansion and Coexistence: Soviet Foreign Policy, 1917–73*. 2d ed. New York: Praeger, 1974.

United Nations, General Assembly. *Report of the Special Committee on the Problem of Hungary*. New York: United Nations, 1957.

United States, Department of State. *Foreign Relations of the United States, 1945: The Conferences at Malta and Yalta*. Washington, D.C.: U.S. Government Printing Office, 1955.

———. *Foreign Relations of the United States: Diplomatic Papers, 1946*. Vol. 6. Washington, D.C.: U.S. Government Printing Office, 1969.

United States, House of Representatives. *Fifth Interim Report on Hungary*. Washington, D.C.: U.S. Government Printing Office, 1954.

———, ———, Committee on Un-American Activities. *International Communism (Revolt in the Satellites)*. Washington, D.C.: U.S. Government Printing Office, 1957.

Vágó, Béla, and Mosse, George L., eds. *Jews and Non-Jews in Eastern Europe, 1918–1945*. New York: Wiley, 1974.

Vajda, Imre. *Van e harmadik út?* Budapest: Kunfi-gárda, 1947.

Váli, Ferenc A. *Rift and Revolt in Hungary: Nationalism versus Communism*. Cambridge, Mass.: Harvard University Press, 1961.

Varga, Jenő. *Die Agrarfrage in der ungarischen proletarischen Revolution*, Reichenberg: Runge, 1921.

———. *Die wirtschaftpolitischen Probleme der proletarischen Diktatur*. Vienna: Neue Erde, 1920.

Varga, Károly. *Magyar egyetemi hallgatók életfelfogása (nemzetközi összehasonlitás)*. Budapest: Akadémiai, 1968.

Varga, László. *Human Rights in Hungary*. Gainesville, Fla.: Danubian Research and Information Center, 1967.

Varga, Rózsa. *Keressétek, ami összeköt: Népfrontpolitika, irodalom, és a Magyar Nap*. Budapest: Kossuth, 1971.

Vargyai, Gyula. *Katonai közigazgatás és kormányzoi jogkör, 1919–1921*. Budapest: Közgazdasági és Jogi, 1971.

Várkonyi, Péter. *Magyar-amerikai kapcsolatok, 1945–1948*. Budapest: Kossuth, 1971.

Váry, Albert. *A vörösuralom áldozatai Magyarországon*. Budapest: n.p., 1923.

Vas, Zoltán. *Hazatérés 1944*. Budapest: Szépirodalmi, 1970.

Vass, Henrik, ed. *A kommunista párt szövetségi politikája, 1936–1962.* Budapest: Kossuth, 1966.

Vass, Henrik; Bassa, Endre; and Betlen, Oszkár, eds. *Munkásmozgalomtörténeti Lexikon.* Budapest: Kossuth, 1972.

Veres, Péter. *Mit ér az ember ha magyar: Levelek egy parasztfiuhoz.* 5th ed. Budapest: Magyar Élet, 1946.

————. *Az ország útján.* Budapest: Szépirodalmi, 1966.

Vértes, György. *József Attila és az illegális Kommunista Párt.* Budapest: Magvető, 1964.

Vértes, Róbert, and Acs, Mrs. András, eds. *A magyar szakszervezetek kongresszusainak krónikája.* Budapest: Táncsics, 1971.

Vincze, Edit S. *Küzdelem az önálló proletárpárt megteremtéséért Magyarországon, 1848–1890.* Budapest: Kossuth, 1963.

————. *A Magyarországi Szociáldemokrata Párt megalakulása és tevékenységének első évei, 1890–1896.* Budapest: Kossuth, 1961.

Vogeler, Robert. *I Was Stalin's Prisoner.* New York: Harcourt, Brace, 1952.

Völgyes, Iván. *The Hungarian Soviet Republic, 1919: An Evaluation and a Bibliography.* Stanford: Hoover Institution Press, 1970.

————, ed. *Hungary in Revolution, 1918–1919: Nine Essays.* Lincoln: University of Nebraska Press, 1971.

————. *Political Socialization in Eastern Europe: A Comparative Framework.* New York: Praeger, 1975.

Vonsik, Gyula, and Pál, László. *Ujfajta had.* Salgótarján: n.p., 1970.

Vörös, Sándor. *American Commissar.* Philadelphia: Chilton, 1961.

Wagner, Francis S., ed. *The Hungarian Revolution in Perspective.* Washington, D.C.: F.F. Memorial Foundation, 1967.

Weis, István. *A mai magyar társadalom.* Budapest: Magyar Szemle, 1930.

Weit, Erwin. *Eyewitness.* London: Deutsch, 1973.

Zágoni, Ernő. *A magyar kommunisták a munkásegységért, 1939–1942.* Budapest: Kossuth, 1963.

Zamercev, I. T. *Emlékek, arcok, Budapest . . . .* Budapest: Zrinyi, 1969.

Zinner, Paul E. *Revolution in Hungary.* New York: Columbia University Press, 1962.

————, ed. *National Communism and Popular Revolt in Eastern Europe.* New York: Columbia University Press, 1956.

Zinoviev, Grigori, and Radek, Karl, eds. *Mit mond a III. Internacionálé a magyarországi proletárforradalomról.* Vienna: A Kommunisták Németausztriai Pártja, 1920.

Zitta, Victor. *Georg Lukacs' Marxism.* The Hague: Nijhoff, 1964.

Zsoldos, László. *The Economic Integration of Hungary into the Soviet Bloc: Foreign Trade Experience.* Columbus: Bureau of Business Research, Ohio State University, 1963.

# Index